"I immediately went to my nurse manager after I failed the NCLEX® and she referred me to ATI. I was able to discover the areas I was weak in, and focused on those areas in the review modules and online assessments.

I was much more prepared the second time around!"

Terim Richards
Nursing student

Danielle Platt

Nurse Manager • Children's Mercy Hospital • Kansas City, MO

"The year our hospital did not use the ATI program, we experienced a 15% decrease in the NCLEX® pass rates. We reinstated the ATI program the following year and had a 90% success rate."

"As a manager, I have witnessed graduate nurses fail the NCLEX® and the devastating effects it has on their morale. Once the nurses started using ATI, it was amazing to see the confidence they had in themselves and their ability to go forward and take the NCLEX® exam."

Mary Moss

Associate Dean of Nursing - Service and Health Division • Mid-State Technical College • Wisconsin Rapids, WI

"I like that ATI lets students know what to expect from the NCLEX®, helps them plan their study time and tells them what to do in the days and weeks before the exam. It is different from most of the NCLEX® review books on the market."

Editor

Jeanne Wissmann, PhD, RN, CNE
Director Nursing Curriculum and Educational Services
Assessment Technologies Institute®, LLC

Associate Editors

Audrey Knippa, MS, MPH, RN, CNE
Curriculum Project Coordinator

Jamie Easum, BSN, RN
Educational Services Coordinator

Kristen M. Lawler, MBA
Director of Development

Derek Prater, MS Journalism
Product Developer

Important Notice to the Reader of this Publication

Preface

Overview

The overall goal of this Assessment Technologies Institute®, LLC (ATI) Content Mastery Series module is to provide nursing students with an additional resource for the focused review of "Adult Medical-Surgical Nursing" content relevant to NCLEX-PN® preparation and entry level nursing practice. Content within this review module is provided in a key point plus rationale format in order to focus recall and application of relevant content. Unit and chapter selections are reflective of the adult medical-surgical nursing-relevant content categories and explanations of the NCLEX-PN® test plan, the ATI "Adult Medical-Surgical Nursing" assessment test plans, and standard nursing curricular content. Each chapter begins with an overview of some of the topic-relevant nursing activities outlined by the NCLEX-PN® test plan in an effort to guide the learner's review and application of chapter content.

Contributors

ATI would like to extend appreciation to the nurse educators and nurse specialists who contributed content for this review module. The names of contributors are noted in the chapter bylines. We would also like to thank those talented individuals who reviewed, edited, and developed this module. In the summer and fall of 2005, two focus groups of committed nurse educators gave invaluable input and feedback regarding the format and purposes of review modules. Their input and ideas were instrumental to the development of this review module, and we are very appreciative. Additionally, we would like to recognize and extend appreciation to the multiple nursing students and educators who have contacted us in the past year with comments and ideas regarding the content of this review module. And finally, we want to recognize and express appreciation to all of the contributors, reviewers, production developers, and editors of previous editions of this Content Mastery Series module.

Suggestions for Effective Utilization

Δ   Understanding the organizational framework of this review module will facilitate focused review. Unit 1 focuses on general principles and nursing skills of "Emergency Care and Triage." The chapters within units 2 to 12 focus on nursing care for clients with system-specific disorders. Within each unit are sections relevant to the nursing care of clients 1) undergoing system-specific diagnostic and therapeutic procedures; 2) with a specific disorder; and 3) experiencing system-specific medical emergencies. And finally, unit 13 focuses on "Perioperative Nursing Care."

Δ   Some suggested uses of this review module include:

•   As a review of NCLEX-PN® relevant adult medical-surgical content in developing and assessing your readiness for the NCLEX-PN®.

•   As a focused review resource based on the results of an ATI "Adult Medical-Surgical" or "Comprehensive Predictor" assessment. "Topics to Review" identified upon completion of these assessments can be used to focus your efforts to a review of content within specific chapter(s) of this review module. For example, an identified "Topic to Review" of "Signs and Symptoms of Acute Pain" suggests that a review of chapter 79, "Pain Management," and completion of the application exercises at the end of the chapter would be helpful.

Δ   To foster long-term recall and development of an ability to apply knowledge to a variety of situations, learners are encouraged to take a comprehensive approach to topic review. Using this review module along with other resources (class notes, course textbooks, nursing reference texts, instructors, ATI DVD series), consider addressing questions for each specific disorder, such as:

•   What are the presenting signs and symptoms? What techniques are used to monitor for these signs and symptoms?

•   Identify client findings that need to be reported immediately to the primary care provider.

- What are relevant diagnostic and therapeutic procedures? What are the risks associated with the procedure? Identify appropriate client preparation for the procedure and information to be reinforced prior to and following the procedure. Identify appropriate nursing care prior to, during, and following the procedure. Identify appropriate monitoring and actions to take to prevent or minimize the risk of complications of procedures.

- What are appropriate nursing diagnoses and interventions (including medication administration)?

- What are the desired client outcomes or goals and how would they be prioritized?

- What are possible complications associated with the disorder? What are signs and symptoms of these complications? Identify appropriate nursing interventions in response to these complications.

- Evaluate the client's response to interventions and progress toward recovery.

- What client teaching should be reinforced (e.g., appropriate dietary alterations, symptoms to report, and appropriate use of medications)?

Δ   Complete application exercises at the end of each chapter after a review of the topic. Answer questions fully and note rationales for answers. Complete exercises initially without looking for the answers within the chapter or consulting the answer key. Use these exercises as an opportunity to assess your readiness to apply knowledge. When reviewing the answer key, in addition to identifying the correct answer, examine why you missed or answered correctly each item—was it related to ability to recall, recognition of a common testing principle, or perhaps attention to key words?

Feedback

All feedback is welcome – suggestions for improvement, reports of mistakes (small or large), and testimonials of effectiveness. Please address feedback to: comments@atitesting.com

Table of Contents

Unit 3 Nursing Care of Clients with Cardiovascular or Hematologic Disorders

Section: Diagnostic and Therapeutic Procedures: Cardiovascular or Hematologic

Section: Nursing Care of Clients with Hematologic Disorders

Section: Nursing Care of Clients with Vascular Disorders

Section: Nursing Care of Clients with Cardiac Failure

Section: Medical Emergencies: Cardiovascular

Unit 4 Nursing Care of Clients with Fluid and Electrolyte Needs

Section: Nursing Care of Clients with Fluid and Electrolyte Imbalances

Section: Nursing Care of Clients Receiving Infusion Therapy

Unit 10 Nursing Care of Clients with Lymph, Immune, or Infectious Disorders

Unit 11 Nursing Care of Clients with Integumentary Disorders

Unit 12 Nursing Care of Clients with Reproductive Disorders

Section: Diagnostic and Therapeutic Procedures: Reproductive

Section: Nursing Care of Clients with Reproductive Cancers

Section: Nursing Care of Clients with Select Reproductive Disorders

Unit 13 Perioperative Nursing care

Section: Diagnostic and Therapeutic Procedures: Surgical

Section: Perioperative Nursing

Unit 1   Emergency Care and Triage

Chapter 1:   Emergency Nursing Principles
Contributor: Lori A. Budd, BS, RN

⟳ NCLEX-PN® Connections:

> **Learning Objective**: Review and apply knowledge within "**Emergency Nursing Principles**" in readiness for performance of the following nursing activities as outlined by the NCLEX-PN® test plan:
>
> Δ   Recognize and take appropriate actions in life-threatening situations, including notifying the primary care provider of the client's emergency situation.
>
> Δ   Review the client's response to emergency interventions and complete the proper documentation.
>
> Δ   Suggest changes in emergency treatment based upon evaluation of the client's response to interventions.

📖 Key Points

Δ   Nurses must have the ability to **identify emergent situations**.

Δ   Nurses must be able to **rapidly assess** and **intervene** when life-threatening conditions exist.

Δ   Emergency care is guided by the principle of **ABCDE**.

- **A**irway/Cervical Spine
- **B**reathing
- **C**irculation
- **D**isability
- **E**xposure

Δ   Emergent conditions are common to all nursing environments.

Nursing Assessments and Interventions

Primary Survey

Δ The primary survey is a **rapid assessment** of life-threatening conditions. It should take **no longer than 60 seconds** to perform.

Δ The primary survey should be **completed systematically**, so conditions are not missed.

Δ **Standard precautions attire** – such as gloves, gowns, eye protection, face masks, and shoe covers – must be worn to prevent contamination with bodily fluids.

Δ The **ABCDE** principle guides the primary survey.

ABCDE Principle

Δ **Airway/Cervical Spine**

- This is the most important step in performing the primary survey. If a **patent airway** is not established, subsequent steps of the primary survey are futile.

- If the client is awake and responsive, the airway is open.

- If the client's ability to maintain an airway is lost, it is important to **inspect for blood**, **broken teeth**, **vomitus**, or **other foreign materials** in the airway that may cause an obstruction.

- Unresponsive *without* suspicion of trauma

    ◊ The airway should be opened with a **head-tilt-chin-lift maneuver.**

    ◊ This is the most effective manual technique for opening a client's airway.

    ◊ It must **NOT** be performed on clients who have a potential cervical spine injury.

    ◊ **Technique:** The nurse should assume a position at the head of the client, place one hand on the forehead, and the other on the chin. The head should be tilted while the chin is lifted superiorly. This lifts the tongue out of the laryngopharynx and provides for a patent airway.

- **Unresponsive with suspicion of trauma**

    ◊ The airway should be opened with a **modified jaw thrust maneuver.**

    ◊ **Technique:** The nurse should assume a position at the head of the client, and place both hands on the side of the client's head. Locate the connection between the maxilla and the mandible. Lift the jaw superiorly while maintaining alignment of the cervical spine.

- Once the airway is opened, it should be inspected for blood, broken teeth, vomitus, and secretions. If present, obstructions should be cleared with **suction** or a **finger sweep** method.

- The open airway can be maintained with **airway adjuncts**, such as an oropharyngeal or nasopharyngeal airway.

- **Bag-valve-mask** with a 100% oxygen source is indicated for clients who need additional support during resuscitation.

Δ **Breathing**

- Once a patent airway is achieved, the **presence** and **effectiveness** of breathing should be assessed.

- Breathing **assessment** includes:

  ◊ Auscultation of breath sounds.

  ◊ Observation of chest expansion and respiratory effort.

  ◊ Notation of rate and depth of respirations.

  ◊ Identification of chest trauma.

- If the client is not breathing or is breathing inadequately, **manual ventilation** should be performed by a bag-valve-mask with supplemental oxygen or mouth-to-mask ventilation until a bag-valve-mask can be obtained.

Δ **Circulation**

- Once adequate ventilation is accomplished, circulation is assessed.

- Nurses should assess **heart rate, blood pressure, and perfusion.**

- **Interventions** geared toward restoring effective circulation include:

  ◊ Cardiopulmonary resuscitation.

  ◊ Hemorrhage control (direct pressure should be applied to visible, significant external bleeding).

  ◊ Obtaining intravenous (IV) access.

  ◊ Infusion of fluids and/or blood.

- **IV access** should be achieved with a large-bore line in the antecubital fossa (bend of the elbow). Lactated Ringer's (LR) and 0.9% normal saline (NS) are typical resuscitation fluids.

- **Shock** may develop if circulation is compromised. Shock is the body's response to inadequate tissue perfusion and oxygenation. It manifests with an increased heart rate and hypotension and may result in tissue ischemia and necrosis.

- **Interventions to alleviate shock** include:
  - ◊ Administer oxygen.
  - ◊ Apply pressure to obvious bleeding.
  - ◊ Elevate the client's feet to shunt blood to vital organs.
  - ◊ Administer fluids and blood products as ordered.
  - ◊ Monitor vital signs.
  - ◊ Remain with the client and provide reassurance and support for anxiety.

Δ **Disability**

- Disability is a rapid assessment of a client's **neurological status**.
- The **AVPU** mnemonic is useful.
  - ◊ A: Alert
  - ◊ V: Responsive to voice
  - ◊ P: Responsive to pain
  - ◊ U: Unresponsive
- The **Glasgow Coma Scale** is another widely used method.
  - ◊ Components include **eye opening**, **verbal response**, and **motor response**.
- Frequent re-assessment must be done to identify improvements or deteriorations.

Δ **Exposure**

- The nurse should remove all of the client's clothing for a complete physical assessment.
- Clothing should be cut away during a resuscitation situation.
- **Evidence** such as bullets, drugs, or weapons may need to be preserved.
- **Hypothermia** is a primary concern for clients. Hypothermia leads to vasoconstriction and impaired oxygenation.
- To **prevent hypothermia**, the nurse should:
  - ◊ Remove wet clothing from the client.
  - ◊ Cover the client with blankets.
  - ◊ Increase the temperature of the room.
  - ◊ Infuse warmed fluids as ordered.

Triage Guidelines

Δ **Triage Under Usual Conditions**

- Triage guidelines ensure that clients with the **highest acuity needs** receive the **quickest treatment**.

- Clients are categorized based upon their acuity. One example of a triage framework is the **Emergent, Urgent, Nonurgent model.**

   ◊ Emergent triage indicates a life- or limb-threatening situation.

   ◊ Urgent triage indicates that the client should be treated soon, but that the risk posed is not life-threatening.

   ◊ Nonurgent cases can generally wait for several hours without serious deterioration.

Δ **Triage Under Mass Casualty Conditions**

- A military form of triage is implemented with a focus of achieving **the greatest good for the greatest number of people.**

- Classifications include:

   ◊ **Emergent or Class I** – identified with a **red tag** indicating an immediate threat to life.

   ◊ **Urgent or Class II** – identified with a **yellow tag** indicating major injuries that require immediate treatment.

   ◊ **Nonurgent or Class III** – identified with a **green tag** indicating minor injuries that do not require immediate treatment.

   ◊ **Expectant or Class IV** – identified with a **black tag** indicating one who is expected and allowed to die.

Basic First-Aid

Δ Complete the primary survey before performing first-aid.

Δ **Bleeding**

- Identify any sources of external bleeding and apply **direct pressure** to the wound site.

- DO NOT remove **impaled** objects.

- **Internal bleeding** may require intravascular volume replacement with fluids and/or blood products or surgical intervention.

Δ **Fractures & Splinting**

- Assess the site for **swelling, deformity,** and **skin integrity**.

- Assess **temperature, distal pulses,** and **mobility**.

- Apply a splint to **immobilize** the fracture. Cover any open areas with a sterile cloth if available.

- Reassess neurovascular status after splinting.

Δ   Sprains

- Refrain from **weight-bearing**.

- Apply **ice** to decrease inflammation.

- Apply a **compression dressing** to minimize swelling.

- **Elevate** the affected limb.

Δ   **Heat Stroke**

- Heat stroke must be recognized and treated immediately and aggressively.

- **Signs** and **symptoms** include hypotension, tachypnea, tachycardia, anxiety, confusion, bizarre behavior, seizures, and coma.

- **Rapid cooling** must be achieved. Methods include:

  ◊   Remove the client's clothing.

  ◊   Place ice packs over the major arteries (axillae, chest, groin, neck).

  ◊   Immerse the victim in cold water if possible.

  ◊   Wet the client's body, then fan with rapid movement of air.

Δ   **Frostnip and Frost Bite**

- **Frostnip** does not lead to tissue injury and is easily remedied with application of warmth.

- **Frostbite** presents as a white, waxy appearance to exposed skin, and tissue injury occurs.

- Frostbite may be **full-** or **partial-thickness**.

- The affected area should be warmed in a **water bath** (38° to 41° C).

- **Pain medication** should be provided.

- A **tetanus vaccination** should be provided.

Δ   **Burns**

- Burns may result from **electrical current**, **chemicals**, **radiation**, or **flames**.

- **Remove the agent** (electrical current, radiation source, chemical).

- Smother any flames that are present.

- Perform a primary survey.

- Cover the client and maintain nothing by mouth (**NPO**) status.

- **Elevate extremities** if not contraindicated (presence of a fracture).
- Perform a head-to-toe **assessment** and estimate the **surface area** and **thickness** of burns.
- Administer **fluids** and **tetanus toxoid**.

Δ   **Altitude-Related Illnesses**

- Clients may become **hypoxic** in **high altitudes**.
- **Signs and symptoms** include:
  ◊   Throbbing headache.
  ◊   Nausea.
  ◊   Vomiting.
  ◊   Dyspnea.
  ◊   Anorexia.
- **Interventions** for these clients include:
  ◊   Administer oxygen.
  ◊   Descend to a lower altitude.
  ◊   Provide pharmacological therapy, such as steroids and diuretics if indicated.
- Altitude sickness can progress to **cerebral** and **pulmonary edema** and should be treated immediately.

Primary Reference:

Ignatavicius, D. D., & Workman, M. L. (2006). *Medical-surgical nursing* (5th ed.). St. Louis, MO: Saunders.

Additional Resources:

NANDA International (2004). *NANDA nursing diagnoses: Definitions and classification 2005-2006*. Philadelphia: NANDA.

Taylor, C., Lillis, C., & LeMone, P. (2005). *Fundamentals of nursing: The art and science of nursing care* (5th ed.). Philadelphia: Lippincott Williams & Wilkins.

Chapter 1: Emergency Nursing Principles

Application Exercises

Scenario: A client arrives in the emergency department after falling off his mountain bike. He is alert, oriented, and able to move all extremities. He has a compound fracture to his left tibia, as well as several scrapes and bruises. He was not wearing a helmet. Vital signs are: blood pressure 98/60 mm Hg, heart rate 104 beats/min, respiratory rate 24/min, and temperature 37.2° C (99° F).

1. What should the nurse's assessment include? How should the interventions be prioritized?

2. Several minutes later, the client's vital signs have changed. They now read: blood pressure 78/45 mm Hg, heart rate 131 beats/min, respiratory rate 34/min, and temperature 37° C (99° F). He is unable to answer questions and is mumbling incoherently. What is the likely explanation for the change in his status? What should the nurse expect to do next?

3. A client presents to the emergency department after being involved in a motor vehicle crash and is unresponsive. The nurse should open the airway with what technique?

   A. Head tilt chin lift

   B. Modified jaw thrust

   C. Hyperextension of the head and placement of an endotracheal tube

   D. Flexion of the head and placement of an endotracheal tube

4. What techniques can be used to provide manual ventilation for a client who is not breathing or who is breathing inadequately?

5. Which of the following are appropriate interventions for a client with heat stroke? (Check all that apply.)

   _____   Immerse the victim in cold water.

   _____   Encourage the client to walk it off.

   _____   Apply ice packs to the groin and axillae.

   _____   Keep clothing on to avoid sun exposure.

   _____   Administer a tetanus vaccination.

Chapter 1: Emergency Nursing Principles

Application Exercises Answer Key

Scenario: A client arrives in the emergency department after falling off his mountain bike. He is alert, oriented, and able to move all extremities. He has a compound fracture to his left tibia, as well as several scrapes and bruises. He was not wearing a helmet. Vital signs are: blood pressure 98/60 mm Hg, heart rate 104 beats/min, respiratory rate 24/min, and temperature 37.2° C (99° F).

1. What should the nurse's assessment include? How should the interventions be prioritized?

   The nurse should start with a primary survey utilizing the ABCDE mnemonic. The client has a patent airway and is breathing, evidenced by the fact that he is talking. Since the client was not wearing a helmet and did fall, his head and neck should be immobilized until a cervical spine injury can be ruled out. The nurse should next assess circulation. IV access should be obtained, and perfusion should be assessed with blood pressure and pulse. The AVPU mnemonic can be used to assess the client's disability or neurological status. Lastly, the client's clothing should be removed to allow for a complete physical assessment. However, the room should be kept warm to prevent hypothermia.

2. Several minutes later, the client's vital signs have changed. They now read: blood pressure 78/45 mm Hg, heart rate 131 beats/min, respiratory rate 34/min, and temperature 37° C (99° F). He is unable to answer questions and is mumbling incoherently. What is the likely explanation for the change in his status? What should the nurse expect to do next?

   It is possible that internal bleeding is occurring from hidden injuries. The nurse should expect to administer warmed fluids and/or blood products to replenish his intravascular volume. The client may also require a surgical intervention to stop the bleeding.

3. A client presents to the emergency department after being involved in a motor vehicle crash and is unresponsive. The nurse should open the airway with what technique?

      A. Head tilt chin lift

      B. Modified jaw thrust

      C. Hyperextension of the head and placement of an endotracheal tube

      D. Flexion of the head and placement of an endotracheal tube

The modified jaw thrust is the correct technique for a client who is unresponsive following a motor vehicle crash. The head tilt chin lift is used for a client who is unresponsive without suspicion of trauma. Hyperextension and flexion of the head can cause further injury.

4. What techniques can be used to provide manual ventilation for a client who is not breathing or who is breathing inadequately?

Bag-valve-mask with supplemental oxygen or mouth-to-mask ventilation

5. Which of the following are appropriate interventions for a client with heat stroke? (Check all that apply.)

    __X__   Immerse the victim in cold water.

    _____   Encourage the client to walk it off.

    __X__   Apply ice packs to the groin and axillae.

    _____   Keep clothing on to avoid sun exposure.

    _____   Administer a tetanus vaccination.

Immersing the client in cold water and applying ice packs to the groin and axillae are appropriate interventions for heat stroke. The client should stop all activity to conserve energy. All clothing should be removed prior to immersing the client in cold water. A tetanus vaccination is not indicated for heatstroke, but is indicated for frostnip and frostbite.

Unit 1   Emergency Care and Triage

Chapter 2:   Cardiopulmonary Resuscitation (CPR)

Contributor: Linda Turchin, MSN, RN

NCLEX-PN® Connections:

Learning Objective: Review and apply knowledge within "**Cardiopulmonary Resuscitation (CPR)**" in readiness for performance of the following nursing activities as outlined by the NCLEX-PN® test plan:

Δ   Recognize life-threatening situations and intervene appropriately.

Δ   Perform CPR according to current neonate/infant/child/adult guidelines.

Δ   Alert the primary care provider to the client's medical emergency.

Key Points

Δ   **Cardiac arrest,** the sudden cessation of breathing and adequate circulation of blood, results in the termination of cardiac output and is characterized by the **absence of a pulse** in an unconscious victim who is not breathing (respiratory arrest).

Δ   **Ventricular fibrillation (VF)** is the cause of sudden, non-traumatic cardiac arrest in 80 to 90% of victims.

Δ   Without sufficient cardiac output, the brain will suffer **cell anoxia** (cell death) within 4 to 6 min, with death following shortly thereafter.

Δ   An **interdisciplinary team** will provide care during in-hospital cardiac arrests. This team should include nurses, physicians, respiratory therapists, laboratory personnel, and chaplain services.

Δ   **Management** of cardiac arrest depends on **prompt recognition** of signs and symptoms and the introduction of therapeutic interventions directed at **artificially sustaining circulation and ventilation.**

Δ   The **goals for management** of a cardiac arrest include:

- Rapid identification of the signs and symptoms of cardiac arrest.

- Quick initiation of both circulatory and respiratory support.

- Activation of the emergency medical system (EMS).

- Utilization of emergency equipment and cardiac monitoring.

- Stabilization of the client following the arrest.

- Diagnosis and treatment of the cause of the cardiac arrest.

Δ CPR is the process of **externally supporting the circulation and respirations** of an individual who has experienced a cardiac arrest. CPR significantly increases the chances of survival when initiated immediately.

Δ Prehospital care greatly improves the chance of survival for cardiac arrest victims.

Cardiopulmonary Resuscitation (CPR)

Δ CPR is a combination of basic interventions designed to **sustain oxygen and circulation to vital organs** until more advanced interventions can be initiated to correct the root cause of the cardiac arrest.

Δ Basic interventions can be delivered by trained citizens, but advanced interventions require more sophisticated training and certification and the use of emergency equipment.

Δ CPR is a series of emergency procedures directed at artificially providing a client with **circulation (chest compressions) and oxygenation (ventilations)** in the absence of cardiac output.

Δ CPR is a component of **basic life support (BLS)** and **advanced cardiac life support (ACLS)**.

Δ The **goal of BLS** is to provide oxygen to the vital organs until appropriate advanced resuscitation measures can be initiated or until resuscitative efforts are ordered to be stopped. BLS involves the **ABCs of CPR**:

- **Airway**

  ◊ Confirm the absence of spontaneous respirations.

  ◊ Establish a patent airway.

  ◊ Provide the Heimlich maneuver if the airway is obstructed with a foreign object.

  ◊ Use abdominal thrusts for unconscious clients.

- **Breathing**

  ◊ Provide artificial respirations (**ventilations**) to deliver oxygen into the blood in an attempt to prevent cell anoxia.

- **Circulation**
  ◊ Confirm the absence or presence of a pulse.
  ◊ Provide external support of circulation (**chest compressions**) to transport oxygenated blood to the brain.

Δ The **goal of ACLS** is the return of spontaneous breathing and circulation. In addition to the ABCs of BLS, ACLS involves:

- **Diagnosis** of underlying cardiac **dysrhythmias**. Pharmacological interventions are dependent upon the rhythm identified.
  ◊ **Defibrillation** may be required. This involves delivering a pre-measured **shock** to the heart in order to interrupt the aberrant rhythm and allow the natural pacemaker of the heart to initiate beats.
- Insertion of an oropharyngeal or endotracheal **airway** with **bag ventilation** and supplemental oxygen.
- Administration of **IV fluids**.
- Administration of **IV antidysrhythmic drugs**.

Δ The **chain of survival** is a series of interventions directed at the resuscitation of the cardiac arrest victim. It involves:

- Early activation of the emergency medical services.
- Early CPR/early defibrillation.
- Early ACLS care.

Nursing Responsibilities during a Cardiac Arrest

Δ The nurse assisting during a cardiac arrest must:

- Utilize the current BLS and ACLS guidelines from the **American Heart Association (AHA)**.
- Be knowledgeable about institutional **policies/procedures** and the location and operation of **emergency equipment** (crash cart).
- Have current **certification** for BLS and/or ACLS skills.

Δ Nursing responsibilities include:

- Maintain **airway patency**.
- Assess the depth and rate of **respirations**.
- Provide **chest compressions** at the appropriate rate and depth for age (see the chart on the following page).
- Assess **vital signs** for effectiveness of chest compressions and ventilations.

- **Defibrillate** the client when indicated.
- Obtain and maintain **IV access**.
- Provide **medications** as ordered.
- Monitor **laboratory values** (for example, ABGs, CBC, electrolytes).
- **Document** all interventions and medications.

AHA Guidelines: BLS for Infants, Children, and Adults*

Maneuver	Adult (adolescent and up)	Child (1 year to adolescent)	Infant (under 1 year)
Activate Emergency Response Number	Activate when victim found unresponsive. If asphyxial arrest is likely, call after 5 cycles (2 min) of CPR.	Activate after performing 5 cycles of CPR. For sudden, witnessed collapse, activate after verifying that the victim is unresponsive.	
Airway	Head tilt chin lift (for suspected trauma, use jaw thrust)		
Breaths Initial	2 breaths at 1 second/breath	2 effective breaths at 1 second/breath	
Rescue Breaths without chest compressions	10 to 12 breaths/min (approx. 1 breath every 5-6 sec)	12 to 20 breaths/min (approx. 1 breath every 3 to 5 sec)	
Rescue Breaths for CPR with advanced airway	8 to 10 breaths/min (approx. 1 breath every 6 to 8 sec)		
Foreign-Body Airway Obstruction	Abdominal thrusts		Back slaps and chest thrusts
Circulation	Carotid	Carotid or femoral	Brachial or femoral
Compression Landmarks	Center of chest, between nipples		Just below nipple line
Compression Method	2 hands: heel of one hand, other hand on top	2 hands: heel of one hand, other hand on top 1 hand: heel of one hand only	1 rescuer: 2 fingers 2 rescuers: 2 thumb-encircling hands
Compression Depth	1 ½ to 2 in	Approx. 1/3 to 1/2 the depth of the chest	
Compression Rate	Approx. 100/min		
Compression-Ventilation Ratio	30:2 (1 or 2 rescuers)	30:2 (1 rescuer) 15:2 (2 rescuers)	

*Table based on AHA guidelines for healthcare providers.

Source: American Heart Association. American Heart Association 2005 Guidelines for CPR and ECC. Retrieved May 10, 2006, from: http://www.americanheart.org/presenter.jhtml?identifier=3035517.

AHA ACLS Protocols

Δ   **VF or Pulseless Ventricular Tachycardia (VT)**

- Perform CPR (stop when the defibrillator is ready).
- Provide oxygen.
- Defibrillate: 200 joules.
- Defibrillate: 300 joules.
- Defibrillate: 360 joules.
- Establish IV access.
- Administer **epinephrine** 1 mg IV push every 3 to 5 min OR vasopressin 40 units IV x 1 only (switch to epinephrine if no response).
- Defibrillate: 360 joules within 30 to 60 seconds.
- Consider the following medications:
  ◊ Amiodarone
  ◊ Lidocaine
  ◊ Magnesium sulfate
  ◊ Procainamide
  ◊ Bicarbonate

Δ   **Pulseless Electrical Activity (PEA)**

- Perform CPR.
- Provide oxygen.
- Defibrillate for VF or pulseless VT.
- Establish IV access.
- Consider the most common causes:
  ◊ 5 H's
    ° Hypovolemia
    ° Hypoxia
    ° Hydrogen ion accumulation, resulting in acidosis
    ° Hyperkalemia or hypokalemia
    ° Hypothermia

◊ 5 T's

º Tables (accidental or deliberate drug overdose)

º Tamponade (cardiac)

º Tension pneumothorax

º Thrombosis (coronary)

º Thrombosis (pulmonary)

- Administer epinephrine 1 mg IV push every 3 to 5 min.

- If PEA rate is slow (bradycardic), administer **atropine** 1 mg IV every 3 to 5 min (maximum total dose 0.04 mg/kg).

Δ **Asystole**

- Perform CPR.

- Provide oxygen.

- Defibrillate for VF or pulseless VT.

- Confirm true asystolic rhythm.

- Establish IV access.

- Begin immediate transcutaneous pacing, if possible.

- Administer epinephrine 1 mg push every 3 to 5 min.

- Administer atropine 1 mg IV every 3 to 5 min (maximum total dose 0.04 mg/kg).

- Consider ceasing resuscitation if asystole persists.

Using Conventional Defibrillators

Δ The following steps represent the **safe and effective method** for delivering shocks to a client with VF.

- Turn on the defibrillator.

- Select energy level at 200 joules for monophasic defibrillators (or clinically equivalent for biphasic energy level).

- Set the "lead select" switch on the paddles (or Lead I, II, or III if monitor leads are used).

- Apply gel to paddles, or position conductor pads on the client's chest.

- Position paddles or remote defibrillation pads on the client's sternum apex.

- Visually check the monitor display and assess the rhythm (subsequent steps assume that VF/VT is present).

- Announce to the team members, "**Charging defibrillator. Stand clear!**"

- Press the **"Charge"** button on the apex paddle (right hand) or on the defibrillator controls.

- When the defibrillator is fully charged, state in a forceful voice the following chant (or some suitable equivalent) before each shock:

  "I'm going to shock on three. One, I'm clear." (Check to be sure that you are clear of contact with the client, the stretcher, and the equipment.)

  "Two, you're clear." (Make a visual check to ensure that no one continues to touch the client or stretcher. In particular, do not forget about the person providing ventilations. That person's hands should not be touching the ventilatory adjuncts, including the tracheal tube.)

  "Three, everybody's clear." (Check yourself one more time before pressing the "shock" buttons.)

- Apply 25 lb of pressure on both paddles.

- Press the two paddle **"discharge"** buttons simultaneously.

- Check the monitor. If VF/VT remains, recharge the defibrillator at once. Check for a pulse if there is any question about rhythm display (if, for example, a lead has been dislodged or the paddles are not displaying the correct signal).

- Shock at 200 to 300 joules, then at 360 joules for monophasic defibrillators (or clinically equivalent biphasic energy level), repeating the same verbal statements previously described.

Primary Reference:

Ignatavicius, D. D., & Workman, M. L. (2006). *Medical-surgical nursing* (5th ed.). St. Louis, MO: Saunders.

Additional Resources:

ECG facts made incredibly quick! (2005). Philadelphia: Lippincott Williams & Wilkins.

Lewis, Heitkemper, and Dirksen (2004). *Medical-surgical nursing: Assessment and management of clinical problems* (6th ed.). St. Louis, MO: Mosby.

NANDA International (2004). *NANDA nursing diagnoses: Definitions and classification 2005-2006*. Philadelphia: NANDA.

Potter, P. A., & Perry, A. G. (2005). *Fundamentals of nursing* (6th ed.). St. Louis, MO: Mosby.

For more information, visit the American Heart Association at: *www.americanheart.org*.

Chapter 2: Cardiopulmonary Resuscitation (CPR)

Application Exercises

Scenario: A 62-year-old male client has been hospitalized for abdominal pain. He has a history of type 2 diabetes mellitus, hypertension, and coronary artery disease, and he is currently taking medication for a sinus infection. The client is found by the nurse on the floor next to his bed.

1. Which of the following actions should the nurse take first?

> A. Check the client's blood glucose.
>
> B. Assess the patency of his airway.
>
> C. Check for a carotid pulse.
>
> D. Note the depth and rate of his respirations.

2. Number the following steps in the correct order to reflect the proper performance of CPR for this adult client.

Position client.	
Perform ventilations.	
Open airway.	
Start compressions.	
Check for breathing.	
Check for spontaneous pulse.	
Check for unresponsiveness.	
Call for help.	
Check circulation (carotid pulse/signs of circulation).	

3. **True or False:** ACLS can be performed by average citizens.

4. **True or False:** The American Heart Association provides the guidelines for BLS and ACLS.

5. **True or False:** Documentation is not an important duty for the nurse during a cardiac arrest.

6. For each of the following dysrhythmias, identify the appropriate interventions.

Dysrhythmia	Interventions
1. VF or pulseless VT	
2. Pulseless Electrical Activity (PEA)	
3. Asystole	

Interventions:

A.   Perform CPR.

B.   Administer epinephrine 1 mg IV push every 3 to 5 min.

C.   Obtain IV access.

D.   Consider the 5 H's and 5 T's.

E.   Administer atropine 1 mg IV every 3 to 5 min (max total dose 0.04 mg/kg).

F.   Defibrillate up to three times:

- Defibrillate: 200 joules.

- Defibrillate: 300 joules.

- Defibrillate: 360 joules.

G.   Consider administering:

- Amiodarone.

- Lidocaine.

- Magnesium sulfate.

- Procainamide.

- Bicarbonate.

H.   Provide oxygen.

Chapter 2: Cardiopulmonary Resuscitation (CPR)

Application Exercises Answer Key

Scenario: A 62-year-old male client has been hospitalized for abdominal pain. He has a history of type 2 diabetes mellitus, hypertension, and coronary artery disease, and he is currently taking medication for a sinus infection. The client is found by the nurse on the floor next to his bed.

1. Which of the following actions should the nurse take first?

> A. Check the client's blood glucose.
> **B. Assess the patency of his airway.**
> C. Check for a carotid pulse.
> D. Note the depth and rate of his respirations.

> **Using the ABCs (airway, breathing, circulation) of CPR, the nurse should first check the patency of the airway.**

2. Number the following steps in the correct order to reflect the proper performance of CPR for this adult client.

Position client.	3
Perform ventilations.	6
Open airway.	4
Start compressions.	8
Check for breathing.	5
Check for spontaneous pulse.	9
Check for unresponsiveness.	1
Call for help.	2
Check circulation (carotid pulse/signs of circulation).	7

3. **True or False:** ACLS can be performed by average citizens.

> **False: ACLS duties may be performed only by specially trained and certified individuals. These individuals include physicians, nurses, and paramedics.**

4. **True or False:** The American Heart Association provides the guidelines for BLS and ACLS.

True

5. **True or False:** Documentation is not an important duty for the nurse during a cardiac arrest.

False: Documentation is extremely important during any emergency situation. Details are often difficult to accurately recall following an emergency.

6. For each of the following dysrhythmias, identify the appropriate interventions.

Dysrhythmia	Interventions
1. VF or pulseless VT	A, B, C, F, G, H
2. Pulseless Electrical Activity (PEA)	A, B, C, D, E, F, H
3. Asystole	A, B, C, E, F, H

Interventions:

A. Perform CPR.

B. Administer epinephrine 1 mg IV push every 3 to 5 min.

C. Obtain IV access.

D. Consider the 5 H's and 5 T's.

E. Administer atropine 1 mg IV every 3 to 5 min (max total dose 0.04 mg/kg).

F. Defibrillate up to three times:

- Defibrillate: 200 joules.
- Defibrillate: 300 joules.
- Defibrillate: 360 joules.

G. Consider administering:

- Amiodarone.
- Lidocaine.
- Magnesium sulfate.
- Procainamide.
- Bicarbonate.

H. Provide oxygen.

Unit 2   Nursing Care of Clients with Respiratory Disorders
Section: Diagnostic and Therapeutic Procedures: Respiratory

Chapter 3:   Arterial Blood Gases
Contributor: Lori A. Budd, BS, RN

⟳ NCLEX-PN® Connections:

Learning Objective: Review and apply knowledge within **"Arterial Blood Gases"** in readiness for performance of the following nursing activities as outlined by the NCLEX-PN® test plan:

Δ   Perform/assist with relevant laboratory, diagnostic, and therapeutic procedures within the nursing role, including:

- Preparation of the client for the procedure.

- Reinforcement of client teaching (before and following the procedure).

- Accurate collection of specimens.

- Monitoring procedure results (compare to norms) and appropriate notification of the primary care provider.

- Monitoring the client's response (expected, unexpected adverse response, comparison to baseline) to the procedure.

- Monitoring and taking actions, including reinforcing client teaching, to prevent or minimize the risk of complications.

- Recognizing signs of potential complications and reporting to the primary care provider.

- Recommending changes in the test/procedure as needed based on client findings.

📖 Key Points

Δ   An **arterial blood gas (ABG)** sample reports the status of **oxygenation** and **acid-base balance** of the blood.

Δ   An ABG measures:

- **pH** – the amount of free hydrogen ions in the arterial blood (H^+).

- **PaO$_2$** – the partial pressure of oxygen.

- **PaCO$_2$** – the partial pressure of carbon dioxide.

- **HCO$_3^-$** – the concentration of bicarbonate in arterial blood.

- **SaO$_2$** – percentage of oxygen bound to hemoglobin as compared to the total amount that can be possibly carried.

ABG measure	Normal range
pH	7.35-7.45
PaO$_2$	80-100 mm Hg
PaCO$_2$	35-45 mm Hg
HCO$_3^-$	22-26 mEq/L
SaO$_2$	95-100%

Δ   Blood pH levels may be affected by any number of disease processes (respiratory, endocrine, or neurologic).

Δ   Blood pH levels **below 7.35** reflect **acidosis**, while levels **above 7.45** reflect **alkalosis.**

Δ   ABGs can be obtained by an arterial puncture or through an arterial line.

Key Factors

Δ   These assessments are helpful in monitoring the effectiveness of various treatments (such as acidosis interventions), in guiding oxygen therapy, and in evaluating client responses to weaning from mechanical ventilation.

Nursing Interventions

Δ   Obtaining an Arterial Blood Gas Sample

Arterial Puncture	Arterial Line
• Obtain a heparinized syringe for the sample collection. • Explain and reinforce the procedure with the client. • Perform an Allen's test prior to arterial puncture to verify patent radial and ulnar circulation. The nurse should compress the ulnar and radial arteries simultaneously while instructing the client to form a fist. Then, have the client relax the hand while releasing pressure on the radial artery. The hand should turn pink quickly, indicating patency of the radial artery. Repeat this process for the ulnar artery.	• Verify that the arterial line may be used for specimen collection. • Obtain a heparinized syringe for the sample collection and a standard syringe for waste. • Explain and reinforce the procedure to the client.
• Perform an arterial puncture using surgical aseptic technique and collect a specimen into a heparinized syringe. • Place the collected and capped specimen into a basin of ice and water to preserve pH levels and oxygen pressure. The specimen should be transported to the laboratory immediately.	• Follow specific institutional protocols for collection procedures. • Collect waste and specimen. Place on ice for transport to the laboratory immediately. • Flush the arterial line with the pre-connected flushing system.
• Immediately after an arterial puncture, hold direct pressure over the site for at least 5 min. Pressure must be maintained for at least 20 min if the client is receiving anti-coagulant therapy. Ensure that bleeding has stopped prior to removing direct pressure.	• Assess the arterial waveform upon completion
• Monitor the ABG sampling site for bleeding, loss of pulse, swelling, and changes in temperature and color.	

Δ   **Document** all interventions and client response.

Δ   **Report results** to the provider as soon as they are available.

Δ   **Administer oxygen** as prescribed. Change ventilator settings as ordered or notify a respiratory therapist.

Complications and Nursing Implications

Δ   **Hematoma, arterial occlusion**

- Observe for changes in temperature, swelling, color, loss of pulse, or pain.

- Notify the primary care provider immediately if symptoms persist.

- Apply pressure to the hematoma site.

Δ   **Air embolism**

- Monitor the client for a sudden onset of shortness of breath, decreases in SaO_2 levels, chest pain, anxiety, and air hunger.

- Notify the primary care provider immediately if symptoms occur, administer oxygen therapy, and obtain ABGs. Continue to assess respiratory status for any deterioration.

Meeting the Needs of Older Adults

Δ   Accessing the radial artery for sampling may be more difficult with older adult clients because of impaired peripheral vasculature.

Primary Reference:

Ignatavicius, D. D., & Workman, M. L. (2006). *Medical-surgical nursing* (5th ed.). St. Louis, MO: Saunders.

Additional Resources:

NANDA International (2004). *NANDA nursing diagnoses: Definitions and classification 2005-2006.* Philadelphia: NANDA.

Williams, L. S. & Hopper, P. D. (2003). *Understanding medical surgical nursing* (2nd ed.). Philadelphia: F.A. Davis Company.

Chapter 3: Arterial Blood Gases

Application Exercises

1. A nurse performs an ABG sampling at 0930 on a client who has a heparin drip infusing. At what time will it be appropriate for the nurse to discontinue holding pressure on the puncture site?

    A. 0935

    B. 0940

    C. 0945

    D. 0950

2. Which of the following signs and symptoms should be reported to the primary care provider following an arterial puncture?

    A. Slight pain

    B. Small hematoma

    C. Ashen fingers and hand

    D. Scab formation

3. Place the following steps for obtaining an arterial blood gas in the correct order.

	Immediately after an arterial puncture, hold direct pressure over the site for at least 5 min. Pressure must be maintained for at least 20 min if the client is receiving anti-coagulant therapy. Ensure that bleeding has stopped prior to removing direct pressure.
	Document all interventions and client response.
	Explain and reinforce the procedure to the client.
	Place the collected and capped specimen into a basin of ice and water to preserve pH levels and oxygen pressure. The specimen should be transported to the laboratory immediately.
	Perform an Allen's test prior to arterial puncture to verify patent radial and ulnar circulation.
	Perform an arterial puncture using surgical aseptic technique and collect a specimen into a heparinized syringe.
	Obtain a heparinized syringe for the sample collection.
	Report results to the primary care provider as soon as they are available.
	Monitor the ABG sampling site for bleeding, loss of pulse, swelling, and changes in temperature and color.

Chapter 3: Arterial Blood Gases

Application Exercises Answer Key

1. A nurse performs an ABG sampling at 0930 on a client who has a heparin drip infusing. At what time will it be appropriate for the nurse to discontinue holding pressure on the puncture site?

    A. 0935

    B. 0940

    C. 0945

    D. 0950

    Immediately after arterial puncture, hold direct pressure over the site for at least 5 min. Pressure must be maintained for at least 20 min if the client is receiving anti-coagulant therapy. Ensure that bleeding has stopped prior to removing direct pressure.

2. Which of the following signs and symptoms should be reported to the primary care provider following an arterial puncture?

    A. Slight pain

    B. Small hematoma

    C. Ashen fingers and hand

    D. Scab formation

    These are signs of poor tissue perfusion, which suggests a possible arterial occlusion.

3. Place the following steps for obtaining an arterial blood gas in the correct order.

6	Immediately after an arterial puncture, hold direct pressure over the site for at least 5 min. Pressure must be maintained for at least 20 min if the client is receiving anti-coagulant therapy. Ensure that bleeding has stopped prior to removing direct pressure.
8	Document all interventions and client response.
2	Explain and reinforce the procedure to the client.
5	Place the collected and capped specimen into a basin of ice and water to preserve pH levels and oxygen pressure. The specimen should be transported to the laboratory immediately.
3	Perform an Allen's test prior to arterial puncture to verify patent radial and ulnar circulation.
4	Perform an arterial puncture using surgical aseptic technique and collect a specimen into a heparinized syringe.
1	Obtain a heparinized syringe for the sample collection.
9	Report results to the primary care provider as soon as they are available.
7	Monitor the ABG sampling site for bleeding, loss of pulse, swelling, and changes in temperature and color.

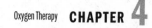

Unit 2
Section:

Nursing Care of Clients with Respiratory Disorders
Diagnostic and Therapeutic Procedures: Respiratory

Chapter 4: Oxygen Therapy
Contributor: Lori A. Budd, BS, RN

NCLEX-PN® Connections:

Learning Objective: Review and apply knowledge within "**Oxygen Therapy**" in readiness for performance of the following nursing activities as outlined by the NCLEX-PN® test plan:

Δ   Recognize the client's need for and correct use of oxygen.

Δ   Perform/assist with relevant laboratory, diagnostic, and therapeutic procedures within the nursing role, including:

   •   Preparation of the client for the procedure.

   •   Reinforcement of client teaching (before and following the procedure).

   •   Accurate collection of specimens.

   •   Monitoring procedure results (compare to norms) and appropriate notification of the primary care provider.

   •   Monitoring the client's response (expected, unexpected adverse response, comparison to baseline) to the procedure.

   •   Monitoring and taking actions, including reinforcing client teaching, to prevent or minimize the risk of complications.

   •   Recognizing signs of potential complications and reporting to the primary care provider.

   •   Recommending changes in the test/procedure as needed based on client findings.

Δ   Monitor therapeutic devices (drainage/irrigating devices, chest tubes), if inserted, for proper functioning.

📖 Key Points

Δ   Oxygen is a **tasteless and colorless gas** that accounts for 21% of atmospheric air.

Δ   Oxygen is used to maintain **adequate cellular oxygenation.** It is used in the treatment of many acute and chronic respiratory problems.

Δ   Adequate cellular oxygenation is usually achieved when the **hemoglobin saturation (SaO_2) is $\geq$ 90%.**

Δ   Oxygen **flow rates** are varied in an attempt to maintain a SaO_2 of 90% by using the **lowest amount to achieve the goal** without the development of complications.

Δ   **Supplemental oxygen** may be delivered by a **variety of methods** that are dependent upon individual client circumstances.

Key Factors

Δ   **Hypoxemia** is a condition of inadequate levels of oxygen in the blood. Hypovolemia, hypoventilation, and interruption of arterial flow can lead to hypoxemia.

Δ   Clinical **Signs and Symptoms** of Hypoxemia

- **Early**
  ◊   Tachypnea
  ◊   Tachycardia
  ◊   Restlessness
  ◊   Pallor of the skin and mucous membranes
  ◊   Elevated blood pressure
  ◊   Symptoms of respiratory distress (use of accessory muscles, nasal flaring, tracheal tugging, adventitious lung sounds)

- **Late**
  ◊   Confusion and stupor
  ◊   Cyanosis of skin and mucous membranes
  ◊   Bradypnea
  ◊   Bradycardia
  ◊   Hypotension
  ◊   Cardiac dysrhythmias

Low-Flow Oxygen Delivery Systems

System	Advantages	Disadvantages
Nasal cannulas • Provide 24 to 40% FiO_2 at a flow rate of 1 to 6 L/min. • Often used for clients who require long-term oxygen therapy.	• Allow for eating, drinking, or speaking. • Often are least frightening for the client.	• Can be easily dislodged. • Cause nasal mucosa drying.
Simple face masks – for increased flow rates • Provide 40 to 60% FiO_2 at a flow rate of 5 to 8 L/min. • Minimum flow rate is 5 L/min to ensure flushing of CO_2 from the mask.	• More comfortable than nasal cannulas for administration of higher amounts of oxygen.	• Can be uncomfortable for clients because they must fit snuggly against the face. • Eating, drinking, and talking are impaired. • Can be frightening, especially for the client with a history of claustrophobia. • If flow rates are not adequate, rebreathing of carbon dioxide can become an issue.
Non-rebreather masks – high concentrations of oxygen • Provide 80 to 95% FiO_2 at a flow rate of 10 to 15 L/min. • The reservoir bag must be at least two-thirds full. • Often used for clients in respiratory distress who may require intubation.	• Prevent the influx of nearly all atmospheric air, so clients inspire nearly 100% oxygen. • Can be used for the administration of other gases.	• Can be uncomfortable for clients because they must fit snuggly against the face. • Eating, drinking, and talking are impaired. • Can be frightening, especially for the client with a history of claustrophobia. • If the oxygen supply is inadequate, suffocation can occur.

High-Flow Systems Oxygen Delivery Systems

System	Advantages	Disadvantages
Venturi masks (Venti masks) deliver the most accurate oxygen concentration.	• Deliver accurate flow, so they are best for clients with chronic lung disease.	• May be uncomfortable. • Interfere with eating, drinking, and talking. • May be frightening.
Aerosol masks, face tents, and tracheostomy collars are used to provide high humidity with oxygen.	• Face tents may be used for clients with facial trauma or burns. • Aerosol masks are often used following extubation, upper airway surgery, or with conditions that produce thick secretions, such as cystic fibrosis.	• May be uncomfortable. • Interfere with eating, drinking, and talking. • May be frightening.

Nursing Interventions

Δ   Assess and monitor the client for **signs and symptoms of hypoxemia** (tachypnea, restlessness, anxiety, pallor of skin and mucous membranes, confusion) that indicate a need for supplemental oxygen therapy.

Δ   Apply the oxygen delivery device as ordered.

Δ   Monitor the client's **SaO$_2$**.

Δ   Place the client in a **high- or semi-Fowler's position** to facilitate breathing.

Δ   Promote good oral hygiene and provide as needed.

Δ   Promote **pulmonary toileting** to include: turning, coughing, deep breathing, and use of incentive spirometry to prevent atelectasis.

Δ   **Promote rest** and decrease environmental stimuli.

Δ   **Provide support** for anxious clients.

Δ   Monitor and **document the client's response** to oxygen therapy.

Δ   Assess and monitor the client's **skin integrity**. Provide moisture and pressure relief devices as needed.

Δ   **Educate** the client about the oxygen-delivery device and the need for it.

Δ   Educate the client and support system to **avoid smoking** and the use of any **open flame** in the presence of the oxygen.

Δ   Monitor for any **deterioration in client status** and **notify the primary care provider**.

Complications and Nursing Implications

Δ   **Oxygen Toxicity**

- **Signs and symptoms** include a non-productive cough, substernal pain, nasal stuffiness, nausea and vomiting, fatigue, headache, sore throat, and hypoventilation.

- Use the lowest level of oxygen necessary to maintain adequate **SaO$_2$**.

- Monitor ABGs and notify the primary care provider if SaO$_2$ levels rise above expected parameters.

- Use of an oxygen mask with continuous positive airway pressure (CPAP), bilevel positive airway pressure (BiPAP), or positive end-expiratory pressure (PEEP) while a client is on a mechanical ventilator may decrease the amount of needed oxygen.

- The oxygen amount should be decreased as soon as client conditions permits.

Δ   **Oxygen-induced hypoventilation** may occur in **clients with chronic obstructive pulmonary disease (COPD)** who have chronic hypoxemia and hypercarbia (elevated levels of CO_2). Clients with COPD rely on low levels of arterial oxygen as their primary drive for breathing. Providing supplemental oxygen at high levels can decrease or eliminate their respiratory drive.

- Monitor for **signs and symptoms** of respiratory depression (decreased respiratory rate, decreased level of consciousness).

- Provide oxygen therapy at the lowest liter flow that will correct hypoxemia.

- If tolerated, use a Venturi mask to delivery precise oxygen levels.

- Monitor the client's respiratory rate and pattern, level of consciousness, and SaO_2 levels.

- Notify the primary care provider of impending respiratory depression.

Meeting the Needs of Older Adults

Δ   **Calcification** of bone and cartilage in the rib cage impairs the ability to ventilate.

Δ   Changes in the **curvature of the spine** decrease thoracic volume and affect ventilation.

Δ   **Loss of alveoli** and the **decreased elasticity of alveoli and bronchioles** lead to problems with ventilation.

Δ   Older adult clients are often at an **increased risk for alterations in skin integrity**.

Primary Reference:

Ignatavicius, D. D., & Workman, M. L. (2006). *Medical-surgical nursing* (5th ed.). St. Louis, MO: Saunders.

Additional Resources:

NANDA International (2004). *NANDA nursing diagnoses: Definitions and classification 2005-2006*. Philadelphia: NANDA.

Taylor, C., Lillis, C., & LeMone, P. (2005). *Fundamentals of nursing: The art and science of nursing care* (5th ed.). Philadelphia: Lippincott Williams & Wilkins.

Chapter 4: Oxygen Therapy

Application Exercises

1. Which of the following is the most appropriate flow rate setting for a client receiving supplemental oxygen by nasal cannula?

        A. 2 to 4 L/min

        B. 5 to 8 L/min

        C. 10 to 12 L/min

        D. 13 to 15 L/min

2. Which of the following is a late sign of hypoxemia?

        A. Tachycardia

        B. Stupor

        C. Tachypnea

        D. Restlessness

3. Which of the following are symptoms of oxygen toxicity? (Check all that apply.)

      _____   Hypoventilation

      _____   Nausea and vomiting

      _____   Report of sore throat

      _____   Restlessness

      _____   Tachycardia

      _____   Headache

      _____   Confusion and stupor

4. Which of the following application devices is most appropriate for a client with a history of claustrophobia?

        A. Nasal cannula

        B. Simple mask

        C. Non-rebreather mask

        D. Partial rebreather mask

Chapter 4: Oxygen Therapy

Application Exercises Answer Key

1. Which of the following is the most appropriate flow rate setting for a client receiving supplemental oxygen by nasal cannula?

    A. **2 to 4 L/min**
    B. 5 to 8 L/min
    C. 10 to 12 L/min
    D. 13 to 15 L/min

Flow rates should not exceed 6 L/min for clients receiving supplemental oxygen by nasal cannula. 5 to 8 L/min is an appropriate flow rate for a client on a simple face mask. 10 to 12 L/min and 13 to 15 L/min are appropriate flow rates for a client on a non-rebreather mask.

2. Which of the following is a late sign of hypoxemia?

    A. Tachycardia
    B. Stupor
    C. Tachypnea
    D. Restlessness

Neurologic changes are late-developing signs of hypoxemia.

3. Which of the following are symptoms of oxygen toxicity? (Check all that apply.)

_x_	Hypoventilation
_x_	Nausea and vomiting
_x_	Report of sore throat
___	Restlessness
___	Tachycardia
_x_	Headache
___	Confusion and stupor

4. Which of the following application devices is most appropriate for a client with a history of claustrophobia?

       A. Nasal cannula

       B. Simple mask

       C. Non-rebreather mask

       D. Partial rebreather mask

A nasal cannula is the only device listed that does not cover the face and is therefore less frightening for clients who are claustrophobic.

Unit 2

Section:

Nursing Care of Clients with Respiratory Disorders

Diagnostic and Therapeutic Procedures: Respiratory

Chapter 5:   Suctioning

Contributor: Lori A. Budd, BS, RN

NCLEX-PN® Connections:

Learning Objective: Review and apply knowledge within "**Suctioning**" in readiness for performance of the following nursing activities as outlined by the NCLEX-PN® test plan:

Δ   Recognize the client's need for suctioning.

Δ   Intervene (suction) to improve the client's respiratory status.

Δ   Perform/assist with relevant laboratory, diagnostic, and therapeutic procedures within the nursing role, including:

- Preparation of the client for the procedure.

- Reinforcement of client teaching (before and following the procedure).

- Accurate collection of specimens.

- Monitoring procedure results (compare to norms) and appropriate notification of the primary care provider.

- Monitoring the client's response (expected, unexpected adverse response, comparison to baseline) to the procedure.

- Monitoring and taking actions, including reinforcing client teaching, to prevent or minimize the risk of complications.

- Recognizing signs of potential complications and reporting to the primary care provider.

- Recommending changes in the test/procedure as needed based on client findings.

Δ   Monitor therapeutic devices (drainage/irrigating devices, chest tubes), if inserted, for proper functioning.

Key Points

Δ   Suctioning can be accomplished **orally, nasally, or endotracheally**.

Δ   **Surgical aseptic technique** must be maintained when performing any form of **tracheal suctioning** to avoid bacterial contamination of the airway.

Δ   Suctioning should **never** be performed for **more than 15 seconds at a time**. Suctioning for longer periods of time may induce **hypoxemia** and stimulate a **vagal response**. Stimulation of the vagus nerve can occur through irritation of the larynx or trachea and results in hypotension and bradycardia.

Key Factors

Δ   Indications for suctioning include: early signs of hypoxemia (restlessness, tachypnea, tachycardia), decreased SaO_2 levels, adventitious breath sounds, visualization of secretions, cyanosis, absence of spontaneous cough.

Δ   **Mucosal secretion** buildup or aspiration of **emesis** can cause a client's airway to become obstructed or reduced.

Δ   An **effective cough** is necessary to **maintain airway patency**. Clients without an effective cough are at risk of airway compromise from secretions or emesis.

Δ   **Clients at risk** for developing airway compromise include: infants, clients with neuromuscular disorders, clients who are quadriplegic, and clients with cystic fibrosis.

Δ   Whenever possible, the client should be encouraged to cough. **Coughing is more effective than artificial suctioning** at moving secretions into the upper trachea or laryngopharynx.

Therapeutic Procedures and Nursing Interventions

Δ   If suctioning is indicated, it is best to usually **begin with oropharyngeal suctioning** since it is better tolerated by clients.

Δ   **Preparation for All Types of Suctioning**

   •   Explain the procedure to ALL clients, conscious or unconscious.

   •   Wear necessary **protective clothing**.

   •   **Encourage** the client to **cough** prior to suctioning to aid with expectoration.

   •   Use **surgical aseptic technique** when **opening suction catheter kits**.

   •   Medical aseptic technique can be used to suction the mouth (oropharyngeal), whereas surgical aseptic technique must be used for all other types of suctioning.

   •   Place a sterile drape or towel on the client's chest.

- Open a sterile basin and fill with approximately 100 mL of sterile water or normal saline.

- Connect suction tubing to wall canister.

- Set suction pressure at 80 to 120 mm Hg.

- **Test the suction setup** by aspirating sterile water/normal saline from the cup. If the unit is operating properly, continue with the procedure.

- Limit each suction attempt to **no longer than 10 to 15 seconds** to avoid hypoxemia and the vagal response. Limit suctioning to two to three attempts.

- Once suctioning is complete, **clear the suction tubing** by aspirating sterile water/normal saline solution.

Δ   **Oropharyngeal Suctioning**

- **Encourage** the client to **deep breathe and cough** in an attempt to clear the secretions without artificial suction.

- If secretions remain, continue with the procedure.

- Place the client in **semi- or high-Fowler's position** for suctioning, if possible.

- Oropharyngeal suctioning is most often performed using a Yankauer or tonsil-tipped rigid suction catheter.

- Insert the catheter into the client's mouth.

- **Apply suction** and move the catheter around the mouth, gumline, and pharynx.

- Monitor the client's **SaO_2 level**.

- Clear the catheter and tubing.

- Repeat as needed.

- Replace oxygen mask, if applicable.

- Store the catheter in a clean, dry place for reuse.

- Allow the client to perform own suction if possible.

Δ   **Nasopharyngeal and Nasotracheal Suctioning**

- Suctioning is performed with a **flexible catheter**.

- **Catheter size** is based upon the diameter of the client's nostrils and the thickness of the secretions.

- **Hyperoxygenate** the client during equipment preparation with 100% FiO_2.

- Lubricate the distal 8 cm of the suction catheter with **water-soluble lubricant**.

- Remove the oxygen delivery device with the nondominant hand, if applicable.

- **Insert** the catheter into the nare **during inhalation.**

- Do not apply suction while inserting the catheter.

- **Follow the natural course of the nare** and slightly slant the catheter downward as you advance it.

- Advance the catheter the approximate distance from nose tip to base of earlobe.

- **Intermittent suction** is only applied during catheter withdrawal, lasting no longer than 10 to 15 seconds at a time. Suction is performed by covering and releasing the suction port with the thumb while concurrently withdrawing the catheter, rotating it between the thumb and forefinger.

- Clear catheter and tubing.

- Allow the client time for recovery between sessions, 20 to 30 seconds. Hyperoxygenate the client before each suctioning pass.

- Repeat as necessary.

- **Document** client response.

- Do not reuse the suction catheter.

Δ   **Endotracheal Suctioning (ETS)**

- ETS is performed through a tracheostomy or endotracheal tube.

- This procedure may require an assistant.

- **Sterility must be maintained** during endotracheal suctioning.

- The outer diameter of the suction catheter should be less than ½ the internal diameter of the endotracheal tube.

- **Hyperoxygenate** the client utilizing a bag-valve-mask (BVM) or specialized ventilator function with 100% FiO_2.

- Immediately after the BVM or ventilator is removed from the tracheostomy or endotracheal tube, **insert the catheter into the lumen of the airway. Advance until resistance is met.** The catheter should reach the level of the carina (location of bifurcation into the main stem bronchi).

- **Intermittent suction** is only applied during catheter withdrawal, lasting no longer than 10 to 15 seconds at a time. Suction is performed by covering and releasing the suction port with the thumb while concurrently withdrawing the catheter, rotating it between the thumb and forefinger.

- **Reattach the BVM or ventilator** and supply the client with 100% inspired oxygen.

- Clear the catheter and tubing.

- Allow time for client recovery between sessions.

- Repeat as necessary.

- Many mechanical ventilators have **in-line suction devices**. This may eliminate the need for an assistant. Follow institution protocols for these systems. Always maintain surgical aseptic technique.

Complications and Nursing Implications

Δ **Hypoxemia**

- Limit each suction attempt to **no longer than 10 to 15 seconds.**

- Limit suctioning to two to three attempts.

- Allow client time for recovery between sessions, 20 to 30 seconds.

- Hyperoxygenate the client before each suctioning pass.

Δ **Anxiety**

- Explain the procedure to all clients prior to suctioning.

- Provide reassurance before, during, and after the procedure.

- Maintain a calm manner.

Meeting the Needs of Older Adults

Δ Older adult clients are at a greater risk of developing hypoxemia than younger clients. Suctioning times may need to be decreased in older adult clients.

Δ Older adult clients have a greater incidence of obstructive diseases that cause copious amounts of thick secretions.

Δ Older adult clients often have diminished immunity and are at a greater risk of developing infections. The nurse must ensure that medical and surgical aseptic techniques are rigidly maintained.

Primary Reference:

Ignatavicius, D. D., & Workman, M. L. (2006). *Medical-surgical nursing* (5th ed.). St. Louis, MO: Saunders.

Additional Resources:

deWit, S. C. (2005). *Fundamental concepts and skills for nursing* (2nd ed.). Philadelphia: Saunders.

NANDA International (2004). *NANDA nursing diagnoses: Definitions and classification 2005-2006*. Philadelphia: NANDA.

Potter, P.A., & Perry, A.G., (2005). *Fundamentals of nursing* (6th ed.) St. Louis: MO: Mosby.

Chapter 5: Suctioning

Application Exercises

1. Which of the following are indications for suctioning a client? (Check all that apply.)

_____ Spontaneous cough

_____ Cyanosis

_____ $SaO_2 > 95\%$

_____ Tachypnea

_____ Visualization of secretions

2. Which of the following is the most effective method for clearing secretions in the airway?

A. Endotracheal suction

B. Oropharyngeal suction

C. Deep breathing and coughing

D. Nasopharyngeal suction

3. Airway depth for oropharyngeal suctioning is measured by

A. determining the distance from the nares to the occipital condyle.

B. determining the distance from the corner of the mouth to the earlobe.

C. determining the distance from the nares to the earlobe.

D. inserting the catheter until resistance is met.

Scenario: A nurse is caring for a 36-year-old male client diagnosed with pneumonia who is currently receiving mechanical ventilation. Initial assessment reveals crackles bilaterally and an SaO_2 of 92%. The client is coughing vigorously.

4. The nurse prepares to perform endotracheal suctioning. Which of the following are appropriate guidelines? (Check all that apply.)

_____ Set wall suction at 150 mm Hg to ensure adequate suction.

_____ Apply intermittent suction while inserting and withdrawing the catheter.

_____ Provide hyperoxygenation to the client with 100% FiO_2 before suctioning.

_____ Clear the catheter and tubing and save for later use.

_____ Maintain surgical aseptic technique.

5. What client findings indicate improved oxygenation as a result of suctioning?

6. **True or False:** It is not necessary to educate unconscious clients when preparing to suction them.

Chapter 5: Suctioning

Application Exercises Answer Key

1. Which of the following are indications for suctioning a client? (Check all that apply.)

	Spontaneous cough
x	Cyanosis
	SaO$_2$ > 95%
x	Tachypnea
x	Visualization of secretions

    Cyanosis, tachypnea, and visualization of secretions are signs of respiratory distress and are indications of the need to suction the client. Spontaneous cough indicates the client's ability to clear secretions. SaO$_2$ > 95% indicates adequate oxygenation.

2. Which of the following is the most effective method for clearing secretions in the airway?

    A. Endotracheal suction

    B. Oropharyngeal suction

    C. Deep breathing and coughing

    D. Nasopharyngeal suction

3. Airway depth for oropharyngeal suctioning is measured by

    A. determining the distance from the nares to the occipital condyle.

    B. determining the distance from the corner of the mouth to the earlobe.

    C. determining the distance from the nares to the earlobe.

    D. inserting the catheter until resistance is met.

Scenario: A nurse is caring for a 36-year-old male client diagnosed with pneumonia who is currently receiving mechanical ventilation. Initial assessment reveals crackles bilaterally and an SaO_2 of 92%. The client is coughing vigorously.

4. The nurse prepares to perform endotracheal suctioning. Which of the following are appropriate guidelines? (Check all that apply.)

_____	Set wall suction at 150 mm Hg to ensure adequate suction.
_____	Apply intermittent suction while inserting and withdrawing the catheter.
__x__	Provide hyperoxygenation to the client with 100% FiO_2 before suctioning.
_____	Clear the catheter and tubing and save for later use.
__x__	Maintain surgical aseptic technique.

Providing hyperoxygenation prior to suctioning the client minimizes the risk of hypoxia. Endotracheal suctioning requires surgical aseptic technique to prevent contamination of the respiratory tract. Suction pressure should be at 80 mm Hg. Intermittent suction is applied only when the catheter is withdrawn. A sterile catheter is required for each suctioning attempt.

5. What client findings indicate improved oxygenation as a result of suctioning?

SaO_2 > 95%

Decrease or absence of crackles

Cessation of coughing

Decrease in client anxiety

6. **True or False:** It is not necessary to educate unconscious clients when preparing to suction them.

False: This procedure should be explained to ALL clients. Clients with an altered mental status or cognitive impairment are still able to experience environmental stimuli, and they experience anxiety during procedures.

Unit 2 — Nursing Care of Clients with Respiratory Disorders

Section: Diagnostic and Therapeutic Procedures: Respiratory

Chapter 6:   Bronchoscopy

Contributor: Sharon Kumm, MN, MS, RN, CCRN

⟳ NCLEX-PN® Connections:

Learning Objective: Review and apply knowledge within "**Bronchoscopy**" in readiness for performance of the following nursing activities as outlined by the NCLEX-PN® test plan:

Δ Perform/assist with relevant laboratory, diagnostic, and therapeutic procedures within the nursing role, including:

- Preparation of the client for the procedure.

- Reinforcement of client teaching (before and following the procedure).

- Accurate collection of specimens.

- Monitoring procedure results (compare to norms) and appropriate notification of the primary care provider.

- Monitoring the client's response (expected, unexpected adverse response, comparison to baseline) to the procedure.

- Monitoring and taking actions, including reinforcing client teaching, to prevent or minimize the risk of complications.

- Recognizing signs of potential complications and reporting to the primary care provider.

- Recommending changes in the test/procedure as needed based on client findings.

Δ Recognize the client's recovery from anesthesia, if used.

Δ Monitor therapeutic devices (drainage/irrigating devices, chest tubes), if inserted, for proper functioning.

Key Points

Δ   Bronchoscopy permits visualization of **the larynx, trachea, and bronchi** via an endoscope.

Δ   Bronchoscopy can be performed as an outpatient procedure, in a surgical suite under general anesthesia, or at the bedside under local anesthesia and conscious sedation.

Δ   Bronchoscopy can also be performed on clients who are receiving **mechanical ventilation** by inserting the scope through the endotracheal tube.

Key Factors

Δ   **Diagnostic indications for a bronchoscopy**

- Visualization of abnormalities such as tumors, inflammation, and strictures.

- Biopsy of suspicious tissue (lung cancer)

- Aspiration of deep sputum or lung abscesses for culture and sensitivity and/or cytology (pneumonia)

Δ   **Therapeutic indications for a bronchoscopy**

- Control of bronchial bleeding

- Removal of aspirated foreign bodies

- Removal of mucous plugs

- Endobronchial brachytherapy

- Laser treatment of neoplastic obstruction

Δ   Clients undergoing a **bronchoscopy with biopsy** have additional risks for **bleeding** and/or **perforation**.

Δ   **Contraindications for a bronchoscopy**

- Severe tracheal stenosis

Nursing Interventions

Δ   **Prior to the Procedure**

- Determine if the client/family/significant other understands the relevant information prior to the procedure. **Provide education as needed**.

- **Assess for allergies** to anesthetic agents or routine use of anticoagulants.

- Ensure that **a consent form** is signed prior to the procedure.

- **Remove** the client's **dentures**, if applicable, prior to the procedure.

- **Maintain NPO status** prior to the procedure as ordered, usually 8 to 12 hr.

- Administer preprocedure medications as prescribed, such as viscous lidocaine or **local anesthetic** throat sprays.

Δ **During the Procedure**

- Position client in a sitting or supine position.

- Administer **medications** as prescribed, such as sedatives, antianxiety agents, and/or atropine to reduce oral secretions.

- Assist in the collecting and labeling of **specimens.** Ensure prompt delivery to the laboratory.

- Monitor the client's **vital signs, respiratory pattern, and oxygenation status** throughout the procedures.

Δ **Following the Procedure**

- Continuously monitor the client's **respirations, blood pressure, pulse oximetry, heart rate,** and **level of consciousness** during the recovery period.

- Assess the client's level of consciousness, **presence of gag reflex, and ability to swallow** prior to resuming oral intake (usually takes about 2 hr).

- Monitor for development of significant fever (mild fever for less than 24 hr is not uncommon), productive cough, significant **hemoptysis indicative of hemorrhage** (a small amount of blood-tinged sputum is expected), hypoxemia.

- **Be prepared to intervene** for unexpected responses (for example, aspiration, laryngospasm).

- Provide oral hygiene.

- Encourage the client to limit or eliminate activities that may irritate the airway, such as talking, coughing, and smoking.

- Evaluate and document the client's response to the procedure (stable vital signs, return of gag reflex)

- Provide/reinforce teaching to clients before discharge.

  ◊ Instruct clients to **notify primary care provider** for:

    ° Hoarseness, wheezing, or stridor.

    ° Coughing up of more than a little blood-tinged sputum.

    ° Shortness of breath or difficulty getting breath.

    ° Fever beyond 24 hr.

- Instruct clients that **gargling with salt water or use of throat lozenges** may provide comfort.

- Inform clients of expected length of time for biopsy and culture reports.

Complications and Nursing Implications

Δ **Laryngospasm**

- Continuously monitor for signs of **respiratory distress.**

- **Maintain patent airway** by positioning the client or inserting an oral or nasopharyngeal airway as appropriate.

- Administer **oxygen therapy** as prescribed. Humidification can decrease the likelihood of laryngeal edema.

Δ **Aspiration**

- **Prevent** aspiration by **withholding oral fluids or food until gag reflex returns** (usually 2 hr).

- Perform **suctioning** as needed.

Meeting the Needs of Older Adults

Δ **Sedation** given to older adult clients with respiratory insufficiency may precipitate respiratory arrest.

Δ Allow adequate time for the **cough and gag reflex** to return prior to resuming oral intake. The cough reflex may be slower to return in older adult clients receiving local anesthesia due to impaired laryngeal reflex.

Δ Encourage **coughing and deep breathing** every 2 hr. There is an increased risk of respiratory infection and pneumonia in older adult clients due to decreased cough effectiveness and decreased secretion clearance. Respiratory infections may be more severe and last longer in older adult clients.

Δ Assess the client's **level of consciousness** while recognizing that older adult clients may develop confusion or lethargy due to the effects of medications given during the bronchoscopy.

Primary Reference:

Ignatavicius, D. D., & Workman, M. L. (2006). *Medical-surgical nursing* (5th ed.). St. Louis, MO: Saunders.

Additional Resources:

NANDA International (2004). *NANDA nursing diagnoses: Definitions and classification 2005-2006.* Philadelphia: NANDA.

Potter, P. A., & Perry, A. G. (2005). *Fundamentals of nursing* (6th ed.). St. Louis, MO: Mosby.

Chapter 6: Bronchoscopy

Application Exercises

1. List four indications for a therapeutic bronchoscopy.

2. A nurse is preparing a client for a bronchoscopy. What should the nurse assess?

3. A client is to receive conscious sedation during a bronchoscopy. What equipment should the nurse make sure is present?

4. A client has just undergone a bronchoscopy. The client is sleepy and requests some water to drink. What assessments should the nurse perform to determine if the client can have a drink?

5. A nurse is caring for a client following a bronchoscopy. Which of the following client findings should the nurse report to the primary care provider immediately?

   A. Blood-tinged sputum

   B. Dry nonproductive cough

   C. Fever of 37.2° C (99° F)

   D. Bronchospasm

6. In caring for a client immediately following a bronchoscopy, the nurse should take which of the following actions? (Check all that apply.)

   _____ Encourage additional fluids for the next 24 hr.

   _____ Ensure the return of the gag reflex prior to offering fluids or foods.

   _____ Monitor vital signs and pulse oximetry every 15 min.

   _____ Notify the primary care provider of any observed complications.

   _____ Assess breath sounds.

7. Which of the actions identified in question 6 can be delegated by the primary nurse to assistive personnel?

Chapter 6: Bronchoscopy

Application Exercises Answer Key

1. List four indications for a therapeutic bronchoscopy.

   Diagnostic indications for a bronchoscopy

   > **Visualization of abnormalities such as tumors, inflammation, and strictures.**

   > **Biopsy of suspicious tissue (lung cancer)**

   > **Aspiration of deep sputum or lung abscesses for culture and sensitivity and/or cytology (pneumonia)**

   Therapeutic indications for a bronchoscopy

   > **Control of bronchial bleeding**

   > **Removal of aspirated foreign bodies**

   > **Removal of mucous plugs**

   > **Endobronchial brachytherapy**

   > **Laser treatment of neoplastic obstruction**

2. A nurse is preparing a client for a bronchoscopy. What should the nurse assess?

   The client/family/significant other has adequate information and all questions have been answered.

   The permit has been signed.

   The client has remained NPO for prescribed period.

   The client has removed jewelry, contact lenses, and dentures.

   Vital signs, breath sounds, pulse oximetry.

   Presence of allergies.

3. A client is to receive conscious sedation during a bronchoscopy. What equipment should the nurse make sure is present?

   The client will need at least one patent IV, as well as:

   > **Oxygen (face mask, nasal cannula)**

   > **Suctioning equipment**

   > **Emergency medications**

   > **Pulse oximetry**

   > **Cardiac monitor**

4. A client has just undergone a bronchoscopy. The client is sleepy and requests some water to drink. What assessments should the nurse perform to determine if the client can have a drink?

   The nurse should assess the level of consciousness and the presence of gag reflex.

5. A nurse is caring for a client following a bronchoscopy. Which of the following client findings should the nurse report to the primary care provider immediately?

   > A. Blood-tinged sputum
   > B. Dry nonproductive cough
   > C. Fever of 37.2° C (99° F)
   > **D. Bronchospasms**

   Mild fever and a small amount of blood-tinged sputum are expected findings. Bronchospasms pose an airway concern and should be reported to the primary care provider immediately.

6. In caring for a client immediately following a bronchoscopy, the nurse should take which of the following actions? (Check all that apply.)

    ____ Encourage additional fluids for the next 24 hr.

    _x_ Ensure the return of the gag reflex prior to offering fluids or foods.

    _x_ Monitor vital signs and pulse oximetry every 15 min.

    _x_ Notify the primary care provider of any observed complications.

    _x_ Assess breath sounds.

A bronchoscopy does not involve contrast dye; therefore, additional fluids are not necessary.

7. Which of the actions identified in question 6 can be delegated by the primary nurse to assistive personnel?

Monitoring of vital signs and pulse oximetry measurements are tasks that can be delegated to assistive personnel. Assessment of breath sounds, interpretation of vital signs and pulse oximetry measurements, assessment of presence of gag reflex, and notification of primary care provider are responsibilities of the primary nurse.

Unit 2   Nursing Care of Clients with Respiratory Disorders
Section: Diagnostic and Therapeutic Procedures: Respiratory

Chapter 7:   Chest Tube Insertion and Monitoring
Contributor: Sharon Kumm, MN, MS, RN, CCRN

⟳ NCLEX-PN® Connections:

Learning Objective: Review and apply knowledge within "**Chest Tube Insertion and Monitoring**" in readiness for performance of the following nursing activities as outlined by the NCLEX-PN® test plan:

Δ   Provide care for the client with a chest tube drainage device.

Δ   Monitor functioning of the chest tube drainage device.

Δ   Maintain chest tube patency.

Δ   Document the client's response to chest tube treatment.

Δ   Perform/assist with relevant laboratory, diagnostic, and therapeutic procedures within the nursing role, including:

  • Preparation of the client for the procedure.

  • Reinforcement of client teaching (before and following the procedure).

  • Accurate collection of specimens.

  • Monitoring procedure results (compare to norms) and appropriate notification of the primary care provider.

  • Monitoring the client's response (expected, unexpected adverse response, comparison to baseline) to the procedure.

  • Monitoring and taking actions, including reinforcing client teaching, to prevent or minimize the risk of complications.

  • Recognizing signs of potential complications and reporting to the primary care provider.

  • Recommending changes in the test/procedure as needed based on client findings.

Δ   Recognize the client's recovery from anesthesia, if used.

📖 Key Points

Δ   Chest tubes are inserted in the pleural space to **drain fluid, blood, or air; re-establish a negative pressure; facilitate lung expansion; and restore normal intrapleural pressure.**

Δ   Chest tubes can be inserted in the emergency department, at the client's bedside by placing the client in a sitting or lying position, or in the operating room through a thoracotomy incision.

Δ   Types of chest drainage systems:

- **Single chamber systems** have water seal and drainage collection in the same chamber.

- **Two chamber systems** have water seal and collection of drainage in separate chambers, which allows for collection of larger amounts of drainage.

- **Three chamber systems** have water seal, collection of drainage, and suction control in separate chambers.

Δ   **Water seals** are created by adding sterile fluid to a chamber up to the 2 cm line. The water seal allows air to exit from the pleural space on exhalation and prevents air from entering with inhalation.

- To maintain the water seal, the **chamber must be kept upright and below the chest tube insertion site at all times.** The nurse should routinely monitor the water level due to the possibility of evaporation. The nurse should add fluid as needed to maintain the 2 cm water seal.

- **Tidaling** (movement of water level with respiration) **is expected** in the water seal chamber. With spontaneous respirations, the water level will rise with inspiration (increase in negative pressure in lung) and will fall with expiration. With positive pressure mechanical ventilation, the water level will rise with expiration and fall with inspiration.

- **Continuous bubbling is a sign of an air leak.**

- **Cessation of tidaling** in the water seal chamber signals **lung re-expansion or an obstruction** within the system.

Δ   **The height of the water in the suction control chamber determines the amount of suction** transmitted to the pleural space. A suction pressure of -20 cm H_2O is common. The application of suction results in continuous bubbling in the suction chamber. The nurse should monitor the fluid level and add fluid as needed to maintain prescribed level of suctioning.

Δ   Chest tubes are **removed when the lungs have re-expanded** and/or there is no more fluid drainage.

Δ Due to the risk of causing a tension pneumothorax, **chest tubes are only clamped** per a primary care provider order in specific circumstances.

- While assessing for an air leak

- During a drainage system change

- When there is accidental disconnection of drainage tubing

- When there is damage to collection device

- While assessing readiness for tube removal

Δ **Do not strip or milk tubing routinely**; only do so by primary care provider order. Stripping creates a high negative pressure and may damage lung tissue.

Key Factors

Δ **Client indications** for chest tube insertion include:

- **Pneumothorax.**

- **Hemothorax.**

- **Postoperative chest drainage** (thoracotomy procedures, coronary artery bypass graft).

- Pleural effusion.

- Lung abscess.

Δ **Severe thrombocytopenia is a possible contraindication** to chest tube insertion or removal due to the risk for excessive bleeding.

Nursing Interventions

Δ **Prior to the Procedure**

- Verify **consent form** is signed.

- Assess the client's understanding of the procedure and provide education as needed.

- Assess for **allergies** to local anesthetics.

- **Assist the client into the desired position** (supine or semi-Fowler's).

- Prepare the chest drainage system in advance of insertion per protocol (for example, fill the water seal chamber).

- Administer **pain and sedation medications** as prescribed.

- Prep the insertion site with Betadine. Drape insertion site.

Δ   **During the Procedure**

- Assist the provider with insertion of chest tubes, application of a dressing to the insertion site, and set-up of the drainage system.

  ◊ The chest tube tip is positioned up toward the shoulder (pneumothorax) or down toward posterior (hemothorax or pleural effusion).

  ◊ The chest tube is then **sutured to the chest wall** and an **airtight dressing** is placed over the puncture wound.

  ◊ The chest tube is then attached to drainage tubing that leads to a collection device.

  ◊ **Place the chest drainage system below chest level** with tubing coiled on the bed. Ensure that the tubing from the bed to the drainage system is straight to promote drainage by gravity.

Δ   **Throughout the procedure, the nurse should continually monitor vital signs and the client's response to the procedure.**

Δ   **After the Procedure**

- Assess the client's vital signs and respiratory status at least every 4 hr.

- Encourage **coughing** and **deep breathing** every 2 hr.

- Keep the drainage system below chest level, including during ambulation.

- **Monitor chest tube placement and function.**

  ◊ Check the water seal level every 2 hr and add water as needed.

  ◊ **Document the amount and characteristics of drainage** every 8 hr by marking the date, hour, and drainage level on the container at the end of each shift. Report excessive drainage to the primary care provider. Drainage will often increase with position changes or coughing.

  ◊ **Monitor the fluid in the suction control chamber and refill as needed.**

  ◊ Check for expected findings of tidaling in water seal chamber and continuous bubbling in suction chamber.

- Routinely monitor tubing for kinks, occlusions, or loose connections.

- Monitor the chest tube insertion site for redness, pain, infection, and crepitus (air leakage in subcutaneous tissue).

- **Position the client to promote lung expansion.** Place the client in the semi-Fowler's position to evacuate air and in the high-Fowler's position to drain fluid.

- **Administer pain medications** as prescribed.

- Obtain chest x-ray to verify chest tube placement.

- Keep two covered hemostats, a bottle of sterile water, and occlusive dressing visible at bedside at all times.

Δ   **Chest Tube Removal**

- **Provide pain medication** one-half hour before removing chest tubes.

- Assist with **suture removal.**

- Instruct client to take a **deep breath, exhale, and bear down (Valsalva maneuver) or to take a deep breath and hold it** (increases intrathoracic pressure and reduces risk of air emboli) **during chest tube removal.**

- **Apply airtight sterile petroleum jelly gauze dressing.** Secure in place with Elastoplast tape.

- **Obtain chest x-rays as prescribed.** This is done to verify continued resolution of the pneumothorax, hemothorax, or pleural effusion.

- Monitor the client for **excessive wound drainage, signs of infection, or recurrent pneumothorax.**

Complications and Nursing Implications

Δ   **Air Leaks**

- Prevention: All connections should be taped. Check connections regularly. Protect connections from accidental disconnection.

- Monitor water seal chamber for continuous bubbling (air leak finding). If observed, locate source of air leak and intervene accordingly (tighten connection, replace drainage system).

  ◊   Check all connections

  ◊   Cross clamp close to client's chest. If bubbling stops, the leak is at insertion site or within thorax. If bubbling doesn't stop, methodically move clamps down the drainage tubing toward the collection device, moving one clamp at a time. When the bubbling stops, the leak is within the section of tubing or at the connection distal to the clamp.

Δ   **Accidental disconnection, system breakage, or removal**

- **If the tubing separates**, the client is instructed to exhale as much as possible and to cough to remove as much air as possible from the pleural space. The nurse cleanses the tips and reconnects the tubing.

- **If the chest tube drainage system breaks**, the nurse immerses the end of the tube in sterile water to restore the water seal.

- If a **chest tube** is **accidentally removed**, an occlusive dressing taped on only three sides should be immediately placed over the insertion site. This allows air to escape and reduces risk for development of a tension pneumothorax.

Δ   Tension pneumothorax

- **Sucking chest wounds, prolonged clamping** of the tubing, **kinks** in the tubing, or **obstruction** may cause a tension pneumothorax.

Meeting the Needs of Older Adults

Δ   Poor oxygenation can quickly lead to serious consequences in an older adult because many have decreased pulmonary reserves.

Δ   The clinical presentation of pneumothorax is similar to the older adult with congestive heart failure: dyspnea, distended neck veins, pallor with poor circulatory perfusion, and coughing. The distinguishing characteristic of pneumothorax and hemothorax from heart failure is a rapid deterioration in respiratory status.

Δ   Changes in fat deposition in many older adults may make it difficult for the provider to identify the landmarks for insertion of the chest tube.

Primary Reference:

Ignatavicius, D. D., & Workman, M. L. (2006). *Medical-surgical nursing* (5th ed.). St. Louis, MO: Saunders.

Additional Resources:

LeMone, P. & Burke, K. (2004). *Medical-surgical nursing: Critical thinking in client care* (3rd ed.). Upper Saddle River, NJ: Prentice-Hall.

NANDA International (2004). *NANDA nursing diagnoses: Definitions and classification 2005-2006.* Philadelphia: NANDA.

Potter, P. A., & Perry, A. G. (2005). *Fundamentals of nursing* (6th ed.). St. Louis, MO: Mosby.

Chapter 7: Chest Tube Insertion and Monitoring

Application Exercises

Scenario: A nurse is preparing to receive a client who has had a chest tube placed.

1. What equipment should the nurse make sure is in the room?

2. Describe actions to take if the connecting tubing is disconnected.

3. A nurse is assessing the functioning of a chest drainage system. Which of the following are expected client findings? (Check all that apply.)

    ___ Continuous bubbling in the water seal chamber

    ___ Gentle constant bubbling in the suction control chamber

    ___ Rise and fall in the level of water in the water seal chamber with inspiration and expiration

    ___ Exposed sutures without dressing

    ___ Drainage system is upright at chest level

4. A nurse is assisting a primary care provider with the removal of a chest tube. The nurse should instruct the client to

    A. lie on his left side during removal.

    B. hold his breath.

    C. inhale deeply during removal.

    D. perform Valsalva maneuver during removal.

Chapter 7: Chest Tube Insertion and Monitoring

Application Exercises Answer Key

Scenario: A nurse is preparing to receive a client who has had a chest tube placed.

1. What equipment should the nurse make sure is in the room?

   Oxygen

   Sterile water: If the tubing becomes disconnected, the end connected to the client can be placed in water to restore the water seal.

   Covered hemostat clamps: Used to check for air leaks.

   Occlusive dressing

   Suction source

2. Describe actions to take if the connecting tubing is disconnected.

   Place the tubing connected to the client into sterile water to restore the water seal.

   Cleanse ends of the tubing and reconnect.

   Tape or clamp all connections.

   Assess the client's respiratory status.

   Assess that the system is intact – no air leaks.

   Document actions taken and the client's response to the event.

   Notify the primary care provider.

3. A nurse is assessing the functioning of a chest drainage system. Which of the following are expected client findings? (Check all that apply.)

    ___ Continuous bubbling in the water seal chamber

    _x_ Gentle constant bubbling in the suction control chamber

    _x_ Rise and fall in the level of water in the water seal chamber with inspiration and expiration

    _x_ Exposed sutures without dressing

    ___ Drainage system is upright at chest level

Continuous bubbling in the water seal chamber indicates an air leak. The insertion site is covered with an airtight dressing. The drainage system should be maintained upright and below chest level.

4. A nurse is assisting a primary care provider with removal of a chest tube. The nurse should instruct the client to

    A. lie on his left side during removal.

    B. hold his breath.

    C. inhale deeply during removal.

    D. perform Valsalva maneuver during removal.

The client should be instructed to take a deep breath, exhale, and bear down (Valsalva maneuver) or to take a deep breath and hold it during tube removal. An airtight dressing is applied following removal.

Unit 2   **Nursing Care of Clients with Respiratory Disorders**

Section: Diagnostic and Therapeutic Procedures: Respiratory

Chapter 8:   Thoracentesis

Contributor: Sharon Kumm, MN, MS, RN, CCRN

NCLEX-PN® Connections

Learning Objective: Review and apply knowledge within "**Thoracentesis**" in readiness for performance of the following nursing activities as outlined by the NCLEX-PN® test plan:

Δ   Perform/assist with relevant laboratory, diagnostic, and therapeutic procedures within the nursing role, including:

- Preparation of the client for the procedure.

- Reinforcement of client teaching (before and following the procedure).

- Accurate collection of specimens.

- Monitoring procedure results (compare to norms) and appropriate notification of the primary care provider.

- Monitoring the client's response (expected, unexpected adverse response, comparison to baseline) to the procedure.

- Monitoring and taking actions, including client education, to prevent or minimize the risk of complications.

- Recognizing signs of potential complications and reporting to the primary care provider.

- Recommending changes in the test/procedure as needed based on client findings.

Δ   Recognize the client's recovery from anesthesia, if used.

Δ   Monitor therapeutic devices (drainage/irrigating devices, chest tubes), if inserted, for proper functioning.

Key Points

Δ   Thoracentesis is the **surgical perforation of the chest wall and pleural space** with a large bore needle. It is performed to:

- **Obtain specimens for diagnostic evaluation.**

- **Instill medication into the pleural space.**

- **Remove fluid** (effusion) **or air** from the pleural space **for therapeutic relief of pleural pressure.**

Δ   **Large amounts of fluid** in the pleural space **compress lung tissue** and can cause pain, shortness of breath, cough, and other **symptoms of pleural pressure.**

Δ   Thoracentesis is performed under local anesthesia by a physician at the client's bedside, in a procedure room, or in a primary care provider's office.

Δ   **Percussion, auscultation, radiography, or sonography is used to locate the effusion and needle insertion site.**

Δ   **Assessment** of the effusion area may reveal **decreased breath sounds, dull percussion sounds, and decreased chest wall expansion.** Pain may occur due to inflammatory process.

Δ   **Aspirated fluid is analyzed** for general appearance, cell counts, protein and glucose content, the presence of enzymes such as lactate dehydrogenase (LDH) and amylase, abnormal cells, and culture.

Δ   **The amount of fluid removed is limited to 1 L** at a time to prevent cardiovascular collapse.

Δ   **Recurrent pleural effusions** can be **managed by instilling an irritant** into the pleural space **to cause scarring.**

Δ   As an alternative to repeated thoracentesis, **a chest tube may be inserted to permit further drainage of fluid.**

Key Factors

Δ   **Client indications for a thoracentesis include:**

- Transudates (congestive heart failure, cirrhosis, nephritic syndrome).

- Exudates (inflammatory, infectious, neoplastic conditions).

  ◊ **Empyema**

  ◊ **Pneumonia**

- Blunt, crushing or penetrating **chest injuries/trauma** or **invasive thoracic procedures**, such as lung and/or cardiac surgery.

Δ   **Severe thrombocytopenia is a possible contraindication** to thoracentesis due to the risk for excessive bleeding.

Nursing Interventions

Δ **Prior to the Procedure**

- Ensure that **informed consent** has been obtained.

- **Provide additional explanation** to the client and family as indicated.

- Gather all needed supplies.

- Obtain **pre-procedure x-ray** as prescribed to locate pleural effusion and to determine needle insertion site.

- **Position the client sitting upright with arms and shoulders raised and supported** on pillows and/or on an overbed table and with feet and legs well supported.

- Instruct the client to **remain absolutely still** (risk of accidental needle damage) during the procedure **and to not to cough or talk** unless instructed by the primary care provider.

Δ **During the Procedure**

- Assist the primary care provider with the procedure (**strict surgical aseptic technique**).

- Prepare the client for a **feeling of pressure** with needle insertion and fluid removal.

- Monitor the client's **vital signs, skin color, and oxygen saturation** throughout the procedure.

- **Measure and record the amount of fluid removed** from the chest.

- **Label specimens at the bedside** and promptly send to the laboratory.

Δ **Following the Procedure**

- **Apply a dressing** over the puncture site **and position the client on the unaffected side for 1 hr.**

- **Monitor** the client's **vital signs and respiratory status** (respiratory rate and rhythm, breath sounds, oxygenation status) **hourly** for the first several hours after the thoracentesis.

- **Encourage deep breathing** to assist with **lung expansion.**

- Normal activity can usually be resumed after 1 hr if no signs of complications are present.

- Obtain a **post-procedure chest x-ray** (check resolution of effusions, rule out pneumothorax).

- **Provide/reinforce client teaching** regarding **manifestations of recurrent effusion or complications** following a thoracentesis. Instruct the client to **report** increasing **dyspnea**, **cough**, and **hemoptysis** to the primary care provider.

Complications and Nursing Implications

Δ   **Shock**

- Monitor for **hypotension, reflex bradycardia, diaphoresis, faintness** during or following the procedure. If occurs during procedure, slow the rate of fluid removal.

Δ   **Pneumothorax**

- Monitor the client for signs and symptoms of pneumothorax, such as diminished breath sounds.

- Monitor post procedure chest x-ray results.

Δ   **Bleeding.**

- Monitor the client for **coughing** and/or **hemoptysis**.

- Monitor vital signs and laboratory results for **evidence of bleeding** (hypotension, reduced hemoglobin level).

Meeting the Needs of Older Adults

Δ   Poor oxygenation can quickly lead to serious consequences in an older adult client because many have decreased pulmonary reserves.

Δ   Changes in fat deposition in many older adult clients may make it difficult for the provider to identify the landmarks for insertion of the thoracentesis needle.

Primary Reference:

Ignatavicius, D. D., & Workman, M. L. (2006). *Medical-surgical nursing* (5th ed.). St. Louis, MO: Saunders.

Additional Resources:

NANDA International (2004). *NANDA nursing diagnoses: Definitions and classification 2005-2006*. Philadelphia: NANDA.

Potter, P. A., & Perry, A. G. (2005). *Fundamentals of nursing* (6th ed.). St. Louis, MO: Mosby.

Chapter 8: Thoracentesis

Application Exercises

1. What equipment should a nurse ensure is available prior to a thoracentesis?

2. Write an example of a brief nurse's note following a thoracentesis.

3. What complications might occur if a client moves, talks, or coughs during a thoracentesis?

4. Which of the following are causes for concern following a thoracentesis? (Check all that apply.)

_____   Dyspnea
_____   Localized bloody drainage contained on the dressing
_____   Fever
_____   Hypotension
_____   SaO$_2$ of 95%
_____   Soreness around puncture site

Chapter 8: Thoracentesis

Application Exercises Answer Key

1. What equipment should a nurse ensure is available prior to a thoracentesis?

   Oxygen

   Pulse oximeter

   Thoracentesis tray

   Collecting tubing and container

   Sterile container with lid

   Local anesthetic, if not on tray

   Dressing

2. Write an example of a brief nurse's note following a thoracentesis.

   The note should include date, time, amount of fluid removed, specimen sent to laboratory, dressing applied, and client response.

   Example:

   Date and time

   Left lower lobe thoracentesis performed by (name of physician) with client sitting on side of bed, leaning on overbed table. 1 L of purulent fluid removed with specimen sent to lab. Dressing applied. Client reports breathing easier; denies shortness of breath or pain. Vital signs stable, pulse oximetry improved from 90% to 93% after procedure. Oxygen remains at 2 L per nasal cannula. Increased breath sounds noted in left lower lung. Chest x-ray completed.

3. What complications might occur if a client moves, talks, or coughs during a thoracentesis?

   Pneumothorax or intrathoracic bleeding due to inadvertent needle damage.

4. Which of the following are causes for concern following a thoracentesis? (Check all that apply.)

__x__	Dyspnea
_____	Localized bloody drainage contained on the dressing
__x__	Fever
__x__	Hypotension
_____	SaO$_2$ of 95%
_____	Soreness around puncture site

Dyspnea can indicate pneumothorax or reaccumulation of fluid. Fever can indicate infection. Hypotension can indicate intrathoracic bleeding. Localized bloody drainage contained on band-aid/dressing and soreness around puncture site are expected findings. SaO$_2$ of 95% indicates good oxygenation.

Unit 2   Nursing Care of Clients with Respiratory Disorders

Section: Diagnostic and Therapeutic Procedures: Respiratory

Chapter 9:	Tracheostomy

Contributor: Sharon Kumm, MN, MS, RN, CCRN

NCLEX-PN® Connections:

Learning Objective: Review and apply knowledge within **"Tracheostomy"** in readiness for performance of the following nursing activities as outlined by the NCLEX-PN® test plan:

Δ   Perform/assist with relevant laboratory, diagnostic, and therapeutic procedures within the nursing role, including:

- Preparation of the client for the procedure.

- Reinforcement of client teaching (before and following the procedure).

- Accurate collection of specimens.

- Monitoring procedure results (compare to norms) and appropriate notification of the primary care provider.

- Monitoring the client's response (expected, unexpected adverse response, comparison to baseline) to the procedure.

- Monitoring and taking actions, including reinforcing client teaching, to prevent or minimize the risk of complications.

- Recognizing signs of potential complications and reporting to the primary care provider.

- Recommending changes in the test/procedure as needed based on client findings.

Δ   Recognize the client's recovery from anesthesia, if used.

Δ   Monitor therapeutic devices (drainage/irrigating devices, chest tubes), if inserted, for proper functioning.

📖 Key Points

Δ   **Tracheotomy** is a **sterile surgical incision** into the **trachea** for the purpose of **establishing an airway.**

Δ   A tracheotomy can be performed as an **emergency procedure or as a scheduled surgical procedure**; it can be **permanent or temporary.**

Δ   **Tracheostomy** is the **stoma/opening** that results from a tracheotomy and the insertion and maintenance of a cannula.

Δ   A **double lumen tracheostomy** tube has **three major parts:**

- **Outer cannula:**

  ◊   Fits into the stoma and **keeps the airway open.**

  ◊   The **faceplate indicates the size and type of tube** and has small holes on both sides for securing the tube with tracheostomy ties.

- **Inner cannula:**

  ◊   **Fits snugly into the outer cannula** and locks into place.

  ◊   Can be withdrawn for brief periods and **cleaned (reusable) or replaced (disposable).**

- **Obturator:**

  ◊   The obturator can be placed inside the tracheostomy to **ease outer cannula insertion.**

  ◊   It is **removed immediately after outer cannula insertion and is always kept with the client and at the bedside** in case of accidental decannulation.

Δ   **Air flow in and out of a tracheostomy** without air leakage (for example, a cuffed tracheostomy tube) **bypasses the vocal cords** resulting in an **inability to produce sound or speech.**

Δ   Uncuffed tubes and fenestrated tubes that are in place or capped allow the client to speak. Clients with a cuffed tube, who can be off mechanical ventilation and breathe around the tube, can use a special valve to allow for speech. The cuff is deflated and the valve occludes the opening.

Δ   Swallowing is possible with a tracheostomy tube in place; however, laryngeal elevation is affected and it is important to **assess the client's risk for aspiration prior to intake.**

Key Factors

Δ   **Client indications** for a **tracheostomy:**

- Bypass an **upper airway obstruction.**

- **Edema** (anaphylaxis, burns, trauma, head/neck surgery)

- **Facilitate removal of secretions.**

- Permit **long-term mechanical ventilation.**

- Provide **airway reconstruction after laryngeal trauma or laryngeal cancer surgery.**

- Treat **obstructive sleep apnea** refractory to conventional therapy.

- **Permit oral intake and speech** in the client who requires long-term mechanical ventilation.

Δ   **Signs and symptoms** necessitating tracheostomy include:

- Inability to oxygenate through the nasopharynx due to obstruction evidenced by **dyspnea, poor SaO_2, poor arterial blood gas (ABG) values.**

- **Inability to wean from mechanical ventilation** within 2 weeks.

- Sleep apnea not improved by noninvasive mechanical ventilation (CPAP).

Δ   **Advantages of a tracheostomy** as the choice for long-term therapy include:

- **Less risk of long-term damage** to the airway.

- **Increased client comfort** because no tube is present in the mouth.

- **Decreased incidence of pressure ulcers** in the oral cavity and upper airway.

- The client can eat with a tracheostomy because the tube enters lower in the airway.

- Allows the client to talk.

Δ   Types of Tracheostomy Tubes: Description and Selection Factors

Cuffed	Cuffed tracheostomy tubes **protect the lower airway by producing a seal between the upper and lower airway.** A cuffed tube is used for **clients receiving mechanical ventilation.**
Uncuffed	A cuffless tracheostomy tube is **used when the client can protect the airway from aspiration** and in **children under 8 years.**
Single-lumen tube	A long tube used **for clients with long or extra-thick necks.**
Tracheostomy tube with cuff and pilot balloon	Low-pressure, high-volume cuff distributes cuff pressure over large area, **minimizing pressure on tracheal wall.**
Uncuffed fenestrated tracheostomy tube	**Has openings on the surface of the outer cannula that permit air from the lungs to flow over the vocal cords;** allows the client to breathe spontaneously through the larynx, speak, and cough up secretions while the tracheostomy remains in place; often used to **wean the client from a tracheostomy tube** by ensuring that the client can tolerate breathing through his/her natural airway before the entire tube is removed.
Cuffed fenestrated tracheostomy tube	Facilitates mechanical ventilation and speech. Often used for clients with **spinal cord paralysis or neuromuscular disease who do not require ventilation at all times.** When not on the ventilator, the client can have the cuff deflated and the tube capped for speech.
Metal tracheostomy tube	Used for **permanent tracheostomy.** It is a cuffless double-lumen tube and can be cleaned and reused indefinitely.
Talking/speaking tracheostomy tube	Has two pigtail tubings. One tubing connects to the cuff and is used for cuff inflation, and the second connects to an opening just above the cuff. When **the second tubing is connected to a low-flow air source, sufficient air moves up over the vocal cords to permit speech.** The client can then speak, although the cuff is inflated.
Foam-filled cuff	The cuff is filled with plastic foam. Before insertion, the cuff is deflated. After insertion, the cuff is allowed to fill passively with air, the pilot tubing is not capped, and no cuff pressure monitoring is required.

Nursing Interventions

Δ   Assess/Monitor

- Oxygenation and ventilation (**respiratory rate, effort, SaO$_2$**) and vital signs hourly

- Thickness, quantity, odor, and color of **mucous secretions**

- **Stoma and skin surrounding stoma** for signs of inflammation or infection (**redness, swelling, or drainage**)

Δ   Provide adequate **humidification and hydration to thin secretions and decrease risk of mucus plugging.**

Δ   **Maintain surgical aseptic technique when suctioning** to prevent infection.

Δ **Provide the client with an emergency call system**, as well as a call light.

Δ When appropriate, notify staff that the client cannot speak due to the tracheostomy.

Δ **Provide the client with methods to communicate** with staff (paper and pen, chalk board, dry erase board).

Δ **Provide emotional support** to the client and family.

Δ For cuffed tubes, keep pressure below 20 mm Hg to reduce the risk of tracheal necrosis due to prolonged compression of tracheal capillaries.

Δ **Provide tracheostomy care** every 8 hr.

- **Suction the tracheostomy tube**, if necessary, using sterile suctioning supplies.

- **Remove old dressings and excess secretions.**

- **Apply the oxygen source loosely if the client desaturates during the procedure.**

- Use cotton-tipped applicators and gauze pads to clean exposed outer cannula surfaces. Begin with **hydrogen peroxide followed by normal saline.** Clean in **circular motion from stoma site outward.**

- **Using surgical aseptic technique, remove and clean the inner cannula** (use hydrogen peroxide to clean the cannula and sterile saline to rinse it). **Replace the inner cannula if it is disposable.**

- **Clean the stoma site** and then **the tracheostomy plate** with hydrogen peroxide followed by sterile saline.

- Place **split 4 x 4 dressing** around tracheostomy.

- **Change tracheostomy ties if they are soiled.** Secure new ties in place before removing soiled ones to prevent accidental decannulation.

- If a knot is needed, tie a square knot that is visible on the side of the neck. **One or two fingers should be able to be placed between the tie tape and the neck.**

- **Document the type and amount of secretions**, the general **condition of the stoma and surrounding skin**, the **client's response** to the procedure, and any teaching or learning that occurred.

Δ **Change non-disposable tracheostomy tubes** every 6 to 8 weeks or **per protocol.**

Δ **Reposition the client** every 2 hr to **prevent atelectasis and pneumonia.**

Δ **Provide oral hygiene** every 2 hr to maintain mucosal integrity.

Δ Minimize dust in the client's room; do not shake bedding.

Δ   If the client is permitted to eat, **position the client in an upright position and tip the client's chin to chest to enable swallowing.** Assess for aspiration.

Δ   Administer prescribed medications.

- Anti-inflammatory drugs to reduce edema
- Antibiotics as indicated for prophylaxis or infection treatment
- Aerosolized **bronchodilators** to relieve bronchospasm
- **Mucous liquefying agents**, such as guaifenesin

Δ   Provide discharge teaching.

- Tracheostomy care
- Signs and symptoms that the client should immediately report to the primary care provider (signs of infection, copious secretions)

Δ   Consider **referral** of the client to a home healthcare agency and community support groups.

Complications and Nursing Implications

Δ   **Accidental Decannulation**

- Keep the **tracheostomy obturator** and a **spare tracheostomy tube at the bedside**.
- **Call for assistance.**
- Accidental decannulation in the first 72 hr after surgery is an emergency because the tracheostomy tract has not matured and replacement may be difficult.
- After the tracheostomy tract has matured, if decannulation occurs the nurse should immediately **insert the obturator into the tracheostomy tract and insert a new tracheostomy tube around the obturator.**
- If unable to replace the tracheostomy tube, **administer oxygen through the stoma**. If unable to administer oxygen through the stoma, occlude the stoma and administer oxygen through the nose and mouth.

Meeting the Needs of Older Adults

Δ   There is an **increased risk of respiratory infection and pneumonia** in older adult clients due to the **decrease in cough effectiveness and secretion clearance**. Respiratory infections may be more severe and last longer.

Δ   Older adult clients may be **at risk for dehydration** (due to limited mobility, decrease in appetite, medications) **contributing to thick, dried secretions** that can occlude the airways.

Δ   **Maintaining good hydration** in older adult clients, as well as **providing humidification** (as ordered), is important to **reduce the viscosity of secretions**.

Primary Reference:

Ignatavicius, D. D., & Workman, M. L. (2006). *Medical-surgical nursing* (5th ed.). St. Louis, MO: Saunders.

Additional Resources:

LeMone, P. & Burke, K. (2004). *Medical-surgical nursing: Critical thinking in client care* (3rd ed.). Upper Saddle River, NJ: Prentice-Hall.

NANDA International (2004). *NANDA nursing diagnoses: Definitions and classification 2005-2006.* Philadelphia: NANDA.

Potter, P. A., & Perry, A. G. (2005). *Fundamentals of nursing* (6th ed.). St. Louis, MO: Mosby.

Chapter 9: Tracheostomy

Application Exercises

1. What equipment should a nurse make sure is in the room of a client being admitted following a tracheotomy?

2. If a tracheostomy cleaning kit is not available, what equipment should the nurse obtain to perform tracheostomy care?

3. Write a brief nursing note documenting tracheostomy care.

4. A nurse is caring for a client following a tracheotomy 2 days ago. The nurse enters the room and notices that the tracheostomy tube is no longer in place. Describe the actions the nurse should take.

5. Which of the following interventions should be included when caring for a client with a tracheostomy? (Check all that apply.)

   _____ Use medical aseptic technique when performing tracheostomy care.
   _____ Change tracheostomy ties each time tracheostomy care is given.
   _____ Provide the client with materials for non-verbal communication.
   _____ Keep pressure > 20 mm Hg.
   _____ Clean the stoma site with hydrogen peroxide followed by normal saline.

Chapter 9: Tracheostomy

Application Exercises Answer Key

1. What equipment should a nurse make sure is in the room of a client being admitted following a tracheotomy?

   Humidified oxygen

   Pulse oximeter

   Suction equipment and catheters

   Spare tracheostomy tube

   Extra tracheostomy ties

   Normal saline

   Split 4 x 4 dressings

2. If a tracheostomy cleaning kit is not available, what equipment should the nurse obtain to perform tracheostomy care?

   Normal saline

   Hydrogen peroxide

   Sterile container to house normal saline and hydrogen peroxide

   Cotton-tipped applicators

   Tracheostomy ties (if needed to replace)

   4 x 4 gauze for cleaning

   Split 4 x 4 gauze for dressing

   Two containers: one for cleaning, one for rinse

   Suction supplies (if not at bedside)

3. Write a brief nursing note documenting tracheostomy care.

   The note should include date, time, care performed, description of secretions, and the appearance of the stoma.

   Example:

   Date & time: Tracheostomy care performed. Client has productive cough of thick light yellow secretions. Scant, thin, white secretions from stoma. Site cleansed with hydrogen peroxide and normal saline. Sterile dressing applied. Tracheostomy ties changed. Stoma healing well without redness or edema.

4. A nurse is caring for a client following a tracheotomy 2 days ago. The nurse enters the room and notices that the tracheostomy tube is no longer in place. Describe the actions the nurse should take.

   This is a medical emergency. The nurse should:

   Call for assistance.

   Assess respiratory rate and effort, SaO$_2$ color/cyanosis.

   Obtain an obturator and a spare tracheostomy tube from the head of the bed and reinsert, if possible.

   If unable to insert a tracheostomy tube, administer oxygen through the stoma. If unable to administer oxygen through the stoma, occlude the stoma and use a mask or bag-valve-mask to administer through the nose and mouth.

5. Which of the following interventions should be included when caring for a client with a tracheostomy? (Check all that apply.)

_____	Use medical aseptic technique when performing tracheostomy care.
_____	Change tracheostomy ties each time tracheostomy care is given.
_x_	Provide the client with materials for non-verbal communication.
_____	Keep pressure > 20 mm Hg.
_x_	Clean the stoma site with hydrogen peroxide followed by normal saline.

   Use surgical aseptic technique when performing tracheostomy care. Suction pressures should be less than 20 mm Hg. Ties only need to be changed when soiled.

Unit 2   Nursing Care of Clients with Respiratory Disorders
Section: Diagnostic and Therapeutic Procedures: Respiratory

Chapter 10:   Mechanical Ventilation
Contributor: Sharon Kumm, MN, MS, RN, CCRN

NCLEX-PN® Connections:

Learning Objective: Review and apply knowledge within "**Mechanical Ventilation**" in readiness for performance of the following nursing activities as outlined by the NCLEX-PN® test plan:

Δ   Provide care to the client receiving mechanical ventilation.

Δ   Perform/assist with relevant laboratory, diagnostic, and therapeutic procedures within the nursing role, including:

- Preparation of the client for the procedure.

- Reinforcement of client teaching (before and following the procedure).

- Accurate collection of specimens.

- Monitoring procedure results (compare to norms) and appropriate notification of the primary care provider.

- Monitoring the client's response (expected, unexpected adverse response, comparison to baseline) to the procedure.

- Monitoring and taking actions, including reinforcing client teaching, to prevent or minimize the risk of complications.

- Recognizing signs of potential complications and reporting to the primary care provider.

- Recommending changes in the test/procedure as needed based on client findings.

Δ   Recognize the client's recovery from anesthesia, if used.

Δ   Monitor therapeutic devices (drainage/irrigating devices, chest tubes), if inserted, for proper functioning.

📖 Key Points

Δ Mechanical ventilation **provides breathing support until lung function is restored.**

Δ Mechanical ventilation delivers warm (body temperature 37° C), 100% humidified oxygen at **FiO$_2$ levels of 21 to 100%.**

Δ Positive-pressure ventilators **deliver air to lungs under pressure** throughout inspiration and/or expiration to keep alveoli open during inspiration and to prevent alveolar collapse during expiration. Benefits include:

- Forced/enhanced **lung expansion.**

- **Improved gas exchange** (oxygenation)

- **Decreased work of breathing**

Δ Mechanical ventilation can be delivered via:

- An endotracheal tube.

- A tracheostomy tube.

- A nasal or face mask (non-invasive modes such as CPAP, BiPAP).

Δ **Following extubation, monitor the client for signs of respiratory distress** or airway obstruction, such as **ineffective cough, dyspnea,** and **stridor.**

Δ Mechanical ventilators may be **cycled** based on **pressure, volume, time,** or **flow.**

Δ Ventilators have **alarms** to signal that the client is not receiving correct ventilation.

- If the nurse cannot determine the cause of a ventilator dysfunction, the client is disconnected from the ventilator and manually ventilated with an Ambu bag.

- Ventilator **alarms should never be turned off.**

- There are three types of ventilator alarms: **volume, pressure,** and **apnea alarms.**

  ◊ **Volume** (low pressure) **alarms** indicate low exhaled volume due to **disconnection, cuff leak,** and **tube displacement.**

  ◊ **Pressure** (high pressure) **alarms** indicate **excess secretions, client biting** the tubing, **kinks** in the tubing, client **coughing,** pulmonary edema, bronchospasm, and pneumothorax.

  ◊ **Apnea alarms** indicate that the ventilator **does not detect spontaneous respiration** in a preset time period.

Δ   Common Modes of Ventilation

Assist-Control (AC)	**Preset ventilator rate and tidal volume.** The **client** can **initiate breaths;** however, the **ventilator takes over and delivers preset tidal volume.** Hyperventilation can result in respiratory alkalosis. The client may require sedation to decrease respiratory rate.
Synchronized Intermittent Mandatory Ventilation (SIMV)	**Preset ventilator rate and tidal volume.** For **client-initiated breaths, tidal volume depends on the client's effort. Ventilator-initiated breaths are synchronized to reduce competition between the ventilator and the client.** SIMV is used as a regular mode of ventilation and as a weaning mode (rate decreased to allow more spontaneous ventilation). It may increase the work of breathing and respiratory muscle fatigue.
Pressure Support Ventilation (PSV)	**Preset pressure delivered during spontaneous inspiration to reduce work of breathing.** The client controls rate and tidal volume. Often used as a weaning mode. PSV decreases the work of breathing and promotes respiratory muscle conditioning. No ventilator breaths are delivered. PSV does not guarantee minimal minute ventilation. It is often combined with other modes of ventilation (SIMV, AC).
Positive End Expiratory Pressure (PEEP)	**Positive pressure applied at end of expiration to increase functional residual and improve oxygenation by opening collapsed alveoli.** PEEP must be used in conjunction with AC or SIMV; it **cannot be used alone.** PEEP decreases cardiac output and may cause volutrauma (trauma to lung tissue caused by tidal volumes that are too high) and increased intracranial pressure (ICP).
Volume Assured Pressure Support Ventilation (VAPSV)	**Similar to PSV with minimal set tidal volume for each breath.** VAPSV optimizes inspiratory flow, reduces the work of breathing, decreases volutrauma and ensures minimal minute ventilation. VAPSV is used with clients who have severe respiratory disease or those who are difficult to wean.
Independent Lung Ventilation (ILV)	**Double lumen endotracheal tube allows each lung to be ventilated separately.** ILV is used in clients with unilateral lung disease. It requires two ventilators, sedation, and/or neuromuscular blocking agents.
High Frequency Ventilation	**Delivers a small amount of gas at very rapid rates** (60 to 3,000 cycles/min). **High frequency ventilation is used frequently in children.** The client must be **sedated and/or receiving neuromuscular blocking agents.** Breath sounds are difficult to assess.
Inverse Ratio Ventilation (IRV)	**Lengthens inspiratory phase of respiration to maximize oxygenation.** IRV is used for hypoxemia refractory to PEEP. It is **uncomfortable for clients and requires sedation and/or neuromuscular blocking agents.** There is a high risk of volutrauma and decreased cardiac output due to air trapping.

Continuous Positive Airway Pressure (CPAP)	**Positive pressure supplied during spontaneous breaths**. No ventilator breaths are delivered unless they are in conjunction with SIMV. Risks include volutrauma, decreased cardiac output, and increased ICP. CPAP may be invasive or noninvasive. It is often used for **obstructive sleep apnea**.
Bi-level Positive Airway Pressure (BiPAP)	**Positive pressure delivered during spontaneous breaths. Different pressures are delivered for inspiration and expiration**. No spontaneous breaths are delivered. BiPAP is a noninvasive mode.

Δ Clients receiving mechanical ventilation **may require sedation or paralytic agents to prevent competition** between extrinsic and intrinsic breathing and the resulting effects of hyperventilation.

Δ **Weaning** from mechanical ventilation to spontaneous breathing usually involves:

- Increasing periods of spontaneous breathing to increase respiratory muscle strength.

- Use of pressure support to augment inspiration and increase client endurance.

- Monitoring throughout the weaning process for tolerance. Clients are frequently extubated if they can sustain 1 hr of spontaneous breathing.

Key Factors

Δ **Client Indications** for **Mechanical Ventilation**

- **Hypoxemia, hypoventilation with respiratory acidosis**

  ◊ Airway **trauma**

  ◊ **Exacerbation of COPD**

  ◊ **Acute pulmonary edema** due to myocardial infarction, congestive heart failure

  ◊ **Asthma attack**

  ◊ **Head injuries**, stroke, coma

  ◊ **Neurological disorders** (multiple sclerosis, myasthenia gravis, Guillain-Barré syndrome)

  ◊ Obstructive **sleep apnea**

- **Respiratory support** following **surgery** (decrease workload)

- **Respiratory support** while under **general anesthesia** or **heavy sedation**

Nursing Interventions

Δ **Maintain a patent airway.**

- Assess position and integrity of tube.

- Document tube placement in centimeters at the teeth or lips.

- Use two staff members for repositioning and re-securing tube.

- Apply protective barriers (soft wrist restraints) according to hospital protocol to prevent self-extubation.

- Use caution when moving the client.

- Suction oral and tracheal secretions to maintain tube patency.

- Support ventilator tubing to prevent mucosal erosion and displacement.

Δ **Assess respiratory status** every 1 to 2 hr: breath sounds, respiratory effort, spontaneous breaths.

- **Monitor** and **document ventilator settings hourly.**

   ◊ Rate, FiO_2, tidal volume

   ◊ Mode of ventilation

   ◊ Use of adjuncts (PEEP, CPAP)

   ◊ Plateau or peak inspiratory pressure (PIP)

   ◊ Alarm settings

Δ **Suction** tracheal tube to **clear secretions**, as needed. **Reposition** the client to promote **mobility of secretions.**

Δ **Maintain adequate** (but not excessive) **volume in cuff** of endotracheal tube.

- Assess **cuff pressure** at least every 8 hr. Maintain cuff pressure below 20 mm Hg to reduce risk of tracheal necrosis.

- Assess for **air leak** around the cuff (client speaking, air hiss, decreasing SaO_2). Inadequate cuff pressure can result in inadequate oxygenation and/or accidental extubation.

Δ Administer medications as prescribed.

- **Analgesics** – morphine sulfate, fentanyl

- **Sedatives** – propofol (Diprivan), diazepam (Valium), lorazepam (Ativan), midazolam (Versed), haloperidol (Haldol)

- **Neuromuscular blocking agents** – pancuronium bromide, atracurium, vecuronium

- **Ulcer-preventing agents** – famotidine (Pepcid) or lansoprazole (Prevacid)

- **Antibiotics** for established infections

Δ   Provide an alternate **method of communication** (yes/no questions, clipboard, dry erase board, magic slate, picture communication board, lip reading).

Δ   **Reposition the oral endotracheal** tube every 24 hr or according to protocol. Assess for skin breakdown.

Δ   **Provide adequate nutrition.**

   • Assess gastrointestinal functioning every 8 hr.

   • Monitor bowel habits.

   • Administer enteral or parenteral feedings as prescribed.

Δ   Continually monitor the client during the weaning process for signs of weaning intolerance.

   • Respiratory rate greater than 30/min or less than 8/min

   • Blood pressure or heart rate changes more than 20% of baseline

   • SaO_2 less than 90%

   • Dysrhythmias, elevated ST segment

   • Significant decrease in tidal volume

   • Labored respirations, increased use of accessory muscles, diaphoresis

   • Restlessness, anxiety, decreased level of consciousness

Δ   **Suction** the oropharynx and trachea **prior to extubation.**

Complications and Nursing Implications

Δ   **Fluid retention**

   • Due to decreased cardiac output, activation of renin-angiotensin-aldosterone system, and ventilator humidification

   • Monitor the client's intake and output and weight.

Δ   **Oxygen toxicity**

   • Risk higher if prolonged ventilation at a $FiO_2 > 50\%$. Provide minimal amount of oxygen needed.

   • Monitor for signs (fatigue, restlessness, severe dyspnea, tachycardia, tachypnea, crackles, cyanosis).

Δ   **Hemodynamic compromise**

   • Risk of increased thoracic pressure (positive pressure) and resulting decreased venous return

   • Monitor for tachycardia, hypotension, urine output less than or equal to 30 mL/hr, cool clammy extremities, decreased peripheral pulses, and decreased level of consciousness.

Δ   **Risk for Aspiration**

- Keep the head of the bed elevated 30° at all times to decrease the risk of **aspiration.**

- Check residuals every 4 hr if the client is receiving enteral feedings to decrease the risk of aspiration.

Δ   GI ulceration (**stress ulcers**)

- Monitor gastrointestinal drainage and stools for **occult bleeding.**

- Administer **ulcer** prevention medications (Carafate, sucralfate, histame$_2$ blockers) as prescribed.

Meeting the Needs of Older Adults

Δ   Older adult clients have **decreased respiratory muscle strength and chest wall compliance,** making them more susceptible to aspiration, atelectasis, and pulmonary infections. The older adult client will require more frequent position changes to mobilize secretions.

Δ   **Older adult clients have fragile skin and are more prone to skin and mucous membrane breakdown.** Older adult clients have decreased oral secretions. They require frequent, gentle skin and oral care.

Primary Reference:

Ignatavicius, D. D., & Workman, M. L. (2006). *Medical-surgical nursing* (5th ed.). St. Louis, MO: Saunders.

Additional Resources:

NANDA International (2004). *NANDA nursing diagnoses: Definitions and classification 2005-2006.* Philadelphia: NANDA.

Chapter 10: Mechanical Ventilation

Application Exercises

1. Which of the following modes of ventilation can increase conditioning of the respiratory muscles? (Check all that apply.)

    _____ AC – Assist-Control
    _____ SIMV – Synchronized intermittent mandatory ventilation
    _____ CPAP – Continuous positive airway pressure
    _____ PSV – Pressure support ventilation

2. What is the difference between pressure support and positive end expiratory pressure?

3. List three complications of mechanical ventilation and one nursing intervention to prevent each complication.

4. What assessments should the nurse routinely perform for a client receiving mechanical ventilation?

5. The high pressure alarm sounds on the ventilator. What should the nurse assess for?

6. The low pressure/low volume alarm sounds on the ventilator. What should the nurse assess for?

7. Provide a rationale for each of the following nursing interventions.

Nursing Intervention	Rationale
Record level of oral or nasal tubes every 8 hr.	
Provide oral care every 2 hr.	
Measure cuff pressure every 8 hr. Maintain pressure less than 20 mm Hg.	
Keep the head of the bed elevated 30° at all times.	
Continuously monitor oxygen saturation.	
Assess skin integrity around the tube every 4 hr.	
Reposition the client every 2 hr.	
Support ventilator tubing.	

Chapter 10: Mechanical Ventilation

Application Exercises Answer Key

1. Which of the following modes of ventilation can increase conditioning of the respiratory muscles? (Check all that apply.)

_____	AC – Assist-Control
_x_	SIMV – Synchronized intermittent mandatory ventilation
_x_	CPAP – Continuous positive airway pressure
_x_	PSV – Pressure support ventilation

In AC mode, the ventilator takes over the work of breathing. Any breaths initiated by the client are augmented by the ventilator at full tidal volume. In the other modes, the client must generate the force to take spontaneous breaths.

2. What is the difference between pressure support and positive end expiratory pressure?

Pressure support ventilation provides pressure on spontaneous ventilation to decrease the work of breathing. Positive end expiratory pressure maintains a small amount of pressure in the lungs to keep alveoli open and prevent atelectasis.

3. List three complications of mechanical ventilation and one nursing intervention to prevent each complication.

Tracheal erosion by cuff: Secure the tracheal tube, keep cuff pressure less than 20 mm Hg, and measure cuff pressure every 8 hr.

Mucosal erosion by oral or nasal tracheal tube: For oral tubes, change to the other side of the mouth every 24 hr, secure tube, and support tubing to prevent weight of tubing and/or pulling on the tube.

Unplanned extubation: Monitor the client closely, provide soft restraints per protocol, and sedate the client as needed.

Lack of synchrony between the client and the ventilator: Decrease the client's anxiety and pain. Provide analgesia and sedation.

Aspiration: Keep the head of the bed elevated 30° and use nasogastric suctioning to prevent distention and vomiting.

Infection (pneumonia, sinusitis): Use surgical aseptic technique with suctioning, monitor temperature every 4 hr, elevate the head of the bed, and monitor nasal and tracheal secretions (color, odor, amount, consistency).

4. What assessments should the nurse routinely perform for a client receiving mechanical ventilation?

   Oxygen saturation levels

   Respiratory rate (ventilator and spontaneous), FiO$_2$, tidal volume, ventilator mode and adjuncts, plateau or peak inspiratory pressure, and alarms

   Heart rate and rhythm, urine output, and blood pressure hourly

   Assess breath sounds every 2 to 4 hr.

   Monitor serial chest x-rays and ABGs.

5. The high pressure alarm sounds on the ventilator. What should the nurse assess for?

   Client biting of the tube

   Breath sounds – indicating the need for suctioning

   Kinks in the tubing

6. The low pressure/low volume alarm sounds on the ventilator. What should the nurse assess for?

   Tubing disconnections

   Air leak around the cuff

7. Provide a rationale for each of the following nursing interventions.

Nursing Intervention	Rationale
Record level of oral or nasal tubes every 8 hr.	This allows the nurse to assess if the tube has been dislodged during repositioning, chest x-rays, etc.
Provide oral care every 2 hr.	The client is unable to eat or drink. This intervention preserves the integrity of oral mucosa.
Measure cuff pressure every 8 hr. Maintain pressure less than 20 mm Hg.	This prevents tracheal necrosis.
Keep the head of the bed elevated 30° at all times.	This prevents aspiration of gastric contents.
Continuously monitor oxygen saturation.	This provides information about oxygenation and the effectiveness of mechanical ventilation.
Assess skin integrity around the tube every 4 hr.	This intervention provides for early detection of skin breakdown or necrosis.
Reposition the client every 2 hr.	This mobilizes secretions and reduces risk for loss of skin integrity.
Support ventilator tubing.	This lessens the pressure and pull on mucosa and decreases the risk of unplanned extubation.

Unit 2   Nursing Care of Clients with Respiratory Disorders
Section: Nursing Care of Clients with Airflow Limitations

Chapter 11:   **Asthma**
Contributor: Wendy Buenzli, MSN, RN

⟳ **NCLEX-PN® Connections:**

Learning Objective: Review and apply knowledge within "**Asthma**" in readiness for performance of the following nursing activities as outlined by the NCLEX-PN® test plan:

Δ   Assist with relevant laboratory, diagnostic, and therapeutic procedures within the nursing role, including:

- Preparation of the client for the procedure.
- Accurate collection of specimens.
- Monitoring client status during and after the procedure.
- Reinforcing client teaching (before and following the procedure).
- Recognizing the client's response (expected, unexpected adverse response) to the procedure.
- Monitoring results.
- Monitoring and taking actions to prevent or minimize the risk of complications.
- Notifying the primary care provider of signs of complications.

Δ   Recognize signs and symptoms of the client's problem and complete the proper documentation.

Δ   Provide and document care based on the client's health alteration.

Δ   Monitor and document vital signs changes.

Δ   Interpret data that need to be reported immediately.

Δ   Reinforce client education on managing the client's health problem.

Δ   Recognize and respond to emergency situations, including notification of the primary care provider.

Δ   Review the client's response to emergency interventions and complete the proper documentation.

Δ   Provide care that meets the age-related needs of clients 65 years of age or older, including recognizing expected physiological changes.

📖 Key Points

Δ   Asthma is a **chronic inflammatory disorder of the airways.** It is an **intermittent** and **reversible** airflow obstruction that **affects the bronchioles.**

Δ   The obstruction occurs either by **inflammation** or **airway hyper-responsiveness.**

Δ   **Manifestations** of Asthma

   • **Mucosal edema**

   • **Bronchoconstriction**

   • **Excessive secretion production**

Δ   Asthma diagnoses are based on symptoms and classified into one of the following four categories.

   • **Mild intermittent:** Symptoms occur less than twice a week.

   • **Mild persistent:** Symptoms occur more than twice a week but not daily.

   • **Moderate persistent:** Daily symptoms occur in conjunction with exacerbations twice a week.

   • **Severe persistent:** Symptoms occur continually, along with frequent exacerbations that limit the client's physical activity and quality of life.

Δ   **Goals of Asthma Management**

   • Improve airflow.

   • Relieve symptoms.

   • Prevent acute attacks.

Δ   Reducing asthma morbidity is a goal of Healthy People 2010.

Key Factors

Δ   **Common Triggers** for Asthma Attacks

   • Environmental factors, such as **changes in temperature and humidity**

   • Pollutants

   • **Smoke**

   • **Strong odors** (for example, perfume)

   • **Allergens** (feathers, dust, animal dander, dust mites, molds, foods treated with sulfites)

   • **Exercise**

- **Stress or being emotionally upset**
- **Medications** (aspirin, NSAIDS, beta-blockers, cholinergic drugs)
- Enzymes, including those in laundry detergents
- **Chemicals** (for example, household cleaners)

Diagnostic Procedures and Nursing Interventions

Δ **Pulmonary function tests** are the most accurate tests for **diagnosing asthma and its severity.**

- **Forced vital capacity (FVC)** is the volume of air exhaled from full inhalation to full exhalation.

- **Forced expiratory volume in the first second (FEV$_1$)** is the volume of air blown out as hard and fast as possible during the first second of the most forceful exhalation after the greatest full inhalation.

- **Peak expiratory rate flow (PERF)** is the fastest airflow rate reached during exhalation.

- A decrease in FEV$_1$ or PERF by 15 to 20% below the expected value is common in clients with asthma. An increase in these values by 12% following the administration of bronchodilators is diagnostic for asthma.

Δ **Arterial Blood Gases (ABGs)**

- Decreased PaO$_2$

- PaCO$_2$ may be decreased in early stages of an attack due to the client's increased work of breathing. It will rise as fatigue sets in.

Δ **Chest x-ray** is used to diagnose **changes in chest structure** over time.

Assessments

Δ Clients with mild to moderate asthma may experience few or no symptoms between asthma attacks. During attacks, **monitor for signs and symptoms.**

- Dyspnea
- Chest tightness
- Coughing
- Wheezing
- Mucus production
- Use of accessory muscles
- Poor oxygen saturation (low SaO$_2$)

Δ   **Assess/Monitor**

- Client's respiratory status (airway patency, breath sounds, respiratory rate, use of accessory muscles, oxygenation status) before and following intervention

- Client's history regarding current and previous asthma exacerbations

  ◊   Onset and duration

  ◊   Precipitating factors (stress, exercise, exposure to irritant)

  ◊   Changes in medication regimen

  ◊   Medications that relieve symptoms

  ◊   Other medications taken

  ◊   Self-care methods used to relieve symptoms

- General appearance (enlargement of chest wall/anteroposterior diameter)

- Laboratory findings (arterial blood gases, sputum culture results)

NANDA Nursing Diagnoses

Δ   Impaired gas exchange

Δ   Ineffective airway clearance

Δ   Ineffective breathing pattern

Δ   Anxiety

Nursing Interventions

Δ   **Administer oxygen therapy** as prescribed.

Δ   Place the client in **high-Fowler's position** to facilitate air exchange.

Δ   **Monitor cardiac rate and rhythm** for changes during an acute attack.

Δ   Initiate and maintain **IV access**.

Δ   **Administer medications** as prescribed.

- **Bronchodilators**

  ◊   **Short-acting beta$_2$ agonists**, such as albuterol (Proventil, Ventolin), provide rapid relief.

  ◊   **Cholinergic antagonists** (anticholinergic drugs), such as ipratropium (Atrovent), block the parasympathetic nervous system. This allows for the sympathetic nervous system effects of increased bronchodilation and decreased pulmonary secretions.

- ◊ **Methylxanthines**, such as theophylline (Theo-Dur), require close monitoring of serum medication levels due to narrow therapeutic range.

- **Anti-inflammatories** decrease airway inflammation.

  - ◊ **Corticosteroids**, such as fluticasone (Flovent) and prednisone; if given systemically, monitor for serious side effects (immunosuppression, fluid retention, hyperglycemia, hypokalemia, poor wound healing).

  - ◊ **Leukotriene antagonists**, such as montelukast (Singulair)

  - ◊ **Mast cell stabilizers**, such as cromolyn sodium (Intal)

  - ◊ **Monoclonal antibodies**, such as omalizumab (Xolair)

- **Combination agents** (bronchodilator and anti-inflammatory)

  - ◊ Ipratropium and albuterol (Combivent)

  - ◊ Fluticasone and salmeterol (Advair)

  - ◊ If prescribed separately for inhalation administration at the same time, administer the bronchodilator first in order to increase the absorption of the anti-inflammatory agent.

Δ Maintain a **calm and reassuring demeanor**.

Δ **Client Education**

- Instruct the client how to **recognize and avoid triggering agents**, such as:

  - ◊ Smoke.

  - ◊ Dust.

  - ◊ Mold.

  - ◊ Sudden weather changes (especially warm to cold).

- Instruct the client how to properly **self-administer medications** (nebulizers and inhalers).

- Educate the client regarding **infection prevention techniques**.

  - ◊ Encourage the client to get a pneumonia vaccine, if not previously administered, and to get annual influenza **vaccinations**.

  - ◊ Promote good **nutrition**.

  - ◊ Reinforce importance of good hand **hygiene**.

- If the client smokes, discuss the effects of smoking on asthma and possible smoking cessation strategies.

- Encourage **regular exercise** as part of asthma therapy.

  - ◊ Promotes ventilation and perfusion.

  - ◊ Maintains cardiac health.

◊   Enhances skeletal muscle strength.

◊   Clients may require pre-medication.

- Provide referral to **support groups** as needed.

Complications and Nursing Implications

Δ   **Respiratory Failure**

- Persistent hypoxemia

- Monitor oxygenation levels and acid-base balance.

- Prepare for intubation and mechanical ventilation as indicated.

Δ   **Status Asthmaticus**

- Life-threatening episode of airway obstruction that is often unresponsive to common treatment.

- Extreme wheezing, labored breathing, use of accessory muscles, distended neck veins, and risk for cardiac and/or respiratory arrest.

- Prepare for emergency intubation.

- As prescribed, administer potent systemic bronchodilators, such as epinephrine, and initiate systemic steroid therapy.

Meeting the Needs of Older Adults

Δ   Older adult clients have **decreased pulmonary reserves** due to physiological lung changes that occur with the aging process.

Δ   **Provide rest periods** for older adult clients with dyspnea. Design room and walkways with opportunities for rest. Incorporate rest into activities of daily living.

Δ   The **sensitivity of beta-adrenergic receptors decreases with age**. As the beta receptors age and lose sensitivity, they are less able to respond to agonists, which can result in bronchospasm.

Δ   Older adult clients are **more susceptible to infections**. Encourage prompt medical attention for infections and appropriate vaccinations.

Primary Reference:

Ignatavicius, D. D., & Workman, M. L. (2006). *Medical-surgical nursing* (5th ed.). St. Louis, MO: Saunders.

Additional Resources:

Monahan, F. D., Sands, J. K., Neighbors, M., Marek, F. J., & Green, C. J. (Eds.). (2007). *Phipps' medical-surgical nursing: Health and illness perspectives* (8th ed.). St. Louis, MO: Mosby.

NANDA International (2004). *NANDA nursing diagnoses: Definitions and classification 2005-2006*. Philadelphia: NANDA.

Chapter 11: Asthma

Application Exercises

Scenario: A client presents to an emergency department with an admitting diagnosis of acute asthma attack.

1. Which of the following parameters indicate deterioration in the client's respiratory status? (Check all that apply.)

   _____ SaO_2 95%

   _____   Wheezing

   _____   Retraction of sternal muscles

   _____   Warm and pink extremities and mucous membranes

   _____   Premature ventricular complexes (PVCs)

   _____   Respiratory rate of 34/min

   _____   Anxiety

2. Two hours after arriving on the medical-surgical unit, the client develops dyspnea. SaO_2 is 91%, and the client is exhibiting audible wheezing and use of accessory muscles. Which classification of medication should the nurse expect to administer and why?

3. A nurse in an outpatient clinic is discussing with a client who is from Mississippi her plans for a trip to Washington state this winter. This client has asthma and is a runner. Which of the following statements is the most appropriate to relay to the client?

   A. "Take your asthma medication on your trip."

   B. "You should not travel to Washington as it is bad for individuals with asthma."

   C. "There is nothing for you to worry about."

   D. "It is important to know that weather changes can trigger an attack."

4. **True or False:** Older adults require smaller doses of beta$_2$ agonists because their receptors are more sensitive to the medication.

5. **True or False:** Asthma attacks can be the result of airway inflammation or airway hyper-responsiveness.

6. **True or False:** Chest x-rays are the most accurate test for diagnosing asthma and its severity.

Chapter 11: Asthma

Application Exercises Answer Key

Scenario: A client presents to an emergency department with an admitting diagnosis of acute asthma attack.

1. Which of the following parameters indicate deterioration in the client's respiratory status? (Check all that apply.)

    _____ SaO_2 95%

    ___x___ Wheezing

    ___x___ Retraction of sternal muscles

    _____ Warm and pink extremities and mucous membranes

    ___x___ Premature ventricular complexes (PVCs)

    ___x___ Respiratory rate of 34/min

    ___x___ Anxiety

2. Two hours after arriving on the medical-surgical unit, the client develops dyspnea. SaO_2 is 91%, and the client is exhibiting audible wheezing and use of accessory muscles. Which classification of medication should the nurse expect to administer and why?

    The nurse should expect to administer a beta$_2$ agonist. Beta$_2$ agonists are used for relief of acute symptoms.

3. A nurse in an outpatient clinic is discussing with a client who is from Mississippi her plans for a trip to Washington state this winter. This client has asthma and is a runner. Which of the following statements is the most appropriate to relay to the client?

    A. "Take your asthma medication on your trip."

    B. "You should not travel to Washington as it is bad for individuals with asthma."

    C. "There is nothing for you to worry about."

    D. "It is important to know that weather changes can trigger an attack."

    Sudden weather changes, especially from warm to cold, can trigger an asthma exacerbation.

4. **True or False:** Older adults require smaller doses of beta$_2$ agonists because their receptors are more sensitive to the medication.

   False: Older adults have a DECREASED sensitivity to beta$_2$ agonists.

5. **True or False:** Asthma attacks can be the result of airway inflammation or airway hyper-responsiveness.

   True: Inflammation and hyper-responsiveness can cause bronchial obstruction, resulting in an asthma exacerbation.

6. **True or False:** Chest x-rays are the most accurate test for diagnosing asthma and its severity.

   False: Pulmonary function tests are used for diagnosing asthma and assessing its severity, while chest x-rays show long-term changes in chest wall structure.

Unit 2
Section:

Nursing Care of Clients with Respiratory Disorders
Nursing Care of Clients with Airflow Limitations

Chapter 12:   Chronic Obstructive Pulmonary Disease (COPD)
Contributor: Wendy Buenzli, MSN, RN

NCLEX-PN® Connections:

Learning Objective: Review and apply knowledge within **"Chronic Obstructive Pulmonary Disease (COPD)"** in readiness for performance of the following nursing activities as outlined by the NCLEX-PN® test plan:

Δ   Assist with relevant laboratory, diagnostic, and therapeutic procedures within the nursing role, including:

- Preparation of the client for the procedure.
- Accurate collection of specimens.
- Monitoring client status during and after the procedure.
- Reinforcing client teaching (before and following the procedure).
- Recognizing the client's response (expected, unexpected adverse response) to the procedure.
- Monitoring results.
- Monitoring and taking actions to prevent or minimize the risk of complications.
- Notifying the primary care provider of signs of complications.

Δ   Recognize signs and symptoms of the client's problem and complete the proper documentation.

Δ   Provide and document care based on the client's health alteration.

Δ   Monitor and document vital signs changes.

Δ   Interpret data that need to be reported immediately.

Δ   Reinforce client education on managing the client's health problem.

Δ   Recognize and respond to emergency situations, including notification of the primary care provider.

Δ   Review the client's response to emergency interventions and complete the proper documentation.

Δ   Provide care that meets the age-related needs of clients 65 years of age or older, including recognizing expected physiological changes.

Key Points

Δ **COPD** encompasses two diseases: **emphysema and chronic bronchitis**. Most clients who have emphysema also have chronic bronchitis.

Δ **Emphysema** is characterized by the **loss of lung elasticity and hyperinflation of lung tissue.** Emphysema causes **destruction of the alveoli**, leading to decreased surface area for gas exchange, carbon dioxide retention, and respiratory acidosis.

Δ **Chronic bronchitis is an inflammation of the bronchi and bronchioles** due to chronic exposure to irritants.

Δ COPD typically affects middle age to older adults.

Key Factors

Δ **Risk Factors**

• **Cigarette smoking** is the primary risk factor for the development of COPD.

• **Alpha$_1$-antitrypsin (AAT) deficiency**

• Exposure to **air pollution**

Diagnostic and Therapeutic Procedures and Nursing Interventions

Δ **Pulmonary Function Tests**

• Comparisons of forced expiratory volume (FEV) to forced vital capacity (FVC) are used to classify COPD as mild to very severe.

• As COPD advances, the FEV to FVC ratio decreases.

Δ **Chest X-ray**

• Reveals **hyperinflation** and **flattened diaphragm** in late stages of emphysema.

• Often not useful for diagnosis of early or moderate disease.

Δ **Arterial Blood Gases (ABGs)**

• Serial ABGs are monitored to evaluate respiratory status.

• **Increased PaCO$_2$ and decreased PaO$_2$**

• Respiratory acidosis, metabolic alkalosis (compensation)

Δ **Pulse Oximetry**

• Monitor oxygen saturation levels.

• Less than normal (normal = 94 to 98%) oxygen saturation levels

Δ   **Peak Expiratory Flow Meters**

  • Used to monitor treatment effectiveness.

  • Decreased with obstruction; increased with relief of obstruction

Δ   AAT levels are used to assess for AAT deficiency.

Δ   Monitor hemoglobin and hematocrit to recognize polycythemia (compensation to chronic hypoxia).

Δ   Evaluate sputum cultures and white blood cell counts for diagnosis of acute respiratory infections.

Δ   **Chest physiotherapy** uses percussion and vibration to mobilize secretions, and positioning is optimized to facilitate drainage and removal of secretions by gravity.

Assessments

Δ   Monitor for **signs and symptoms.**

  • Chronic **dyspnea**

  • Chronic **cough**

  • **Hypoxemia**

  • **Hypercarbia (increased $PaCO_2$)**

  • **Respiratory acidosis** and compensatory metabolic alkalosis

  • **Crackles**

  • Rapid and **shallow respirations**

  • Use of **accessory muscles**

  • **Barrel chest** or increased chest diameter

  • **Hyperresonance** on percussion due to "trapped air" (emphysema)

  • Asynchronous breathing

  • Thin extremities and enlarged neck muscles

  • Dependent edema secondary to right-sided heart failure

  • **Pallor** and **cyanosis** of nail beds and mucous membranes (late stages of the disease)

Δ   **Assess/Monitor**

  • Client's history (occupational history, smoking history)

  • Respiratory rate, symmetry, and effort

  • Breath sounds

- Activity tolerance level and dyspnea

- Nutrition and weight loss

- General appearance

- **Vital signs**

- **Heart rhythm**

- Pallor and cyanosis

- ABGs, SaO_2, CBC, WBC, and chest x-ray results

NANDA Nursing Diagnoses

Δ   Impaired gas exchange

Δ   Ineffective breathing pattern

Δ   Ineffective airway clearance

Δ   Imbalanced nutrition

Δ   Anxiety

Δ   Activity intolerance

Δ   Fatigue

Nursing Interventions

Δ   Position the client to maximize ventilation (**high-Fowler's).**

Δ   Encourage effective **coughing**, or **suction** to remove secretions.

Δ   Encourage **deep breathing** and use of incentive spirometer.

Δ   Administer **breathing treatments and medications** as prescribed.

- **Bronchodilators**

    ◊   **Short-acting beta$_2$ agonists**, such as albuterol (Proventil, Ventolin), provide rapid relief.

    ◊   **Cholinergic antagonists** (anticholinergic drugs), such as ipratropium (Atrovent), block the parasympathetic nervous system. This allows for the sympathetic nervous system effects of increased bronchodilation and decreased pulmonary secretions.

    ◊   **Methylxanthines**, such as theophylline (Theo-Dur), require close monitoring of serum medication levels due to narrow therapeutic range.

- **Anti-inflammatories** decrease airway inflammation.

  ◊ **Corticosteroids**, such as fluticasone (Flovent) and prednisone. If given systemically, monitor for serious side effects (immunosuppression, fluid retention, hyperglycemia, hypokalemia, poor wound healing).

  ◊ **Leukotriene antagonists**, such as montelukast (Singulair)

  ◊ **Mast cell stabilizers**, such as cromolyn sodium (Intal)

  ◊ **Monoclonal antibodies**, such as omalizumab (Xolair)

- **Combination agents** (bronchodilator and anti-inflammatory)

  ◊ Ipratropium and albuterol (Combivent)

  ◊ Fluticasone and salmeterol (Advair)

  ◊ If prescribed separately for inhalation administration at the same time, administer the bronchodilator first in order to increase the absorption of the anti-inflammatory agent.

Δ Administer **heated** and **humidified oxygen therapy** as prescribed. Monitor for **skin breakdown** from the oxygen device.

Δ Instruct clients to practice breathing techniques to control dyspneic episodes.

- **Diaphragmatic or abdominal breathing**

- **Pursed-lip breathing**

Δ Provide oxygen therapy as prescribed to relieve hypoxemia.

- Clients with COPD may need 2 to 4 L/min per nasal cannula or up to 40% per Venturi mask.

- Clients with **chronic hypercarbia** usually require **1 to 2 L/min** via nasal cannula. It is important to recognize that low arterial levels of oxygen serve as their primary drive for breathing.

Δ Determine the client's physical limitations and structure activity to **include periods of rest.**

Δ Promote **adequate nutrition.**

- Increased work of breathing increases caloric demands.

- Proper nutrition aids in the prevention of secondary respiratory infections.

Δ Provide support to the client and family.

Δ Encourage verbalization of feelings.

Δ Encourage **smoking cessation** if applicable. Smoking and other flame sources must be avoided by clients on supplemental oxygen (enhances combustion) in the home.

Complications and Nursing Implications

Δ **Respiratory Infection**

- Results from increased **mucus production** and poor oxygenation.
- Administer **oxygen therapy**.
- Monitor oxygenation.
- **Administer antibiotics** and other medications as prescribed.

Δ **Right-sided Heart Failure (cor pulmonale)**

- Air trapping, airway collapse, and stiff alveoli lead to **increased pulmonary pressures**.
- **Blood flow through lung tissue is difficult**. This increased work load leads to **enlargement** and **thickening** of the **right atrium and ventricle**.
- **Manifestations** include:
  ◊ **Hypoxia**, hypoxemia.
  ◊ **Cyanotic lips**.
  ◊ Enlarged and **tender liver**.
  ◊ Distended neck veins.
  ◊ **Dependent edema**.
- **Nursing Interventions**
  ◊ Monitor **respiratory status** and **administer oxygen** therapy.
  ◊ Monitor **heart rate** and **rhythm**.
  ◊ Administer positive **inotropic** and **contractility medications** as prescribed.
  ◊ Administer **IV fluids** and **diuretics** to maintain fluid balance.

Meeting the Needs of Older Adults

Δ COPD is debilitating for older adult clients. Referrals to assistance programs such as Meals on Wheels may be indicated.

Δ Influenza and pneumonia vaccinations are important for all clients with COPD, but especially for the older adult client.

Δ Older adult clients have decreased pulmonary reserves due to normal lung changes.

Δ Provide rest periods for older adult clients with dyspnea. Design room and walkways with opportunities for relaxation. Incorporate rest into activities of daily living.

Δ   The sensitivity of beta-adrenergic receptors decreases with age. As the receptors age and lose sensitivity, they are less able to respond to agonists and prevent bronchospasm.

Δ   Older adult clients are more susceptible to infections. Encourage prompt medical attention for infections.

Primary Reference:

Ignatavicius, D. D., & Workman, M. L. (2006). *Medical-surgical nursing* (5th ed.). St. Louis, MO: Saunders.

Additional Resources:

NANDA International (2004). *NANDA nursing diagnoses: Definitions and classification 2005-2006*. Philadelphia: NANDA.

Chapter 12: Chronic Obstructive Pulmonary Disease (COPD)

Application Exercises

1. Match the interventions listed below with the appropriate COPD management techniques in the table.

Airway Management	Cough Enhancement	Oxygen Therapy	Energy Management

    A. Encourage the client to take deep breaths.

    B. Monitor the position of the oxygen delivery device.

    C. Promote bedrest.

    D. Position the client to maximize ventilation potential.

    E. Assist with incentive spirometry.

    F. Determine the client's physical limitations.

    G. Instruct the client to breathe deeply, hold breath for 2 seconds, and then cough two to three times.

Scenario: A 59-year-old client comes to the emergency department. She is newly diagnosed with emphysema. She currently smokes one pack of cigarettes a day and has been smoking since she was 19. She presents with symptoms of dyspnea, chronic cough, and sputum production. The client lives alone and is on a fixed income. During the assessment, the nurse notices a strong cigarette smell on the client's clothing and belongings. When the nurse talks about smoking cessation programs, the client doesn't believe quitting will help because the damage is already done.

2. How should the nurse respond to this client?

3. What nursing diagnoses are appropriate for this client?

4. When discharging a client with home oxygen, which of the following is most important for the nurse to teach?

        A. Smoking cessation

        B. Equipment maintenance

        C. Incorporating rest into ADLs

        D. Anger management

5. Which of the following assessment data is most important for a nurse to report to the primary care provider?

        A. SaO_2 90% on room air

        B. Pulse 110 beats/min after lunch

        C. Clubbing of fingers and cyanotic lips

        D. Blood pressure 149/88 mm Hg

6. A client is concerned that he will never be able to leave his house once he is on oxygen therapy. What should the nurse tell him?

Chapter 12: Chronic Obstructive Pulmonary Disease (COPD)

Application Exercises Answer Key

1. Match the interventions listed below with the appropriate COPD management techniques in the table.

Airway Management	Cough Enhancement	Oxygen Therapy	Energy Management
D. Position the client to maximize ventilation potential. E. Assist with incentive spirometry.	A. Encourage the client to take deep breaths. G. Instruct the client to breathe deeply, hold breath for 2 seconds, and then cough two to three times.	B. Monitor the position of the oxygen delivery device.	C. Promote bedrest. F. Determine the client's physical limitations.

A. Encourage the client to take deep breaths.

B. Monitor the position of the oxygen delivery device.

C. Promote bedrest.

D. Position the client to maximize ventilation potential.

E. Assist with incentive spirometry.

F. Determine the client's physical limitations.

G. Instruct the client to breathe deeply, hold breath for 2 seconds, and then cough two to three times.

Scenario: A 59-year-old client comes to the emergency department. She is newly diagnosed with emphysema. She currently smokes one pack of cigarettes a day and has been smoking since she was 19. She presents with symptoms of dyspnea, chronic cough, and sputum production. The client lives alone and is on a fixed income. During the assessment, the nurse notices a strong cigarette smell on the client's clothing and belongings. When the nurse talks about smoking cessation programs, the client doesn't believe quitting will help because the damage is already done.

---

2. How should the nurse respond to this client?

The nurse should inform the client that smoking cessation at any point improves her prognosis.

3. What nursing diagnoses are appropriate for this client?

Impaired gas exchange

Ineffective airway clearance

---

4. When discharging a client with home oxygen, which of the following is most important for the nurse to teach?

    A. Smoking cessation
    B. Equipment maintenance
    C. Incorporating rest into ADLs
    D. Anger management

Oxygen enhances combustion; therefore, all flames, including lit cigarettes and candles, should be kept away from oxygen flow.

5. Which of the following assessment data is most important for a nurse to report to the primary care provider?

    A. SaO_2 90% on room air
    B. Pulse 110 beats/min after lunch
    C. Clubbing of fingers and cyanotic lips
    D. Blood pressure 149/88 mm Hg

Clubbed fingers and circumoral cyanosis are late signs of serious hypoxemia.

6. A client is concerned that he will never be able to leave his house once he is on oxygen therapy. What should the nurse tell him?

The nurse should inform the client that there are portable oxygen delivery systems.

Unit 2   Nursing Care of Clients with Respiratory Disorders

Section: Nursing Care of Clients with Infectious Respiratory Diseases

Chapter 13:   Pneumonia
Contributor: Wendy Buenzli, MSN, RN

↻ NCLEX-PN® Connections:

Learning Objective: Review and apply knowledge within **"Pneumonia"** in readiness for performance of the following nursing activities as outlined by the NCLEX-PN® test plan:

Δ   Assist with relevant laboratory, diagnostic, and therapeutic procedures within the nursing role, including:

- Preparation of the client for the procedure.
- Accurate collection of specimens.
- Monitoring client status during and after the procedure.
- Reinforcing client teaching (before and following the procedure).
- Recognizing the client's response (expected, unexpected adverse response) to the procedure.
- Monitoring results.
- Monitoring and taking actions to prevent or minimize the risk of complications.
- Notifying the primary care provider of signs of complications.

Δ   Recognize signs and symptoms of the client's problem and complete the proper documentation.

Δ   Provide and document care based on the client's health alteration.

Δ   Monitor and document vital signs changes.

Δ   Interpret data that need to be reported immediately.

Δ   Reinforce client education on managing the client's health problem.

Δ   Recognize and respond to emergency situations, including notification of the primary care provider.

Δ   Review the client's response to emergency interventions and complete the proper documentation.

Δ   Provide care that meets the age-related needs of clients 65 years of age or older, including recognizing expected physiological changes.

Key Points

Δ   Pneumonia is an **inflammatory process** in the lungs that **produces excess fluid.** Pneumonia is **triggered by infectious organisms** or by the **aspiration of an irritant.**

Δ   The inflammatory process in the lung parenchyma results in **edema and exudate that fills the alveoli.**

Δ   Pneumonia may be a **primary disease or a complication** of another disease or condition. It affects people of all ages, but the **young, older adult clients, and clients who are immunocompromised** are more susceptible. Immobility can be a contributing factor in the development of pneumonia.

Δ   There are two types of pneumonia. **Community acquired pneumonia (CAP)** is the most common type and often occurs as a complication of influenza. **Hospital acquired pneumonia (HAP),** also known as nosocomial pneumonia, has a higher mortality rate and is **more likely to be resistant to antibiotics.**

Key Factors

Δ   **Common Risk Factors for Pneumonia**

- **Advanced age**

- **Recent exposure** to viral or influenza infections

- **Tobacco use**

- **Chronic lung disease** (for example, asthma)

- **Aspiration**

- **Mechanical ventilation** (ventilator acquired pneumonia)

- **Impaired ability to mobilize secretions** (decreased level of consciousness, immobility, recent abdominal or thoracic surgery)

- Immunocompromised status

Diagnostic Procedures and Nursing Interventions

Δ   **Chest X-ray**

- Shows consolidation of lung tissue.

Δ   **Pulse Oximetry**

- Decreased oxygen saturation levels

Δ   CBC

- Elevated white blood cell count (may not be present in older adult clients)

Δ   **Sputum Culture**

- Obtain specimen by suctioning if the client is unable to cough.

- The responsible organism is only identified about 50% of the time.

Δ   **Arterial Blood Gases (ABGs)**

- Decreased PaO_2 and increased $PaCO_2$ due to impaired gas exchange in the alveoli

Assessments

Δ   Monitor for **signs and symptoms.**

- **Fever**

- **Dyspnea, tachypnea**

- **Pleuritic chest pain**

- **Sputum** production

- **Crackles** and wheezes

- **Coughing**

- **Dull chest percussion** over areas of consolidation

- Poor oxygen saturation (low SaO_2)

Δ   **Assess/Monitor**

- Respiratory status (airway patency, breath sounds, respiratory rate, use of accessory muscles, oxygenation status) before and following interventions

- Sputum (amount, color)

- History of smoking and chronic lung conditions

- Recent exposure to influenza or other viral agents

- Factors that increase the risk of aspiration (for example, following a stroke)

- Difficulty mobilizing secretions (for example, with generalized weakness)

- General appearance (temperature, skin color)

    ◊   Laboratory findings (arterial blood gases, sputum culture results, white blood cell count)

NANDA Nursing Diagnoses

Δ   Impaired gas exchange

Δ   Ineffective airway clearance

Δ   Activity intolerance

Δ   Imbalanced nutrition: Less than body requirements

Δ   Acute pain

Nursing Interventions

Δ   Administer **heated and humidified oxygen** therapy as prescribed.

Δ   Position the client in **high-Fowler's position** to facilitate air exchange.

Δ   Encourage **coughing**, or **suction** to remove secretions.

Δ   Encourage **deep breathing** with an incentive spirometer to prevent alveolar collapse.

Δ   **Administer medications** as prescribed.

  •   **Antibiotics** are given to destroy the infectious pathogens.

    ◊   Commonly used antibiotics include the penicillins and cephalosporins.

    ◊   They are often initially given by IV and then switched to an oral form as the client's condition improves.

    ◊   It is important to obtain any culture specimens prior to giving the first dose of the antibiotic. Once the specimen has been obtained, the antibiotics can be given while waiting for the results of the ordered culture.

  •   **Bronchodilators**

    ◊   **Short-acting beta$_2$ agonists**, such as albuterol (Proventil, Ventolin), quickly provide bronchodilation.

    ◊   **Methylxanthines**, such as theophylline (Theo-Dur), require close monitoring of serum medication levels due to narrow therapeutic range.

  •   **Corticosteroids**, such as prednisone, decrease airway inflammation. If given systemically, monitor for serious side effects (immunosuppression, fluid retention, hyperglycemia, hypokalemia, poor wound healing).

- **Immunizations** can decrease a client's risk of developing CAP.

  ◊ **Influenza vaccine** is recommended annually for clients at risk of complications from influenza, especially older adult clients and those with chronic illnesses.

  ◊ **Pneumococcal vaccine** is administered one time and helps prevent pneumococcal infections, including pneumonia. It is also recommended for older adult clients and those with chronic illnesses.

Δ Determine the client's physical limitations and structure activity to **include periods of rest**.

Δ Promote **adequate nutrition**.

- Increased work of breathing increases caloric demands.

- Proper nutrition aids in the prevention of secondary respiratory infections.

Δ **Provide support** to the client and family.

Δ **Encourage verbalization** of feelings.

Complications and Nursing Implications

Δ **Atelectasis**

- Airway inflammation and edema leads to alveolar collapse and increases the risk of hypoxemia.

- Diminished or absent breath sounds over affected area.

- Chest x-ray shows area of density.

Δ **Acute Respiratory Failure**

- Persistent hypoxemia

- Monitor oxygenation levels and acid-base balance.

- Prepare for intubation and mechanical ventilation as indicated.

Δ **Bacteremia (sepsis)** can occur if pathogens enter the bloodstream from the infection in the lungs.

Meeting the Needs of Older Adults

Δ Older adult clients have decreased pulmonary reserves due to normal lung changes including decreased lung elasticity and thickening alveoli.

Δ Provide rest periods for older adult clients with dyspnea.

Δ Older adult clients are more susceptible to infections. Encourage prompt medical attention when signs of infection occur.

Δ   Older adult clients have a weak cough reflex and decreased muscle strength. Therefore, older adult clients have trouble expectorating, which may lead to difficulty in breathing and make specimen retrieval more difficult.

Δ   Neurologic changes associated with stroke and other conditions increase the risk for aspiration pneumonia.

Δ   Inactivity and immobility increase the risk of secretions pooling, thereby increasing the risk for pneumonia.

Δ   Signs and symptoms are often atypical.

•   Confusion from hypoxia is the most common manifestation of pneumonia in older adult clients.

•   Fever, cough, and purulent sputum are often absent.

•   Chest x-ray is an important diagnostic tool because the early signs and symptoms of pneumonia are often vague in older adult clients.

Primary Reference:

Ignatavicius, D. D., & Workman, M. L. (2006). *Medical-surgical nursing* (5th ed.). St. Louis, MO: Saunders.

Additional Resources:

NANDA International (2004). *NANDA nursing diagnoses: Definitions and classification 2005-2006*. Philadelphia: NANDA.

For more information on pneumonia, visit the Centers for Disease Control and Prevention at *www.cdc.gov* and the World Health Organization at *www.who.int*.

Chapter 13: Pneumonia

Application Exercises

1. Which of the following criteria indicate an increased risk for pneumonia? (Check all that apply.)

   _____   Stroke victim with dysphasia

   _____   34-year-old male client with AIDS

   _____   64-year-old woman who was vaccinated for pneumococcus and influenza 6 months ago

   _____   Postoperative client who received local anesthesia only

   _____   17-year-old female client with a closed head injury receiving mechanical ventilation

   _____   Client with myasthenia gravis

Scenario: A nurse working in an outpatient clinic observes a 76-year-old female client who is brought in by her husband. The husband states that his wife woke up this morning and did not recognize him or know where she was. She reports chills and chest pain that worsens with inspiration.

2. Which of the following is the highest priority nursing task?

   A. Obtain baseline vital signs and oxygen saturation.

   B. Obtain sputum culture.

   C. Obtain complete history from the client.

   D. Provide pneumococcal vaccination.

3. Further assessment yields the following vital signs: temperature 37.3° C (99.1° F), respiratory rate 30/min, blood pressure 130/76 mm Hg, pulse 110 beats/min, and SaO_2 91% on room air. Prioritize the following nursing interventions with 1 being the highest priority.

   _____   Administer antibiotics as prescribed.

   _____   Administer oxygen therapy.

   _____   Perform sputum culture.

   _____   Administer an anti-pyretic medication for client comfort.

4. **True or False:** A client who develops a fever and productive cough 6 hr after admission to the hospital may be developing hospital-acquired pneumonia.

5. **True or False:** Decreased lung elasticity is a physiologic change that is normal with aging.

6. **True or False:** Sepsis can occur in a client with pneumonia if the pathogens enter the blood stream.

Chapter 13: Pneumonia

Application Exercises Answer Key

1. Which of the following criteria indicate an increased risk for pneumonia? (Check all that apply.)

__x__	Stroke victim with dysphasia
__x__	34-year-old male client with AIDS
_____	64-year-old woman who was vaccinated for pneumococcus and influenza 6 months ago
_____	Postoperative client who received local anesthesia only
__x__	17-year-old female client with a closed head injury receiving mechanical ventilation
__x__	Client with myasthenia gravis

A client with difficulty swallowing is at increased risk of aspiration, which increases the risk of pneumonia. A client with AIDS is immunocompromised, which increases the risk of opportunistic infections such as pneumonia. Mechanical ventilation is invasive and increases the risk of respiratory infections. A client with myasthenia gravis has generalized weakness and will have difficulty clearing secretions from the airway, which increases the risk of infection.

Scenario: A nurse working in an outpatient clinic observes a 76-year-old female client who is brought in by her husband. The husband states that his wife woke up this morning and did not recognize him or know where she was. She reports chills and chest pain that worsens with inspiration.

2. Which of the following is the highest priority nursing task?

A. Obtain baseline vital signs and oxygen saturation.

B. Obtain sputum culture.

C. Obtain complete history from the client.

D. Provide pneumococcal vaccination.

Assessment is the first step of the nursing process and an essential first step in planning client care. Another important concept in prioritizing care is to meet the client's physiologic needs first, which is the respiratory system in this case.

3. Further assessment yields the following vital signs: temperature 37.3° C (99.1° F), respiratory rate 30/min, blood pressure 130/76 mm Hg, pulse 110 beats/min, and SaO_2 91% on room air. Prioritize the following nursing interventions with 1 being the highest priority.

    __3__   Administer antibiotics as prescribed.

    __1__   Administer oxygen therapy.

    __2__   Perform sputum culture.

    __4__   Administer an anti-pyretic medication for client comfort.

The client's respiratory and heart rates are elevated and her oxygen saturation is 91% on room air. These signs indicate that her oxygenation needs are not being met, so that is the highest priority of care. After starting the oxygen, it is important to obtain the sputum specimen and then start the antibiotics.

4. **True or False:** A client who develops a fever and productive cough 6 hr after admission to the hospital may be developing hospital-acquired pneumonia.

False: In general, it takes 24 to 48 hr from the time the client is exposed to pathogens to when the client begins to show signs of infection. A client with signs of infection 6 hours after admission was most likely exposed to those pathogens prior to admission.

5. **True or False:** Decreased lung elasticity is a physiologic change that is normal with aging.

True: Lung elasticity decreases and the alveolar walls thicken as part of the expected physiological changes that occur with aging. These changes increase the risk of respiratory infections in older adult clients.

6. **True or False:** Sepsis can occur in a client with pneumonia if the pathogens enter the blood stream.

True: Sepsis is a potential complication of pneumonia.

Unit 2 Nursing Care of Clients with Respiratory Disorders

Section: Nursing Care of Clients with Infectious Respiratory Diseases

Chapter 14: Tuberculosis

Contributor: Wendy Buenzli, MSN, RN

NCLEX-PN® Connections:

Learning Objective: Review and apply knowledge within "**Tuberculosis**" in readiness for performance of the following nursing activities as outlined by the NCLEX-PN® test plan:

Δ Assist with relevant laboratory, diagnostic, and therapeutic procedures within the nursing role, including:

- Preparation of the client for the procedure.

- Accurate collection of specimens.

- Monitoring client status during and after the procedure.

- Reinforcing client teaching (before and following the procedure).

- Recognizing the client's response (expected, unexpected adverse response) to the procedure.

- Monitoring results.

- Monitoring and taking actions to prevent or minimize the risk of complications.

  - Notifying the primary care provider of signs of complications.

Δ Recognize signs and symptoms of the client's problem and complete the proper documentation.

Δ Provide and document care based on the client's health alteration.

Δ Monitor and document vital signs changes.

Δ Interpret data that need to be reported immediately.

Δ Reinforce client education on managing the client's health problem.

Δ Recognize and respond to emergency situations, including notification of the primary care provider.

Δ Review the client's response to emergency interventions and complete the proper documentation.

Δ Provide care that meets the age-related needs of clients 65 years of age or older, including recognizing expected physiological changes.

📖 Key Points

Δ Tuberculosis (TB) is an **infectious disease** caused by *Myobacterium tuberculosis*.

Δ TB is **transmitted through aerosolization** (airborne route). A droplet becomes airborne when an individual coughs, sneezes, laughs, etc. Inhalation of this droplet allows transmission of the bacteria.

Δ Once inside the lung, the body **encases the TB bacillus** with collagen and other cells. This may appear as a **Ghon tubercle** on a chest x-ray.

Δ Only a small percentage of people infected with TB actually develop an active form of the infection. The tuberculosis bacillus may **lie dormant for many years** before producing the disease.

Δ **TB primarily affects the lungs** but can spread to any organ through the blood.

Δ An infected person is **not contagious until signs and symptoms of the infection are present.** The risk of transmission decreases after 2 to 3 weeks of antibiotic therapy.

Δ An intradermal TB test is a common screening tool to assess for TB infection. A client's TB test will be **positive within 2 to 10 weeks** of exposure to the infection.

Δ Early detection and treatment are vital. TB has a slow onset, and the client may not be aware until the symptoms and disease are advanced. TB diagnosis should be considered for any client with a persistent cough, weight loss, anorexia, hemoptysis, dyspnea, fever, or chills.

Δ Increasing the percentage of clients who complete treatment for TB is a goal of Healthy People 2010.

Key Factors

Δ **Common Risk Factors for TB**

• Clients in **frequent and close contact with an untreated individual**

• Clients who are **immunocompromised** (HIV, chemotherapy)

• Clients **living in crowded facilities** (prisons, long-term care facilities)

• Clients from a **lower socioeconomic status** and clients who are **homeless**

• **Immigrants** from countries with a high incidence of TB

Diagnostic Procedures and Nursing Interventions

Δ **Mantoux Skin Test** (read in 48 to 72 hr)

• **Induration of 10 mm** or greater in diameter indicates a **positive** skin test.

• **Induration of 5 mm** is considered a positive test for immunocompromised clients.

- A **positive Mantoux test** indicates either exposure to TB or presence of the inactive disease. It does not confirm that active disease is present.

- Clients who have received a **BCG vaccine** within the past 10 years may have a **false-positive Mantoux test**. These clients will need a chest x-ray to evaluate the presence of an active TB infection.

Δ   **Chest x-ray** may be ordered to detect active lesions in the lungs.

Δ   **Sputum Smear and Culture**

Δ   A positive **acid-fast test** suggests an active infection. **TB precautions should be followed** until the diagnosis is confirmed or ruled out.

Δ   The **diagnosis** is **confirmed** by a **positive culture** for *M. tuberculosis*.

Assessments

Δ   Monitor for **signs and symptoms.**

- **Persistent cough**

- Purulent **sputum**, possibly **blood-streaked**

- **Fatigue**, lethargy

- **Weight loss**, anorexia

- **Night sweats**, fever

Δ   **Assess/Monitor**

- Respiratory status (airway patency, breath sounds, respiratory rate, use of accessory muscles, oxygenation status) before and following interventions

- Cough and sputum (amount, color)

- Recent exposure to TB

- Factors that increase the risk of infection (immunocompromise, advanced age)

- Factors that increase the risk of exposure (crowded living conditions, recent travel outside of the U.S.)

- General appearance (temperature, skin color)

- Laboratory findings (Mantoux test, sputum culture, chest x-ray results)

- Recent exposure to TB

- Overall nutrition and recent weight loss

NANDA Nursing Diagnoses

Δ   Impaired gas exchange

Δ   Ineffective airway clearance

Δ   Imbalanced nutrition: Less than body requirements

Δ   Fatigue

Δ   Social Isolation

Nursing Interventions

Δ   Administer heated and humidified **oxygen therapy** as prescribed.

Δ   Obtain **sputum samples.** The first morning specimen is most accurate and is preferred.

Δ   **Prevent infection transmission.**

- Wear an **N95 or HEPA respirator** when caring for the hospitalized TB client.

- Place the client in a **negative airflow room** and implement **airborne precautions.**

- Use **barrier protection** when the risk of hand or clothing contamination exists.

- Have the client wear a mask if transportation to another department is necessary. The client should be transported using the shortest and least busy route.

Δ   **Administer medications** as prescribed.

- **Isoniazid** (INH) should be taken on an empty stomach; monitor for **hepatitis** and **neurotoxicity. Vitamin B$_6$** (pyridoxine) is used to prevent toxicity from isoniazid.

- **Rifampin** (RIF): Inform the client that urine and other secretions will be orange; observe for **hepatotoxicity.**

- **Pyrazinamide** (PZA): Observe for **hepatotoxicity.**

- **Ethambutol** (EMB): Obtain baseline **visual acuity tests**; determine color discrimination ability.

- **Streptomycin** is not widely used due to resistance; it can cause **ototoxicity,** so monitor hearing function.

- To decrease the development of **drug resistance,** newer drugs contain a combination of rifampin and isoniazid (Rifamate) or rifampin, isoniazid, and pyrazinamide (Rifater). Drug **non-compliance** is a major contributing factor in the development of resistant strains of TB.

Δ **Promote adequate nutrition.**

- **Encourage fluid intake** and a well-balanced diet for adequate caloric intake.

- Encourage foods that are rich in **protein, iron, and vitamin C.**

Δ **Provide client and family education** since TB is often treated in the home setting.

- Teach the client and family about the **importance of the medication regimen.**

- **Exposed family members** should be **tested for TB.**

- Educate the client and family to **continue drug therapy for its full duration of at least 6 months.** Emphasize that failure to take the medications could lead to a resistant strain of TB.

- Instruct the client to continue with **follow-up care for 1 full year.**

- Inform the client that **sputum samples** are needed every **2 to 4 weeks** to monitor therapy effectiveness. Clients are no longer considered infectious after **three negative sputum cultures.**

- Encourage proper **handwashing.**

- Instruct the client to **cover the mouth and nose when coughing or sneezing.**

- Contaminated tissues should be disposed of in plastic bags.

- Clients with active TB should **wear masks when in public places.**

Δ **Provide emotional support.**

Complications and Nursing Implications

Δ **Miliary TB:** The organism invades the blood stream and can spread to multiple body organs with complications including:

- **Meningitis** (headaches, neck stiffness, and drowsiness) can be life-threatening.

- **Pericarditis** (dyspnea, swollen neck veins, pleuritic pain, and hypotension due to an accumulation of fluid in pericardial sac that inhibits the heart's ability to pump effectively).

Meeting the Needs of Older Adults

Δ   Older adult clients have decreased pulmonary reserves due to normal lung changes including decreased lung elasticity and thickening alveoli.

Δ   Older adult clients have a weak cough reflex and muscle strength. Therefore, older adult clients have trouble expectorating, which may lead to difficulty in breathing and make specimen retrieval more difficult.

Δ   Older adult clients often present with atypical symptoms of the disease, such as altered mentation or unusual behavior, fever, anorexia, and weight loss.

Primary Reference:

Ignatavicius, D. D., & Workman, M. L. (2006). *Medical-surgical nursing* (5th ed.). St. Louis, MO: Saunders.

Additional Resources:

NANDA International (2004). *NANDA nursing diagnoses: Definitions and classification 2005-2006*. Philadelphia: NANDA.

For more information on TB, visit the Centers for Disease Control and Prevention at *www.cdc.gov* and the World Health Organization at *www.who.int.*

Chapter 14: Tuberculosis

Application Exercises

1. Which of the following clients is at the greatest risk for developing TB?

> A. 23-year-old male living in a double room dormitory
>
> B. 52-year-old retired school teacher living with her husband
>
> C. 45-year-old alcoholic homeless woman who occasionally lives in a shelter
>
> D. 33-year-old banker who works in an office and drives his car to work

2. A nurse is caring for a client who recently traveled to South America on a mission trip. He traveled through the countryside on a small, crowded bus for several days. As he coughs, the nurse notices what appears to be blood on the tissue. Which of the following actions should the nurse take?

> A. Initiate universal respiratory precautions.
>
> B. Consult the primary care provider and isolate the client.
>
> C. Give the client a breathing treatment and a mask.
>
> D. Continue with the client's physical assessment.

Scenario: A home health nurse is caring for a 72-year-old female client who has active TB. She lives at home with her 78-year-old husband. She is prescribed the following medication regimen:

Isoniazid (INH) 250 mg PO daily
Rifampin (RIF) 500 mg PO daily
Pyrazinamide (PZA) 750 mg PO daily

---

3. Which of the following statements indicate her understanding of appropriate care measures? (Check all that apply.)

> _____ "It is okay to substitute one medication for another when I run out since they all fight the infection."
>
> _____ "I will wash my hands each time I cough or sneeze."
>
> _____ "I will increase my intake of citrus fruits, red meat, and whole grains."
>
> _____ "I am glad that I don't have to collect any more sputum specimens."
>
> _____ "I will make sure that I wear a mask when I am in a public place."
>
> _____ "I do not need to worry about where I go once I start taking my medications."

4. Should her husband be tested for TB?

5. **True or False:** A positive Mantoux test indicates the presence of active TB.

6. **True or False:** TB should be considered as a possible diagnosis for any client experiencing weight loss, anorexia, fever, and cough with sputum production.

Chapter 14: Tuberculosis

Application Exercises Answer Key

1. Which of the following clients is at the greatest risk for developing TB?

      A. 23-year-old male living in a double room dormitory

      B. 52-year-old retired school teacher living with her husband

      C. 45-year-old alcoholic homeless woman who occasionally lives in a shelter

      D. 33-year-old banker who works in an office and drives his car to work

Alcoholism, homelessness, and living in crowded areas place clients at an increased risk for contracting TB.

2. A nurse is caring for a client who recently traveled to South America on a mission trip. He traveled through the countryside on a small, crowded bus for several days. As he coughs, the nurse notices what appears to be blood on the tissue. Which of the following actions should the nurse take?

      A. Initiate universal respiratory precautions.

      B. Consult the primary care provider and isolate the client.

      C. Give the client a breathing treatment and a mask.

      D. Continue with the client's physical assessment.

The client's travel history and blood-tinged sputum indicate that TB is a likely possibility. Isolation precautions should be taken until the diagnosis is confirmed. The provider should be consulted to determine further management.

Scenario: A home health nurse is caring for a 72-year-old female client who has active TB. She lives at home with her 78-year-old husband. She is prescribed the following medication regimen:

Isoniazid (INH) 250 mg PO daily
Rifampin (RIF) 500 mg PO daily
Pyrazinamide (PZA) 750 mg PO daily

3. Which of the following statements indicate her understanding of appropriate care measures? (Check all that apply.)

_____ "It is okay to substitute one medication for another when I run out since they all fight the infection."

__x__ "I will wash my hands each time I cough or sneeze."

__x__ "I will increase my intake of citrus fruits, red meat, and whole grains."

_____ "I am glad that I don't have to collect any more sputum specimens."

__x__ "I will make sure that I wear a mask when I am in a public place."

_____ "I do not need to worry about where I go once I start taking my medications."

The correct statements demonstrate understanding by the client on how to prevent infection and promote nutrition. The remaining statements are direct contradictions for appropriate care practices, such as adhering to the medication regimen and continuing sputum collection to monitor disease progression.

4. Should her husband be tested for TB?

Yes, any exposed family members should be tested for TB.

5. **True or False:** A positive Mantoux test indicates the presence of active TB.

False: A positive Mantoux test indicates either exposure to TB or the presence of inactive disease.

6. **True or False:** TB should be considered as a possible diagnosis for any client experiencing weight loss, anorexia, fever, and cough with sputum production.

True: These are all possible signs of active TB.

Nursing Care of Clients with Respiratory Disorders
Nursing Care of Clients with Cancers of the Respiratory System

Chapter 15: Laryngeal Cancer

Contributor: Gayla H. Love, BSN, RN, CCM

NCLEX-PN® Connections:

Learning Objective: Review and apply knowledge within "**Laryngeal Cancer**" in readiness for performance of the following nursing activities as outlined by the NCLEX-PN® test plan:

Δ   Assist with relevant laboratory, diagnostic, and therapeutic procedures within the nursing role, including:

  • Preparation of the client for the procedure.

  • Accurate collection of specimens.

  • Monitoring client status during and after the procedure.

  • Reinforcing client teaching (before and following the procedure).

  • Recognizing the client's response (expected, unexpected adverse response) to the procedure.

  • Monitoring results.

  • Monitoring and taking actions to prevent or minimize the risk of complications.

  • Notifying the primary care provider of signs of complications.

Δ   Recognize signs and symptoms of the client's problem and complete the proper documentation.

Δ   Provide and document care based on the client's health alteration.

Δ   Monitor and document vital signs changes.

Δ   Interpret data that need to be reported immediately.

Δ   Reinforce client education on managing the client's health problem.

Δ   Recognize and respond to emergency situations, including notification of the primary care provider.

Δ   Review the client's response to emergency interventions and complete the proper documentation.

Δ   Provide care that meets the age-related needs of clients 65 years of age or older, including recognizing expected physiological changes.

Key Points

Δ   Laryngeal cancer can be devastating because of its impact on a client's ability to breath, eat, and speak, as well as the client's appearance.

Δ   Most laryngeal cancers are squamous cell carcinomas and are slow growing.

Δ   Men are three times more likely to be affected than women, and most cancers occur after age 60.

Δ   Treatment includes laryngectomy, radiation, and/or chemotherapy.

Key Factors

Δ   **Risk Factors** for Laryngeal Cancer

- **Tobacco** and **alcohol use** are the primary risk factors. Their effects are synergistic when used in combination.

- Chronic exposure to harmful chemicals.

Diagnostic Procedures and Nursing Interventions

Δ   **X-rays** of skull, sinuses, neck, and chest; **Computed Tomography (CT)**; **Magnetic Resonance Imaging (MRI)**

- Help to determine the **extent** and exact **location of the tumor** and level of soft tissue invasion.

- Prepare the client for the procedure (informed consent, NPO) as appropriate; monitor the client and maintain client safety following the procedure (vital signs, return of gag reflex).

Δ   **Laryngoscopy**

- Used to visualize tumor and obtain **tumor biopsy**, which definitively **determines cell type and staging**.

- Prepare the client for the procedure (informed consent, NPO) as appropriate.

- Monitor the client and maintain client safety following the procedure (vital signs, return of gag reflex, monitor excision site for bleeding).

Δ   **Bone Scan and Positron Emission Tomography (PET) Scan**

- Determines presence of metastasis.

- Assess for client allergies to contrast dye and adequate renal function (ability to excrete dye).

Assessments

Δ Monitor for **signs and symptoms.**

- Persistent or **recurrent hoarseness or sore throat**
- Mouth sores or **lesions that fail to heal**
- **Lump** in throat, mouth, or neck
- **Dysphagia**
- Persistent, unilateral ear pain
- Weight loss, anorexia

Δ **Assess/Monitor**

- Respiratory status (airway patency, breath sounds, respiratory rate, use of accessory muscles, oxygenation status) before and following interventions
- Swallowing ability
- Pain (location, intensity, severity, precipitating factors, self-care methods to relieve symptoms)
- Overall nutrition and recent weight loss
- History of smoking and/or alcohol use
- Laboratory and diagnostic findings (chest x-ray, laryngoscopy, bone scan, PET results)

NANDA Nursing Diagnoses

Δ Risk for aspiration

Δ Acute pain or chronic pain

Δ Impaired verbal communication

Δ Disturbed body image

Nursing Interventions

Δ **Maintain a patent airway.**

- **Suction** the client as needed.
- **Position** the client as **upright** as possible to facilitate ventilation.
- Assess **cough reflex, level of consciousness,** and **ability to swallow.**

Δ Monitor respiratory status.

- Monitor **vital signs, SaO$_2$.**

Δ   Administer **medications** as prescribed.

- **Crush pills** to aid in swallowing.

- Obtain **elixirs** when possible.

Δ   **Provide pain relief.**

- **Administer analgesics** as prescribed.

- Consider **alternative pain relief methods**, such as massage or distraction, in conjunction with medications.

Δ   **Prevent infection.**

- **Cleanse** and **dress surgical sites** as prescribed.

- Perform proper **handwashing**.

- Use **appropriate technique** when **suctioning**.

- **Administer antibiotics** as prescribed.

Δ   **Promote nutrition.**

- Feed in **small amounts**.

- **Increase caloric intake** (whole milk, supplements).

- Use **thickened liquids** if swallowing is impaired.

Δ   **Provide oral care.**

Δ   **Provide education.**

- Instruct the client on the importance of **smoking cessation** if applicable. Provide **nicotine replacement** as prescribed.

- Instruct the client on **appropriate techniques** for **stoma care** and **suctioning**.

- Instruct the client to **report any signs of infection** (fever, purulent drainage, redness, or swelling).

- Refer to group programs or **support groups**.

- Encourage the client to consume a **diet high in protein and calories**.

Δ   **Provide emotional support.**

- **Encourage verbalization** of feelings regarding the prognosis and changes in self-image.

- Consider a **social work consult** for the client and family.

Δ   **Surgical Management**

* **Laryngectomy**

  ◊   May be partial or total.

  ◊   Clients undergoing **total laryngectomies will lose their natural voice.**

  ◊   **Tracheostomies** are created for clients undergoing laryngectomy. They are **permanent for total laryngectomy clients. A laryngectomy tube is inserted** into the stoma. This **prevents contractures** from forming. Care for this is similar to tracheostomy tube care.

  ◊   **Esophageal speech, mechanical devices, and tracheoesophageal fistulas** are methods of speech communication that can be explored and developed following a total laryngectomy. These will allow the client to speak but the quality of the client's speech will sound different.

* If a **nodal neck dissection** ("radical neck") is done, the 11th cranial nerve will be cut, resulting in **shoulder drop** following surgery.

* **Cordectomy** (excision of a vocal cord) may be performed.

* A **tracheostomy** is created for clients undergoing laryngectomy.

* **Provide preoperative teaching** regarding:

  ◊   The use of **alternate forms of communication** (dry erase board, pen and paper, alphabet board). Determine the client's preference.

  ◊   **Self-care of the airway,** including tracheostomy care and suctioning techniques.

  ◊   **Pain control methods.**

* Postoperative care

  ◊   Monitor **airway patency** and vital signs. Avoid suctioning near the surgical site to prevent trauma.

  ◊   Monitor **hemodynamic status** and observe the surgical site for **hemorrhage.**

  ◊   Monitor **pain level** and **administer analgesics** as prescribed (morphine, fentanyl).

  ◊   **Cleanse** and **dress** wounds as prescribed. Wound breakdown is common postoperatively.

  ◊   **Initiate nutritional intake** as ordered.

  ◊   Consider **speech therapy consultation.**

Complications and Nursing Implications

Δ   **Airway Obstruction**

- Monitor **respiratory status** (SaO_2, breath sounds).

- **Suction** the **client** when needed.

- Encourage **deep breathing and coughing** to aid in secretion removal.

- Have airway insertion materials at bedside (tracheostomy kit, endotracheal tubes).

Δ   **Aspiration**

- Maintain **upright positioning.**

- Use **thickened liquids.**

- **Cut food** into small pieces.

- Provide **foods that can be formed into a bolus** before swallowing (meats, bread).

- **Notify the primary care provider** if aspiration is suspected. Place the client on NPO status until swallowing ability can be determined.

- Aspiration **may lead to the development of pneumonia.**

Primary Reference:

Ignatavicius, D. D., & Workman, M. L. (2006). *Medical-surgical nursing* (5th ed.). St. Louis, MO: Saunders.

Additional Resources:

NANDA International (2004). *NANDA nursing diagnoses: Definitions and classification 2005-2006*. Philadelphia: NANDA.

White, L. (2005). *Foundations of nursing*. (2nd ed.). New York: Thomson Delmar Learning.

Chapter 15: Laryngeal Cancer

Application Exercises

1. Which of the following may increase the risk for the development of laryngeal cancer? (Check all that apply.)

_____ A client who paints houses for a living

_____ A client who uses chewing tobacco

_____ A radiology technician who takes x-rays of clients daily

_____ A client who smokes only cigars, not cigarettes

_____ A client who consumes two glasses of red wine per week and lives with a spouse who smokes cigarettes

Scenario: A nurse is assessing a 62-year-old male client with a history of prolonged smoking and alcoholism. The client's chief symptom is hoarseness that has persisted for more than 2 months. The client reports that he has difficulty swallowing due to the feeling that he has a lump in his throat. The admitting provider orders diagnostic studies to rule out laryngeal cancer. Laryngoscopy reveals enlarged cervical nodes, and a CT scan reveals a subglottic lesion with lymph node enlargement. Multiple biopsy specimens confirm the presence of malignancy. The client is diagnosed with laryngeal cancer and is admitted for a total laryngectomy.

2. The decision is made to move forward with a total laryngectomy, radiation, and chemotherapy. The client asks the nurse if he will be able to speak after surgery. Which of the following is the most appropriate response?

A. "We will have to assess your ability to speak following the procedure, but there is a good chance that you will be able to speak in your natural voice."

B. "No, you will not be able to speak, so you will have to use written forms of communication."

C. "Since you are having a total laryngectomy, you will not be able to speak again with your natural voice. However, there are options for re-establishing speech communication that you can consider as your healing progresses."

D. "The primary concern is to remove the cancer, so you shouldn't worry about your voice at this time."

3. The client has been approved to resume his oral intake. The nurse prepares a snack for the client. Which of the following foods represent an appropriate choice for this client? (Check all that apply.)

_____ Mashed potatoes and gravy
_____ Orange juice
_____ Turkey sandwich
_____ Chicken noodle soup
_____ Tuna salad
_____ Oatmeal

4. The nurse enters the room and observes the client lying in bed coughing forcefully. The client's wife states that he began coughing when trying to swallow some water. What should the nurse do first?

5. What education is important to provide to this client?

6. Why is providing emotional support to clients with laryngeal cancer so important?

Chapter 15: Laryngeal Cancer

Application Exercises Answer Key

1. Which of the following may increase the risk for the development of laryngeal cancer? (Check all that apply.)

__x__	A client who paints houses for a living
__x__	A client who uses chewing tobacco
_____	A radiology technician who takes x-rays of clients daily
__x__	A client who smokes only cigars, not cigarettes
__x__	A client who consumes two glasses of red wine per week and lives with a spouse who smokes cigarettes

   Clients who use tobacco or alcohol, or are exposed to harmful chemicals, are at risk for laryngeal cancer.

Scenario: A nurse is assessing a 62-year-old male client with a history of prolonged smoking and alcoholism. The client's chief symptom is hoarseness that has persisted for more than 2 months. The client reports that he has difficulty swallowing due to the feeling that he has a lump in his throat. The admitting provider orders diagnostic studies to rule out laryngeal cancer. Laryngoscopy reveals enlarged cervical nodes, and a CT scan reveals a subglottic lesion with lymph node enlargement. Multiple biopsy specimens confirm the presence of malignancy. The client is diagnosed with laryngeal cancer and is admitted for a total laryngectomy.

2. The decision is made to move forward with a total laryngectomy, radiation, and chemotherapy. The client asks the nurse if he will be able to speak after surgery. Which of the following is the most appropriate response?

   A. "We will have to assess your ability to speak following the procedure, but there is a good chance that you will be able to speak in your natural voice."

   B "No, you will not be able to speak, so you will have to use written forms of communication."

   C. **"Since you are having a total laryngectomy, you will not be able to speak again with your natural voice. However, there are options for re-establishing speech communication that you can consider as your healing progresses."**

   D. "The primary concern is to remove the cancer, so you shouldn't worry about your voice at this time."

   There are several methods and devices that can be used to help the client communicate through speech.

3. The client has been approved to resume his oral intake. The nurse prepares a snack for the client. Which of the following foods represent an appropriate choice for this client? (Check all that apply.)

__X__	Mashed potatoes and gravy
_____	Orange juice
__X__	Turkey sandwich
_____	Chicken noodle soup
__X__	Tuna salad
__X__	Oatmeal

A client with laryngeal cancer is at risk for aspiration. Clients at risk for aspiration should sit upright for meals, avoid liquids unless a thickener has been added, and choose foods that can be formed into a bolus.

4. The nurse enters the room and observes the client lying in bed coughing forcefully. The client's wife states that he began coughing when trying to swallow some water. What should the nurse do first?

The nurse should assist the client to an upright position and then assess his respiratory status by checking his SaO_2. The client should then be suctioned if secretions are detected. Place the client on NPO status. Lastly, the nurse should notify the primary care provider, because aspiration should be suspected.

5. What education is important to provide to this client?

The nurse should inform the client and his wife of the risk for aspiration following his procedure. Instruct the client to consume foods and liquids in an upright position, cut food into small pieces, and to consume thickened liquids or semi-liquid foods once oral intake is approved.

6. Why is providing emotional support to clients with laryngeal cancer so important?

Clients with this diagnosis deal with a great amount of loss. Often, their speech is altered or their ability to talk may be completely eliminated. Surgical procedures can leave the client very disfigured depending upon the degree of tumor invasion into the soft tissues.

Unit 2   **Nursing Care of Clients with Respiratory Disorders**
Section: Nursing Care of Clients with Cancers of the Respiratory System

Chapter 16:   Lung Cancer
Contributor: Gayla H. Love, BSN, RN, CCM

NCLEX-PN® Connections:

Learning Objective: Review and apply knowledge within **"Lung Cancer"** in readiness for performance of the following nursing activities as outlined by the NCLEX-PN® test plans:

Δ   Assist with relevant laboratory, diagnostic, and therapeutic procedures within the nursing role, including:

- Preparation of the client for the procedure.
- Accurate collection of specimens.
- Monitoring client status during and after the procedure.
- Reinforcing client teaching (before and following the procedure).
- Recognizing the client's response (expected, unexpected adverse response) to the procedure.
- Monitoring results.
- Monitoring and taking actions to prevent or minimize the risk of complications.
- Notifying the primary care provider of signs of complications.

Δ   Recognize signs and symptoms of the client's problem and complete the proper documentation.

Δ   Provide and document care based on the client's health alteration.

Δ   Monitor and document vital signs changes.

Δ   Interpret data that need to be reported immediately.

Δ   Reinforce client education on managing the client's health problem.

Δ   Recognize and respond to emergency situations, including notification of the primary care provider.

Δ   Review the client's response to emergency interventions and complete the proper documentation.

Δ   Provide care that meets the age-related needs of clients 65 years of age or older, including recognizing expected physiological changes.

📘 Key Points

Δ Lung cancer is a **leading cause of cancer-related deaths**. The 5-year survival rate for lung cancer is less than 15%.

Δ Lung cancer is often diagnosed in an advanced stage when metastasis is present. **Palliative care**, or treatment geared toward relieving symptoms, is often the focus of lung cancer therapy when metastasis is present.

Δ **Bronchogenic carcinomas** (arising from the bronchial epithelium) account for 90% of primary lung cancers.

Δ Histologic **cell type determines** lung cancer **classification**. Categories include:

- **Non-small cell lung cancer (NSCLC).**

  ◊ Most lung cancers are from this category.

  ◊ Includes squamous, adeno, and large cell carcinomas.

- **Small cell lung cancer (SCLC).**

  ◊ Fast growing

  ◊ Almost always associated with history of cigarette smoking

Δ **Staging** of lung cancer is defined with the **TMN system.**

- T = tumor

- N = nodes

- M = metastasis

Δ Chemotherapy is the primary choice of treatment for lung cancers. It is often used in combination with radiation and/or surgery.

Key Factors

Risk Factors

- Cigarette, cigar, and pipe **smoking** or exposure to **second-hand smoke.**

- Chronic exposure to inhaled environmental irritants.

Diagnostic Procedures and Nursing Interventions

Δ **Chest x-ray** and **Computed Tomography (CT) Scan**

- Provides **initial identification** of tumor.

Δ **Bronchoscopy**

- May provide **direct visibility** of tumor.

- Allows for **specimen** and **biopsy collection**.

- Prepare the client for the procedure (informed consent, NPO) as appropriate, monitor the client, and maintain client safety following the procedure (vital signs, **return of gag reflex**, administer sedatives and supplemental oxygen as needed).

Assessments

Δ   Monitor for **signs and symptoms.**

◊   Clients with lung cancer may experience few symptoms early in the disease. Monitor for signs and symptoms that often appear late in the disease:

° Persistent **cough**, with or without rust-colored or **blood-tinged sputum.**

° **Dyspnea.**

° **Unilateral wheezing**, if the airway is obstructed.

° Chest wall **pain.**

° Muffled heart sounds.

° Fatigue, weight loss, anorexia.

Δ   **Assess/Monitor**

- Client's respiratory status (airway patency, lung sounds, respiratory rate, use of accessory muscles, oxygenation status) before and following interventions.

- Client's history regarding use of tobacco products.

◊   Determine the **pack-year history**, which is the number of packs of cigarettes smoked per day times the number of years smoked.

◊   Evaluate use of other tobacco products, such as cigars, pipes, and chewing tobacco.

◊   Ask about exposure to secondhand smoke.

- Nutritional status, weight loss, anorexia.

NANDA Nursing Diagnoses

Δ   Ineffective airway clearance

Δ   Impaired gas exchange

Δ   Imbalanced nutrition: Less than body requirements

Δ   Anxiety

Nursing Interventions

Δ   Maintain a **patent airway and monitor respiratory status**.

- Suction the client as needed.

- Place in upright or **high-Fowler's** position to facilitate ventilation.

- Assist with therapeutic procedures (intubation, tumor removal/resection, thoracentesis).

- Assess breathing pattern and auscultate lung sounds.

- Assess SaO_2, ABG values.

Δ   **Administer oxygen** as prescribed.

Δ   Promote **high-calorie, high-protein diet**.

Δ   Provide information for **smoking cessation** classes.

Δ   **Surgical Intervention**

- Often involves removal of a lung (**pneumonectomy**), lobe (**lobectomy**), segment (**segmentectomy**), or peripheral lung tissue (**wedge resection**).

- **Preoperative** care

  ◊   Teach the client about the **surgical incision and chest tube**.

  ◊   Relieve client anxiety and **encourage verbalization of feelings**.

- **Postoperative** care

  ◊   Monitor **vital signs, oxygenation** (SaO_2, ABG values), and for signs of **hemorrhage**.

  ◊   Manage **chest tube and drainage system**.

  ◊   **Administer oxygen** and manage the ventilator if appropriate.

Δ   **Palliative Care**

- Includes medication, radiation, and laser therapy; thoracentesis; pain management; and hospice referral and care. Nursing care should include:

  ◊   **Administer humidified oxygen** for hypoxemia, dyspnea, and anxiety.

  ◊   Administer **bronchodilators and corticosteroids** to decrease inflammation, bronchospasm, and edema; administer mucolytics to aid with expectoration of sputum.

  ◊   Assist with **thoracentesis**.

  ◊   **Monitor the client for complications from radiation** therapy.

  ◊   Assess **onset, quality, duration, and severity of the pain**.

◊ **Administer opioid analgesics** (morphine, fentanyl, OxyContin); consider patient-controlled analgesia (PCA) **pump**.

◊ Provide **emotional support** to the client and family; **encourage verbalization** of feelings.

◊ Refer to **hospice care**.

Complications and Nursing Implications

Δ **Superior Vena Cava Syndrome**

• Results from pressure placed on the vena cava by a tumor. This is a medical emergency.

• Monitor for signs:

◊ **Early signs** include facial edema, tightness of shirt collars, nosebleeds, peripheral edema, and dyspnea.

◊ **Late signs** include mental status changes, cyanosis, hemorrhage, and hypotension.

• **Notify the primary care provider immediately.**

• **Radiation** and **stent placement** provide temporary relief. Prepare the client for procedure (informed consent, NPO if possible, client transport).

• **Monitor client status** (vital signs, oxygenation) during and after the procedure.

Δ **Metastasis**

• Metastasis to the **bones** can cause bone pain and increase the risk of pathologic fractures. Encourage client to ambulate carefully.

• Metastasis to the **central nervous system** can lead to changes in mentation, lethargy, and bowel and bladder malfunction. Reorient client as needed.

Meeting the Needs of Older Adults

Δ Older adult clients have **decreased pulmonary reserves** due to normal lung changes including decreased lung elasticity and thickening alveoli. This contributes to impaired gas exchange.

Δ **Structural changes in the skeletal system** decrease diaphragmatic expansion and therefore **restrict ventilation**.

Primary Reference:

Ignatavicius, D. D., & Workman, M. L. (2006). *Medical-surgical nursing* (5th ed.). St. Louis, MO: Saunders.

Additional Resources:

NANDA International (2004). *NANDA nursing diagnoses: Definitions and classification 2005-2006*. Philadelphia: NANDA.

White, L. (2005). *Foundations of nursing* (2nd ed.). New York: Thomson Delmar Learning.

For more information, visit the American Cancer Society at: *www.cancer.org*.

Chapter 16: Lung Cancer

Application Exercises

Scenario: A nurse is caring for a 68-year-old male client who presented to the emergency department with dyspnea and rust-colored sputum that has persisted for nearly 3 weeks. Lung cancer is suspected, and diagnostic tests are ordered.

1. Which of the following would the nurse most likely find in this client's history?

   A. Chronic alcohol abuse

   B. Family history of breast cancer

   C. Smokes 2 packs of cigarettes/day

   D. History of asthma

2. The CT scan reveals the presence of a mass at the base of the bronchial tree. The client is expected to undergo a bronchoscopy. What actions should the nurse expect to take?

Scenario: A client is admitted to the emergency department with a diagnosis of advanced lung cancer. The client reports dyspnea on exertion and at rest, and her family states that she has become disoriented over the last 72 hr. A chest x-ray reveals a baseball-sized mediastinal tumor. Vital signs are: heart rate 104 beats/min, blood pressure 88/42 mm Hg, respiratory rate 38/min, temperature 37.9° C (100.2° F). The client's SaO_2 is 89% on room air.

3. What do these signs and symptoms indicate?

4. Which of the following is the most important intervention for the nurse to perform initially?

   A. Notify the primary care provider.

   B. Obtain CT scan to determine exact location of the tumor.

   C. Administer oxygen.

   D. Provide family support.

5. **True or False:** Most clients with bronchogenic cancer have small cell lung cancer.

6. **True or False:** A client has just returned to the unit following a bronchoscopy and lung biopsy. It is important for the nurse to assess the client's gag reflex prior to offering oral fluids.

Chapter 16: Lung Cancer

Application Exercises Answer Key

Scenario: A nurse is caring for a 68-year-old male client who presented to the emergency department with dyspnea and rust-colored sputum that has persisted for nearly 3 weeks. Lung cancer is suspected, and diagnostic tests are ordered.

1. Which of the following would the nurse most likely find in this client's history?

> A. Chronic alcohol abuse
>
> B. Family history of breast cancer
>
> **C. Smokes 2 packs of cigarettes/day**
>
> D. History of asthma

> **The most significant history finding in a client with lung cancer is a history of cigarette smoking. The longer the client smoked and the more he smoked, the greater the risk of developing lung cancer.**

2. The CT scan reveals the presence of a mass at the base of the bronchial tree. The client is expected to undergo a bronchoscopy. What actions should the nurse expect to take?

> **The nurse should prepare the client for the procedure by making him NPO, obtaining informed consent, and educating the client regarding the procedure. During the procedure, the nurse should administer prescribed medications and monitor the client's vital signs and oxygenation status. Post procedure, the nurse should expect to continue monitoring the client's vital signs and oxygenation. In addition, the client must be assessed for the return of his gag reflex and signs of complications, such as hemorrhage. The nurse should appropriately label the specimen and transport it to the laboratory.**

Scenario: A client is admitted to the emergency department with a diagnosis of advanced lung cancer. The client reports dyspnea on exertion and at rest, and her family states that she has become disoriented over the last 72 hr. A chest x-ray reveals a baseball-sized mediastinal tumor. Vital signs are: heart rate 104 beats/min, blood pressure 88/42 mm Hg, respiratory rate 38/min, temperature 37.9° C (100.2° F). The client's SaO_2 is 89% on room air.

3. What do these signs and symptoms indicate?

> **The client's signs and symptoms indicate that she is experiencing superior vena cava syndrome.**

4. Which of the following is the most important intervention for the nurse to perform initially?

        A. Notify the primary care provider.

        B. Obtain CT scan to determine exact location of the tumor.

        C. Administer oxygen.

        D. Provide family support.

5. **True or False:** Most clients with bronchogenic cancer have small cell lung cancer.

False: Non-small cell cancer is the most common category of bronchogenic cancers.

6. **True or False:** A client has just returned to the unit following a bronchoscopy and lung biopsy. It is important for the nurse to assess the client's gag reflex prior to offering oral fluids.

True: A local anesthetic is applied to the upper airway prior to a bronchoscopy to suppress the gag reflex during the procedure. It is very important for the nurse to assess the client's gag reflex following the procedure and to decrease the risk of aspiration.

Unit 2   Nursing Care of Clients with Respiratory Disorders

Section: Medical Emergencies: Respiratory

Chapter 17:   Pulmonary Embolism
Contributor: Gayla H. Love, BSN, RN, CCM

NCLEX-PN® Connections:

Learning Objective: Review and apply knowledge within **"Pulmonary Embolism"** in readiness for performance of the following nursing activities as outlined by the NCLEX-PN® test plan:

Δ   Assist with relevant laboratory, diagnostic, and therapeutic procedures within the nursing role, including:

- • Preparation of the client for the procedure.
- • Accurate collection of specimens.
- • Monitoring client status during and after the procedure.
- • Reinforcing client teaching (before and following the procedure).
- • Recognizing the client's response (expected, unexpected adverse response) to the procedure.
- • Monitoring results.
- • Monitoring and taking actions to prevent or minimize the risk of complications.
- • Notifying the primary care provider of signs of complications.

Δ   Recognize signs and symptoms of the client's problem and complete the proper documentation.

Δ   Provide and document care based on the client's health alteration.

Δ   Monitor and document vital signs changes.

Δ   Interpret data that need to be reported immediately.

Δ   Reinforce client education on managing the client's health problem.

Δ   Recognize and respond to emergency situations, including notification of the primary care provider.

Δ   Review the client's response to emergency interventions and complete the proper documentation.

Δ   Provide care that meets the age-related needs of clients 65 years of age or older, including recognizing expected physiological changes.

📖 **Key Points**

Δ A pulmonary embolism (PE) occurs when a **substance (solid, gaseous, or liquid) enters venous circulation and terminates in the pulmonary vasculature.**

Δ Emboli originating from **deep vein thrombosis (DVT)** are the most common cause.

Δ Large emboli lead to decreased oxygenation, pulmonary tissue hypoxia, and possibly death. **A PE is a medical emergency.**

Δ **Prevention, rapid recognition, and treatment** of a PE are essential for a positive outcome.

Key Factors

Δ **Risk Factors for PE**

- Long-term **immobility**

- **Oral contraceptive use, estrogen therapy**

- **Smoking**

- **Hypercoagulability** (for example elevated platelet count)

- **Obesity**

- **Surgery**

- Heart failure or chronic **atrial fibrillation**

- Autoimmune hemolytic anemia such as **sickle cell disease**

- **Long bone fractures**

- Advanced age

Diagnostic Procedures and Nursing Interventions

Δ Radiological Assessment

- **Spiral Computed Tomography** (CT) is commonly used to diagnose a PE.

- **Chest x-ray** may show a large PE.

- **Ventilation and Perfusion Scan (V/Q scan), Pulmonary Angiography**

  ◊ May be used to support diagnosis of PE.

  ◊ Monitor client status (vital signs, SaO_2, anxiety, informed consent and bleeding with angiography) during and after the procedure.

Δ   Laboratory Assessment

• **ABG analysis**

◊ $PaCO_2$ levels are low due to initial hyperventilation (**respiratory alkalosis**).

◊   As hypoxemia progresses, **respiratory acidosis** ensues.

◊   Obtain specimen, apply appropriate pressure to puncture site, place specimen in a heparinized syringe and ice, ensure timely transport, and communicate results.

Assessments

Δ   Clients with a PE often experience a sudden onset of signs and symptoms. Monitor for signs and symptoms of a PE:

• Dyspnea, air hunger

• Pleurisy

• **Tachycardia**

• Hypotension

• **Tachypnea**

• **Anxiety**, apprehension

• Adventitious breath sounds (crackles), cough

• S_3, S_4

• Diaphoresis

• **Decreased SaO$_2$**

• Petechiae, cyanosis

• Pleural effusion

Δ   **Assess/Monitor**

• Client's respiratory status (airway patency, breath sounds, respiratory rate, use of accessory muscles, oxygenation status) before and following intervention

• Client's history regarding risk factors for a PE

• General appearance

• Laboratory and diagnostic findings (arterial blood gases, CT scan)

NANDA Nursing Diagnoses

 Δ   Impaired gas exchange

 Δ   Decreased cardiac output

 Δ   Risk for injury

 Δ   Anxiety

Nursing Interventions

 Δ   Assess and monitor **respiratory status** (breath sounds, vital signs, SaO_2).

- • **Administer oxygen therapy** as prescribed.

- • Place the client in **high-Fowler's** position to facilitate gas exchange.

- • Collect and interpret **ABG values**.

 Δ   Assess and monitor **cardiovascular status** (heart rate and rhythm, cardiac output if available, pulmonary pressures if available).

 Δ   **Assess** and monitor **pain**.

 Δ   Initiate and maintain **IV access**.

 Δ   Administer medications as prescribed.

- • **Anticoagulants**: Enoxaparin (Lovenox), heparin, warfarin (Coumadin)

  ◊   Used to prevent clot from getting larger or other clots from forming.

  ◊   Assess for **contraindications** (active bleeding, peptic ulcer disease, history of stroke, recent trauma).

  ◊   **Monitor bleeding times** – prothrombin time (PT), activated partial thromboplastin time (aPTT), international normalized ratio (INR), complete blood count (CBC).

  ◊   Monitor for **side effects of anticoagulants** (thrombocytopenia, anemia, hemorrhage).

- • **Fibrinolytic therapy:** Alteplase, Streptokinase

  ◊   Used to break up blood clots.

  ◊   Similar side effects and contraindications as anticoagulants.

Δ   Provide **education** to client for the **treatment and prevention of a PE.**

- **Avoid** long periods of **immobility.**

- Monitor intake of foods high in vitamin K (for example, green leafy vegetables) if the client is taking warfarin. Vitamin K can reduce the anticoagulant effects of warfarin.

- **Adhere to a schedule for monitoring of PT and INR** and follow instructions regarding medication dosage adjustments (for clients on warfarin).

Δ   Provide **emotional support and comfort** to control client anxiety.

Δ   Surgical management

- **Embolectomy** (removal of the embolus)

- **Insertion of a filter** in the vena cava to prevent further emboli from reaching the pulmonary vasculature.

  ◊   Prepare the client for the procedure (NPO status, informed consent).

  ◊   Monitor postoperatively (vital signs, SaO_2, incision drainage, pain management).

Complications and Nursing Implications

Δ   **Decreased Cardiac Output**

- Monitor for **hypotension, tachycardia,** cyanosis, jugular venous distention, and syncope.

- S_3 or S_4 may occur.

- Initiate and maintain **IV access.**

- **Administer IV fluids** (crystalloids) to replace vascular volume.

- Continuously monitor **electrocardiogram** (ECG).

- Monitor **pulmonary pressures.** IV fluids may contribute to pulmonary hypertension for clients with right-sided heart failure (cor pulmonale).

- Administer **inotropic agents,** such as milrinone (Primacor) and dobutamine (Dobutrex), to increase myocardial contractility.

- **Vasodilators** may be needed if pulmonary artery (PA) pressure is high enough that it interferes with cardiac contractility.

Δ   **Hemorrhage**

- **Assess** for oozing, bleeding, or bruising from **injection and surgical sites.**

- Monitor **cardiovascular status** (blood pressure, heart rate and rhythm).

- Monitor **CBC** (hemoglobin, hematocrit, platelets) and **bleeding times** (PT, aPTT, INR).

- Administer **IV fluids and blood products** as required.

- Test stools, urine, nasogastric drainage, and vomit for **occult blood**.

- Monitor for **internal bleeding** (measure abdominal girth, abdominal or flank pain).

- **Avoid intramuscular injections when possible.** Use small gauge needles for necessary injections.

- **Avoid rectal temperatures and enemas**; utilize electric shavers and soft-bristled toothbrushes.

Meeting the Needs of Older Adults

Δ   Older adult clients have **decreased pulmonary reserves** due to normal lung changes including decreased lung elasticity and thickening alveoli. **Older adult clients may decompensate more quickly.**

Δ   Certain pathological conditions and procedures that **predispose** clients to **DVT** formation (peripheral vascular disease, hypertension, hip and knee replacements) are more prevalent in the older adult population.

Δ   Many older adult clients experience decreased physical activity levels, thus predisposing them to DVT formation and pulmonary emboli.

Primary Reference:

Ignatavicius, D. D., & Workman, M. L. (2006). *Medical-surgical nursing* (5th ed.). St. Louis, MO: Saunders.

Additional Resources:

Burke, K. M., LeMone, P., & Mohn-Brown, E. L. (2003). *Medical-surgical nursing care*. Upper Saddle River, NJ: Prentice-Hall.

Kowalak, J.P., & Hughes, A. S. (Eds.). (2002). *Atlas of Pathophysiology*. Philadelphia: Lippincott Williams & Wilkins.

NANDA International (2004). *NANDA nursing diagnoses: Definitions and classification 2005-2006*. Philadelphia: NANDA.

Chapter 17: Pulmonary Embolism

Application Exercises

1. Which of the following clients are at risk for a PE? (Check all that apply.)

_____ 28-year-old female taking birth control pills

_____ Female client who is postmenopausal

_____ 14-year-old male with a fractured femur

_____ Client who smokes one pipe daily

_____ 32-year-old marathon runner

_____ Client with congestive heart failure with chronic atrial fibrillation

---

Scenario: A 54-year-old woman is admitted to the coronary care unit with acute dyspnea and diaphoresis. The client states that she is anxious because she feels that she can't get enough air. Vital signs are: heart rate 117 beats/min, respiratory rate 38/min, temperature 38.4° C (101.2° F), and blood pressure 100/54 mm Hg.

---

2. Prioritize the following provider orders. Designate "1" as the highest priority.

_____ Obtain an ABG.

_____ Initiate a heparin drip.

_____ Administer oxygen therapy.

_____ Obtain a spiral CT scan.

3. Which of the following client statements poses an immediate concern for the nurse?

A. "I am allergic to morphine."

B. "I take antacids several times a day."

C. "I had a blood clot in my leg several years ago."

D. "It hurts to take a deep breath."

4. Vital signs now include: heart rate 138 beats/min, temperature 38.6° C (101.4° F), blood pressure 78/46 mm Hg, and SaO_2 88% on 2 L per nasal cannula. What do these signs indicate?

---

5. Match the following interventions with their associated rationale.

_____ Administer crystalloids.   A. Improve cardiac contractility.

_____ Administer dobutamine.   B. Restore intravascular volume.

_____ Monitor platelet count.   C. Assess for thrombocytopenia.

6. Which of the following is a contraindication to fibrinolytic therapy?

    A. Recent surgery
    B. Motor vehicle crash 2 months ago
    C. History of asthma
    D. Elevated platelet count

Chapter 17: Pulmonary Embolism

Application Exercises Answer Key

1. Which of the following clients are at risk for a PE? (Check all that apply.)

   __x__   28-year-old female taking birth control pills

   _____   Female client who is postmenopausal

   __x__   14-year-old male with a fractured femur

   __x__   Client who smokes one pipe daily

   _____   32-year-old marathon runner

   __x__   Client with congestive heart failure with chronic atrial fibrillation

   Estrogen use and smoking can cause hypercoagulability, which increases the risk of a blood clot. A client with turbulent blood flow in the heart, such as with a dysrhythmia, is also at increased risk of a blood clot. A fractured bone, particularly in a long bone such as the femur, increases the risk of fat emboli.

   Scenario: A 54-year-old woman is admitted to the coronary care unit with acute dyspnea and diaphoresis. The client states that she is anxious because she feels that she can't get enough air. Vital signs are: heart rate 117 beats/min, respiratory rate 38/min, temperature 38.4° C (101.2° F), and blood pressure 100/54 mm Hg.

2. Prioritize the following provider orders. Designate "1" as the highest priority.

   __2__   Obtain an ABG.

   __3__   Initiate a heparin drip.

   __1__   Administer oxygen therapy.

   __4__   Obtain a spiral CT scan.

   Meeting the client's oxygenation needs is the highest priority. The nurse should administer oxygen as needed.

3. Which of the following client statements poses an immediate concern for the nurse?

    A. "I am allergic to morphine."

    B. "I take antacids several times a day."

    C. "I had a blood clot in my leg several years ago."

    D. "It hurts to take a deep breath."

Option B indicates that this client may have peptic ulcer disease. Further assessment should be completed as this may place the client at an increased risk for hemorrhage once the heparin drip is started.

4. Vital signs now include: heart rate 138 beats/min, temperature 38.6° C (101.4° F), blood pressure 78/46 mm Hg, and SaO$_2$ 88% on 2 L per nasal cannula. What do these signs indicate?

These signs could be due to decreased cardiac output. This may have resulted from hemorrhage or progressing pulmonary hypertension.

5. Match the following interventions with their associated rationale.

    __B__ Administer crystalloids.   A. Improve cardiac contractility.

    __A__ Administer dobutamine.   B. Restore intravascular volume.

    __C__ Monitor platelet count.   C. Assess for thrombocytopenia.

Crystalloids will help restore fluid volume and prevent shock. Dobutamine may be used if cardiac output is low and IV therapy is not effective in preventing shock. A decreasing platelet count could be related to heparin-induced thrombocytopenia.

6. Which of the following is a contraindication to fibrinolytic therapy?

    A. Recent surgery

    B. Motor vehicle crash 2 months ago

    C. History of asthma

    D. Elevated platelet count

Clients who have recently had surgery should not receive fibrinolytic therapy because of the risk of hemorrhage from the surgical site.

Unit 2 Nursing Care of Clients with Respiratory Disorders
Section: Medical Emergencies: Respiratory

Chapter 18: ARF/ARDS/SARS
Contributor: Gayla H. Love, BSN, RN, CCM

NCLEX-PN® Connections:

Learning Objective: Review and apply knowledge within "**ARF/ARDS/SARS**" in readiness for performance of the following nursing activities as outlined by the NCLEX-PN® test plan:

Δ   Assist with relevant laboratory, diagnostic, and therapeutic procedures within the nursing role, including:

  • Preparation of the client for the procedure.

  • Accurate collection of specimens.

  • Monitoring client status during and after the procedure.

  • Reinforcing client teaching (before and following the procedure).

  • Recognizing the client's response (expected, unexpected adverse response) to the procedure.

  • Monitoring results.

  • Monitoring and taking actions to prevent or minimize the risk of complications.

  • Notifying the primary care provider of signs of complications.

Δ   Recognize signs and symptoms of the client's problem and complete the proper documentation.

Δ   Provide and document care based on the client's health alteration.

Δ   Monitor and document vital signs changes.

Δ   Interpret data that need to be reported immediately.

Δ   Reinforce client education on managing the client's health problem.

Δ   Recognize and respond to emergency situations, including notification of the primary care provider.

Δ   Review the client's response to emergency interventions and complete the proper documentation.

Δ   Provide care that meets the age-related needs of clients 65 years of age or older, including recognizing expected physiological changes.

📖 Key Points

Δ   **Acute Respiratory Failure (ARF)**

- Classification of acute respiratory failure is **based upon arterial blood gas (ABG) values.**

- ABGs that may be diagnostic for ARF are: PaO_2 < 60 mm Hg, SaO_2 < 90%, or $PaCO_2$ > 50 mm Hg in conjunction with a pH < 7.30.

- Acute respiratory failure is often the result of a **failure to adequately ventilate and/or oxygenate.**

- **Ventilatory failure** may be due to a mechanical abnormality of the lungs or chest wall, impaired muscle function (for example, the diaphragm), or a malfunction in the respiratory control center of the brain.

- **Oxygenation failure** may result from a lack of perfusion to the pulmonary capillary bed (for example, a pulmonary embolism) or a condition that alters the gas exchange medium (pulmonary edema, pneumonia).

- A **combination of ventilatory and oxygenation failure occurs in individuals with abnormal lungs** (asthma, emphysema). Diseased lung tissue leads to oxygenation failure, and the increased work of breathing eventually results in respiratory muscle fatigue and ventilatory failure.

- Clients with **acute respiratory failure are always hypoxemic.**

Δ   **Acute Respiratory Distress Syndrome (ARDS)**

- ARDS is a state of **acute respiratory failure.**

- The following **indicators** must be present for ARDS:

  ◊   Persistent hypoxemia despite administration of 100% oxygen

  ◊   Decreased pulmonary compliance

  ◊   Dyspnea

  ◊   Bilateral pulmonary edema that is noncardiac

  ◊   Dense pulmonary infiltrates (often appear as "ground glass" on chest x-ray)

- ARDS carries a 50 to 60% mortality rate.

- A systemic inflammatory response **injures the alveolar-capillary membrane.** It becomes permeable to large molecules, and the lung space is filled with fluid.

- **Surfactant activity is reduced**, thus alveoli become unstable and collapse, leading to worsening edema.

Δ   **Severe Acute Respiratory Syndrome (SARS)**

- SARS is the result of a viral infection from a family of viruses known as the **coronaviruses.**

- The virus invades the pulmonary tissue, which leads to an inflammatory response.

- It is spread easily through **airborne droplets** from sneezing, coughing, or talking.

- The virus does not spread to the bloodstream because it flourishes at temperatures slightly below normal core body temperature.

Key Factors

Δ   **Risk factors for ARF**

- **Ventilatory failure**
  ◊ Neuromuscular disorders, such as multiple sclerosis, Guillain-Barré, spinal cord injuries and stroke, that impair the client's rate and depth of respiration
  ◊ Elevated intracranial pressure (closed head injuries, cerebral edema, hemorrhagic stroke)
  ◊ COPD
  ◊ Asthma
  ◊ Pulmonary embolism, pneumothorax
  ◊ ARDS
  ◊ Pulmonary edema
  ◊ Fibrosis of lung tissue

- **Oxygenation failure**
  ◊ Low concentrations of oxygen (carbon monoxide poisoning, high altitude, smoke inhalation)
  ◊ Pneumonia
  ◊ Pulmonary edema
  ◊ Hypoventilation
  ◊ Hypovolemic shock
  ◊ Low hemoglobin
  ◊ ARDS

Δ   **Risk Factors for ARDS**

- May result from **direct injury to lung tissue** or effects of **other systemic problems**.
  ◊ Aspiration
  ◊ Pulmonary emboli (fat or amniotic fluid)
  ◊ Pneumonia and other pulmonary infections
  ◊ Sepsis
  ◊ Trauma
  ◊ Nervous system injury
  ◊ Smoke or toxic gas inhalation
  ◊ Drug ingestion (heroin, opioids, aspirin)
  ◊ Near-drowning victims

Δ   **Risk Factors for SARS**

- Exposure to an infected individual
- Immunocompromised individuals (chemotherapy, AIDS)

Diagnostic Procedures and Nursing Interventions

Δ **Arterial Blood Gas (ABG)**

- Place the specimen in a heparinized syringe on ice.

- Transport the specimen to the laboratory.

- Interpret and communicate results to appropriate personnel in a timely manner.

Δ **Chest X-ray**

- ARDS shows white-out or "ground-glass" appearance.

- Infiltrates seen in SARS.

- Assist with client positioning before and after the x-ray.

- Interpret and communicate results to appropriate personnel in a timely manner.

Assessments

Δ Monitor for **signs and symptoms.**

- Dyspnea

- Hypoxia, hypercarbia

- Hypoxemia (Low PaO_2 despite delivery of a high concentration of oxygen)

- Infiltrates on chest x-ray

- Decreased SaO_2

- Adventitious breath sounds

- Orthopnea

- Elevated white blood cell count (infection and inflammation)

Δ **Assess/Monitor**

- Client's respiratory status (airway patency, lung sounds, respiratory rate, use of accessory muscles, oxygenation status) before and following intervention

- Client's history of risk factors

- General appearance

- Laboratory findings and diagnostic findings

NANDA Nursing Diagnoses

Δ Impaired gas exchange

Δ Decreased cardiac output

Δ Anxiety

Δ Risk for infection

Δ Imbalanced nutrition: Less than body requirements

Nursing Interventions

Δ   **Mechanical ventilation** is often required. Positive end expiratory pressure (PEEP) is often used to prevent alveolar collapse during expiration.

Δ   Maintain **patent airway** and monitor **respiratory status**.

- Suction the client as needed.
- Assess breath sounds every 4 hr and as needed.
- Document ventilator settings hourly.
- Obtain ABGs as ordered.
- Continually monitor vital signs, including SaO_2.

Δ   Position the client to facilitate ventilation and perfusion ("good lung down"). Administer **medications** as prescribed.

- **Sedatives** for client anxiety.
    - ◊ Lorazepam (Ativan), midazolam (Versed)
    - ◊ Propofol (Diprivan): Contraindicated for clients with hyperlipidemia and egg allergies; monitor ECG; drip must be slowed to assess the client's neurological status (follow institution protocol).
    - ◊ Monitor for hypoventilation and hypotension.
- **Analgesia**
    - ◊ Morphine, fentanyl (Duragesic)
    - ◊ Assess the client's pain level and response to medication.
    - ◊ Document the client's pain level.
- **Neuromuscular blocking agents**
    - ◊ Vecuronium (Norcuron)
    - ◊ Give pain medication and sedate with neuromuscular blocking agents.
    - ◊ Often used to facilitate painful ventilatory modes (inverse ratio ventilation and PEEP).
- **Corticosteroids**
    - ◊ Decrease white blood cell (WBC) migration and help to stabilize the alveolar-capillary membrane during ARDS.
    - ◊ Cortisone, methylprednisone, dexamethasone
- **Antibiotics** are used to treat identified organisms.

Δ   **Prevent infection** through:

- Handwashing.
- Using appropriate suctioning technique.
- Providing oral care every 2 hr and as needed.
- Wearing protective clothing (gown, gloves, mask) when appropriate.

Δ **Promote nutrition** through:

- Administering enteral and/or parenteral feedings as prescribed.
- Assessing bowel sounds.
- Monitoring elimination patterns.
- Obtaining daily weight.
- Recording urine output.
- Preventing aspiration with enteral feedings (elevate head of bed 30 to 45°).

Δ **Provide emotional support** to the client and family.

- Encourage verbalization of feelings.
- Provide alternative communication means (dry erase board, pen and paper).

Complications and Nursing Implications

Δ **Decreased cardiac output and fluid retention**

- **Positive pressure** (e.g., PEEP) increases intrathoracic pressure and leads to a decreased blood return to the heart, resulting in a **decreased cardiac output**.
- Hypotension results.
- Kidneys sense decreased cardiac output and activate renin-angiotensin-aldosterone system, leading to **fluid retention**.
  - ◊ Monitor intake and output, weight, and hydration status.
  - ◊ Teach the client to **avoid the Valsalva** maneuver (e.g., straining with bowel movement).

Δ **Barotrauma**

- Ventilation with positive pressure causes **damage to the lungs** (pneumothorax, subcutaneous emphysema).
  - ◊ Monitor oxygenation status and x-ray.
  - ◊ Document all ventilator changes made.

Meeting the Needs of Older Adults

Δ Older adult clients have **decreased pulmonary reserves** due to normal lung changes, including decreased lung elasticity and thickening alveoli. **Older adult clients may decompensate more quickly.**

Primary Reference:

Ignatavicius, D. D., & Workman, M. L. (2006). *Medical-surgical nursing* (5th ed.). St. Louis, MO: Saunders.

Additional Resources:

Burke, K. M., LeMone, P., & Mohn-Brown, E. L. (2003). *Medical-surgical nursing care.* Upper Saddle River, NJ: Prentice-Hall.

NANDA International (2004). *NANDA nursing diagnoses: Definitions and classification 2005-2006.* Philadelphia: NANDA.

For more information about SARS, visit the Centers for Disease Control and Prevention at *www.cdc.gov* and the World Health Organization at *www.who.int.*

Chapter 18: ARF/ARDS/SARS

Application Exercises

Scenario: A 40-year-old male client is admitted to the emergency department following a motor vehicle crash. Physical assessment reveals absent breath sounds in the left lower lobe. He is dyspneic and vital signs are: blood pressure 111/68 mm Hg, heart rate 124 beats/min, respiratory rate 38/min, temperature 38.6° C (101.4° F), and SaO$_2$ 92% on room air.

1. Which of the following actions should the nurse take first?

>   A. Obtain a chest x-ray.
>
>   B. Prepare for chest tube insertion.
>
>   C. Administer oxygen via a high-flow mask.
>
>   D. Obtain IV access.

2. The client is now on 15 L/min of oxygen by a non-rebreather mask. The client's ABG results are as follows: pH 7.25, PaO$_2$ 55 mm Hg, PaCO$_2$ 58 mm Hg, and HCO$_3^-$ 34 mEq/L. Interpret this ABG.

3. What medical intervention should the nurse anticipate next?

4. The client is started on mechanical ventilation. Explain why PEEP would be useful for this client.

5. This client is receiving vecuronium (Norcuron). What other medications should the client receive? (Check all that apply.)

>   _____ Fentanyl (Duragesic)
>
>   _____ Furosemide (Lasix)
>
>   _____ Midazolam (Versed)
>
>   _____ Famotidine (Pepcid)

6. Which of the following clients is/are at risk for the development of acute respiratory failure and/ or ARDS? (Check all that apply.)

_____ A 14-year-old boy who received 2 min of CPR following a near-drowning

_____ A client post coronary artery bypass graft with two chest tubes

_____ A client with a hemoglobin level of 14.5 mg/dL

_____ A client with an exacerbation of cystic fibrosis

_____ A client with dysphagia

_____ A client with a sinus infection

7. **True or False:** Sepsis is a primary concern for clients infected with SARS.

Chapter 18: ARF/ARDS/SARS

Application Exercises Answer Key

Scenario: A 40-year-old male client is admitted to the emergency department following a motor vehicle crash. Physical assessment reveals absent breath sounds in the left lower lobe. He is dyspneic and vital signs are: blood pressure 111/68 mm Hg, heart rate 124 beats/min, respiratory rate 38/min, temperature 38.6° C (101.4° F), and SaO_2 92% on room air.

1. Which of the following actions should the nurse take first?

> A. Obtain a chest x-ray.
>
> B. Prepare for chest tube insertion.
>
> **C. Administer oxygen via high-flow mask.**
>
> D. Obtain IV access.

2. The client is now on 15 L/min of oxygen by a non-rebreather mask. The client's ABG results are as follows: pH 7.25, PaO_2 55 mm Hg, $PaCO_2$ 58 mm Hg, and HCO_3^- 34 mEq/L. Interpret this ABG.

This client is in a state of uncompensated respiratory acidosis.

3. What medical intervention should the nurse anticipate next?

The nurse should prepare the client for endotracheal intubation and mechanical ventilation.

4. The client is started on mechanical ventilation. Explain why PEEP would be useful for this client.

PEEP exerts pressure at the end of expiration to prevent alveolar collapse and facilitate gas exchange.

5. This client is receiving vecuronium (Norcuron). What other medications should the client receive? (Check all that apply.)

    __x__   Fentanyl (Duragesic)

    _____   Furosemide (Lasix)

    __x__   Midazolam (Versed)

    _____   Famotidine (Pepcid)

Pain medication and sedation are often used when a client is on a ventilator along with a neuromuscular blocking agent, because a neuromuscular blocking agent does not block pain impulses. The client may be in pain and anxious but unable to communicate this.

---

6. Which of the following clients is/are at risk for the development of acute respiratory failure and/or ARDS? (Check all that apply.)

    __x__   A 14-year-old boy who received 2 min of CPR following a near-drowning

    __x__   A client post coronary artery bypass graft with two chest tubes

    _____   A client with a hemoglobin level of 14.5 mg/dL

    __x__   A client with an exacerbation of cystic fibrosis

    __x__   A client with dysphagia

    _____   A client with a sinus infection

7. **True or False:** Sepsis is a primary concern for clients infected with SARS.

False: The virus that causes SARS, the coronavirus, flourishes in temperatures just below core body temperature, and therefore resides in the lung parenchyma.

Unit 2   Nursing Care of Clients with Respiratory Disorders
Section: Medical Emergencies: Respiratory

Chapter 19:   Hemothorax/Pneumothorax
                Contributor: Gayla H. Love, BSN, RN, CCM

◯ NCLEX-PN® Connections:

Learning Objective: Review and apply knowledge within "**Hemothorax/ Pneumothorax**" in readiness for performance of the following nursing activities as outlined by the NCLEX-PN® test plans:

Δ   Assist with relevant laboratory, diagnostic, and therapeutic procedures within the nursing role, including:

•   Preparation of the client for the procedure.

•   Accurate collection of specimens.

•   Monitoring client status during and after the procedure.

•   Reinforcing client teaching (before and following the procedure).

•   Recognizing the client's response (expected, unexpected adverse response) to the procedure.

•   Monitoring results.

•   Monitoring and taking actions to prevent or minimize the risk of complications.

    •   Notifying the primary care provider of signs of complications.

Δ   Recognize signs and symptoms of the client's problem and complete the proper documentation.

Δ   Provide and document care based on the client's health alteration.

Δ   Monitor and document vital signs changes.

Δ   Interpret data that need to be reported immediately.

Δ   Reinforce client education on managing the client's health problem.

Δ   Recognize and respond to emergency situations, including notification of the primary care provider.

Δ   Review the client's response to emergency interventions and complete the proper documentation.

Δ   Provide care that meets the age-related needs of clients 65 years of age or older, including recognizing expected physiological changes.

Key Points

Δ   A **pneumothorax** is the presence of **air or gas in the pleural space** that causes **lung collapse.**

Δ   **Tension pneumothorax** occurs when air enters the pleural space during inspiration through a one-way valve created by blunt chest trauma, and is not able to exit upon expiration. The increase in pressure compresses blood vessels and limits venous return, leading to a decrease in cardiac output. **Death can quickly ensue if left untreated.**

Δ   A **hemothorax** is an **accumulation of blood** in the pleural space.

Key Factors

Δ   **Common risk factors for a hemothorax or pneumothorax include:**

- Blunt **chest trauma.**

- Penetrating chest wounds.

- Closed/**occluded chest tube.**

Diagnostic Procedures and Nursing Interventions

Δ   **Arterial Blood Gas (ABG)**

- Place the specimen in a heparinized syringe on ice.

- Transport the specimen to the laboratory.

- Interpret and communicate results to appropriate personnel in a timely manner.

Δ   **Chest X-ray**

- Assist with client placement before and after the x-ray.

- Interpret and communicate results to appropriate personnel in a timely manner.

Δ   **Thoracentesis** may be used to confirm **hemothorax.**

- Assist with client positioning, specimen transport, and monitor client status (vital signs, SaO_2, injection site).

Assessments

Δ   Monitor for **signs and symptoms.**

- Pleuritic pain

- Signs of **respiratory distress** (tachypnea, tachycardia, hypoxia, cyanosis, dyspnea, and use of accessory muscles)

- **Tracheal deviation** to the unaffected side (tension pneumothorax)
- Reduced or **absent breath sounds** on the affected side
- **Asymmetrical chest wall movement**
- **Anxiety**
- Hyperresonance on percussion (pneumothorax)
- Dull percussion (hemothorax)
- **Subcutaneous emphysema** (air accumulating in subcutaneous tissue)

Δ **Assess/Monitor**

- Client's respiratory status (airway patency, lung sounds, respiratory rate, use of accessory muscles, oxygenation status) before and following intervention
- Client's history of risk factors
- General appearance
- Laboratory and diagnostic findings

NANDA Nursing Diagnoses

Δ Impaired gas exchange

Δ Ineffective breathing pattern

Δ Decreased cardiac output

Δ Anxiety

Δ Risk for infection

Nursing Interventions

Δ Assess and monitor **respiratory status**.

- Administer oxygen therapy.
- Assess breath sounds and signs of respiratory distress.
- Document ventilator settings hourly.
- Obtain ABGs as ordered.
- Continually monitor vital signs, including SaO_2.
- Position the client to facilitate ventilation and perfusion.

Δ Monitor **chest tube drainage**.

Δ **Administer medications** as prescribed.

- **Anxiolytics**
  - ◊ Lorazepam (Ativan) or midazolam (Versed) may be used to decrease the client's anxiety.
  - ◊ Monitor for hypoventilation and hypotension.
- **Analgesia**
  - ◊ Morphine or fentanyl may be used for pain management.
  - ◊ Assess the client's pain level and response to medication.
  - ◊ Document the client's pain level.

Δ **Provide emotional support** to the client and family.

Δ **Surgical Management**

- Chest tube insertion
  - ◊ Obtain informed consent, gather supplies, monitor client status (vital signs, SaO_2, chest tube drainage), report abnormalities to the primary care provider, and administer pain medications.
  - ◊ Insertion of large-bore needle into the 2nd intercostal space may be done to **alleviate pressure before chest tube insertion** with a tension pneumothorax.

Complications and Nursing Implications

Δ **Decreased Cardiac Output**

- Results as intrathoracic pressures rise.
- **Hypotension** develops.
- Administer **IV fluids and blood products** as prescribed.
- Monitor **heart rate and rhythm**.
- Monitor intake and output (**chest tube drainage**).

Δ **Respiratory Failure**

- Prepare for **mechanical ventilation**.
- Continue respiratory assessment.

Meeting the Needs of Older Adults

Δ Older adult clients have **decreased pulmonary reserves** due to normal lung changes including decreased lung elasticity and thickening alveoli.

Δ **Provide rest periods** for older adult clients with dyspnea.

Δ Older adult clients are **more susceptible to infections**. Encourage prompt medical attention when signs of infection occur.

Primary Reference:

Ignatavicius, D. D., & Workman, M. L. (2006). *Medical-surgical nursing* (5th ed.). St. Louis, MO: Saunders.

Additional Resources:

Burke, K. M., LeMone, P., & Mohn-Brown, E. L. (2003). *Medical-surgical nursing care*. Upper Saddle River, NJ: Prentice Hall.

NANDA International (2004). *NANDA nursing diagnoses: Definitions and classification 2005-2006*. Philadelphia: NANDA.

Chapter 19: Hemothorax/Pneumothorax

Application Exercises

Scenario: A 24-year-old male client is admitted to the emergency department suffering from a gunshot wound. Vital signs are: blood pressure 108/55 mm Hg, heart rate 124 beats/min, respiratory rate 36/min, temperature 38.6° C (101.4° F), and SaO$_2$ 95% on 15 L/min by a nonrebreather mask. He reports dyspnea and pain.

1. The nurse reassesses the client 30 min later. The nurse should report which of the following assessment findings to the primary care provider? (Check all that apply.)

    _____ SaO$_2$ of 90%

    _____ Tracheal deviation

    _____ Headache

    _____ Blood pressure 104/54 mm Hg

    _____ Heart rate 154 beats/min

    _____ Hemoptysis

    _____ Distended neck veins

    _____ Nausea

2. A chest x-ray is performed, and tracheal deviation is observed. Vital signs are: blood pressure 82/48 mm Hg, heart rate 158 beats/min, respiratory rate 42/min, temperature 38.7° C (101.6° F), and SaO$_2$ 87%. What do these vital signs indicate?

3. Prioritize the following provider orders. Designate "1" as the most important intervention.

    _____ Document interventions.

    _____ Obtain large-bore IV needle for immediate decompression.

    _____ Administer lorazepam (Ativan).

    _____ Prepare for chest tube insertion.

4. As a result of a tension pneumothorax, air continues to accumulate and the intrapleural pressure rises, which

    A. causes the lung to collapse on the affected side, resulting in increased lung capacity.

    B. allows air to flow freely through the chest wall during inspiration and expiration.

    C. causes less air to enter on inspiration and exceed the barometric pressure.

    D. will cause the mediastinum to shift away from the affected side and decrease venous return.

5. **True or False:** A client should be assessed closely for the development of a pneumothorax following the removal of a chest tube.

6. **True or False:** Older adult clients with a pneumothorax tend to deteriorate more slowly.

Chapter 19: Hemothorax/Pneumothorax

Application Exercises Answer Key

Scenario: A 24-year-old male client is admitted to the emergency department suffering from a gunshot wound. Vital signs are: blood pressure 108/55 mm Hg, heart rate 124 beats/min, respiratory rate 36/min, temperature 38.6° C (101.4° F), and SaO_2 95% on 15 L/min by a nonrebreather mask. He reports dyspnea and pain.

1. The nurse reassesses the client 30 min later. The nurse should report which of the following assessment findings to the primary care provider? (Check all that apply.)

    __x__ SaO_2 of 90%

    __x__   Tracheal deviation

    _____   Headache

    _____   Blood pressure 104/54 mm Hg

    __x__   Heart rate 154 beats/min

    __x__   Hemoptysis

    __x__   Distended neck veins

    _____   Nausea

    Signs of respiratory distress indicate the client's condition is worsening and needs to be reported to the primary care provider.

2. A chest x-ray is performed, and tracheal deviation is observed. Vital signs are: blood pressure 82/48 mm Hg, heart rate 158 beats/min, respiratory rate 42/min, temperature 38.7° C (101.6° F), and SaO_2 87%. What do these vital signs indicate?

    The client is experiencing a tension pneumothorax. The tracheal deviation is a definitive sign of tension pneumothorax. The hypotension, tachycardia, tachypnea, and decreasing SaO_2 indicate that the client is progressing toward respiratory failure.

3. Prioritize the following provider orders. Designate "1" as the most important intervention.

   _4_   Document interventions.

   _1_   Obtain large-bore IV needle for immediate decompression.

   _3_   Administer lorazepam (Ativan).

   _2_   Prepare for chest tube insertion.

Establishing and maintaining the client's respiratory function is the highest priority. The nurse should obtain the supplies to do a needle aspiration, or decompression, to prepare for chest tube insertion. The client will likely be anxious and an anxiolytic medication may be ordered. Finally, the nurse should document the interventions.

4. As a result of a tension pneumothorax, air continues to accumulate and the intrapleural pressure rises, which

    A. causes the lung to collapse on the affected side, resulting in increased lung capacity.

    B. allows air to flow freely through the chest wall during inspiration and expiration.

    C. causes less air to enter on inspiration and exceed the barometric pressure.

    D. will cause the mediastinum to shift away from the affected side and decrease venous return.

A tension pneumothorax causes air trapping in the pleural space, which compresses the local blood vessels and ultimately decreases venous return.

5. **True or False:** A client should be assessed closely for the development of a pneumothorax following the removal of a chest tube.

True: Air can leak into the thoracic cavity at the chest tube insertion site following removal. This could cause the client's lung to collapse.

6. **True or False:** Older adult clients with a pneumothorax tend to deteriorate more slowly.

False: Older adult clients have fewer reserves and tend to develop significant respiratory complications more quickly than younger adults.

Unit 3   Nursing Care of Clients with Cardiovascular or Hematologic Disorders

Section: Diagnostic and Therapeutic Procedures: Cardiovascular or Hematologic

Chapter 20:   Dysrhythmias: Monitoring and Intervening
Contributor: Sharon Kumm, MN, MS, RN, CCRN

↻ NCLEX-PN® Connections:

Learning Objective: Review and apply knowledge within "**Dysrhythmias: Monitoring and Intervening**" in readiness for performance of the following nursing activities as outlined by the NCLEX-PN® test plan:

Δ   Perform electrocardiogram (ECG).

Δ   Perform/assist with relevant laboratory, diagnostic, and therapeutic procedures within the nursing role, including:

- Preparation of the client for the procedure.

- Reinforcement of client teaching (before and following the procedure).

- Accurate collection of specimens.

- Monitoring procedure results (compare to norms) and appropriate notification of the primary care provider.

- Monitoring the client's response (expected, unexpected adverse response, comparison to baseline) to the procedure.

- Monitoring and taking actions, including reinforcing client teaching, to prevent or minimize the risk of complications.

- Recognizing signs of potential complications and reporting to the primary care provider.

- Recommending changes in the test/procedure as needed based on client findings.

Δ   Monitor therapeutic devices (drainage/irrigating devices, chest tubes), if inserted, for proper functioning.

📖 **Key Points**

Δ   Cardiac electrical activity can be monitored by using an electrocardiogram (ECG). The heart's electrical activity can be monitored by a standard 12-lead ECG (resting ECG), ambulatory ECG (Holter monitoring), continuous cardiac monitoring, or by telemetry.

Δ   Continuous cardiac monitoring requires the client to be in close proximity to the monitoring system, and telemetry allows the client to ambulate while maintaining proximity to the monitoring system.

Δ   Cardiac dysrhythmias are **heartbeat disturbances** (beat formation, beat conduction, myocardial response to beat).

Δ   Dysrhythmias are classified by the:

- **Site of origin:** SA node, atria, atrioventricular (AV) node, or ventricle.

- **Effect on heart's rate and rhythm**: Bradycardia, tachycardia, heart block, premature beat, flutter, fibrillation, or asystole.

Δ   Dysrhythmias may be **benign or life-threatening.**

Δ   The life-threatening effects of dysrhythmias are generally related to **decreased cardiac output and ineffective tissue perfusion.**

Δ   Cardiac dysrhythmias are a primary **cause of death in clients suffering acute myocardial infarction (MI)** and other sudden death disorders.

Δ   **Rapid recognition** and **treatment** of serious dysrhythmias **is essential** to preserve life.

Δ   Dysrhythmia **treatment is based on the client's symptoms** and the cardiac rhythm.

Δ   **Cardioversion** is the delivery of **synchronized direct countershock** to the heart for the elective treatment of atrial dysrhythmias or ventricular tachycardia with pulse.

Δ   **Defibrillation** is the delivery of an **unsynchronized, direct countershock** to the heart during ventricular fibrillation or pulseless ventricular tachycardia. **Defibrillation stops all electrical activity of the heart**, allowing the sinoatrial (SA) node to take over and reestablish a perfusing rhythm.

Δ   **Electrophysiological study (EPS)** determines the area of the heart causing the dysrhythmia. Ablation of the area is possible.

Dysrhythmia	Medication	Electrical Management
Bradycardia (any rhythm < 60 beats/min) Treat if client is symptomatic	Atropine, isoproterenol	Pacemaker
Atrial Fibrillation, Supraventricular Tachycardia (SVT), or Ventricular Tachycardia with pulse	Amiodarone, adenosine, verapamil	Synchronized cardioversion
Ventricular Tachycardia without pulse or Ventricular Fibrillation	Amiodarone, lidocaine, epinephrine	Defibrillation

Key Factors

Δ   **Risk Factors for Dysrhythmias**

- **Cardiovascular disease**

- **Myocardial infarction**

- Hypoxia

- Acid-base imbalances

- **Electrolyte** disturbances

- Chronic renal, hepatic, or lung disease

- Pericarditis

- **Drug use or abuse**

- **Hypovolemia**

- **Shock**

Nursing Interventions

Δ   Perform 12-lead ECG by:

- Positioning the client in supine position with chest exposed.

- Washing the client's skin to remove excess oils.

- Attaching one electrode to each extremity by applying electrodes to flat surfaces above the wrists and ankles and the other six electrodes to the chest, avoiding chest hair.

- Instructing the client to remain still and breathe normally.

Δ   Apply leads, and monitor for dysrhythmias for the client on continuous cardiac monitoring.

Δ   **Monitor for signs and symptoms of decreased perfusion** (chest pain, decreased level of consciousness, shortness of breath) and **hypoxia**.

Δ   Prevention

- **Reduce risk factors** for **coronary artery disease.**

- Correct **electrolyte imbalances.**

- Treat substance abuse.

- **Manage stress**, fever, and anxiety.

Δ   Assess/monitor for signs of **decreased cardiac output (hypotension, irregular heart beats**, fatigue, dyspnea, chest pain, syncope).

Δ   Monitor for pulmonary or systemic **emboli following cardioversion.**

Δ   Administer **oxygen.**

Δ   Administer prescribed **antidysrhythmic agent** or other prescribed medications.

Δ   Perform **CPR** for cardiac asystole or other **pulseless rhythms.**

Δ   Defibrillate immediately for **ventricular fibrillation.**

Δ   Prepare the client for cardioversion if prescribed.

- Cardioversion is the treatment of choice for symptomatic clients.

- **Clients with atrial fibrillation of unknown duration must receive adequate anticoagulation prior to cardioversion therapy to prevent dislodgement of thrombi into the bloodstream.**

    ◊   Administer **oxygen** and **sedation** as prescribed.

    ◊   Monitor the client in a lead that provides an **upright QRS complex.**

    ◊   Cardioversion requires activation of the **synchronizer button** in addition to charging the machine. This allows the shock to be in "sync" with the client's underlying rhythm. **Failure to synchronize can lead to development of a lethal dysrhythmia,** such as ventricular fibrillation.

Δ   After defibrillation or cardioversion, check vital signs, assess airway patency, and obtain an ECG.

Δ   **Provide reassurance** and emotional support to the client and family.

Δ   **Document**

- Client's condition prior to intervention

- Pre- and postprocedure rhythm

- Number of defibrillation or cardioversion attempts, energy settings, time, and response

- Vital signs

- Emergency medications administered including times and dosages
- The client's condition and state of consciousness following the procedure

Δ Teach the client and family regarding the need for **compliance with prescribed medication regimen.**

Δ Teach the client and family how to **assess pulse.**

Complications and Nursing Implications

Δ **Embolism**

- **Pulmonary embolism** – dyspnea, chest pain, air hunger, decreasing SaO_2
- **Stroke, cerebral vascular accident (CVA)** – decreased level of consciousness, slurred speech, muscle weakness/paralysis
- **Myocardial infarction (MI)** – chest pain, ST segment depression or elevation
- Provide **therapeutic anticoagulation** for clients with dysrhythmias.

Δ **Decreased Cardiac Output** and Heart Failure

- Monitor for signs of decreased cardiac output (hypotension, syncope, increased heart rate) and of heart failure (dyspnea, productive cough, edema, venous distention).
- Provide medications to increase output (inotropic agents) and to decrease cardiac workload.

Meeting the Needs of Older Adults

Δ Dysrhythmias may present atypically in older adult clients.

Δ Ischemia and infarction may present asymptomatically or atypically.

Δ Risks for heart disease, hypertension, dysrhythmias, and atherosclerosis increase with age.

Δ Increased risk for heart failure is related to long-standing atrial fibrillation often associated with chronic obstructive pulmonary disease (COPD) and status postoperative coronary artery bypass grafting (CABG).

Δ Heart rate variability decreases with age.

Primary Reference:

Ignatavicius, D. D., & Workman, M. L. (2006). *Medical-surgical nursing* (5th ed.). St. Louis, MO: Saunders.

Additional Resources:

Black, J. M., & Hawks, J. H. (2005). *Medical-surgical nursing: Clinical management for positive outcomes* (7th ed.). St. Louis, MO: Saunders.

NANDA International (2004). *NANDA nursing diagnoses: Definitions and classification 2005-2006*. Philadelphia: NANDA.

For more information, visit the American Heart Association at: *www.americanheart.org*.

Chapter 20: Dysrhythmias: Monitoring and Intervening

Application Exercises

Scenario: A client reports feeling lightheaded. Assessment of his vital signs reveals: heart rate 144 beats/min and irregular, blood pressure 84/49 mm Hg, and SaO_2 95%. An ECG reveals atrial fibrillation with a rapid ventricular response. Synchronized cardioversion is performed at 50 joules.

1. What should the nurse document following the cardioversion?

2. Two hours after his cardioversion, the client develops ventricular fibrillation. What action should the nurse take first?

3. Which of the following clients are at risk for the development of dysrhythmias? (Check all that apply.)

   _____ A client with ABG results of: pH 7.26, PaO_2 75 mm Hg, $PaCO_2$ 58 mm Hg, HCO_3^- 32 mEq/L

   _____ A client with a serum potassium level of 4.3 mEq/L

   _____ A client with an SaO_2 of 96%

   _____ A client with COPD

   _____ A client 3 hr post myocardial infarction

4. **True or False:** Atrial fibrillation is primarily treated with defibrillation.

Chapter 20: Dysrhythmias: Monitoring and Intervening

Application Exercises Answer Key

Scenario: A client reports feeling lightheaded. Assessment of his vital signs reveals: heart rate 144 beats/min and irregular, blood pressure 84/49 mm Hg, and SaO_2 95%. An ECG reveals atrial fibrillation with a rapid ventricular response. Synchronized cardioversion is performed at 50 joules.

1. What should the nurse document following the cardioversion?

   The nurse should document:

   The client's condition prior to the intervention.

   The number of cardioversion attempts, energy settings, time, and response.

   The client's postprocedure vital signs.

   The client's level of consciousness following the procedure.

   Medications administered.

2. Two hours after his cardioversion, the client develops ventricular fibrillation. What action should the nurse take first?

   Defibrillation is the first treatment for ventricular fibrillation.

3. Which of the following clients are at risk for the development of dysrhythmias? (Check all that apply.)

     _X_   A client with ABG results of: pH 7.26, PaO_2 75 mm Hg, $PaCO_2$ 58 mm Hg, HCO_3^- 32 mEq/L

     ___   A client with a serum potassium level of 4.3 mEq/L

     ___   A client with an SaO_2 of 96%

     _X_   A client with COPD

     _X_   A client 3 hr post myocardial infarction

4. **True or False:** Atrial fibrillation is primarily treated with defibrillation.

   False: Atrial fibrillation may be treated with medications or synchronized cardioversion. Defibrillation is not a recognized treatment.

Unit 3 Nursing Care of Clients with Cardiovascular or Hematologic Disorders

Section: Diagnostic and Therapeutic Procedures: Cardiovascular or Hematologic

Chapter 21: Hemodynamic Monitoring
Contributor: Sharon Kumm, MN, MS, RN, CCRN

NCLEX-PN® Connections:

Learning Objective: Review and apply knowledge within **"Hemodynamic Monitoring"** in readiness for performance of the following nursing activities as outlined by the NCLEX-PN® test plan:

Δ   Perform electrocardiogram (ECG).

Δ   Perform/assist with relevant laboratory, diagnostic, and therapeutic procedures within the nursing role, including:

- Preparation of the client for the procedure.

- Reinforcement of client teaching (before and following the procedure).

- Accurate collection of specimens.

- Monitoring procedure results (compare to norms) and appropriate notification of the primary care provider.

- Monitoring the client's response (expected, unexpected adverse response, comparison to baseline) to the procedure.

- Monitoring and taking actions, including reinforcing client teaching, to prevent or minimize the risk of complications.

- Recognizing signs of potential complications and reporting to the primary care provider.

- Recommending changes in the test/procedure as needed based on client findings.

Δ   Monitor therapeutic devices (drainage/irrigating devices, chest tubes), if inserted, for proper functioning.

Key Points

Δ   Hemodynamic monitoring involves special **indwelling catheters** to **provide information about blood volume and perfusion, fluid status, and how well the heart is pumping.**

Δ   Hemodynamic status is assessed with several parameters.

- **Central venous pressure (CVP)**

- **Pulmonary artery pressure (PAP)**

- **Pulmonary artery wedge pressure (PAWP)**

- **Cardiac output (CO)**

- **Intra-arterial pressure**

Δ   **Mixed venous oxygen saturation (SvO$_2$)** indicates the balance between oxygen supply and demand. It is measured by a pulmonary artery catheter with fiberoptics.

Δ   A pressure-monitoring system comprised of a catheter with an infusion system, a transducer, and a monitor is used to display a client's hemodynamic information.

Δ   Hemodynamic pressure lines must be calibrated to read atmospheric pressure as zero and the transducer should be positioned at the right atrium (phlebostatic axis).

Δ   **Components** of Hemodynamic Monitoring Systems

- Pressure transducer

- Pressure tubing

- Monitor

- Pressure bag and flush device

Δ   **Arterial Lines**

- Arterial lines are **placed in the radial (most common), brachial, or femoral artery.**

- Arterial lines provide continuous information about changes in blood pressure and permit the withdrawal of samples of arterial blood. Intra-arterial pressures may differ from cuff pressures.

- The integrity of the arterial waveform should be assessed to verify the accuracy of blood pressure readings.

- **Monitor circulation** in the limb with the arterial line (capillary refill, temperature, color).

- Arterial lines are not to be used for intravenous fluid infusion.

Δ   **Pulmonary Artery Catheters**

- Pulmonary artery (PA) catheters have **multiple ports** and components that enable a variety of hemodynamic measurements, the collection of blood samples, and the infusion of intravenous fluids.

- The PA catheter is **inserted into a large vein** (internal jugular, femoral, subclavian, brachial) and threaded through the right atria and ventricle into a branch of the pulmonary artery.

- Pulmonary artery catheters have multiple lumens.

   ◊   **Proximal lumen** can be used to measure right atrial pressure (CVP), infuse intravenous fluids, and to obtain venous blood samples.

   ◊   **Distal lumen** can be used to measure pulmonary artery pressures (PA systolic, PA diastolic, mean pulmonary artery pressure, and pulmonary artery wedge pressure). This lumen is not to be used for intravenous fluid infusion.

   ◊   **Balloon inflation port** is intermittently used for PAWP measurements. When not in use, it should be left deflated and in the 'locked' position.

   ◊   **Thermistor** measures temperature differences between the right atrium and the pulmonary artery in order to determine cardiac output.

   ◊   Additional infusion ports, depending on the brand.

Δ   **Normal Values of Hemodynamic Readings**

Central Venous Pressure (CVP)	1-8 mm Hg
Pulmonary Artery Systolic (PAS)	15-26 mm Hg
Pulmonary Artery Diastolic (PAD)	5-15 mm Hg
Pulmonary Artery Wedge Pressure (PAWP)	4-12 mm Hg
Cardiac Output (CO)	4-6 L/min
Mixed venous oxygen saturation (SvO_2)	60-80%

Key Factors

Δ   **Client Indications** for **Hemodynamic Monitoring**

- Serious or critical illness

- **Congestive heart failure**

- Post coronary artery bypass graft (CABG) **clients**
- ARDS
- Acute renal failure
- **Burn victims**
- **Trauma victims**

Nursing Interventions

Δ   **Line Insertion**

- Obtain **informed consent**.
- **Gather equipment** and supplies.
- Assemble pressure monitoring system. **Purge all air** from system.
- **Maintain sterility** of connections.
- Place client in **supine** or **Trendelenburg** position.
- **Monitor client status** during and after the procedure (vital signs, SaO_2, heart rhythm).
- Administer **sedation** and **pain medications** as prescribed.
- Obtain **chest x-ray** following the procedure to confirm catheter placement.
- **Level transducer with phlebostatic axis** (4th intercostal space, mid-axillary line).
- **Zero system** with atmospheric pressure.
- **Obtain initial readings** as prescribed. Compare arterial blood pressure to non-invasive cuff pressure (NIBP).
- **Document** the client's response.

Δ   Monitor symptoms of altered hemodynamics.

Preload		Afterload	
Right heart - CVP Left heart - PAWP		Right heart – Peripheral Vascular Resistance (PVR) Left heart – Systemic Vascular Resistance (SVR)	
Elevated	Decreased	Elevated	Decreased
• Crackles in lungs • Jugular vein distention • Hepatomegaly • Peripheral edema • Taut skin turgor	• Poor skin turgor • Dry mucous membranes	• Cool extremities • Weak peripheral pulses	• Warm extremities • Bounding peripheral pulses

Δ   Continually **monitor respiratory and cardiac status** (vital signs, heart rhythm, SaO_2).

- Observe respiratory pattern and effort.

- Compare NIBP to arterial blood pressure.

Δ   Maintain **line placement and integrity**.

- Observe and document waveforms. Report changes in waveforms to the provider as this may indicate catheter migration or displacement.

- Document catheter placement each shift and as needed (for example, after movement or transport).

- Monitor and secure connections between pressure tubing, transducers, and catheter ports.

Δ   **Obtain readings** from hemodynamic catheter as prescribed.

- Place the client in **supine position** prior to recording hemodynamic values. Head of bed may be elevated 15° to 30°.

- Level the transducer at the phlebostatic axis before readings and with all position changes.

- Zero system to atmospheric pressure.

- Compare hemodynamic findings to physical assessment.

- Monitor trends in values obtained over time.

- Change flushing solution and tubing according to institution policy.

- Flush pressure lines after blood samples to maintain line patency.

Δ   **Prevent infection**.

- Change dressings per hospital protocol and as needed.

- Use surgical aseptic technique with all dressing changes (mask, sterile gloves, maintain sterile field).

- Observe catheter site for swelling, redness, or drainage.

- Practice thorough handwashing.

Complications and Nursing Implications

Δ   **Infection/Sepsis**

- Monitor the insertion site.

- Monitor for evidence of infection (elevated white blood cell count, increased temperature).

- Perform thorough handwashing.

- Collect specimens (blood cultures, catheter tip cultures) and deliver to the laboratory.

- Administer antibiotic therapy as prescribed.

- Administer intravenous fluids for intravascular support.

- Administer vasopressors (for example, dopamine) for vasodilation secondary to sepsis.

Δ **Embolism**

- Use heparinized solution for flushing system to prevent thromboembolism.

- Avoid introduction of air into flushing system to prevent air embolism.

- There is a risk of **pneumothorax** with insertion of the line.

- There is a risk of **dysrhythmias** with insertion/movement of the line.

Meeting the Needs of Older Adults

Δ The intravascular volume in older adult clients is often reduced; therefore, the nurse should anticipate lower hemodynamic readings, particularly if dehydration is a complication.

Primary Reference:

Ignatavicius, D. D., & Workman, M. L. (2006). *Medical-surgical nursing* (5th ed.). St. Louis, MO: Saunders.

Additional Resources:

Black, J. M., & Hawks, J. H. (2005). *Medical-surgical nursing: Clinical management for positive outcomes* (7th ed.). St. Louis, MO: Saunders.

NANDA International (2004). *NANDA nursing diagnoses: Definitions and classification 2005-2006*. Philadelphia: NANDA.

Chapter 21: Hemodynamic Monitoring

Application Exercises

1. Which hemodynamic pressures should the nurse monitor to determine the following parameters?

   Preload: _____

   Afterload: _____

2. What actions are necessary to obtain an accurate hemodynamic reading?

3. List three complications of hemodynamic monitoring. Provide one nursing intervention to prevent or detect each complication.

Complication	Intervention

4. A nurse receives an order to administer normal saline (NS) at 50 mL/hr. Which of the following lines may be used for administration? (Check all that apply.)

   _____ Peripheral IV site

   _____ Arterial line

   _____ Proximal (CVP) lumen of PA catheter

   _____ Distal lumen of PA catheter

5. A nurse has just obtained the following hemodynamic readings for a client:

> PAS 34 mm Hg
>
> PAD 21 mm Hg
>
> PAWP 16 mm Hg
>
> CVP 12 mm Hg

Which of the following conditions support these hemodynamic values? (Check all that apply.)

_____ Congestive heart failure

_____ Cor pulmonale

_____ Hypovolemic shock

_____ Pulmonary hypertension

Chapter 21: Hemodynamic Monitoring

Application Exercises Answer Key

1. Which hemodynamic pressures should the nurse monitor to determine the following hemodynamic parameters?

   Preload: **PAWP, CVP**

   Afterload: **SVR, PVR**

2. What actions are necessary to obtain an accurate hemodynamic reading?

   Place the client in supine position, head elevated no more than 30°.

   Level transducer to phlebostatic axis.

   Zero transducer to room air.

   Record readings.

   Compare readings to physical assessment.

3. List three complications of hemodynamic monitoring. Provide one nursing intervention to prevent or detect each complication.

Complication	Intervention
Neurovascular compromise (arterial line)	Assess distal pulses; skin temperature and color; sensation; and movement.
Pneumothorax (pulmonary artery catheter)	Obtain chest x-ray after insertion. Assess breath sounds every 4 hr.
Infection at point of insertion	Assess insertion site every 8 hr. Use surgical aseptic technique when changing dressing.

4. A nurse receives an order to administer normal saline (NS) at 50 mL/hr. Which of the following lines may be used for administration? (Check all that apply.)

    __x__   Peripheral IV site

    _____   Arterial line

    __x__   Proximal (CVP) lumen of PA catheter

    _____   Distal lumen of PA catheter

Arterial lines and the distal lumens of pulmonary artery catheters are used for hemodynamic measurements and the collection of blood samples. They are not to be used for intravenous fluid administration.

5. A nurse has just obtained the following hemodynamic readings for a client:

    PAS 34 mm Hg

    PAD 21 mm Hg

    PAWP 16 mm Hg

    CVP 12 mm Hg

Which of the following conditions support these hemodynamic values? (Check all that apply.)

    __x__   Congestive heart failure

    __x__   Cor pulmonale

    _____   Hypovolemic shock

    __x__   Pulmonary hypertension

These elevated hemodynamic measurements are consistent with left ventricular failure and pulmonary problems. Hypovolemic shock is characterized by low hemodynamic values.

Unit 3

Section:

Nursing Care of Clients with Cardiovascular or Hematologic Disorders

Diagnostic and Therapeutic Procedures: Cardiovascular or Hematologic

Chapter 22: Pacemakers

Contributor: Sharon Kumm, MN, MS, RN, CCRN

NCLEX-PN® Connections:

Learning Objective: Review and apply knowledge within "**Pacemakers**" in readiness for performance of the following nursing activities as outlined by the NCLEX-PN® test plan:

Δ   Perform electrocardiogram (ECG).

Δ   Perform/assist with relevant laboratory, diagnostic, and therapeutic procedures within the nursing role, including:

- Preparation of the client for the procedure.

- Reinforcement of client teaching (before and following the procedure).

- Accurate collection of specimens.

- Monitoring procedure results (compare to norms) and appropriate notification of the primary care provider.

- Monitoring the client's response (expected, unexpected adverse response, comparison to baseline) to the procedure.

- Monitoring and taking actions, including reinforcing client teaching, to prevent or minimize the risk of complications.

- Recognizing signs of potential complications and reporting to the primary care provider.

- Recommending changes in the test/procedure as needed based on client findings.

Δ   Recognize the client's recovery from anesthesia, if used.

Δ   Monitor therapeutic devices (drainage/irrigating devices, chest tubes), if inserted, for proper functioning.

Key Points

Δ   A pacemaker is a battery-operated device that **electrically stimulates the heart** when the natural pacemaker of the heart fails to maintain an acceptable rhythm.

Δ   Pacemakers are composed of three parts:

- **Pulse generator** – houses energy source and control center.

- **Lead** – provides communication between the generator and electrode.

- **Electrode** – direct contact with the myocardial muscle.

Δ   Pacemakers may be **temporary or permanent**. Temporary pacemakers have an external battery pack; permanent pacemakers have an internal pacing unit.

Δ   **Temporary Pacemakers**

- **External (transcutaneous)**

  ◊   Involves energy delivery through the thoracic musculature to the heart through two electrode patches placed on the skin.

  ◊   Requires large amounts of electricity, which can be painful for the client.

  ◊   Used only in emergency resuscitation of a client who does not have pacing wires inserted.

- **Epicardial**

  ◊   Involves energy delivery through the thoracic musculature to the heart through lead wires.

  ◊   Commonly used during and immediately following open heart surgery.

- **Endocardial (transvenous)**

  ◊   Involves energy delivered through lead wires that are threaded through a large central vein (subclavian, jugular, or femoral) and lodged into the wall of the right ventricle.

Δ   **Permanent Pacemakers**

- Permanent pacemakers are indicated for **chronic or recurrent dysrhythmias** due to sinus or atrioventricular (AV) node malfunction.

- **Pacemaker modes**

  ◊   **Fixed rate (asynchronous)** – fires at a constant rate without regard for the heart's electrical activity.

  ◊   **Demand mode (synchronous)** – senses the heart's electrical activity and fires at preset rate if the heart's intrinsic rate is below a certain level.

  ◊   **Antidysrhythmic function** – can overpace a tachydysrhythmia or deliver an electrical shock.

- Pacemakers can be programmed to pace the atria, ventricles, or both (AV sequential pacing).

- Inter-Society Commission for Heart Disease (ICHD) codes are used for **pacemaker identification**.

  ◊ First letter – chamber paced

  ◊ Second letter – chamber sensed

  ◊ Third letter – mode of response

  ◊ Fourth letter – programmable functions

  ◊ Fifth letter – tachydysrhythmic functions

  ◊ Response to sensing determines the pacemaker's activity when intrinsic activity is sensed.

    ° Inhibited – pacemaker activity is inhibited/does not fire.

    ° Triggered – pacemaker activity is triggered/fires when intrinsic activity is sensed.

Chamber paced	Chamber sensed	Response to sensing	Programmability	Anti-tachy dysrhythmia ability
O - None	O - None	O - None	O - None	O - None
A – Atria	A - Atria	T - Triggered	P - Simple Programmable	P- Pacing (anti-tachydysrhythmia)
V – Ventricle	V - Ventricle	I - Inhibited	M – Multiple Programmable	S - Shock
D - Dual (AV)	D - Dual (AV)	D - Dual (AV)	C - Communicating	D - Dual (P + S)
			R - Rate Modulation	

Key Factors

Δ **Client Indications** for Pacemaker Placement

- **Symptomatic bradycardia**

- **Complete heart block**

- **Sick sinus syndrome**

- Sinus arrest

- Asystole

- Atrial **tachydysrhythmias**

- Ventricular tachydysrhythmias

Nursing Interventions

Δ   **Before the Procedure**

- Assess the client/family/significant other's knowledge of the procedure and need for pacemaker (if non-emergent situation).

- Obtain **informed consent.**

- **Transcutaneous pacing**

  ◊   Cleanse skin with soap and water. Do not shave or rub skin or apply alcohol. Trim excess hair.

  ◊   Apply the **posterior electrode between the spine and the left scapula.** Avoid placing it over bone, as bone is a poor conductor of electricity.

  ◊   Place the **anterior electrode over the heart, between the V_2 and V_5** positions. Displace female breast tissue and position under the breast.

Δ   **During the Procedure**

- Monitor **client status** (vital signs, SaO_2, comfort).

- Administer **medications** as prescribed (analgesia, anxiolytics, anti-arrhythmics).

- Set pacemaker settings as ordered. Establish threshold (lowest stimulation that achieves capture).

Δ   **Following the Procedure**

- **Document**: time and date of insertion, model (permanent pacemaker), settings, rhythm strip, presence of adequate pulse and blood pressure, client response.

- Continually monitor heart rate and rhythm.

- Obtain **chest x-ray** as prescribed to assess lead placement and for pneumothorax, hemothorax, or pleural effusion.

- Provide **analgesia** as prescribed.

- **Minimize shoulder movement initially** and provide a sling (if prescribed) to allow leads to anchor. Provide gentle, passive range-of-motion exercise three times daily after 24 hr (permanent pacemaker).

Δ   **Maintain safety.**

- Ensure all **electrical equipment has grounded connections.**

- Remove any electrical equipment that is damaged.

- Secure pacemaker battery pack. Take care when moving the client. Ensure there is enough wire slack.

- Temporary pacemaker

  ◊ Wear gloves when handling pacemaker leads.

  ◊ Insulate pacemaker terminals and leads with non-conductive material when not in use (rubber gloves).

  ◊ Keep spare generator, leads, and batteries at bedside.

- Permanent pacemaker

  ◊ **Provide the client with a pacemaker identification card** including the manufacturer's name, model number, mode of function, rate parameters, and expected battery life.

Δ Monitor the site for **redness, drainage, pain, swelling,** and **hematoma.**

Δ Assess the client for **hiccups,** which may indicate that the generator is pacing the diaphragm.

Δ **Permanent pacemaker** discharge **teaching** includes:

- Instruct the client to **carry a pacemaker identification card at all times.**

- Teach that batteries last 10 years on average.

- Wear a sling when out of bed, if prescribed.

- Teach the client to **take pulse daily at the same time.**

- Tell the client the set rate of the pacemaker and to **notify the primary care provider if the heart rate is less than 5 beats below pacer rate.**

- Report signs of **dizziness, fainting, fatigue, weakness, chest pain, hiccupping, or palpitations.**

- For clients with pacer-defibrillators, inform the client and family that anyone touching the client when the device delivers a shock will feel a slight electrical impulse but that the impulse will not harm the person.

- The client should follow activity restrictions as prescribed, including **no contact sports or heavy lifting for 2 months.**

- The client should avoid direct blows or injury to the generator site.

- The client can **resume sexual activity as desired**, avoiding positions that put stress on the incision site.

- Household appliances should not affect pacemaker function unless held directly over pacer generator. This includes garage door openers, burglar alarms, microwave ovens, and antitheft devices.

- Pacemakers will set off airport security detectors and officials should be notified. The airport security device should not affect pacemaker functioning.

- Instruct the client to **inform other providers and dentists about the pacemaker.** Some tests, such as MRI, may be contraindicated.

Complications and Nursing Implications

Δ **Failure to Capture**

- Occurs when the **pacemaker initiates a stimulus, but depolarization of the myocardium does not happen.**

- ECG shows pacing spikes without the expected P wave or QRS complex.

- **Causes** include:

  ◊ Dislodgement of the electrode.

  ◊ Myocardial ischemia or infarction.

  ◊ Antidysrhythmic medications.

  ◊ Electrolyte imbalances (hypokalemia, hyperkalemia).

- **Treatment** involves:

  ◊ Increasing the voltage delivered (mA).

Δ **Failure to Sense**

- Occurs when the **pacemaker fails to sense the heart's intrinsic electrical activity, resulting in the delivery of unnecessary stimulus.**

- ECG shows pacemaker spikes at intervals different from the programmed interval.

- **Discharge of an impulse during the T wave can lead to life-threatening ventricular dysrhythmias.**

- **Treatment** involves:

  ◊ Decreasing the amplitude at which the pacemaker recognizes intrinsic electrical activity (mV).

Δ **Stimulation of Chest Wall or Diaphragm**

- Indicated by **muscle twitching or hiccups.**

- Often caused by lead wire perforation with high electrical current.

- **Can lead to cardiac tamponade.**

- **Notify the provider,** as it requires repositioning of the lead wires by the provider.

Δ **Microshock** (epicardial pacing)

- Cover wires with non-conductive insulation (rubber gloves) and non-conductive tape.

- Ground all equipment with a 3-pronged plug.

- Wear rubber gloves when handling pacing wires.

Meeting the Needs of Older Adults

Δ   Conduction of electrical impulses is delayed as persons age.

Δ   Ischemia, infarction, and mitral or tricuspid valve surgery can impair blood flow to the AV node, resulting in temporary or permanent heart block.

Primary Reference:

Ignatavicius, D. D., & Workman, M. L. (2006). *Medical-surgical nursing* (5th ed.). St. Louis, MO: Saunders.

Additional Resources:

Black, J. M., & Hawks, J. H. (2005). *Medical-surgical nursing: Clinical management for positive outcomes* (7th ed.). St. Louis, MO: Saunders.

Kidd, P. S., & Wagner, K. D. (2001). *High acuity nursing* (3rd ed.). Upper Saddle River, NJ: Prentice Hall.

NANDA International (2004). *NANDA nursing diagnoses: Definitions and classification 2005-2006*. Philadelphia: NANDA.

Chapter 22: Pacemakers

Application Exercises

1. List several safety measures to implement when a client has a temporary pacemaker in place.

Scenario: A nurse is caring for a client who has been admitted to the coronary care unit from the emergency department. The client's vital signs are: heart rate 34 beats/min, blood pressure 83/48 mm Hg, respiratory rate 30/min, and temperature 38.6° C (101.4° F). The client is lethargic and unable to complete sentences. The heart rhythm strip indicates complete heart block.

2. Which of the following interventions should the nurse perform first?

     A. Obtain informed consent.

     B. Prepare the client for permanent pacemaker insertion.

     C. Attach transcutaneous pacing pads and obtain threshold.

     D. Obtain a 12-lead ECG to confirm heart rhythm.

3. A temporary venous pacemaker is inserted until a permanent pacemaker can be inserted. It is set as a VVI pacemaker at a rate of 70/min. Which of the following signs and symptoms pose a concern for the nurse? (Check all that apply.)

     _____   Cool and clammy foot with capillary refill of 5 seconds

     _____   Observed pacing spike followed by a QRS complex

     _____   Twitching of intercostal muscle

     _____   Heart rate of 84 beats/min

     _____   Blood pressure of 104/62 mm Hg

4. The client has now received a permanent pacemaker. Which of the following statements indicates a need for further teaching?

     A. "I will notify the airport screeners about my pacemaker."

     B. "I will call if I notice hiccups or muscle twitching."

     C. "I need to disconnect my garage door opener."

     D. "I will take my pulse every morning when I awake."

Chapter 22: Pacemakers

Application Exercises Answer Key

1. List several safety measures to implement when a client has a temporary pacemaker in place.

   Wear rubber gloves when touching exposed wires.

   Check that all electrical equipment has adequate grounding.

   Limit motion of the extremity near the insertion site.

   Secure the battery pack.

   Make sure wires are loose enough to reposition the client.

   Keep spare batteries at bedside.

Scenario: A nurse is caring for a client who has been admitted to the coronary care unit from the emergency department. The client's vital signs are: heart rate 34 beats/min, blood pressure 83/48 mm Hg, respiratory rate 30/min, and temperature 38.6° C (101.4° F). The client is lethargic and unable to complete sentences. The heart rhythm strip indicates complete heart block.

---

2. Which of the following interventions should the nurse perform first?

   A. Obtain informed consent.
   B. Prepare the client for permanent pacemaker insertion.
   C. Attach transcutaneous pacing pads and obtain threshold.
   D. Obtain 12-lead ECG to confirm heart rhythm.

   This client is clearly symptomatic, so transcutaneous pacing should be used to stabilize the client's heart rate, rhythm, and blood pressure.

3. A temporary venous pacemaker is inserted until a permanent pacemaker can be inserted. It is set as a VVI pacemaker at a rate of 70/min. Which of the following signs and symptoms pose a concern for the nurse? (Check all that apply.)

    __x__   Cool and clammy foot with capillary refill of 5 seconds
    _____   Observed pacing spike followed by a QRS complex
    __x__   Twitching of intercostal muscle
    _____   Heart rate of 84 beats/min
    _____   Blood pressure of 104/62 mm Hg

Pacing spike followed by a QRS complex, heart rate of 84/min, and blood pressure of 104/62 mm Hg are expected findings. A cool and clammy foot may be an indication of a hematoma secondary to insertion via the femoral vein. Twitching of intercostal muscle may be a sign of lead wire perforation and stimulation of the diaphragm.

4. The client has now received a permanent pacemaker. Which of the following statements indicates a need for further teaching?

A. "I will notify the airport screeners about my pacemaker."
B. "I will call if I notice hiccups or muscle twitching."
C. **"I need to disconnect my garage door opener."**
D. "I will take my pulse every morning when I awake."

This indicates that the client does not understand that household appliances, such as microwaves and garage door openers, will not affect his pacemaker.

Unit 3   Nursing Care of Clients with Cardiovascular or Hematologic Disorders
Section: Diagnostic and Therapeutic Procedures: Cardiovascular or Hematologic

Chapter 23:   **Angiography and Angioplasty**

Contributor: Sharon Kumm, MN, MS, RN, CCRN

NCLEX-PN® Connections:

Learning Objective: Review and apply knowledge within "**Angiography and Angioplasty**" in readiness for performance of the following nursing activities as outlined by the NCLEX-PN® test plan:

Δ   Perform/assist with relevant laboratory, diagnostic, and therapeutic procedures within the nursing role, including:

- Preparation of the client for the procedure.

- Reinforcement of client teaching (before and following the procedure).

- Accurate collection of specimens.

- Monitoring procedure results (compare to norms) and appropriate notification of the primary care provider.

- Monitoring the client's response (expected, unexpected adverse response, comparison to baseline) to the procedure.

- Monitoring and taking actions, including reinforcing client teaching, to prevent or minimize the risk of complications.

- Recognizing signs of potential complications and reporting to the primary care provider.

- Recommending changes in the test/procedure as needed based on client findings.

Δ   Recognize the client's recovery from anesthesia, if used.

Δ   Monitor therapeutic devices (drainage/irrigating devices, chest tubes), if inserted, for proper functioning.

📖 Key Points

Δ   A **coronary angiogram**, also called a **cardiac catheterization**, is an invasive diagnostic procedure used to **evaluate the presence and degree of coronary artery blockage.**

Δ   **Angiography** involves the insertion of a **catheter** into a femoral (sometimes a brachial) vessel and threading it into the right or left side of the heart. Coronary artery narrowings and occlusions are identified by the injection of **contrast media under fluoroscopy.**

Δ   Percutaneous transluminal coronary angioplasty (PTCA) involves inflating a **balloon** to **dilate the arterial lumen** and the adhering plaque, thus widening the arterial lumen. A **stent** (mesh-wire device) is often placed to prevent restenosis of the artery.

Δ   **PTCA** is used as an **alternative to coronary artery bypass graft (CABG) surgery** approximately 50% of the time.

Δ   PTCA can be performed on an elective basis to treat coronary artery disease (CAD) or on an emergency basis to treat myocardial infarction.

Key Factors

Δ   **Client Indications for Angiography**

- **Unstable angina and ECG changes** (T wave inversion, ST segment elevation, and depression)

- **Confirmation and determination of location and extent of heart disease**

- **Evaluation** of **treatment effectiveness** (medication therapy, PTCA)

Δ   **Client Indications for PTCA**

- Single or double vessel disease with a discrete proximal lesion

- Evolving acute myocardial infarction (along with thrombolytic therapy)

- Because acute vessel closure is a risk, PTCA is **contraindicated for treatment of left main coronary artery lesions.**

Nursing Interventions

Δ   **Before the Procedure**

- Ensure that the **consent** form is signed.

- Maintain the client on **NPO** status for at least 8 hr (risk for aspiration when lying flat for the procedure).

- Assess that the client and family understand the procedure.

- Assess for **iodine/shellfish allergy** (contrast media).

- Assess renal function prior to introduction of contrast dye.

- **Administer premedications** as ordered (Solu-Medrol, diphenhydramine).

Δ **During the Procedure**

- Administer **sedatives** and **analgesia** as prescribed.

- Monitor for **chest pain** during angioplasty.

- Continually **monitor vital signs** and **heart rhythm**.

- Be prepared to intervene for **dysrhythmias.**

Δ **Following the Procedure**

- Assess **vital signs** every 15 min x4, every 30 min x2, every hour x4, and then every 4 hr (follow hospital protocol).

- Assess the **groin site** at the same intervals for:

  ◊ Bleeding and hematoma formation.

  ◊ Thrombosis; document pedal pulse, color, temperature.

- Maintain **bedrest** in supine position with leg straight for prescribed time.

- Conduct **continuous cardiac monitoring** for dysrhythmias (reperfusion following angioplasty may cause dysrhythmias).

- Administer **antiplatelet** or **thrombolytic** agents as prescribed to prevent clot formation and restenosis.

  ◊ Aspirin

  ◊ Clopidogrel (Plavix), ticlopidine (Ticlid)

  ◊ Heparin

  ◊ Low molecular weight heparin (Enoxaparin)

  ◊ GP IIb/IIIa inhibitors, such as eptifibatide (Integrilin)

- Administer **anxiolytics** and **analgesia** as needed.

- Monitor **urine output and administer IV fluids** for hydration.

  ◊ Contrast media acts as an osmotic diuretic.

- Perform/assist with **sheath removal** from vessel.

  ◊ Apply pressure to arterial/venous sites for the prescribed period of time (varies depending upon the method used for vessel closure).

  ◊ Observe for vagal response (hypotension, bradycardia) from compression of nerves.

  ◊ Apply pressure dressing.

Δ   **Discharge Teaching**

- Instruct the client to:

    ◊   **Avoid strenuous exercise** for the prescribed period of time.

    ◊   **Immediately report** bleeding from the insertion site, chest pain, shortness of breath, and changes in the color or temperature of the extremity.

    ◊   **Restrict lifting** (< 10 lb) for the prescribed period of time.

- Clients with stent placement will receive **anticoagulation therapy** for 6 to 8 weeks. Instruct the client to:

    ◊   Take the medication at the same time each day.

    ◊   Have regular laboratory tests to determine therapeutic levels.

    ◊   Avoid activities that could cause bleeding (use soft toothbrush, wear shoes when out of bed).

- Encourage the client to follow **lifestyle guidelines** (manage weight, consume a low-fat/low-cholesterol diet, get regular exercise, stop smoking, decrease alcohol intake).

Complications and Nursing Implications

Δ   **Cardiac tamponade** can result from fluid accumulation in the pericardial sac.

- **Signs** include hypotension, jugular venous distention, muffled heart sounds, and paradoxical pulse (variance of 10 mm Hg or more in systolic blood pressure between expiration and inspiration).

- Hemodynamic monitoring will reveal intracardiac and pulmonary artery pressures similar and elevated (plateau pressures).

- **Notify the primary care provider immediately**.

- Administer **IV fluids** to combat hypotension as ordered.

- Obtain a chest x-ray or echocardiogram to confirm diagnosis.

- Prepare the client for **pericardiocentesis** (informed consent, gather materials, administer medications as appropriate).

    ◊   Monitor hemodynamic pressures as they normalize.

    ◊   Monitor heart rhythm; changes indicate improper positioning of the needle.

    ◊   Monitor for reoccurrence of signs after the procedure.

Δ   **Hematoma Formation**

- Assess the groin at prescribed intervals and as needed.

- Hold pressure for uncontrolled oozing/bleeding.

- Monitor peripheral circulation.
- Notify the primary care provider.

Δ **Restenosis** (of treated vessel)

- Assess ECG patterns and for occurrence of chest pain.
- **Notify the primary care provider immediately.**
- Prepare the client for return to the cardiac catheterization laboratory.

Δ **Retroperitoneal Bleeding**

- Assess for flank pain and hypotension.
- **Notify the primary care provider immediately.**
- Administer IV fluids and blood products as ordered.

Meeting the Needs of Older Adults

Δ Older adult clients may have **arthritis**, which can make lying in bed for 4 to 6 hr after the procedure painful.

Δ Older adult clients with coronary artery disease may also have **peripheral artery disease**, increasing the risk for occlusion or bleeding.

Primary Reference:

Ignatavicius, D. D., & Workman, M. L. (2006). *Medical-surgical nursing* (5th ed.). St. Louis, MO: Saunders.

Additional Resources:

Black, J. M., & Hawks, J. H. (2005). *Medical-surgical nursing: Clinical management for positive outcomes* (7th ed.). St. Louis, MO: Saunders.

NANDA International (2004). *NANDA nursing diagnoses: Definitions and classification 2005-2006*. Philadelphia: NANDA.

Chapter 23: Angiography and Angioplasty

Application Exercises

Scenario: A nurse is caring for a client who is scheduled to undergo a cardiac catheterization and possible PTCA with stent placement.

1. Which of the following client statements indicates a need for further teaching?

    A. "I will need to lie flat for several hours following the procedure."

    B. "I will avoid taking my daily aspirin to prevent bleeding from my groin."

    C. "I should call you following the procedure if I notice a wet feeling in my groin."

    D. "You will monitor my blood pressure closely following the procedure."

2. The nurse performs the vital signs and groin site assessment 30 min following the catheterization. Which of the following should pose a concern for the nurse? (Check all that apply.)

    _____ Capillary refill of 2 seconds in affected extremity

    _____ Cool, clammy feel to affected extremity

    _____ Thready pedal pulse in affected limb

    _____ Blood pressure of 110/68 mm Hg

    _____ Groin site that is soft with some oozing and a +2 pedal pulse

    _____ ST elevation that is lower than before catheterization

    _____ Occasional premature ventricular complexes (PVCs) that occur in singlets

3. Two hours after the catheterization, the client reports feeling dizzy and lightheaded. Vital signs are: heart rate 127 beats/min and regular, blood pressure 88/46 mm Hg, respiratory rate 34/min, temperature 38.9° C (102° F), and SaO_2 92% on oxygen at 2 L/min. Heart sounds are muffled. What do these symptoms likely indicate?

4. What discharge teaching should a nurse provide to a client following an angioplasty?

5. What additional teaching is required for a client who has received a coronary artery stent?

Chapter 23: Angiography and Angioplasty

Application Exercises Answer Key

Scenario: A nurse is caring for a client who is scheduled to undergo a cardiac catheterization and possible PTCA with stent placement.

1. Which of the following client statements indicates a need for further teaching?

    A. "I will need to lie flat for several hours following the procedure."

    B. "I will avoid taking my daily aspirin to prevent bleeding from my groin."

    C. "I should call you following the procedure if I notice a wet feeling in my groin."

    D. "You will monitor my blood pressure closely following the procedure."

Anticoagulant therapy is continued following angiography to minimize the risk of restenosis.

2. The nurse performs the vital signs and groin site assessment 30 min following the catheterization. Which of the following should pose a concern for the nurse? (Check all that apply.)

_____	Capillary refill of 2 seconds in affected extremity
__x__	Cool, clammy feel to affected extremity
__x__	Thready pedal pulse in affected limb
_____	Blood pressure of 110/68 mm Hg
_____	Groin site that is soft with some oozing and a +2 pedal pulse
_____	ST elevation that is lower than before catheterization
_____	Occasional premature ventricular complexes (PVCs) that occur in singlets

These findings suggest reduced circulation to the affected extremity possibly related to hematoma formation. Brisk capillary refill, BP within normal range, and positive pedal pulses are expected findings. A decreased ST elevation is a sign of treatment effectiveness. Occasional PVCs are fairly commonly during and following catheterization.

3. Two hours after the catheterization, the client reports feeling dizzy and lightheaded. Vital signs are: heart rate 127 beats/min and regular, blood pressure 88/46 mm Hg, respiratory rate 34/min, temperature 38.9° C (102° F), and SaO_2 92% on oxygen at 2 L/min. Heart sounds are muffled. What do these symptoms likely indicate?

These symptoms are indicative of cardiac tamponade. The nurse should notify the primary care provider immediately and prepare for a pericardiocentesis.

4. What discharge teaching should a nurse provide to a client following an angioplasty?

Avoid strenuous activity.

Avoid lifting more than 10 lb until follow-up visit.

Immediately report bleeding from the insertion site, chest pain or shortness of breath, decreased pulses, or color/temperature changes in the affected extremity.

Lifestyle changes (smoking cessation, low-fat and low-cholesterol diet, exercise) to reduce redevelopment or worsening of plaque deposits.

5. What additional teaching is required for a client who has received a coronary artery stent?

Clients with stent placement will receive anticoagulation therapy for 6 to 8 weeks. Therefore, clients should be told to take the medication at the same time each day, have regular laboratory tests to determine therapeutic levels, and avoid activities that could cause bleeding (use soft toothbrush, wear shoes when out of bed).

Unit 3
Section:

Nursing Care of Clients with Cardiovascular or Hematologic Disorders

Diagnostic and Therapeutic Procedures: Cardiovascular or Hematologic

Chapter 24:   Bypass Grafts

Contributor: Sharon Kumm, MN, MS, RN, CCRN

NCLEX-PN® Connections:

Learning Objective: Review and apply knowledge within "**Bypass Grafts**" in readiness for performance of the following nursing activities as outlined by the NCLEX-PN® test plan:

Δ   Identify signs/symptoms of potential circulatory complications and intervene.

Δ   Monitor for signs and symptoms of bleeding.

Δ   Perform/assist with relevant laboratory, diagnostic, and therapeutic procedures within the nursing role, including:

- Preparation of the client for the procedure.

- Reinforcement of client teaching (before and following the procedure).

- Accurate collection of specimens.

- Monitoring procedure results (compare to norms) and appropriate notification of the primary care provider.

- Monitoring the client's response (expected, unexpected adverse response, comparison to baseline) to the procedure.

- Monitoring and taking actions, including reinforcing client teaching, to prevent or minimize the risk of complications.

- Recognizing signs of potential complications and reporting to the primary care provider.

- Recommending changes in the test/procedure as needed based on client findings.

Δ   Recognize the client's recovery from anesthesia, if used.

Δ   Monitor therapeutic devices (drainage/irrigating devices, chest tubes), if inserted, for proper functioning.

Coronary Artery Bypass Grafts

 Key Points

Δ   Coronary artery bypass grafting (CABG) is **the most common form of cardiac surgery** performed on adults. It is performed to bypass an obstruction in one or more of the coronary arteries.

Δ   Left ventricular function is the most important indicator for long-term survival. **Successful CABGs occur most often when a client has good ventricular function remaining** (ejection fraction 40 to 50%).

Δ   CABG **does not alter the atherosclerotic process**.

Δ   CABG **improves the quality of life** of most clients:

•   80 to 90% of clients are pain-free 1 year after CABG.

•   70% remain pain-free after 5 years.

Δ   CABG is an **invasive surgical procedure** that aims to **restore vascularization** of the myocardium.

•   It involves utilizing an **extracardiac vein** (saphenous vein) or artery (usually the mammary artery) **to bypass an obstruction** in one or more of the coronary arteries.

•   Most often, a **median sternotomy incision** is made to visualize the heart and the great vessels.

•   The client is placed on **cardiopulmonary bypass**, and the client's core **temperature is lowered** to **decrease the rate of metabolism** and the **demand for oxygen**.

•   A **cardioplegic solution is used to stop the heart**. This prevents myocardial ischemia and allows for a motionless operative field.

•   The artery or vein to be used is harvested. When a **saphenous vein** is used, it is **reversed to prevent the valves from interfering with blood flow**.

•   The **harvested vessel is anastomosed to the aorta** and the affected coronary artery distal to the occlusion.

•   Once the bypass is complete, the **client is rewarmed** by the bypass machine. The **grafts are observed for patency and leakage** as the client is weaned from the bypass machine and **blood is redirected through the coronary vasculature**.

•   Lastly, **pacemaker wires** are sutured into the myocardium, and **chest tubes** are placed. The incision is closed with wire sutures, and the client is transported to the intensive care unit.

Key Factors

Δ   **Indications for CABG**

- Coronary artery disease that is nonresponsive to medical management
- Angina with greater than 50% occlusion of the left main coronary artery
- Unstable angina with severe two-vessel disease
- Triple-vessel disease
- Ischemia with heart failure (may not be reasonable for clients with poor ejection fractions)
- Persistent ischemia or likely myocardial infarction (MI) following coronary angiography, percutaneous transluminal coronary angioplasty (PTCA), or stent placement
- Clients with vessels unsuitable for PTCA (for example, narrow or calcified)
- Valvular disease

Nursing Interventions

Δ   **Before the Procedure**

- CABG may be a **planned or emergent procedure**. When planned, preparation begins before the client comes to the hospital for the procedure.
- **Provide instruction** to the client and family **about the procedure and the postsurgical environment.**
  - ◊ Inform the client of the importance of **coughing and deep breathing after the procedure to prevent complications.**
  - ◊ Instruct the client to **splint the incision** when coughing and deep breathing. Perform a return demonstration.
  - ◊ Instruct the client to **report any pain** to the nursing staff. The majority of pain stems from the harvest site for the vein.
  - ◊ Inform the client to expect to be on a **ventilator** for several hours following surgery.
  - ◊ Encourage the client to **breathe with the ventilator.**
  - ◊ Inform the client and family that **talking will not be possible** with the endotracheal tube in place.
  - ◊ Inform the client to expect the following postoperatively:
    - ° **Sternal incision** and possible leg incision.
    - ° **1 to 2 chest tubes.**
    - ° **Foley catheter.**

- ° **Pacemaker wires.**

- ° **Hemodynamic monitoring devices** (pulmonary artery catheter, arterial line).

◊ Instruct the client to **alter or discontinue regular medications as prescribed by the primary care provider.** Medications frequently discontinued for CABG include:

- ° Digitalis (Digoxin) 12 hr prior to surgery.

- ° Diuretics 2 to 3 days before surgery.

- ° Aspirin and other anticoagulants 1 week before surgery.

◊ **Medications** often **continued** for CABG include:

- ° Potassium supplements.

- ° Scheduled antidysrhythmics, such as amiodarone (Cordarone).

- ° Scheduled antihypertensives, such as beta-blockers and calcium-channel blockers.

◊ Assess client and family **anxiety** levels surrounding the procedure.

- ° Reassure the client and family that the high level of care and sophisticated equipment are standard and routine for CABG.

- ° Encourage verbalization of feelings.

- Verify that **informed consent** is signed.

- Administer **preoperative medications** as prescribed.

  ◊ **Anxiolytics**, such as lorazepam (Ativan) and diazepam (Valium)

  ◊ Prophylactic **antibiotics**

  ◊ **Cholinergic blocker**, such as scopolamine (a central nervous system depressant that reduces secretions)

- Provide **safe transport** of the client to the operating room. Monitor heart rate and rhythm, oxygenation, and other vital indicators.

Δ **Following the Procedure**

- Maintain a **patent airway** and **adequate ventilation** and **prevent atelectasis.**

  ◊ Monitor **respiratory rate** and **effort.**

  ◊ Auscultate **breath sounds.** Report crackles.

  ◊ Monitor **SaO$_2$**.

  ◊ Document **ventilator settings.**

  ◊ **Suction** as needed. (*For information, refer to chapter 5, Suctioning.*)

  ◊ **Assist** with **extubation.**

- Encourage the client to **splint the incision** while deep breathing and coughing.

- **Dangle** and **turn the client** side to side as tolerated **within 2 hr** following extubation. Assist the client **to a chair within 48 hr. Ambulate the client** 25 to 100 ft by the first postoperative day.

- Continually **monitor the client's heart rate and rhythm. Treat dysrhythmias** per protocol.

- Maintain an **adequate circulating blood** volume.

  ◊ Monitor **blood pressure.**

    ° **Hypotension** may result in **graft collapse.**

    ° **Hypertension** may result in **bleeding from the grafts** and sutures.

    ° Titrate **IV drips** – dobutamine, milrinone, sodium nitroprusside (Nipride) – per protocol to control blood pressure.

  ◊ Monitor **hemodynamic pressures.** Monitor **catheter placement.** Observe waveforms and markings on the catheter.

  ◊ Monitor the client's **level of consciousness.** Assess **neurological status** every 30 to 60 min until the client awakens from anesthesia, then every 2 to 4 hr, or per institutional policy.

  ◊ **Notify the surgeon** of significant changes in values.

- Monitor **chest tube patency and drainage.**

  ◊ **Measure** drainage at least **hourly.**

  ◊ Volume **exceeding 150 mL/hr could be a sign of possible hemorrhage and should be reported to the surgeon.**

  ◊ **Avoid dependent loops** in tubing to facilitate drainage.

Δ **Assess and control pain.**

- Determine the **source** of the pain (angina, incisional pain).

  ◊ **Anginal pain** often radiates and is unaffected by breathing.

  ◊ **Incisional pain** is localized, sharp, aching, burning, and often worsens with deep breathing.

- Administer **analgesia** as prescribed (morphine, fentanyl).

  ◊ Pain will stimulate the sympathetic nervous system, resulting in increased heart rate and systemic vascular resistance (SVR).

  ◊ Provide frequent and adequate doses to control pain.

Δ   Monitor **fluid** and **electrolyte status**.

- **Fluid administration** is determined by blood pressure, pulmonary artery wedge pressure, right atrial pressure (CVP), cardiac output and index, systemic vascular resistance (SVR), blood loss, and urine output.

- Follow provider or unit-specific orders for fluid administration.

- Monitor for **electrolyte imbalances**, especially for hypokalemia and hyperkalemia.

Δ   Prevent and monitor for **infection**.

- Practice proper **handwashing**.

- Use **surgical aseptic technique** during procedures such as dressing changes and suctioning.

- Administer **antibiotics**.

- Monitor white blood cell (WBC) counts, incisional redness and drainage, and fever.

Discharge Teaching

Δ   Instruct the client to monitor and **report signs of infection**, such as fever, incisional drainage, and redness.

Δ   Instruct the client to **treat angina**.

- Maintain a fresh supply of sublingual **nitroglycerin**.

- Store the nitroglycerin in a **light-resistant** container.

- Discontinue activity and rest with the onset of pain.

Δ   Instruct the client to adhere to the pharmacological regimen.

Δ   Instruct clients with diabetes to closely **monitor blood glucose levels**.

Δ   Encourage the client to consume a **heart-healthy diet** (low-fat, low-cholesterol, high-fiber, low-salt).

Δ   Encourage the client to **quit smoking** if applicable. Provide resources on smoking cessation.

Δ   Encourage **physical activity**. Consult the cardiac rehabilitation program or a physical therapist to devise a specific program.

Δ   Instruct the client to remain **home during the first week after surgery** and to resume normal activities slowly.

- Week 2 – possible return to work part time, increase in social activities.

- Week 3 – lifting of up to 15 lb, avoidance of heavier lifting for 6 to 8 weeks.

Δ Clients can **resume sexual activity based on the advice of the primary care provider.**

- Walking 1 block or climbing 2 flights of stairs symptom-free generally indicates that it is safe to resume normal sexual activity.

Δ Encourage verbalization of feelings.

Complications and Nursing Implications

Δ **Pulmonary Complications**

- **Atelectasis** (main complication experienced by CABG clients)

- Pneumonia

- Pulmonary edema

Δ **Decreased Cardiac Output**

- **Dysrhythmias**

  ◊ Treat dysrhythmias as prescribed.

  ◊ Utilize **pacemaker wires**, if heart block is present.

- **Cardiac tamponade**

  ◊ Cardiac tamponade results from bleeding and mediastinal **chest tubes with inadequate drainage**.

  ◊ Cardiac tamponade compresses the heart chambers and **inhibits effective pumping**.

  ◊ **Signs** include a sudden decrease/cessation of chest-tube drainage following heavy drainage, jugular-venous distension (JVD) with clear lung sounds, and equal PAWP and CVP values.

  ◊ **Treatment** involves volume expansion (fluid administration) and emergency sternotomy with drainage. Pericardiocentesis is avoided because blood may have clotted.

- **Myocardial infarction**

Δ **Electrolyte Disturbances**

- **Potassium** and **magnesium depletion** is common.

  ◊ Always dilute potassium supplements in adequate fluid (40 to 80 mEq in 100 mL of IV solution).

  ◊ Administer with an infusion pump to control the rate of delivery.

  ◊ Administer through a central catheter.

Meeting the Needs of Older Adults

Δ Mortality rates for older adult clients undergoing CABG are higher than those of younger clients.

Δ Older adult clients are more likely to have transient neurological changes.

Δ Toxic effects from cardiac medications are more likely to occur in older adult clients.

Δ Older adult clients are more prone to dysrhythmias.

Δ Recovery from CABG is slower for the older adult client.

Peripheral Bypass Grafts

 Key Points

Δ The femoral-popliteal area is the site most commonly affected by chronic peripheral artery disease (PAD) in clients who do not have diabetes.

Δ **PAD is caused by atherosclerosis** and causes a **gradual thickening of the intima** and media of the arteries, ultimately resulting in the **progressive narrowing** of the vessel lumen.

Δ Progressive stiffening of the arteries and narrowing of the lumen **decreases the blood supply to affected tissues and increases resistance to blood flow.**

Δ **Bypass graft surgery aims to restore adequate blood flow** to the affected area.

Δ If bypass surgery fails to restore circulation, the client may need to undergo amputation of the limb.

Δ **A peripheral bypass graft involves suturing graft material or autogenous saphenous veins before and after an occluded area of an artery.** This procedure improves blood supply to the area normally served by the blocked artery.

Key Factors

Δ Client Indications for Peripheral Artery Bypass Grafts (arterial revascularization)

- **Acute circulatory compromise in limb**
- **Severe pain at rest that interferes with ability to work**

Nursing Interventions

Δ **Before the Procedure**

- Assess **client** and **family understanding** of the procedure.
- Verify that **consent** form is signed.
- Assess for **allergies.**
- Document **baseline vital signs and peripheral pulses.**
- Administer **prophylactic antibiotic therapy** as prescribed.
- Maintain **NPO status** for at least 8 hr prior to surgery.

Δ **Following the Procedure**

- Assess and monitor **vital signs every 15 min for 1 hr and then hourly after the first hour.**
- Assess and monitor the **operative limb every 15 min for 1 hr and then hourly after that,** paying particular attention to the following:
  - ◊ Incision site for **bleeding.**
  - ◊ **Peripheral pulses and skin color/temperature** for signs of bypass graft occlusion.
  - ◊ If the peripheral pulse is difficult to locate, mark the site with indelible marker.
- Administer **intravenous fluids** as ordered.
- **Assess the type of pain experienced.**
  - ◊ Throbbing pain is experienced due to increased blood flow to the extremity.
  - ◊ Ischemic pain is often difficult to relieve with narcotic administration.
- Administer **analgesics,** such as morphine and fentanyl, to provide pain relief.
- Administer **antibiotics** as prescribed.
- Use **surgical aseptic technique** for dressing changes.
- Monitor incision sites for signs of **infection,** such as erythema, tenderness, and drainage.
- Administer **anticoagulant therapy,** such as warfarin (Coumadin), heparin, and enoxaparin, to **prevent reocclusion.**
- Administer **antiplatelet therapy,** such as clopidogrel (Plavix), ticlopidine (Ticlid), and aspirin.
- Help the **client turn, cough, and deep breathe every 2 hr.**

- Assist the client to get out of bed and **ambulate**. Encourage the use of a walker initially.

- **Discourage sitting** for **long periods of time**.

- Apply **support stockings** to promote venous return.

- Set up a progressive **exercise program** that includes walking. Consider a **physical therapy consult**.

- **Discharge Teaching**

  ◊ Advise the client to completely **abstain from smoking**. Suggest community services that help smokers abstain.

  ◊ Reinforce **activity restrictions**.

  ◊ Remind the client to **avoid crossing legs**.

  ◊ Advise the client to **avoid risk factors for atherosclerosis** (smoking, sedentary life style, uncontrolled diabetes).

  ◊ Teach the client techniques of **foot inspection and care**. Encourage the client to:

    ° Keep feet dry and clean.

    ° Avoid extreme temperatures.

    ° Use lotion.

    ° Avoid constraining garments.

    ° Wear clean, white, cotton socks.

Complications and Nursing Implications

  Δ **Graft Occlusion**

  - Notify the provider immediately for any noted **changes in pedal pulse, extremity color, or temperature**.

  - Prepare the client for thrombectomy or thrombolytic therapy.

  Δ **Compartment Syndrome**

  - This occurs with increased pressure in tissues that are confined, which leads to a decrease in blood flow.

  - Assess for **worsening pain, swelling, and tense or taut skin**.

  - Report abnormal findings to the primary care provider immediately.

Bypass Grafts

Δ   **Infection**

- Monitor **white blood cell count and temperature**.

- Collect specimens (wound or blood cultures).

- Administer antibiotic therapy.

Primary Reference:

Ignatavicius, D. D., & Workman, M. L. (2006). *Medical-surgical nursing* (5th ed.). St. Louis, MO: Saunders.

Additional Resources:

NANDA International (2004). *NANDA nursing diagnoses: Definitions and classification 2005-2006*. Philadelphia: NANDA.

For more information, visit the American Heart Association at: *www.americanheart.org*.

Medical Surgical

227

Chapter 24: Bypass Grafts

Application Exercises

Scenario: A nurse is caring for a client in the immediate postoperative period following CABG surgery.

1. Which of the following signs and/or symptoms pose an immediate concern to the nurse? (Check all that apply.)

    _____ Chest tube drainage of 200 mL over 2 hr

    _____ Client report of pain that originates in mediastinal area with radiation to the neck and shoulder

    _____ Blood pressure of 164/92 mm Hg

    _____ Serum potassium level of 2.9 mEq/L

    _____ Blood pressure of 82/44 mm Hg

    _____ Chest tube drainage of 10 mL during the second postoperative hour (drainage was 110 mL the first postoperative hour)

    _____ Client rating of pain, with deep breathing, at level 2 on a scale of 1 to 10

2. The client is 4 hr post extubation. He has refused to cough because he is tired and it hurts too much. He is only able to inspire 200 mL with the incentive spirometer. Which of the following is an appropriate nursing intervention?

    A. Let the client rest for now and return in 1 hr to try again.

    B. Administer morphine 4 mg IV per provider order, and return in 10 to 15 min to try again.

    C. Document the 200 mL as an appropriate volume.

    D. Tell the client that he will have to learn to breathe through the pain if he does not want to get pneumonia.

3. Upon discharge, which of the following statements indicates a need for further teaching? (Check all that apply.)

    _____ "I will take my nitroglycerin tablets every 5 min, up to 3 times, before calling for transport to the hospital."

    _____ "I don't need to watch my diet as closely, since the surgery eliminated my heart disease."

    _____ "I can anticipate returning to work within a few weeks."

    _____ "I will avoid participating in an exercise program, so that it won't stress my heart."

    _____ "I can lift objects less than 15 pounds if I am careful."

Scenario: A nurse is caring for a client in the immediate postoperative period following peripheral bypass graft surgery.

4. Provide rationales for the following interventions.

Nursing Intervention	Rationale
Assess the incision for bleeding.	
Assess distal pulse.	
Place an "X" on the site of the pulse.	
Discourage sitting for prolonged periods of time.	
Wrap legs with elastic bandages.	
Encourage participation in a walking program.	

5. Which of the following client signs/symptoms pose an immediate concern? (Check all that apply.)

_____ Trace of bloody drainage on first dressing change
_____ Capillary refill of affected limb of 6 seconds
_____ Cool feel and mottled appearance of the limb
_____ Temperature of 37.4° C (99.3° F)
_____ Throbbing pain of affected limb that is decreased with morphine
_____ Pulse of 2+ in the affected limb

6. List three of the most important topics for discharge teaching. Provide rationales for your choices.

Topic	Rationale

Chapter 24: Bypass Grafts

Application Exercises Answer Key

Scenario: A nurse is caring for a client in the immediate postoperative period following CABG surgery.

1. Which of the following signs and/or symptoms pose an immediate concern to the nurse? (Check all that apply.)

   _____ Chest tube drainage of 200 mL over 2 hr

   __X__ Client report of pain that originates in mediastinal area with radiation to the neck and shoulder

   __X__ Blood pressure of 164/92 mm Hg

   __X__ Serum potassium level of 2.9 mEq/L

   __X__ Blood pressure of 82/44 mm Hg

   __X__ Chest tube drainage of 10 mL during the second postoperative hour (drainage was 110 mL the first postoperative hour)

   _____ Client rating of pain, with deep breathing, at level 2 on a scale of 1 to 10

   Mediastinal pain with radiation is indicative of further ischemia and potential myocardial infarction. Hypotension and hypertension are damaging to new grafts, because the grafts may collapse or leak. A sudden decrease in chest tube drainage may indicate an accumulation of blood in the mediastinum, which can lead to cardiac tamponade.

2. The client is 4 hr post extubation. He has refused to cough because he is tired and it hurts too much. He is only able to inspire 200 mL with the incentive spirometer. Which of the following is an appropriate nursing intervention?

   A. Let the client rest for now and return in 1 hr to try again.

   B. Administer morphine 4 mg IV per provider order, and return in 10 to 15 min to try again.

   C. Document the 200 mL as an appropriate volume.

   D. Tell the client that he will have to learn to breathe through the pain if he does not want to get pneumonia.

   Pain medication should be administered to aid the client with deep breathing and coughing.

3. Upon discharge, which of the following statements indicates a need for further teaching? (Check all that apply.)

_____ "I will take my nitroglycerin tablets every 5 min, up to 3 times, before calling for transport to the hospital."

__x__ "I don't need to watch my diet as closely, since the surgery eliminated my heart disease."

_____ "I can anticipate returning to work within a few weeks."

__x__ "I will avoid participating in an exercise program, so that it won't stress my heart."

_____ "I can lift objects less than 15 pounds if I am careful."

The second and fourth options are contraindications for postoperative CABG clients. CABG does not cure heart disease, so measures to maintain heart health should still be practiced.

Scenario: A nurse is caring for a client in the immediate postoperative period following peripheral bypass graft surgery.

4. Provide rationales for the following interventions.

Nursing Intervention	Rationale
Assess the incision for bleeding.	Arteries were involved in the bypass graft. An arterial bleed is life-threatening.
Assess distal pulse.	Distal pulse is an indicator of adequate circulation.
Place an "X" on the site of the pulse.	This allows for easier assessment of distal pulse.
Discourage sitting for prolonged periods of time.	Sitting puts pressure on vessels and increases risk of venous stasis and edema.
Wrap legs with elastic bandages.	This intervention decreases edema by increasing interstitial hydrostatic pressure.
Encourage participation in a walking program.	Exercise improves blood circulation.

5. Which of the following client signs/symptoms pose an immediate concern? (Check all that apply.)

_____	Trace of bloody drainage on first dressing change
__x__	Capillary refill of affected limb of 6 seconds
__x__	Cool feel and mottled appearance of the limb
_____	Temperature of 37.4° C (99.3° F)
_____	Throbbing pain of affected limb that is decreased with morphine
_____	Pulse of 2+ in the affected limb

6. List three of the most important topics for discharge teaching. Provide rationales for your choices.

Topic	Rationale
Smoking cessation	Nicotine causes vasoconstriction, which will decrease perfusion and delay healing. Smoking will also increase progression of atherosclerosis.
Following medication regimen	Medications will increase circulation, prevent reocclusion, and prevent or treat infection.
Activity restrictions	This will prevent disruption of sutures.
Foot inspection	Skin remains fragile. Wounds will not heal well if circulation is compromised.
Dietary modification	An appropriate diet will slow the progression of atherosclerosis.

Unit 3 Nursing Care of Clients with Cardiovascular or Hematologic Disorders

Section: Diagnostic and Therapeutic Procedures: Cardiovascular or Hematologic

Chapter 25: **Blood Transfusions**

Contributor: Sharon Kumm, MN, MS, RN, CCRN

NCLEX-PN® Connections:

Learning Objective: Review and apply knowledge within "**Blood Transfusions**" in readiness for performance of the following nursing activities as outlined by the NCLEX-PN® test plan:

Δ Monitor the client during blood transfusions.

Δ Perform/assist with relevant laboratory, diagnostic, and therapeutic procedures within the nursing role, including:

- Monitoring the client's response (expected, unexpected adverse response, comparison to baseline) to the procedure.

- Monitoring and taking actions, including reinforcing client teaching, to prevent or minimize the risk of complications.

- Recognizing signs of potential complications and reporting to the primary care provider.

- Recommending changes in the test/procedure as needed based on client findings.

Key Points

Δ Whole blood or components of whole blood can be transfused. Blood **components** include packed red blood cells (RBCs), plasma, albumin, clotting factors, prothrombin complex, cryoprecipitate, and platelets.

Δ **Incompatibility is a major concern** when administering blood or blood products.

Δ **Blood is typed based on the presence of antigens.**

Blood Type	Antigen	Antibodies Against	Compatible With
A	A	B	A, O
B	B	A	B, O
AB	AB	O	A, B, AB, O
O	O	A, B	O

- Another consideration is the Rh factor: Blood that contains D antigen makes the Rh factor positive. **Rh positive blood given to an Rh negative person will cause hemolysis.**

Δ **Transfusion Types**

- Transfusion **from blood donors**

- **Autologous transfusion**: The client's own blood is collected in anticipation of future transfusions (elective surgery). This blood is designated for and can be used only by the client.

- **Intraoperative blood salvage**: Blood loss during certain surgeries can be recycled through a cell-saver machine and transfused intraoperatively or postoperatively (orthopedic surgeries, CABG).

Key Factors

Δ **Indications for Transfusions**

- Excessive **blood loss** (hemoglobin 6 to 10 g/dL and depending on symptoms) – whole blood

- **Anemia** (hemoglobin 6 to 10 g/dL and depending on symptoms) – packed RBCs

- **Chronic renal failure** – packed RBCs

- Coagulation factor deficiencies such as **hemophilia** – fresh frozen plasma (FFP)

- **Thrombocytopenia**/platelet dysfunction (platelets < 20,000 or < 80,000 and actively bleeding) – platelets

Nursing Interventions

Δ **Before the Transfusion**

- Assess **laboratory values**, such as hemoglobin and hematocrit.

- **Verify order** for specific blood product.

- **Obtain blood samples** for **compatibility determination**.

- Initiate **large-bore IV** access.

- Assess for a **history** of blood-transfusion **reactions**.

- Obtain blood products from the blood bank. **Inspect the blood for discoloration, excessive bubbles, or cloudiness.**

- Following specific institution protocol, confirm the **client's identity, blood compatibility, and expiration time** of the blood product with another nurse.

- Prime the blood administration set with **normal saline (NS)**. Blood products are only infused with NS. **NEVER add medications to blood products.**

- **Ascertain** whether or not a **filter** should be used.

- Obtain baseline vital signs.

- Begin the transfusion. Use a blood warmer if indicated.

Δ **During the Transfusion**

- **Remain with the client for the first 15 min of the infusion** (reactions occur most often during first 15 min) and monitor:

  ◊ **Vital signs.**

  ◊ **Rate of infusion.**

  ◊ **Respiratory status.**

  ◊ Sudden increase in anxiety.

  ◊ Breath sounds.

  ◊ Neck-vein distention.

- **Notify the primary care provider immediately for any signs of reaction.**

- Complete the transfusion within a 2 to 4 hr time frame to avoid bacterial growth.

Δ **Following the Transfusion**

- Obtain **vital signs** upon completion of the transfusion.

- Dispose of the blood-administration set appropriately **(biohazard bags)**.

- **Monitor blood values** as prescribed (CBC, hemoglobin, hematocrit).

    ◊ Hemoglobin levels should rise by approximately 1 g/dL with each unit transfused.

- Complete paperwork and file in the appropriate places.

- **Document** the client's response.

Complications and Nursing Implications

Δ   **Transfusion Reactions**

Type of reaction	Onset	Signs and symptoms
Acute hemolytic	Immediate	This reaction may be mild or life-threatening. Symptoms include: **chills, fever, low back pain, tachycardia, flushing, hypotension, chest tightening or pain, tachypnea, nausea, anxiety, and hemoglobinuria.** This reaction may cause **cardiovascular collapse, acute renal failure, disseminated intravascular coagulation, shock, and death.**
Febrile	30 min to 6 hr after transfusion	Symptoms include: **chills, fever, flushing,** headache, and anxiety. Use white blood cell filter. Administer **antipyretics.**
Mild allergic	During or up to 24 hr after transfusion	Symptoms include: **itching,** urticaria, and **flushing.** Administer **antihistamines,** such as diphenhydramine (Benadryl).
Anaphylactic	Immediate	Symptoms include: **wheezing, dyspnea, chest tightness, cyanosis, and hypotension.** Maintain **airway;** administer **oxygen, IV fluids, antihistamines, corticosteroids, vasopressors.**

- **Stop the transfusion immediately** if a reaction is suspected.

- Initiate a saline infusion. The **saline infusion** should be initiated with a separate line, so as not to give more blood from the transfusion tubing.

- **Save the blood bag** with the remaining blood and the blood tubing for testing.

Δ   **Circulatory Overload**

- Symptoms include: dyspnea, chest tightness, tachycardia, tachypnea, headache, hypertension, jugular-vein distention, peripheral edema, orthopnea, sudden anxiety, and crackles in the base of the lungs.

- Administer **oxygen,** monitor vital signs, **slow the infusion rate,** and **administer diuretics as ordered.**

- **Notify the primary care provider immediately.**

Δ   **Sepsis and Septic Shock**

- Symptoms include: fever, nausea, vomiting, abdominal pain, chills, hypotension.

- Maintain patent **airway** and administer **oxygen.**

- Administer **antibiotic** therapy as ordered.

- Obtain samples for blood cultures.

- Administer **vasopressors**, such as dopamine, to combat vasodilation in the late phase.

- Elevate the client's feet.

- If disseminated intravascular coagulation (**DIC**) occurs:

    ◊   Administer anticoagulants, such as heparin, in the early phase.

    ◊   Administer clotting factors and blood products during the late phase (clotting factors are used up in the early stage).

    ◊   Administer activated protein C (Xigris) to control inflammatory response.

Meeting the Needs of Older Adults

Δ   Older adult clients with cardiac or renal dysfunction are at an **increased risk for heart failure** and fluid-volume excess when receiving a blood transfusion.

Δ   Venous access for blood transfusions may be limited due to **age-related vascular and skin changes.**

Δ   Assess vital signs more frequently because changes in pulse, blood pressure, and respiratory rate may indicate fluid overload or may be the sole indicators of a transfusion reaction.

Primary Reference:

Ignatavicius, D. D., & Workman, M. L. (2006). *Medical-surgical nursing* (5th ed.). St. Louis, MO: Saunders.

Additional Resources:

Black, J. M., & Hawks, J. H. (2005). *Medical-surgical nursing: Clinical management for positive outcomes* (7th ed.). St. Louis, MO: Saunders.

NANDA International (2004). *NANDA nursing diagnoses: Definitions and classification 2005-2006*. Philadelphia: NANDA.

Chapter 25: Blood Transfusions

Application Exercises

1. Fill in the types of blood that each of the following clients may receive.

Client's Blood Type	Compatible Blood Types
A⁺	
A⁻	
B⁺	
B⁻	
AB⁺	
AB⁻	
O⁺	
O⁻	

2. What checks should a nurse make prior to administering blood products?

3. Why should a nurse remain with the client for the first 15 min after starting a blood transfusion?

4. What actions should a nurse take if there is a possible transfusion reaction?

5. Which of the following signs or symptoms should pose an immediate concern for a nurse? (Check all that apply.)

_____ Temperature change from 37° C (98.6° F) pretransfusion to 37.2° C (99.0° F) post-transfusion

_____ Dyspnea

_____ Anxiety

_____ Flank pain

_____ Heart rate increase: 74 beats/min pretransfusion, 81 beats/min post-transfusion

_____ Client report of itching

_____ Flushed appearance

Chapter 25: Blood Transfusions

Application Exercises Answer Key

1. Fill in the types of blood that each of the following clients may receive.

Client's Blood Type	Compatible Blood Types
A⁺	A⁺, A⁻, O⁺, O⁻
A⁻	A⁻, O⁻
B⁺	B⁺, B⁻, O⁺, O⁻
B⁻	B⁻, O⁻
AB⁺	AB⁺, AB⁻, A⁺, A⁻, B⁺, B⁻, O⁺, O⁻
AB⁻	AB⁻, A⁻, B⁻, O⁻
O⁺	O⁺, O⁻
O⁻	O⁻

2. What checks should a nurse make prior to administering blood products?

Two nurses should check the order.

Verify the client's name, blood type, and cross match on the blood bag with another nurse.

Indicate the expiration date on the blood bag.

Examine the unit of blood for gas bubbles, discoloration, or cloudiness.

Obtain vital signs.

3. Why should a nurse remain with the client for the first 15 min after starting a blood transfusion?

This is the time period when transfusion reactions most often occur.

4. What actions should a nurse take if there is a possible transfusion reaction?

Stop the transfusion.

Remove the blood bag and tubing.

Maintain the IV with NS.

Assess vital signs, breath sounds, and airway patency frequently.

Notify the primary care provider.

Return the blood bag and tubing to the laboratory.

A blood and urine sample may be sent to the laboratory.

Complete all appropriate documentation.

5. Which of the following signs or symptoms should pose an immediate concern for a nurse? (Check all that apply.)

_____	Temperature change from 37° C (98.6° F) pretransfusion to 37.2° C (99.0° F) post-transfusion
__X__	Dyspnea
__X__	Anxiety
__X__	Flank pain
_____	Heart rate increase: 74 beats/min pretransfusion, 81 beats/min post-transfusion
__X__	Client report of itching
__X__	Flushed appearance

These are signs or symptoms of blood transfusion reactions. Slight changes in temperature, such as from 37° C (98.6° F) pretransfusion to 37.2° C (99.0° F) post-transfusion, and variations in pulse rate, such as from 74 beats/min pretransfusion to 81 beats/min post transfusion, are not unexpected findings during a transfusion.

Unit 3   Nursing Care of Clients with Cardiovascular or Hematologic Disorders
Section: Nursing Care of Clients with Hematologic Disorders

Chapter 26:   Anemias
Contributor: Sharon Kumm, MN, MS, RN, CCRN

⟳ NCLEX-PN® Connections:

Learning Objective: Review and apply knowledge within "**Anemias**" in readiness for performance of the following nursing activities as outlined by the NCLEX-PN® test plan:

Δ   Assist with relevant laboratory, diagnostic, and therapeutic procedures within the nursing role, including:

- Preparation of the client for the procedure.

- Accurate collection of specimens.

- Monitoring client status during and after the procedure.

- Reinforcing client teaching (before and following the procedure).

- Recognizing the client's response (expected, unexpected adverse response) to the procedure.

- Monitoring results.

- Monitoring and taking actions to prevent or minimize the risk of complications.

- Notifying the primary care provider of signs of complications.

Δ   Recognize signs and symptoms of the client's problem and complete the proper documentation.

Δ   Provide and document care based on the client's health alteration.

Δ   Monitor and document vital signs changes.

Δ   Interpret data that need to be reported immediately.

Δ   Reinforce client education on managing the client's health problem.

Δ   Recognize and respond to emergency situations, including notification of the primary care provider.

Δ   Review the client's response to emergency interventions and complete the proper documentation.

Δ   Provide care that meets the age-related needs of clients 65 years of age or older, including recognizing expected physiological changes.

Key Points

Δ   Anemia is an abnormally **low amount of circulating red blood cells (RBCs), hemoglobin concentration, or both.**

Δ   Anemia results in **diminished oxygen-carrying capacity and delivery to tissues** and organs. The goal of treatment is to restore and maintain adequate tissue oxygenation.

Δ   Anemias are due to:

- **Blood loss.**

- **Inadequate** RBC **production.**

- **Increased** RBC **destruction.**

- **Insufficient** or **defective hemoglobin.**

Δ   **Iron deficiency anemia** is the **most common** anemia.

Key Factors

Δ   Common **Risk Factors** for Anemia

- Acute or chronic **blood loss**
  - ◊   Menorrhagia
  - ◊   Gastrointestinal bleed (ulcers, tumor)

- Increased **hemolysis**
  - ◊   Defective hemoglobin (**sickle cell disease**) – RBCs become malformed during periods of hypoxia and obstruct capillaries in joints and organs.
  - ◊   Impaired **glycolysis** – glucose-6-phosphate-dehydrogenase (G6PD) deficiency anemia
  - ◊   Immune disorder or destruction (**transfusion reactions, autoimmune diseases**)
  - ◊   **Mechanical trauma** to RBCs (mechanical heart valve, cardiopulmonary bypass)

- **Dietary** inadequacy
  - ◊   **Iron deficiency**
  - ◊   **Vitamin B$_{12}$ deficiency** – Pernicious anemia due to deficiency of intrinsic factor produced by gastric mucosa, which is necessary for absorption of vitamin B$_{12}$

◊ **Folic acid** deficiency

◊ **Pica,** or persistent eating of substances not normally considered as food (nonnutritive substances), for at least 1 month, which may limit the amount of healthy food choices a client makes

- **Bone-marrow suppression**

  ◊ Exposure to radiation or chemicals

  ◊ **Aplastic anemia** results in a decreased number of red blood cells as well as decreased platelets and white blood cells.

Diagnostic Procedures and Nursing Interventions

Δ Laboratory Assessment

- **Complete blood count (CBC)**

  ◊ Red blood cells (RBCs) are the major carriers of hemoglobin in the blood.

  ◊ Hemoglobin (Hgb) transports oxygen and carbon dioxide to and from the cells and can be used as an index of the oxygen-carrying capacity of the blood.

  ◊ Hematocrit (Hct) is the percentage of RBCs in relation to the total blood volume.

  ◊ White blood cells (WBCs) destroy organisms in the body.

  ◊ Platelets are important for clot formation.

- **RBC indices to determine the type and cause of most anemias:**

  ◊ **Mean corpuscular volume (MCV):** size of red blood cells

    ° Normocytic – normal size

    ° Microcytic – small cells

    ° Macrocytic – large cells

  ◊ **Mean corpuscular hemoglobin (MCH):** to determine the amount of hemoglobin per RBC

    ° Normochromic – normal amount of Hgb per cell

    ° Hypochromic – decreased Hgb per cell

  ◊ **Mean corpuscular hemoglobin concentration (MCHC):** to indicate hemoglobin amount relative to the size of the cell

RBC indices	Classification	Possible causes
Normal MCV, MCH, MCHC	Normocytic, normochromic anemia	• Acute blood loss • Sickle cell disease
Decreased MCV, MCH, MCHC	Microcytic, hypochromic anemia	• Iron deficiency anemia • Anemia of chronic illness • Chronic blood loss
Increased MCV	Macrocytic anemia	• Vitamin B_{12} deficiency • Folic acid deficiency

- **Iron studies**

  ◊ Total iron-binding capacity (**TIBC**) reflects an indirect measurement of serum transference.

  ◊ **Serum ferritin** is an indicator of total body iron stores.

  ◊ **Serum iron** measures the amount of iron in the blood. Low serum iron and elevated TIBC indicates iron deficiency anemia.

- **Hemoglobin electrophoresis** separates normal hemoglobin from abnormal. It is used to detect thalassemia and **sickle cell disease**.

- **Sickle cell test** evaluates the sickling of red blood cells in the presence of decreased oxygen tension.

- **Schilling test** measures vitamin B_{12} absorption with and without intrinsic factor. It is used to differentiate between malabsorption and pernicious anemia.

- **Bone marrow examination** diagnoses aplastic anemia (failure of bone marrow to produce RBCs as well as platelets and WBCs). After **bone marrow aspiration**:

  ◊ **Apply pressure** to the site for 5 to 10 min.

  ◊ **Assess vital signs** frequently.

  ◊ Apply **pressure dressing**.

  ◊ **Monitor for signs of bleeding** and **infection** for 24 hr.

Assessments

Δ Monitor for **signs and symptoms**.

- May be **asymptomatic in mild cases**

- **Pallor**

- **Fatigue**

- Irritability

- **Numbness and tingling** of extremities

- **Dyspnea** on exertion

- Impaired skin healing

- Brittle, spoon-shaped nails

- **Cheilosis**

- **Smooth, sore, bright red tongue**

- Sensitivity to cold

- Brittle and ridged nails

- Pain and hypoxia with sickle cell crisis

Δ **Assess/Monitor**

- Client's respiratory status, activity tolerance, fatigue

- Client's history regarding risk factors for anemia

- General appearance

- Laboratory and diagnostic findings

NANDA Nursing Diagnoses

Δ Risk for injury

Δ Activity intolerance

Δ Fatigue

Δ Self-care deficit

Δ Risk for infection

Nursing Interventions

Δ Assess and monitor **laboratory results**.

Δ Assess and monitor **activity intolerance**.

Δ Encourage **increased dietary intake of the deficient nutrient** (iron, vitamin B_{12}, folic acid).

Δ **Administer medications** as prescribed. Instruct the client on side effects.

- Iron supplements

   ◊ Oral iron supplements (ferrous sulfate, ferrous fumarate, ferrous gluconate)

   ◊ Parenteral iron supplements (iron dextran)

   ◊ **Take with meals** if gastrointestinal side effects occur.

◊ **Vitamin C** improves absorption.

◊ Do not take within 2 hr of **milk or antacids**.

◊ **Stools will be black.**

◊ May cause **constipation**; increase intake of fluids and foods high in fiber.

◊ Use a straw with liquid iron to avoid **staining of teeth**.

◊ Administer parenteral iron using **Z-track method**.

• Erythropoietin (Procrit)

• Cobalamin (vitamin B_{12}) parenterally or intranasally

• Folic acid supplements

• Oxygen

• Vitamin C supplements (to enhance iron absorption)

• Intravenous fluids (sickle cell crisis, G6PD anemia)

Δ Teach the client and family about **energy conservation**.

Δ Teach the client the time frame for resolution.

• **Transfusions** – lead to an **immediate improvement** in blood cell counts and client signs and symptoms.

◊ Typically only used when the client has significant symptoms of anemia because of the risk of blood-borne infections.

• **Oral** supplements – **4 to 6 weeks** for increase in RBCs

• **Vitamin B_{12}** supplements – increased **RBCs in 1 week**

• **Vitamin B_{12}** supplementation

◊ B_{12} supplementation can be given orally if the deficit is due to poor dietary intake. However, with **pernicious anemia it must be given parenterally** because it won't be absorbed if given orally.

◊ Administer **parenteral forms intramuscularly or deep subcutaneous** to decrease irritation. Do not mix other medications in the syringe.

◊ Pernicious anemia must be **treated for life.**

• **Folic acid** supplementation

◊ Can be given **orally or parenterally.**

◊ Large doses will stain **urine dark yellow.**

Complications and Nursing Implications

Δ   Monitor the client for signs of **hypoxemia**: dyspnea, decreased oxygen saturation, central cyanosis.

   •   Administer oxygen therapy. Monitor SaO_2.

   •   Administer blood transfusions as ordered.

Δ   Assess the **neurologic status** of clients with **macrocytic anemias**.

   •   Vitamin B_{12} is essential for neurological function. Administer supplements.

   •   Notify the provider of any changes in mentation.

Δ   **Sickle Cell Crisis**

   •   Sickle cell disease is an autosomal recessive condition, which means a client inherited at least one affected gene from each parent.

   •   At least 40% of total hemoglobin is the abnormal hemoglobin S (HbS) in sickle cell disease.

   •   When HbS is exposed to hypoxic environments, it contracts and clusters together within the cell.

   •   Cells become rigid, forming a "sickle" or "C" shape which causes them to clump together and impede blood flow. This leads to further tissue hypoxia.

   •   Signs and symptoms include cyanosis, abdominal pain, leg and back pain, low-grade fever, seizures, and stroke manifestations (weakness, paresthesia).

   •   Administer oxygen and hydration therapy.

   •   Administer analgesia.

   •   Organ failure can result if left untreated.

Meeting the Needs of Older Adults

Δ   Older adult clients are at risk for nutritional-deficient anemias (iron, vitamin B_{12}, folate).

Δ   Anemia may be misdiagnosed as depression or debilitation.

Δ   Gastrointestinal bleeding is a common cause of anemia in older adult clients.

Primary Reference:

Ignatavicius, D. D., & Workman, M. L. (2006). *Medical-surgical nursing* (5th ed.). St. Louis, MO: Saunders.

Additional Resources:

NANDA International (2004). *NANDA nursing diagnoses: Definitions and classification 2005-2006*. Philadelphia: NANDA.

For more information on sickle cell disease, visit the American Sickle Cell Anemia Association at: *www.ascaa.org*.

Chapter 26: Anemias

Application Exercises

1. Provide assessment findings indicating anemia in the following body systems:

Integumentary	
Gastrointestinal	
Cardiovascular	
Respiratory	
Musculoskeletal	
Neurologic	

2. What should a nurse teach a client about taking oral iron supplementation?

3. Suggest three energy-conservation methods for a client with chronic anemia.

4. Complete the following table:

Laboratory Values	Type of Anemia	Common Causes
Increased MCV, normal MCH & MCHC		
Decreased MCV, MCH, MCHC		
Normal MCV, MCH, MCHC		

5. Which anemias are the following clients most at risk to develop?

Toddlers:

Teenagers:

Pregnant women:

Women of childbearing age:

Older adult clients:

6. A nurse is caring for a client in sickle cell crisis. Which of the following interventions should the nurse expect to perform? (Check all that apply.)

_____   Administer morphine.

_____   Administer normal saline.

_____   Provide blood transfusion to replace hemoglobin.

_____   Assess hand-grip strength.

Chapter 26: Anemias

Application Exercises Answer Key

1. Provide assessment findings indicating anemia in the following body systems:

Integumentary	Pallor of skin, mucous membranes, conjunctiva & nail beds; petechiae, purpura, cheilosis, spoon-shaped nail, sore beefy red tongue
Gastrointestinal	Anorexia, diarrhea, nausea, abdominal pain
Cardiovascular	Tachycardia, palpitations
Respiratory	Tachypnea, dyspnea on exertion
Musculoskeletal	Fatigue, weakness, night cramps, joint pain
Neurologic	Paresthesias, headache, dizziness, forgetfulness, pain, pica

2. What should a nurse teach a client about taking oral iron supplementation?

Stools will be black.

May cause gastrointestinal distress. Take with food if this occurs.

Take with vitamin C to increase absorption.

Take 2 hr before or after milk or antacids.

Increase fiber and fluids in diet to manage constipation.

3. Suggest three energy-conservation methods for a client with chronic anemia.

Sit to bathe, dress, prepare food.

Schedule rest periods between activities.

Establish priorities for tasks.

Perform priority tasks when rested.

Decide which tasks can be performed by family and friends.

4. Complete the following table:

Laboratory Values	Type of Anemia	Common Causes
Increased MCV, normal MCH & MCHC	Macrocytic anemia	Vitamin B_{12} deficiency Folic acid deficiency Alcoholism
Decreased MCV, MCH, MCHC	Microcytic, hypochromic anemia	Chronic blood loss Iron deficiency anemia Anemia of chronic disease
Normal MCV, MCH, MCHC	Normocytic, normochromic anemia	Acute blood loss Sickle cell disease

5. Which anemias are the following clients most at risk to develop?

Toddlers:	Iron deficiency anemia
Teenagers:	Iron deficiency anemia
Pregnant women:	Iron deficiency anemia
Women of childbearing age:	Iron deficiency anemia, chronic blood loss
Older adult clients:	Iron deficiency anemia, chronic blood loss, vitamin B_{12} and folate deficiencies

6. A nurse is caring for a client in sickle cell crisis. Which of the following interventions should the nurse expect to perform? (Check all that apply.)

   __x__   Administer morphine.

   __x__   Administer normal saline.

   _____   Provide blood transfusion to replace hemoglobin.

   __x__   Assess hand-grip strength.

The key interventions for a client in sickle cell crisis is to promote and maintain oxygenation and tissue perfusion, hydrate the client to prevent excessive sickling of the red blood cells, manage the client's pain, and promote neurological function. Clients with sickle cell anemia have problems with the shape of the red blood cells, not the number, so a blood transfusion would not be indicated.

Unit 3

Section:

Nursing Care of Clients with Cardiovascular or Hematologic Disorders

Nursing Care of Clients with Hematologic Disorders

Chapter 27:   Cancers: Leukemia and Lymphomas

Contributor: Dana Bartlett, MSN, RN, CSPI

NCLEX-PN® Connections:

Learning Objective: Review and apply knowledge within "**Cancers: Leukemia and Lymphomas**" in readiness for performance of the following nursing activities as outlined by the NCLEX-PN® test plan:

Δ   Assist with relevant laboratory, diagnostic, and therapeutic procedures within the nursing role, including:

- Preparation of the client for the procedure.
- Accurate collection of specimens.
- Monitoring client status during and after the procedure.
- Reinforcing client teaching (before and following the procedure).
- Recognizing the client's response (expected, unexpected adverse response) to the procedure.
- Monitoring results.
- Monitoring and taking actions to prevent or minimize the risk of complications.
- Notifying the primary care provider of signs of complications.

Δ   Recognize signs and symptoms of the client's problem and complete the proper documentation.

Δ   Provide and document care based on the client's health alteration.

Δ   Monitor and document vital signs changes.

Δ   Interpret data that need to be reported immediately.

Δ   Reinforce client education on managing the client's health problem.

Δ   Recognize and respond to emergency situations, including notification of the primary care provider.

Δ   Review the client's response to emergency interventions and complete the proper documentation.

Δ   Provide care that meets the age-related needs of clients 65 years of age or older, including recognizing expected physiological changes.

📖 Key Points

Δ **Leukemias are cancers of white blood cells** or of cells that will develop into white blood cells.

- In leukemia, the white blood cells are not functional. They invade and destroy bone marrow, and they can metastasize to the liver, spleen, lymph nodes, testes, and brain.

- Leukemias are divided into acute (**acute lymphocytic leukemia** and **acute myelogenous leukemia**) and chronic (**chronic lymphocytic leukemia** and **chronic myelogenous leukemia**) and are further classified by the type of white blood cells primarily affected.

- Clients with leukemia are vulnerable to infection and can develop anemia secondary to bone marrow destruction.

- The goal of treatment is to eliminate all leukemia cells.

Δ **Lymphomas are cancers of lymphocytes**, which are white blood cells in the bone marrow and lymph nodes that fight infection and produce antibodies.

- There are two types of lymphomas: Hodgkin's lymphoma (HL) and non-Hodgkin's lymphoma (NHL).

- Lymphomas can metastasize to almost any organ.

Key Factors

Δ **Leukemia**

- The exact cause of leukemia is not known.

- Factors involved in the development of leukemia include:

  ◊ **Ionizing radiation** (radiation therapy, environmental).

  ◊ Exposure to certain **chemicals and drugs** (chemotherapy agents and drugs that suppress bone marrow).

  ◊ **Genetic factors** (for example, hereditary conditions).

  ◊ Immunologic factors (for example, immunosuppression).

- Incidence and Cure Rates

  ◊ **Acute lymphocytic leukemia (ALL):** various factors influence the prognosis for children (age at diagnosis, gender, cell type involved); less than 50% of adults can be cured.

  ◊ **Acute myelocytic leukemia (AML):** Most common leukemia among adults; prognosis is poor.

◊ **Chronic lymphocytic leukemia (CLL):** Most cases involve people older than 60. This disease does not occur in children.

◊ **Chronic myelocytic leukemia (CML):** Most cases involve adults. The disease is uncommon in children.

Δ **Lymphoma**

• Hodgkin's Lymphoma

◊ Most cases involve adults.

◊ Possible causes include viral infections and exposure to chemical agents.

• Non-Hodgkin's Lymphoma

◊ More common in clients older than 50 years.

◊ Possible causes include gene damage, viral infections, autoimmune disease, and exposure to radiation or to toxic chemicals.

Diagnostic Procedures and Nursing Interventions

Δ **Leukemia**

• **White Blood Cell (WBC) Count:** Often elevated (20,000 to 100,000/mm³) with leukemia prior to treatment; decreased with treatment

• **Hemoglobin, hematocrit, and platelets: Decreased**

• **Bleeding times: Increased**

• **Bone marrow aspiration and biopsy:** Identification of prolific quantities of immature leukemic blast cells and protein markers indicating the specific type of leukemia – lymphoid or myeloid. After **bone marrow aspiration:**

◊ **Apply pressure** to the site for 5 to 10 min.

◊ **Assess vital signs** frequently.

◊ Apply **pressure dressing.**

◊ **Monitor for signs of bleeding** and **infection** for 24 hr.

Δ **Lymphoma**

• **Lymph node biopsy:**

◊ Hodgkin's lymphoma (HL): The presence of Reed-Sternberg cells (B-lymphocytes that have become cancerous) is diagnostic for Hodgkin's disease.

Therapeutic Procedures and Nursing Interventions

Δ **Surgical Management of Leukemia**

- Bone marrow transplantation

  ◊ Used as a treatment for leukemia.

  ◊ Closely matched donor stem cells are used.

    ° **Autologous cells** are the client's own cells that are collected before chemotherapy.

    ° **Syngeneic cells** are donated from the client's identical twin.

    ° **Allogenic cells** are obtained from an HLA-matched donor, such as a relative or from umbilical cord blood.

  ◊ Following transplantation, the client is at high risk for infection and bleeding until the transfused stem cells grow.

Assessments

Δ Monitor for **signs and symptoms.**

- **Acute leukemia**

  ◊ **Bone pain**

  ◊ Joint swelling

  ◊ Enlarged liver and spleen

  ◊ Weight loss

  ◊ Fever

  ◊ Poor wound healing (for example, infected lesions)

  ◊ Signs of **anemia** (fatigue, pallor, tachycardia, dyspnea on exertion)

  ◊ Signs of **bleeding** (ecchymoses, hematuria, bleeding gums)

- **HL and NHL:**

  ◊ Some clients may only experience an **enlarged lymph node** (usually in the neck with HL).

  ◊ Other possible symptoms include fever, fatigue, and infections.

Δ **Monitor/Assess**

- **Immune function and bone marrow function** assessments are critical.

- Make an initial assessment of the client's health status, such as nutritional status, risk-related behaviors (smoking, alcohol, drug use), tolerance for exercise, and vital signs.

- Perform a systematic assessment. Pay close attention to the client's skin (bruising, bleeding, lesions, enlarged and painful lymph nodes), oral cavity, gastrointestinal status (pain, diarrhea, constipation, character and frequency of bowel movements, rectal bleeding), genitourinary system (dysuria, hematuria), and central nervous system.

- **Monitor for ANY signs of infection and report immediately.**

NANDA Nursing Diagnoses

Δ   Risk for infection

Δ   Risk for injury

Δ   Fatigue

Nursing Interventions

Δ   **Prevent infection.**

- Frequent, thorough handwashing is a priority intervention.

- Place the client in a private room.

- Screen visitors carefully.

- Encourage good nutrition (low-bacteria diet, avoid salads, raw fruits, and vegetables) and fluid intake.

- Monitor WBC counts.

- Encourage good personal hygiene.

- Avoid crowds if possible.

- **These interventions are especially important during chemotherapy induction and for clients who have received a bone marrow transplant.**

Δ   **Prevent injury.**

- Monitor platelet counts.

- Assess the client frequently for obvious and occult signs of bleeding.

- Protect the client from trauma (avoid injections and venipunctures, apply firm pressure, increase vitamin K intake).

- Teach the client how to avoid trauma (use electric shaver, soft bristled toothbrush, avoid contact sports).

Δ   **Conserve the client's energy.**

- Encourage rest, good nutrition, and fluid intake.

- Try to ensure the client gets adequate sleep.

- Assess the client's energy resources/capability.

- Try to plan activities as appropriate.

Complications and Nursing Implications

Δ   **Pancytopenia**

- **Neutropenia** secondary to disease and/or treatment, which **greatly increases the client's risk for infection**

    ◊   Nurses must maintain a hygienic environment and encourage the client to do the same.

    ◊   Vigilantly monitor the client for signs of infection (cough, alterations in breath sounds, urine, or feces). **Report temperature greater than 37.8° C (100° F).**

    ◊   Administer antimicrobial, antiviral, and antifungal medications as prescribed.

    ◊   **An absolute neutrophil count (ANC) less than 2,000/mm³ suggests an increased risk of infection. ANC of less than 500/mm³ indicates a severe risk of infection.**

    ◊   Administer blood products (for example, granulocytes) as needed.

- **Thrombocytopenia** secondary to disease and/or treatment, which **greatly increases the client's risk for bleeding**

    ◊   Nurses must minimize the risk of trauma (safe environment).

    ◊   **The greatest risk is at platelet counts less than 50,000/mm³, and spontaneous bleeds can occur at less than 20,000/mm³.**

    ◊   Administer blood products (for example, platelets) as needed.

- **Anemia** secondary to disease and/or treatment, which **greatly increases the client's risk for hypoxemia**

    ◊   Nurses must maintain an environment that does not overly tax the client's energy resources/capability.

    ◊   Monitor red blood cell counts.

    ◊   Provide a diet **high in protein and carbohydrates**.

    ◊   Administer colony-stimulating factors, such as **epoetin alfa (Procrit)**, as prescribed.

    ◊   Administer blood products (e.g., packed red blood cells) as needed.

Δ   **Bone Marrow Transplant Complications**

- Failure of stem cells to engraft

- Graft-versus-host disease

- Phlebitis

Meeting the Needs of Older Adults

Δ   Older adult clients often have **diminished immune function and decreased bone marrow function,** which increases their risk of complications of leukemia and lymphoma.

Δ   Older adult clients also have decreased energy reserves and will tire more easily during treatment. Safety is a concern with ambulation.

Primary Reference:

Ignatavicius, D. D., & Workman, M. L. (2006). *Medical-surgical nursing* (5th ed.). St. Louis, MO: Saunders.

Additional Resources:

Hockenberry, M. J. (2005). *Wong's Essentials of Pediatric Nursing* (7th ed.). St. Louis, MO: Mosby.

NANDA International (2004). *NANDA nursing diagnoses: Definitions and classification 2005-2006.* Philadelphia: NANDA.

For more information about leukemia or lymphoma, visit the American Cancer Society at: *www.cancer.org.*

Chapter 27: Cancers: Leukemia and Lymphomas

Application Exercises

1. A client with leukemia develops thrombocytopenia following chemotherapy. Based on this specific finding, which of the following nursing interventions is the highest priority?

   A. Encourage the client to turn, cough, and deep breathe every 2 hr.

   B. Monitor the client's temperature every 4 hr.

   C. Monitor the client's platelet counts.

   D. Encourage the client to ambulate several times a day.

2. Which of the following nursing interventions and client instructions are appropriate in caring for a client with pancytopenia? (Check all that apply and identify the rationale for each option.)

   _____ Restrict fresh fruits and vegetables in the diet.

   _____ Restrict all visitors.

   _____ Insert a Foley catheter to monitor intake and output.

   _____ Restrict fluids.

   _____ Report low-grade temperature.

   _____ Hold firm pressure for 5 min following necessary venipunctures.

   _____ Report an ANC of 2,500/mm³.

   _____ Administer epoetin alfa (Procrit) as prescribed.

3. A client's platelet count is 10,000/mm³. Based on this laboratory value, which of the following is the priority nursing assessment?

   A. Level of consciousness

   B. Skin turgor

   C. Bowel sounds

   D. Breath sounds

4. Match the following.

   _____ Hodgkin's lymphoma   A. Most common leukemia in adults

   _____ Acute myelocytic leukemia (AML)   B. Most cases are in adults over the age of 60

   _____ Chronic lymphocytic leukemia (CLL)   C. Reed-Sternberg cells

Chapter 27: Cancers: Leukemia and Lymphomas

Application Exercises Answer Key

1. A client with leukemia develops thrombocytopenia following chemotherapy. Based on this specific finding, which of the following nursing interventions is the highest priority?

    A. Encourage the client to turn, cough, and deep breathe every 2 hr.

    B. Monitor the client's temperature every 4 hr.

    C. Monitor the client's platelet counts.

    D. Encourage the client to ambulate several times a day.

    Thrombocytopenia is a decrease in platelet counts with a risk of bleeding. Bleeding precautions are generally implemented for counts less than 50,000/mm³.

2. Which of the following nursing interventions and client instructions are appropriate in caring for a client with pancytopenia? (Check all that apply and identify the rationale for each option.)

__x__	Restrict fresh fruits and vegetables in the diet.
_____	Restrict all visitors.
_____	Insert a Foley catheter to monitor intake and output.
_____	Restrict fluids.
__x__	Report low-grade temperature.
__x__	Hold firm pressure for 5 min following necessary venipunctures.
_____	Report an ANC of 2,500/mm³.
__x__	Administer epoetin alfa (Procrit) as prescribed.

Fresh fruits and vegetables pose a greater risk for introduction of bacteria into the gastrointestinal systems. Clients with low WBC counts need to follow a low-bacteria diet.

Not all visitors need to be restricted. Only those individuals who pose a significant risk, such as individuals with infections, should be restricted.

Invasive procedures and indwelling catheters pose a risk for injury and for infection. Limit whenever possible.

Fluids should be encouraged to maintain good renal function and to assist in elimination of medications. Dehydration poses a greater risk for infection.

Clients are immunosuppressed, so a low-grade temperature may represent an immune response to an infection. Nurses must be vigilant.

Due to low platelet counts, clients are at greater risk for bleeding. Firm pressure for longer periods of time is indicated following invasive procedures.

An absolute neutrophil count (ANC) of 2,500/mm³ does not indicate a high risk for infection. An ANC of less than 2,000/mm³ suggests an increased risk of infection. ANC of less than 500/mm³ indicates a severe risk of infection.

Anemia is a probable consequence of the disease and/or treatment. Administration of a colony stimulating factor can be vital in RBC production to counter disease/treatment-induced anemia.

3. A client's platelet count is 10,000/mm³. Based on this laboratory value, which of the following is the priority nursing assessment?

    A. Level of consciousness
    B. Skin turgor
    C. Bowel sounds
    D. Breath sounds

The client is at a high risk for spontaneous bleeding, including the risk for a fatal cerebral bleed, due to a platelet count less than 20,000/mm³. A change in level of consciousness can be an early sign of cerebral hemorrhage.

4. Match the following.

__C__ Hodgkin's lymphoma	A. Most common leukemia in adults
__A__ Acute myelocytic leukemia (AML)	B. Most cases are in adults over the age of 60
__B__ Chronic lymphocytic leukemia (CLL)	C. Reed-Sternberg cells

Unit 3 Nursing Care of Clients with Cardiovascular or Hematologic Disorders

Section: Nursing Care of Clients with Vascular Disorders

Chapter 28: **Hypertension**

Contributor: Martha Ann Fiese, MSN, RN, BC

⟲ **NCLEX-PN® Connections:**

Learning Objective: Review and apply knowledge within "**Hypertension**" in readiness for performance of the following nursing activities as outlined by the NCLEX-PN® test plan:

Δ Assist with relevant laboratory, diagnostic, and therapeutic procedures within the nursing role, including:

• Preparation of the client for the procedure.

• Accurate collection of specimens.

• Monitoring client status during and after the procedure.

• Reinforcing client teaching (before and following the procedure).

• Recognizing the client's response (expected, unexpected adverse response) to the procedure.

• Monitoring results.

• Monitoring and taking actions to prevent or minimize the risk of complications.

• Notifying the primary care provider of signs of complications.

Δ Recognize signs and symptoms of the client's problem and complete the proper documentation.

Δ Provide and document care based on the client's health alteration.

Δ Monitor and document vital signs changes.

Δ Interpret data that need to be reported immediately.

Δ Reinforce client education on managing the client's health problem.

Δ Recognize and respond to emergency situations, including notification of the primary care provider.

Δ Review the client's response to emergency interventions and complete the proper documentation.

Δ Provide care that meets the age-related needs of clients 65 years of age or older, including recognizing expected physiological changes.

Key Points

Δ   **Normal adult blood pressure is less than 120 mm Hg systolic and 80 mm Hg diastolic.**

Δ   Clients with a **systolic blood pressure of 120 to 139 mm Hg or a diastolic blood pressure of 80 to 89 mm Hg are considered prehypertensive. Lifestyle changes** are needed for these clients to help prevent cardiovascular disease.

Δ   Hypertension is a **systolic blood pressure above 140 mm Hg or a diastolic blood pressure above 90 mm Hg.**

Δ   Hypertension is **directly related to the development of cardiovascular disorders** with or without the presence of other risk factors.

Δ   One in four adults is hypertensive.

Δ   The **risk** of developing coronary, cerebral, renal, and peripheral vascular disease **increases as blood pressure increases.**

Δ   Blood pressure is **regulated by four bodily mechanisms:**

- **Arterial baroreceptors.**

  ◊   Baroreceptors are located in the carotid sinus, aorta, and left ventricle.

  ◊   They control blood pressure by altering the heart rate and/or causing vasoconstriction or vasodilation.

- **Regulation of body-fluid volume.**

  ◊   Properly functioning kidneys either retain fluid when the client is hypotensive or excrete fluid when the client is hypertensive.

- **Renin-angiotensin system.**

  ◊   Angiotensin II vasoconstricts and controls aldosterone release, which causes the kidneys to reabsorb sodium and inhibit fluid loss.

- **Vascular autoregulation.**

  ◊   This maintains consistent levels of tissue perfusion.

Δ   **Essential hypertension**, also called primary hypertension, accounts for most cases of hypertension. There is no known cause. **Secondary hypertension** may be caused by certain disease states such as renal disease or as a side effect of some medications.

Δ   Improving compliance with treatment for hypertension is a goal of Healthy People 2010.

Key Factors

Δ   **Risk Factors** for **Essential Hypertension**

- Positive family history
- Excessive sodium intake
- Physical inactivity
- Obesity
- High alcohol consumption
- African-American descent
- Smoking
- Hyperlipidemia
- Stress

Δ   **Risk Factors** for **Secondary Hypertension**

- Renal disease
- Cushing's disease (excessive glucocorticoid secretion)
- Primary aldosteronism (causes hypertension and hypokalemia)
- Pheochromocytoma (excessive catecholamine release)
- Brain tumors, encephalitis
- Medications such as estrogen, steroids, sympathomimetics

Diagnostic Procedures and Nursing Interventions

Δ   No laboratory tests exist to diagnose hypertension; however, **several laboratory tests can identify the causes of secondary hypertension**.

- **BUN**, **creatinine**: Elevation indicative of renal disease
- **Elevated serum corticoids** to detect Cushing's disease

Δ   **ECG** may help to determine the level of cardiac involvement.

- Tall R-waves are often seen with **left ventricular hypertrophy**.

Δ   **Chest** x-ray may show **cardiomegaly**.

Assessments

Δ   Clients with hypertension may experience few or no symptoms. The nurse should **monitor for signs and symptoms**.

- **Headaches**

- **Dizziness**

- **Fainting**

- Retinal changes, visual disturbances

Δ   **Assess/Monitor**

- Blood pressure

- Factors that increase the risk of hypertension (age, ethnic origin and race, dietary intake, exercise habits, current medications)

- General appearance (temperature, skin color)

- Laboratory findings (BUN, creatinine)

NANDA Nursing Diagnoses

Δ   Deficient knowledge

Δ   Ineffective therapeutic regimen management

Δ   Ineffective tissue perfusion

Δ   Sexual dysfunction

Nursing Interventions

Δ   Treatment involves **lifestyle changes**. Some clients will also require **pharmacologic therapy**. **Secondary hypertension** may be treated by **removing the cause** (adrenal tumor, medication).

Δ   **Lifestyle Changes**

- **Sodium restriction**

  ◊   Monitor potassium with salt substitutes (may interfere with some medications).

  ◊   Consume less than 2.3 g/day of sodium.

- **Weight reduction**

  ◊   Consume a diet low in fat, saturated fat, and cholesterol.

  ◊   Control alcohol intake (2 oz liquor, 8 oz wine, 24 oz beer per day).

- **Exercise**
  - ◊ Begin slowly and gradually and advance the program with the guidance of the primary care provider and physical therapist.

- **Smoking cessation**
  - ◊ Smoking is not directly linked to hypertension, but it should be avoided due to its high association with the development of cardiovascular diseases.

- **Stress reduction**
  - ◊ Encourage the client to try yoga, massage, hypnosis, or other forms of relaxation.

Δ **Medication Therapy**

- Medications are added to treat hypertension not responsive to lifestyle changes alone. Diuretics are often used as the first line drugs. However, clients may require a combination of drugs to control hypertension.

- **Diuretics**
  - ◊ **Thiazide diuretics**, such as hydrochlorothiazide (HydroDIURIL), prevent water and sodium reabsorption and promote potassium excretion.
  - ◊ **Other diuretics** may be used to treat hypertension not responsive to the thiazide diuretics.
    - ° **Loop diuretics**, such as furosemide (Lasix), decrease sodium reabsorption and promote potassium excretion. Monitor the client closely for **hypokalemia**.
    - ° **Potassium-sparing diuretics**, such as spironolactone (Aldactone), affect the distal tubule and prevent reabsorption of sodium in exchange for potassium. Monitor the client closely for **hyperkalemia**.

- **Calcium-Channel Blockers**
  - ◊ **Verapamil hydrochloride (Calan), amlodipine (Norvasc), and diltiazem (Cardizem)** alter the movement of calcium ions through the cell membrane, which causes vasodilation, resulting in lowering of the blood pressure.

- **Angiotensin-converting enzyme (ACE) inhibitors** prevent the conversion of angiotensin I to angiotensin II, which prevents vasoconstriction.

- **Angiotensin II receptor antagonists**, also called angiotensin receptor blockers (ARBs), such as **candesartan (Atacand), losartan (Cozaar), and telmisartan (Micardis)**, are a good option for clients on ACE inhibitors reporting cough and those with hyperkalemia. Also, ARBs do not require a dosage adjustment for older adult clients.

- **Aldosterone receptor antagonists,** such as **eplerenone (Inspra)**, block aldosterone action. Hypertriglyceridemia, hyponatremia, and hyperkalemia can occur as the dose increases.

- **Beta-blockers,** such as **metoprolol (Lopressor) and atenolol (Tenormin)**, are indicated for clients with unstable angina or myocardial infarction.

- **Central alpha agonists,** such as **clonidine (Catapres)**, prevent reuptake of norepinephrine, which lowers peripheral vascular resistance (PVR) and blood pressure.

- **Alpha-adrenergic agonists,** such as **prazosin (Minipress)**, dilate arterioles and veins. Use of these medications should be limited.

Drug	Nursing Implications	Rationale
Diuretics (Thiazide and Loop)	• Monitor K+ levels and watch for muscle weakness, irregular pulse, and dehydration.	• Hypokalemia is a common occurrence.
Potassium-Sparing Diuretics	• Monitor K+ levels and watch for muscle weakness and irregular pulse.	• Hypokalemia or hyperkalemia may occur.
Calcium-Channel Blockers (CCB)	• Monitor blood pressure and pulse; change positions slowly. • Encourage intake of foods high in fiber. Use protective clothing or sunscreen when exposed to sun. • Teach clients to avoid grapefruit juice.	• Hypotension is a common side effect. • Decreased heart rate and photosensitivity may occur. • Grapefruit juice potentiates medication effects, increases hypotensive effects, and increases the risk of drug toxicity. • CCBs should be used cautiously with clients with heart failure.
Angiotensin-Converting Enzyme (ACE) Inhibitors	• Monitor blood pressure and pulse. • Teach the client to change positions slowly. • Monitor for and teach the client to report signs of heart failure such as edema. • Teach the client to report a cough.	• Hypotension is a common side effect. • This drug may cause heart and renal complications. • Coughing is a common side effect. • Encourage the client to rise slowly due to possible orthostatic hypotension.
Angiotensin II Receptor Antagonists (ARBs)	• Monitor blood pressure and pulse. • Teach the client to change positions slowly. • Monitor for and teach the client to report signs of angioedema (swollen lips or face) or of heart failure (edema).	• Hypotension is a common side effect. • Angioedema is a serious but uncommon adverse effect. • Heart failure can result from taking this medication.

Drug	Nursing Implications	Rationale
Aldosterone Receptor Antagonist	• Monitor renal function. • Monitor triglycerides • Monitor sodium levels. • Monitor K+ levels every 2 weeks for first few months and every 2 months thereafter. • Teach the client about potential drug and herbal interactions. • Caution the client to be careful when getting out of bed, driving, and climbing stairs until medication effects are fully known.	• The risk of adverse effects increases with deteriorating renal function. • Hyponatremia and hyperkalemia may occur with this medication. • Do not give with K+ supplements and K+-sparing diuretics. • Do not take salt substitutes with K+ or other foods rich in K+. • Grapefruit juice and St. John's Wort can increase adverse effects. • Orthostatic hypotension may occur, especially in older adult clients.
Beta Adrenergic Blockers	• Monitor blood pressure and pulse. • Teach the client to change positions slowly. • Advise the client not to suddenly stop taking the medication without the advice of the provider.	• Stopping suddenly may cause rebound hypertension. • The medication may cause fatigue, weakness, depression, and sexual dysfunction. • It may mask hypoglycemia in diabetics.
Central Alpha Agonists (Clonidine)	• Monitor blood pressure and pulse. • Teach the client to change positions slowly. • Caution the client to be careful when getting out of bed, driving, and climbing stairs until medication effects are fully known.	• Side effects include sedation, orthostatic hypotension, and impotence. • This medication is not indicated for first-line management of hypertension.

Δ   Encourage the **client and family to participate in the lifestyle changes** outlined above.

Δ   Express to the client and family the **importance of adhering to the medication regimen, even if the client is asymptomatic.**

Δ   Provide **verbal and written education regarding medications** and their side effects.

Δ   Encourage the client to have **regular provider appointments** to monitor hypertension and cardiovascular status.

Δ   Encourage the client to **report symptoms or side effects** as they may be indicative of additional problems. Medications can often be changed to alleviate side effects.

Complications and Nursing Implications

Δ **Hypertensive Crisis** (malignant hypertension)

- Malignant hypertension often occurs when clients do **not follow the medication therapy** regimen.

- Signs and symptoms include:

    ◊ Severe **headache.**

    ◊ Extremely high blood pressure (generally, **systolic blood pressure greater than 240 mm Hg, diastolic greater than 120 mm Hg**).

    ◊ **Blurred vision, dizziness, and disorientation.**

- Administer **IV antihypertensive** therapies, such as nitroprusside (Nipride), nicardipine (Cardene IV), and labetalol (Normodyne).

Meeting the Needs of Older Adults

Δ Older adult clients are more likely to experience medication interactions.

Δ Older adult clients are more likely to experience orthostatic hypotension.

Primary Reference:

Ignatavicius, D. D., & Workman, M. L. (2006). *Medical-surgical nursing* (5th ed.). St. Louis, MO: Saunders.

Additional Resources:

Lewis, Heitkemper, and Dirksen (2004). *Medical-surgical nursing: Assessment and management of clinical problems* (6th ed.). St. Louis, MO: Mosby.

NANDA International (2004). *NANDA nursing diagnoses: Definitions and classification 2005-2006*. Philadelphia: NANDA.

Potter, P. A., & Perry, A. G. (2005). *Fundamentals of nursing* (6th ed.). St. Louis, MO: Mosby.

Chapter 28: Hypertension

Application Exercises

1. Which of the following practices should be avoided by clients predisposed to or with hypertension? (Check all that apply.)

   _____ Drinking 8 oz of red wine three times per week

   _____ Eating popcorn at the movie theater

   _____ Walking 1 mile daily at 12-min/mile pace

   _____ Consuming three cans of beer daily

   _____ Smoking a pipe

2. A client diagnosed with hypertension is prescribed spironolactone (Aldactone) 25 mg/day. Which of the following statements indicates a need for further teaching?

   A. "I will eat a lot of fruits and vegetables, especially bananas and potatoes."

   B. "I will report any changes in heart rate or rhythm."

   C. "I will buy a salt substitute that is low in potassium."

   D. "I am okay to take this medication because I do not have lung problems."

3. Explain why clients should be encouraged to follow their prescribed treatment for hypertension therapy.

4. A client is admitted to the emergency department with a blood pressure of 266/147 mm Hg. The client reports a headache and states that she is seeing double. The client states that she ran out of her diltiazem (Cardizem) 3 days ago, and she has not been able to purchase more. Which of the following nursing interventions should the nurse expect to perform first?

   A. Administer Tylenol for her headache.

   B. Administer an oral dose of diltiazem (Cardizem).

   C. Obtain IV access and prepare to administer an IV antihypertensive.

   D. Call the local pharmacy to arrange for prescription delivery.

5. A client has a prescription for furosemide (Lasix) 40 mg by mouth daily. The nurse is providing discharge instructions. What time of day should the client be encouraged to take this medication? Why?

6. **True or False:** Angiotensin II causes the body to excrete sodium.

Chapter 28: Hypertension

Application Exercises Answer Key

1. Which of the following practices should be avoided by clients predisposed to or with hypertension? (Check all that apply.)

_____	Drinking 8 oz of red wine three times per week
__X__	Eating popcorn at the movie theater
_____	Walking 1 mile daily at 12-min/mile pace
__X__	Consuming three cans of beer daily
__X__	Smoking a pipe

Popcorn at a movie theater contains a large amount of sodium, which should be limited in a client with hypertension. Consuming more than one drink or can of beer per day can contribute to hypertension and cardiovascular disease and should be avoided in a client with hypertension. Smoking causes vasoconstriction, which can increase a client's blood pressure.

2. A client diagnosed with hypertension is prescribed spironolactone (Aldactone) 25 mg/day. Which of the following statements indicates a need for further teaching?

   A. "I will eat a lot of fruits and vegetables, especially bananas and potatoes."
   B. "I will report any changes in heart rate or rhythm."
   C. "I will buy a salt substitute that is low in potassium."
   D. "I am okay to take this medication because I do not have lung problems."

   Potatoes and bananas are high in potassium, and spironolactone is a potassium-sparing diuretic. Consuming these foods may lead to hyperkalemia.

3. Explain why clients should be encouraged to follow their prescribed treatment for hypertension therapy.

   Clients should be encouraged to adhere to their therapy because uncontrolled hypertension can lead to the development of vascular complications, such as stroke, heart attack, and retinal damage. Although clients may not experience symptoms, it is important that they understand that the pathology of the disease continues and can lead to poor outcomes.

4. A client is admitted to the emergency department with a blood pressure of 266/147 mm Hg. The client reports a headache and states that she is seeing double. The client states that she ran out of her diltiazem (Cardizem) 3 days ago, and she has not been able to purchase more. Which of the following nursing interventions should the nurse expect to perform first?

> A. Administer Tylenol for her headache.
>
> B. Administer an oral dose of diltiazem (Cardizem).
>
> **C. Obtain IV access and prepare to administer an IV antihypertensive.**
>
> D. Call the local pharmacy to arrange for prescription delivery.

A blood pressure of 266/147 mm Hg can be life-threatening. The highest priority is to decrease the client's blood pressure as quickly as possible. An IV should be started for IV access. Medications given by the IV route will be absorbed and distributed much faster than by the oral route.

5. A client has a prescription for furosemide (Lasix) 40 mg by mouth daily. The nurse is providing discharge instructions. What time of day should the client be encouraged to take this medication? Why?

The client should take the furosemide in the morning so that the peak action and duration of the medication occurs during waking hours. If the client takes the furosemide at bedtime, the peak action and duration will occur at night and will most likely interrupt the client's sleep.

6. **True or False:** Angiotensin II causes the body to excrete sodium.

False: Angiotensin II causes the kidneys to reabsorb sodium through the release of aldosterone.

Unit 3   Nursing Care of Clients with Cardiovascular or Hematologic Disorders
Section: Nursing Care of Clients with Vascular Disorders

Chapter 29:   **Aneurysms**

Contributor: Martha Ann Fiese, MSN, RN, BC

↻ NCLEX-PN® Connections:

Learning Objective: Review and apply knowledge within "**Aneurysms**" in readiness for performance of the following nursing activities as outlined by the NCLEX-PN® test plan:

Δ   Assist with relevant laboratory, diagnostic, and therapeutic procedures within the nursing role, including:

- Preparation of the client for the procedure.

- Accurate collection of specimens.

- Monitoring client status during and after the procedure.

- Reinforcing client teaching (before and following the procedure).

- Recognizing the client's response (expected, unexpected adverse response) to the procedure.

- Monitoring results.

- Monitoring and taking actions to prevent or minimize the risk of complications.

- Notifying the primary care provider of signs of complications.

Δ   Recognize signs and symptoms of the client's problem and complete the proper documentation.

Δ   Provide and document care based on the client's health alteration.

Δ   Monitor and document vital signs changes.

Δ   Interpret data that need to be reported immediately.

Δ   Reinforce client education on managing the client's health problem.

Δ   Recognize and respond to emergency situations, including notification of the primary care provider.

Δ   Review the client's response to emergency interventions and complete the proper documentation.

Δ   Provide care that meets the age-related needs of clients 65 years of age or older, including recognizing expected physiological changes.

Key Points

Δ   An aneurysm is **a permanent dilation of an artery** to at least two times its normal diameter.

Δ   An aneurysm can be diffuse, affecting the circumference of an artery (**fusiform**), or it can be an out-pouching, affecting only a specific portion of the artery (**saccular**).

Δ   Aneurysms can occur in any central or peripheral artery; however, **the most common is within the abdominal aorta** between the renal arteries and the aortic bifurcation (75% of all aneurysms).

Δ   **Aortic dissection** can occur when blood accumulates within the aortic wall (hematoma) following a tear in the lining of the aorta (usually due to hypertension).

Key Factors

Δ   **Causes/Risk Factors**

*   The most common cause of aneurysms is atherosclerosis.

*   The **most significant risk factor** for the development and the rupture/dissection of an aneurysm is **uncontrolled hypertension**.

*   Cigarette smoking is also a risk factor.

Δ   **Risk for Rupture**

*   Aneurysms greater than 6 cm (2.4 in) in diameter have a 50% chance of rupture within 1 year.

*   Aneurysms less than 6 cm (2.4 in) have a 15 to 20% chance of rupture in 1 year.

Diagnostic Procedures and Nursing Interventions

Δ   **X-rays** can reveal the classic **"eggshell"** appearance of an aneurysm. Aneurysms are often discovered when examining the client for some other clinical possibility.

Δ   **Computed tomography** (CT) imaging scans and **ultrasonography** are used to assess the size and location of aneurysms and are often repeated at periodic intervals to monitor the progression of an aneurysm.

Therapeutic Procedures and Nursing Interventions

Δ   **Abdominal aortic aneurysm (AAA) resection** involves the excision of the aneurysm and the placement of a Dacron graft. Surgical management may be either elective or emergency. A rupturing aneurysm requires prompt emergency surgery. AAA of 6 cm or greater in diameter may be managed with elective surgery. Mortality rates are 2 to 5% for elective AAA resections and 50% when rupture has occurred. Risks include significant blood loss and the consequences of reduced cardiac output and tissue ischemia (myocardial infarction, renal failure, respiratory distress, paralytic ileus). Monitoring the client's arterial pressure, heart rhythm, and hemodynamic values as well as for signs of graft occlusion or rupture postoperatively are priority interventions.

Δ **Percutaneous insertion of endothelial stent grafts** for aneurysm repair avoids abdominal incision and a prolonged postoperative period. Nursing care after the procedure is similar to care following an arteriogram (for example, pedal pulse checks).

Assessments

Δ Monitor for **signs and symptoms.**

- Clients are often asymptomatic initially.

- With AAA:

  ◊ Gnawing constant abdominal, flank, or back pain

  ◊ Pulsating abdominal mass

  ◊ Bruit

  ◊ Elevated blood pressure (unless in cardiac tamponade or rupture of aneurysm)

- With AAA rupture:

  ◊ Sudden onset of "tearing," "ripping," and "stabbing" abdominal or back pain

  ◊ **Hypovolemic shock**

    ° Diaphoresis, nausea, vomiting, faintness, apprehension

    ° Decreased or absent peripheral pulses

    ° Neurological deficits

    ° Hypotension and tachycardia (initial)

- Of graft occlusion or rupture:

  ◊ Changes in pulses

  ◊ Coolness and/or cyanosis of extremities below graft

  ◊ Severe pain

  ◊ Decrease in urinary output

Δ Assess/Monitor

- Vital signs

- Baseline peripheral pulse assessments and observe for changes

- Color, temperature, and capillary refill in the extremities and monitor for changes

- Alteration in sensation and movement of the extremities

- Increased pain level (indicator of altered peripheral perfusion)

- Renal function

NANDA Nursing Diagnoses

Δ   Ineffective tissue perfusion

Δ   Decreased cardiac output

Δ   Anxiety

Δ   Deficient knowledge

Δ   Acute pain

Δ   Ineffective therapeutic regimen management

Nursing Interventions

Δ   **The priority intervention is to reduce (and maintain) systolic blood pressure between 100 and 120 mm Hg.** Administer antihypertensive agents as prescribed. Often more than one is prescribed (for example, beta blockers and calcium blockers).

Δ   **Postoperative Interventions**

- Monitor vital signs and circulation (pulses distal to graft) every 15 min.

- Avoid flexion of the graft (keep the head of bed less than 45°).

- Monitor and maintain normal blood pressure. **Prolonged hypotension can cause thrombi to form within the graft**, and **severe hypertension can cause leakage or rupture at the arterial anastomosis suture line**.

- Administer IV fluids at prescribed rates to ensure adequate hydration and renal perfusion.

- Any signs of graft occlusion or rupture should be reported immediately (changes in pulses, coolness of extremity below graft, white or blue extremities or flanks, severe pain, abdominal distention, decreased urine output).

- Maintain a warm environment to prevent temperature-induced vasoconstriction.

- Monitor urinary output (report less than 50 mL/hr), daily weights, BUN, and serum creatinine to detect signs of altered renal perfusion and renal failure (secondary to surgical clamping of aorta).

- Turn, cough, and deep breathe every 2 hr and auscultate breath sounds. Encourage splinting with coughing.

- Monitor and intervene for pain (for example, administer opioids as prescribed).

- Monitor bowel sounds and for abdominal distention. Maintain nasogastric suction as prescribed.

- Take measures to reduce the risk of thromboembolism (sequential compression devices, early ambulation, administer prescribed antiplatelet or anticoagulant medications).

- Monitor for signs of infection such as elevated body temperature, WBC count, heart rate, and respiratory rate; decreased blood pressure; erythema and warmth along the incision line; persistent drainage from incisions as well as at sites of invasive lines; and separation of wound edges.

- Administer a broad-spectrum antibiotic as ordered to maintain adequate blood levels of the drug.

- Ensure adequate nutrition – specifically a diet high in protein, vitamin C, vitamin A, and zinc – to promote healing.

- Provide client teaching regarding postoperative activity restrictions (avoidance of lifting more than 15 lb, strenuous activity).

Δ **Client Education on Non-Surgical Management**

- Emphasize the importance of monitoring and controlling blood pressure.

- Emphasize the importance of following through on scheduled tests to monitor growth.

- Encourage smoking cessation.

- Encourage a low-fat, low-cholesterol diet.

- Explain manifestations of aneurysm rupture that need to be promptly reported (abdominal fullness or pain, chest or back pain, shortness of breath, difficulty swallowing, hoarseness).

Complications and Nursing Implications

Δ **Rupture** is the most frequent complication and is life-threatening, leading to abrupt massive hemorrhagic shock. It requires simultaneous resuscitation and immediate surgical repair.

Δ **Thrombi** within the wall of the aneurysm can be a source of emboli in distal arteries below the aneurysm, causing ischemia and shut down of other body systems.

Meeting the Needs of Older Adults

Δ   With the aging process, there is arterial stiffening caused by loss of elastin in arterial walls, thickening of intima of arteries, and progressive fibrosis of media. Older adult clients are more prone to aneurysms and have a higher mortality rate from aneurysms than younger individuals.

Primary Reference:

Ignatavicius, D. D., & Workman, M. L. (2006). *Medical-surgical nursing* (5th ed.). St. Louis, MO: Saunders.

Additional Resources:

Lewis, Heitkemper, and Dirksen (2004). *Medical-surgical nursing: Assessment and management of clinical problems* (6th ed.). St. Louis, MO: Mosby.

NANDA International (2004). *NANDA nursing diagnoses: Definitions and classification 2005-2006*. Philadelphia: NANDA.

Chapter 29: Aneurysms

Application Exercises

Scenario: A 56-year-old client presents with reports of a persistent, chronic cough unrelieved by sinus and cold medications or antacids. On assessment, the nurse notes that the client's voice sounds hoarse, blood pressure is 164/98 mm Hg, pulse 96 beats/min, and respirations 22/min. The client confirms episodes of epigastric discomfort. Chest x-ray results indicate a 5-cm enlargement of the ascending aorta.

1. What do these findings indicate?

2. What should the priority goal for treatment be for this client?

3. Identify appropriate nursing interventions for the care of this client.

4. Four months later, the client has dutifully complied with treatments as prescribed. The client arrives by ambulance into the emergency department with a blood pressure of 86/30 mm Hg, diaphoresis, mental obtundation, an irregular heart rhythm, severe back pain, and bilateral bruising in the flanks. What findings indicate that this is a medical emergency?

5. What course of action should the nurse anticipate in the care of this client at this time?

6. What are priority nursing interventions postoperatively? (Check all that apply.)

_____ Assess, establish baseline data, and observe for changes.

_____ Assess for diminished or absent peripheral pulses in the extremities.

_____ Assess for color or temperature changes in the extremities.

_____ Monitor and report increased pain as an indication of altered peripheral perfusion.

_____ Compare extremities for warmth, capillary refill, and color because differences may indicate impaired blood flow.

_____ Maintain a warm environment to prevent temperature-induced vasoconstriction.

_____ Restrict fluids due to risk of pulmonary congestion.

_____ Administer anticoagulants and/or antiplatelet agents as prescribed to prevent thrombus formation.

_____ Report a WBC of 9,700/mm^3.

_____ Report an hourly urine output of 60 mL.

_____ Use surgical aseptic technique to care for the incision and any indwelling IV line, tubing, or catheter because these sites are potential portals of entry for infection.

_____ Ensure adequate nutrition, specifically a diet high in protein, vitamin C, vitamin A, and zinc to promote healing.

Chapter 29: Aneurysms

Application Exercises Answer Key

Scenario: A 56-year-old client presents with reports of a persistent, chronic cough unrelieved by sinus and cold medications or antacids. On assessment, the nurse notes that the client's voice sounds hoarse, blood pressure is 164/98 mm Hg, pulse 96 beats/min, and respirations 22/min. The client confirms episodes of epigastric discomfort. Chest x-ray results indicate a 5-cm enlargement of the ascending aorta.

1. What do these findings indicate?

   The client demonstrates uncontrolled hypertension, which may be a significant contributing factor to these conditions. This client is experiencing symptoms resulting from pressure from the 5-cm aneurysm on surrounding structures. The client is probably experiencing hoarseness as a result of pressure on the laryngeal nerve. Pressure on pulmonary structures can result in coughing, dyspnea, and airway obstruction. Epigastric discomfort is probably a result of pressure on the esophagus and stomach. Pressure on the esophagus can cause dysphagia. Pressure on the superior vena cava can result in decreased venous drainage resulting in distended neck veins and edema of the head and arms.

2. What should the priority goal for treatment be for this client?

   The primary goal for non-surgical management is to monitor the growth of the aneurysm and maintain the blood pressure at normal levels to decrease the risk of rupture. The client's hypertension (an important risk factor for rupture) is treated with antihypertensives to decrease the rate of enlargement and the risk of rupture.

3. Identify appropriate nursing interventions for the care of this client.

   Emphasize the importance of following through on scheduled CT scans, which are used to monitor the growth of the aneurysm.

   Explain manifestations of the aneurysm that need to be promptly reported.

   Assess for indications of rupture (paleness, weakness, tachycardia, hypotension, abdominal, back, or groin pain, changes in sensorium, or a pulsating abdominal mass).

   Assess for normal tissue perfusion and intact motor and sensory function.

   Provide client education on controlling hypertension, the medication regimen, smoking cessation, and a low-fat, low-cholesterol diet.

4. Four months later, the client has dutifully complied with treatments as prescribed. The client arrives by ambulance into the emergency department with a blood pressure of 86/30 mm Hg, diaphoresis, mental obtundation, an irregular heart rhythm, severe back pain, and bilateral bruising in the flanks. What findings indicate that this is a medical emergency?

Symptoms of shock (BP of 86/30 mm Hg, diaphoresis, mental obtundation, dysrhythmia) and of rupture of the aneurysm (severe back pain, and bilateral bruising in the flanks) are indicative of a critical, immediate, life-threatening situation.

5. What course of action should the nurse anticipate in the care of this client at this time?

Immediate surgical intervention to control bleeding and repair the aorta. Large volumes of IV fluids would be required to maintain tissue perfusion.

6. What are priority nursing interventions postoperatively? (Check all that apply.)

__x__	Assess, establish baseline data, and observe for changes.
__x__	Assess for diminished or absent peripheral pulses in the extremities.
__x__	Assess for color or temperature changes in the extremities.
__x__	Monitor and report increased pain as an indication of altered peripheral perfusion.
__x__	Compare extremities for warmth, capillary refill, and color because differences may indicate impaired blood flow.
__x__	Maintain a warm environment to prevent temperature-induced vasoconstriction.
_____	Restrict fluids due to risk of pulmonary congestion.
__x__	Administer anticoagulants and/or antiplatelet agents as prescribed to prevent thrombus formation.
_____	Report a WBC of 9,700/mm³.
_____	Report an hourly urine output of 60 mL.
__x__	Use surgical aseptic technique to care for the incision and any indwelling IV line, tubing, or catheter because these sites are potential portals of entry for infection.
__x__	Ensure adequate nutrition, specifically a diet high in protein, vitamin C, vitamin A, and zinc to promote healing.

Unit 3   Nursing Care of Clients with Cardiovascular or Hematologic Disorders
Section: Nursing Care of Clients with Vascular Disorders

Chapter 30:   Peripheral Arterial Disease
Contributor: Martha Ann Fiese, MSN, RN, BC

↻ **NCLEX-PN® Connections:**

Learning Objective: Review and apply knowledge within **"Peripheral Arterial Disease"** in readiness for performance of the following nursing activities as outlined by the NCLEX-PN® test plan:

Δ   Provide care for the client with impaired tissue perfusion.

Δ   Assist with relevant laboratory, diagnostic, and therapeutic procedures within the nursing role, including:

- Preparation of the client for the procedure.

- Accurate collection of specimens.

- Monitoring client status during and after the procedure.

- Reinforcing client teaching (before and following the procedure).

- Recognizing the client's response (expected, unexpected adverse response) to the procedure.

- Monitoring results.

- Monitoring and taking actions to prevent or minimize the risk of complications.

- Notifying the primary care provider of signs of complications.

Δ   Recognize signs and symptoms of the client's problem and complete the proper documentation.

Δ   Provide and document care based on the client's health alteration.

Δ   Monitor and document vital signs changes.

Δ   Interpret data that need to be reported immediately.

Δ   Reinforce client education on managing the client's health problem.

Δ   Recognize and respond to emergency situations, including notification of the primary care provider.

Δ   Review the client's response to emergency interventions and complete the proper documentation.

Δ   Provide care that meets the age-related needs of clients 65 years of age or older, including recognizing expected physiological changes.

Key Points

Δ   Peripheral arterial disease (PAD) **results from atherosclerosis** in the arteries of the lower extremities and is characterized by inadequate flow of blood. PAD is classified as inflow (distal aorta, iliac arteries) or outflow (femoral, popliteal, and tibial artery) and may range from mild to severe. Tissue damage occurs below the arterial obstruction.

Δ   **Acute arterial occlusion** is a sudden occlusion of an artery by an embolus or a local thrombus (more common in lower extremities). Acute occlusion may cause severe ischemia manifested by sensory and motor loss.

Δ   Buerger's disease, subclavian steal syndrome, thoracic outlet syndrome, Raynaud's disease and Raynaud's phenomenon, and popliteal entrapment are examples of peripheral arterial diseases.

Key Factors

Δ   The most common cause of PAD is atherosclerosis.

Δ   **Risk Factors** (same as for atherosclerosis)

- Hypertension
- Hyperlipidemia
- Diabetes mellitus
- Cigarette smoking
- Obesity
- Familial predisposition
- Age

Δ   **In acute arterial occlusion**, the embolus is most often derived from the heart (recent myocardial infarction, atrial fibrillation). The history includes sudden onset of severe pain, coldness, numbness, and pallor in an extremity with absent pulses distal to the obstruction.

Diagnostic Procedures and Nursing Interventions

Δ   **Arteriography** of lower extremities (invasive and not commonly performed today) involves arterial injection of contrast medium to visualize areas of decreased arterial flow on an x-ray.

Δ   **Exercise Tolerance Testing**: Stress test or treadmill with measurement of pulse volumes and blood pressures prior to and following the onset of symptoms or 5 min of exercise. Delays in return to normal pressures and pulse waveforms indicate arterial disease. Used to evaluate claudication without rest pain.

Δ **Plethysmography**: Used to determine the variations of blood passing through an artery, thus identifying abnormal arterial flow in the affected limb.

Δ **Segmental Systolic Blood Pressure (BP) Measurements**: The use of a Doppler probe to take various BP measurements (thigh, calf, ankle, brachial) for comparison. With arterial disease, the pressures in the thigh, calf, and ankle are lower than brachial pressures (normally higher).

Therapeutic Procedures and Nursing Interventions

Δ **Percutaneous Transluminal Angioplasty (PTA)**: An invasive intra-arterial procedure using a balloon and stent to open and help maintain the patency of the vessel. It is used for poor surgical candidates or in cases where amputation is inevitable.

Δ **Laser-Assisted Angioplasty**: An invasive procedure in which a laser probe is advanced through a cannula to the site of stenosis. The laser is used to vaporize atherosclerotic plaque and open the artery. The priority for postoperative care is observing for bleeding at the puncture site. Close observation of vital signs, peripheral pulses, and capillary refill is indicated, as well as bedrest with the limb straight for 6 to 8 hr before ambulation. Anticoagulant therapy is used during the operative procedure, followed by antiplatelet therapy for 1 to 3 months following the procedure. Acetylsalicylic acid (ASA) therapy is used thereafter for maintenance therapy.

Δ **Atherectomy** involves the use of a high-speed rotary metal burr to scrape plaque out of affected arteries and improve blood flow to ischemic limbs.

Δ **Arterial revascularization** surgery is used when the severity threatens the loss of a limb or for clients with severe pain at rest or claudication interfering with their ability to work.

Δ **Bypass Grafts**

- Inflow procedures (more successful, less chance of reocclusion or postoperative ischemia) include aortoiliac, aortofemoral, and axillofemoral bypasses.

- Outflow procedures (less successful in relieving ischemic pain and higher incidence of reocclusion) include femoropopliteal and femorotibial bypasses.

- Graft materials can be autogenous (harvested) or synthetic materials. Postoperatively, it is essential to monitor the client's circulation and for any evidence of graft occlusion.

Assessments

Δ   Monitor for **signs and symptoms.**

	Inflow	Outflow
Discomfort	Lower back, buttocks, or thighs	**Claudication** (burning or cramping in calves, ankles, feet, and toes)
Onset of pain after walking	Mild: 2 blocks Moderate: 1-2 blocks Severe: less than 1 block and at rest	Mild: 5 blocks Moderate: 2 blocks; intermittent pain at rest Severe: ½ block and at rest
Pain relief	With rest and/or legs in dependent position	With rest and/or legs in dependent position
Physical findings	<ul><li>Bruits</li><li>Increased capillary refill of toes (> 3 sec)</li><li>Decreased or nonpalpable pulses</li><li>Loss of hair on lower calf, ankle, and foot</li><li>Dry, scaly, mottled skin</li><li>Thick toenails</li><li>Cold and cyanotic extremity</li><li>Pallor of extremity with elevation</li><li>Dependent rubor</li><li>Muscle atrophy</li><li>Ulcers and possible gangrene of toes</li></ul>	

Δ   **Assess/Monitor**

- Peripheral pulses

- Fluid status

- Coagulation status

- Pain

- Exercise tolerance

NANDA Nursing Diagnoses

Δ   Chronic pain

Δ   Ineffective tissue perfusion (peripheral)

Δ   Risk for injury

Δ   Risk for peripheral neurovascular dysfunction

Nursing Interventions

Δ **Nonsurgical Nursing Interventions**

- Encourage exercise to build up collateral circulation – initiate gradually, increase slowly. **Instruct the client to walk until the point of pain, stop and rest, and then walk a little farther.**

- Positioning

  ◊ **Avoid crossing legs.**

  ◊ Refrain from wearing restrictive garments.

  ◊ Elevate to reduce swelling but do not elevate legs above the level of the heart because extreme elevation slows arterial blood flow to the feet.

- **Promote vasodilation and avoid vasoconstriction.**

  ◊ Provide warm environment.

  ◊ Wear insulated socks.

  ◊ Never apply direct heat to the affected extremity as sensitivity is decreased and the client may inadvertently be burned.

  ◊ Avoid exposure to cold (causes vasoconstriction and decreased arterial flow).

  ◊ Avoid stress, caffeine, and nicotine, which also cause vasoconstriction. Complete abstinence from smoking or chewing tobacco is the most effective method of preventing vasoconstriction (vasoconstrictive effects last up to 1 hr after each cigarette smoked).

- Administer medications as prescribed.

  ◊ Hemorheologic drugs, such as pentoxifylline (Trental), to increase the flexibility of red blood cells and to decrease blood viscosity by inhibiting platelet aggregation and decreasing fibrinogen, thus increasing blood flow in the extremities.

  ◊ Antiplatelet agents, such as aspirin (acetylsalicylic acid) and clopidogrel (Plavix).

  ◊ Antihypertensives to improve tissue perfusion by maintaining pressures that are adequate to perfuse the periphery but not constrict the vessels.

Δ **Postoperative Nursing Interventions**

- Immediately postoperative, mark the site where the distal (dorsalis pedis or posterior tibial) pulse is best palpated or heard by Doppler.

- Assess the extremity and compare to the contralateral extremity (every 15 min for the first hour, then hourly) for changes in color, temperature, pulse intensity, circulatory refill, and pain (type, intensity, location, duration).

- Warmth, redness, and edema of the affected limb are expected outcomes of surgery as a result of increased blood flow.

- Monitor for pain. Pain from occlusion may be masked by patient-controlled analgesia.

- Monitor blood pressure and notify the surgeon if pressure increases or decreases beyond normal limits. Hypotension may indicate hypovolemia, which can increase the risk of clotting or graft collapse. Hypertension poses a risk for bleeding from sutures.

- Limit range of motion of the affected limb (bending of hip and knee is contraindicated) to decrease the risk of clot formation.

Complications and Nursing Implications

Δ **Graft occlusion** is a serious complication of arterial revascularization and often occurs within the first 24 hr following surgery. Promptly notify the surgeon of signs and symptoms of occlusion. Treatment may include emergency thrombectomy (removal of clot) and/or local intra-arterial thrombolytic therapy with an agent such as tissue plasminogen activator (t-PA) or an infusion of platelet inhibitor such as abciximab (ReoPro). Other antiplatelet drugs such as glycoprotein IIb/IIIa inhibitors tirofiban (Aggrastat) or eptifibatide (Integrilin) may be used as alternatives. With these treatments, closely assess the client for manifestations of bleeding.

Δ **Compartment syndrome** is considered an emergency. Tissue pressure within a confined body space becomes elevated and restricts blood flow. Resultant ischemia can lead to irreversible tissue damage within 4 to 6 hr and eventually tissue death. Symptoms include tingling, numbness, worsening pain, edema, pain on passive movement, and uneven pulses. Report symptoms immediately. Loosen dressings. Fasciotomy (surgical opening into the tissues) may be necessary to prevent further injury and to save the limb.

Δ **Acute arterial occlusion** is a sudden occlusion of an artery by an embolus or a local thrombus (more common in lower extremities). Assess for severe pain below the level of the occlusion, even at rest. The extremity may become cool, pulseless, and mottled. Minute areas on toes may be blackened or gangrenous. The client presents with the six P's of ischemia: pain, pallor, pulselessness, paresthesia, paralysis, and poikilothermia (coolness). Prompt treatment is required to prevent ischemic damage or loss of the extremity. Treatments may include anticoagulant therapy with unfractionated heparin to prevent further clot formation. The client may also undergo angiography, surgical thrombectomy, or embolectomy with local anesthesia to remove the occlusion. Local intra-arterial thrombolytic therapy with a thrombolytic such as alteplase (Activase) and the use of platelet inhibitors such as abciximab (ReoPro) may also be used as an alternative to surgical treatment.

Δ **Ulcer formation**: Monitor peripheral circulation. Employ measures to prevent. Treat promptly.

Meeting the Needs of Older Adults

Δ   With the aging process, there is arterial stiffening caused by the loss of elastin in arterial walls, thickening of intima of arteries, and progressive fibrosis of media. Advancing age also increases the risk of disease related to the development of atherosclerosis.

Δ   Older adult clients have a higher incidence of peripheral arterial disease (rate of occurrence is increased in men over 45 and in postmenopausal women) and have a higher mortality rate from complications than younger individuals.

Primary Reference:

Ignatavicius, D. D., & Workman, M. L. (2006). *Medical-surgical nursing* (5th ed.). St. Louis, MO: Saunders.

Additional Resources:

Lewis, Heitkemper, and Dirksen (2004). *Medical-surgical nursing: Assessment and management of clinical problems* (6th ed.). St. Louis, MO: Mosby.

NANDA International (2004). *NANDA nursing diagnoses: Definitions and classification 2005-2006*. Philadelphia: NANDA.

Chapter 30: Peripheral Arterial Disease

Application Exercises

1. A nurse performing an assessment with a client who has chronic peripheral arterial disease should expect to find

    A. edema around the ankles and feet.

    B. ulceration around the medial malleoli.

    C. scaling eczema of the lower legs with stasis dermatitis.

    D. pallor on elevation of limbs and rubor when limbs are dependent.

2. A nurse identifies the nursing diagnosis of ineffective peripheral perfusion related to decreased arterial blood flow for a client with chronic peripheral arterial disease. Following client teaching, the nurse determines a need for further instruction when the client says,

    A. "I will wear loose clothing that does not bind across my legs or waist."

    B. "I will change positions every hour, avoid sitting with my legs crossed, and avoid long periods of sitting with my legs down."

    C. "I will sleep with a heating pad on my feet at night to increase the circulation and warmth in my feet."

    D. "For 30 min to an hour each day, I will walk to the point of pain, rest, and then walk again until I develop pain."

3. A client who has just undergone a femoral-popliteal bypass graft procedure is returning to the medical-surgical floor from postanesthesia recovery. The nurse should first

    A. assess the client's level of pain using a standard pain scale.

    B. encourage the client to ambulate to improve circulation and avoid graft occlusion.

    C. assess the client's circulation in the operative leg as compared with the nonoperative leg.

    D. teach the client to utilize an incentive spirometer every hour to improve lung expansion.

4. For a client with severe PAD, the nurse should expect that the client may sleep most comfortably in which of the following positions?

    A. Affected limb hanging from bed

    B. Affected limb elevated on pillows

    C. Head of bed raised on blocks

    D. Side-lying recumbent position

Chapter 30: Peripheral Arterial Disease

Application Exercises Answer Key

1. A nurse performing an assessment with a client who has chronic peripheral arterial disease should expect to find

   A. edema around the ankles and feet.

   B. ulceration around the medial malleoli.

   C. scaling eczema of the lower legs with stasis dermatitis.

   D. pallor on elevation of limbs and rubor when limbs are dependent.

   Findings depend on the severity of PAD. Observe for loss of hair on lower calf, ankle, and foot; dry, scaly, dusky, pale, or mottled skin; and thickened toenails. Severe disease: The extremity is cold and gray-blue (cyanotic) or darkened. In chronic disease, pallor may occur when the extremity is elevated; dependent rubor may occur when the extremity is lowered. Muscle atrophy can accompany prolonged chronic arterial disease. Edema around the ankles and feet, ulceration around the medial malleoli, and scaling eczema of the lower legs with stasis dermatitis are seen with venous stasis.

2. A nurse identifies the nursing diagnosis of ineffective peripheral perfusion related to decreased arterial blood flow for a client with chronic peripheral arterial disease. Following client teaching, the nurse determines a need for further instruction when the client says,

   A. "I will wear loose clothing that does not bind across my legs or waist."

   B. "I will change positions every hour, avoid sitting with my legs crossed, and avoid long periods of sitting with my legs down."

   C. "I will sleep with a heating pad on my feet at night to increase the circulation and warmth in my feet."

   D. "For 30 min to an hour each day, I will walk to the point of pain, rest, and then walk again until I develop pain."

   Never apply direct heat to the extremity as sensitivity is decreased and the client may inadvertently be burned. The client should be instructed to walk until point of pain, stop and rest, and then walk a little farther. The client should change positions frequently, avoid crossing legs, and refrain from wearing restrictive garments. Sitting with legs in the dependent position for long periods of time leads to swelling, which impedes circulation.

3. A client who has just undergone a femoral-popliteal bypass graft procedure is returning to the medical-surgical floor from postanesthesia recovery. The nurse should first

    A. assess the client's level of pain using a standard pain scale.

    B. encourage the client to ambulate to improve circulation and avoid graft occlusion.

    C. assess the client's circulation in the operative leg as compared with the nonoperative leg.

    D. teach the client to utilize an incentive spirometer every hour to improve lung expansion.

Postoperative care includes assessment of the client's circulation in the operative leg as compared with the nonoperative leg (pulse, capillary refill, temperature, color, and motor and neurological functioning) and compared to baseline data to evaluate arterial blood flow. Changes and variations should be reported to the surgeon immediately. Pulse sites should be marked for identification and continuity of care. In general, range of motion of the affected extremity is limited postoperatively to decrease the risk of graft occlusion. While pain assessment and use of an incentive spirometer are important interventions, they are not the highest priority at this point.

4. For a client with severe PAD, the nurse should expect that the client may sleep most comfortably in which of the following positions?

    A. Affected limb hanging from bed

    B. Affected limb elevated on pillows

    C. Head of bed raised on blocks

    D. Side-lying recumbent position

Clients with severe PAD may find comfort with the affected limb in a dependent position.

Unit 3   Nursing Care of Clients with Cardiovascular or Hematologic Disorders
Section: Nursing Care of Clients with Vascular Disorders

Chapter 31:   Peripheral Venous Disease

Contributor: Martha Ann Fiese, MSN, RN, BC

NCLEX-PN® Connections:

Learning Objective: Review and apply knowledge within "**Peripheral Venous Disease**" in readiness for performance of the following nursing activities as outlined by the NCLEX-PN® test plan:

Δ   Assist with relevant laboratory, diagnostic, and therapeutic procedures within the nursing role, including:

- Preparation of the client for the procedure.

- Accurate collection of specimens.

- Monitoring client status during and after the procedure.

- Reinforcing client teaching (before and following the procedure).

- Recognizing the client's response (expected, unexpected adverse response) to the procedure.

- Monitoring results.

- Monitoring and taking actions to prevent or minimize the risk of complications.

- Notifying the primary care provider of signs of complications.

Δ   Recognize signs and symptoms of the client's problem and complete the proper documentation.

Δ   Provide and document care based on the client's health alteration.

Δ   Monitor and document vital signs changes.

Δ   Interpret data that need to be reported immediately.

Δ   Reinforce client education on managing the client's health problem.

Δ   Recognize and respond to emergency situations, including notification of the primary care provider.

Δ   Review the client's response to emergency interventions and complete the proper documentation.

Δ   Provide care that meets the age-related needs of clients 65 years of age or older, including recognizing expected physiological changes.

Key Points

Δ   Peripheral venous disease is **a disease of the veins that interferes with adequate flow of blood from the extremities.** This includes both venous thromboembolism (VTE) and venous insufficiency.

Δ   Three distinct phenomena alter blood flow in veins: thrombus formation, defective valves, and lack of skeletal muscle contractility.

Δ   **VTE** is the blocking of a blood vessel by a thrombus that has become detached from its site of formation. It is the current term that includes both deep vein thrombosis (DVT) and pulmonary embolism (PE).

•   A **thrombus** (thrombosis) is a blood clot believed to result from an endothelial injury, venous stasis, or hypercoagulability (Virchow's triad). Thrombus formation can lead to PE, a life-threatening complication.

•   **Thrombophlebitis** refers to a thrombus that is associated with inflammation. This can occur in any vein, but most frequently occurs in deep veins in lower extremities. **DVT** and thrombophlebitis present a greater risk of PE.

•   **PE** is when a dislodged blood clot travels to the pulmonary artery. It is a life-threatening situation.

Δ   **Venous insufficiency** is sequelae of edema, stasis pigmentation, stasis dermatitis, and stasis ulceration. Venous insufficiency occurs as a result of prolonged venous hypertension, which stretches the veins and damages the valves. Defective valves lead to venous insufficiency and varicose veins, which are problematic but not life-threatening. Treatment for venous stasis focuses on decreasing edema and promoting venous return.

Δ   **Varicose veins** are enlarged, twisted superficial veins that may occur in any part of the body, but are most commonly observed in the lower extremities and in the esophagus.

Key Factors

Δ   **Risk Factors: Venous Thromboembolism**

•   Hip surgery, total knee replacement, open prostate surgery

•   Heart failure

•   Immobility

•   Pregnancy

Δ   **Risk Factors: Venous Insufficiency**

•   Sitting or standing in one position for a long period of time

•   Obesity

- Pregnancy

- Thrombophlebitis

Δ   **Risk Factors: Varicose Veins**

- Older than 30 with an occupation requiring prolonged standing

- Pregnancy

- Obesity

- Systemic diseases (for example, heart disease)

- Family history

Diagnostic Procedures and Nursing Interventions: Deep Vein Thrombosis and Thrombophlebitis

Δ   Venous duplex ultrasonography, Doppler flow studies, and impedance plethysmography are noninvasive procedures that can confirm a DVT, although they are dependent on the technical skill of the professional performing the test and each is better at detecting DVT within various locations.

Δ   If the above tests are negative but a DVT is still suspected, a **venogram** may be needed for accurate diagnosis.

Δ   A magnetic resonance imaging (MRI) scan is noninvasive and useful for finding DVTs in inferior vena cava or pelvic veins.

Δ   A **D-dimer test** measures fibrin degradation products produced from fibrinolysis. It can be very useful as an adjunct to noninvasive testing. A negative D-dimer test can exclude a DVT without an ultrasound.

Diagnostic Procedures and Nursing Interventions: Varicose Veins

Δ   The **Trendelenburg test** assists with a diagnosis of varicose veins.

- Place the client in a supine position with legs elevated.

- When the client sits up, the veins will fill from the proximal end if varicosities are present (veins normally fill from the distal end).

Therapeutic Procedures and Nursing Interventions: Varicose Veins

Δ   **Sclerotherapy**

- A solution is injected into the vein, followed by the application of a pressure dressing.

- An incision and drainage of the trapped blood in the sclerosed vein are preformed 14 to 21 days after the injection, followed by the application of a pressure dressing for 12 to 18 hr.

Δ   **Vein Stripping**

- Varicose veins are removed if they are larger than 4 mm in diameter or if they are in clusters.

- Preoperatively

  ◊   Assist the physician with vein marking.

  ◊   Evaluate pulses as baseline for comparison postoperatively.

- Postoperatively

  ◊   Maintain elastic bandages on the client's legs.

  ◊   Monitor the groin and leg for bleeding through the elastic bandages.

  ◊   Monitor the extremity for edema, warmth, color, and pulses.

  ◊   Elevate the legs above the level of the heart.

  ◊   Encourage range of motion exercises of the legs.

  ◊   Instruct the client to elevate the legs when sitting and avoid leg dangling or chair sitting.

  ◊   Emphasize the importance of wearing elastic stockings after bandage removal.

Δ   Application of **Radiofrequency** (RF) Energy: The vein is heated from the inside by the RF and shrinks. Collateral veins take over.

Δ   **Laser Treatment**: Endovenous laser treatment uses a laser fiber to heat and close the main vessel that is contributing to the varicosity.

Assessments

Δ   **Deep Vein Thrombosis and Thrombophlebitis**

- The client may be asymptomatic.

- Classic signs are calf or groin pain or tenderness and sudden onset of swelling of the leg.

- Pain in the calf on dorsiflexion of the foot (positive Homans' sign) is **NOT ADVISED** for diagnosis because it only occurs in 10% of cases. May represent false positive.

- Examine the area, compare the site to the contralateral limb, gently palpate the site, and observe for induration along the blood vessel and for warmth and edema.

- Measure, record, and compare right and left calf and thigh circumferences for changes over time; observe for localized edema.

- Monitor for shortness of breath and chest pain, which can indicate pulmonary emboli.

Δ **Venous Insufficiency**

- Stasis dermatitis or brown discoloration along the ankles and extending up to the calf

- Edema

- Ulcer formation

Δ **Varicose Veins**

- Distended, protruding veins that appear darkened and tortuous

- Pain in legs with dull aching after standing

- A feeling of fullness in the legs

- Ankle edema

NANDA Nursing Diagnoses

Δ Risk for ineffective tissue perfusion (peripheral)

Δ Acute pain

Δ Risk for injury

Nursing Interventions

Δ **Deep Vein Thrombosis and Thrombophlebitis**

- Encourage **REST**.

  ◊ Facilitate bedrest and elevation of the extremity above the level of the heart as ordered (avoid using a knee gatch or pillow under knees).

  ◊ Administer intermittent or continuous warm moist compresses as ordered (to prevent thrombus from dislodging and becoming an embolus, do NOT massage the affected limb).

  ◊ Provide thigh-high compression or antiembolism stockings as prescribed to reduce venous stasis and to assist in venous return of blood to the heart.

- Administer medications as prescribed.

  ◊ Anticoagulants

    ° **Unfractionated heparin** (UFH) IV based on body weight is given to prevent formation of other clots and to prevent enlargement of the existing clot, followed by oral anticoagulation with warfarin (Coumadin). Hospital admission is required for laboratory value monitoring and dose adjustment. Monitor activated partial thromboplastin time (aPTT) to allow for adjustments of heparin dosage. Monitor platelet counts for heparin-induced thrombocytopenia. Ensure that protamine sulfate, the antidote for heparin, is available if needed for excessive bleeding. Monitor for hazards and side effects associated with anticoagulant therapy.

- ° **Low-molecular weight heparin** (LMWH) is given subcutaneously. Enoxaparin (Lovenox), dalteparin (Fragmin), and ardeparin (Normiflo) have consistent action and are approved for the prevention and treatment of DVT. Some may be managed at home with daily visits from a home care nurse. The client must have stable DVT or PE, low risk for bleeding, adequate renal function, and normal vital signs. The client must be willing to learn self-injection or have family/friend/home care nurse administer the subcutaneous injections. Monitor the client for evidence of bleeding (blood in stools). The aPTT is not checked on an ongoing basis because the doses of LMWH are not adjusted.

- ° **Warfarin** works in the liver to inhibit synthesis of the four vitamin K-dependent clotting factors and takes 3 to 4 days before it can exert therapeutic anticoagulation. Heparin is continued until the warfarin therapeutic anticoagulation effect is achieved, then IV heparin may be discontinued. If the client is on LMWH, warfarin is added after the first dose of LMWH. Therapeutic levels are measured by international normalized ratio (INR), which is more consistently accurate than prothrombin time (PT) for warfarin levels. Most laboratories report both results. Monitor for bleeding. Ensure that vitamin K (the antidote for warfarin) is available in case of excessive bleeding.

◊ **Thrombolytic Therapy**

- ° Thrombolytic therapy is effective in dissolving thrombi quickly and completely. It must be initiated within 5 days after the onset of symptoms to be most effective.

- ° The advantage is the prevention of valvular damage and consequential venous insufficiency, or "postphlebitis syndrome."

- ° It is contraindicated during pregnancy and following surgery, childbirth, trauma, a cerebrovascular accident, or spinal injury.

- ° Tissue plasminogen activator (t-PA), a thrombolytic agent, and platelet inhibitors such as abciximab (ReoPro), tirofiban (Aggrastat), and eptifibatide (Integrilin) may be effective in dissolving a clot or preventing new clots during the first 24 hr. They can be given by catheter directly into the thrombus, and therefore less concentration is needed. This reduces the chance of bleeding.

- ° The primary complication of thrombolytic therapy is serious bleeding (for example, intracerebral bleeding). Closely monitor the client for bleeding.

◊ **Analgesics:** Administer as ordered to reduce pain.

- Prepare the client for an inferior vena cava interruption surgery (a filter traps emboli and prevents them from reaching the heart) as indicated.

Δ **Venous Insufficiency**

- Consult with a dietician and wound care specialist as needed.

- Instruct the client:

  ◊ To **elevate legs** for at least 20 min four to five times a day.

  ◊ To elevate legs above the level of the heart.

  ◊ To avoid prolonged sitting or standing, constrictive clothing, or crossing legs when seated.

  ◊ To wear **elastic or compression stockings** during the day and evening as prescribed.

    ° Put elastic stockings on before getting out of bed after sleep.

    ° Clean the elastic stockings each day, keep the seams to the outside, and do not wear bunched up or rolled down.

    ° Replace worn out compression stockings as needed.

  ◊ On using an **intermittent sequential pneumatic compression system**, if prescribed.

    ° Instruct the client to apply the compression system twice daily for 1 hr in the morning and evening.

    ° Advise the client with an open ulcer that the compression system is applied over a dressing.

Δ **Varicose Veins**

- Emphasize the importance of antiembolism stockings as prescribed.

- Instruct the client to elevate legs as much as possible.

- Instruct the client to avoid constrictive clothing and pressure on the legs.

Complications and Nursing Implications

Δ **Ulcer Formation**: Typically over malleolus, more often medially than laterally. Ulcers are chronic, hard to heal, and recurrence is common. They may lead to amputation and/or death. Apply occlusive dressings, such as a hydrocolloid dressing, or artificial skin products (secrete growth factors to speed healing) as prescribed. An Unna boot may be applied to provide a healing environment for the ulcer. Topical agents such as Accuzyme may be prescribed to chemically debride the ulcer, eliminating necrotic tissue and promoting healing. Apply topical agents to the wound as prescribed to debride the ulcer, eliminate necrotic tissue, and promote healing. Administer systemic antibiotics as prescribed.

△ **Pulmonary Embolism**: Occurs when a thrombus is dislodged, becomes emboli, and lodges in the pulmonary vessels. This may lead to obstruction of pulmonary blood flow, decreased systemic oxygenation, pulmonary tissue hypoxia, and potential death. Symptoms include sudden onset dyspnea, pleuritic chest pain, restlessness and apprehension, feelings of impending doom, cough and hemoptysis. Signs include, tachypnea, crackles, pleural friction rub, tachycardia, S_3 or S_4 heart sound, diaphoresis, low-grade fever, petechiae over chest and axillae, and decreased arterial oxygen saturation. Notify the provider immediately, reassure the client, and assist the client to a position of comfort with the head of the bed elevated. Prepare for oxygen therapy and blood gas analysis while continuing to monitor and assess for other manifestations.

Meeting the Needs of Older Adults

△ Pedal pulses in older adults may be more difficult to find. Thin, shiny skin, thick ridged nails, and loss of hair on the lower legs are signs of arterial insufficiency associated with normal aging.

Primary Reference:

Ignatavicius, D. D., & Workman, M. L. (2006). *Medical-surgical nursing* (5th ed.). St. Louis, MO: Saunders.

Additional Resources:

Lewis, Heitkemper, and Dirksen (2004). *Medical-surgical nursing: Assessment and management of clinical problems* (6th ed.). St. Louis, MO: Mosby.

NANDA International (2004). *NANDA nursing diagnoses: Definitions and classification 2005-2006*. Philadelphia: NANDA.

Chapter 31: Peripheral Venous Disease

Application Exercises

Scenario: A 56-year-old client with a diagnosis of deep vein thrombosis and thrombophlebitis of the left lower extremity is admitted to a medical-surgical unit. Reported symptoms include left calf pain and tenderness with a sudden onset of swelling in the affected extremity.

1. To monitor for the progression of the DVT, the nurse should

   A. place the client in the knee-chest position.

   B. measure, record, and compare right and left calf and thigh circumferences.

   C. perform passive range of motion in the affected extremity.

   D. encourage the client to walk to the point of pain, rest, and then walk again until the point of pain.

2. The provider has ordered thigh-high compression stockings to prevent chronic venous insufficiency. The nurse should instruct the client to

   A. massage both legs firmly with lotion prior to applying the stockings.

   B. apply the stockings in the morning upon awakening and before getting out of bed.

   C. roll the stockings down to the knees if they will not stay up on the thighs.

   D. remove the stockings while out of bed for 1 hr four times a day to allow the legs to rest.

3. On day 2, the client becomes restless and agitated. The nurse notes that the client appears diaphoretic and is demonstrating shortness of breath. The client apologetically admits that she is experiencing chest pain. The nurse should

   A. tell the client, "It's OK, everyone gets grouchy at times."

   B. immediately call the primary care provider while elevating the head of the bed and administering oxygen.

   C. promptly elevate the client's legs by placing pillows under her knees.

   D. assist the client to the Trendelenburg position.

4. The client has been on IV unfractionated heparin (UFH) for 1 week, and her condition is resolving. Two days ago, the primary care provider also prescribed warfarin (Coumadin). The client expresses concern and questions the nurse about receiving both heparin and warfarin concurrently. An appropriate response by the nurse is,

> A. "The provider must have forgotten that you were already on heparin."
>
> B. "Your blood was so thick that two anticoagulants were needed."
>
> C. "You will probably have to stay on both IV heparin and warfarin for the rest of your life."
>
> D. "Warfarin takes 3 to 4 days to achieve therapeutic anticoagulant effects, so heparin is continued until the warfarin can take over."

Chapter 31: Peripheral Venous Disease

Application Exercises Answer Key

Scenario: A 56-year-old client with a diagnosis of deep vein thrombosis and thrombophlebitis of the left lower extremity is admitted to a medical-surgical unit. Reported symptoms include left calf pain and tenderness with a sudden onset of swelling in the affected extremity.

1. To monitor for the progression of the DVT, the nurse should

    A. place the client in the knee-chest position.

    B. measure, record, and compare right and left calf and thigh circumferences.

    C. perform passive range of motion in the affected extremity.

    D. encourage the client to walk to the point of pain, rest, and then walk again until the point of pain.

    Measure, record, and compare right and left calf and thigh circumferences to monitor for changes and the progression of DVT. The client should be on bedrest, and the extremity should be elevated above the level of the heart as ordered. Avoid using a knee gatch or pillow under the knees. Manipulation of the affected extremity should be avoided to prevent disruption and embolism of the clot. Walking to the point of pain, resting, and then walking again until the point of pain is the intervention for intermittent claudication with arterial insufficiency.

2. The provider has ordered thigh-high compression stockings to prevent chronic venous insufficiency. The nurse should instruct the client to

    A. massage both legs firmly with lotion prior to applying the stockings.

    B. apply the stockings in the morning upon awakening and before getting out of bed.

    C. roll the stockings down to the knees if they will not stay up on the thighs.

    D. remove the stockings while out of bed for 1 hr four times a day to allow the legs to rest.

    Apply stockings in the morning upon awakening and before getting out of bed to reduce venous stasis and to assist in the venous return of blood to the heart. Legs are less edematous at this time. Massage of affected area may dislodge a clot and cause embolism. Rolling stockings down may restrict circulation and cause edema.

3. On day 2, the client becomes restless and agitated. The nurse notes that the client appears diaphoretic and is demonstrating shortness of breath. The client apologetically admits that she is experiencing chest pain. The nurse should

    A. tell the client, "It's OK, everyone gets grouchy at times."

    B. immediately call the primary care provider while elevating the head of the bed and administering oxygen.

    C. promptly elevate the client's legs by placing pillows under her knees.

    D. assist the client to the Trendelenburg position.

The client is likely experiencing a potentially fatal complication of pulmonary embolism. All efforts must be made to facilitate the client's respiratory process.

4. The client has been on IV unfractionated heparin (UFH) for 1 week, and her condition is resolving. Two days ago, the primary care provider also prescribed warfarin (Coumadin). The client expresses concern and questions the nurse about receiving both heparin and warfarin concurrently. An appropriate response by the nurse is,

    A. "The provider must have forgotten that you were already on heparin."

    B. "Your blood was so thick that two anticoagulants were needed."

    C. "You will probably have to stay on both IV heparin and warfarin for the rest of your life."

    D. "Warfarin takes 3 to 4 days to achieve therapeutic anticoagulant effects, so heparin is continued until the warfarin can take over."

Warfarin takes 3 to 4 days to achieve therapeutic anticoagulant effects because it depresses synthesis of clotting factors but does not have any effect on clotting factors that are already present. Effects are delayed until the clotting factors that are present decay.

Unit 3   Nursing Care of Clients with Cardiovascular or Hematologic Disorders
Section: Nursing Care of Clients with Cardiac Failure

Chapter 32:   Heart Failure and Cardiomyopathy
Contributor: Sharon Kumm, MN, MS, RN, CCRN

NCLEX-PN® Connections:

Learning Objective: Review and apply knowledge within "**Heart Failure and Cardiomyopathy**" in readiness for performance of the following nursing activities as outlined by the NCLEX-PN® test plan:

Δ   Assist with relevant laboratory, diagnostic, and therapeutic procedures within the nursing role, including:

- Preparation of the client for the procedure.
- Accurate collection of specimens.
- Monitoring client status during and after the procedure.
- Reinforcing client teaching (before and following the procedure).
- Recognizing the client's response (expected, unexpected adverse response) to the procedure.
- Monitoring results.
- Monitoring and taking actions to prevent or minimize the risk of complications.
- Notifying the primary care provider of signs of complications.

Δ   Recognize signs and symptoms of the client's problem and complete the proper documentation.

Δ   Provide and document care based on the client's health alteration.

Δ   Monitor and document vital signs changes.

Δ   Interpret data that need to be reported immediately.

Δ   Reinforce client education on managing the client's health problem.

Δ   Recognize and respond to emergency situations, including notification of the primary care provider.

Δ   Review the client's response to emergency interventions and complete the proper documentation.

Δ   Provide care that meets the age-related needs of clients 65 years of age or older, including recognizing expected physiological changes.

📖 **Key Points**

Δ   Heart failure is the **inability of the heart to maintain adequate circulation to meet tissue needs for oxygen and nutrients.** Heart failure occurs when the heart muscle is unable to pump effectively, resulting in inadequate cardiac output, myocardial hypertrophy, and pulmonary/systemic congestion. Heart failure is the result of an acute or chronic cardiopulmonary problem, such as systemic hypertension, myocardial infarction, pulmonary hypertension, dysrhythmias, valvular heart disease, pericarditis, and cardiomyopathy.

Δ   **Severity of heart failure** is graded on the New York Heart Association's functional classification scale indicating how little, or how much, activity it takes to make the client symptomatic (chest pain, shortness-of-breath).

   •   Class I: Client exhibits no symptoms with activity.

   •   Class II: Client has symptoms with ordinary exertion.

   •   Class III: Client displays symptoms with minimal exertion.

   •   Class IV: Client has symptoms at rest.

Δ   **Cardiomyopathy** is a change in the structure of cardiac muscle fibers that causes impaired cardiac function leading to heart failure. Blood circulation is impaired to the lungs or body when the cardiac pump is compromised. There are three main types:

   •   **Dilated** – decreased contractility and increased ventricular filling pressures.

   •   **Hypertrophic** – increased thickness of ventricular and/or septal muscles.

   •   **Restrictive** – ventricles become rigid and lose their compliance.

Δ   **Low output heart failure** can initially occur on either the left or right side of the heart.

   •   **Left-sided heart (ventricular) failure** results in inadequate left ventricle (cardiac) output and consequently in inadequate tissue perfusion. Forms include:

      ◊   Systolic heart (ventricular) failure (ejection fraction below 40%, pulmonary and systemic congestion).

      ◊   Diastolic heart (ventricular) failure (inadequate relaxation or "stiffening" prevents ventricular filling).

   •   **Right-sided heart (ventricular) failure** results in inadequate right ventricle output and systemic venous congestion (for example, peripheral edema).

Δ   An uncommon form of heart failure is **high-output failure**, in which cardiac output is normal or above normal.

Key Factors

Δ **Risk Factors/Causes: Left-Sided Heart (Ventricular) Failure**

- Hypertension
- Coronary artery disease, angina, myocardial infarction (MI)
- Valvular disease (mitral and aortic)

Δ **Risk Factors/Causes: Right-Sided Heart (Ventricular) Failure**

- Left-sided heart (ventricular) failure
- Right ventricular myocardial infarction
- Pulmonary problems (COPD, ARDS)

Δ **Risk Factors/Causes: High-Output Heart Failure**

- Increased metabolic needs
- Septicemia (fever)
- Anemia
- Hyperthyroidism

Δ **Risk Factors/Causes: Cardiomyopathy**

- Coronary artery disease
- Infection or inflammation of the heart muscle
- Various cancer treatments
- Prolonged alcohol abuse
- Heredity

Diagnostic Procedures and Nursing Interventions

Δ **Human B-type Natriuretic Peptides** (BNP): Elevated in heart failure. Used to differentiate dyspnea related to heart failure versus respiratory problem and to monitor the need for and the effectiveness of aggressive heart failure intervention. BNP levels below 100 pg/mL indicate no heart failure; BNP levels of 100 to 300 pg/mL suggest heart failure is present; BNP levels above 300 pg/mL indicate mild heart failure; BNP levels above 600 pg/mL indicate moderate heart failure; and BNP levels above 900 pg/mL indicate severe heart failure.

Δ **Hemodynamic Monitoring**: Increased central venous pressure (CVP), increased right arterial pressure, increased pulmonary capillary wedge pressure (PCWP), increased pulmonary artery pressure (PAP), decreased cardiac output (CO)

Δ **Ultrasound** (also called cardiac ultrasound or echocardiogram): 2D (2-dimensional) or 3D (3-dimensional), to measure both systolic and diastolic function of the heart.

- Left ventricular ejection fraction (LVEF): The volume of blood pumped from the left ventricle into the arteries upon each beat. Normal is 55 to 70%.

- Right ventricular ejection fraction (RVEF): The volume of blood pumped from the right ventricle to the lungs upon each beat. Normal is 45 to 60%.

Δ **Chest x-ray** can reveal cardiomegaly and pleural effusions.

Δ **Electrocardiogram** (ECG), cardiac enzymes, electrolytes, and arterial blood gases: Assess factors contributing to heart failure and/or the impact of heart failure.

Therapeutic Procedures and Nursing Interventions

Δ A **ventricular assist device** (VAD) is a mechanical pump that assists a heart that is too weak to pump blood through the body. A VAD is used in clients who are eligible for heart transplants or who have severe end-stage congestive heart failure and are not candidates for heart transplants. Heart transplantation is the treatment of choice for clients with severe dilated cardiomyopathy.

Δ **Heart transplantation** is a possible option for clients with end-stage heart failure. Immunosuppressant therapy is required post transplantation to prevent rejection.

Assessments

Δ Monitor for **signs and symptoms.**

- **Left-sided failure**
  ◊ **Dyspnea**, orthopnea, nocturnal dyspnea
  ◊ Fatigue
  ◊ Displaced apical pulse (hypertrophy)
  ◊ S_3 heart sound (gallop)
  ◊ Pulmonary congestion (**dyspnea**, **cough**, bibasilar crackles)
  ◊ Frothy sputum (may be blood-tinged)
  ◊ Altered mental status
  ◊ Symptoms of organ failure, such as oliguria
  ◊ Hemodynamic findings:
    ° CVP/right atrial pressure (normal = 1 to 8 mm Hg): Normal or elevated
    ° PAP (normal = 15 to 26 mm Hg/5 to 15 mm Hg): Elevated
    ° PAWP (normal = 4 to 12 mm Hg): Elevated
    ° CO (normal = 4 to 7 L/min): Decreased

- **Right-sided failure**
  - ◊ Jugular vein distention
  - ◊ **Ascending dependent edema** (legs, ankles, sacrum)
  - ◊ Abdominal distention, ascites
  - ◊ Fatigue, weakness
  - ◊ Nausea and anorexia
  - ◊ Polyuria at rest (for example, nocturnal)
  - ◊ Liver enlargement (hepatomegaly) and tenderness
  - ◊ Weight gain
  - ◊ Hemodynamic findings
    - ° CVP/right atrial pressure (normal = 1 to 8 mm Hg): Elevated
- **Cardiomyopathy**
  - ◊ Fatigue, weakness
  - ◊ Heart failure (left with dilated type, right with restrictive type)
  - ◊ Dysrhythmias (for example, heart block)
  - ◊ S_3 gallop
  - ◊ Cardiomegaly

Δ **Assess/Monitor**

- Oxygen saturation
- Vital signs
- Heart rhythm
- Lung sounds for crackles, wheezes
- Level of dyspnea upon exertion
- Serum electrolytes (especially potassium if receiving diuretics)
- Daily weight
- Changes in level of consciousness
- Intake and output
- For signs of drug toxicity
- Coping ability of client and family

NANDA Nursing Diagnoses

Δ   Impaired gas exchange

Δ   Decreased cardiac output

Δ   Activity intolerance

Δ   Excess fluid volume

Δ   Ineffective tissue perfusion (cerebral)

Δ   Risk for ineffective tissue perfusion (renal)

Nursing Interventions

Δ   If a client is experiencing respiratory distress, place the client in **high-Fowler's position** and administer **oxygen** as prescribed.

Δ   Encourage bedrest until the client is stable.

Δ   Encourage **energy conservation** by assisting with care and activities of daily living.

Δ   Maintain dietary restrictions as prescribed (**restricted fluid intake, restricted sodium intake**).

Δ   Administer medications as prescribed.

- **Diuretics**: To decrease preload
  - ◊   Loop diuretics, such as furosemide (Lasix), bumetanide (Bumex)
  - ◊   Thiazide diuretics, such as hydrochlorothiazide (HydroDIURIL)
  - ◊   Potassium-sparing diuretics, such as spironolactone (Aldactone)
  - ◊   Teach the client taking loop or thiazide diuretics to ingest foods and drinks that are high in potassium to counter hypokalemia effect. Potassium supplementation may be required. Administer IV furosemide (Lasix) no faster than 20 mg/min.

- **Afterload-Reducing Agents**
  - ◊   Angiotensin converting enzyme (ACE) inhibitors, such as enalapril (Vasotec), captopril (Capoten); monitor for initial dose hypotension.
  - ◊   Beta-blockers, such as carvedilol (Coreg), metoprolol (Lopressor XL)
  - ◊   Angiotensin receptor II blockers, such as losartan (Cozaar)

- **Inotropic agents**, such as digoxin (Lanoxin), dopamine, dobutamine (Dobutrex), milrinone (Primacor): To increase contractility and thereby improve cardiac output

- **Vasodilators**, such as nitrates: To decrease preload and afterload

- **Human B-Type Natriuretic Peptides** (hBNP), such as nesiritide (Natrecor): To treat acute heart failure by causing natriuresis (loss of sodium and vasodilation)

- **Anticoagulants**, such as warfarin (Coumadin), heparin, clopidogrel: To prevent thrombus formation (risk associated with congestion/stasis and associated atrial fibrillation)

Δ Teach clients who are **self-administering digoxin** (Lanoxin) to:

- Count pulse for one full minute before taking the medication. If the pulse rate is irregular or the pulse rate is outside of the limitations set by the provider (usually less than 60 or greater than 100), instruct the client to hold the dose and to contact the primary care provider.

- Take digoxin (Lanoxin) dose at same time each day (for example, 0900).

- Do not take digoxin at the same time as antacids. Separate by 2 hr.

- Report signs of toxicity, including fatigue, muscle weakness, confusion, and loss of appetite.

- Regularly have digoxin and potassium levels checked.

Δ Provide emotional support to the client and family.

Δ **Client Education**

- Take medications as prescribed.

- Take **diuretics in early morning and early afternoon**.

- **Maintain fluid and sodium restriction** – a dietary consult may be useful.

- Increase dietary intake of potassium (cantaloupe, bananas) if taking potassium-losing diuretics such as loop diuretics and thiazide diuretics.

- Weigh self daily at the same time and **notify the primary care provider for weight gain of 2 lb in 24 hr or 5 lb in 1 week**.

- Schedule regular follow-ups with the primary care provider.

- Get vaccinations (pneumococcal vaccine and yearly influenza vaccine).

Complications and Nursing Implications

Δ **Acute pulmonary edema** is a life-threatening medical emergency. Symptoms include anxiety, tachycardia, acute respiratory distress, dyspnea at rest, change in level of consciousness, and an ascending fluid level within lungs (crackles, cough productive of frothy, blood-tinged sputum). Prompt response to this emergency includes:

- Positioning the client in high-Fowler's position.

- Administration of oxygen, positive airway pressure, and/or intubation and mechanical ventilation.

- IV morphine (to decrease anxiety, respiratory distress, and decrease venous return).

- IV administration of rapid-acting loop diuretics, such as furosemide (Lasix).

- Effective intervention should result in diuresis (carefully monitor output), reduction in respiratory distress, improved lung sounds, and adequate oxygenation.

Δ **Cardiogenic shock** is a serious complication of pump failure, commonly following a myocardial infarction of 40% or more of the left ventricle. It is a class IV heart failure. Symptoms include tachycardia, hypotension (BP less than 90 mm Hg or less than 30 mm Hg from baseline BP), inadequate urinary output (less than 30 mL/hr), altered level of consciousness, respiratory distress (crackles, tachypnea), cool clammy skin, decreased peripheral pulses, and chest pain. Intervention includes administration of oxygen; possible intubation and ventilation; IV administration of morphine, diuretics, and/or nitroglycerin to decrease preload; and IV administration of vasopressors and/or positive inotropes to increase cardiac output and to maintain organ perfusion. Other possible emergency interventions include use of an intra-aortic balloon pump and/or emergency coronary artery bypass surgery.

Δ **Pericardial effusion and pericardial tamponade** is an accumulation of fluid within the pericardial sac. Immediate intervention, such as a pericardiocentesis, sternotomy, and creation of a pericardial window, may be necessary in addition to measures to improve cardiac output. Administer anti-inflammatory medications as prescribed.

Δ **Systemic and pulmonary emboli** are possible complications due to decreased cardiac output and systemic congestion. New onsets of atrial fibrillation need to be reported.

Δ **Organ failure**, such as renal failure, is possible due to tissue ischemia.

Meeting the Needs of Older Adults

Δ Systolic blood pressure is elevated in older adults, putting them at risk for coronary artery disease and heart failure.

Δ The risk for valvular complications is increased in older adults with heart failure.

Δ There is an increased risk for exercise intolerance in older adults with heart failure.

Δ The presence of other chronic illnesses may mask the presence of heart failure.

Δ An increased risk of electrolyte disturbances is related to frequent diuretic use by older adults.

Primary Reference:

Ignatavicius, D. D., & Workman, M. L. (2006). *Medical-surgical nursing* (5th ed.). St. Louis, MO: Saunders.

Additional Resources:

Black, J. M., & Hawks, J. H. (2005). *Medical-surgical nursing: Clinical management for positive outcomes* (7th ed.). St. Louis, MO: Saunders.

NANDA International (2004). *NANDA nursing diagnoses: Definitions and classification 2005-2006.* Philadelphia: NANDA.

Chapter 32: Heart Failure and Cardiomyopathy

Application Exercises

1. List the signs and symptoms of heart failure.

Right-sided heart failure	Left-sided heart failure

2. Provide the rationale for each of the following therapies.

Therapy	Rationale
Oxygen administration	
Diuretics	
Bedrest	
Inotropic agents	
Vasodilators	
Fluid restriction	
Sodium restriction	

3. What should a nurse include when planning discharge teaching for a client with heart failure?

4. A client with a diagnosis of heart failure reports increased shortness of breath. The nurse increases the oxygen per protocol. Which of the following should be the nurse's next action?

   A. Notify the primary care provider.

   B. Assist the client into high-Fowler's position.

   C. Auscultate the lungs, listening for increased crackles.

   D. Check oxygen saturation with pulse oximeter.

5. A client with a diagnosis of heart failure asks how to limit fluid intake to 2,000 mL/day. The nurse's best response would be,

   A. "This is the same as a 2 L bottle of soda. Pour the amount of fluid you drink into an empty soda bottle to keep tract of how much you drink."

   B. "Each glass contains 8 oz. There are 30 mL per ounce, so you can have a total of 8 glasses or cups of fluid each day."

   C. "This is the same as 2 quarts or about the same as two pots of coffee."

   D. "Just take sips of water or ice chips. That way you will not take in too much fluid."

6. A client with a diagnosis of heart failure reports not taking diuretics on days that activities are scheduled to prevent having to go to the bathroom all the time. Which of the following statements by the nurse assesses the effect of this action?

   A. "Do you take the medication later in the day when you return home?"

   B. "Do you have more difficulty breathing or swelling in your legs the next day?"

   C. "You should take the medicine earlier so its effect is gone before the activity begins."

   D. "That is why you had to be admitted to the hospital again to remove excess water."

7. Which of the following client findings might suggest digitalis toxicity or a risk for digitalis toxicity? (Check all that apply.)

   _____ Serum potassium level of 3.2 mEq/L

   _____ Apical heart rate of 54/min

   _____ Blurred vision

   _____ Dysrhythmia

   _____ Renal failure

   _____ Weight gain of 2 lb in 1 day

   _____ Leg cramps

   _____ Slurred speech

   _____ Shortness of breath

   _____ Anorexia

   _____ Altered mental status

8. Identify which of the following food selections are high in sodium (mark with an S) and which are high in potassium (mark with a P). In general, clients with heart failure may need to reduce sodium intake and to increase potassium intake.

	Cheese (cheddar, cottage cheese)
	Cantaloupe
	Milk
	Soy sauce
	Cured meats (pork)
	White potatoes
	Avocado
	Banana
	Raisins
	Meats (beef, pork, chicken, veal)
	Codfish, salmon, tuna

Chapter 32: Heart Failure and Cardiomyopathy

Application Exercises Answer Key

1. List the signs and symptoms of heart failure.

Right-sided heart failure	Left-sided heart failure
Peripheral edema Jugular vein distention Liver enlargement (right upper quadrant pain) Ascites Fatigue Weight gain	Dyspnea, orthopnea, dyspnea on exertion Crackles in lungs S_3 heart sound Cough Frothy sputum Fatigue

2. Provide the rationale for each of the following therapies.

Therapy	Rationale
Oxygen administration	Increase myocardial and systemic oxygen supply
Diuretics	Decrease preload
Bedrest	Conserve energy, decrease cellular oxygen demand
Inotropic agents	Increase contractility
Vasodilators	Decrease preload and afterload
Fluid restriction	Decrease vascular volume – preload
Sodium restriction	Decrease vascular volume – preload

3. What should a nurse include when planning discharge teaching for a client with heart failure?

Follow fluid and sodium restrictions.

Conserve energy – schedule rest periods between periods of activity.

Adhere to medication regimen.

Weigh self daily – notify provider of weight gain of 2 lb in 24 hr or 5 lb in 1 week.

Get influenza vaccine yearly.

If prescribed digoxin, take pulse for 1 minute, notify the provider if pulse is below set limit.

Take diuretics in early morning and early afternoon (if prescribed twice daily) to allow for uninterrupted sleep.

Notify the provider of increased dyspnea, orthopnea, and inability to wear rings or shoes.

4. A client with a diagnosis of heart failure reports increased shortness of breath. The nurse increases the oxygen per protocol. Which of the following should be the nurse's next action?

    A. Notify the primary care provider.

    B. Assist the client into high-Fowler's position.

    C. Auscultate the lungs, listening for increased crackles.

    D. Check oxygen saturation with pulse oximeter.

Assisting the client into a high-Fowler's position will decrease venous return to the heart (preload) and will help relieve lung congestion. The other actions are appropriate but are not the first action nor will they directly improve the client's oxygenation or relieve symptoms.

5. A client with a diagnosis of heart failure asks how to limit fluid intake to 2,000 mL/day. The nurse's best response would be,

    A. "This is the same as a 2 L bottle of soda. Pour the amount of fluid you drink into an empty soda bottle to keep tract of how much you drink."

    B. "Each glass contains 8 oz. There are 30 mL per ounce, so you can have a total of 8 glasses or cups of fluid each day."

    C. "This is the same as 2 quarts or about the same as two pots of coffee."

    D. "Just take sips of water or ice chips. That way you will not take in too much fluid."

This will give the client a visual guide to how much fluid is consumed and how much is left. Glasses and cups vary in size. Quarts, pots of coffee, sips of water, and ice chips are not concrete methods to determine intake.

6. A client with a diagnosis of heart failure reports not taking diuretics on days that activities are scheduled to prevent having to go to the bathroom all the time. Which of the following statements by the nurse assesses the effect of this action?

    A. "Do you take the medication later in the day when you return home?"

    B. "Do you have more difficulty breathing or swelling in your legs the next day?"

    C. "You should take the medicine earlier so its effect is gone before the activity begins."

    D. "That is why you had to be admitted to the hospital again to remove excess water."

The question asks for assessment of the effect. Option B evaluates the effect of skipping a dose of medicine. Options A and C do not assess the effect of skipping a dose. Option D blames the client and may cause resistance to recommendations of alternate actions.

7. Which of the following client findings might suggest digitalis toxicity or a risk for digitalis toxicity? (Check all that apply.)

__x__	Serum potassium level of 3.2 mEq/L
__x__	Apical heart rate of 54/min
__x__	Blurred vision
__x__	Dysrhythmia
__x__	Renal failure
_____	Weight gain of 2 lb in 1 day
__x__	Leg cramps
_____	Slurred speech
_____	Shortness of breath
__x__	Anorexia
__x__	Altered mental status

Hypokalemia increases the risk of digitalis toxicity. Leg cramps are a possible sign of hypokalemia. Renal failure increases the risk for digitalis toxicity due to reduced elimination. Slowed pulse, blurred vision, dysrhythmias, anorexia, and altered mental status are signs of digitalis toxicity. Weight gain and shortness of breath are signs of heart failure. Slurred speech could be a sign of a cerebrovascular accident.

8. Identify which of the following food selections are high in sodium (mark with an S) and which are high in potassium (mark with a P). In general, clients with heart failure may need to reduce sodium intake and to increase potassium intake.

S	Cheese (cheddar, cottage cheese)
P	Cantaloupe
S	Milk
S	Soy sauce
S, P	Cured meats (pork)
P	White potatoes
P	Avocado
P	Banana
P	Raisins
P	Meats (beef, pork, chicken, veal)
P	Codfish, salmon, tuna

Unit 3 Nursing Care of Clients with Cardiovascular or Hematologic Disorders
Section: Nursing Care of Clients with Cardiac Failure

Chapter 33: Valvular Heart Disease
Contributor: Sharon Kumm, MN, MS, RN, CCRN

⟳ NCLEX-PN® Connections:

Learning Objective: Review and apply knowledge within "**Valvular Heart Disease**" in readiness for performance of the following nursing activities as outlined by the NCLEX-PN® test plan:

Δ   Assist with relevant laboratory, diagnostic, and therapeutic procedures within the nursing role, including:

- Preparation of the client for the procedure.
- Accurate collection of specimens.
- Monitoring client status during and after the procedure.
- Reinforcing client teaching (before and following the procedure).
- Recognizing the client's response (expected, unexpected adverse response) to the procedure.
- Monitoring results.
- Monitoring and taking actions to prevent or minimize the risk of complications.
- Notifying the primary care provider of signs of complications.

Δ   Recognize signs and symptoms of the client's problem and complete the proper documentation.

Δ   Provide and document care based on the client's health alteration.

Δ   Monitor and document vital signs changes.

Δ   Interpret data that need to be reported immediately.

Δ   Reinforce client education on managing the client's health problem.

Δ   Recognize and respond to emergency situations, including notification of the primary care provider.

Δ   Review the client's response to emergency interventions and complete the proper documentation.

Δ   Provide care that meets the age-related needs of clients 65 years of age or older, including recognizing expected physiological changes.

📖 **Key Points**

Δ   Valvular heart disease may have congenital or acquired causes.

Δ   **Valves on the left side are most commonly affected** due to higher pressures.

Δ   Valvular disease is classified as:

  •   **Stenosis** – narrowed opening that impedes blood moving forward.

  •   **Insufficiency** – improper closure – some blood flows backward (regurgitation).

Δ   Congenital valvular disease may affect all four valves and cause either stenosis or insufficiency.

Δ   Acquired valvular disease is classified as one of three types:

  •   **Degenerative disease** – due to damage over time from mechanical stress. The most common cause is hypertension.

  •   **Rheumatic disease** – gradual fibrotic changes, calcification of valve cusps. The mitral valve is most commonly affected.

  •   **Infective endocarditis** – infectious organisms destroy the valve. Streptococcal infections are a common cause.

Δ   A **murmur** is heard with turbulent blood flow. The location of the murmur and timing (diastolic versus systolic) help determine the valve involved. Murmurs are graded on a scale of I (very faint) to VI (extremely loud).

Key Factors

Δ   **Risk Factors** for Valvular Heart Disease

  •   Hypertension

  •   Rheumatic fever (mitral stenosis and insufficiency)

  •   Infective endocarditis

  •   Congenital malformations

  •   Marfan syndrome

Diagnostic Procedures and Nursing Interventions

Δ   Chest x-ray shows chamber enlargement, pulmonary congestion, and valve calcification.

Δ   12-lead electrocardiogram (ECG) shows chamber hypertrophy.

Δ   Echocardiogram shows chamber size, hypertrophy, specific valve dysfunction, ejection function, and amount of regurgitant flow.

Δ   Exercise tolerance testing/stress echocardiography is used to assess the impact of the valve problem on functioning during stress.

Δ   Radionuclide studies determine ejection fraction during activity and rest.

Δ   Angiography reveals chamber pressures, ejection fraction, regurgitation, and pressure gradients.

Therapeutic Procedures and Nursing Interventions

Δ   **Percutaneous balloon valvuloplasty** may open the stenotic aortic or mitral valves. A catheter is inserted through the femoral artery and advanced to the heart. A balloon is inflated at the stenotic lesion to open the fused commissures and improve leaflet mobility.

Δ   Surgical management includes valve repair, chordae tendineae reconstruction, commissurotomy (relieve stenosis on leaflets), annuloplasty ring insertion (correct dilatation of valve annulus), and prosthetic valve replacement.

     •   Prosthetic valves may be mechanical or tissue. Mechanical valves last longer but require anticoagulation. Tissue valves last 10 to 15 years.

Assessments

Δ   Monitor for **signs and symptoms.**

Left-sided valve damage results in dyspnea, fatigue, increased pulmonary artery pressure, and decreased cardiac output.			
Mitral stenosis	**Mitral insufficiency**	**Aortic stenosis**	**Aortic insufficiency**
• Palpitations • Hemoptysis • Hoarseness • Dysphagia • Jugular vein distention • Orthopnea • Cough • Diastolic murmur • Atrial fibrillation	• Proximal nocturnal Dyspnea • Orthopnea • Palpitations • S_3 and/or S_4 • Crackles in lungs • Systolic murmur • **Atrial fibrillation**	• Angina • Syncope • Decreased SVR • S_3 and/or S_4 • Systolic murmur • Narrowed pulse pressure	• Angina • S_3 • Diastolic murmur • Widened pulse pressure
Right-sided valve damage results in dyspnea, fatigue, increased right atrial pressure, peripheral edema, jugular vein distention, and hepatomegaly			
Tricuspid stenosis	**Tricuspid insufficiency**	**Pulmonic stenosis**	**Pulmonic insufficiency**
• Atrial dysrhythmias • Diastolic murmur • Decreased cardiac output	• Conduction delays • Supraventricular tachycardia • Systolic murmur	• Cyanosis • Systolic murmur	• Diastolic murmur

Δ **Assess/Monitor**

- Oxygen status
- Vital signs
- Cardiac rhythm
- Hemodynamics
- Heart and lung sounds
- Exercise tolerance

NANDA Nursing Diagnoses

Δ Decreased cardiac output

Δ Impaired gas exchange

Δ Activity intolerance

Δ Acute pain

Nursing Interventions

Δ Administer **oxygen** as prescribed to improve myocardial oxygenation.

Δ Maintain fluid and sodium restriction.

Δ Administer **medications** as prescribed.

- Diuretics to decrease preload.
- Antihypertensive agents (beta-blockers, calcium-channel blockers, ACE inhibitors) to reduce afterload.
- Inotropic agents to increase contractility – digoxin (Lanoxin), dobutamine.
- Anticoagulation therapy for clients with mechanical valve replacement, atrial fibrillation, or severe left ventricle dysfunction.

Δ Assist the client to conserve energy and decrease myocardial oxygen consumption.

Δ Post-surgery care is similar to coronary artery bypass surgery (care for sternal incision, activity limits for 6 weeks, report fever).

Δ **Client Education**

- **Prophylactic antibiotics are recommended prior to dental work, surgery, or other invasive procedures**.
- Encourage the client to follow the prescribed exercise program.

- Encourage adherence to dietary restrictions; consider nutritional consultation.

- Teach the client energy conservation.

Complications and Nursing Implications

Δ **Heart failure** is the inability of the heart to maintain adequate circulation to meet tissue needs for oxygen and nutrients. Ineffective valves result in heart failure. Monitoring a client's heart failure class (I to IV) is often the gauge for surgical intervention for valvular problems.

Meeting the Needs of Older Adults

Δ With age, fibrotic thickening occurs in the mitral and aortic valves.

Δ The aorta is stiffer in older adult clients, increasing systolic blood pressure and stress on the mitral valve.

Δ In older adult clients, the predominant causes of valvular heart disease are degenerative calcification, papillary muscle dysfunction, and infective endocarditis.

Δ Medical management is appropriate for many older adult clients; surgery is indicated when symptoms interfere with daily activities.

Δ The goal of surgery may be to improve the quality of life rather than to prolong life.

Primary Reference:

Ignatavicius, D. D., & Workman, M. L. (2006). *Medical-surgical nursing* (5th ed.). St. Louis, MO: Saunders.

Additional Resources:

Black, J. M., & Hawks, J. H. (2005). *Medical-surgical nursing: Clinical management for positive outcomes* (7th ed.). St. Louis, MO: Saunders.

NANDA International (2004). *NANDA nursing diagnoses: Definitions and classification 2005-2006*. Philadelphia: NANDA.

For more information, visit the American College of Cardiology Foundation at *www.acc.org* or the American Heart Association at *www.americanheart.org*.

Chapter 33: Valvular Heart Disease

Application Exercises

1. Identify which specific valve problems can cause each of the following client findings.

Client Finding	Associated Valve Problem
Atrial dysrhythmias (for example, atrial fibrillation)	
Pulmonary edema	
Systolic murmurs	
Diastolic murmurs	
Angina	

2. Provide the rationale for each of the following interventions performed for a client admitted with valvular heart disease.

Nursing Intervention	Rationale
Administer oxygen	
Monitor heart rhythm	
Encourage rest periods	
Administer diuretics	
Administer inotropes	
Administer beta-blockers	
Gradual increase in exercise	

3. What assessments should a nurse perform immediately postoperative for a client with a mitral valve replacement?

4. What discharge teaching should a nurse provide a client with a mechanical valve replacement?

5. A client reports that a parent has been diagnosed with valvular heart disease and asks what can be done to prevent getting the disease. The nurse informs the client that one of the most common causes of valvular heart disease is

    A. hypertension.

    B. tobacco smoking.

    C. diabetes.

    D. alcoholism.

6. A nurse notes that a client has a history of mitral insufficiency. The nurse should assess the client for

    A. angina.

    B. bilateral ankle edema.

    C. crackles in lung bases.

    D. jugular vein distention.

Chapter 33: Valvular Heart Disease

Application Exercises Answer Key

1. Identify which specific valve problems can cause each of the following client findings.

Client Finding	Associated Valve Problem
Atrial dysrhythmias (for example, atrial fibrillation)	Mitral stenosis, mitral insufficiency, tricuspid stenosis, tricuspid insufficiency
Pulmonary edema	Mitral stenosis, mitral insufficiency
Systolic murmurs	Tricuspid insufficiency, pulmonic stenosis, mitral insufficiency, aortic stenosis
Diastolic murmurs	Tricuspid stenosis, pulmonic insufficiency, mitral stenosis, aortic insufficiency
Angina	Aortic stenosis, aortic insufficiency

2. Provide the rationale for each of the following interventions performed for a client admitted with valvular heart disease.

Nursing Intervention	Rationale
Administer oxygen	Increase myocardial oxygen supply.
Monitor heart rhythm	Atrial dysrhythmias and heart blocks are common in valve disease, dysrhythmias can decrease cardiac output.
Encourage rest periods	Decreases energy consumption and helps manage fatigue.
Administer diuretics	Decrease preload.
Administer inotropes	Increase contractility.
Administer beta-blockers	Decrease afterload.
Gradual increase in exercise	Increase endurance.

3. What assessments should a nurse perform immediately postoperative for a client with a mitral valve replacement?

Vital signs, cardiac rhythm, oxygen saturation, hemodynamics (cardiac output, PAWP, SVR), urine output, chest tube output, heart and lung sounds, peripheral pulses

4. What discharge teaching should a nurse provide a client with a mechanical valve replacement?

Prophylactic antibiotics are recommended prior to dental work, surgery, or other invasive procedures.

Stress the importance of follow-up appointments.

Inform the client of support groups in the area.

Instruct the client to follow medication regimen.

Encourage the client to follow the prescribed exercise program.

Encourage adherence to dietary restrictions; consider nutritional consultation.

Inform the client of when to notify the provider.

5. A client reports that a parent has been diagnosed with valvular heart disease and asks what can be done to prevent getting the disease. The nurse informs the client that one of the most common causes of valvular heart disease is

A. hypertension.
B. tobacco smoking.
C. diabetes.
D. alcoholism.

The high flow turbulence of uncontrolled hypertension has a degenerative effect on valves.

6. A nurse notes that a client has a history of mitral insufficiency. The nurse should assess the client for

A. angina.
B. bilateral ankle edema.
C. crackles in lung bases.
D. jugular vein distention.

Mitral insufficiency initially results in dyspnea, orthopnea, and pulmonary congestion.

Unit 3
Section:

Nursing Care of Clients with Cardiovascular or Hematologic Disorders
Medical Emergencies: Cardiovascular

Chapter 34: **Angina and Myocardial Infarction**

Contributor: Sharon Kumm, MN, MS, RN, CCRN

🗘 NCLEX-PN® Connections:

> **Learning Objective**: Review and apply knowledge within "**Angina and Myocardial Infarction**" in readiness for performance of the following nursing activities as outlined by the NCLEX-PN® test plan:
>
> Δ   Assist with relevant laboratory, diagnostic, and therapeutic procedures within the nursing role, including:
>
> •   Preparation of the client for the procedure.
>
> •   Accurate collection of specimens.
>
> •   Monitoring client status during and after the procedure.
>
> •   Reinforcing client teaching (before and following the procedure).
>
> •   Recognizing the client's response (expected, unexpected adverse response) to the procedure.
>
> •   Monitoring results.
>
> •   Monitoring and taking actions to prevent or minimize the risk of complications.
>
> •   Notifying the primary care provider of signs of complications.
>
> Δ   Recognize signs and symptoms of the client's problem and complete the proper documentation.
>
> Δ   Provide and document care based on the client's health alteration.
>
> Δ   Monitor and document vital signs changes.
>
> Δ   Interpret data that need to be reported immediately.
>
> Δ   Reinforce client education on managing the client's health problem.
>
> Δ   Recognize and respond to emergency situations, including notification of the primary care provider.
>
> Δ   Review the client's response to emergency interventions and complete the proper documentation.
>
> Δ   Provide care that meets the age-related needs of clients 65 years of age or older, including recognizing expected physiological changes.

📖 Key Points

- Δ   The continuum from angina to myocardial infarction (MI) is termed **acute coronary syndrome**. Symptoms of acute coronary syndrome are due to an **imbalance between myocardial oxygen supply and demand**.

- Δ   Angina pectoris is a warning sign for acute MI.

- Δ   Women and older adults may not always experience symptoms typically associated with angina or MI.

- Δ   The majority of deaths from an MI occur within 1 hr of symptom onset. The average time for a person seeking treatment is 4 hr. Early recognition and treatment of acute MI is essential to prevent death.

- Δ   Research shows improved outcomes following an MI in clients treated with aspirin, beta-blockers, and angiotensin-converting enzyme (ACE) inhibitors.

- Δ   When blood flow to the heart is compromised, ischemia causes chest pain. Anginal pain is often described as a tight squeezing, heavy pressure, or constricting feeling in the chest. The pain may radiate to the jaw, neck, or arm.

- Δ   The three types of angina are:

  - **Stable angina** (exertional angina) occurs with exercise or emotional stress and is relieved by rest or nitroglycerin.

  - **Unstable angina** (preinfarction angina) occurs with exercise or emotional stress, but it increases in occurrence, severity, and duration over time.

  - **Variant angina** (Prinzmetal's angina) is due to coronary artery spasm, often occurring at rest.

- Δ   **Pain unrelieved by rest or nitroglycerine and lasting for more than 15 min differentiates MI from angina.**

- Δ   An abrupt interruption of oxygen to the heart muscle produces myocardial ischemia. **Ischemia may lead to tissue necrosis (infarction) if blood supply and oxygen are not restored.** Ischemia is reversible; infarction results in permanent damage.

- Δ   When the cardiac muscle suffers ischemic injury, cardiac enzymes are released into the bloodstream, providing specific markers of MI.

- Δ   MIs are classified based on:

  - The affected area of the heart (anterior, anterolateral).

  - The depth of involvement (transmural versus nontransmural).

  - The EKG changes produced (Q wave, non-Q wave). Non-Q-wave MIs are more common in older adults, women, and clients with diabetes.

Key Factors

Δ   **Risk Factors** for Angina and MI

- Male gender
- Hypertension
- Smoking history
- Increased age
- Hyperlipidemia
- Metabolic disorders: Diabetes mellitus, hyperthyroidism
- Methamphetamine or cocaine use
- Stress: Occupational, physical exercise, sexual activity

Diagnostic Procedures and Nursing Interventions

Δ   **Electrocardiograms** (ECG): Check for changes on serial ECGs.

- Angina: ST depression and/or T-wave inversion (ischemia)
- MI: T-wave inversion (ischemia), ST-segment elevation (injury), and an abnormal Q wave (necrosis)

Δ   Clients with non-ST elevation MIs have other indicators.

- ST segment depression that resolves with relief of chest pain
- New development of left bundle branch block
- T-wave inversion in all chest leads

Δ   **Serial Cardiac Enzymes**: Typical pattern of elevation and decrease back to baseline occurs with MI.

Cardiac Enzyme	Normal Levels	Elevated Levels First Detectable Following Myocardial Injury	Expected Duration of Elevated Levels
Creatinine kinase MB isoenzyme (CK-MB) – more sensitive to myocardium	0% of total CK (30-170 units/L)	4-6 hr	3 days
Troponin T	< 0.2 ng/L	3-5 hr	14-21 days
Troponin I	< 0.03 ng/L	3 hr	7-10 days
Myoglobin	< 90 mcg/L	2 hr	24 hr

Δ   **Thallium scans** assess for ischemia or necrosis. Radioisotopes cannot reach areas with decreased or absent perfusion and they appear as "cold spots."

Δ   **Cardiac catheterization** reveals the exact location of coronary artery obstructions and provides an assessment of the degree of ischemia and necrosis.

Therapeutic Procedures and Nursing Interventions

Δ   **Percutaneous transluminal coronary angioplasty** (PTCA) uses a balloon at the tip of a catheter guided under fluoroscopy to press plaque against the vessel wall and to dilate the obstructed coronary artery to increase/restore tissue perfusion. Stents may be placed to maintain patency. Following a PTCA, monitor for bleeding (heparin used), acute vessel closure (emergency coronary artery bypass graft), and dysrhythmias (reperfusion).

Δ   **Coronary artery bypass graft** (CABG) surgery restores myocardial tissue perfusion by the addition of grafts bypassing the obstructed coronary arteries.

Assessments

Δ   Monitor for **signs and symptoms.**

- May be asymptomatic
- Chest pain (substernal or precordial, may radiate to the neck, arms, shoulders or jaw; tight squeezing or heaviness in the chest, burning, aching, dull, constant)
- Dyspnea
- Pallor and cool, clammy skin
- Tachycardia and/or palpitations
- Anxiety/fear, feeling of doom
- Sweating (diaphoresis)
- Nausea and vomiting
- Dizziness, decreased level of consciousness

Δ   Differentiate angina from MI.

Angina	Myocardial Infarction
Precipitated by **exertion** or stress	Occurs without cause, often in the morning after rest
Relieved by **rest or nitroglycerine**	Relieved only by **opioids**
< 15 min	**> 30 min**
Not associated with nausea, epigastric distress, dyspnea, anxiety, diaphoresis	Associated with nausea, epigastric distress, dyspnea, anxiety, diaphoresis

Δ   **Assess/Monitor**

- Vital signs every 15 min until stable, then every hour
- Serial ECG, continuous ST segment monitoring
- Location, severity, quality, and duration of pain
- Continuously monitor cardiac rhythm
- Oxygen saturation levels
- Hourly urine output – greater than 30 mL/ hr indicates renal perfusion
- Laboratory data: Cardiac enzymes, electrolytes, ABGs

NANDA Nursing Diagnoses

Δ   Ineffective tissue perfusion

Δ   Decreased cardiac output

Δ   Acute pain

Δ   Anxiety/fear

Δ   Activity intolerance

Nursing Interventions

Δ   Administer **oxygen** (4 to 6 L), as prescribed.

Δ   Obtain and maintain IV access.

Δ   Promote energy conservation (for example, cluster nursing interventions).

Δ   Administer **medications** as prescribed.

- Vasodilators oppose coronary artery vasospasm and reduce preload and afterload, decreasing myocardial oxygen demand. Nitroglycerin is the medication of choice.

- Analgesics reduce pain, which decreases sympathetic stress leading to preload reduction. Morphine is the medication of choice.

- Beta-blockers have antidysrhythmic and antihypertensive properties and decrease the imbalance between myocardial oxygen supply and demand by reducing afterload. In acute MI, beta-blockers decrease infarct size and improve short- and long-term survival rates.

- Thrombolytic agents can be effective in dissolving thrombi if administered within the first 6 hr following an MI. Contraindications include recent surgery, recent head trauma, and any other situation that poses an additive risk for bleeding internally.

- Antiplatelet agents inhibit cyclooxygenase, which produces thromboxane A2, a potent platelet activator. Aspirin is the medication of choice.

- Anticoagulants (heparin, low molecular weight heparins) are used to prevent the recurrence of a clot after fibrinolysis.

- Glycoprotein IIB/IIIA inhibitors (thrombolytic agents) prevent the binding of fibrogen and thus block platelet aggregation. In combination with aspirin therapy, IIB/IIA inhibitors are standard therapy.

Δ Teach the client to avoid straining, strenuous exercise, or emotional stress when possible.

Δ Client education regarding **response to chest pain**:

- Stop activity and rest.

- Place nitroglycerin tablet under tongue to dissolve (quick absorption).

- Repeat every 5 min if the pain is not relieved.

- Call 911 if the pain is not relieved in 15 min.

Δ Prepare the client for diagnostic examinations as prescribed and revascularization procedures (angiography, angioplasty, CABG).

Δ Encourage lifestyle modifications to lower incidence of recurrence: smoking cessation, limiting saturated fat/cholesterol, weight management, and blood pressure control. Make appropriate referrals (for example, dietician).

Complications and Nursing Implications

Δ **Acute MI** is a complication of angina not relieved by rest or nitroglycerin.

Δ **Cardiogenic shock** is a serious complication of pump failure, commonly following an MI of 40% or more of the left ventricle. It is Class IV heart failure. Symptoms include tachycardia, hypotension (blood pressure less than 90 mm Hg or less than 30 mm Hg from baseline blood pressure), inadequate urinary output (less than 30 mL/hr), altered level of consciousness, respiratory distress (crackles, tachypnea), cool, clammy skin, decreased peripheral pulses, and chest pain. Intervention includes administration of oxygen; possible intubation and ventilation; IV administration of morphine, diuretics, and/or nitroglycerin to decrease preload; and IV administration of vasopressors and/or positive inotropes to increase cardiac output and to maintain organ perfusion. Other possible emergency interventions include use of an intra-aortic balloon pump and/or emergency coronary artery bypass surgery.

Δ **Ischemic mitral regurgitation** due to myocardial ischemia may be evidenced by the development of new cardiac murmur.

Δ **Dysrhythmias** due to myocardial hypoperfusion require vigilant continuous cardiac monitoring.

Δ **Ventricular aneurysms/rupture** due to myocardial necrosis may present as sudden chest pain, dysrhythmias, and severe hypotension.

Meeting the Needs of Older Adults

Δ An increased risk of coronary artery disease exists for older adult clients who are physically inactive, have one or more chronic diseases (hypertension, heart failure, and diabetes mellitus), and/or have lifestyle (smoking and diet) habits that contribute to atherosclerosis.

Δ The incidence of cardiac disease increases with age, especially in the presence of hypertension, diabetes mellitus, hypercholesterolemia, elevated homocystine, and highly sensitive C-reactive protein (HS-CRP).

Δ Older adult clients often do not feel the intense crushing pain because of an altered release of neurotransmitters that occurs in the aging process; therefore, many have atypical symptoms.

Δ Atherosclerotic changes related to aging predispose the heart to poor blood perfusion and oxygen delivery.

Δ Older adult clients with atherosclerosis typically have well-established collateral circulation in the blood vessels of the heart. For this reason, they are often saved the lethal complications associated with MI.

Primary Reference:

Ignatavicius, D. D., & Workman, M. L. (2006). *Medical-surgical nursing* (5th ed.). St. Louis, MO: Saunders.

Additional Resources:

Black, J. M., & Hawks, J. H. (2005). *Medical-surgical nursing: Clinical management for positive outcomes* (7th ed.). St. Louis, MO: Saunders.

NANDA International (2004). *NANDA nursing diagnoses: Definitions and classification 2005-2006.* Philadelphia: NANDA.

Chapter 34: Angina and Myocardial Infarction

Application Exercises

1. What assessments can a nurse perform to distinguish angina from MI?

2. What is the rationale for each of the following interventions?

Intervention	Rationale
Oxygen	
Beta-blocker	
ACE inhibitor	
Stool softener	
Nitroglycerin	
Morphine	
Thrombolytic agent	

3. When are the following cardiac enzymes first detectable?

Cardiac Enzyme	First detectable
CK-MB	
Troponin I or T	
Myoglobin	

4. A client with a diagnosis of MI reports that dyspnea began 2 weeks ago. Which of the following cardiac enzymes should the nurse assess to determine if the infarction occurred 14 days ago?

    A. CK-MB

    B. Troponin I

    C. Troponin T

    D. Myoglobin

5. A client asks why one aspirin per day has been prescribed. Which of the following is the nurse's best response?

      A. "Aspirin reduces the formation of blood clots that could cause a heart attack."

      B. "Aspirin will decrease any pain due to myocardial ischemia."

      C. "Aspirin will dissolve any clots that are forming in your coronary arteries."

      D. "Aspirin will relieve any headaches that are caused by your other medications."

6. A client with angina reports not being able to make all of the lifestyle changes recommended. Which of the following changes should the nurse suggest the client work on first?

      A. Diet modification

      B. Relaxation exercises

      C. Smoking cessation

      D. Taking omega-3 capsules

Chapter 34: Angina and Myocardial Infarction

Application Exercises Answer Key

1. What assessments can a nurse perform to distinguish angina from MI?

Angina can be relieved by rest and nitroglycerin.

2. What is the rationale for each of the following interventions?

Intervention	Rationale
Oxygen	Increases myocardial oxygen supply.
Beta-blocker	Antidysrhythmic, antihypertensive, reduces afterload to decrease myocardial oxygen consumption, decreases infarct size, and improves survival rates.
ACE inhibitor	Decreases afterload and therefore myocardial oxygen consumption.
Stool softener	Reduces straining which could precipitate MI, vasovagal effect.
Nitroglycerin	Reduces preload and afterload and dilates coronary arteries, increases myocardial oxygen supply and reduces oxygen consumption.
Morphine	Reduces preload by venous vasodilation decreasing myocardial oxygen consumption, relieves pain, decreases sympathetic nervous system stimulation.
Thrombolytic agent	Removes clot that is causing ischemia/infarction.

3. When are the following cardiac enzymes first detectable?

Cardiac Enzyme	First detectable
CK-MB	4-6 hr
Troponin I or T	3 hr
Myoglobin	2 hr

4. A client with a diagnosis of MI reports that dyspnea began 2 weeks ago. Which of the following cardiac enzymes should the nurse assess to determine if the infarction occurred 14 days ago?

    A. CK-MB

    B. Troponin I

    C. Troponin T

    D. Myoglobin

The Troponin T level does not disappear until after 14 to 21 days. CK-MB disappears after 3 days. Troponin I disappears after 7 days. Myoglobin levels disappear after 24 hr.

5. A client asks why one aspirin per day has been prescribed. Which of the following is the nurse's best response?

    A. "Aspirin reduces the formation of blood clots that could cause a heart attack."

    B. "Aspirin will decrease any pain due to myocardial ischemia."

    C. "Aspirin will dissolve any clots that are forming in your coronary arteries."

    D. "Aspirin will relieve any headaches that are caused by your other medications."

Aspirin decreases platelet aggregation. One aspirin a day is not sufficient to alleviate ischemic pain. Aspirin does not dissolve clots. Other medications may cause headaches, but one aspirin per day is not administered as an analgesic.

6. A client with angina reports not being able to make all of the lifestyle changes recommended. Which of the following changes should the nurse suggest the client work on first?

    A. Diet modification

    B. Relaxation exercises

    C. Smoking cessation

    D. Taking omega-3 capsules

Nicotine causing vasoconstriction, elevating blood pressure and narrowing coronary arteries.

Unit 3
Section:

Nursing Care of Clients with Cardiovascular or Hematologic Disorders
Medical Emergencies: Cardiovascular

Chapter 35: **Shock**

Contributors: Susan Holcomb, PhD, ARNP, BC
Sharon Kumm, MN, MS, RN, CCRN

NCLEX-PN® Connections:

Learning Objective: Review and apply knowledge within "**Shock**" in readiness for performance of the following nursing activities as outlined by the NCLEX-PN® test plan:

Δ   Assist with relevant laboratory, diagnostic, and therapeutic procedures within the nursing role, including:

- Preparation of the client for the procedure.
- Accurate collection of specimens.
- Monitoring client status during and after the procedure.
- Reinforcing client teaching (before and following the procedure).
- Recognizing the client's response (expected, unexpected adverse response) to the procedure.
- Monitoring results.
- Monitoring and taking actions to prevent or minimize the risk of complications.
- Notifying the primary care provider of signs of complications.

Δ   Recognize signs and symptoms of the client's problem and complete the proper documentation.

Δ   Provide and document care based on the client's health alteration.

Δ   Monitor and document vital signs changes.

Δ   Interpret data that need to be reported immediately.

Δ   Reinforce client education on managing the client's health problem.

Δ   Recognize and respond to emergency situations, including notification of the primary care provider.

Δ   Review the client's response to emergency interventions and complete the proper documentation.

Δ   Provide care that meets the age-related needs of clients 65 years of age or older, including recognizing expected physiological changes.

Key Points

Δ   Shock is a **state of inadequate tissue perfusion** that impairs maintenance of normal cellular metabolism. Any condition that compromises oxygen delivery to tissues and organs can cause shock.

Δ   Shock is identified by its underlying cause:

- **Cardiogenic** – pump failure or heart failure.

- **Hypovolemic** – decrease in intravascular volume of 10 to 15% or more.

- **Distributive** – widespread vasodilation and increased capillary permeability.

- **Obstructive** – mechanical blockage in the heart or great vessels.

Δ   All types of shock progress through the same stages and produce similar effects on body systems.

- **Initial** – no visible changes in client parameters, changes on the cellular level only.

- **Compensatory** – measures to increase cardiac output to restore tissue perfusion and oxygenation.

- **Progressive** – compensatory mechanisms begin to fail.

- **Refractory** – irreversible shock, total body failure.

Δ   The cause of shock, category of shock, and the stage of shock (initial, compensatory, progressive, or refractory) direct treatment.

Key Factors

Δ   **Risk Factors for Shock**

- **Cardiogenic** – **pump failure** due to myocardial infarction, heart failure, cardiomyopathy, dysrhythmias, cardiac tamponade, and valvular rupture or stenosis.

- **Hypovolemic** – **excessive fluid loss** from diuresis; vomiting/diarrhea; blood loss secondary to surgery, trauma, or gynecologic/obstetric causes; burns; and diabetic ketoacidosis.

- **Distributive** is divided into three types:

  ◊   **Septic** – endotoxins and other mediators causing massive vasodilation. The most common cause is gram-negative bacteria.

  ◊   **Neurogenic** – loss of sympathetic tone (vasoconstriction) causing massive vasodilation. Trauma, spinal shock, and epidural anesthesia are among the causes.

◊ **Anaphylactic** – antigen-antibody reaction causing massive vasodilation. Allergens inhaled, swallowed, contacted, or introduced intravenously are causes.

- **Obstructive – blockage of great vessels.** Cardiac valve stenosis, pulmonary embolism, and aortic dissection are among the causes.

Diagnostic Procedures and Nursing Interventions

Δ **Arterial Blood Gases** (ABGs): Decreased tissue oxygenation (for example, acidosis)

Δ **Hemodynamic Monitoring**: Decreased cardiac output, pressures within various cardiac chambers

Δ **Cardiogenic**

- Electrocardiogram (ECG)
- Cardiac echocardiogram
- Computerized tomography (CT)
- Cardiac catheterization
- Chest x-ray
- Cardiac enzymes – creatine phosphokinase (CPK), troponin

Δ **Hypovolemic**

- Hemoglobin and hematocrit – decreased with hemorrhage, increased with dehydration
- Type and cross match for possible blood transfusion
- Investigate possible sources of bleeding
    - ◊ Blood in nasogastric drainage or stools
    - ◊ Esophogastroduodenoscopy
    - ◊ CT scan of abdomen

Δ **Septic**

- Cultures: blood, urine, wound
- Coagulation tests: prothrombin time (PT), international normalized ratio (INR), activated partial thromboplastin time (aPTT)

Δ Obstructive

- Echocardiogram
- CT scan

Assessments

Δ   Monitor for **signs and symptoms.**

- Hypoxia

- Hypotension (mean arterial pressure < 60 mm Hg)

- Tachycardia, weak thready pulse

	Initial	Compensatory	Progressive	Refractory
Heart rate (beats/min)	≤ 100	> 100	≥ 120	≥ 140
Systolic blood pressure	Normal	Normal/ Increased	70-90 mm Hg	< 50-60 mm Hg
Respiratory rate (per minute)	Normal	20-30	30-40	> 40
Urine output (mL/hr)	≥ 30	20-30	5-20	Negligible
Skin	Cool, pink, dry	Cold, pale, dry/ moist	Cold, pale, moist	Cold, mottled, cyanotic, dry
Capillary refill	Normal	Slightly delayed	Delayed	Not noted
Miscellaneous	May see rashes with septic or anaphylactic shock. May see angioedema with anaphylactic shock. Rales are possible with cardiogenic shock. Seizures may occur with all forms of shock. Fever may occur with all forms of shock, but especially with septic shock.			

Δ   Assess/Monitor

- **Oxygenation status (priority)**

- Vital signs

- Urinary output

- Level of consciousness

- Cardiac rhythm (if monitored)

- Skin color, temperature, moisture, capillary refill, turgor

- Symptoms indicating body system compromise: chest pain; changes in heart tones, lung sounds, bowel sounds, neurological status

NANDA Nursing Diagnoses

Δ   Decreased cardiac output

Δ   Impaired gas exchange

Δ   Ineffective tissue perfusion

Δ   Deficient fluid volume

Δ   Anxiety

Nursing Interventions

Δ   Identify clients at risk for developing shock based on risk factors.

Δ   If shock process is suspected:

- Obtain vital signs, including pulse oximetry.

- Obtain any laboratory or diagnostic work per protocol that may help identify shock.

- Calculate urine output and begin monitoring hourly output. Report output less than 30 mL/hr.

- Perform a complete assessment.

Δ   **Place the client on high-flow oxygen, such as a 100% nonrebreather face mask.** If the client has chronic obstructive pulmonary disease, place on a 2 L nasal cannula; increase the oxygen flow as needed.

Δ   Be sure patent IV access is available.

Δ   For **hypotension**, place the client flat, flat with legs elevated, or in Trendelenburg position to increase venous return.

Δ   Notify the primary care provider of findings.

Δ   Initiate orders to intervene with shock, including transfer to the intensive care unit, surgery, other specialty unit, or diagnostic area.

Δ   Explain procedures and findings to the client and family and reassure the client and family.

Δ   If in the intensive care unit:

- Prepare for and carry out hemodynamic monitoring.

- Administer medications as ordered.

- Be sure IV access is patent.

- Place the client on continuous cardiac monitoring.

Δ   Administer **medications** as prescribed

- Hypovolemic

  ◊   Volume replacement: isotonic crystalloids or colloids (including blood products)

  ◊   Vasopressors to increase blood pressure. **ALERT**: *In hypovolemic shock, replace volume first to enhance blood pressure before using vasopressors.*

- **Cardiogenic**

  ◊   Afterload reducers

  ◊   Inotropic agents

  ◊   Vasopressors

- **Anaphylactic**

  ◊   Antihistamines

  ◊   Epinephrine

- **Septic**

  ◊   Antibiotics sensitive to cultured organism(s)

  ◊   Norepinephrine to decrease vasodilation

  ◊   Heparin initially and then clotting factors, platelets, and plasma

- **Neurogenic**

  ◊   Volume replacement

  ◊   Norepinephrine to decrease vasodilation

- **All types of shock**

  ◊   Proton pump inhibitors (PPIs) possible for all clients in shock to protect against stress ulcer development

  ◊   Deep vein thrombosis (DVT) prophylaxis (heparin, low-molecular weight heparin) possible with all shock clients

Δ   Prevention

- Educate the client about risk factors for accidents, myocardial infarction, diabetes mellitus, urinary tract infection, etc.

- Educate the client about interventions to avoid dehydration with gastrointestinal illness, genitourinary infections, etc.

Complications and Nursing Implications

Δ **Organ Dysfunction**, such as myocardial infarction, acute/adult respiratory distress syndrome (ARDS), renal failure, and liver failure due to inadequate tissue perfusion. Assess organ function and take interventions to compensate for dysfunction (administration of clotting factors, dialysis).

Δ **Disseminated intravascular coagulation (DIC)** is a complication of septic shock. Thousands of small clots form within organ capillaries (liver, kidney, heart, brain) creating hypoxia and anaerobic metabolism. As circulation becomes more compromised, skin becomes cool and pale/cyanotic. As a result of massive clot formation, fibrinogen resources are taxed and the client is at increased risk for hemorrhage. The client develops diffuse petechiae and ecchymoses, and blood oozes from membranes and puncture sites.

Meeting the Needs of Older Adults

Δ Older adult clients will be less likely to have the ability to stay in the compensatory stage of shock for very long. They may not be able to easily increase their cardiac output by increasing pumping ability. They also have more problems with the vasoconstriction necessary for maintenance of blood pressure due to decreased effectiveness of baroreceptors in the carotids and aortic arch.

Δ Older adult clients are more at risk for myocardial infarction and cardiomyopathy.

Δ Older adult clients are more prone to dehydration due to decreased fluid intake, protein intake, and use of medications, such as diuretics. It will not take as much in the way of fluid losses through vomiting/diarrhea, for older adult clients to become dehydrated.

Δ Urosepsis is more frequent in older adult clients, since they seem to have diminished sensations of burning and urgency to trigger the recognition of a urinary tract infection (UTI). Many older adult clients live in extended care facilities, where urinary catheters are used, increasing the likelihood of urosepsis.

Primary Reference:

Ignatavicius, D. D., & Workman, M. L. (2006). *Medical-surgical nursing* (5th ed.). St. Louis, MO: Saunders.

Additional Resources:

LeMone, P. & Burke, K. (2004). *Medical-surgical nursing: Critical thinking in client care* (3rd ed.). Upper Saddle River, NJ: Prentice Hall.

NANDA International (2004). *NANDA nursing diagnoses: Definitions and classification 2005-2006*. Philadelphia: NANDA.

Chapter 35: Shock

Application Exercises

1. Identify the impact of each of the following classifications of shock on the given hemodynamic values (increased or decreased).

	Hypovolemic	Cardiogenic	Septic	Neurogenic	Anaphylactic
Heart rate					
Blood pressure					
Preload					
Afterload					

Scenario: A client is admitted following a colon resection. The client is receiving oxygen at 3 L/min per nasal cannula and has a right forearm IV with lactated Ringer's infusing at 125 mL/hr, a saline lock in the left forearm, a urinary catheter, and an epidural catheter for pain management. The abdominal dressing is dry and intact. Orders include:

Cefotaxime 1 g IV every 12 hr

Metronidazole 1 g IV every 12 hr

Dextrose 5% ½ normal saline at 125 mL/hr

2. What types of shock is the client at risk to develop?

3. What should the nurse monitor to determine if each type of shock is developing?

4. A nurse should anticipate the use of afterload-reducing agents in which of the following types of shock?

   A. Cardiogenic
   B. Obstructive
   C. Hypovolemic
   D. Distributive

5. The focus of the collaborative management of septic shock is aimed toward

    A. limiting fluids to minimize the possibility of heart failure.

    B. finding and eradicating the cause of the infection.

    C. discontinuing all IV lines as a possible cause of sepsis.

    D. administering vasoactive substances to increase blood flow to vital organs.

6. The nursing measure that can best enhance management of hypovolemic shock is

    A. insertion of large-diameter peripheral intravenous catheters.

    B. positioning the client in Trendelenburg position.

    C. forcing at least 240 mL of fluid orally each hour.

    D. administering IV antibiotics to control the source of the shock.

7. A client is brought to the emergency department with an allergic reaction to a bee sting. The client experiences wheezing and swelling of the tongue. Which of the following medications should the nurse expect to administer?

    A. Corticosteroids

    B. Antihistamine

    C. Epinephrine

    D. Albuterol inhaler

8. An older adult client is admitted with suspected hypovolemic shock. Which of the following assessment findings supports the diagnosis?

    A. Temperature 38.4° C (101.1° F)

    B. Urine output 20 mL/hr, dark amber color

    C. Skin on forearm tents

    D. Oral mucous membranes moist

Chapter 35: Shock

Application Exercises Answer Key

1. Identify the impact of each of the following classifications of shock on the given hemodynamic values (increased or decreased).

	Hypovolemic	Cardiogenic	Septic	Neurogenic	Anaphylactic
Heart rate	Increased	Increased	Increased	Decreased	Increased
Blood pressure	Decreased	Decreased	Decreased	Decreased	Decreased
Preload	Decreased	Increased	Decreased	Decreased	Decreased
Afterload	Increased	Increased	Decreased	Decreased	Decreased

Scenario: A client is admitted following a colon resection. The client is receiving oxygen at 3 L/min per nasal cannula and has a right forearm IV with lactated Ringer's infusing at 125 mL/hr, a saline lock in the left forearm, a urinary catheter, and an epidural catheter for pain management. The abdominal dressing is dry and intact. Orders include:

Cefotaxime 1 g IV every 12 hr

Metronidazole 1 g IV every 12 hr

Dextrose 5% ½ normal saline at 125 mL/hr

2. What types of shock is the client at risk to develop?

Hypovolemic – due to bleeding and fluid collection in peritoneal cavity

Septic – due to colon surgery

Anaphylactic – due to antibiotics

Neurogenic – due to epidural analgesia

Obstructive – due to pulmonary emboli if deep vein thrombosis develops

3. What should the nurse monitor to determine if each type of shock is developing?

Hypovolemic – vital signs, intake and output, skin turgor, abdominal girth

Septic – vital signs, temperature, wound

Anaphylactic – vital signs, lung sounds

Neurogenic – vital signs, movement and sensation of legs, peripheral pulses

Obstructive – for deep vein thrombosis

---

4. A nurse should anticipate the use of afterload-reducing agents in which of the following types of shock?

  A. Cardiogenic
  B. Obstructive
  C. Hypovolemic
  D. Distributive

Reducing afterload will allow the heart to pump more effectively. The high afterload is due to obstruction of blood flow, and afterload-reducing agents will not remove the obstruction. Fluid replacement and reduction of further fluid loss are the focus of management of hypovolemic shock. All three forms of distributive shock result in decreased afterload from vasodilation.

5. The focus of the collaborative management of septic shock is aimed toward

  A. limiting fluids to minimize the possibility of heart failure.
  B. finding and eradicating the cause of the infection.
  C. discontinuing all IV lines as a possible cause of sepsis.
  D. administering vasoactive substances to increase blood flow to vital organs.

Septic shock is caused by some form of infection. Large amounts of fluid may be given to fill the increased vascular space caused by the vasodilation. IV lines may be cultured to determine if they are the source of infection, but the client will need IV fluids. Vasoactive substances may be administered, but the focus is on removing the cause of the shock.

6. The nursing measure that can best enhance management of hypovolemic shock is

A. insertion of large-diameter peripheral intravenous catheters.

B. positioning the client in Trendelenburg position.

C. forcing at least 240 mL of fluid orally each hour.

D. administering IV antibiotics to control the source of the shock.

Management involves replacing lost fluid. Raising the legs above the level of the heart is a temporary measure for hypotension. The client requires IV fluid replacement in hypovolemic shock. The gastrointestinal tract is one of the first body systems to have reduced perfusion in shock states. Hypovolemic shock is due to fluid loss. IV antibiotics are one of the primary treatment strategies of septic shock.

7. A client is brought to the emergency department with an allergic reaction to a bee sting. The client experiences wheezing and swelling of the tongue. Which of the following medications should the nurse expect to administer?

A. Corticosteroids

B. Antihistamine

C. Epinephrine

D. Albuterol inhaler

Epinephrine will treat both symptoms. Clients with allergic reactions are given prescriptions for epinephrine pens that they should carry with them at all times. Corticosteroids may be administered during allergic reactions to decrease respiratory inflammation. Antihistamines will decrease some swelling, but will not improve bronchospasms. This bronchodilator will improve wheezing, but will not affect the angioedema causing the tongue swelling.

8. An older adult client is admitted with suspected hypovolemic shock. Which of the following assessment findings supports the diagnosis?

A. Temperature 38.4° C (101.1° F)

B. Urine output 20 mL/hr, dark amber color

C. Skin on forearm tents

D. Oral mucous membranes moist

Urine is concentrated with fluid deficit. This suggests septic shock, but might be due to severe dehydration. The skin of older adults has poor elasticity; skin turgor should be tested on the forehead or over the sternum. Fluid deficits cause dry mucous membranes.

Unit 3   Nursing Care of Clients with Cardiovascular or Hematologic Disorders

Section: Medical Emergencies: Cardiovascular

Chapter 36:   Acute Pulmonary Edema

Contributor: Sharon Kumm, MN, MS, RN, CCRN

NCLEX-PN® Connections:

Learning Objective: Review and apply knowledge within "**Acute Pulmonary Edema**" in readiness for performance of the following nursing activities as outlined by the NCLEX-PN® test plan:

Δ   Assist with relevant laboratory, diagnostic, and therapeutic procedures within the nursing role, including:

- Preparation of the client for the procedure.

- Accurate collection of specimens.

- Monitoring client status during and after the procedure.

- Reinforcing client teaching (before and following the procedure).

- Recognizing the client's response (expected, unexpected adverse response) to the procedure.

- Monitoring results.

- Monitoring and taking actions to prevent or minimize the risk of complications.

- Notifying the primary care provider of signs of complications.

Δ   Recognize signs and symptoms of the client's problem and complete the proper documentation.

Δ   Provide and document care based on the client's health alteration.

Δ   Monitor and document vital signs changes.

Δ   Interpret data that need to be reported immediately.

Δ   Reinforce client education on managing the client's health problem.

Δ   Recognize and respond to emergency situations, including notification of the primary care provider.

Δ   Review the client's response to emergency interventions and complete the proper documentation.

Δ   Provide care that meets the age-related needs of clients 65 years of age or older, including recognizing expected physiological changes.

Key Points

- Δ Pulmonary edema is a severe, **life-threatening accumulation of fluid in the alveoli and interstitial spaces of the lung**.

- Δ **Severe left ventricular failure** causes blood to back up into the left atrium and the pulmonary circulation, which leads to hypoxemia.

- Δ Cardiogenic factors are the most common cause of pulmonary edema. It is a complication of various heart and lung diseases and usually occurs from increased pulmonary vascular pressure secondary to severe cardiac dysfunction.

- Δ Non-cardiac pulmonary edema can occur due to barbiturate or opiate overdose, inhalation of irritating gases, rapid administration of intravenous fluids, and after a pneumonectomy evacuation of pleural effusion.

- Δ Neurogenic pulmonary edema develops after a head injury.

Key Factors

- Δ **Risk Factors for Pulmonary Edema**

  - **Acute myocardial infarction** (MI)

  - **Fluid volume overload**

  - Hypertension

  - **Valvular heart disease**

  - Post pneumonectomy

  - Post evacuation of pleural effusion

  - Acute respiratory failure

  - Left-sided heart failure

  - High altitude exposure or deep sea diving

  - Trauma

  - Sepsis

  - Drug overdose

Diagnostic Procedures and Nursing Interventions

- Δ PaO_2 and SaO_2 are significantly decreased.

- Δ Chest x-rays will show fluid in or around the lung space or an enlarged heart.

- Δ Hemodynamic testing: Increased pulmonary artery pressure, increased pulmonary artery wedge pressure, decreased cardiac output

Assessments

Δ   Monitor for **signs and symptoms.**

- **Persistent cough with pink, frothy sputum (cardinal sign)**
- Tachypnea, dyspnea, **orthopnea**
- Restlessness, anxiety, inability to sleep
- Hypoxemia
- Cyanosis (later stage)
- Crackles
- Tachycardia
- Confusion, stupor
- S_3 heart sound
- Increased pulmonary artery occlusion pressure

Δ   **Assess/Monitor**

- Vital signs every 15 min until stable
- Pulse oximetry (continuously)
- Respiratory status for respiratory compromise
- Intake and output
- Hemodynamic status (pulmonary capillary wedge pressures, cardiac output)
- Blood work as indicated

NANDA Nursing Diagnoses

Δ   Impaired gas exchange

Δ   Fluid volume excess

Δ   Decreased cardiac output

Δ   Anxiety

Δ   Fatigue

Δ   Activity intolerance

Nursing Interventions

Δ **Maintain a patent airway. Suction as needed.**

Δ Position the client in **high-Fowler's position** with feet and legs dependent or sitting on the side of the bed to decrease preload.

Δ **Administer oxygen** using a high-flow rebreather mask. BiPAP or intubation/ventilation may become necessary. Be prepared to intervene quickly.

Δ Restrict fluid intake (slow or discontinue infusing IV fluids).

Δ Administer **medications** as prescribed.

- **Rapid-acting diuretics**, such as furosemide (Lasix) and bumetanide, to promote fluid excretion

- **Morphine** to decrease sympathetic nervous system response and anxiety and to promote mild vasodilation

- Vasodilators (nitroglycerin, sodium nitroprusside) to decrease preload and afterload

- Inotropic agents, such as digoxin (Lanoxin) and dobutamine, to improve cardiac output

- Antihypertensives, such as angiotensin-converting enzyme (ACE) inhibitors and beta-blockers

Δ Monitor hourly urine output. Report intake greater than output and/or hourly urine output less than 30 mL/hr.

Δ Monitor laboratory values, such as serial ABGs and serum potassium (hypokalemia risk with rapid-acting diuretics).

Δ Provide emotional support for the client and family.

Δ **Client Education** (include family members if this is a long-term problem)

- Instruct the client on effective breathing techniques.

- Instruct the client on medications.

  ◊ Stress the importance of continuing to take medications even if the client is feeling better.

  ◊ Teach common side effects and reasons to contact the primary care provider.

- Instruct the client on a low-sodium diet and fluid restriction.

- **The client should measure weight daily at the same time. Notify the primary care provider of a gain of more than 2 lb in 1 day or 5 lb in 1 week.**

Meeting the Needs of Older Adults

Δ   Increased risk for pulmonary edema occurs related to decreased cardiac output and congestive heart failure (CHF).

Δ   Increased risk for fluid and electrolyte imbalances occurs when the older adult client receives treatment with diuretics.

Δ   Intravenous infusions must be administered at a slower rate to prevent circulatory overload.

Primary Reference:

Ignatavicius, D. D., & Workman, M. L. (2006). *Medical-surgical nursing* (5th ed.). St. Louis, MO: Saunders.

Additional Resources:

Black, J. M., & Hawks, J. H. (2005). *Medical-surgical nursing: Clinical management for positive outcomes* (7th ed.). St. Louis, MO: Saunders.

NANDA International (2004). *NANDA nursing diagnoses: Definitions and classification 2005-2006*. Philadelphia: NANDA.

Chapter 36: Acute Pulmonary Edema

Application Exercises

1. Provide the rationale for each of the following interventions for a client with pulmonary edema.

Nursing Intervention	Rationale
Administer oxygen.	
High-Fowler's position	
Administer morphine sulfate IV.	
Restrict fluid intake.	
Monitor pulse oximetry.	
Administer diuretic.	
Daily weight	
Oral care	

2. A client is being admitted for pulmonary edema. What equipment should the nurse have at the bedside?

3. A family member of a client admitted with pulmonary edema asks why the nurse is administering morphine sulfate when the client does not have pain. Which of the following is the nurse's best response?

      A. "Morphine decreases anxiety and will help the client get some rest."

      B. "After breathing so rapidly, the muscles in the chest will begin to hurt."

      C. "The blood pressure is too high and this will help lower it so that breathing is easier."

      D. "Morphine dilates veins and decreases blood returning to the heart and lungs."

4. Which of the following assessment findings is the best indicator that the client may be developing pulmonary edema?

      A. Dyspnea

      B. Orthopnea

      C. Tachypnea

      D. Tachycardia

5. Which of the following clients should the nurse monitor closely for the development of pulmonary edema?

   A. 76-year-old client with history of heart failure
   B. 33-year-old client with asthma attack
   C. 46-year-old client with abdominal surgery
   D. 51-year-old client with leg fracture

6. A nurse hears crackles throughout the chest and an S_3 heart sound. The client has a productive cough of frothy sputum, and pulse oximetry reveals oxygen saturation of 76%. Which of the following should the nurse do next?

   A. Order a chest x-ray to assess if fluid is accumulating in the lungs.
   B. Notify the primary care provider and prepare to insert a chest tube.
   C. Percuss the posterior chest to mark areas of dullness.
   D. Sit the client at the side of bed with legs dependent and feet supported.

Chapter 36: Acute Pulmonary Edema

Application Exercises Answer Key

1. Provide the rationale for each of the following interventions for a client with pulmonary edema.

Nursing Intervention	Rationale
Administer oxygen.	Increase oxygen supply.
High-Fowler's position	Decrease the amount of fluid returning to heart (preload) to improve cardiac output.
Administer morphine sulfate IV.	Decrease anxiety, relieve feeling of shortness of breath, decrease amount of fluid returning to the heart (preload).
Restrict fluid intake.	Decrease fluid volume.
Monitor pulse oximetry.	Evaluate success of therapeutic management.
Administer diuretic.	Decrease fluid volume.
Daily weight	Best indicator of total body fluid volume.
Oral care	Promote integrity of oral mucosa – the client has fluid restriction and may be breathing through the mouth.

2. A client is being admitted for pulmonary edema. What equipment should the nurse have at the bedside?

Oxygen

Suction equipment, including catheters

Pillows for support

Oral swabs

3. A family member of a client admitted with pulmonary edema asks why the nurse is administering morphine sulfate when the client does not have pain. Which of the following is the nurse's best response?

      A. "Morphine decreases anxiety and will help the client get some rest."

      B. "After breathing so rapidly, the muscles in the chest will begin to hurt."

      C. "The blood pressure is too high and this will help lower it so that breathing is easier."

      D. "Morphine dilates veins and decreases blood returning to the heart and lungs."

Morphine causes vasodilation resulting in decreased preload, slightly decreased afterload, and decreased sympathetic nervous system stimulation. Although morphine will decrease anxiety, the goal is not to help the client rest. Chest muscles may hurt after rapid breathing, but this is not the reason for giving morphine. Morphine may decrease the blood pressure slightly, but it has more effect on venous dilation.

4. Which of the following assessment findings is the best indicator that the client may be developing pulmonary edema?

      A. Dyspnea

      B. Orthopnea

      C. Tachypnea

      D. Tachycardia

Orthopnea means the client cannot breathe while lying down, frequently due to fluid accumulation. Dyspnea occurs when any respiratory compromise occurs, not specifically pulmonary edema. Rapid respirations are not a specific indicator of pulmonary edema. Tachypnea occurs whenever the body needs to increase oxygen or to reduce carbon dioxide. A rapid heart rate occurs whenever the body needs an increase in oxygen or with sympathetic nervous system stimulation. This may be due to exercise, anxiety, or fever.

5. Which of the following clients should the nurse monitor closely for the development of pulmonary edema?

   A. 76-year-old client with history of heart failure
   B. 33-year-old client with asthma attack
   C. 46-year-old client with abdominal surgery
   D. 51-year-old client with leg fracture

Both age and history of heart failure put this client at risk for development of pulmonary edema. Asthma causes narrowing of airways, but will not cause pulmonary edema unless pulmonary hypertension develops. Fluid volume deficit is more of a concern with abdominal surgery than fluid overload. A client with a leg fracture may be at risk for pulmonary embolism, but not for pulmonary edema.

6. A nurse hears crackles throughout the chest and an S_3 heart sound. The client has a productive cough of frothy sputum, and pulse oximetry reveals oxygen saturation of 76%. Which of the following should the nurse do next?

   A. Order a chest x-ray to assess if fluid is accumulating in the lungs.
   B. Notify the primary care provider and prepare to insert a chest tube.
   C. Percuss the posterior chest to mark areas of dullness.
   D. Sit the client at the side of bed with legs dependent and feet supported.

The first action should be to improve breathing by administering oxygen as prescribed and positioning the client upright with legs dependent. A prescription is required to order a chest x-ray. The nurse will notify the primary care provider at a later time. At this time, something needs to be done to improve breathing.

Unit 4
Nursing Care of Clients with Fluid and Electrolyte Needs

Section: Nursing Care of Clients with Fluid and Electrolyte Imbalances

Chapter 37:   Fluid Imbalances
Contributor: Linda Turchin, MSN, RN

⟳ NCLEX-PN® Connections:

Learning Objective: Review and apply knowledge within **"Fluid Imbalances"** in readiness for performance of the following nursing activities as outlined by the NCLEX-PN® test plan:

Δ   Assist with laboratory, diagnostic, and therapeutic procedures related to the treatment of fluid imbalances within the nursing role, including:

  • Preparation of the client for the procedure.

  • Accurate collection of specimens.

  • Monitoring client status during and after procedure.

  • Reinforcing client teaching (before and following procedure).

  • Recognizing the client's response (expected, unexpected adverse response) to the procedure.

  • Monitoring results.

  • Monitoring and taking actions to prevent or minimize the risk of complications.

  • Notifying the primary care provider of signs of complications.

Δ   Recognize signs and symptoms of the client's problem – fluid imbalances – and complete the proper documentation.

Δ   Provide and document care based on the client's health alteration – fluid imbalances.

Δ   Monitor and document vital signs changes.

Δ   Interpret data that need to be reported immediately.

Δ   Reinforce client education on managing the client's health problem – fluid imbalances.

Δ   Recognize and respond to emergency situations, including notification of the primary care provider.

Δ   Review the client's response to emergency interventions and complete the proper documentation.

Δ   Provide care that meets the age-related needs of clients 65 years of age or older, including recognizing expected physiological changes.

Fluid Volume Deficits

📖 Key Points

Δ   Body fluids are distributed between **intracellular (ICF)** and **extracellular (ECF) fluid compartments.**

Δ   Fluid can move between compartments (through **selectively permeable membranes**) by a variety of methods **(diffusion, active transport, filtration, and osmosis)** in order to maintain homeostasis.

Δ   **Fluid volume deficits (FVDs)** include **hypovolemia** (body loses both water and electrolytes from the ECF) and **dehydration** (water is lost from the body, but there is no loss of electrolytes).

Δ   **Hypovolemia** can lead to **hypovolemic shock.**

Key Factors

Δ   **Risk Factors/Causes** of Hypovolemia

  •   Abnormal **gastrointestinal (GI) losses:** Vomiting, nasogastric suctioning, diarrhea

  •   Abnormal **skin losses:** Diaphoresis

  •   Abnormal **renal losses:** Diuretic therapy, diabetes insipidus, renal disease, adrenal insufficiency, osmotic diuresis

  •   **Third spacing:** Peritonitis, intestinal obstruction, ascites, burns

  •   **Hemorrhage**

  •   **Altered intake**, such as nothing by mouth (NPO)

Δ   **Risk Factors/Causes** of Dehydration

  •   Hyperventilation

  •   Diabetic ketoacidosis

  •   Enteral feeding without sufficient water intake

Δ   **Compensatory mechanisms** include sympathetic nervous system responses of increased thirst, antidiuretic hormone (ADH) release, and aldosterone release.

Diagnostic Procedures and Nursing Interventions

Δ **Expected Findings**

- **Hemoglobin (Hgb) and hematocrit (Hct)**

  ◊ Hypovolemia: **Increased Hgb and Hct**

  ◊ Dehydration: Increased (**hemoconcentration**)

- **Serum osmolarity**

  ◊ Dehydration: Increased (**hemoconcentration**) osmolarity (> 300 mOsm/L) — increased protein, blood urea nitrogen (BUN), electrolytes, glucose

- **Urine specific gravity and osmolarity**

  ◊ Dehydration: Increased (**concentration**)

- **Serum sodium**

  ◊ Dehydration: Increased (**hemoconcentration**)

Δ **Nursing Interventions**

- **Report abnormal findings** to the primary care provider.

Assessments

Δ **Expected Client Findings**

- **Vital signs:** Hyperthermia, **tachycardia**, thready pulse, **hypotension**, orthostatic hypotension, decreased central venous pressure

- **Neuromusculoskeletal:** Dizziness, **syncope**, **confusion**, **weakness**, fatigue

- **GI:** Thirst, dry furrowed tongue, nausea/vomiting, anorexia, acute weight loss

- **Renal: Oliguria**

- **Other signs:** Diminished capillary refill, cool clammy skin, diaphoresis, sunken eyeballs, flattened neck veins

NANDA Nursing Diagnoses

Δ **Decreased cardiac output**

Δ Ineffective tissue perfusion

Δ Deficient fluid volume

Δ Risk for injury

Δ Impaired oral mucous membrane

Nursing Interventions

Δ Place the client in **shock position** (on back with legs elevated).

Δ **Fluid replacement:** Administer oral and IV fluids (crystalloid solutions such as Ringer's lactate; blood transfusions) as ordered.

Δ Monitor intake and output. Alert the primary care provider to urine output less than 0.5 mL/kg/hr for two consecutive hours.

Δ Monitor vital signs and heart rhythm.

Δ Monitor level of consciousness and maintain client safety.

Δ Treat underlying cause of fluid volume deficit.

Δ Encourage the client to change positions slowly.

Complications and Nursing Implications

Δ **Hypovolemic Shock**

- **Vital organ hypoxia/anoxia – decreased** hemoglobin **oxygen saturation** and **pulse pressure** (systolic-diastolic blood pressure)

- Administer **oxygen.**

- Provide **fluid replacement** with:

  ◊ Colloids (whole blood, packed RBCs, plasma, synthetic plasma expanders).

  ◊ Crystalloids (Ringer's lactate, normal saline).

- Administer **vasoconstrictors,** such as **dopamine** (Intropin) and norepinephrine (Levophed); **coronary vasodilators,** such as sodium nitroprusside (Nipride); and/or **positive inotropic medications,** such as dobutamine (Dobutrex).

- Perform hemodynamic monitoring.

Fluid Volume Excess

 Key Points

Δ Fluid volume excesses (FVEs) include **hypervolemia** (occurs when both water and sodium are retained in abnormally high proportions) and **overhydration** (occurs when more water is gained than electrolytes).

Key Factors

Δ   **Risk Factors/Causes** of **Overhydration**

- Water replacement without electrolyte replacement (for example, strenuous exercise with profuse diaphoresis)

Δ   **Risk Factors/Causes** of **Hypervolemia**

- **Chronic stimulus** to the kidney to **conserve sodium and water** (heart failure, cirrhosis, glucocorticosteroids)

- **Abnormal renal function** with reduced excretion of sodium and water (renal failure)

- Interstitial to plasma **fluid shifts** (hypertonic fluids, burns)

- **Age-related changes** in cardiovascular and renal function

- **Excessive sodium intake**

Δ   **Compensatory mechanisms** include increased release of natriuretic peptides, resulting in increased loss of sodium and water by the kidneys and the decreased release of aldosterone.

Diagnostic Procedures and Nursing Interventions

Δ   **Expected Findings**

- **Hemoglobin (Hgb) and hematocrit (Hct)**

  ◊   Overhydration: Decreased (**hemodilution**)

- **Serum osmolarity**

  ◊   Overhydration: Decreased (**hemodilution**) osmolarity (< 270 mOsm/L) — decreased protein and electrolytes

- **Serum sodium**

  ◊   Overhydration: Decreased (**hemodilution**)

- **Electrolytes, BUN, and creatinine**

  ◊   Hypervolemia: **Increased electrolytes, BUN, and creatinine**

Δ   **Nursing Interventions**

- **Report abnormal findings** to the primary care provider.

Assessments

Δ   **Expected Client Findings**

- **Vital signs: Tachycardia**, bounding pulse, **hypertension, tachypnea**, increased central venous pressure

- **Neuromusculoskeletal: Confusion**, muscle weakness

- **GI: Weight gain**, ascites
- **Respiratory: Dyspnea, orthopnea, crackles**
- **Other signs: Edema**, distended neck veins

NANDA Nursing Diagnoses

Δ Excess fluid volume

Δ Impaired gas exchange

Δ Impaired skin integrity

Nursing Interventions

Δ Assess breath sounds.

Δ Monitor arterial blood gases for hypoxemia and respiratory alkalosis.

Δ Position the client in **semi-Fowler's** position.

Δ Administer **oxygen** as needed.

Δ **Reduce IV flow rates.**

Δ Administer **diuretics** (osmotic, loop) as ordered.

Δ Monitor daily intake and output and weight.

- **Limit fluid and sodium** intake as ordered.

Δ Monitor and document presence of edema (pretibial, sacral, periorbital).

- Monitor and document circulation to the extremities.
- Turn and position the client at least every 2 hr.
- Support arms and legs to **decrease dependent edema** as appropriate.
- Monitor for/treat skin breakdown.

Complications and Nursing Implications

Δ **Pulmonary Edema**

- Signs and symptoms include **ascending crackles, dyspnea at rest**, and confusion.
- Position the client in **high-Fowler's**.
- Administer **IV morphine**.
- Administer IV diuretic.
- Prepare for **possible intubation** and mechanical ventilation.

Primary Reference:

Ignatavicius, D. D., & Workman, M. L. (2006). *Medical-surgical nursing* (5th ed.). St. Louis, MO: Saunders.

Additional Resources:

Heitz, U., & Horne, M. M. (2005). *Pocket guide to fluid, electrolyte, and acid-base balance* (5th ed.). St. Louis, MO: Mosby.

NANDA International (2004). *NANDA nursing diagnoses: Definitions and classification 2005-2006*. Philadelphia: NANDA.

Chapter 37: Fluid Imbalances

Application Exercises

Scenario: A 35-year-old male client is seen in the emergency department with reports of nausea, vomiting, dizziness, and weakness. History reveals that he had just completed a 10-mile run in preparation for an upcoming marathon when the onset of symptoms occurred. Physical assessment reveals dry oral mucous membranes, temperature 38.5° C (101.3° F), pulse 92 beats/min and thready, respirations 20/min, skin cool and diaphoretic, and blood pressure 102/64 mm Hg. His urine is concentrated with a high specific gravity.

1. What client findings are consistent with the presence of fluid volume deficit?

2. What history is supportive of the diagnosis?

3. Identify some examples of appropriate diagnostic interventions.

4. What collaborative actions are appropriate for addressing the client's altered fluid volume?

5. Provide examples of nursing diagnoses appropriate for this client.

Scenario: An 83-year-old female client is admitted to an acute care facility with dyspnea, weakness, weight gain of 2 lb, 1+ pitting edema of both lower extremities to mid calf, and bilateral crackles in lung bases. Assessment findings include: temperature 37.2° C (99° F), pulse 96 beats/min and bounding, respirations 26/min, pulse oximetry 94% on 3 L oxygen, and blood pressure 152/96 mm Hg. She is diagnosed with congestive heart failure (CHF) and fluid volume excess. IV furosemide (Lasix) is prescribed.

6. What data supports the presence of fluid volume excess?

7. Why is fluid volume excess a common complication of CHF?

8. What is the gerontological consideration regarding this client?

9. Which electrolyte should the nurse carefully monitor in this client and why?

Scenario: An 81-year-old male client living in an assisted living facility has become weak and confused. Usually a good eater, today he has eaten only 40% of his breakfast and lunch. He has required constant encouragement to drink. Assessment findings include: temperature 38.3° C (100.9° F), pulse rate 92 beats/min, respirations 20/min, and blood pressure 108/60 mm Hg. He has lost ¾ lb and he reports dizziness when assisted to the bathroom. He also has a nonproductive cough with diminished breath sounds in the right lower lobe. His urine is dark yellow.

10. Which of the above data supports fluid volume deficit?

11. Identify several appropriate nursing interventions for this client.

12. Identify several additional signs of fluid deficit that the nurse should be watching for in this client.

13. A client receiving 0.9% normal saline should be monitored for signs of

       A. fluid overload.
       B. fluid deficit.

14. An older adult client reports thirst, weakness, and dizziness. Assessment findings reveal dark yellow urine and dry oral mucous membranes. Based on these findings, what laboratory value alterations should be expected for each of the following?

       Hemoglobin and hematocrit:
       Serum electrolytes:
       Urine specific gravity:
       Electrocardiogram:

15. Which of the following sets of vital signs should be expected for this client?

       A. Temperature 37.2° C (99° F), respirations 14/min, pulse 86 beats/min, pulse oximetry 96% on 2 L oxygen, blood pressure 138/92 mm Hg

       B. Temperature 38.2° C (100.8° F), respirations 24/min, pulse 96 beats/min, pulse oximetry 92% on room air, blood pressure 102/62 mm Hg

       C. Temperature 37.8° C (100° F), respirations 18/min, pulse 88 beats/min, pulse oximetry 93% on 2 L oxygen, blood pressure 115/92 mm Hg

       D. Temperature 37.2° C (99° F), respirations 16/min, pulse 76 beats/min, pulse oximetry 95% on room air, blood pressure 138/80 mm Hg

Chapter 37: Fluid Imbalances

Application Exercises Answer Key

Scenario: A 35-year-old male client is seen in the emergency department with reports of nausea, vomiting, dizziness, and weakness. History reveals that he had just completed a 10-mile run in preparation for an upcoming marathon when the onset of symptoms occurred. Physical assessment reveals dry oral mucous membranes, temperature 38.5° C (101.3° F), pulse 92 beats/min and thready, respirations 20/min, skin cool and diaphoretic, and blood pressure 102/64 mm Hg. His urine is concentrated with a high specific gravity.

1. What client findings are consistent with the presence of fluid volume deficit?

   Dry oral mucous membranes, elevated temperature, hypotensive and tachycardic, concentrated urine with high specific gravity, diaphoretic

2. What history is supportive of the diagnosis?

   Nausea, vomiting, dizziness, strenuous exercise

3. Identify some examples of appropriate diagnostic interventions.

   Serum electrolytes (sodium), BUN: Creatinine ratio

4. What collaborative actions are appropriate for addressing the client's altered fluid volume?

   Identification and treatment of the underlying cause, encouraging oral intake of fluids, and administration of isotonic intravenous fluids

5. Provide examples of nursing diagnoses appropriate for this client.

Deficient fluid volume related to abnormal fluid loss – diaphoresis

Impaired oral mucous membrane related to dehydration

Hyperthermia related to dehydration

Risk for injury

Scenario: An 83-year-old female client is admitted to an acute care facility with dyspnea, weakness, weight gain of 2 lb, 1+ pitting edema of both lower extremities to mid calf, and bilateral crackles in lung bases. Assessment findings include: temperature 37.2° C (99° F), pulse 96 beats/min and bounding, respirations 26/min, pulse oximetry 94% on 3 L oxygen, and blood pressure 152/96 mm Hg. She is diagnosed with congestive heart failure (CHF) and fluid volume excess. IV furosemide (Lasix) is prescribed.

6. What data supports the presence of fluid volume excess?

Dyspnea, weakness, weight gain, 1+ pitting edema of both lower extremities to mid calf, bilateral crackles in lung bases, temperature 37.2° C (99 ° F), pulse 96 beats/min and bounding, respirations 26/min, pulse oximetry 94% on 3 L oxygen, and blood pressure 152/96 mm Hg

7. Why is fluid volume excess a common complication of CHF?

CHF occurs when the cardiac muscle is too weak to maintain adequate cardiac output. This results in decreased renal blood flow and renal perfusion. This prompts the retention of sodium and water. Poor myocardial contraction also results in insufficient ventricle emptying resulting in pulmonary and/or peripheral edema.

8. What is the gerontological consideration regarding this client?

There is an increased risk for fluid volume excess related to changes in cardiac and/or renal function.

9. Which electrolyte should the nurse carefully monitor in this client and why?

Potassium, because furosemide (Lasix) administration may result in hypokalemia.

Scenario: An 81-year-old male client living in an assisted living facility has become weak and confused. Usually a good eater, today he has eaten only 40% of his breakfast and lunch. He has required constant encouragement to drink. Assessment findings include: temperature 38.3° C (100.9° F), pulse rate 92 beats/min, respirations 20/min, and blood pressure 108/60 mm Hg. He has lost ¾ lb and he reports dizziness when assisted to the bathroom. He also has a nonproductive cough with diminished breath sounds in the right lower lobe. His urine is dark yellow.

10. Which of the above data supports fluid volume deficit?

Weak and confused, ate only 40% of his breakfast and lunch, requires encouragement to drink, temperature 38.3° C (100.9° F), pulse rate 92 beats/min, respirations 20/min, blood pressure 108/60 mm Hg, ¾ lb weight loss, dizziness, nonproductive cough with diminished breath sounds in the right lower lobe, dark yellow urine

11. Identify several appropriate nursing interventions for this client.

Monitor and report intake and output, monitor vital signs and report any deterioration in status, monitor respirations for indication of shortness of breath, encourage fluids, provide a safe environment, and monitor for confusion.

12. Identify several additional signs of fluid deficit that the nurse should be watching for in this client.

Stupor, dry oral mucous membranes, dry, furrowed tongue, sunken eyeballs, flat neck veins, marked decrease in urine output

13. A client receiving 0.9% normal saline should be monitored for signs of

> **A. fluid overload.**
> B. fluid deficit.

Rationale: 0.9% normal saline is an isotonic solution. Hypertonic fluids pose a risk for fluid volume deficits.

14. An older adult client reports thirst, weakness, and dizziness. Assessment findings reveal dark yellow urine and dry oral mucous membranes. Based on these findings, what laboratory value alterations should be expected for each of the following?

> Hemoglobin and hematocrit: **increased**
> Serum electrolytes: **increased**
> Urine specific gravity: **increased**
> Electrocardiogram: **dysrhythmias**

These client findings are indicative of fluid volume deficit related to dehydration. Hemoconcentration occurs with dehydration, resulting in increases of Hgb, Hct, serum electrolytes, and urine specific gravity. Electrolyte imbalances pose a risk for dysrhythmias.

15. Which of the following sets of vital signs should be expected for this client?

> A. Temperature 37.2° C (99° F), respirations 14/min, pulse 86 beats/min, pulse oximetry 96% on 2 L oxygen, blood pressure 138/92 mm Hg
> **B. Temperature 38.2° C (100.8° F), respirations 24/min, pulse 96 beats/min, pulse oximetry 92% on room air, blood pressure 102/62 mm Hg**
> C. Temperature 37.8° C (100° F), respirations 18/min, pulse 88 beats/min, pulse oximetry 93% on 2 L oxygen, blood pressure 115/92 mm Hg
> D. Temperature 37.2° C (99° F), respirations 16/min, pulse 76 beats/min, pulse oximetry 95% on room air, blood pressure 138/80 mm Hg

Hyperthermia, tachycardia, hypotension, and hypoxia are expected vital signs with fluid volume deficits.

Unit 4
Section:

Nursing Care of Clients with Fluid and Electrolyte Needs
Nursing Care of Clients with Fluid and Electrolyte Imbalances

Chapter 38: Electrolyte Imbalances

Contributor: Linda Turchin, MSN, RN

NCLEX-PN® Connections:

Learning Objective: Review and apply knowledge within "**Electrolyte Imbalances**" in readiness for performance of the following nursing activities as outlined by the NCLEX-PN® test plan:

Δ   Assist with laboratory, diagnostic, and therapeutic procedures related to the treatment of electrolyte imbalances within the nursing role, including:

- Preparation of the client for the procedure.
- Accurate collection of specimens.
- Monitoring client status during and after procedure.
- Reinforcing client teaching (before and following procedure).
- Recognizing the client's response (expected, unexpected adverse response) to the procedure.
- Monitoring results.
- Monitoring and taking actions to prevent or minimize the risk of complications.
- Notifying the primary care provider of signs of complications.

Δ   Recognize signs and symptoms of the client's problem – electrolyte imbalances – and complete the proper documentation.

Δ   Provide and document care based on the client's health alteration – electrolyte imbalances.

Δ   Monitor and document vital signs changes.

Δ   Interpret data that need to be reported immediately.

Δ   Reinforce client education on managing the client's health problem – electrolyte imbalances.

Δ   Recognize and respond to emergency situations, including notification of the primary care provider.

Δ   Review the client's response to emergency interventions and complete the proper documentation.

Δ   Provide care that meets the age-related needs of clients 65 years of age or older, including recognizing expected physiological changes.

Electrolytes

 Key Points

Δ Electrolytes are **minerals** (sometimes called salts) that are present in all body fluids. They **regulate fluid balance** and hormone production, strengthen skeletal structures, and act as **catalysts in nerve response, muscle contraction**, and the metabolism of nutrients.

Δ When dissolved in water or other solvent, electrolytes separate into ions and then conduct either a positive (cations – magnesium, potassium, sodium, calcium) or negative (anions – phosphate, sulfate, chloride, bicarbonate) electrical current.

Δ Electrolytes are distributed between **intracellular (ICF)** and **extracellular (ECF) fluid compartments**. While laboratory tests can accurately reflect the electrolyte concentrations in plasma, it is **not possible to directly measure** electrolyte concentrations **within cells**.

Sodium Imbalances

Key Points

Δ **Sodium (Na⁺)** is the major electrolyte found in extracellular fluid.

Δ Sodium is essential for maintenance of acid-base balance, active and passive transport mechanisms, and maintaining irritability and conduction of nerve and muscle tissue.

Δ **Normal serum sodium levels** are between **135 to 145 mEq/L.**

Hyponatremia

Key Points

Δ **Hyponatremia** is a serum sodium level **less than 135 mEq/L.**

Δ Hyponatremia is a **net gain of water** or **loss of sodium**-rich fluids.

Δ Delays and **slows the depolarization** of membranes.

Δ Water moves from ECF into the ICF, which causes **cells to swell** (for example, cerebral edema).

Key Factors

Δ **Risk Factors/Causes** of Hyponatremia

- Deficient ECF volume

- **Abnormal gastrointestinal (GI) losses:** Vomiting, nasogastric suctioning, diarrhea, tap water enemas

- **Renal losses:** Diuretics, kidney disease, adrenal insufficiency

- **Skin losses:** Burns, wound drainage, gastrointestinal obstruction, peripheral edema, ascites

- **Increased or normal ECF volume**

  ◊ Excessive oral water intake

  ◊ Syndrome of inappropriate antidiuretic hormone (SIADH) – excess secretion of antidiuretic hormone (ADH)

- **Edematous states:** Congestive heart failure, cirrhosis, nephrotic syndrome

- Excessive **hypotonic IV fluids**

- **Inadequate sodium** intake (for example, nothing by mouth status)

- **Age-related risk factors:** Older adult clients are at greater risk due to **increased incidence of chronic illnesses**, use of **diuretic medications**, and risk for **insufficient sodium intake.**

Δ **Compensatory mechanisms** include the renal excretion of sodium-free water.

Diagnostic Procedures and Nursing Interventions

Δ **Expected Findings**

- **Serum sodium**

  ◊ **Decreased:** < 135 mEq/L

- **Serum osmolarity**

  ◊ **Decreased:** < 270 mOsm/L

Δ **Nursing Interventions**

- **Report abnormal findings** to the primary care provider.

Assessments

Δ **Expected Client Findings**

- Clinical indicators depend on whether it is associated with a normal, decreased, or increased ECF volume.

- **Vital signs:** Hypothermia, **tachycardia**, thready pulse, **hypotension**, orthostatic hypotension

- **Neuromusculoskeletal:** Headache, confusion, lethargy, **muscle weakness to the point of possible respiratory compromise,** fatigue, **decreased deep muscle reflexes (DTR)**

- **GI: Increased motility, hyperactive** bowel sounds, abdominal cramping, nausea

NANDA Nursing Diagnoses

Δ   Excess fluid volume

Δ   Deficient fluid volume

Δ   Impaired memory

Nursing Interventions

Δ   Fluid overload: Restrict water intake as ordered.

Δ   Acute hyponatremia:

- Administer hypertonic oral and IV fluids as ordered.

- Encourage foods and fluids high in sodium (cheeses, milk, condiments).

Δ   Restoration of normal ECF volume: Administer isotonic IV therapy (0.9% normal saline, Ringer's lactate).

Δ   Monitor intake and output and daily weight.

Δ   Monitor vital signs and level of consciousness — report abnormal findings.

Δ   Encourage the client to change positions slowly.

Complications and Nursing Implications

Δ   Seizures, coma, and respiratory arrest

- Seizure precautions and management

- Life support interventions

Hypernatremia

Key Points

Δ   **Hypernatremia** is a serum sodium **greater than 145 mEq/L.**

Δ   Hypernatremia is a serious electrolyte imbalance. It can cause significant neurological, endocrine, and cardiac disturbances.

Δ   Increased sodium causes **hypertonicity** of the serum. This causes a shift of water out of the cells, making the **cells dehydrated.**

Key Factors

Δ **Risk Factors/Causes** of **Hypernatremia**

- Water deprivation (for example, nothing by mouth)

- **Excessive sodium intake:** Dietary sodium intake, hypertonic IV fluids, bicarbonate intake

- **Excessive sodium retention:** Renal failure, Cushing's syndrome, aldosteronism, some medications (glucocorticosteroids)

- **Fluid losses: Fever,** diaphoresis, burns, respiratory infection, diabetes insipidus, hyperglycemia, watery diarrhea

- **Age-related changes,** specifically **decreased total body water content** and **inadequate fluid intake** related to **altered thirst mechanism**

Δ **Compensatory mechanisms** include increased thirst and increased production of ADH.

Diagnostic Procedures and Nursing Interventions

Δ **Expected Findings**

- **Serum sodium**

  ◊ **Increased:** > 145 mEq/L

- **Serum osmolarity**

  ◊ **Increased:** > 300 mOsm/L

Δ **Nursing Interventions**

- **Report abnormal findings** to the primary care provider.

Assessments

Δ **Expected Client Findings**

- **Vital signs:** Hyperthermia, tachycardia, orthostatic hypotension

- **Neuromusculoskeletal:** Restlessness, **irritability, muscle twitching** to the point of muscle weakness including respiratory compromise, **increased deep muscle reflexes (DTR)** to the point of absent DTRs, seizures, coma

- **GI: Thirst,** dry mucous membranes, **increased motility, hyperactive** bowel sounds, abdominal cramping, nausea

- **Other signs:** Edema, warm flushed skin, oliguria

NANDA Nursing Diagnoses

- Δ Deficient fluid volume

- Δ Impaired memory

- Δ Risk for injury

- Δ Impaired oral mucous membrane

Nursing Interventions

- Δ Fluid loss:

  - Based on serum osmolarity:

    - ◊ Administer hypotonic IV fluids (0.45% sodium chloride).

    - ◊ Administer isotonic IV fluids (0.9% sodium chloride).

- Δ Excess sodium

  - Encourage water intake and discourage sodium intake.

  - Administer diuretics (for example, loop diuretics).

- Δ Monitor level of consciousness and maintain client safety.

- Δ Provide oral hygiene and other comfort measures to decrease thirst.

- Δ Monitor intake and output and alert the primary care provider of inadequate renal output.

Complications and Nursing Implications

- Δ Cellular dehydration, convulsions, and death

  - Seizure precautions and management

  - Life support interventions

Potassium Imbalances

Key Points

- Δ **Potassium (K^+)** is the major cation in the intracellular fluid (ICF).

- Δ Potassium plays a vital role in cell metabolism, transmission of nerve impulses, **functioning of cardiac**, lung, and muscle tissues, and **acid-base balance**.

- Δ Potassium has **reciprocal** action with sodium.

- Δ **Normal serum potassium levels** are **3.5 to 5.0 mEq/L.**

Hypokalemia

Key Points

Δ Hypokalemia is a serum potassium **less than 3.5 mEq/L.**

Δ Hypokalemia is the result of **increased loss of potassium** from the body or **movement of potassium into the cells.**

Key Factors

Δ **Risk Factors/Causes** of **Hypokalemia**

- Decreased total body potassium

    ◊ Abnormal GI losses: Vomiting, nasogastric suctioning, diarrhea, inappropriate laxative use

    ◊ Renal losses: Excessive use of diuretics such as furosemide (Lasix), corticosteroids

    ◊ Skin losses: Diaphoresis, wound losses

- Insufficient potassium

    ◊ Inadequate dietary intake (rare)

    ◊ Prolonged administration of non-electrolyte containing IV solutions such as D_5W

- Intracellular shift: Metabolic alkalosis, after correction of acidosis, during periods of tissue repair (burns, trauma, starvation), total parenteral nutrition

- **Age-related risk factors:** Older adult clients are at greater risk due to **increased use of diuretics and laxatives.**

Diagnostic Procedures and Nursing Interventions

Δ **Expected Findings**

- **Serum potassium**

    ◊ Decreased: < 3.5 mEq/L

- Arterial Blood Gases

    ◊ Metabolic **alkalosis**: pH > 7.45

- **Electrocardiogram**

    ◊ Dysrhythmias

Δ **Nursing Interventions**

- **Report abnormal findings** to the primary care provider.

Assessments

Δ **Expected Client Findings**

- **Vital signs:** Hyperthermia, **weak irregular pulse**, hypotension, respiratory distress

- **Neuromusculoskeletal: Weakness** to the point of respiratory collapse and paralysis, **muscle cramping**, decreased muscle tone and **hypoactive reflexes, paresthesias, mental confusion**

- **ECG: Premature ventricular contractions (PVCs), bradycardia**, blocks, **ventricular tachycardia**, inverted T waves, and ST depression

- **GI: Decreased motility**, abdominal distention, **constipation**, ileus, nausea, vomiting, anorexia

- **Other signs:** Polyuria (dilute urine)

NANDA Nursing Diagnoses

Δ Decreased cardiac output

Δ Ineffective breathing pattern

Δ Risk for injury

Δ Constipation

Nursing Interventions

Δ Treat underlying cause.

Δ **Replacement of potassium:**

- Encourage foods high in potassium (avocados, broccoli, dairy products, dried fruit, cantaloupe, bananas).

- Provide oral potassium supplementation.

- IV potassium supplementation:

  ◊ **Never IV push** (high risk of **cardiac arrest**).

  ◊ The maximum recommended rate is **5 to 10 mEq/hr**.

  ◊ Monitor for **phlebitis** (tissue irritant).

  ◊ Monitor for and maintain adequate urine output.

Δ Monitor for shallow ineffective respirations and diminished breath sounds.

Δ Monitor the client's cardiac rhythm and intervene promptly as needed.

Δ Monitor level of consciousness and maintain client safety.

Δ Monitor bowel sounds and abdominal distention and intervene as needed.

Complications and Nursing Implications

Δ **Respiratory Failure**

- Monitor for hypoxemia and hypercapnia.

- Intubation and mechanical ventilation may be required.

Δ **Cardiac Arrest**

- Perform continuous cardiac monitoring.

- Treat life-threatening dysrhythmias.

Hyperkalemia

Key Points

Δ **Hyperkalemia** is a serum potassium **greater than 5.0 mEq/L.**

Δ Hyperkalemia is the result of **increased intake** of potassium, **movement of potassium out of the cells,** or **inadequate renal excretion.**

Key Factors

Δ **Risk Factors/Causes** of Hyperkalemia

- **Increased total body potassium**: IV potassium administration, salt substitute.

- **Extracellular shift**: Decreased insulin, acidosis (for example, diabetic ketoacidosis), tissue catabolism (sepsis, trauma, surgery, fever, myocardial infarction)

- **Hypertonic states**: Uncontrolled diabetes

- **Decreased excretion of potassium**: Renal failure, severe dehydration, potassium-sparing diuretics, ACE Inhibitors, NSAIDs, adrenal insufficiency

- **Age-related risk factors**: Older adult clients are at greater risk due to **increased use of: salt substitutes, ACE inhibitors**, and potassium-sparing diuretics.

Diagnostic Procedures and Nursing Interventions

Δ **Expected Findings**

- **Serum potassium**
  - ◊ Increased: > 5.0 mEq/L
- Arterial Blood Gases
  - ◊ Metabolic **acidosis**: pH < 7.35
- **Electrocardiogram**
  - ◊ Dysrhythmias

Δ **Nursing Interventions**

- **Report abnormal findings** to the primary care provider.

Assessments

Δ **Expected Client Findings**

- **Vital signs: Slow, irregular pulse, hypotension**
- **Neuromusculoskeletal**: Restlessness, irritability, **weakness** to the point of ascending flaccid paralysis, **paresthesias**
- **ECG: Ventricular fibrillation, peaked T waves**, and widened QRS
- **Gastrointestinal**: Nausea, vomiting, **increased motility, diarrhea, hyperactive bowel sounds**
- **Other signs**: Oliguria

NANDA Nursing Diagnoses

Δ Decreased cardiac output

Δ Risk for injury

Δ Diarrhea

Nursing Interventions

Δ Decrease potassium intake:

- Stop infusion of IV potassium.
- Withhold oral potassium.
- Provide potassium restricted diet (avoid foods high in potassium such as avocados, broccoli, dairy products, dried fruit, cantaloupe, bananas).

Δ   Increase potassium excretion:

- Administer loop diuretics, such as furosemide (Lasix), if renal function is adequate.

- Administer cation exchange resins such as sodium polystyrene sulfonate (Kayexalate).

- Perform dialysis.

Δ   Promote movement of potassium from ECF to ICF:

- Administer IV fluids with dextrose (glucose) and Regular insulin.

- Administer sodium bicarbonate (reverse acidosis).

Δ   Monitor the client's cardiac rhythm and intervene promptly as needed.

Complications and Nursing Implications

Δ   **Cardiac Arrest**

- Perform continuous cardiac monitoring.

- Treat life-threatening dysrhythmias.

Other Electrolyte Imbalances

Key Points

Δ   **Hypocalcemia**

- Hypocalcemia is a **serum calcium** level **less than 9.0 mg/dL**.

- **Risk factors/causes** of hypocalcemia

    ◊   Malabsorption syndromes such as Crohn's disease

    ◊   End-stage renal disease

    ◊   Post thyroidectomy

- **Clinical indications** of hypocalcemia

    ◊   Neuromuscular

        °   Muscle twitches/tetany

        °   Frequent, painful muscle spasms at rest

        °   Hyperactive deep tendon reflexes

        °   Positive Chvostek's sign (tap on facial nerve triggers facial twitching)

        °   Positive Trousseau's sign (hand/finger spasms with sustained blood pressure cuff inflation)

◊ Cardiovascular

  ° Decreased myocardial contractility: Decreased heart rate and hypotension

  ° ECG changes: Prolonged QT interval

◊ GI: Hyperactive bowel sounds, diarrhea, abdominal cramping

- **Nursing interventions**

◊ Administer oral or IV calcium supplements.

◊ Seizure precautions.

◊ Emergency equipment on standby.

◊ Encourage foods high in calcium including dairy products and dark green vegetables.

Δ **Hypomagnesemia**

- Hypomagnesemia is a **serum magnesium** level **less than 1.2 mg/dL.**

- **Risk factors/causes** of hypomagnesemia

◊ Malnutrition (insufficient magnesium intake)

◊ Alcohol ingestion (magnesium excretion)

- **Clinical indications** of hypomagnesemia

◊ Neuromuscular: Increased nerve impulse transmission (hyperactive deep tendon reflexes, paresthesias, muscle tetany), positive Chvostek's and Trousseau's signs

◊ GI: Hypoactive bowel sounds, constipation, abdominal distention, paralytic ileus

- **Nursing interventions**

◊ Discontinue magnesium-losing medications (e.g., loop diuretics).

◊ Administer oral or IV magnesium sulfate following safety protocols.

◊ Encourage foods high in magnesium including dairy products and dark green vegetables.

Primary Reference:

Ignatavicius, D. D., & Workman, M. L. (2006). *Medical-surgical nursing* (5th ed.). St. Louis, MO: Saunders.

Additional Resources:

Heitz, U., & Horne, M. M. (2005). *Pocket guide to fluid, electrolyte, and acid-base balance* (5th ed.). St. Louis, MO: Mosby.

NANDA International (2004). *NANDA nursing diagnoses: Definitions and classification 2005-2006*. Philadelphia: NANDA.

Chapter 38: Electrolyte Imbalances

Application Exercises

1. For each of the following client findings, note which electrolyte imbalance(s) is/are supported by the finding.

Client Findings	Hyponatremia	Hypernatremia	Hypokalemia	Hyperkalemia
Serum sodium = 125 mEq/L				
Serum sodium = 150 mEq/L				
Serum potassium = 5.4 mEq/L				
Serum potassium = 3.1 mEq/L				
Hypotension/orthostatic hypotension				
Muscle weakness				
Oliguria				
Dry oral mucous membranes				
Thirst				
Vital sign alterations				
Dysrhythmias				
Paresthesias/numbness				
Vomiting and diarrhea				
Administration of non-potassium-sparing diuretics				
Chronic renal failure				
Hyperactive bowel sounds				
Decreased deep tendon reflexes				

2. A client has the following electrolyte results: Na+ 133 mEq/L, K+ 3.4 mEq/L. Which of the following treatments likely resulted in these results?

  A. Three tap water enemas

  B. Normal saline 50 cc/hr

  C. D_5W with 20 K+ 80 mL/hr

  D. Administration of glucocorticoids

3. A potassium level of 5.4 mEq/L should alert the nurse to assess the client for

  A. ECG changes.

  B. constipation.

  C. polyuria.

  D. hypertension.

4. The nurse should closely monitor a client who has a nasogastric tube for suctioning for which of the following electrolyte imbalances?

  A. Hypokalemia

  B. Hyponatremia

  C. Hypokalemia and hyponatremia

  D. Hypomagnesemia

5. Hyperkalemia can be triggered by which of the following conditions?

  A. Diabetic ketoacidosis

  B. CHF

  C. Diabetes insipidus

  D. Thyroidectomy

6. When testing for Chvostek's sign, where should the nurse tap?

Chapter 38: Electrolyte Imbalances

Application Exercises Answer Key

1. For each of the following client findings, note which electrolyte imbalance(s) is/are supported by the finding.

Client Findings	Hyponatremia	Hypernatremia	Hypokalemia	Hyperkalemia
Serum sodium = 125 mEq/L	X			
Serum sodium = 150 mEq/L		X		
Serum potassium = 5.4 mEq/L				X
Serum potassium = 3.1 mEq/L			X	
Hypotension/ orthostatic hypotension	X	X	X	
Muscle weakness	X	X	X	X
Oliguria		X		X
Dry oral mucous membranes		X		
Thirst		X		
Vital sign alterations	X	X	X	X
Dysrhythmias			X	X
Paresthesias/numbness				X
Vomiting and diarrhea	X		X	
Administration of non- potassium-sparing diuretics			X	
Chronic renal failure	X			X
Hyperactive bowel sounds		X		X
Decreased deep tendon reflexes	X		X	

2. A client has the following electrolyte results: Na+ 133 mEq/L, K+ 3.4 mEq/L. Which of the following treatments likely resulted in these results?

> **A. Three tap water enemas**
> B. Normal saline 50 cc/hr
> C. D$_5$W with 20 K+ 80 mL/hr
> D. Administration of glucocorticoids

Tap water is hypotonic. GI losses are isotonic. This creates an imbalance and solute dilution.

3. A potassium level of 5.4 mEq/L should alert the nurse to assess the client for

> **A. ECG changes.**
> B. constipation.
> C. polyuria.
> D. hypertension.

Constipation and polyuria are signs of hypokalemia. Hypotension is a sign of hyperkalemia.

4. The nurse should closely monitor a client who has a nasogastric tube for suctioning for which of the following electrolyte imbalances?

> A. Hypokalemia
> B. Hyponatremia
> **C. Hypokalemia and hyponatremia**
> D. Hypomagnesemia

Nasogastric losses are isotonic, containing both sodium and potassium.

5. Hyperkalemia can be triggered by which of the following conditions?

>   **A. Diabetic ketoacidosis**
>   B. CHF
>   C. Diabetes insipidus
>   D. Thyroidectomy

6. When testing for Chvostek's sign, where should the nurse tap?

>   **The nurse should tap on the facial nerve just below and anterior to the ear. A positive response is facial twitching of the mouth, nose, and cheek on the side being tested.**

Unit 4   Nursing Care of Clients with Fluid and Electrolyte Needs
Section: Nursing Care of Clients with Fluid and Electrolyte Imbalances

Chapter 39:	Acid-Base Imbalances
	Contributor: Linda Turchin, MSN, RN

NCLEX-PN® Connections:

Learning Objective: Review and apply knowledge within "**Acid-Base Imbalances**" in readiness for performance of the following nursing activities as outlined by the NCLEX-PN® test plan:

Δ   Assist with laboratory, diagnostic, and therapeutic procedures related to the treatment of acid-base imbalances within the nursing role, including:

- Preparation of the client for the procedure.

- Accurate collection of specimens.

- Monitoring client status during and after procedure.

- Reinforcing client teaching (before and following procedure).

- Recognizing the client's response (expected, unexpected adverse response) to the procedure.

- Monitoring results.

- Monitoring and taking actions to prevent or minimize the risk of complications.

- Notifying the primary care provider of signs of complications.

Δ   Recognize signs and symptoms of the client's problem – acid/base imbalances – and complete the proper documentation.

Δ   Provide and document care based on the client's health alteration – acid/base imbalances.

Δ   Monitor and document vital signs changes.

Δ   Interpret data that need to be reported immediately.

Δ   Reinforce client education on managing the client's health problem – acid/base imbalances.

Δ   Recognize and respond to emergency situations, including notification of the primary care provider.

Δ   Review the client's response to emergency interventions and complete the proper documentation.

Δ   Provide care that meets the age-related needs of clients 65 years of age or older, including recognizing expected physiological changes.

Key Points

Δ   For cells to function optimally, metabolic processes must maintain a steady balance between the acids and the bases found in the body.

Δ   **Acid-base balance** represents homeostasis of **hydrogen (H^+) ion** concentration in body fluids. Hydrogen shifts between the extracellular and intracellular compartments to compensate for acid-base imbalances.

Δ   Minor changes in hydrogen concentration have major effects on normal cellular function.

Δ   **Arterial pH** is an indirect measurement of hydrogen ion concentration and is a result of respiratory and renal compensational function. **Arterial blood gases (ABGs)** are most commonly used to evaluate acid-base balance.

Δ   The **pH** is the expression of the balance between **carbon dioxide (CO_2)**, which is regulated by the lungs, and **bicarbonate (HCO_3^-)**, a base regulated by the kidneys.

-   The **greater the concentration of hydrogen**, the more **acidic** the body fluids and the **lower the pH.**

-   The **lower the concentration of hydrogen**, the more **alkaline** the body fluids and the **higher the pH.**

Δ   Acid-base balance is maintained by **chemical, respiratory,** and **renal processes.**

-   **Chemical** and **protein buffers:**

    ◊   Are the first line of defense.

    ◊   Either **bind or release hydrogen ions** as needed.

    ◊   **Respond quickly to changes in pH.**

-   **Respiratory buffers:**

    ◊   Are the second line of defense.

    ◊   **Control** the level of **hydrogen ions** in the blood through the **control of CO_2 levels.**

    ◊   When **chemoreceptors** sense a change in the level of CO_2, they signal the brain to **alter the rate and depth of respirations.**

        °   **Hyperventilation = decrease in hydrogen ions**

        °   **Hypoventilation = increase in hydrogen ions**

-   **Renal buffers:**

    ◊   The kidneys are the third line of defense.

    ◊   This buffering system is much **slower to respond,** but it is the **most effective buffering system** with the longest duration.

◊   The **kidneys control the movement of bicarbonate in the urine**. Bicarbonate can be reabsorbed into the bloodstream or excreted in the urine in response to blood levels of hydrogen.

◊   The kidneys may also **produce more bicarbonate** when needed.

    °   High hydrogen ions = bicarbonate reabsorption and production

    °   Low hydrogen ions = bicarbonate excretion

Δ   **Compensation** refers to the process by which the **body attempts to correct changes and imbalances in pH levels.**

•   **Full compensation** occurs when the **pH level of the blood returns to normal (7.35 to 7.45).**

•   If the pH is not able to normalize, then it is referred to as **partial compensation.**

Δ   **Metabolic alkalosis, metabolic acidosis, respiratory alkalosis,** and **respiratory acidosis** are examples of acid-base imbalances.

Key Factors

Δ   **Acid-base imbalances** are a result of **insufficient compensation.** Respiratory and renal function play a large role in the body's ability to effectively compensate for acid-base alterations. **Organ dysfunction negatively affects** acid-base compensation.

Respiratory Compensation   Metabolic Compensation

$$H_2O + CO_2 \longleftrightarrow H_2CO_3 \longleftrightarrow H^+ + HCO_3^-$$

Water   Carbon dioxide   Carbonic acid   Hydrogen ion   Bicarbonate

Expelled by lungs   Expelled by kidneys

Δ   Risk Factors/Causes of Acid-Base Imbalances

Respiratory Acidosis - Hypoventilation	Respiratory Alkalosis - Hyperventilation
• **Respiratory acidosis** results from: ◊ Respiratory depression from poisons, anesthetics, trauma, or neurological diseases, such as myasthenia gravis or Guillain-Barré. ◊ Inadequate chest expansion due to muscle weakness, pneumothorax/ hemothorax, flail chest, obesity, tumors, or deformities. ◊ Airway obstruction that occurs in laryngospasm, asthma, and some cancers. ◊ Alveolar-capillary blockage secondary to a pulmonary embolus, thrombus, cancer, or pulmonary edema. ◊ Inadequate mechanical ventilation. • **Respiratory acidosis** results in: ◊ Increased CO_2. ◊ Increased H^+ concentration.	• **Respiratory alkalosis** results from: ◊ Hyperventilation due to fear, anxiety, intracerebral trauma, salicylate toxicity, or excessive mechanical ventilation. ◊ Hypoxemia from asphyxiation, high altitudes, shock, or early-stage asthma or pneumonia. • **Respiratory alkalosis** results in: ◊ Decreased CO_2. ◊ Decreased H^+ concentration.

Metabolic Acidosis	Metabolic Alkalosis

• **Metabolic acidosis** results from:
 	
◊ Excess production of hydrogen ions
 	
  ° DKA
  ° Lactic acidosis
  ° Starvation
  ° Heavy exercise
  ° Seizure activity
  ° Fever
  ° Hypoxia
  ° Intoxication with ethanol or salicylates
 	
◊ Inadequate elimination of hydrogen ions
 	
  ° Renal failure
 	
◊ Inadequate production of bicarbonate
 	
  ° Renal failure
  ° Pancreatitis
  ° Liver failure
  ° Dehydration
 	
◊ Excess elimination of bicarbonate
 	
  ° Diarrhea, ileostomy
 	
• **Metabolic acidosis** results in:
 	
◊ Decreased HCO_3^-.
 	
◊ Increased H+ concentration.
	• **Metabolic alkalosis** results from:
	
	◊ Base excess
	
	  ° Oral ingestion of bases **(antacids)**
	  ° **Venous administration** of bases (blood transfusions, TPN, or sodium bicarbonate)
	
	◊ Acid deficit
	
	  ° **Loss of gastric** secretions such as through prolonged **vomiting or NG suction**
	  ° **Potassium depletion** due to, for example, thiazide diuretics, laxative abuse, Cushing's syndrome
	
	• **Metabolic alkalosis** results in:
	
	◊ Increased HCO_3^-.
	
	◊ Decreased H+ concentration.

Diagnostic and Therapeutic Procedures and Nursing Interventions

    Δ   See chapter 3 regarding **ABG analysis** and associated nursing interventions.

Assessments

    Δ   To determine the type of imbalance, follow these steps:

Step 1   Look at pH.   If < 7.35, diagnose as acidosis.

                                         If > 7.45, diagnose as alkalosis.

Step 2   Look at $PaCO_2$ and HCO_3^- simultaneously.

                         Determine which one is in the normal range.

                         Then, conclude that the other is the indicator of imbalance.

                         Diagnose < 35 or > 45 $PaCO_2$ as respiratory in origin.

                         Diagnose < 22 or > 26 HCO_3^- as metabolic in origin.

Step 3   Combine diagnoses of Steps 1 and 2 to name the type of imbalance

The following are the five classic types of ABG results demonstrating balance and imbalance.

Step 1	Step 2		Step 3
If	*Determine which is in normal range*		*Combine names*
pH	**PaCO$_2$**	**HCO$_3^-$**	**Diagnosis**
7.35-7.45	35-45	22-26	Homeostasis
< 7.35	> 45	22-26	Respiratory acidosis
< 7.35	35-45	< 22	Metabolic acidosis
> 7.45	< 35	22-26	Respiratory alkalosis
> 7.45	35-45	> 26	Metabolic alkalosis

Step 4   Evaluate the PaO$_2$ and the SaO$_2$.

If the results are below the normal range, the client is hypoxic.

Step 5   Determine compensation as follows:

◊ **Uncompensated**: The pH will be abnormal and either the HCO$_3^-$ or the PaCO$_2$ will be abnormal.

◊ **Partially compensated**: The pH, HCO$_3^-$, and PaCO$_2$ will be abnormal.

◊ **Fully compensated**: The pH will be normal, but the PaCO$_2$ and HCO$_3^-$ will both be abnormal. Then, looking back at the pH will provide a clue as to which system initiated the problem, respiratory or metabolic. If the pH is < 7.40, think "acidosis" and determine which system has the acidosis value. If the pH is > 7.40, think "alkalosis" and determine which system has the alkalosis value.

Δ   **Assessment Findings of Acid-Base Imbalances**

Respiratory Acidosis - Hypoventilation	Respiratory Alkalosis - Hyperventilation
• Vital signs: Tachycardia, tachypnea	• Vital Signs: Tachypnea
• Dysrhythmias	• Neurological: Anxiety, tetany, convulsions, tingling, numbness
• Neurological: Anxiety, irritability, confusion, coma	• CV: Palpitations, chest pain, dysrhythmias
Metabolic Acidosis	**Metabolic Alkalosis**
• Vital Signs: Bradycardia, tachypnea, hypotension	• Vital Signs: Tachycardia, hypotension
• Dysrhythmias	• Dysrhythmias
• Neurological: Fatigue, weakness, lethargy, confusion	• Neurological: Numbness, tingling, tetany, muscle weakness, hyporeflexia, confusion, convulsion
• GI: Anorexia, nausea, vomiting, diarrhea	• Polyuria, polydipsia

NANDA Nursing Diagnoses

- Δ Respiratory acidosis/alkalosis
  - Impaired gas exchange
  - Ineffective breathing pattern
- Δ Metabolic acidosis/alkalosis
  - Decreased cardiac output

Nursing Interventions

- Δ For all acid-base imbalances, it is imperative to treat the underlying cause.

- Δ Respiratory acidosis: Oxygen therapy, maintain patent airway, and enhance gas exchange (positioning and breathing techniques, ventilatory support, bronchodilators, mucolytics).

- Δ Respiratory alkalosis: Oxygen therapy, anxiety reduction interventions, rebreathing techniques.

- Δ Metabolic acidosis: Varies with causes. For example, if DKA, administer insulin; if related to GI losses, administer antidiarrheals and provide rehydration; if serum bicarbonate is low, administer sodium bicarbonate (1 mEq/kg).

- Δ Metabolic alkalosis: Varies with causes. For example, if GI losses, administer antiemetics, fluids, and electrolyte replacements; if related to potassium depletion, discontinue causative agent or potassium-sparing diuretic.

Complications and Nursing Implications

- Δ Convulsions, Coma, and Respiratory Arrest
  - Seizure precautions and management
  - Life-support interventions

Primary Reference:

Ignatavicius, D. D., & Workman, M. L. (2006). *Medical-surgical nursing* (5th ed.). St. Louis, MO: Saunders.

Additional Resources:

Heitz, U., & Horne, M. M. (2005). *Pocket guide to fluid, electrolyte, and acid-base balance* (5th ed.). St. Louis, MO: Mosby.

NANDA International (2004). *NANDA nursing diagnoses: Definitions and classification 2005-2006*. Philadelphia: NANDA.

Potter, P. A., & Perry, A. G. (2005). *Fundamentals of nursing* (6th ed.). St. Louis, MO: Mosby.

Chapter 39: Acid-Base Imbalances

Application Exercises

Scenario: A 62-year-old male client who is a widower, retired, and living alone, enters the emergency department reporting shortness of breath and tingling in his fingers. His breathing is shallow and rapid (30/min). He denies diabetes and his blood glucose is normal. There are no ECG changes. He has no significant respiratory or cardiac history. He takes several anti-anxiety medications. He says he has had anxiety attacks before. While the client is being worked up for chest pain, an ABG is done. Results are: pH 7.48, $PaCO_2$ 28 mm Hg, PaO_2 85 mm Hg, HCO_3^- 22 mEq/L.

1. What, if any, acid-base imbalance is the client experiencing?

2. Which client findings support this conclusion?

3. What nursing interventions are appropriate for this client?

4. Interpret each of the following ABG results.

Possible interpretations: Respiratory acidosis, respiratory alkalosis, metabolic acidosis, metabolic alkalosis, partially compensated metabolic acidosis, partially compensated metabolic alkalosis, partially compensated respiratory acidosis, partially compensated respiratory alkalosis, normal.

pH 7.28 $PaCO_2$ 56 mm Hg HCO_3^- 25 mEq/L SaO_2 89% Interpretation: _____	pH 7.49 $PaCO_2$ 30 mm Hg HCO_3^- 23 mEq/L SaO_2 96% Interpretation: _____
pH 7.28 $PaCO_2$ 43 mm Hg HCO_3^- 20 mEq/L SaO_2 96% Interpretation: _____	pH 7.40 $PaCO_2$ 40 mm Hg HCO_3^- 24 mEq/L SaO_2 98% Interpretation: _____
pH 7.50 $PaCO_2$ 36 mm Hg HCO_3^- 27 mEq/L SaO_2 97% Interpretation: _____	pH 7.33 $PaCO_2$ 29 mm Hg HCO_3^- 16 mEq/L SaO_2 95% Interpretation: _____
pH 7.35 $PaCO_2$ 42 mm Hg HCO_3^- 26 mEq/L SaO_2 95% Interpretation: _____	pH 7.12 $PaCO_2$ 60 mm Hg HCO_3^- 29 mEq/L SaO_2 94% Interpretation: _____
pH 7.48 $PaCO_2$ 33 mm Hg HCO_3^- 24 mEq/L SaO_2 96% Interpretation: _____	pH 7.62 $PaCO_2$ 47 mm Hg HCO_3^- 30 mEq/L SaO_2 95% Interpretation: _____
pH 7.36 $PaCO_2$ 44 mm Hg HCO_3^- 24 mEq/L SaO_2 98% Interpretation: _____	pH 7.30 $PaCO_2$ 59 mm Hg HCO_3^- 38 mEq/L SaO_2 94% Interpretation: _____

5. A 24-year-old female client who has a history of depression is admitted with confusion and lethargy. She was found at home with an empty bottle of aspirin next to her in the bed, along with a suicide note. Vital signs reveal a blood pressure of 104/72 mm Hg, pulse rate of 116 beats/min with a regular rhythm, and a respiratory rate of 42/min and deep. Which of the following arterial blood gas results should the nurse expect?

A. pH 7.38, PaO_2 96 mm Hg, $PaCO_2$ 38 mm Hg, HCO_3^- 24 mEq/L

B. pH 7.48, PaO_2 100 mm Hg, $PaCO_2$ 28 mm Hg, HCO_3^- 23 mEq/L

C. pH 6.98, PaO_2 100 mm Hg, $PaCO_2$ 30 mm Hg, HCO_3^- 18 mEq/L

D. pH 7.58, PaO_2 96 mm Hg, $PaCO_2$ 38 mm Hg, HCO_3^- 29 mEq/L

6. An adult male client was involved in a single-vehicle car crash. He is reporting chest pain and difficulty breathing, A chest x-ray reveals a pneumothorax. Blood gas analysis is obtained. Which of the following results should the nurse expect?

A. pH 7.06, PaO_2 96 mm Hg, $PaCO_2$ 52 mm Hg, HCO_3^- 24 mEq/L

B. pH 7.42, PaO_2 100 mm Hg, $PaCO_2$ 38 mm Hg, HCO_3^- 23 mEq/L

C. pH 6.98, PaO_2 100 mm Hg, $PaCO_2$ 30 mm Hg, HCO_3^- 18 mEq/L

D. pH 7.58, PaO_2 96 mm Hg, $PaCO_2$ 38 mm Hg, HCO_3^- 29 mEq/L

7. A female client is in the first trimester of pregnancy. She has experienced approximately 1 week of severe nausea with frequent vomiting. Which of the following conditions should the nurse expect to find if an arterial blood gas is analyzed?

A. Respiratory acidosis

B. Respiratory alkalosis

C. Metabolic acidosis

D. Metabolic alkalosis

Chapter 39: Acid-Base Imbalances

Application Exercises Answer Key

Scenario: A 62-year-old male client who is a widower, retired, and living alone, enters the emergency department reporting shortness of breath and tingling in his fingers. His breathing is shallow and rapid (30/min). He denies diabetes and his blood glucose is normal. There are no ECG changes. He has no significant respiratory or cardiac history. He takes several anti-anxiety medications. He says he has had anxiety attacks before. While the client is being worked up for chest pain, an ABG is done. Results are: pH 7.48, $PaCO_2$ 28 mm Hg, PaO_2 85 mm Hg, HCO_3^- 22 mEq/L.

1. What, if any, acid-base imbalance is the client experiencing?

This client is experiencing respiratory alkalosis. His pH is high, which supports a diagnosis of alkalosis, and the $PaCO_2$ is low, which indicates that the alkalosis is due to respiratory alterations.

2. Which client findings support this conclusion?

Shortness of breath, tingling in fingers, shallow rapid breathing, and history of anxiety attacks are findings consistent with respiratory alkalosis.

3. What nursing interventions are appropriate for this client?

If he is hyperventilating from an anxiety attack, the simplest solution is to have him breathe into a paper bag. He will rebreathe some exhaled CO_2. This will increase $PaCO_2$ and trigger his normal respiratory drive to take over breathing control. Please note this will not work on a person with chronic CO_2 retention, such as a client with COPD. These individuals develop a hypoxic drive and do not respond to CO_2 changes.

Provide supportive care for the underlying cause as ordered:

Stay with the client during periods of extreme stress and anxiety, offer reassurance, and maintain a calm, quiet environment.

Monitor/report signs of neuromuscular, respiratory, or cardiovascular dysfunction.

Monitor and report any variations in ABG and serum electrolyte levels.

4. Interpret each of the following ABG results.

Possible interpretations: Respiratory acidosis, respiratory alkalosis, metabolic acidosis, metabolic alkalosis, partially compensated metabolic acidosis, partially compensated metabolic alkalosis, partially compensated respiratory acidosis, partially compensated respiratory alkalosis, normal.

pH 7.28 $PaCO_2$ 56 mm Hg HCO_3^- 25 mEq/L SaO_2 89% Interpretation: **Respiratory acidosis**	pH 7.49 $PaCO_2$ 30 mm Hg HCO_3^- 23 mEq/L SaO_2 96% Interpretation: **Respiratory alkalosis**
pH 7.28 $PaCO_2$ 43 mm Hg HCO_3^- 20 mEq/L SaO_2 96% Interpretation: **Metabolic acidosis**	pH 7.40 $PaCO_2$ 40 mm Hg HCO_3^- 24 mEq/L SaO_2 98% Interpretation: **Normal**
pH 7.50 $PaCO_2$ 36 mm Hg HCO_3^- 27 mEq/L SaO_2 97% Interpretation: **Metabolic alkalosis**	pH 7.33 $PaCO_2$ 29 mm Hg HCO_3^- 16 mEq/L SaO_2 95% Interpretation: **Partially compensated metabolic acidosis**
pH 7.35 $PaCO_2$ 42 mm Hg HCO_3^- 26 mEq/L SaO_2 95% Interpretation: **Normal**	pH 7.12 $PaCO_2$ 60 mm Hg HCO_3^- 29 mEq/L SaO_2 94% Interpretation: **Partially compensated respiratory acidosis**
pH 7.48 $PaCO_2$ 33 mm Hg HCO_3^- 24 mEq/L SaO_2 96% Interpretation: **Respiratory alkalosis**	pH 7.62 $PaCO_2$ 47 mm Hg HCO_3^- 30 mEq/L SaO_2 95% Interpretation: **Partially compensated metabolic alkalosis**
pH 7.36 $PaCO_2$ 44 mm Hg HCO_3^- 24 mEq/L SaO_2 98% Interpretation: **Normal**	pH 7.30 $PaCO_2$ 59 mm Hg HCO_3^- 38 mEq/L SaO_2 94% Interpretation: **Partially compensated respiratory acidosis**

5. A 24-year-old female client who has a history of depression is admitted with confusion and lethargy. She was found at home with an empty bottle of aspirin next to her in the bed, along with a suicide note. Vital signs reveal a blood pressure of 104/72 mm Hg, pulse rate of 116 beats/min with a regular rhythm, and a respiratory rate of 42/min and deep. Which of the following arterial blood gas results should the nurse expect?

      A. pH 7.38, PaO_2 96 mm Hg, $PaCO_2$ 38 mm Hg, HCO_3^- 24 mEq/L

      B. pH 7.48, PaO_2 100 mm Hg, $PaCO_2$ 28 mm Hg, HCO_3^- 23 mEq/L

      C. pH 6.98, PaO_2 100 mm Hg, $PaCO_2$ 30 mm Hg, HCO_3^- 18 mEq/L

      D. pH 7.58, PaO_2 96 mm Hg, $PaCO_2$ 38 mm Hg, HCO_3^- 29 mEq/L

An aspirin overdose would result in metabolic acidosis.

6. An adult male client was involved in a single-vehicle car crash. He is reporting chest pain and difficulty breathing, A chest x-ray reveals a pneumothorax. Blood gas analysis is obtained. Which of the following results should the nurse expect?

      A. pH 7.06, PaO_2 96 mm Hg, $PaCO_2$ 52 mm Hg, HCO_3^- 24 mEq/L

      B. pH 7.42, PaO_2 100 mm Hg, $PaCO_2$ 38 mm Hg, HCO_3^- 23 mEq/L

      C. pH 6.98, PaO_2 100 mm Hg, $PaCO_2$ 30 mm Hg, HCO_3^- 18 mEq/L

      D. pH 7.58, PaO_2 96 mm Hg, $PaCO_2$ 38 mm Hg, HCO_3^- 29 mEq/L

Pneumothorax can cause alveolar hypoventilation and increased carbon dioxide levels, resulting in a state of respiratory acidosis.

7. A female client is in the first trimester of pregnancy. She has experienced approximately 1 week of severe nausea with frequent vomiting. Which of the following conditions should the nurse expect to find if an arterial blood gas is analyzed?

      A. Respiratory acidosis

      B. Respiratory alkalosis

      C. Metabolic acidosis

      D. Metabolic alkalosis

Excessive vomiting causes a loss of gastric acids and an accumulation of bicarbonate in the blood, resulting in metabolic alkalosis.

Unit 4   Nursing Care of Clients with Fluid and Electrolyte Needs
Section: Nursing Care of Clients Receiving Infusion Therapy

Chapter 40:   Vascular Access
Contributor: Polly Gerber Zimmermann, MSN, MBA, RN, CEN

⟳ NCLEX-PN® Connections:

Learning Objective: Review and apply knowledge within **"Vascular Access"** in readiness for performance of the following nursing activities as outlined by the NCLEX-PN® test plan:

Δ Assist in preparing the client for insertion of a vascular access device (VAD).

Δ Perform/assist with relevant laboratory, diagnostic, and therapeutic procedures within the nursing role, including:

 • Preparation of the client for the procedure.

 • Reinforcement of client teaching (before and following the procedure).

 • Accurate collection of specimens.

 • Monitoring procedure results (compare to norms) and appropriate notification of the primary care provider.

 • Monitoring the client's response (expected, unexpected adverse response, comparison to baseline) to the procedure.

 • Monitoring and taking actions, including reinforcing client teaching, to prevent or minimize the risk of complications.

 • Recognizing signs of potential complications and reporting to the primary care provider.

 • Recommending changes in the test/procedure as needed based on client findings.

Δ Recognize the client's recovery from anesthesia, if used.

Δ Monitor therapeutic devices (drainage/irrigating devices, chest tubes), if inserted, for proper functioning.

📖 Key Factors

    Δ   **Characteristics of therapy** (medication type, pH and osmolality, length of time for therapy) **determine the site** and **type of vascular access**.

    Δ   **Type of fluid** and **length of need determine type of catheter** with the goal of minimizing the number of catheter insertions and adverse reactions.

Peripheral Catheters: Short-Term and Long-Term Dwell Catheters

Short-Term Dwell Catheters: Short Peripheral Catheters

    Δ   **Description:** Short (¾ to 1¼ inches) plastic cannula around a sharp stylet

    Δ   **Length of use: 72 to 96 hr per insertion**; appropriate if IV therapy is planned for up to 7 days

    Δ   **Insertion location:** Superficial veins in the **dorsal venous network**, basilic, cephalic, and median veins and their branches

    Δ   **Location selection factors**

- **Avoid the hand veins** in older adult clients or active clients receiving therapy.

- Avoid palm-side veins and veins 4 to 5 inches proximal to the wrist.

- Avoid veins in the fingers and thumb; their smaller diameter allows little blood flow and they easily infiltrate.

- **Avoid veins** on an **extremity with lymphedema** (for example, post CVA or mastectomy), paralysis, or a dialysis graft/fistula.

- Start with **most distal** location and **move proximally** when selecting site for insertion.

    Δ   Insertion technique

- **Limit the number of attempts to two** attempts before obtaining another healthcare provider to try.

- Immediately stop and remove the catheter if the client reports a new onset of paresthesia, numbness, or sharp shooting pain.

Long-Term Dwell Catheters: Midline Catheters (MLC)

    Δ   **Description: 6 to 8 inches** in length

    Δ   **Length of use: 1 to 4 weeks**

    Δ   **Insertion location:** Antecubital fossa into the basilica, cephalic, or median cubital veins

△ **MLC selection factors**: Infused fluids and medications delivered by a MLC should:

- Have a pH between 5 and 9.

- Have a final osmolarity of less than 500 mOsm/L.

- Not be vesicants.

△ MLC are not appropriate for TPN infusion or routine blood sampling.

Documentation of Peripheral Catheter Insertion

△ Date and time of insertion

△ Type and gauge of catheter

△ Name of the vein cannulated

△ Number and location of attempts

△ Type of dressing

△ How the client tolerated the procedure

Monitoring and Maintaining Peripheral IV Catheters

△ If used intermittently, flush with NS at least every 8 to 12 hr to prevent occlusion.

△ Monitor for signs of phlebitis (redness, warmth, induration) and infiltration (localized swelling, coolness, does not stop with pressure over the tip).

Central Catheters

△ **Indication**: Appropriate for **any fluids** due to rapid hemodilution in the superior vena cava (SVC).

△ Requires **x-ray** for verification of tip placement **prior to use.**

△ **All central catheters,** other than PICC lines, require a **primary care provider for insertion.** Insertion occurs in the OR, the client's hospital room, or in an outpatient facility.

△ **Tunneled** and **implanted catheters** require **surgical removal.**

△ Risk of air embolism. Treat by placing client in Trendelenburg on left side (air rises).

Nontunneled Percutaneous Central Catheters (Triple Lumen)

△ **Description**: 15 to 20 cm in length with 1 to 3 lumens

△ **Length of use:** Up to 3 months

△ **Insertion location:** Subclavian vein, jugular vein; tip in the distal third of the superior vena cava

Peripherally Inserted Central Catheter (PICC)

Δ   **Description**: 40 to 65 cm with single or multiple lumens

Δ   **Length of use**: Up to **12 months**

Δ   **Insertion location**: Basilic or cephalic vein at least one finger's breadth below or above the antecubital fossa; the catheter advanced until the tip is positioned in the lower one-third of the superior vena cava.

Δ   Apply local anesthetic at insertion site and insert catheter using surgical aseptic technique.

- Initial dressing of gauze should be replaced with a transparent dressing within 24 hr.
- An initial x-ray should be taken to ensure proper placement.
- Nurses require special training to perform this procedure.

Δ   Indications include: administration of blood, long-term administration of chemotherapeutic agents, antibiotics, and total parenteral nutrition.

Δ   Care of a PICC line includes:

- Assess the site at least every 8 hr. Note redness, swelling, drainage, tenderness, and condition of the dressing.
- Change tube and positive pressure cap per facility protocol (e.g., usually minimum of every 3 days for the hospitalized client).
- Use 10 mL or larger syringe to flush the line.
- Clean insertion port with alcohol for 3 sec and allow to dry completely prior to accessing.
- Perform flush for intermittent medication administration per facility protocol, usually with 10 mL of normal saline before, between, and after medications.
- Use transparent dressing. Follow facility protocol for dressing changes, usually every 7 days and when indicated (wet, loose, soiled).
- Advise the client to avoid excessive physical activity with the involved extremity.

Tunneled Percutaneous Central Catheters (brand names Hickman, Groshong)

Δ   **Indication**: Need for vascular access is long-term and frequent.

Δ   **Description: 48 to 104 cm (19 to 41 inches) in length.** No dressing is needed since entrance into skin and vein are separate and tissue granulates into catheter cuff, providing a barrier. Groshong catheters have pressure-sensitive valves to prevent blood reflux and do not require a clamp.

Δ   **Length of use:** Years

Δ   **Insertion location:** A portion of the catheter lies in a subcutaneous tunnel separating the point where the catheter enters the vein from where it enters the skin with a cuff. Tissue granulates into the cuff to provide a mechanical barrier to organisms and an anchoring for the catheter.

Implanted port

Δ   **Indication: Need** for **vascular access is long-term** (a year or more). Commonly used for chemotherapy.

Δ   **Description:** Port is comprised of a small reservoir covered by a thick septum.

Δ   **Insertion location:** Port is surgically implanted into chest wall pocket; the catheter is inserted into the subclavian vein with the tip in the superior vena cava.

Δ   Procedure to access implanted port includes:

- Apply local anesthetic to skin if indicated. Palpate skin to locate the port body septum to ensure proper insertion of the needle.

- Clean the skin with alcohol for at least 3 sec and allow to dry prior to insertion of the needle.

- Access with noncoring needle (Huber).

- Flush after every use and at least once a month.

- Follow facility protocol to flush when deaccessing port (e.g., flush with 10 mL of normal saline followed by 5 mL of 100 units/mL of heparin).

Dialysis catheter

Δ   **Description:** Very large lumen, shorter, less flexible, may be tunneled or nontunneled.

Δ   Do not use dialysis catheters for other fluids/medications unless in an emergency.

Complications and Nursing Implications

Δ   **Phlebitis** – chemical (osmolarity or pH is different, veins too small for substance), bacterial, or mechanical irritation (excess IV manipulation)

- Monitor for **signs and symptoms.**
  ◊   Erythema at the site (usual initial sign)
  ◊   Pain or burning at the site and the length of the vein
  ◊   Discomfort when the skin over the tip is touched
  ◊   Warmth over the site

◊ Edema at the site

◊ Vein indurated (hard), red streak, and/or cordlike

◊ Slowing infusion rate

◊ Temperature elevation of 1° F or more

◊ Infection appearing 7 to10 days after insertion

- **Preventive Measures**

  ◊ **Observe site** every 2 hr for signs of **infection or infiltration**.

  ◊ Nontunneled catheters require an intact sterile dressing (tunneled catheters do not).

  ◊ Use the smallest gauge in the largest vein possible to minimize mechanical and chemical irritation to the vein wall.

  ◊ Clean the site with 2% chlorhexidine-based preparation, 70% alcohol, or tincture of iodine per protocol **with friction**. Let preparation air dry before insertion.

  ◊ Change IV sites every 3 days.

- **Treatment**

  ◊ Discontinue the IV.

  ◊ Apply warm compresses.

  ◊ Restart with new tubing/infusate.

Δ **Catheter Thrombosis/Emboli**

- Flush the line per hospital protocol.

- Do not force fluid if resistance is encountered (may dislodge thrombosis).

- Use a large-barrel syringe (10 cc or bigger) to avoid excess pressure per square inch (PSI) that could cause catheter fracture/rupture.

Δ **Infiltration** (fluid leaking into surrounding subcutaneous tissue)/**Extravasation** (unintentional infiltration of a vesicant medication that causes tissue damage)

- **Causes**

  ◊ Improper IV insertion

  ◊ Improper vein selection (too small, too fragile, poor location)

  ◊ Irritating infusates that weaken and rupture the vein wall

  ◊ Overmanipulation of the IV catheter

  ◊ Improper taping that allows IV catheter movement and vein compromise

  ◊ Tape too tight, becoming a tourniquet

- Monitor for **signs and symptoms.**

  ◊ Swelling around the site and proximal or distal to the IV

  ◊ Edema "puffiness" in the dependent area underneath

  ◊ Skin taut or rigid with blanching

  ◊ Sensation of coolness

  ◊ Pressure on the vein just beyond the tip of the catheter should stop the IV flow. If flow is not affected, the fluid is probably going into the subcutaneous tissue.

  ◊ Rate slows; IV alarms due to occlusion. (Do not rely on the pump alarm because pressure must be significant to activate).

  ◊ "Leaking" at the site after confirming tube connections

  ◊ Blood return is not considered a reliable indicator.

- **Preventive Measures**

  ◊ Do not use arm with MLC or PICC for blood pressure or phlebotomy.

  ◊ Do not use hand veins in older adult clients who have lost subcutaneous tissue.

  ◊ Do not use hand veins for vesicant medication.

  ◊ Use a hand board for sites affected by the motion of a joint.

- **Treatment**

  ◊ Remove with direct pressure with gauze sponge until bleeding stops.

  ◊ Cool, rather than warm, compresses are recommended.

  ◊ Elevation is now considered optional.

  ◊ Avoid starting a new IV site in the same extremity.

Δ **Occlusion**

- Flush the line at least every 12 hr (3 cc for peripheral, 10 cc for central lines) to maintain patency.

- Studies show that normal saline solution (0.9% sodium chloride) is as effective as heparinized flush solutions to maintain catheter patency. Follow institutional policy.

- Flush ports after every use and at least once a month while implanted.

- Urokinase to lyse obstructions per protocol.

Δ **Air embolism**

- Leave central lines clamped when not in use.

- Have the client hold breath while the tubing is changed.

- If the client has sudden shortness of breath, place in Trendelenburg on left side, give oxygen, and notify the provider (to trap and aspirate air).

Δ   **Accidental dislodgement**

- Cover extremity site with stretch netting.

- Wrap a washcloth folded in thirds around the arm before applying a needed restraint. This prevents the restraint from sliding and dislodging the catheter.

- Only tape the catheter hub to minimize manipulation.

- If it is necessary to remove the dressing, pull from distal to proximal.

- If the skin is oily, "defat" oils with alcohol and air-dry before antiseptic cleansing.

Δ   **Mesh damage on port catheters**

- Use only a noncoring needle (Huber).

Δ   **Catheter migration**

- Note length; notify the provider of any changes in length.

Meeting the Needs of Older Adults

Δ   Age-related loss of skin turgor and poor vein conditions pose challenges to vascular access.

Δ   Hand veins are not appropriate in older adult clients.

Δ   Use 24- to 22-gauge catheters for peripheral insertions.

Primary Reference:

Ignatavicius, D. D., & Workman, M. L. (2006). *Medical-surgical nursing* (5th ed.). St. Louis, MO: Saunders.

Additional Resources:

Bowe-Geddes, L. A., & Nichols, H. A. (2005, August 17). An overview of peripherally inserted central catheters. *Medscape Nurses*, Article 508939. Retrieved April 24, 2007, from http://www.medscape.com/viewarticle/508939

Moureau, N. (2001, July). Preventing complications with vascular access. *Nursing2001*, 31(7): 52-55.

NANDA International (2004). *NANDA nursing diagnoses: Definitions and classification 2005-2006*. Philadelphia: NANDA.

For more information, visit the Infusion Nurses Society at: *www.ins1.org*.

Chapter 40: Vascular Access

Application Exercises

1. Which of the following describes proper nursing management of a venous access device?

   A. The nurse flushes a PICC line with 3 cc normal saline every 8 hr.

   B. The nurse meets with some resistance when attempting to flush a PICC line. The nurse proceeds with a push/pull motion with the syringe before a "power push" or forceful push.

   C. The nurse applies a sterile transparent dressing to a tunneled catheter.

   D. The nurse flushes a dialysis catheter line with 10 cc normal saline before starting an IVPB antibiotic.

   E. The nurse inserts a 20-gauge peripheral catheter in the client's right basilic vein.

   F. The nurse inserts a peripheral catheter into the superficial visible vein located on the dorsal side of the wrist.

   G. An implanted port is accessed with a small gauge (25-gauge) needle to avoid damaging the port's silicone septum mesh.

   H. The nurse starts a peripheral line in the left arm's cephalic vein. The nurse charts: "Peripheral IV 20 gauge started in left forearm dorsal side."

2. Discuss which type of vascular access device is a good selection for each of the following clients.

   Client A is to complete a 6-week course of IV antibiotics at home.

   Client B is going to receive a full course of chemotherapy for ovarian cancer.

   Client C is hospitalized in the ICU for sepsis.

   Client D has chronic renal failure and will be dialyzed three times a week.

3. List what a nurse should observe for when checking a peripheral IV site every 2 hr.

4. A nurse is starting a nontunneled peripheral catheter in a client's right cephalic vein. The client screams out, reporting pain that is shooting up his arm. Which of the following is the best action for the nurse to take first?

   A. Reassure the client that discomfort sometimes occurs but will lessen.

   B. Flush the catheter with 3 cc normal saline to check placement.

   C. Apply a topical anesthetic, such as EMLA, to numb the region.

   D. Remove the catheter and use a different site.

5. A nurse is changing the IV line on a client's central catheter line. The client is laughing at a joke. The client suddenly becomes short of breath with rapid respirations and diaphoresis. Which of the following is the best action for the nurse to take first?

    A. Raise the head of the bed and have the client breathe into a paper bag to help the client's anxiety-induced hyperventilation.

    B. Coach the client to take slow, deep breaths with pursed lips and apply oxygen at 6 L per nasal cannula.

    C. Place the client in Trendelenburg position, lying on the left side.

    D. Listen to the client's breath sounds for bilateral wheezing and the need for an as-needed nebulizer.

6. A client is receiving intravenous infusion of $D_5\frac{1}{2}NS$ with 20 mEq KCl through a nontunneled peripheral intravenous line, and the nurse is assessing the site every 2 hr. Which of the following findings is most important for the nurse to follow up?

    A. The client reports that the arm is a little sore along the vein.

    B. The IV flow does not stop when the nurse presses her finger against the catheter tip.

    C. The tape for the IV tubing is covering the catheter.

    D. The transparent dressing over the site is loose on one corner.

Chapter 40: Vascular Access

Application Exercises Answer Key

1. Which of the following describes proper nursing management of a venous access device?

   A. The nurse flushes a PICC line with 3 cc normal saline every 8 hr.

   B. The nurse meets with some resistance when attempting to flush a PICC line. The nurse proceeds with a push/pull motion with the syringe before a "power push" or forceful push.

   C. The nurse applies a sterile transparent dressing to a tunneled catheter.

   D. The nurse flushes a dialysis catheter line with 10 cc normal saline before starting an IVPB antibiotic.

   E. The nurse inserts a 20-gauge peripheral catheter in the client's right basilic vein.

   F. The nurse inserts a peripheral catheter into the superficial visible vein located on the dorsal side of the wrist.

   G. An implanted port is accessed with a small gauge (25-gauge) needle to avoid damaging the port's silicone septum mesh.

   H. The nurse starts a peripheral line in the left arm's cephalic vein. The nurse charts: "Peripheral IV 20 gauge started in left forearm dorsal side."

Option E is correct: Proper sites are superficial veins in the dorsal venous network (the basilic, cephalic, and median veins and their branches).

A is incorrect because PICC lines are up to 60 cm in length and require a minimum of at least 10 cc of solution.

B is incorrect because force should never be used in flushing a line. It could dislodge a clot or break off the tip of the catheter and cause an embolism.

C is incorrect because tunneled catheters have the cuff and two entrance sites (one for the skin and one for the vein) that serve as a barrier for microorganisms. No dressing is needed.

D is incorrect because a dialysis catheter should not be used for other fluids or medications unless an extreme emergency exists.

F is incorrect because wrist veins are to be avoided. The veins are fragile, painful to access, have a higher risk of nerve injury, and are more likely to infiltrate during normal client activity.

G is incorrect because a non-coring needle (Huber-point) must be used.

H is incorrect because proper documentation (per the Infusion Nurses Society) includes the name of the vein cannulated (as well as the time, number and location of attempts, type of dressing, and how the client tolerated the procedure).

2. Discuss which type of vascular access device is a good selection for each of the following clients.

Client A is to complete a 6-week course of IV antibiotics at home.

Client A would benefit from a PICC line due to length of treatment and home environment.

Client B is going to receive a full course of chemotherapy for ovarian cancer.

Client B would benefit from an imported port to minimize the risk of extravasation of the vesicant chemotherapy.

Client C is hospitalized in the ICU for sepsis.

Client C would benefit from a multiple-lumen central catheter (jugular or subclavian) for a likely extended course of multiple fluids, antibiotics, and other medications. It will provide rapid hemodilution of potent or incompatible drugs.

Client D has chronic renal failure and will be dialyzed three times a week.

Client D would benefit from a large diameter dialysis catheter for exclusive use for dialysis.

3. List what a nurse should observe for when checking a peripheral IV site every 2 hr.

Assess for:

Signs of phlebitis (redness, warmth, swelling, tenderness, red streaks, hardness).

Signs of infiltration – local swelling, including below the site (due to gravity) especially in older adult clients, local coolness, leaking at the site.

No backflow of blood into the hub if an intermittent site.

No accidental dislodgement.

Intact transparent dressing.

4. A nurse is starting a nontunneled peripheral catheter in a client's right cephalic vein. The client screams out, reporting pain that is shooting up his arm. Which of the following is the best action for the nurse to take first?

    A. Reassure the client that some discomfort sometimes occurs but will lessen.

    B. Flush the catheter with 3 cc normal saline to check placement.

    C. Apply a topical anesthetic, such as EMLA, to numb the region.

    D. Remove the catheter and use a different site.

Discomfort should be relatively minor and not shooting; new severe shooting pain could indicate that a nerve has been struck. Remove the catheter to prevent nerve damage. The other options would not solve the issue. EMLA is applied prior to the insertion.

5. A nurse is changing the IV line on a client's central catheter line. The client is laughing at a joke. The client suddenly becomes short of breath with rapid respirations and diaphoresis. Which of the following is the best action for the nurse to take first?

    A. Raise the head of the bed and have the client breathe into a paper bag to help the client's anxiety-induced hyperventilation.

    B. Coach the client to take slow, deep breaths with pursed lips and apply oxygen at 6 L per nasal cannula.

    C. Place the client in Trendelenburg position, lying on the left side.

    D. Listen to the client's breath sounds for bilateral wheezing and the need for an as-needed nebulizer.

The change in intrathoracic pressure during the procedure could have caused an air embolism. This client placement will help trap air for the provider to aspirate. The client is neither in anxiety-induced hyperventilation nor an asthma attack. Oxygen should not be applied at more than 5 L per nasal cannula.

6. A client is receiving intravenous infusion of $D_5\frac{1}{2}NS$ with 20 mEq KCl through a nontunneled peripheral intravenous line, and the nurse is assessing the site every 2 hr. Which of the following findings is most important for the nurse to follow up?

    A. The client reports that the arm is a little sore along the vein.

    B. The IV flow does not stop when the nurse presses her finger against the catheter tip.

    C. The tape for the IV tubing is covering the catheter.

    D. The transparent dressing over the site is loose on one corner.

The flow should stop when the tip is occluded; continuing to infuse could indicate infiltration. It is normal to feel soreness with potassium infusions. The tape should not cover the catheter because it can result in excessive mechanical manipulation, but it is not a priority. A corner can be loose but not require replacement if the dressing over the site is still intact.

Unit 4
Section:

Nursing Care of Clients with Fluid and Electrolyte Needs
Nursing Care of Clients Receiving Infusion Therapy

Chapter 41: Total Parenteral Nutrition
Contributor: Polly Gerber Zimmermann, MSN, MBA, RN, CEN

↻ NCLEX-PN® Connections:

Learning Objective: Review and apply knowledge within **"Total Parenteral Nutrition"** in readiness for performance of the following nursing activities as outlined by the NCLEX-PN® test plan:

Δ   Perform/assist with relevant laboratory, diagnostic, and therapeutic procedures within the nursing role, including:

- Preparation of the client for the procedure.

- Reinforcement of client teaching (before and following the procedure).

- Accurate collection of specimens.

- Monitoring procedure results (compare to norms) and appropriate notification of the primary care provider.

- Monitoring the client's response (expected, unexpected adverse response, comparison to baseline) to the procedure.

- Monitoring and taking actions, including reinforcing client teaching, to prevent or minimize the risk of complications.

- Recognizing signs of potential complications and reporting to the primary care provider.

- Recommending changes in the test/procedure as needed based on client findings.

Δ   Recognize the client's recovery from anesthesia, if used.

Δ   Monitor therapeutic devices (drainage/irrigating devices, chest tubes), if inserted, for proper functioning.

Key Points

Δ   Total parenteral nutrition (TPN) is a **hypertonic intravenous solution** that provides complete nutrition to a client who does not have a functioning gastrointestinal (GI) tract. The purpose of TPN administration is to **prevent or to correct nutritional deficiencies** to minimize the adverse effects of malnourishment.

Δ   TPN administration is usually through a **central line**, such as a nontunneled triple lumen catheter or a single- or double-lumen peripherally inserted central line (PICC). It is inserted **into a large vein**, such as the subclavian or internal jugular, so that the tip is in the **superior vena cava**, to allow for **rapid dilution**.

Δ   **Partial parenteral nutrition or peripheral parenteral nutrition** (PPN) is less hypertonic and intended for short-term use in a large peripheral vein. Usual **dextrose** concentration is **15 to 20%**. Risks include phlebitis.

Δ   **TPN protocols** often include:

- Gradually increase the administration rate during initiation and wean off the solution during discontinuation.

- Check glucose every 4 to 6 hr the first days of administration.

- Monitor daily laboratory values (for example, electrolytes).

- Individually prepare solutions in sterile conditions for each client.

- Hang a new solution and tubing (with filter) every 24 hr.

Δ   TPN contains complete nutrition, including calories (through a high concentration – 20 to 50% – of dextrose), lipids/essential fatty acids, protein, electrolytes, vitamins, and trace elements. Standard IV therapy is typically ≤ 700 calories a day.

Δ   Administration of TPN involves management/observation for major metabolic, mechanical, and infectious complications.

Δ   Another common term to describe TPN administration is **hyperalimentation**.

Key Factors

Δ   Potential **indications for TPN** include any condition that:

- **Affects the ability to absorb nutrition.**

- Has a prolonged recovery.

- Creates a hypermetabolic state.

- Creates a chronic malnutrition.

Δ **Specific conditions** include:

- Chronic pancreatitis.

- Diffuse peritonitis.

- Short bowel syndrome.

- Gastric paresis from diabetes mellitus.

- Severe burns.

Δ Enteral nutrition requires a functioning bowel and is preferred when possible.

Δ Basic guidelines regarding **when to initiate TPN** are:

- The "5 day rule" (has not eaten for 5 days and is not expected to eat within the next 5 days) or inadequate nutrition for 7 to 10 days.

- A weight loss of 7% body weight and NPO for 5 to 7 days.

- A hypermetabolic state.

Therapeutic Procedures and Nursing Interventions

Δ **Administration Procedures**

- The flow rate is **gradually increased** and **gradually decreased** to allow body adjustment (usually no more than a 10% hourly increase in rate).

- **Never abruptly stop** TPN. Speeding up/slowing down the rate is contraindicated. Abrupt rate changes can alter glucose levels significantly.

- **Check capillary glucose** every 4 to 6 hr for at least the first 24 hr.

  ◊ Clients receiving TPN frequently need **supplemental** sliding scale regular **insulin** until the pancreas can increase its endogenous production of insulin.

  ◊ Keep D_{10} or D_{20} at the bedside in case the solution is unexpectedly ruined. This will minimize the risk of hypoglycemia with abrupt changes in dextrose concentrations.

- Monitor vital signs every 4 to 8 hr.

- Obtain daily laboratory values, including electrolytes. **Solutions are customized** for each client **according to daily laboratory results.**

- Follow sterile procedures to **minimize the risk of sepsis.**

  ◊ TPN solution is prepared by the pharmacy using aseptic technique with a laminar flow hood.

  ◊ Change tubing and solution bag (even if not empty) every 24 hr.

  ◊ A filter is used on the IV line (to collect particles from the solution).

◊ **Do not use the line for other IV solutions** (prevents contamination and interruption of the flow).

◊ Do not add anything to the solution due to risks of contamination and incompatibility.

◊ **Use sterile procedures**, including mask, when changing central line dressing (per facility procedure).

Δ **Effective outcomes** of TPN therapy include:

- Weight gain (≤ 1 kg/day).

- Laboratory values within normal ranges.

- Avoidance of complications.

Complications and Nursing Implications

Δ **Metabolic Complications** (hyperglycemia/hypoglycemia, vitamin deficiencies)

- Daily laboratory work must be ordered and results obtained before new solution is prepared.

- Fluid needs are typically replaced with a separate IV to prevent fluid volume excess.

- Monitor for signs of hyperglycemia (glucose > 100 mg/dL, polyuria).

- Maintain continuous infusion and monitor for signs of hypoglycemia with rate or solution changes.

Δ **Mechanical Complications** (phlebitis, air embolism)

- Discourage the client from talking/laughing when changing tubing to prevent air embolism from pressure change (have the client hold breath).

- Signs and symptoms of **air embolism** (sudden onset of dyspnea, chest pain, anxiety, hypoxia) should be treated emergently by clamping the catheter and placing the client in **Trendelenburg position** and on **left side to trap air**. Administer **oxygen** and get the provider stat so that trapped air can be aspirated.

Δ **Infection** (concentrated glucose is a medium for bacteria)

- Observe the central line insertion site frequently for local infection (erythema, tenderness, exudate).

- Change sterile dressing on central line per protocol (typically every 72 hr).

- Observe the client for signs of systemic infection (fever, increased WBC, chills, malaise).

- Do NOT use TPN line for other IV fluids and medications (repeated access increases the risk for infection).

Δ   **Potential Fluid Imbalance** – particularly fluid volume excess (FVE) due to the hyperosmotic solution (three to six times the osmolarity of blood), which poses a risk for fluid shifts

- Assess lungs for crackles and monitor the client for evidence of respiratory distress.

- Monitor daily weights and intake/output.

- Use a controlled infusion pump to administer TPN at the prescribed rate.

- Do not speed up the infusion to "catch-up."

- Gradually increase the flow rate until the prescribed infusion rate is achieved.

Meeting the Needs of Older Adults

Δ   Older adult clients are more vulnerable to complications, particularly fluid and electrolyte imbalances. Clients with a history of congestive heart failure may need a more concentrated solution to avoid fluid shifts.

Δ   Older adult clients have an increased incidence of glucose intolerance.

Δ   Age-related physiological changes, such as decreased lean muscle mass, influence the reliability of measures used for nutritional assessment.

Primary Reference:

Ignatavicius, D. D., & Workman, M. L. (2006). *Medical-surgical nursing* (5th ed.). St. Louis, MO: Saunders.

Additional Resources:

Metheny, N. M. (2000). *Fluid and electrolyte balance: Nursing considerations* (4th ed.). Philadelphia: Lippincott Williams & Wilkins.

NANDA International (2004). *NANDA nursing diagnoses: Definitions and classification 2005-2006.* Philadelphia: NANDA.

For more information, visit the American Society for Parenteral and Enteral Nutrition at *www.nutritioncare.org.*

Chapter 41: Total Parenteral Nutrition

Application Exercises

1. A client is receiving TPN. Which of the following are the best procedures for the nurse to follow in managing the TPN administration? (Check all that apply.)

_____ Place a mask on the client and have her turn away from the site during a dressing change.

_____ Obtain serum potassium (K^+) level every day.

_____ Flush the line with 30 cc sterile normal saline before using it for IV aminoglycoside administration.

_____ Monitor daily weights.

_____ Teach the client about diabetes control if she has an elevated glucose and requires sliding scale Regular insulin.

2. A client is anorexic and is eating less than 30% of his diet. He had hip surgery 5 days ago. Should TPN be considered for this client? Why or why not?

3. A nurse is assigned at 0700 to care for a client who started receiving TPN yesterday for chronic pancreatitis. Which of the following should be included in the nurse's plan of care for this client? (Check all that apply.)

_____ Obtain a capillary glucose (Accu-Chek®) at 1100.

_____ Add the ordered additional IV potassium to the bag of TPN solution.

_____ Take a set of vital signs two times during the 8-hr shift.

_____ Contact the primary care provider to request an increase in the rate by 10% if the urine is concentrated with a specific gravity of 1.025.

_____ Ensure a daily activated partial thromboplastin time (aPTT) is obtained.

4. A client is started on TPN for chronic pancreatitis. The most important assessments for the nurse to make 24 hr later are

A. blood urea nitrogen and creatinine levels.

B. glucose level and auscultation of lungs for presence of crackles.

C. temperature and white blood cell count.

D. redness and drainage at the central line insertion site.

5. It has been 24 hr since the last bag of TPN was hung for a client. There is 400 mL of TPN solution remaining. Which of the following is the appropriate action for the nurse to take?

    A. Remove the old bag and hang the new bag.

    B. Let the remaining solution infuse at the current rate and hang the new bag when the current bag is empty for cost-effectiveness.

    C. Increase the rate of the TPN infusion so as to administer the remaining solution within the next hour before starting the new bag.

    D. Clarify the procedure with the pharmacy.

6. A nurse is reviewing the laboratory values of a female client with a GI fistula who has been receiving TPN for 3 days. The nurse should follow up first on which of the following laboratory results?

    A. White blood cells 12,000/mm³, neutrophils 88%

    B. Hemoglobin 9.9 g/dL, hematocrit 46%

    C. Potassium 3.5 mEq/L, sodium 140 mg/dL

    D. Blood urea nitrogen 20 mg/dL, creatinine 1.1 mg/dL

7. A client is receiving TPN for short bowel syndrome. He requests that the nurse discontinue the TPN infusion while he takes a shower. Which of the following is the best response by the nurse?

    A. Contact the provider to get an appropriate order.

    B. Discontinue the TPN but emphasize the need to notify nursing to reconnect it as soon as shower is completed.

    C. Explain that the request cannot be met and share the rationale.

    D. Increase the rate for an hour first to compensate for the time the line will be disconnected.

Chapter 41: Total Parenteral Nutrition

Application Exercises Answer Key

1. A client is receiving TPN. Which of the following are the best procedures for the nurse to follow in managing the TPN administration? (Check all that apply.)

   __X__   Place a mask on the client and have her turn away from the site during a dressing change.

   __X__   Obtain serum potassium (K⁺) level every day.

   _____   Flush the line with 30 cc sterile normal saline before using it for IV aminoglycoside administration.

   __X__   Monitor daily weights.

   _____   Teach the client about diabetes control if she has an elevated glucose and requires sliding scale Regular insulin.

   Sterile technique decreases the risk of infection.

   A daily potassium level is needed prior to preparing the next solution and to assess electrolyte balance from the current solution.

   The line is not used for other solutions/medications due to the risk of infection and incompatibilities as well as the fact that it would interrupt the flow of the solution and place the client at risk for hypoglycemia.

   Weight is used to assess fluid balance and as one consideration in the evaluation of the TPN's effectiveness.

   Hyperglycemia is treated with sliding scale insulin, but it is usually a temporary measure until the body can "catch up" in making enough endogenous insulin. There are no permanent changes in the pancreatic function that would result in the client having diabetes mellitus.

2. A client is anorexic and is eating less than 30% of his diet. He had hip surgery 5 days ago. Should TPN be considered for this client? Why or why not?

   Enteral nutrition is always preferred. The enteral route is the most natural for the absorption and use of nutrients. It has less associated complications. TPN is reserved for significant malnutrition, clients without a functioning GI tract, or a hypermetabolic state such as sepsis. It is better to consider other options to improve oral intake when possible.

3. A nurse is assigned at 0700 to care for a client who started receiving TPN yesterday for chronic pancreatitis. Which of the following should be included in the nurse's plan of care for this client? (Check all that apply.)

   __x__   Obtain a capillary glucose (Accu-Chek®) at 1100.

   _____   Add the ordered additional IV potassium to the bag of TPN solution.

   __x__   Take a set of vital signs two times during the 8-hr shift.

   _____   Contact the primary care provider to request an increase in the rate by 10% if the urine is concentrated with a specific gravity of 1.025.

   _____   Ensure a daily activated partial thromboplastin time (aPTT) is obtained.

The client is at risk for hyperglycemia the first 24 hr of administration and may require sliding scale coverage until the body makes enough endogenous insulin.

No additional substances should be added to the bag of TPN on the unit due to the risk of contamination and incompatibility.

Vital signs are recommended every 4 to 8 hr to help assess for FVE and infection.

TPN candidates are at risk for fluid overload. Additional fluid needs are met with a separate IV rather than increasing the hypertonic TPN solution beyond the nutritional requirements. Also, this specific gravity is at the high end of the normal range.

PTT measures the anticoagulation effect of heparin. While some heparin may be added to the solution to help prevent thrombus formation, the amount is too small to require a daily laboratory assessment.

4. A client is started on TPN for chronic pancreatitis. The most important assessments for the nurse to make 24 hr later are

    A. blood urea nitrogen and creatinine levels.

    B. glucose level and auscultation of lungs for presence of crackles.

    C. temperature and white blood cell count.

    D. redness and drainage at the central line insertion site.

Particularly the first 24 hr, the client is prone to hyperglycemia because the pancreas has not yet adjusted from the fasting state to the concentrated solution. Supplemental insulin is frequently needed. The client is at risk for FVE related to the administration of a concentrated solution. FVE is typically first evident as crackles. BUN and creatinine are indications of kidney function and kidney problems are not a complication specific to this intervention. Urine ketones would be more helpful (Option A). It would typically take at least 2 to 3 days to see signs of infection (Options C and D).

5. It has been 24 hr since the last bag of TPN was hung for a client. There is 400 mL of TPN solution remaining. Which of the following is the appropriate action for the nurse to take?

A. Remove the old bag and hang the new bag.

B. Let the remaining solution infuse at the current rate and hang the new bag when the current bag is empty for cost-effectiveness.

C. Increase the rate of the TPN infusion so as to administer the remaining solution within the next hour before starting the new bag.

D. Clarify the procedure with the pharmacy.

The current bag of TPN should not hang more than 24 hr related to the risk of infection. The TPN infusion rate should never be increased/decreased abruptly due to the risk of phlebitis and hyperglycemia.

6. A nurse is reviewing the laboratory values of a female client with a GI fistula who has been receiving TPN for 3 days. The nurse should follow up first on which of the following laboratory results?

A. White blood cells 12,000/mm³, neutrophils 88%

B. Hemoglobin 9.9 g/dL, hematocrit 46%

C. Potassium 3.5 mEq/L, sodium 140 mg/dL

D. Blood urea nitrogen 20 mg/dL, creatinine 1.1 mg/dL

The client is showing signs of an acute infection. As many TPN clients are immunosuppressed or debilitated, they do not respond with the classic dramatic infectious response. Known malnourishment was a probable reason for starting the TPN (Option B). The results in options C and D are borderline normal.

7. A client is receiving TPN for short bowel syndrome. He requests that the nurse discontinue the TPN infusion while he takes a shower. Which of the following is the best response by the nurse?

A. Contact the provider to get an appropriate order.

B. Discontinue the TPN but emphasize the need to notify nursing to reconnect it as soon as shower is completed.

C. Explain that the request cannot be met and share the rationale.

D. Increase the rate for an hour first to compensate for the time the line will be disconnected.

TPN lines should never be abruptly stopped as hypoglycemia can result (the insulin levels are high, anticipating the continuous infusion of the highly concentrated glucose). For the same reason, the rate should never be increased or decreased to compensate.

Unit 5 Nursing Care of Clients with Renal and Urinary Disorders

Section: Diagnostic and Therapeutic Procedures: Renal

Chapter 42: Hemodialysis and Peritoneal Dialysis

Contributor: Carol Green-Nigro, PhD, RN

NCLEX-PN® Connections

Learning Objective: Review and apply knowledge within "**Hemodialysis and Peritoneal Dialysis**" in readiness for performance of the following nursing activities as outlined by the NCLEX-PN® test plan:

- Δ Provide peritoneal dialysis per protocols.
- Δ Provide care for the client undergoing hemodialysis.
- Δ Perform/assist with relevant laboratory, diagnostic, and therapeutic procedures within the nursing role, including:
  - Preparation of the client for the procedure.
  - Reinforcement of client teaching (before and following the procedure).
  - Accurate collection of specimens.
  - Monitoring procedure results (compare to norms) and appropriate notification of the primary care provider.
  - Monitoring the client's response (expected, unexpected adverse response, comparison to baseline) to the procedure.
  - Monitoring and taking actions, including reinforcing client teaching, to prevent or minimize the risk of complications.
  - Recognizing signs of potential complications and reporting to the primary care provider.
  - Recommending changes in the test/procedure as needed based on client findings.
- Δ Monitor therapeutic devices (drainage/irrigating devices, chest tubes), if inserted, for proper functioning.

📖 **Key Points**

Δ **Functions of Dialysis**

- Rid the body of excess fluid and electrolytes.
- Achieve acid-base balance.
- Eliminate waste products.
- Restore internal homeostasis by osmosis, diffusion, and ultrafiltration.

Δ Dialysis can **sustain life** for clients with both **acute** and **chronic renal failure**.

Δ Dialysis does **not replace** the **hormonal functions** of the kidney.

Δ **Hemodialysis**

- Shunts the client's blood from the body through a **dialyzer** and back into the client's circulation.
- **Requires** internal or external **access device**.

Δ **Peritoneal Dialysis**

- Involves instillation of fluid into the peritoneal cavity.
- Peritoneum serves as the filtration membrane.

Key Factors

Δ **Risk Factors for Dialysis**

- Renal insufficiency
- Acute renal failure
- Chronic renal failure
- Drug overdose
- Persistent hyperkalemia
- Hypervolemia unresponsive to diuretics

Therapeutic Procedures and Nursing Interventions

Δ **Hemodialysis (HD)**

- Prior to hemodialysis, assess for **patency of the access site** (presence of bruit, palpable thrill, distal pulses, and circulation).

- Prior to and after hemodialysis monitor/assess:
  ◊ Vital signs.
  ◊ Laboratory values (BUN, serum creatinine, electrolytes, hematocrit).
  ◊ Weight.
  ◊ Decreases in blood pressure, weight, and laboratory values are expected following dialysis.

- After hemodialysis assess:
  ◊ For **complications** (hypotension, access clotting, headache, muscle cramps, bleeding, disequilibrium syndrome, hepatitis).
  ◊ Access site for **indications of bleeding, infection**.
  ◊ For **nausea, vomiting, level of consciousness**.
  ◊ For signs of **hypovolemia**.

- Nursing Interventions
  ◊ Discuss with the primary care provider any **medications to be withheld** until after dialysis. Dialyzable medications and medications that lower blood pressure are usually withheld.
  ◊ Provide **emotional support** prior, during, and after the procedure.
  ◊ **Avoid taking blood pressure, administering injections, performing venipunctures or inserting IV lines on an arm with an access site.**
  ◊ Avoid **invasive procedures** for 4 to 6 hr after dialysis (heparin administered during dialysis).
  ◊ Elevate the extremity following surgical development of AV fistula to reduce swelling.
  ◊ Teach the client to:
    ° **Avoid lifting heavy objects** with access-site arm.
    ° **Avoid carrying objects that compress the extremity.**
    ° **Avoid sleeping with body weight on top of the extremity** with the access device.
    ° Perform hand **exercises that promote fistula maturation**.

Δ **Peritoneal Dialysis (PD)**

- Prior to and after peritoneal dialysis assess/monitor:
  ◊ Weight.
  ◊ Serum electrolytes, creatinine, BUN, blood glucose (as prescribed).

- After peritoneal dialysis assess/monitor:
  - ◊ **Color** (clear, light yellow is expected) **and amount (expected to equal or exceed amount of dialysate inflow) of outflow.**
  - ◊ For signs of **infection** (fever, bloody, cloudy, or frothy dialysate return, drainage at access site).
  - ◊ For **complications** (respiratory distress, abdominal pain, insufficient outflow, discolored outflow).
- Nursing Interventions
  - ◊ Check the access site dressing for wetness (risk of dialysate leakage).
  - ◊ **Warm the dialysate** prior to instilling (avoid use of microwaves which cause uneven heating).
  - ◊ Follow **prescribed times for infusion, dwell, and outflow.**
  - ◊ **Maintain surgical asepsis:**
    - ° Of the catheter insertion site.
    - ° When accessing PD catheter.
  - ◊ Keep the outflow bag **lower than the client's abdomen (drain by gravity, prevent reflux).**
  - ◊ **Reposition** the client if inflow or outflow is inadequate.
  - ◊ Carefully **milk PD catheter if fibrin clot** has formed.
  - ◊ Teach the client **home care of the access site.**
  - ◊ Provide emotional support to the client and family.

Complications and Nursing Implications

Δ **Hemodialysis**

- **Clotting/Infection of Access Site**
  - ◊ Use **surgical aseptic technique** during cannulation.
  - ◊ Avoid compression of access site/extremity.
- **Disequilibrium Syndrome** (too rapid a decrease of BUN)
  - ◊ Early recognition is essential. Signs include nausea, vomiting, change in level of consciousness, seizures, and agitation.
  - ◊ Can be avoided with a slow dialysis exchange rate, especially in older adult clients and those being newly treated with hemodialysis.
  - ◊ Anticonvulsants/barbiturates may be needed.

- **Hypotension**
  - ◊ **Discontinue dialysis**.
  - ◊ Place the client in the **Trendelenburg** position.
- **Anemia**
  - ◊ Administer prescribed medication therapy (**erythropoietin**) to stimulate the production of red blood cells.
- **Infectious Diseases**
  - ◊ HD poses a risk for transmission of bloodborne diseases such as HIV and hepatitis B and C.
  - ◊ Maintain sterility of equipment.
  - ◊ Use standard precautions.

Δ **Peritoneal Dialysis**

- **Peritonitis** (the major complication of PD)
  - ◊ Maintain **meticulous surgical asepsis** during the procedure.
- **Infection** (at access site)
  - ◊ Maintain surgical **asepsis of access site**.
- Protein Loss
  - ◊ Increase dietary intake of protein.
- **Hyperglycemia** (hyperosmolar dialysate)
  - ◊ Insulin for glycemic control.
  - ◊ Lipid therapy for triglyceride control.
- Poor Dialysate Inflow or Outflow
  - ◊ Rotate catheter to facilitate inflow and outflow.
  - ◊ Milk tubing to break up fibrin clot.
  - ◊ Check tubing for kinks or closed clamps.
  - ◊ Avoid constipation (high fiber, stool softeners).

Meeting the Needs of Older Adults

Δ Older age is a risk factor for:

- **Dialysis disequilibrium and hypotension** due to rapid changes in fluid and electrolyte status.
- **Access site complications** related to chronic illnesses and/or fragile veins.

Δ Older adult clients may be unable to care for a peritoneal access site due to cognitive or physical deficits.

Δ   The most common cause of death in older adult clients receiving dialysis is cardiovascular disease followed by withdrawal of dialysis treatment.

Δ   The increasing number of older, debilitated clients receiving dialysis for ESRD has raised ethical concerns about the use of scarce resources in a population with a limited life expectancy.

Primary Reference:

Ignatavicius, D. D., & Workman, M. L. (2006). *Medical-surgical nursing* (5th ed.). St. Louis, MO: Saunders.

Additional Resources:

NANDA International (2004). *NANDA nursing diagnoses: Definitions and classification 2005-2006*. Philadelphia: NANDA.

Thomas, N. (Ed.). (2002). *Renal Nursing* (2nd ed.). St Louis, MO: Elsevier Science.

Chapter 42: Hemodialysis and Peritoneal Dialysis

Application Exercises

Scenario: A 35-year-old male client with a lifetime history of polycystic kidney disease has received hemodialysis for renal failure for the past 7 years. While awaiting a renal transplant, he is receiving hemodialysis three times a week by an arteriovenous fistula created in his left arm. The client was admitted to the acute care facility during the night for reports of fever and flu-like symptoms. He is to receive his scheduled hemodialysis at 0700 this morning. His vital signs are: temperature 38.3° C (101° F) orally, pulse 90 beats/min, respirations 26/min, and blood pressure 160/90 mm Hg.

1. **True or False:** Dialysis sustains the life of clients with renal failure because it restores fluid and electrolyte function, maintains homeostasis, and replaces several important hormonal functions of the kidneys.

2. **True or False:** When a client undergoes peritoneal dialysis, the peritoneum serves as the osmotic membrane.

3. **True or False:** Peritonitis, insertion site infection, hyperglycemia, and protein loss are potential complications of peritoneal dialysis.

4. **True or False:** Hemodialysis requires more frequent exchanges than peritoneal dialysis but has fewer adverse effects.

5. **True or False:** Older adult clients are at increased risk for dialysis complications such as disequilibrium syndrome.

6. Which of the following nursing assessments and interventions should the nurse implement immediately prior to initiating hemodialysis?

_____   Determine current medications being taken by client.

_____   Assess AV fistula for bruit.

_____   Calculate total urine output for the night.

_____   Assess dietary intake.

_____   Obtain blood glucose level.

_____   Obtain client's weight.

_____   Assess hydration status.

_____   Obtain serum electrolytes.

_____   Obtain client's blood pressure reading.

7. Select appropriate pre-dialysis nursing diagnoses. For selected diagnoses, prioritize and provide rationale for your prioritization.

_____   Deficient fluid volume

_____   Potential complications of hemodialysis (clotting, infection, hypotension)

_____   Risk for activity intolerance

_____   Risk for impaired gas exchange

8. Which of the following nursing assessments and interventions should the nurse implement following the client's hemodialysis procedure? (Check all that apply.)

_____   Obtain BUN and serum creatinine.

_____   Assess for headache and/or confusion.

_____   Obtain blood glucose level.

_____   Administer antihypertensive medication for hypertension.

_____   Obtain serum electrolytes.

_____   Assess access site for indications of bleeding.

_____   Monitor access site for indications of bleeding.

9. Provide two nursing actions for each of the following post-hemodialysis nursing diagnoses for this client. Provide a rationale for each identified nursing action.

    A. Potential complications of hemodialysis (infection, clotting of access site, hypotension)

    B. Deficient knowledge: Care of vascular access site

10. What impact, if any, does the client's current fever and flu-like symptoms have on his hemodialysis treatment or nursing care?

Chapter 42: Hemodialysis and Peritoneal Dialysis

Application Exercises Answer Key

Scenario: A 35-year-old male client with a lifetime history of polycystic kidney disease has received hemodialysis for renal failure for the past 7 years. While awaiting a renal transplant, he is receiving hemodialysis three times a week by an arteriovenous fistula created in his left arm. The client was admitted to the acute care facility during the night for reports of fever and flu-like symptoms. He is to receive his scheduled hemodialysis at 0700 this morning. His vital signs are: temperature 38.3° C (101° F) orally, pulse 90 beats/min, respirations 26/min, and blood pressure 160/90 mm Hg.

1. **True or False:** Dialysis sustains the life of clients with renal failure because it restores fluid and electrolyte function, maintains homeostasis, and replaces several important hormonal functions of the kidneys.

   False: Dialysis does sustain the life of clients with renal failure, but it does not replace hormonal functions, which are permanently lost. Medications such as erythropoietin can be given to stimulate the production of red blood cells, a hormonal function that is lost with renal failure.

2. **True or False:** When a client undergoes peritoneal dialysis, the peritoneum serves as the osmotic membrane.

   False: The peritoneum serves as the filtration membrane. Osmosis is the movement of fluid from an area of high to low concentration across a semi-permeable membrane. Osmosis and diffusion are the mechanisms by which waste products are removed during peritoneal dialysis.

3. **True or False:** Peritonitis, insertion site infection, hyperglycemia, and protein loss are potential complications of peritoneal dialysis.

   True

4. **True or False:** Hemodialysis requires more frequent exchanges than peritoneal dialysis but has fewer adverse effects.

False: Hemodialysis may be performed several times daily initially, but once the client is stabilized on therapy, it is generally performed three times weekly. Peritoneal dialysis may be performed as often as every 2 to 3 hr depending on its prescribed frequency. Both hemodialysis and peritoneal dialysis have adverse effects, but peritoneal dialysis has fewer adverse effects than hemodialysis.

5. **True or False:** Older adult clients are at increased risk for dialysis complications such as disequilibrium syndrome.

True

6. Which of the following nursing assessments and interventions should the nurse implement immediately prior to initiating hemodialysis?

_x_	Determine current medications being taken by client.
_x_	Assess AV fistula for bruit.
_____	Calculate total urine output for the night.
_____	Assess dietary intake.
_____	Obtain blood glucose level.
_x_	Obtain client's weight.
_____	Assess hydration status.
_x_	Obtain serum electrolytes.
_x_	Obtain client's blood pressure reading.

7. Select appropriate pre-dialysis nursing diagnoses. For selected diagnoses, prioritize and provide rationale for your prioritization.

     _____   Deficient fluid volume

     _____   Potential complications of hemodialysis (clotting, infection, hypotension)

     __2__   Risk for activity intolerance

     __1__   Risk for impaired gas exchange

Risk for impaired gas exchange is the top priority nursing diagnosis. Fluid overload results in fluid accumulation within tissues and the lungs. If not relieved, the client will develop pulmonary edema and an inability to adequately exchange O_2 and CO_2, which is life-threatening.

The second priority nursing diagnosis is risk for activity intolerance. Fluid overload produces fatigue, which decreases the client's tolerance for activity.

Deficient fluid volume and potential complications of hemodialysis are applicable to the client after receiving dialysis.

8. Which of the following nursing assessments and interventions should the nurse implement following the client's hemodialysis procedure? (Check all that apply.)

     __x__   Obtain BUN and serum creatinine.

     __x__   Assess for headache and/or confusion.

     _____   Obtain blood glucose level.

     _____   Administer antihypertensive medication for hypertension.

     __x__   Obtain serum electrolytes.

     __x__   Assess access site for indications of bleeding.

     __x__   Monitor access site for indications of bleeding.

9. Provide two nursing actions for each of the following post-hemodialysis nursing diagnoses for this client. Provide a rationale for each identified nursing action.

A. Potential complications of hemodialysis (infection, clotting of access site, hypotension)

Monitor the client for hypotension. Rationale: Blood pressure will drop as fluid is removed from the intravascular space. If too much fluid is removed, the client may develop hypotension.

Assess the access site for bleeding. Rationale: The blood is heparinized to prevent clotting during hemodialysis, which increases the client's risk for bleeding at the access site that has been cannulated.

B. Deficient knowledge: Care of vascular access site

Teach the client to avoid restrictive clothing. Rationale: Restrictive clothing, venipunctures, or blood pressures taken in the extremity with venous access may causing clotting of the fistula or graft.

Teach the client to monitor the access site for redness, tenderness, swelling, and warmth. Rationale: These are signs of infection that need to be reported to the primary care provider. Infection of the site can lead to systemic infection and sepsis.

10. What impact, if any, does the client's current fever and flu-like symptoms have on his hemodialysis treatment or nursing care?

Regardless of how the client feels, it is essential that he be dialyzed. His illness does place him at increased risk for complications such as infection, fluid volume deficit, and nausea and vomiting.

Unit 5   Nursing Care of Clients with Renal and Urinary Disorders

Section: Diagnostic and Therapeutic Procedures: Renal

Chapter 43:   Renal Transplantation
                Contributor: Carol Green-Nigro, PhD, RN

NCLEX-PN® Connections:

Learning Objective: Review and apply knowledge within "**Renal Transplantation**" in readiness for performance of the following nursing activities as outlined by the NCLEX-PN® test plan:

Δ   Perform/assist with relevant laboratory, diagnostic, and therapeutic procedures within the nursing role, including:

- Preparation of the client for the procedure.

- Reinforcement of client teaching (before and following the procedure).

- Accurate collection of specimens.

- Monitoring procedure results (compare to norms) and appropriate notification of the primary care provider.

- Monitoring the client's response (expected, unexpected adverse response, comparison to baseline) to the procedure.

- Monitoring and taking actions, including reinforcing client teaching, to prevent or minimize the risk of complications.

- Recognizing signs of potential complications and reporting to the primary care provider.

- Recommending changes in the test/procedure as needed based on client findings.

Δ   Recognize the client's recovery from anesthesia, if used.

Δ   Monitor therapeutic devices (drainage/irrigating devices, chest tubes), if inserted, for proper functioning.

📖 Key Points

Δ Transplantation is a **life-sustaining treatment** for end-stage renal disease, **not a cure**.

Δ Clients with **medical problems** that increase the risks involved with transplantation are **excluded as candidates** (see "Risk Factors" below).

Δ Donors for renal transplantation may be **living**, **non-heart-beating**, or **cadaver** donors.

Δ **Tissue types** are **matched between donor and recipient**. In-depth tissue typing includes assessment of **blood type (ABO) compatibility** and **histocompatibility** (human leukocytic antigen (HLA) and other minor antigens).

Δ The size of the donor kidney does not matter.

Δ Clients receiving a donor kidney from a living, related donor with matching tissue type have the greatest survival rates.

Δ The donor kidney is placed in the **anterior iliac fossa** with the renal artery anteriorly and the renal vein posteriorly. The client's nonfunctioning kidneys may be left in, unless they are infected.

Δ Clients undergoing renal transplant face the possibility of organ rejection within 48 hr of transplantation (**hyperacute** rejection), 1 to 2 weeks following transplantation (**acute** rejection), or months to years following transplantation (**chronic** rejection).

Key Factors

Δ Conditions that **increase the risks involved** in renal transplantation surgery, lifelong immunosuppression, and organ rejection include:

• Age younger than **2 years**.

• Age older than **70 years** (evaluated individually).

• Advanced, untreatable cardiac disease.

• **Active cancer**.

• Severe psychosocial problems, such as chemical dependency.

• Chronic **infectious** or systemic diseases (HIV infection, hepatitis C).

• **Coagulopathies** and certain immune disorders.

Δ   Client indications of end stage renal disease (ESRD) necessitating renal transplantation include:

- Anuria.

- Proteinuria.

- Marked azotemia (elevated BUN and serum creatinine).

- Severe electrolyte imbalance (hyperkalemia, hypernatremia).

- Fluid volume excess conditions (heart failure, pulmonary edema).

- Uremic lung.

Nursing Interventions

Δ   **Preoperative Care**

- Schedule **preoperative laboratory assessments,** including blood chemistry studies, CBC and differential, bleeding times, urine culture, blood type, and crossmatch.

- Prepare the client **mentally and emotionally** for the procedure.

- Advise the client that **compliance** with the post-transplant interventions (e.g., **lifelong immunosuppression**) and **risk factor reduction** (e.g., smoking cessation, blood pressure and blood glucose control) are **crucial to the success** of the transplantation.

  ◊   Administer preoperative medications as prescribed, including prophylactic antibiotics and **induction of immunosuppressant therapy** (e.g., Solu-Medrol, cyclosporine, Neoral).

Δ   **Postoperative Care**

- Assess/Monitor

  ◊   **Vital signs** continually

  ◊   **Intake** and **output** at least **hourly (urine output should be greater than 30 mL/hr)**

  ◊   Urine appearance and odor hourly (initially pink and bloody, gradually returning to normal in a few days to several weeks)

  ◊   **Daily weight**

  ◊   Daily urine tests, including **urinalysis** and **glucose determinations**

  ◊   Renal function, specifically for oliguria (100 to 400 mL output in 24 hr)

  ◊   For fluid and electrolyte imbalances, such as hypervolemia, hypovolemia, hypokalemia, and hyponatremia

  ◊   For signs of **infection** (respiratory, surgical site)

  ◊   For signs of organ **rejection**

- Administer intravenous fluids as prescribed.

- Administer oral fluids and discontinue IVs once bowel function returns and fluids are tolerated.

- Encourage the client to turn, cough, and deep breathe to **prevent atelectasis and pneumonia.**

- Provide urinary catheter care:

  ◊ Attach the **large indwelling urinary catheter** to bedside drainage.

  ◊ Maintain continuous bladder irrigation as prescribed.

  ◊ Remove the urinary catheter as soon as possible to decrease risk of infection (immunosuppressed client).

- Intervene for oliguria as needed. Diuretics and/or dialysis may be necessary until kidney function is satisfactory.

- Administer **immunosuppressive drugs to prevent rejection**:

  ◊ Monitor for **side effects** (infection, fluid retention).

  ◊ Educate the client and family about **the increased risk for infection** during immunosuppressant therapy and **infection control measures**.

- Immediately notify the surgeon if any signs of organ rejection appear.

- Administer stool softeners to prevent straining and constipation (risk associated with bowel manipulation during abdominal surgery and the effects of general anesthetics and analgesics).

- Arrange for counseling for the client and family if necessary.

- Arrange for post-transplant follow-up appointments and interventions.

Complications and Nursing Implications

Δ **Organ Rejection**

- Monitor for and report signs of rejection immediately:

  ◊ **Hyperacute** – occurs within 48 hr after surgery. Symptoms include fever, hypertension, and pain at the transplant site. Treatment is immediate removal of the donor kidney.

  ◊ **Acute** – occurs 1 week to 2 years after surgery. Symptoms include oliguria, anuria, low-grade fever, hypertension, tenderness over the transplanted kidney, lethargy, azotemia, and fluid retention. Treatment involves **increased doses of immunosuppressive drugs**.

  ◊ **Chronic** – occurs gradually over months to years. Symptoms include gradual return of azotemia, fluid retention, electrolyte imbalance, and fatigue. Treatment is conservative until dialysis is required.

Δ   **Acute Tubular Necrosis (ATN)**

- Monitor urine output and serum creatinine and BUN levels to detect failure of the transplanted kidney.

- Report hourly output volumes less than 30 mL/hr.

- Assist with dialysis as indicated.

- Prepare client for renal biopsy to distinguish ATN from organ rejection.

Δ   **Renal Artery Stenosis** (due to scarring of surgical anastomosis)

- Monitor for and report **hypertension, bruit** over artery anastomosis site, and **decreased renal function**.

- Prepare client for renal scan to verify status of renal blood flow.

- Angioplasty and/or surgical intervention may be necessary.

Δ   **Thrombosis**

- Monitor for and report a sudden decease in urine output.

- Prepare the client for emergency surgery.

Δ   **Infection** (the most common cause of first-transplant-year morbidity and mortality)

- Give high priority to infection control measures.

- Monitor for and report signs of **localized** (wound) or **systemic infection** (pneumonia, sepsis).

Meeting the Needs of Older Adults

Δ   Clients older than 70 years of age are poor candidates for renal transplantation.

Δ   Older adult clients are more likely to have **advanced heart disease and malignancies**, which make them less than ideal candidates for renal transplantation surgery.

Primary Reference:

Ignatavicius, D. D., & Workman, M. L. (2006). *Medical-surgical nursing* (5th ed.). St. Louis, MO: Saunders.

Additional Resources:

Monahan, F. D., Sands, J. K., Neighbors, M., Marek, F. J., & Green, C. J. (Eds.). (2007). *Phipps' medical-surgical nursing: Health and illness perspectives* (8th ed.). St. Louis, MO: Mosby.

NANDA International (2004). *NANDA nursing diagnoses: Definitions and classification 2005-2006*. Philadelphia: NANDA.

Chapter 43: Renal Transplantation

Application Exercises

Scenario: A 40-year-old male client with end-stage renal disease underwent a renal transplant 4 days ago. His urinary catheter has been removed, and the client is able to void. He is being started on oral fluids today. If he tolerates fluids, his intravenous electrolyte infusion will be discontinued. The client has not shown any signs of transplant rejection.

1. The client is at risk for which of the following fluid and electrolyte imbalances during this phase of his recovery? (Check all that apply.)

    _____ Hypokalemia   _____ Hypovolemia

    _____ Hypercalcemia   _____ Fluid-volume excess (overload)

    _____ Hypomagnesemia   _____ Hyponatremia

2. The client is placed on the stool softener docusate sodium. Why is this intervention necessary following kidney transplantation?

3. Which of the following nursing diagnoses take priority when caring for the client during this early postoperative phase following kidney transplantation?

    _____ Imbalanced nutrition: Less than body requirements

    _____ Risk for deficient fluid volume

    _____ Deficient knowledge: Medication regimen

    _____ Noncompliance with therapeutic regimen

    _____ Fear

    _____ Risk for infection

    _____ Disturbed body image

    _____ Anxiety

4. Which client findings should cause the nurse to suspect organ rejection? What kind of rejection can occur at this time? What is a priority intervention?

Chapter 43: Renal Transplantation

Application Exercises Answer Key

Scenario: A 40-year-old male client with end-stage renal disease underwent a renal transplant 4 days ago. His urinary catheter has been removed, and the client is able to void. He is being started on oral fluids today. If he tolerates fluids, his intravenous electrolyte infusion will be discontinued. The client has not shown any signs of transplant rejection.

1. The client is at risk for which of the following fluid and electrolyte imbalances during this phase of his recovery? (Check all that apply.)

   __x__ Hypokalemia   __x__ Hypovolemia

   _____ Hypercalcemia   __x__ Fluid-volume excess (overload)

   _____ Hypomagnesemia   __x__ Hyponatremia

   With oliguria, the potential for fluid volume excess and associated complications (hypertension, heart failure, and pulmonary edema) is increased. Hypovolemia is a risk, especially if diuretic therapy is administered to treat oliguria. Diuresis increases the risk for hypokalemia and hyponatremia.

2. The client is placed on the stool softener docusate sodium. Why is this intervention necessary following kidney transplantation?

   Stool softeners such as docusate sodium are necessary to prevent constipation because manipulation of the bowel during surgery and decreased activity after surgery can exacerbate constipation. They also prevent straining at stool, which should be avoided in any postoperative client.

3. Which of the following nursing diagnoses take priority when caring for the client during this early postoperative phase following kidney transplantation?

   __x__ Imbalanced nutrition: Less than body requirements

   __x__ Risk for deficient fluid volume

   _____ Deficient knowledge: Medication regimen

   _____ Noncompliance with therapeutic regimen

   __x__ Fear

   __x__ Risk for infection

   _____ Disturbed body image

   __x__ Anxiety

4. Which client findings should cause the nurse to suspect organ rejection? What kind of rejection can occur at this time? What is a priority intervention?

Signs of organ rejection include malaise, oliguria, anuria, fever, tachycardia, enlarged tender kidney, boggy kidney on palpation, weight gain, hypertension, decreased urine output, abnormal chemistry studies, abnormal renal biopsy, and abnormal radionuclide scan. Rejection after the first 48 hr and up to 2 years following transplant is acute rejection. Administration of increased doses of immunosuppressants is a priority intervention.

Unit 5   Nursing Care of Clients with Renal and Urinary Disorders
Section: Nursing Care of Clients with Select Renal Disorders

Chapter 44:   Urinary Incontinence
Contributor: Gayla H. Love, BSN, RN, CCM

⟳ NCLEX-PN® Connections:

Learning Objective: Review and apply knowledge within "**Urinary Incontinence**" in readiness for performance of the following nursing activities as outlined by the NCLEX-PN® test plan:

Δ   Assist with bladder retraining.

Δ   Perform skin care for the client who is incontinent (wash often, use barrier creams/ointments).

Δ   Assist with relevant laboratory, diagnostic, and therapeutic procedures within the nursing role, including:

- Preparation of the client for the procedure.

- Accurate collection of specimens.

- Monitoring client status during and after the procedure.

- Reinforcing client teaching (before and following the procedure).

- Recognizing the client's response (expected, unexpected adverse response) to the procedure.

- Monitoring results.

- Monitoring and taking actions to prevent or minimize the risk of complications.

- Notifying the primary care provider of signs of complications.

Δ   Recognize signs and symptoms of the client's problem and complete the proper documentation.

Δ   Provide and document care based on the client's health alteration.

Δ   Monitor and document vital signs changes.

Δ   Interpret data that need to be reported immediately.

Δ   Reinforce client education on managing the client's health problem.

Δ   Recognize and respond to emergency situations, including notification of the primary care provider.

Δ   Review the client's response to emergency interventions and complete the proper documentation.

Δ   Provide care that meets the age-related needs of clients 65 years of age or older, including recognizing expected physiological changes.

📖 Key Points

Δ   There are six major types of urinary incontinence:

  • **Stress** – loss of small amounts of urine with sneezing, laughing, or lifting. Stress incontinence is related primarily to weak pelvic muscles, urethra, or surrounding tissues.

  • **Urge** – the inability to stop urine flow long enough to reach the toilet. Urge incontinence is related to an overactive detrusor muscle with increased bladder pressure.

  • **Overflow** – urinary retention associated with bladder overdistention and frequent loss of small amounts of urine. Overflow incontinence is related to obstruction of the urinary outlet or an impaired detrusor muscle.

  • **Reflex** – involuntary loss of a moderate amount of urine usually with warning. Reflex incontinence is related to hyperreflexia of the detrusor muscle, usually from altered spinal cord activity.

  • **Functional** – inability to get to the toilet to urinate. Functional incontinence is related to physical, cognitive, or social impairment.

  • **Total incontinence** – involuntary, unpredictable loss of urine that does not generally respond to treatment.

Δ   Urinary incontinence is a significant **contributing factor to altered skin integrity** and **falls,** especially in older adults.

Key Factors

Δ   **Eighty-five percent of clients** with urinary incontinence are **female.**

Δ   **Risk factors/causes for urinary incontinence**

  • History of **multiple pregnancies** and **vaginal births, aging, renal disease, urinary bladder spasm, chronic urinary retention, and chronic bladder infection (cystitis)**

  • **Neurological disorders** such as Parkinson's disease, brain attack (stroke), multiple sclerosis, and spinal cord injury

  • **Medication therapy:** Diuretics, anticholinergics, sedative/hypnotics, narcotics, calcium channel blockers, and adrenergic antagonists

  • **Obesity**

  • **Confusion, dementia, immobility, depression**

Diagnostic Procedures and Nursing Interventions

Δ **Postvoid residual urine** – to rule out urinary retention (greater than 100 mL retained urine post voiding)

Δ Urinalysis and **urine culture/sensitivity** – to rule out urinary tract infection (presence of RBCs, WBCs, microorganisms)

Δ **Serum creatinine** and **BUN** – to assess renal function (elevated with renal dysfunction)

Δ Voiding **cystourethrography (VCUG)** – to assess the size, shape, support, and function of the urinary bladder; identify obstruction (prostate) and postvoid residual urine

Δ Urodynamic Testing

• **Cystourethroscopy** – visualization of the inside of the bladder

• **Cystometrogram (CMG)** – measures pressure inside the bladder with urine filling

• **Uroflowmetry** – measures rate and degree of bladder emptying

• **Urethral pressure profilometry (UPP)** – compares urethral pressure to bladder pressure during certain activities (coughing, lifting)

Δ **Electromyography (EMG)** – measures strength of pelvic muscle contractions

Δ **Ultrasound** – to detect bladder abnormalities and/or residual urine

Therapeutic Procedures and Nursing Interventions

Δ **Surgical procedures** include anterior vaginal repair, retropubic suspension, pubovaginal sling, and/or insertion of an artificial sphincter. Catheters (suprapubic and/or urinary) are typically inserted and maintained until the client has a postvoid residual of less than 50 mL. Traction (with tape) is applied to the catheter to prevent movement of the bladder.

Δ Periurethral collagen injections to bladder neck

Assessments

Δ Monitor for **signs and symptoms.**

• **Loss of urine** when laughing, coughing, or sneezing

• **Enuresis** (bed-wetting)

• Bladder **spasms**

• Urinary **retention**

• **Frequency, urgency, nocturia**

Δ   **Assess/Monitor**

- **Intake and output**

- **Residual urine** volumes using a pelvis ultrasonographic scanner or postvoid catheterization

- Urinary **patterns**

- **Skin integrity**

- Environmental or other **barriers to toileting**

- Signs of **urinary tract infection**

- Lower abdomen for **suprapubic fullness**

NANDA Nursing Diagnoses

Δ   Urinary incontinence (reflex, stress, urge, functional, overflow, total)

Δ   Anxiety

Δ   Risk for impaired tissue integrity

Δ   Risk for injury: Falls

Nursing Interventions

Δ   Establish a **toileting schedule**.

Δ   Initiate a **bladder training program**.

- **Urinary bladder training** increases the bladder's ability to hold urine and the client's ability to suppress urination.

  ◊   The client is reminded to void at established intervals.

  ◊   Gradually increase voiding intervals if the client has no incontinence episodes for 3 days until the optimal 4-hr interval is achieved.

  ◊   Teach the client to **consciously hold urine** until the scheduled toileting time.

- **Urinary habit training** helps clients with limited cognitive ability to establish a predictable pattern of bladder emptying.

  ◊   Toileting scheduled is based on voiding pattern.

  ◊   Remind the client to void at established intervals.

  ◊   Maintain a voiding schedule according to the pattern in which no incontinence occurs, such as every 2 hr.

- **Intermittent urinary catheterization** is periodic catheterization to empty the bladder.

  ◊ Frequency of catheterization is adjusted to maintain an output of 300 mL or less.

Δ Monitor fluid during the daytime, and **decrease fluid intake prior to bedtime**.

Δ **Remove or control barriers to toileting**.

Δ Apply and monitor **electrical stimulation of the pelvic floor muscles** if ordered.

Δ Provide or suggest **incontinence garments**.

Δ Apply an **external or condom catheter** to males.

Δ **Avoid the use of indwelling urinary catheters**.

Δ Teach the client:

- To keep an incontinence diary.

- **Kegel exercises.** Tighten pelvic muscles for a count of 10; relax slowly for a count of 10; repeat in sequences of 15 in lying-down, sitting, and standing positions.

- **Bladder compression** techniques (Credé, Valsalva, double-voiding, splinting).

- To **avoid caffeine and alcohol** consumption because they produce diuresis and the urge to urinate.

- Regarding the side effects of prescribed medications that may stimulate voiding.

- **Vaginal cone therapy** to strengthen pelvic muscles (stress incontinence).

Δ Teach the client self-administration of prescribed **medications**:

- Antibiotics, if UTI is present.

- Antidepressants, if depression is present.

- Urinary antispasmodics or anticholinergic agents, such as oxybutynin (Ditropan), propantheline (Pro-Banthine), to decrease urgency.

- Calcium channel blockers.

- Alpha-adrenergic antagonists, if benign prostatic hypertrophy (BPH) is present.

- Hormone replacement therapy. This is controversial, but it increases blood supply to the pelvis.

Δ Provide postoperative care as indicated.

Complications and Nursing Implications

Δ   **Skin Breakdown** (related to chronic exposure to urine)

- Keep the skin clean and dry.

- Assess for signs of breakdown.

- Apply protective barrier creams.

- Implement bladder retraining program.

Δ   **Social Isolation**

- Assist the client with measures to conceal urinary leaking (peri-pad, external catheter, adult incontinence garments).

- Offer emotional support.

Meeting the Needs of Older Adults

Δ   Incontinence is not a normal part of aging, but because of physiological changes secondary to aging, the older adult is at greater risk.

Δ   Decreased estrogen levels and decreased pelvic-muscle tone increase the risk for urinary incontinence.

Δ   Increased incontinence risks may be attributed to immobility, chronic degenerative diseases, dementia, diabetes mellitus, stroke, and medications.

Δ   Urinary incontinence is associated with a risk for falls, fractures, pressure ulcers, and depression.

Δ   A decreased number of functioning nephrons increases the risk of renal complications.

Primary Reference:

Ignatavicius, D. D., & Workman, M. L. (2006). *Medical-surgical nursing* (5th ed.). St. Louis, MO: Saunders.

Additional Resources:

Burke, K. M., LeMone, P., & Mohn-Brown, E. L. (2003). *Medical-surgical nursing care.* Upper Saddle River, NJ: Prentice Hall.

NANDA International (2004). *NANDA nursing diagnoses: Definitions and classification 2005-2006.* Philadelphia: NANDA.

Chapter 44: Urinary Incontinence

Application Exercises

Scenario: A 54-year-old woman visits her provider and reports that she cannot go out in public because she loses urine whenever she coughs, laughs, or sneezes. She states that she wears a vaginal pad, but she is afraid that others can smell the urine. The client relates a history of three vaginal births but no serious accidents or illnesses.

1. What type of urinary incontinence is this client experiencing? Explain your answer.

2. Which of the following collaborative interventions are appropriate to control or eliminate the client's incontinence? (Check all that apply.)

    _____   Limit total daily fluid intake.

    _____   Decrease or avoid caffeine.

    _____   Increase intake of calcium supplements.

    _____   Avoid the intake of alcohol.

    _____   Use Credé maneuver.

    _____   Maintain prescribed hormone therapy.

3. Identify the rationale for each of the following nursing interventions for a nursing diagnosis of impaired urinary elimination.

A. Assess intake/output and urination:

B. Teach Kegel exercises:

C. Minimize delays in toileting:

D. Limit beverages after evening meals:

E. If diuretics are prescribed, take them in the morning or mid-afternoon:

4. Why is the use of an indwelling catheter contraindicated for long-term control of urinary incontinence?

Chapter 44: Urinary Incontinence

Application Exercises Answer Key

Scenario: A 54-year-old woman visits her provider and reports that she cannot go out in public because she loses urine whenever she coughs, laughs, or sneezes. She states that she wears a vaginal pad, but she is afraid that others can smell the urine. The client relates a history of three vaginal births but no serious accidents or illnesses.

1. What type of urinary incontinence is this client experiencing? Explain your answer.

Stress incontinence is the loss of small amounts of urine with sneezing, laughing, lifting, or whenever there is an increase in intra-abdominal pressure. It is primarily related to weak pelvic muscles, urethra, or surrounding tissues.

2. Which of the following collaborative interventions are appropriate to control or eliminate the client's incontinence? (Check all that apply.)

	Limit total daily fluid intake.
X	Decrease or avoid caffeine.
	Increase intake of calcium supplements.
X	Avoid the intake of alcohol.
	Use Credé maneuver.
X	Maintain prescribed hormone therapy.

3. Identify the rationale for each of the following nursing interventions for a nursing diagnosis of impaired urinary elimination.

A. Assess intake/output and urination:

This identifies the type and pattern of incontinence.

B. Teach Kegel exercises:

This improves pelvic muscle strength.

C. Minimize delays in toileting:

This reduces the risk of incontinent episodes.

D. Limit beverages after evening meals:

This reduces the risk of nighttime incontinence.

E. If diuretics are prescribed, take them in the morning or mid-afternoon:

This allows the client to have peak effect of medication during awake hours.

4. Why is the use of an indwelling catheter contraindicated for long-term control of urinary incontinence?

Indwelling urinary catheters increase the risk for infection and subsequent urosepsis, especially in older adults. They should be avoided whenever possible.

Unit 5   Nursing Care of Clients with Renal and Urinary Disorders
Section: Nursing Care of Clients with Select Renal Disorders

Chapter 45:   Urinary Tract Infection
Contributor: Gayla H. Love, BSN, RN, CCM

⟳ NCLEX-PN® Connections:

Learning Objective: Review and apply knowledge within "**Urinary Tract Infection**" in readiness for performance of the following nursing activities as outlined by the NCLEX-PN® test plan:

Δ   Assist with relevant laboratory, diagnostic, and therapeutic procedures within the nursing role, including:

- Preparation of the client for the procedure.
- Accurate collection of specimens
- Monitoring the client's status during and after procedure.
- Reinforcing client teaching (before and following the procedure).
- Recognizing the client's response (expected, unexpected adverse response, and comparison to baseline) to the procedure.
- Monitoring results.
- Monitoring and taking actions to prevent or minimize the risk of complications.
- Notifying the primary care provider of signs of complications.

Δ   Recognize signs and symptoms of the client's problem and complete the proper documentation.

Δ   Provide and document care based on the client's health alteration.

Δ   Monitor and document vital signs changes.

Δ   Interpret data that need to be reported immediately.

Δ   Reinforce client education on managing the client's health problem.

Δ   Recognize and respond to emergency situations, including notification of the primary care provider.

Δ   Review the client's response to emergency interventions and complete the proper documentation.

Δ   Provide care that meets the age-related needs of clients 65 years of age or older, including recognizing expected physiological changes.

Key Points

Δ Urinary tract infection (UTI) refers to any portion of the lower urinary tract. This includes conditions such as:

- **Cystitis.**

- **Urethritis.**

- **Prostatitis.**

Δ Upper urinary tract infection refers to conditions such as **pyelonephritis.**

Δ UTIs are caused by **Enterobacteriaceae** microorganisms (such as *Klebsiella* and *Proteus*), *Pseudomonas, Serratia,* and, most commonly, *Escherichia coli.*

Δ Untreated UTIs may lead to **urosepsis,** which can lead to **septic shock** and death.

Key Factors

Δ Risk factors/causes of UTI

- Female gender

  ◊ Short urethra predisposes women to UTIs.

  ◊ Close proximity of the urethra to the rectum increases the risk of infection.

  ◊ Decreased estrogen in aging women promotes atrophy of the urethral opening toward the rectum. This increases the risk of **urosepsis** in women.

  ◊ Sexual intercourse

  ◊ The frequent use of feminine hygiene sprays, tampons, sanitary napkins, and spermicidal jellies

  ◊ Pregnancy

  ◊ Women who are fitted poorly with diaphragms

  ◊ Hormonal influences within the vaginal flora

  ◊ Synthetic underwear and pantyhose

  ◊ Wet bathing suits

  ◊ Frequent submersion into baths or hot tubs

- **Indwelling urinary catheters** (significant source of infection in clients who are hospitalized)

- Stool incontinence

- Bladder distention

- **Urinary** conditions (anomalies, stasis, calculi, and residual urine)
- Possible genetic links
- Disease (for example, diabetes mellitus)

Diagnostic Procedures and Nursing Interventions

Δ **Urinalysis** and urine **culture and sensitivity**

- Expected findings include:
  ◊ Bacteria, sediment, white blood cells (WBC), and red blood cells.
  ◊ Positive **leukocyte esterase** (85 to 90% specific).
  ◊ Positive nitrate (95% specific).
- WBC count and differential if urosepsis is suspected
  ◊ White blood cell count at or above 10,000/mm³ with shift to the left (indicating an increased number of immature cells in response to infection).

Δ Voiding **cystoureterography** or excretory urography is used for complicated UTIs.

Δ Cystoscopy is used for complicated UTIs.

Δ Rule out sexually transmitted diseases.

Assessments

Δ Clinical findings depend on the area of the urinary tract affected by the infecting organism. **Expected client findings** include:

- Urinary frequency with voiding of small amounts: **nocturia**.
- **Dysuria**, bladder cramping, or spasms.
- Perineal itching.
- Warm sensation during urination.
- Urethral discharge.
- Cloudy or foul-smelling urine.
- **Hematuria** (tea- or cola-colored urine).
- Lower back or lower abdominal discomfort and tenderness over the bladder area.
- Fever.
- Pyuria.
- Nausea and vomiting.
- Mental status changes in older adult clients.

Δ **Assess/Monitor**

- Urinary output for color, volume, and odor
- Pain status
- Temperature for fever

NANDA Nursing Diagnoses

Δ Acute pain

Δ Impaired urinary elimination

Δ Anxiety

Δ Deficient knowledge

Nursing Interventions

Δ Female clients should be instructed to:

- Wipe the perineal area from front to back.
- Urinate before and after intercourse.
- Avoid the use of feminine products containing perfumes, bubble baths, and toilet paper containing perfumes.
- Avoid sitting in wet bathing suits.
- Avoid wearing pantyhose with slacks or tight clothing.

Δ Encourage the client to increase fluid intake if not contraindicated.

Δ Instruct the client regarding the proper collection of clean catch urine if specimens are required.

Δ Collect the catheterized urine specimen using a sterile technique.

Δ Provide perineal care to the client prior to the insertion of the urinary catheter.

Δ Teach the client the need to take all of the prescribed antibiotics even if symptoms abate.

- **Fluoroquinolones** (Ciprofloxacin), **nitrofurantoin** (Macrobid), or **sulfonamides** (Bactrim or Septra).

Δ Advise the client that certain urinary analgesics such as **Pyridium** will turn the urine orange.

Complications and Nursing Implications

Δ **Urethral obstruction, pyelonephritis, chronic renal failure, urosepsis,** septic shock, and death.

- Monitor/assess.

- Report abnormal data promptly.

- Maintain medication schedules to assure adequate medication blood levels to eradicate infection.

Meeting the Needs of Older Adult Clients

Δ Older adult clients have an increased risk of bacteremia, sepsis, and shock.

Δ Renal complications increase due to a decreased number of functioning nephrons.

Δ Decreased fluid intake and increased incidence of stool incontinence predisposes older adult clients to UTIs.

Δ Older women are the most susceptible due to the risk for incontinence of stool/urine, changes in urine pH, and relaxation of the pelvic floor.

Δ UTIs may be asymptomatic in older adult clients except for mental status changes.

Primary Reference:

Ignatavicius, D. D., & Workman, M. L. (2006). *Medical-surgical nursing* (5th ed.). St. Louis, MO: Saunders.

Additional Resources:

Kowalak, J. P., & Hughes, A. S. (Eds.). (2002). *Atlas of Pathophysiology*. Philadelphia: Lippincott Williams & Wilkins.

LeMone, P. & Burke, K. (2004). *Medical-surgical nursing: Critical thinking in client care* (3rd ed.). Upper Saddle River, NJ: Prentice-Hall.

NANDA International (2004). *NANDA nursing diagnoses: Definitions and classification 2005-2006*. Philadelphia: NANDA.

Chapter 45: Urinary Tract Infection

Application Exercises

1. Complete the following concept map:

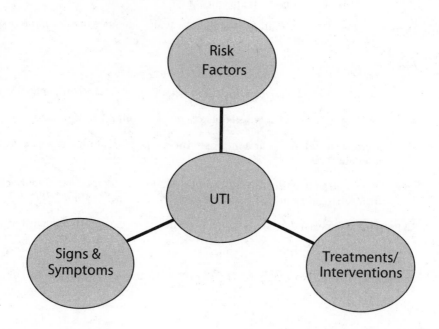

2. Prioritize the following nursing diagnoses for a client who has been diagnosed with UTI, with "1" being the highest priority. Explain the rationale for each prioritization.

_____ Anxiety

_____ Pain

_____ Knowledge deficiency

Chapter 45: Urinary Tract Infection

Application Exercises Answer Key

1. Complete the following concept map:

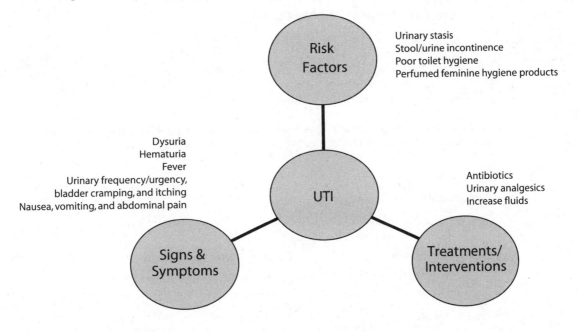

Risk Factors

Urinary stasis
Stool/urine incontinence
Poor toilet hygiene
Perfumed feminine hygiene products

Dysuria
Hematuria
Fever
Urinary frequency/urgency,
bladder cramping, and itching
Nausea, vomiting, and abdominal pain

UTI

Antibiotics
Urinary analgesics
Increase fluids

Signs & Symptoms

Treatments/ Interventions

2. Prioritize the following nursing diagnoses for a client who has been diagnosed with UTI, with "1" being the highest priority. Explain the rationale for each prioritization.

   2   Anxiety

   1   Pain

   3   Knowledge deficiency

The control of pain is the most basic of human needs (Maslow's hierarchy of needs) and, therefore, should be addressed first. Anxiety must be controlled before learning can take place since it interferes with the client's ability to comprehend or learn.

Unit 5   Nursing Care of Clients with Renal and Urinary Disorders
Section: Nursing Care of Clients with Select Renal Disorders

Chapter 46:   Pyelonephritis
Contributor: Gayla H. Love, BSN, RN, CCM

🗘 NCLEX-PN® Connections:

Learning Objective: Review and apply knowledge within "**Pyelonephritis**" in readiness for performance of the following nursing activities as outlined by the NCLEX-PN® test plan:

Δ Assist with relevant laboratory, diagnostic, and therapeutic procedures within the nursing role, including:

- Preparation of the client for the procedure.
- Accurate collection of specimens.
- Monitoring client status during and after the procedure.
- Reinforcing client teaching (before and following the procedure).
- Recognizing the client's response (expected, unexpected adverse response) to the procedure.
- Monitoring results.
- Monitoring and taking actions to prevent or minimize the risk of complications.
- Notifying the primary care provider of signs of complications.

Δ Recognize signs and symptoms of the client's problem and complete the proper documentation.

Δ Provide and document care based on the client's health alteration.

Δ Monitor and document vital signs changes.

Δ Interpret data that need to be reported immediately.

Δ Reinforce client education on managing the client's health problem.

Δ Recognize and respond to emergency situations, including notification of the primary care provider.

Δ Review the client's response to emergency interventions and complete the proper documentation.

Δ Provide care that meets the age-related needs of clients 65 years of age or older, including recognizing expected physiological changes.

Key Points

Δ   Pyelonephritis is an **infection and inflammation of the renal pelvis, calyces, and medulla**. The infection usually **begins in the lower urinary tract** with organisms ascending into the renal pelvis.

Δ   *Escherichia coli* organisms are the cause of most acute cases of pyelonephritis.

Δ   **Repeated infections create scarring** that changes blood flow to the kidney, glomerulus, and tubular structure.

Δ   **Filtration, reabsorption, and secretion are impaired,** and there is a decrease in renal function.

Δ   Acute pyelonephritis is an **active bacterial infection** that can cause:

- Interstitial inflammation.

- Tubular cell necrosis.

- Abscess formation in the capsule, cortex, or medulla.

- Temporarily altered renal function, but this rarely progresses to renal failure.

Δ   **Chronic pyelonephritis** is the result of **repeated infections** that cause progressive inflammation and scarring.

- This can result in thickening of the calyces and postinflammatory fibrosis with permanent renal tissue scarring.

- It is more common with obstructions, urinary anomaly, and vesicoureteral urine reflux.

- Reflux of urine occurs at the junction where the ureter connects to the bladder.

Key Factors

Δ   **Risk Factors**

- **Women over 65 years of age**

- Older men with **prostate problems**

- Chronic **urinary stone** disorders

- **Spinal cord injury**

- **Pregnancy**

- **Congenital malformations**

- **Bladder tumors**

- **Chronic illness** (diabetes mellitus, hypertension, chronic cystitis)

Diagnostic Procedures and Nursing Interventions

Δ **Urinalysis** and urine **culture and sensitivity**

- Monitor for:

  ◊ **Dark color, cloudy appearance, foul odor.**

  ◊ **Bacturia,** sediment, **white blood cells,** and **red blood cells.**

  ◊ Positive **leukocyte esterase** (85 to 90% specific).

  ◊ Positive **nitrate** (95% specific).

Δ **WBC count and differential:** White blood cell count at or **above 10,000/mm³** with **shift to the left** indicates increased number of immature cells in response to infection.

Δ **Blood cultures** will be positive for the presence of **bacteria** if a systemic infection is present.

Δ **Serum creatinine** and blood urea nitrogen **(BUN)** are **elevated** during acute episodes and consistently elevated with chronic infection.

Δ **C-reactive protein is elevated** during exacerbating inflammatory processes.

Δ **Erythrocyte sedimentation rate (ESR)** is elevated during acute or chronic inflammation.

Δ **X-ray of kidneys, ureters, and bladder (KUB)** may demonstrate calculi or structural abnormalities.

Δ **Intravenous pyelogram (IVP)** may demonstrate calculi, structural, or vascular abnormalities.

- Assess renal function and allergy to contrast dye prior to the procedure.

- Bowel preparation may be prescribed prior to the procedure for image clarity.

- Hydration prior to the procedure and diuretic administration following the procedure may be prescribed to reduce the risk of nephrotoxicity.

Δ **Gallium scan** may indicate active pyelonephritis or abscesses.

Therapeutic Procedures and Nursing Interventions

Δ Surgical procedures may be needed to terminate the infectious process.

- **Pyelolithotomy** – removal of a stone from the kidney

- **Nephrectomy** – removal of the kidney

- **Ureteral diversion** or re-implantation of the ureter to restore bladder drainage

- **Ureteroplasty** – repair or revision of the ureter

Assessments

Δ Monitor for **signs and symptoms.**

- **Vital signs: Fever,** tachycardia, tachypnea, hypertension
- **Chills**
- **Costovertebral tenderness**
- **Flank** and back pain
- Colicky-type **abdominal pain**
- **Nausea and vomiting**
- **Malaise, fatigue**
- **Burning, urgency, and frequency** with urination
- **Nocturia**
- **Inability to concentrate urine or conserve sodium** (chronic pyelonephritis)
- Asymptomatic **bacteremia**

Δ **Assess/Monitor**

- Nutritional status
- Intake and output
- Fluid and electrolyte balance
- Pain status

NANDA Nursing Diagnoses

Δ Acute pain

Δ Deficient knowledge

Δ Activity intolerance

Δ Anxiety

Δ Impaired urinary elimination

Nursing Interventions

Δ **Manage pain.**

- Narcotic analgesics
- Non-steroidal anti-inflammatory agents (NSAIDs)

Δ **Administer intravenous antibiotics** after a specimen for urine culture and sensitivity has been obtained.

Δ Maintain antibiotic schedules to maximize medication effectiveness.

Δ Teach self-administration of prescribed medications.

Δ Increase **fluid intake to 2 to 3 L/day** unless contraindicated.

Δ Monitor temperature and administer **antipyretic** as needed.

Δ Provide **emotional support**.

Δ Assist with **personal hygiene**.

Complications and Nursing Implications

Δ **Septic Shock**

- Identify signs, such as hypotension, tachycardia, and fever.

- Initiate life-support interventions as needed.

Δ **Renal Failure**

- Monitor intake and output.

- Monitor renal function studies for elevations in BUN and creatinine.

- Encourage increased fluid intake.

Δ **Hypertension**

- Monitor blood pressure for trends.

- Report changes from baseline.

Meeting the Needs of Older Adults

Δ Older adult clients are at an increased risk for urinary infections related to decreased renal function with aging.

Δ Decrease in vascular flow may decrease blood flow to the kidneys.

Δ Urine pH increases and promotes bacterial growth.

Δ Incomplete bladder emptying is more common among older adult clients.

Δ Older adult clients may exhibit gastrointestinal or pulmonary symptoms instead of febrile responses.

Primary Reference:

Ignatavicius, D. D., & Workman, M. L. (2006). *Medical-surgical nursing* (5th ed.). St. Louis, MO: Saunders.

Additional Resources:

Monahan, F. D., Sands, J. K., Neighbors, M., Marek, F. J., & Green, C. J. (Eds.). (2007). *Phipps' medical-surgical nursing: Health and illness perspectives* (8th ed.). St. Louis, MO: Mosby.

NANDA International (2004). *NANDA nursing diagnoses: Definitions and classification 2005-2006*. Philadelphia: NANDA.

Chapter 46: Pyelonephritis

Application Exercises

Scenario: A female client is being treated for a second occurrence of pyelonephritis. A urine specimen has been collected and blood drawn for culture and sensitivity tests. The client confides that she is fearful of having sexual intercourse in the future because she is sure that is why she has gotten pyelonephritis for the second time.

1. How should the nurse respond to this client?

2. Which of the following findings should the nurse expect when reviewing the client's laboratory reports? (Check all that apply.)

        _____   Elevated BUN

        _____   Decreased C-reactive protein

        _____   Positive leukocyte esterase

        _____   Decreased ESR

        _____   Bacturia

        _____   Decreased serum creatinine

3. Prioritize nursing diagnoses for this client. Provide a rationale for your prioritization.

        _____   Pain

        _____   Deficient knowledge

        _____   Activity intolerance

        _____   Anxiety

4. Which of the following clients is at the greatest risk for developing pyelonephritis? (Check all that apply.)

        _____   A client who just had a catheterized urine specimen obtained

        _____   A client who has not voided for 8 hr postoperatively

        _____   A client with a neurogenic bladder

        _____   A client with diabetes mellitus

5. A client discharged from the hospital is placed on oral antibiotics for treatment of acute pyelonephritis. The client asks if he can stop taking the medication when he starts to feel better. How should the nurse answer this question?

Chapter 46: Pyelonephritis

Application Exercises Answer Key

Scenario: A female client is being treated for a second occurrence of pyelonephritis. A urine specimen has been collected and blood drawn for culture and sensitivity tests. The client confides that she is fearful of having sexual intercourse in the future because she is sure that is why she has gotten pyelonephritis for the second time.

1. How should the nurse respond to this client?

   The nurse should reassure the client that while intercourse increases the risk of bacterial contamination, that risk can be greatly reduced if she voids before and after intercourse. Also, the nurse should explain that there are other risk factors for pyelonephritis in addition to sexual intercourse. Those risk factors should be reviewed with the client.

2. Which of the following findings should the nurse expect when reviewing the client's laboratory reports? (Check all that apply.)

__x__	Elevated BUN
_____	Decreased C-reactive protein
__x__	Positive leukocyte esterase
_____	Decreased ESR
__x__	Bacturia
_____	Decreased serum creatinine

3. Prioritize nursing diagnoses for this client. Provide a rationale for your prioritization.

__1__	Pain
__4__	Deficient knowledge
__3__	Activity intolerance
__2__	Anxiety

   According to Maslow's hierarchy of needs, alleviation of pain is a basic need that must be met before other needs become important. Clients in pain cannot comprehend well or make decisions. Anxiety increases metabolic demand and contributes to fatigue and activity intolerance; thus, it should be addressed after pain. Activity intolerance must then be addressed so that conditions are right for learning. The client is ready to learn when all other basic needs have been met.

4. Which of the following clients is at the greatest risk for developing pyelonephritis? (Check all that apply.)

_____	A client who just had a catheterized urine specimen obtained
_____	A client who has not voided for 8 hr postoperatively
__X__	A client with a neurogenic bladder
__X__	A client with diabetes mellitus

5. A client discharged from the hospital is placed on oral antibiotics for treatment of acute pyelonephritis. The client asks if he can stop taking the medication when he starts to feel better. How should the nurse answer this question?

The nurse should explain that the symptoms may be relieved in a short period of time, but the antibiotic needs to be taken for the length of time prescribed so that all of the bacteria can be eliminated from the urinary tract.

Unit 5   Nursing Care of Clients with Renal and Urinary Disorders
Section: Nursing Care of Clients with Select Renal Disorders

Chapter 47:   Urolithiasis
Contributor: Annette M. Peacock-Johnson, MSN, RN

↻ NCLEX-PN® Connections

Learning Objective: Review and apply knowledge within "**Urolithiasis**" in readiness for performance of the following nursing activities as outlined by the NCLEX-PN® test plan:

Δ   Assist with relevant laboratory, diagnostic, and therapeutic procedures within the nursing role, including:

- Preparation of the client for the procedure.

- Accurate collection of specimens.

- Monitoring client status during and after the procedure.

- Reinforcing client teaching (before and following the procedure).

- Recognizing the client's response (expected, unexpected adverse response) to the procedure.

- Monitoring results.

- Monitoring and taking actions to prevent or minimize the risk of complications.

- Notifying the primary care provider of signs of complications.

Δ   Recognize signs and symptoms of the client's problem and complete the proper documentation.

Δ   Provide and document care based on the client's health alteration.

Δ   Monitor and document vital signs changes.

Δ   Interpret data that need to be reported immediately.

Δ   Reinforce client education on managing the client's health problem.

Δ   Recognize and respond to emergency situations, including notification of the primary care provider.

Δ   Review the client's response to emergency interventions and complete the proper documentation.

Δ   Provide care that meets the age-related needs of clients 65 years of age or older, including recognizing expected physiological changes.

📖 Key Points

Δ   **Urolithiasis** is the presence of **calculi (stones) in the urinary tract.**

Δ   The majority of stones **(75%) are composed of calcium oxalate or calcium phosphate** but may contain other substances such as **uric acid, struvite,** or **cystine.**

Δ   A **diet high in calcium is not believed to increase the risk of stone formation** unless there is a preexisting metabolic disorder or renal tubular defect.

Δ   Reoccurrence is increased (35 to 50%) in individuals with calcium stones who have a **family history, or whose first occurrence of urinary calculi is prior to the age of 25 years.**

Δ   Most clients can expel stones without invasive procedures. Factors that influence whether a stone will pass spontaneously or not include the **composition, size, and location of the stone.**

Key Factors

Δ   The cause of urolithiasis is unknown.

Δ   There is an **increased incidence** of urolithiasis **in males.**

Δ   Urolithiasis formation is associated with:

- **Slow urine flow** with **supersaturation of urine with particles** (for example, calcium).

- **Damage to the lining** of the urinary tract.

- **Decreased inhibitor substances** in the urine.

- **Metabolic defects** including:

  ◊   **Increased intestinal absorption** or **decreased renal excretion of calcium.**

  ◊   **Increased oxalate production** (genetic) or ingestion from foods.

  ◊   Increased **production or decreased clearance of purines** (contributing to increased uric-acid levels).

Δ   High **urine acidity or alkalinity contributes** to stone formation.

Δ   Urinary **stasis,** urinary **retention, immobilization,** and **dehydration** contribute to an environment **favorable for stone formation.**

Diagnostic Procedures and Nursing Interventions

Δ   **Expected Findings**

- **Urinalysis** is used to detect:

  ◊   **Increased RBCs, WBCs, and bacteria** from urinary stasis.

  ◊   **Increased urine turbidity and odor** (if urine is infected).

  ◊   **Crystals** noted on microscopic exam.

  ◊   Abnormal serum **calcium, phosphate, and uric-acid levels** in the presence of metabolic disorders/defects.

  ◊   **Elevated WBC** if infection is present.

- Radiology examination – **KUB** (x-ray of kidney, ureters, bladder), **noncontrast helical CT scan**, or **IVP** (intravenous pyelogram) is used to confirm the presence and location of stones.

  ◊   IVP is **contraindicated if there is urinary obstruction.**

- **CT or MRI** is used to identify **cystine or uric-acid stones**, which cannot be seen on standard x-rays.

- A renal **ultrasound or cystoscopy** may confirm diagnosis.

Therapeutic Procedures and Nursing Interventions

Δ   **Non-surgical Management**

- **Extracorporeal shock wave lithotripsy (ESWL)**

  ◊   Uses sound, laser or shock-wave energies to break the stone into fragments.

  ◊   Requires conscious sedation and ECG monitoring during the procedure.

- **Surgical management**

  ◊   **Stenting** is the placement of a small tube in the ureter during ureteroscopy to dilate the ureter, enlarging the passageway for the stone to be passed.

  ◊   **Retrograde ureteroscopy** uses a basket, forceps, or loop on the end of the ureteroscope to grasp and remove the stone.

  ◊   **Percutaneous ureterolithotomy/nephrolithotomy** is the insertion of an ultrasonic or laser lithotripter into the ureter or kidney to grasp and extract the stone.

  ◊   **Open surgery** uses a surgical incision to remove the stone; this surgery is used for large or impacted stones (such as staghorn calculi), or for stones not removed by other approaches.

  - **Ureterolithotomy** (into the ureter)

  - **Pyelolithotomy** (into the kidney pelvis)

  - **Nephrolithotomy** (into the kidney)

Δ   **Nursing Interventions**

- **Prepare** the client for procedures.

- **Teach** the client about the procedures.

- **Report abnormal findings** to the provider.

- **Teach the client about ESWL.**

  ◊   **Strain urine** following the procedure.

  ◊   **Bruising is normal** at the site where waves are applied.

- Provide preoperative and postoperative care as indicated. (*For information, refer to chapter 126, Preoperative Nursing, and chapter 128, Postoperative Nursing.*)

Assessments

Δ   **Severe pain** (renal colic)

- Pain intensifies as stone moves through ureter.

- Flank pain suggests stones in the kidney or ureter.

- Flank pain that radiates to the abdomen, scrotum, testes, or vulva is suggestive of stones in the ureters or bladder.

Δ   **Nausea/vomiting**

Δ   **Urinary frequency or dysuria (occurs with stones in the bladder)**

Δ   **Pallor**

Δ   **Diaphoresis**

Δ   **Vital signs:** Tachycardia, tachypnea, increased or decreased blood pressure with pain

Δ   **Oliguria/anuria** (occurs with stones that obstruct urinary flow)

Δ   **Hematuria**

NANDA Nursing Diagnoses

Δ   Acute pain

Δ   Risk for infection

Δ   Deficient knowledge

Δ   Risk for injury (renal)

Δ   Fear

Δ   Anxiety

Nursing Interventions

Δ   Assess/Monitor

- **Pain status**
- Intake and output
- **Urinary pH**

Δ   Administer prescribed medications, such as:

- **Analgesics** (opioids such as morphine sulfate, NSAIDS such as Toradol).
- **Spasmolytic drugs:**
  ◊   Oxybutynin chloride (Ditropan).
  ◊   Propantheline bromide (Pro-Banthine).
- **Antibiotics** if infection is present.

Δ   **Strain all urine** to check for passage of the stone; save the stone for laboratory analysis.

Δ   Encourage **increased oral intake to 3,000 mL/day unless contraindicated.**

Δ   Administer **intravenous fluids** as prescribed.

Δ   Encourage **ambulation** to promote passage of the stone.

Δ   Provide **client education** regarding the role of **diet and medications** in the treatment and prevention of urinary stones.

- **Calcium phosphate**
  ◊   Dietary interventions
  - Limit intake of food high in animal protein (Reduction of protein intake decreases calcium precipitation).
  - Limit sodium intake.
  - Reduced calcium intake (dairy products) is individualized.
  ◊   Medications
  - Thiazide diuretics (hydrochlorothiazide) to increase calcium reabsorption
  - Orthophosphates to decrease urine saturation of calcium oxalate
  - Sodium cellulose phosphate to reduce intestinal absorption of calcium

- **Calcium oxalate**
  - ◊ Dietary interventions
    - ° Avoid oxalate sources: Spinach, black tea, rhubarb, cocoa, beets, pecans, peanuts, okra, chocolate, wheat germ, lime peel, Swiss chard
    - ° Limit sodium intake.
  - ◊ Medications
    - ° In addition to those for calcium phosphate, allopurinol (Zyloprim), vitamin B_6 (pyridoxine)
- **Struvite** (magnesium ammonium phosphate)
  - ◊ Dietary interventions
    - ° Avoid high-phosphate foods (dairy products, red and organ meats, whole grains).
- **Uric acid (urate)**
  - ◊ Dietary interventions
    - ° Decrease intake of purine sources (organ meats, poultry, fish, gravies, red wine, sardines).
  - ◊ Medications
    - ° Allopurinol (Zyloprim) to prevent formation of uric acid
    - ° Potassium or sodium citrate or sodium bicarbonate to alkalinize the urine
- **Cystine**
  - ◊ Dietary interventions
    - ° Limit animal protein intake.
  - ◊ Medications
    - ° Alpha mercapto propionylglycine (AMPG) to lower urine cystine
    - ° Captopril (Capoten) to lower urine cystine

Complications and Nursing Implications

- Δ Treat an **obstruction of the ureter** and interruption of urinary flow as an emergency, and report it immediately.

- Δ Monitor for signs of **infection**, and report abnormal findings.

- Δ Monitor for signs of urine outflow obstruction (**hydronephrosis**) of the affected kidney, and report abnormal findings.

- Δ **Renal failure** (*For information, refer to chapter 50, Renal Failure.*)

Meeting the Needs of Older Adults

Δ **Decreased fluid intake** or increased incidence of **dehydration** among older adult clients, may increase the risk of stone formation.

Primary Reference:

Ignatavicius, D. D., & Workman, M. L. (2006). *Medical-surgical nursing* (5th ed.). St. Louis, MO: Saunders.

Additional Resources:

Black, J. M., & Hawks, J. H. (2005). *Medical-surgical nursing: Clinical management for positive outcomes* (7th ed.). St. Louis, MO: Saunders.

NANDA International (2004). *NANDA nursing diagnoses: Definitions and classification 2005-2006*. Philadelphia: NANDA.

Chapter 47: Urolithiasis

Application Exercises

Scenario: A male client is admitted to the nursing unit with a diagnosis of right renal calculus. Upon assessment, the client reports nausea with moderate right flank pain that radiates to his right testicle. His admission vitals are: blood pressure 142/86 mm Hg, heart rate 96/min, respirations 24/min, and temperature 37.2° C (99° F).

1. What additional nursing assessment is indicated specific to this client's diagnosis of renal calculus?

2. Select priority nursing diagnoses for this client. (Check all that apply.)

   _____ Activity intolerance

   _____ Acute Pain

   _____ Nausea

   _____ Risk for infection

   _____ Ineffective individual coping

   _____ Deficient knowledge

3. A client is admitted to the nursing unit with a diagnosis of right renal calculus. He has a Foley catheter and IV of 1,000 mL of 0.9% normal saline infusing at 150 mL/hr. Which of the following assessment findings warrants immediate reporting by the nurse?

   A. Flank pain that radiates to the lower abdomen

   B. Nausea that is controlled with prescribed medication

   C. No urine output for 2 hr

   D. Client reports of feeling "sweaty"

4. A 42-year-old client is scheduled for extracorporeal shock wave lithotripsy (ESWL). Which of the following statements by the client demonstrates correct understanding of the procedure?

   A. "I will be fully awake during the procedure."

   B. "Lithotripsy will reduce my chances of stone reoccurrence."

   C. "I will report any bruising that occurs to my doctor."

   D. "Straining my urine following the procedure is important."

5. A nurse is providing discharge instructions for a client who spontaneously passed a urinary calcium phosphate stone. In teaching the client about dietary modifications, the nurse should teach the client to limit which of the following in the diet? (Check all that apply.)

_____ Organ meats	_____ Fish	_____ Red wines
_____ Tea	_____ Red meat	_____ Dairy products
_____ Cheese	_____ Rhubarb	_____ Whole grains
_____ Soy sauce	_____ Spinach	

6. A client is to be discharged home after spontaneous passage of a calcium phosphate stone. The nurse teaches the client ways to prevent reoccurrence. Which of the following should be included in the discharge plan? (Check all that apply.)

_____ Limit intake of foods high in animal protein.

_____ Reduce sodium intake in diet.

_____ Avoid drinking fluids at bedtime.

_____ Limit physical activity throughout the day.

_____ Report burning or dysuria to the provider.

_____ Increase fluid intake to 3 to 4 L/day.

_____ Strain all urine.

7. Match the appropriate medications to each of the types of calculi listed below.

_____ Calcium phosphate   A. Allopurinol (Zyloprim)

_____ Calcium oxalate   B. Captopril (Capoten)

_____ Uric acid (urate)   C. Thiazide diuretic

_____ Cystine   D. Vitamin B_6 (pyridoxine)

Chapter 47: Urolithiasis

Application Exercises Answer Key

Scenario: A male client is admitted to the nursing unit with a diagnosis of right renal calculus. Upon assessment, the client reports nausea with moderate right flank pain that radiates to his right testicle. His admission vitals are: blood pressure 142/86 mm Hg, heart rate 96/min, respirations 24/min, and temperature 37.2° C (99° F).

1. What additional nursing assessment is indicated specific to this client's diagnosis of renal calculus?

   Diet history and assessment of fluid intake patterns

   A personal or family history of calculi

   Altered patterns of elimination, including dysuria, frequency, or oliguria

   Detailed pain assessment, including intensity, location, character

   Observation of urinary output, including amount and presence of stones, hematuria

2. Select priority nursing diagnoses for this client. (Check all that apply.)

_____	Activity intolerance
__X__	Acute Pain
__X__	Nausea
__X__	Risk for infection
_____	Ineffective individual coping
__X__	Deficient knowledge

3. A client is admitted to the nursing unit with a diagnosis of right renal calculus. He has a Foley catheter and IV of 1,000 mL of 0.9% normal saline infusing at 150 mL/hr. Which of the following assessment findings warrants immediate reporting by the nurse?

  A. Flank pain that radiates to the lower abdomen

  B. Nausea that is controlled with prescribed medication

  C. No urine output for 2 hr

  D. Client reports of feeling "sweaty"

The lack of urine output may indicate obstruction and warrants immediate reporting by the nurse. Nausea, flank pain that radiates to the abdomen, and sweating are all common occurrences associated with a renal calculus.

4. A 42-year-old client is scheduled for extracorporeal shock wave lithotripsy (ESWL). Which of the following statements by the client demonstrates correct understanding of the procedure?

  A. "I will be fully awake during the procedure."

  B. "Lithotripsy will reduce my chances of stone reoccurrence."

  C. "I will report any bruising that occurs to my doctor."

  D. "Straining my urine following the procedure is important."

Straining will allow for analysis of the stone.

5. A nurse is providing discharge instructions for a client who spontaneously passed a urinary calcium phosphate stone. In teaching the client about dietary modifications, the nurse should teach the client to limit which of the following in the diet? (Check all that apply.)

_____ Organ meats	_____ Fish	_____ Red wines
_____ Tea	_x_ Red meat	_____ Dairy products
_x_ Cheese	_____ Rhubarb	_____ Whole grains
_x_ Soy sauce	_____ Spinach	

6. A client is to be discharged home after spontaneous passage of a calcium phosphate stone. The nurse teaches the client ways to prevent reoccurrence. Which of the following should be included in the discharge plan? (Check all that apply.)

__x__	Limit intake of foods high in animal protein.
__x__	Reduce sodium intake in diet.
_____	Avoid drinking fluids at bedtime.
_____	Limit physical activity throughout the day.
__x__	Report burning or dysuria to the provider.
__x__	Increase fluid intake to 3 to 4 L/day.
_____	Strain all urine.

7. Match the appropriate medications to each of the types of calculi listed below.

__C__	Calcium phosphate	A. Allopurinol (Zyloprim)
__A,D__	Calcium oxalate	B. Captopril (Capoten)
__A__	Uric acid (urate)	C. Thiazide diuretic
__B__	Cystine	D. Vitamin B$_6$ (pyridoxine)

Unit 5   Nursing Care of Clients with Renal and Urinary Disorders

Section: Nursing Care of Clients with Select Renal Disorders

Chapter 48:   **Acute/Chronic Glomerulonephritis**

Contributor: Gayla H. Love, BSN, RN, CCM

NCLEX-PN® Connections

Learning Objective: Review and apply knowledge within "**Acute/Chronic Glomerulonephritis**" in readiness for performance of the following nursing activities as outlined by the NCLEX-PN® test plan:

Δ   Assist with relevant laboratory, diagnostic, and therapeutic procedures within the nursing role, including:

- Preparation of the client for the procedure.
- Accurate collection of specimens.
- Monitoring client status during and after the procedure.
- Reinforcing client teaching (before and following the procedure).
- Recognizing the client's response (expected, unexpected adverse response) to the procedure.
- Monitoring results.
- Monitoring and taking actions to prevent or minimize the risk of complications.
- Notifying the primary care provider of signs of complications.

Δ   Recognize signs and symptoms of the client's problem and complete the proper documentation.

Δ   Provide and document care based on the client's health alteration.

Δ   Monitor and document vital signs changes.

Δ   Interpret data that need to be reported immediately.

Δ   Reinforce client education on managing the client's health problem.

Δ   Recognize and respond to emergency situations, including notification of the primary care provider.

Δ   Review the client's response to emergency interventions and complete the proper documentation.

Δ   Provide care that meets the age-related needs of clients 65 years of age or older, including recognizing expected physiological changes.

📖 **Key Points**

Δ Glomerulonephritis is an **inflammation of the glomerular capillaries**, usually following a streptococcal infection. It is an **immune complex disease, not an infection** of the kidney.

Δ Glomerulonephritis exists as an acute, latent, and chronic disease.

Δ **Acute Glomerulonephritis (AGN)**

- Insoluble **immune complexes** develop and become trapped in the **glomerular tissue** producing **swelling and capillary cell death.**

- **Prognosis varies** depending upon specific cause but **spontaneous recovery generally occurs** after the acute illness.

Δ **Chronic Glomerulonephritis (CGN)**

- Can occur **without previous history** or known onset.

- Involves **progressive destruction of glomeruli** and eventual **hardening (sclerosis).**

- CGN is the **third leading cause of end-stage renal disease** (ESRD), with prognosis varying depending on the specific cause.

Key Factors

Δ **Risk Factors**

- **Immunological reactions**

◊ Primary infection with **group A beta-hemolytic streptococcal** infection (most common)

◊ **Systemic lupus erythematosus**

- **Vascular injury** (hypertension)

- **Metabolic disease** (diabetes mellitus)

- **Nephrotoxic** drugs

- Excessively **high protein** and **high sodium** diets

Diagnostic Procedures and Nursing Interventions

Δ **Serum BUN** (elevated: 100 to 200 mg/dL; normal: 10 to 20 mg/dL) and **Creatinine** (elevated: greater than 6 mg/dL; normal: 0.6 to 1.2 mg/dL)

Δ **Creatinine Clearance** (decreased: 50 mL/min; normal 80 to 140 mL/min)

Δ **Urinalysis:** Proteinuria, hematuria, cell debris (red cells and casts), increased urine specific gravity

Δ **Electrolytes:** Hyperkalemia, hypermagnesemia, dilutional hyponatremia if urine output is decreased

Δ **Throat Culture** (to identify possible streptococcus infection)

Δ **Antistreptolysin-O (ASO) titer** (positive indicating the presence of strep antibodies)

Δ **Erythrocyte Sedimentation Rate** (ESR) (elevated indicating active inflammatory response)

Δ **White Blood Cell Count** (elevated indicating inflammation and presence of active strep infection)

Δ **X-ray of Kidney, Ureter, Bladder** (KUB), **Renal Ultrasound** (to detect structural abnormalities such as atrophy)

Δ **Renal Biopsy** (to confirm or rule out diagnosis)

Therapeutic Procedures and Nursing Interventions

Δ **Plasmapheresis** (to **filter antibodies** out of circulating blood volume)

- Monitor the client carefully during and following the procedure.

- Take interventions to reduce the risk of coagulation.

Assessments

Δ Monitor for **signs and symptoms** characteristic of systemic circulatory overload.

- **Renal symptoms**

  ◊ **Decreased urine output**

  ◊ Smoky or **coffee-colored** urine (hematuria)

  ◊ **Proteinuria**

- **Fluid volume excess symptoms**

  ◊ Shortness of breath

  ◊ Orthopnea

  ◊ Bibasilar rales

  ◊ Periorbital edema

  ◊ Mild to severe hypertension

- **Change in level of consciousness**

- Anorexia/nausea

- Headache

- Back pain
- **Fever** (AGN)
- **Pruritus** (CGN)

Δ **Assess/Monitor**

- Dyspnea, orthopnea, lung crackles
- Weight gain
- Edema
- Hypertension
- Intake and output
- Changes in urinary pattern
- Serum electrolytes, BUN, creatinine
- Skin integrity (pruritus)

NANDA Nursing Diagnoses

Δ Fluid volume excess

Δ Fatigue

Δ Acute pain

Δ Fear

Δ Anxiety

Δ Deficient knowledge

Nursing Interventions

Δ Administer prescribed medications:

- Administer **antibiotics on time** to maintain blood levels for effective elimination of strep infection.
- **Diuretics** to reduce edema.
- **Vasodilators** to decrease blood pressure.
- **Corticosteroids** to decrease inflammatory response.

Δ Maintain **bedrest** to decrease metabolic demands.

Δ   Maintain prescribed **dietary restrictions**:

- Fluid restriction (24 hr output + 500 mL).

- Sodium restriction.

- Protein restriction (if azotemia is present).

Δ   Correct electrolyte imbalances.

Complications and Nursing Implications

Δ   **Renal Failure** (*For information, refer to chapter 50, Renal Failure.*)

Δ   **Uremia**

- Symptoms include muscle cramps, fatigue, pruritus, anorexia, metallic taste in mouth.

- Intervene to maintain skin integrity.

- Assist with dialysis.

Δ   **Pulmonary Edema, Congestive Heart Failure, Pericarditis**

- Monitor for dyspnea, crackles, edema, and decreased cardiac output.

- Intervene accordingly (oxygen, diuretics, inotropic medications).

Δ   **Anemia**

- Monitor hemoglobin.

- Administer iron and erythropoietin as indicated.

Meeting the Needs of Older Adults

Δ   Older adult clients may report **vague symptoms** such as nausea, fatigue, or joint aches, which **may mask** glomerular disease.

Δ   Older adult clients tend to have **decreased working nephrons** and are at increased risk for chronic renal failure.

Primary Reference:

Ignatavicius, D. D., & Workman, M. L. (2006). *Medical-surgical nursing* (5th ed.). St. Louis, MO: Saunders.

Additional Resources:

Burke, K. M., LeMone, P., & Mohn-Brown, E. L. (2003). *Medical-surgical nursing care.* Upper Saddle River, NJ: Prentice-Hall.

Kowalak, J.P., & Hughes, A. S. (Eds.). (2002). *Atlas of Pathophysiology.* Philadelphia: Lippincott Williams & Wilkins.

Monahan, F. D., Sands, J. K., Neighbors, M., Marek, F. J., & Green, C. J. (Eds.). (2007). *Phipps' medical-surgical nursing: Health and illness perspectives* (8th ed.). St. Louis, MO: Mosby.

NANDA International (2004). *NANDA nursing diagnoses: Definitions and classification 2005-2006.* Philadelphia: NANDA.

Chapter 48: Acute/Chronic Glomerulonephritis

Application Exercises

1. Many pharmacologic agents may be administered in the treatment of glomerulonephritis. What is the rationale for administering the following medications?

Medication	Rationale
Glucocorticoids	
Penicillin	
Antihypertensives	
Diuretics	

2. Interpret the following laboratory test results:

Test	Result	Normal Range	Interpretation
Serum Creatinine	2.2 mg/dL	0.6 to 1.2 mg/dL	
Serum BUN	30 mg/dL	10 to 20 mg/dL	
24-hr Urine Creatinine Clearance	52 mL/min	80 to 140 mL/min	

3. Number from 1 to 5 the sequence of pathological events that occurs in glomerulonephritis.

_____ Edema

_____ Salt and water retention

_____ Glomerular-capillary membrane damage

_____ Hematuria and proteinuria

_____ Immune response with antibody production

4. Which of the following clinical findings are expected in clients with glomerulonephritis? (Check all that apply.)

_____ Fever   _____ Bradycardia

_____ Peripheral edema   _____ Polyuria

_____ Pulse deficit   _____ Hypotension

_____ Weight gain   _____ Headache

_____ Proteinuria   _____ Dyspnea

Chapter 48: Acute/Chronic Glomerulonephritis

Application Exercises Answer Key

1. Many pharmacologic agents may be administered in the treatment of glomerulonephritis. What is the rationale for administering the following medications?

Medication	Rationale
Glucocorticoids	Glucocorticoids are given to reduce the inflammatory process.
Penicillin	Penicillin is the antibiotic given to clients with post streptococcal glomerulonephritis.
Antihypertensives	Antihypertensives will lower the blood pressure.
Diuretics	Diuretics will lower the blood pressure and reduce edema.

2. Interpret the following laboratory test results:

Test	Result	Normal Range	Interpretation
Serum Creatinine	2.2 mg/dL	0.6 to 1.2 mg/dL	Indicates decreased renal function.
Serum BUN	30 mg/dL	10 to 20 mg/dL	Indicates decreased renal function.
24-hr Urine Creatinine Clearance	52 mL/min	80 to 140 mL/min	Indicates reduced renal blood flow.

3. Number from 1 to 5 the sequence of pathological events that occurs in glomerulonephritis.

5	Edema
4	Salt and water retention
2	Glomerular-capillary membrane damage
3	Hematuria and proteinuria
1	Immune response with antibody production

4. Which of the following clinical findings are expected in clients with glomerulonephritis? (Check all that apply.)

__x__	Fever	_____	Bradycardia
__x__	Peripheral edema	_____	Polyuria
_____	Pulse deficit	_____	Hypotension
__x__	Weight gain	__x__	Headache
__x__	Proteinuria	__x__	Dyspnea

Unit 5   Nursing Care of Clients with Renal and Urinary Disorders
Section: Nursing Care of Clients with Select Renal Disorders

Chapter 49:   Nephrotic Syndrome
Contributor: Gayla H. Love, BSN, RN, CCM

↻ NCLEX-PN® Connections:

Learning Objective: Review and apply knowledge within "**Nephrotic Syndrome**" in readiness for performance of the following nursing activities as outlined by the NCLEX-PN® test plan:

Δ   Assist with relevant laboratory, diagnostic, and therapeutic procedures within the nursing role, including:

- Preparation of the client for the procedure.

- Accurate collection of specimens.

- Monitoring client status during and after the procedure.

- Reinforcing client teaching (before and following the procedure).

- Recognizing the client's response (expected, unexpected adverse response) to the procedure.

- Monitoring results.

- Monitoring and taking actions to prevent or minimize the risk of complications.

- Notifying the primary care provider of signs of complications.

Δ   Recognize signs and symptoms of the client's problem and complete the proper documentation.

Δ   Provide and document care based on the client's health alteration.

Δ   Monitor and document vital signs changes.

Δ   Interpret data that need to be reported immediately.

Δ   Reinforce client education on managing the client's health problem.

Δ   Recognize and respond to emergency situations, including notification of the primary care provider.

Δ   Review the client's response to emergency interventions and complete the proper documentation.

Δ   Provide care that meets the age-related needs of clients 65 years of age or older, including recognizing expected physiological changes.

📖 Key Points

Δ   Nephrotic syndrome is a **group of symptoms, not a disease.**

Δ   **Glomerular capillaries are damaged** from immune complex deposits, nephrotoxic antibodies, or non-immunological insults.

Δ   Damaged glomerular capillaries are **permeable to serum proteins, resulting in decreased serum osmotic pressure.**

Δ   Nephrotic syndrome is characterized by **proteinuria, hypoalbuminemia,** and **edema.**

Key Factors

Δ   **Causes/Risk Factors**

- Immunologic disorders

- Toxic injury to the kidney

- Neoplasms

- Multisystem diseases (for example, diabetes mellitus)

- Infections

- Hyperlipidemia

- Diseases of the vascular system

Diagnostic Procedures and Nursing Interventions

Δ   **Urinalysis**/24-hr urine collection

- Protein as high as +3 or +4 (> 3.5 g in 24 hr)

- Casts

Δ   **Serum lipid levels**

- Elevated serum cholesterol (> 200 mg/dL)

- Elevated triglycerides

- Elevated low-density and very low-density lipoproteins

Δ   **Serum albumin**

- May fall below 2 g/dL

Δ **Kidney biopsy**

- Minimal to extensive damage

- Fatty deposits in tubules

- Epithelium changes

- Hypercellularity

- Glomerular sclerosis

- Immunoglobulins in capillary walls

Δ Serum blood urea nitrogen (**BUN**), **creatinine**, and glomerular filtration rate (**GFR**) levels may indicate **minimal to extensive loss** of kidney function. BUN and creatinine levels rise, and GFR decreases with loss of kidney function.

Nursing Interventions

Δ **Prepare** the client for diagnostic procedures.

Δ Provide client education (before and after the procedure).

Δ **Collect specimens accurately.**

Δ **Report** abnormal findings to the provider.

Assessments

Δ Monitor for **signs and symptoms.**

- Proteinuria

- Hematuria

- Edema (periorbital and dependent)

- Irritability

- Malaise, fatigue

- Hypertension

- Anemia (hemoglobin 12 g/dL)

- Anorexia/nausea

- Azotemia: Elevated serum BUN (> 20 mg/dL) and serum creatinine (> 1.2 mg/dL)

- Uremia (symptoms of renal failure)

Δ **Assess/Monitor**

- Loss of skin integrity related to edema

- Intake and output

- Vital signs (especially blood pressure)

NANDA Nursing Diagnoses

Δ Fluid volume excess

Δ Risk for infection

Δ Deficient knowledge

Δ Anxiety

Δ Fear

Nursing Interventions

Δ Provide periods of rest with activities.

Δ Provide emotional support.

Δ Encourage **adequate nutritional intake** within restriction guidelines.

- Encourage lowering sodium intake.

- Adjust protein intake according to protein loss in urine over 24 hr.

- Provide high biologic value protein (lean meat, fish, poultry, dairy).

- Provide small, frequent feedings because of client's loss of appetite.

Δ Administer **medications** as prescribed.

- Diuretics: Furosemide (Lasix)

- Angiotensin-converting enzyme (ACE) inhibitors

- Glucocorticoids: Prednisone

- Nonsteroidal anti-inflammatory drugs (NSAIDS)

- Anticoagulants: Heparin, warfarin (Coumadin)

- Erythropoietin: Epoetin (Procrit)

Complications and Nursing Implications

Δ **Respiratory Compromise**

- Assess/monitor **breath sounds, respiratory rate**.

Δ Peritonitis

- Assess/monitor **bowel sounds**.

- Monitor **for infection** (rigid, tender abdomen, fever, elevated white blood cell count).

Δ **Renal Failure**

- Assess/monitor **renal status** (BUN, serum creatinine, urinalysis).

- Prepare client for **dialysis**, if indicated.

Δ **Shock/Death**

- Assess/monitor for early indications of shock.

- Implement **life-saving measures**.

Meeting the Needs of Older Adults

Δ Chronic illnesses **increase the potential of nephrotic syndrome** in the older adult client.

Δ **Renal function decreases with aging**, which increases the risk for nephrotic syndrome.

Primary Reference:

Ignatavicius, D. D., & Workman, M. L. (2006). *Medical-surgical nursing* (5th ed.). St. Louis, MO: Saunders.

Additional Resources:

Kowalak, J. P., Welsh, W., & Mayer, B. (Eds.). (2003). *Professional guide to pathophysiology.* Philadelphia: Lippincott Williams & Wilkins.

Monahan, F. D., Sands, J. K., Neighbors, M., Marek, F. J., & Green, C. J. (Eds.). (2007). *Phipps' medical-surgical nursing: Health and illness perspectives* (8th ed.). St. Louis, MO: Mosby.

NANDA International (2004). *NANDA nursing diagnoses: Definitions and classification 2005-2006.* Philadelphia: NANDA.

Chapter 49: Nephrotic Syndrome

Application Exercises

1. Beginning with the first event, identify the sequence of pathological events that occurs in clients with nephrotic syndrome.

   _____ Proteinuria

   _____ Generalized edema

   _____ Renal insult

   _____ Increased glomerular permeability

   _____ Decreased serum protein

2. A client with nephrotic syndrome asks the nurse why her legs and feet are swollen. How can the nurse best address the client's concerns?

3. Explain the rationale for each of the following nursing interventions for a client with nephrotic syndrome:

Intervention	Rationale
Restricting dietary sodium and potassium	
Adjusting protein intake to urine protein loss	
Administering prescribed glucocorticoid drug	
Aggressive treatment of hypertension	
Administering prescribed ACE inhibitors	

4. For which of the following signs and symptoms should the nurse monitor in clients with nephrotic syndrome? (Check all that apply.)

   _____ Malnutrition

   _____ Hematuria

   _____ Infection

   _____ Peritonitis

   _____ Hyperkalemia

   _____ Hypotension

   _____ Fever

Chapter 49: Nephrotic Syndrome

Application Exercises Answer Key

1. Beginning with the first event, identify the sequence of pathological events that occurs in clients with nephrotic syndrome.

    __3__   Proteinuria

    __5__   Generalized edema

    __1__   Renal insult

    __2__   Increased glomerular permeability

    __4__   Decreased serum protein

2. A client with nephrotic syndrome asks the nurse why her legs and feet are swollen. How can the nurse best address the client's concerns?

    The nurse should explain that the client's kidneys are not able to rid her body of excess fluids. Those fluids are collecting in the tissues. The nurse should also reassure the client that interventions will be implemented to help rid her body of fluids while her kidney heals.

3. Explain the rationale for each of the following nursing interventions for a client with nephrotic syndrome:

Intervention	Rationale
Restricting dietary sodium and potassium	Sodium intake is limited because it increases fluid retention. Potassium intake is limited to prevent dangerously elevated levels in clients who do not have adequate renal function to eliminate it.
Adjusting protein intake to urine protein loss	Urinary protein losses can be severe in clients with nephrotic syndrome; however, the waste products of protein loss cannot be adequately eliminated when kidney function is compromised. Therefore, dietary protein intake is adjusted to compensate only for losses.
Administering prescribed glucocorticoid drug	Corticosteroids may help control the inflammatory process occurring in the kidneys.
Aggressive treatment of hypertension	The inability of the kidneys to rid the body of fluid increases intravascular blood pressure, which may be severe in clients with nephrotic syndrome. This places the client at increased risk for brain attack (stroke).
Administering prescribed ACE inhibitors	ACE inhibitors significantly reduce protein loss in the urine.

4. Which of the following signs and symptoms should the nurse monitor for in clients with nephrotic syndrome? (Check all that apply.)

x	Malnutrition
x	Hematuria
x	Infection
x	Peritonitis
x	Hyperkalemia
	Hypotension
x	Fever

Unit 5   Nursing Care of Clients with Renal and Urinary Disorders

Section: Nursing Care of Clients with Select Renal Disorders

Chapter 50:   Renal Failure

Contributor: Carol Green-Nigro, PhD, RN

⟳ NCLEX-PN® Connections

Learning Objective: Review and apply knowledge within "**Renal Failure**" in readiness for performance of the following nursing activities as outlined by the NCLEX-PN® test plan:

Δ   Assist with relevant laboratory, diagnostic, and therapeutic procedures within the nursing role, including:

- Preparation of the client for the procedure.
- Accurate collection of specimens
- Monitoring the client's status during and after the procedure.
- Reinforcing client teaching (before and following the procedure).
- Recognizing the client's response (expected, unexpected adverse response, comparison to baseline) to the procedure.
- Monitoring results.
- Monitoring and taking actions to prevent or minimize the risk of complications.
- Notifying the primary care provider of signs of complications.

Δ   Recognize signs and symptoms of the client's problem and complete the proper documentation.

Δ   Provide and document care based on the client's health alteration.

Δ   Monitor and document vital signs changes.

Δ   Interpret data that need to be reported immediately.

Δ   Reinforce client education on managing the client's health problem.

Δ   Recognize and respond to emergency situations, including notification of the primary care provider.

Δ   Review the client's response to emergency interventions and complete the proper documentation.

Δ   Provide care that meets the age-related needs of clients 65 years of age or older, including recognizing expected physiological changes.

📖 Key Points

Δ   The kidneys regulate fluid, acid-base, and electrolyte balance, as well as eliminating wastes from the body.

Δ   Renal failure may be diagnosed as acute or chronic. Acute renal failure can result in chronic renal failure without aggressive treatment or when complicating pre-existing conditions exist.

Δ   **Acute Renal Failure (ARF)** – the sudden cessation of renal function that occurs when blood flow to the kidneys is significantly compromised.

   •   ARF is a leading cause of mortality among hospitalized clients, 50% of which is due to an iatrogenic cause.

   •   ARF is comprised of three phases:

      ◊   **Oliguria** – begins with the renal insult and continues for 3 weeks.

      ◊   **Diuresis** – begins when the kidneys begin to recover and continues for 7 to 14 days.

      ◊   **Recovery** – continues until renal function is fully restored and requires 3 to 12 months.

   •   Prerenal failure from volume depletion or prolonged reduction of blood pressure is the most common cause of acute renal deterioration and is usually reversible with prompt intervention.

Δ   **Chronic Renal Failure (CRF)** – is a progressive, irreversible kidney disease.

   •   End-stage renal failure exists when 90% of the functioning nephrons have been destroyed and are no longer able to maintain fluid, electrolyte, or acid-base homeostasis.

   •   CRF is comprised of five stages:

      ◊   **Stage 1:** Minimal kidney damage with normal glomerular filtration rate (GFR).

      ◊   **Stage 2:** Mild kidney damage with mildly decreased GFR.

      ◊   **Stage 3:** Moderate kidney damage with moderate decrease in GFR.

      ◊   **Stage 4:** Severe kidney damage with severe decrease in GFR.

      ◊   **Stage 5:** Kidney failure and end-stage renal disease with little or no glomerular filtration taking place.

   •   Dialysis or kidney transplantation can maintain life, but neither are cures for CRF.

Key Factors

Δ   African Americans, Native Americans, and Asians have the highest incidence of end-stage renal disease.

Δ   Risk factors for acute renal failure include prerenal, intrarenal, and postrenal causes.

Δ   **Prerenal** – the insult occurs before damage to the kidney occurs.

- **Hypovolemia** resulting from:
    - ◊ Hemorrhage.
    - ◊ Dehydration.
    - ◊ Burns.
    - ◊ Osmotic diuresis.
    - ◊ Prolonged vomiting or diarrhea.

- **Decreased cardiac output** resulting in reduced renal perfusion can be caused by:
    - ◊ Myocardial infarction.
    - ◊ Cardiogenic shock.
    - ◊ Cardiac arrhythmias.
    - ◊ Congestive heart failure.
    - ◊ Pericardial tamponade.
    - ◊ Open heart surgery.

- **Decreased peripheral vascular resistance** associated with:
    - ◊ Renal artery stenosis.
    - ◊ Septic shock.
    - ◊ Anaphylaxis.
    - ◊ Neurological injury.

- **Renal vascular obstruction** can be caused by:
    - ◊ Thrombosis of renal arteries.
    - ◊ Thrombosis of renal veins.
    - ◊ Embolism.

Δ **Intrarenal** – the insult occurs within the kidney and the damage is usually irreversible (acute tubular necrosis).

- **Nephrotoxic injury** caused by:
  - ◊ Specific antibiotics.
  - ◊ NSAIDs.
  - ◊ Organic solvents.
  - ◊ Contrast dye.
  - ◊ Heavy metals.
  - ◊ Hemolytic transfusion reactions.

- **Acute glomerulonephritis**
  - ◊ Acute pyelonephritis
  - ◊ Toxemia of pregnancy
  - ◊ Malignant hypertension
  - ◊ Systemic lupus erythematosus
  - ◊ Interstitial nephritis

Δ **Postrenal** – obstruction of structures leaving the kidney.

- Renal calculi
- Urinary tract obstruction
- Prostate cancer
- Bladder cancer
- Trauma
- Strictures
- Spinal cord disease

Δ Risk factors/causes of chronic renal failure include:

- Acute renal failure.
- Diabetes mellitus.
- Chronic glomerulonephritis.
- Nephrotoxic medications (gentamicin, NSAIDS) or chemicals.
- Hypertension, especially if African-American.
- Autoimmune disorders (systemic lupus erythematosus).
- Polycystic kidney.

- Pyelonephrosis.

- Renal artery stenosis.

- Recurrent severe infections.

Diagnostic Procedures and Nursing Interventions

Δ **Urinalysis**

- Hematuria, proteinuria, and alterations in specific gravity

- Serum creatinine

  ◊ Gradual increase of 1 to 2 mg/dL per every 24 to 48 hr for acute renal failure (ARF)

  ◊ Gradual increase over months to years for chronic renal failure (CRF) exceeding 4.0 mg/dL

- Blood urea nitrogen (BUN)

  ◊ 80 to 100 mg/dL within 1 week for ARF

  ◊ Gradual increase in concert with elevated serum creatinine over months to years for CRF

Δ **Serum electrolytes**

- Decreased sodium (dilutional), calcium

- Increased potassium, phosphorus, and magnesium

- Complete blood count (CBC)

- Decreased hemoglobin and hematocrit from anemia secondary to loss of erythropoietin in CRF

Δ Radiology

- Renal ultrasound

- Kidneys-ureter-bladder (KUB)

- Computerized tomography (CT)

- Aortorenal angiography

- Cystoscopy

- Retrograde pyelography

- Renal biopsy

- Demonstrates disease processes, obstruction, and arterial defects

Assessments

Δ   Clinical manifestations occur abruptly with ARF.

Δ   Client diagnosed with CRF may be asymptomatic except during periods of stress (infection, surgery, and trauma). As renal failure progresses, clinical manifestations become apparent.

Δ   In most cases, symptoms of renal failure are related to fluid volume overload and include:

- **Renal** – polyuria, nocturia (early), oliguria, anuria (late), proteinuria, hematuria, and dilute urine color when present.

- **Cardiovascular** – hypertension, peripheral edema, pericardial effusion, congestive heart failure, cardiomyopathy, and orthostatic hypotension.

- **Respiratory** – dyspnea, tachypnea, uremic pneumonitis, lung crackles, Kussmaul respirations, and pulmonary edema.

- **Hematologic** – anemia, bruising, and bleeding.

- **Neurologic** – lethargy, insomnia, confusion, encephalopathy, seizures, tremors, ataxia, paresthesias, and coma.

- **Gastrointestinal** – nausea, anorexia, vomiting, metallic taste, stomatitis, diarrhea, uremic halitosis, and gastritis.

- **Skin** – decreased skin turgor, yellow cast to skin, dry, pruritus, bruising, and uremic frost (late).

- **Musculoskeletal** – osteomalacia, muscle weakness, pathologic fractures, and muscle cramps.

- **Reproductive** – erectile dysfunction.

Δ   **Other general symptoms can include:**

- Fatigue.

- Lethargy.

- Restless leg syndrome.

- Depression.

- Intractable hiccups.

Δ   **Abnormal findings** to be reported and monitored include:

- Urinary elimination patterns (amount, color, odor, and consistency).

- Vital signs (especially blood pressure).

- Weight – 1 kg (2.2 lb) daily weight increase is approximately 1 L of fluid retained.

- Assess/monitor vascular access or peritoneal dialysis insertion site.

NANDA Nursing Diagnoses

Δ   Imbalanced nutrition

Δ   Risk for infection

Δ   Impaired gas exchange

Δ   Activity intolerance

Δ   Impaired skin integrity

Δ   Disturbed thought processes

Δ   Deficient knowledge

Nursing Interventions

Δ   Provide high carbohydrate and moderate fat content in the client's diet.

Δ   Restrict the client's intake of fluids (based on urinary output).

Δ   Balance the client's activity and rest.

Δ   Prepare the client for hemodialysis, peritoneal dialysis, and hemofiltration. (*For information, refer to chapter 42, Hemodialysis and Peritoneal Dialysis.*)

Δ   Provide skin care to client to increase comfort and prevent breakdown.

Δ   Protect the client from injury.

Δ   Provide emotional support to the client and family.

Δ   Encourage the client to ask questions and discuss fears.

Δ   Encourage the client to diet, exercise, and take medication to control hyperlipidemia.

Δ   Administer medications as prescribed.

- **Antihypertensives** – ACE inhibitors, calcium channel blockers (avoid dihydropyridine as monotherapy), alpha-adrenergic blockers, beta-adrenergic blockers, and vasodilators)

- **Iron supplements** and **folic acid** as needed

- **Kayexalate** to increased elimination of potassium

- **Erythropoietin alfa** (Epogen, Procrit) to stimulate production of red blood cells

- **Alkalizers** (sodium bicarbonate)

- **Phosphate binders** to prevent calcium loss from bones in clients with CRF

- **Aluminum hydroxide**

- **Calcium carbonate or acetate**

- **Sevelamer hydrochloride** (Renagel)

- **Vitamin D supplements** and **calcium supplements**

- **Stool softeners** (docusate)

- **Diuretics** (except in ESRD)

Δ Clients diagnosed with CRF often require their medication dosages be adjusted based on renal function. Dosages are generally reduced.

Δ For clients with ARF, the nurse should:

- Identify and assist with correcting the underlying cause.

- Prevent prolonged episodes of hypotension and hypovolemia.

- Prepare for fluid challenge and diuretics during prerenal period of azotemia if the client is showing signs of fluid volume deficit.

- Restrict fluid intake during oliguric phase.

- Restrict dietary intake of protein, sodium, and potassium during oliguric phase. This restriction is for the client not requiring dialysis.

Δ For clients with CRF, the nurse should:

- Obtain a detailed medication and herb history to determine the client's risk for continued renal insult.

- Control protein intake based on the client's stage of renal failure and type of dialysis.

- Restrict the client's dietary sodium, potassium, phosphorous, and magnesium.

- Refer the client to a community resource or support group.

- Refer the client to a smoking cessation support group and counseling if needed.

- Encourage the client with diabetes mellitus to adhere to strict blood glucose control since uncontrolled diabetes is a major risk factor for renal failure.

- Encourage the client to obtain a yearly influenza vaccine and to also get the pneumococcal vaccine.

- Teach the client how to measure blood pressure and weight at home.

- Teach the client to avoid antacids containing magnesium.

- Teach the client about the signs and symptoms that require immediate reporting.

Complications and Nursing Implications

Δ   Potential complications of renal failure include: electrolyte imbalance, dysrhythmias, fluid overload, metabolic acidosis, and secondary infection.

Δ   Monitor for and plan interventions for life-threatening complications, including:

- **Hyperkalemia** – Administer Kayexalate or insulin as prescribed.

- **Hypertension** – Administer antihypertensives and diuretics as prescribed.

- **Seizures** – Implement seizure precautions.

- **Cardiac dysrhythmias** – Provide life support interventions for life-threatening dysrhythmias. Monitor the client for and report non-lethal dysrhythmias.

- **Pulmonary edema** – Prepare the client for hemodialysis.

- **Infection** – Maintain the client's surgical asepsis of invasive lines, monitor breath sounds, and turn the client every 2 hr. Monitor the client for signs of localized and systemic infections and report.

- **Metabolic acidosis** – Prepare the client for hemodialysis.

- **Uremia** – Prepare the client for hemodialysis.

Meeting the Needs of Older Adult Clients

Δ   Older adult clients are at an increased risk for renal failure related to the decreased number of functioning nephrons, decreased glomerular filtration rate (GFR), and water and sodium-conserving and compensating mechanisms.

Δ   Increased risk for dehydration is related to inadequate fluid intake secondary to slow loss of thirst mechanism.

Δ   Symptoms may be missed or confused with other chronic illnesses until extensive renal damage has occurred.

Δ   The older adult client generally has a poorer prognosis after an episode of ARF than a younger client.

Δ   There is a 5 to 25% increased mortality rate from ARF for the older adult client.

Δ   ESRD occurs most frequently in persons between 65 to 69 years of age.

Δ   An increased incidence of chronic renal failure may be related to the prevalence of diabetes mellitus, hypertension, and use of NSAIDs in the older adult client.

Primary Reference:

Ignatavicius, D. D., & Workman, M. L. (2006). *Medical-surgical nursing* (5th ed.). St. Louis, MO: Saunders.

Additional Resources:

Monahan, F. D., Sands, J. K., Neighbors, M., Marek, F. J., & Green, C. J. (Eds.). (2007). *Phipps' medical-surgical nursing: Health and illness perspectives* (8th ed.). St. Louis, MO: Mosby.

NANDA International (2004). *NANDA nursing diagnoses: Definitions and classification 2005-2006.* Philadelphia: NANDA.

Thomas, N. (Ed.). (2002). *Renal Nursing* (2nd ed.). St Louis, MO: Elsevier Science.

Chapter 50: Renal Failure

Application Exercises

Scenario: A 64-year-old male client with a history of type 2 diabetes mellitus was admitted to the critical care unit following an automobile crash in which he suffered multiple injuries, blood loss, and hemorrhagic shock. The client underwent surgery for repair of lacerations and removal of his ruptured spleen. His vital signs have stabilized, but he has no urine output in spite of aggressive fluid resuscitation. The client is in acute renal failure.

1. What type of acute renal failure (ARF) is the client experiencing?

2. Based on the client's data, what phase of acute renal failure is the client experiencing, and how long is this phase likely to last?

3. What assessments need to be made while the client is in this phase of acute renal failure to detect possible complications?

4. What risk factors does the client have for ARF?

5. Which of the following assessments need to be made while the client is in acute renal failure? (Check all that apply.)

___ Cardiac enzymes	___ Blood glucose	___ Blood pressure
___ Serum electrolytes	___ Serum creatinine	___ Red blood cells
___ Arterial blood gases	___ Urine output	___ Breath sounds

6. The client's kidney function does not return to normal in spite of the aggressive treatment he has received and he develops chronic renal failure. His output is about 450 mL/day. How does chronic renal failure differ from acute renal failure?

7. Prioritize nursing activities for this client, with "1" representing the most important activity.

_____ Monitor serum potassium level.

_____ Turn client every 2 hr.

_____ Offer emotional support to family.

_____ Assess breath sounds.

8. Which of the following are the two most important collaborative interventions for the client at this time?

_____   Providing adequate pain control

_____   Preventing complications

_____   Correcting electrolyte imbalances

_____   Teaching the client about dialysis

9. What is the relationship between chronic renal failure and diabetes mellitus?

Chapter 50: Renal Failure

Application Exercises Answer Key

Scenario: A 64-year-old male client with a history of type 2 diabetes mellitus was admitted to the critical care unit following an automobile crash in which he suffered multiple injuries, blood loss, and hemorrhagic shock. The client underwent surgery for repair of lacerations and removal of his ruptured spleen. His vital signs have stabilized, but he has no urine output in spite of aggressive fluid resuscitation. The client is in acute renal failure.

1. What type of acute renal failure (ARF) is the client experiencing?

   The client is experiencing prerenal failure related to decreased renal perfusion secondary to hemorrhage (hypovolemia). It is prerenal because the insult did not involve the kidney itself, but loss of blood volume and pressure to the kidney.

2. Based on the client's data, what phase of acute renal failure is the client experiencing, and how long is this phase likely to last?

   The client is in the oliguric phase of ARF with urine production less than 400 mL/day. This phase begins at the time of the insult and lasts for 1 to 3 weeks if corrective action is taken to re-establish blood volume and/or pressure to the kidneys.

3. What assessments need to be made while the client is in this phase of acute renal failure to detect possible complications?

   Vital signs (especially blood pressure), hourly urine output, BUN, serum creatinine, electrolytes, lung sounds, peripheral and dependent edema, arterial blood gases, cardiac rhythm (dysrhythmias), neurological status (seizures), pain (headaches), nausea, vomiting, and signs of infection.

4. What risk factors does the client have for ARF?

   Diabetes mellitus
   Hypovolemic (hemorrhagic) shock
   Age (possibly)

5. Which of the following assessments need to be made while the client is in acute renal failure? (Check all that apply.)

    ___ Cardiac enzymes   _x_ Blood glucose   _x_ Blood pressure

    _x_ Serum electrolytes   _x_ Serum creatinine   ___ Red blood cells

    _x_ Arterial blood gases   _x_ Urine output   _x_ Breath sounds

6. The client's kidney function does not return to normal in spite of the aggressive treatment he has received and he develops chronic renal failure. His output is about 450 mL/day. How does chronic renal failure differ from acute renal failure?

Acute renal failure (ARF) occurs within hours to days and if treated promptly, may be reversible. ARF may not be reversible if other chronic conditions such as diabetes exist. These chronic conditions can complicate recovery. Chronic renal failure (CRF) takes months to years to develop. It is progressive and irreversible. ARF and CRF produce the same signs and symptoms.

7. Prioritize nursing activities for this client, with "1" representing the most important activity.

    __1__   Monitor serum potassium level.

    __3__   Turn client every 2 hr.

    __4__   Offer emotional support to family.

    __2__   Assess breath sounds.

8. Which of the following are the two most important collaborative interventions for the client at this time?

    _____   Providing adequate pain control

    __x__   Preventing complications

    __x__   Correcting electrolyte imbalances

    _____   Teaching the client about dialysis

9. What is the relationship between chronic renal failure and diabetes mellitus?

Chronic hyperglycemia contributes to the development of macrovascular disease, which causes a chronic reduction in blood flow to the kidneys. Over time, renal damage occurs resulting in chronic renal failure.

Unit 6

Nursing Care of Clients with Endocrine Disorders

Section:

Nursing Care of Clients with Thyroid Disorders

Chapter 51:   **Hypothyroidism and Myxedema Coma**

Contributor: Faith Darilek, MSN, RN

NCLEX-PN® Connections:

Learning Objective: Review and apply knowledge within "**Hypothyroidism and Myxedema Coma**" in readiness for performance of the following nursing activities as outlined by the NCLEX-PN® test plan:

Δ   Assist with relevant laboratory, diagnostic, and therapeutic procedures within the nursing role, including:

- Preparation of the client for the procedure.
- Accurate collection of specimens.
- Monitoring client status during and after the procedure.
- Reinforcing client teaching (before and following the procedure).
- Recognizing the client's response (expected, unexpected adverse response) to the procedure.
- Monitoring results.
- Monitoring and taking actions to prevent or minimize the risk of complications.
- Notifying the primary care provider of signs of complications.

Δ   Recognize signs and symptoms of the client's problem and complete the proper documentation.

Δ   Provide and document care based on the client's health alteration.

Δ   Monitor and document vital signs changes.

Δ   Interpret data that need to be reported immediately.

Δ   Reinforce client education on managing the client's health problem.

Δ   Recognize and respond to emergency situations, including notification of the primary care provider.

Δ   Review the client's response to emergency interventions and complete the proper documentation.

Δ   Provide care that meets the age-related needs of clients 65 years of age or older, including recognizing expected physiological changes.

▱ Key Points

Δ **Hypothyroidism** is a condition in which there is an **inadequate** amount of circulating thyroid hormones triiodothyronine (T_3) and thyroxine (T_4), causing a **decrease in metabolic rate** that affects all body systems.

Key Factors

Δ Classifications of hypothyroidism by **etiology**:

- **Primary** – most common, caused by disease or loss of the thyroid gland (iodine deficiency, surgical removal of the gland).

- **Secondary** – caused by failure of the anterior pituitary gland to stimulate the thyroid gland or failure of the target tissues to respond to the thyroid hormones (pituitary tumors).

- **Tertiary** – caused by failure of hypothalamus to produce thyroid-releasing factor.

Δ Hypothyroidism is also classified by **age of onset**.

- **Cretinism** – state of severe hypothyroidism found in infants. When infants do not produce normal amounts of thyroid hormones, their skeletal maturation and central nervous system development are altered, resulting in retardation of physical growth, mental growth, or both.

- **Juvenile hypothyroidism** – most often caused by chronic autoimmune thyroiditis and affects the growth and sexual maturation of the child. Signs and symptoms are similar to adult hypothyroidism, and the treatment reverses most of the clinical manifestations of the disease.

- **Adult hypothyroidism**

Δ The disorder is most prevalent in women, with the incidence rising significantly in persons age 40 to 50.

Δ Many individuals with mild hypothyroidism are frequently undiagnosed, but the hormone disturbance may contribute to an acceleration of atherosclerosis or complication of medical treatment, such as intraoperative hypotension and cardiac complications following surgery.

Diagnostic Procedures and Nursing Interventions

Δ T_3 and T_4 – low

Δ Serum thyroid-stimulating hormone (TSH) – determines etiology. Level is **elevated with primary** hypothyroidism and is **decreased in secondary** hypothyroidism.

Δ Thyrotropin-releasing hormone (TRH) stimulation test – elevated basal, with exaggerated rise in the presence of early hypothyroidism.

Δ Free thyroxine index (FTI) and thyroxine (T_4) levels – decreased

Δ Skull x-ray, CT scan, MRI – locate pituitary or hypothalamic lesions that may be the underlying cause of hypothyroidism.

Δ Radioisotope (^{131} I) scan and uptake – will be less than 10% in a 24-hr period. In secondary hypothyroidism, intake increases with administration of exogenous TSH.

Δ ECG – **sinus bradycardia**, flat or inverted T waves

Δ Serum **cholesterol – elevated**

Δ CBC – **anemia**

Assessments

Δ Hypothyroidism is often characterized by **vague and varied symptoms** that develop slowly over time.

- **Early symptoms**
  - ◊ Weakness
  - ◊ **Fatigue**
  - ◊ Cold intolerance
  - ◊ Constipation
  - ◊ **Weight gain** (unintentional)
  - ◊ Depression
  - ◊ Joint or muscle pain
  - ◊ Thin, brittle fingernails
  - ◊ Thin and brittle hair
  - ◊ Paleness
- **Late symptoms**
  - ◊ Slow speech
  - ◊ Dry flaky skin
  - ◊ Thickening of the skin
  - ◊ Puffy face, hands, and feet
  - ◊ Decreased taste and smell
  - ◊ Thinning of eyebrows
  - ◊ Hoarseness
  - ◊ Abnormal menstrual periods

NANDA Nursing Diagnoses

Δ   Decreased cardiac output

Δ   Ineffective breathing pattern

Δ   Activity intolerance

Δ   Imbalanced nutrition: More than body requirements

Δ   Risk for constipation

Nursing Interventions

Δ   *Caution:* Because of the alteration in metabolism, clients do not tolerate barbiturates or sedatives and therefore **central nervous system depressants are contraindicated**. Also, external warming measures are contraindicated for hypothermia because they can produce vasodilatation and vascular collapse.

Δ   Administer **thyroid hormone therapy**, as ordered.

- Synthetic **levothyroxine** (Synthroid) is the medication most frequently prescribed.

- Because significant cardiovascular disease accompanies hypothyroidism, the client is at risk for cardiac complications if the metabolic rate is increased too quickly. Therefore, the client needs to be **monitored for cardiovascular compromise** (palpitations, chest pain, shortness of breath, rapid heart rate) during early thyroid therapy.

- Treatment **begins slowly** and the dosage **increases every 2 to 3 weeks** until the desired response is obtained. The treatment is considered to be **lifelong**, requiring ongoing medical assessment of thyroid function.

- Clients receiving thyroid replacement therapy must be **monitored for** and taught regarding **signs and symptoms of hyperthyroidism**, which can occur with overmedication. Signs include: irritability, tremors, tachycardia, palpitations, and heat intolerance.

Δ   Increase the client's activity level gradually, and provide **frequent rest** periods to avoid fatigue and **decrease myocardial oxygen demand**.

Δ   Apply **antiembolism** stockings and elevate the client's legs to assist venous return.

Δ   Encourage the client to **cough and breathe deeply** to prevent pulmonary complications.

Δ   Provide a **high-bulk, low-calorie diet** and encourage activity to combat constipation and promote weight loss. Administer cathartics and stool softeners, as needed. The client's intolerance to cold may extend to cold foods, making meal planning more difficult.

Δ   Provide meticulous skin care. **Turn and reposition** the client **every 2 hr** if the client is on extended bed rest. Use alcohol-free skin care products and an emollient lotion after bathing.

Δ   Provide **extra clothing and blankets** for clients with decreased cold tolerance. Dress the client in layers, adjust room temperature, and encourage warm liquids if possible. Caution the client against using electric blankets or other electric heating devices because the combination of vasodilatation, decreased sensation, and decreased alertness may result in unrecognized burns.

Δ   Encourage the client to verbalize feelings and fears about changes in body image. Return to the euthyroid state takes some time. The client may need frequent reassurance that most of the physical manifestations are reversible.

Complications and Nursing Implications

Δ   **Myxedema Coma**

•   A life-threatening condition that occurs when hypothyroidism is untreated or when a stressor such as infection affects an individual with hypothyroidism.

•   Clients with myxedema coma experience:

◊   **Significantly depressed respirations**, so $PaCO_2$ levels may rise.

◊   Decreased cardiac output.

◊   Worsening cerebral hypoxia.

◊   Stupor.

◊   Hypothermia.

◊   Bradycardia.

◊   Hypotension.

Δ   **Nursing Responses to Myxedema Coma**

•   Maintain airway patency with ventilatory support if necessary.

•   Maintain circulation through IV fluid replacement.

•   Provide continuous EKG monitoring.

•   Monitor arterial blood gases (ABGs) to detect hypoxia and metabolic acidosis.

•   Warm the client with blankets.

•   Monitor body temperature until stable.

•   Replace thyroid hormone by administering large IV levothyroxine (Synthroid) doses, as ordered. Monitor vital signs because rapid correction of hypothyroidism can cause adverse cardiac effects.

•   Monitor intake and output and daily weight. With treatment, urine output should increase and body weight decrease; if not, report to the provider.

- Replace fluids and other substances, such as glucose, as needed.

- Administer corticosteroids, as ordered.

- Check for possible sources of infection – such as blood, sputum, or urine – which may have precipitated coma. Treat underlying illness.

Meeting the Needs of Older Adults

Δ   Because older adult clients with hypothyroidism may have confusing signs and symptoms that mimic the aging process, hypothyroidism is often undiagnosed in older adult clients, which can lead to potentially serious side effects from medications such as sedatives, opiates, and anesthetics.

Δ   When starting thyroid hormone replacement, care must be taken with older adult clients and with those who have coronary artery disease to avoid coronary ischemia because of increased oxygen demands of the heart. It is preferable to start with much lower doses and increase gradually, taking 1 to 2 months to reach full replacement doses.

Δ   Polypharmacy is a significant concern for the hypothyroid client. Several classifications of medications are affected by the addition of thyroid supplements, including beta-blockers, oral anticoagulants, bronchodilators, digitalis preparations, tricyclic antidepressants, and cholesterol-lowering agents.

Primary Reference:

Ignatavicius, D. D., & Workman, M. L. (2006). *Medical-surgical nursing* (5th ed.). St. Louis, MO: Saunders.

Additional Resources:

NANDA International (2004). *NANDA nursing diagnoses: Definitions and classification 2005-2006*. Philadelphia: NANDA.

Smeltzer, S. C. & Bare, B. G. (2004). *Brunner and Suddarth's textbook of medical-surgical nursing* (10th ed.). Philadelphia: Lippincott Williams & Wilkins.

Chapter 51: Hypothyroidism and Myxedema Coma

Application Exercises

Scenario: A 46-year-old client visits the outpatient clinic for symptoms of fatigue, cold intolerance, dry scaly skin, hoarseness, weight gain, and fluid retention. Based on her symptoms, thyroid studies are performed and reveal an elevated thyroid stimulating hormone (TSH) and decreased T_3 and T_4 levels. The client is placed on levothyroxine (Synthroid) 0.1 mg by mouth daily and instructed to return to the clinic in 1 month.

    1. What is the significance of the client's laboratory findings?

    2. What does the client need to be taught about her condition and the prescribed medication?

    3. The client feels that she is not losing weight, so she doubles her dose. What are the potential risks of too much thyroid replacement hormone?

Chapter 51: Hypothyroidism and Myxedema Coma

Application Exercises Answer Key

Scenario: A 46-year-old client visits the outpatient clinic for symptoms of fatigue, cold intolerance, dry scaly skin, hoarseness, weight gain, and fluid retention. Based on her symptoms, thyroid studies are performed and reveal an elevated thyroid stimulating hormone (TSH) and decreased T_3 and T_4 levels. The client is placed on levothyroxine (Synthroid) 0.1 mg by mouth daily and instructed to return to the clinic in 1 month.

1. What is the significance of the client's laboratory findings?

   When serum T_3 and T_4 fall below normal, the pituitary gland is stimulated to release TSH in an attempt to raise the T_3 and T_4 back to normal. If the thyroid gland cannot produce T_3 and T_4 because of disease, the TSH will continue to elevate, but production of T_3 and T_4 will not be able to increase.

2. What does the client need to be taught about her condition and the prescribed medication?

   The client should be instructed on: how and when to take her prescribed medication, especially in relationship to food, vitamins, and minerals; the necessity for complying with her medication regimen; side effects of the medication (nervousness, fast or irregular heart beat, heat intolerance, excessive weight loss, diarrhea); that the medication should not be discontinued without the advice of her primary care provider; and the need for follow-up care.

3. The client feels that she is not losing weight, so she doubles her dose. What are the potential risks of too much thyroid replacement hormone?

   Taking too much thyroid replacement hormone could place the client into a hyperthyroid state, potentially placing her at risk for osteoporosis and cardiovascular disease, such as cardiac dysrhythmias and heart failure. Occasionally hair loss or alopecia may occur.

Unit 6   Nursing Care of Clients with Endocrine Disorders
Section: Nursing Care of Clients with Thyroid Disorders

Chapter 52:   **Hyperthyroidism and Thyroid Storm**
              Contributor: Faith Darilek, MSN, RN

NCLEX-PN® Connections:

Learning Objective: Review and apply knowledge within "**Hyperthyroidism and Thyroid Storm**" in readiness for performance of the following nursing activities as outlined by the NCLEX-PN® test plan:

Δ   Assist with relevant laboratory, diagnostic, and therapeutic procedures within the nursing role, including:

- Preparation of the client for the procedure.
- Accurate collection of specimens.
- Monitoring client status during and after the procedure.
- Reinforcing client teaching (before and following the procedure).
- Recognizing the client's response (expected, unexpected adverse response) to the procedure.
- Monitoring results.
- Monitoring and taking actions to prevent or minimize the risk of complications.
- Notifying the primary care provider of signs of complications.

Δ   Recognize signs and symptoms of the client's problem – hyperthyroidism – and complete the proper documentation.

Δ   Provide and document care based on the client's health alteration – hyperthyroidism.

Δ   Monitor and document vital signs changes.

Δ   Interpret data that need to be reported immediately.

Δ   Reinforce client education on managing the client's health problem – hyperthyroidism.

Δ   Recognize and respond to emergency situations – thyroid storm – including notification of the primary care provider.

Δ   Review the client's response to emergency interventions and complete the proper documentation.

Δ   Provide care that meets the age-related needs of clients 65 years of age or older, including recognizing expected physiological changes.

📖 **Key Points**

Δ   The thyroid gland produces three hormones: thyroxine (T_4), triiodothyronine (T_3), and thyrocalcitonin (calcitonin). Secretion of T_3 and T_4 is regulated by the anterior pituitary gland through a negative feedback mechanism.

Δ   When serum T_3 and T_4 levels decrease, thyroid-stimulating hormone (TSH) is released by the anterior pituitary. This stimulates the thyroid gland to secrete more hormones until normal levels are reached.

Δ T_3 and T_4 affect all body systems by **regulating** overall body **metabolism**, energy production, and fluid and electrolyte balance and controlling tissue use of fats, proteins, and carbohydrates.

Δ   Calcitonin inhibits mobilization of calcium from bone and reduces blood calcium levels.

Key Factors

Δ   **Hyperthyroidism** is a clinical syndrome caused by excessive circulating thyroid hormones. Because thyroid activity affects all body systems, excessive thyroid hormone exaggerates normal body functions and produces a **hypermetabolic** state.

Δ   Causes of hyperthyroidism – action of immunoglobulins on the thyroid gland.

•   Graves' disease is the most common cause. Autoimmune antibodies apparently mimic TSH, thus leading to hypersecretion of thyroid hormones.

Diagnostic Procedures and Nursing Interventions

Δ   Serum **TSH** test – **decreased** in the presence of disease.

Δ   Free thyroxine index (FTI) and T_3 – **elevated** in the presence of disease.

Δ   Thyrotropin-releasing hormone (TRH) stimulation test – failure of expected rise in TSH.

Δ   Radioiodine (^{123} I) uptake and thyroid scan – clarifies size of gland and detects presence of hot or cold nodules.

Δ   Take a medication history to determine the use of iodides.

•   Recent contrast media and oral contraceptives may cause falsely elevated serum thyroid hormone levels.

•   Severe illness, malnutrition, and use of aspirin, corticosteroids, and phenytoin sodium may cause a false decrease in serum thyroid hormone levels.

Assessments

Δ   Monitor clients for signs and symptoms of hyperthyroidism, which include:

- Nervousness, **irritability**, hyperactivity, emotional lability, and decreased attention span.

- Weakness, easy fatigability, **exercise intolerance**.

- **Heat intolerance**.

- Weight change (usually loss), **increased appetite**.

- Insomnia, interrupted sleep.

- Frequent stools, diarrhea.

- Menstrual irregularities, decreased libido.

- Warm, sweaty, flushed skin with velvety-smooth texture.

- Tremor, hyperkinesias, hyperreflexia.

- Vision changes, **exophthalmos**, retracted eye lids, staring gaze.

- Hair loss.

- Goiter.

- Bruits over the thyroid gland.

- Elevated systolic blood pressure, widened pulse pressure, S_3 heart sound.

NANDA Nursing Diagnoses

Δ   Hyperthermia

Δ   Activity intolerance

Δ   Imbalanced nutrition: Less than body requirements

Δ   Disturbed thought processes

Nursing Interventions

Δ   Administer antithyroid medications as prescribed, which may include:

- **Propylthiouracil** (PTU) or methimazole (Tapazole) – blocks thyroid hormone synthesis.

- Beta-adrenergic blockers – treats sympathetic nervous system effects (tachycardia, palpitations).

- Iodine-containing medications – inhibits the release of stored thyroid hormone and retards hormone synthesis. Use of these medications is contraindicated in pregnancy.

- Clients receiving antithyroid medications should be monitored for signs of hypothyroidism, which can occur with overmedication.

Δ Promote a calm environment.

Δ **Minimize** the client's **energy expenditure** by assisting with activities as necessary and by encouraging the client to alternate periods of activity with rest.

Δ **Monitor nutritional status**. Provide increased calories, protein, and other nutritional support as necessary.

Δ Assess the client's mental status and decision-making ability. Intervene as needed to ensure safety.

Δ Provide **eye protection** (patches, eye lubricant, taping eyelids closed) for a client with exophthalmos.

Δ Monitor vital signs and hemodynamic parameters (for an acutely ill client) for signs of heart failure.

Δ Reassure the family that any abrupt changes in the client's behavior likely are disease related and should subside with antithyroid therapy.

Δ Prepare the client for total/subtotal thyroidectomy, if the client is unresponsive to antithyroid medications or has an airway-obstructing goiter.

Complications and Nursing Implications

Δ **Thyroid Storm**

- Also known as thyrotoxic crisis, thyroid storm results from a sudden surge of large amounts of thyroid hormones into the bloodstream, causing an even greater **increase in body metabolism**. This is a **medical emergency** with a high mortality rate.

- Precipitating factors include: infection, trauma, and emotional stress, all of which increase demands on body metabolism. It can also occur following subtotal thyroidectomy because of manipulation of the gland during surgery.

- Symptoms include: hyperthermia, hypertension, delirium, vomiting, abdominal pain, and tachydysrhythmias.

Δ **Nursing Responses to Thyroid Storm**

- Maintain a patent airway.

- Monitor continuously for dysrhythmias.

- As prescribed, administer **acetaminophen** to decrease temperature. *Caution*: Aspirin is contraindicated because it releases thyroxine from protein-binding sites and increases free thyroxine levels.

- Provide **cool sponge baths** or apply ice packs to the client's axilla and groin areas to decrease fever. If temperature continues, obtain a prescription for a hypothermia blanket.

- Administer **propylthiouracil (PTU)** as prescribed to prevent further synthesis and release of thyroid hormones.

- Administer **propranolol** (Inderal) as prescribed to block sympathetic nervous system effects.

- Administer **IV fluids** as prescribed to provide adequate hydration and prevent vascular collapse. Fluid volume deficit may occur because of increased fluid excretion by the kidneys or excessive diaphoresis. Carefully monitor intake and output hourly to prevent fluid overload or inadequate replacement.

- Administer sodium iodide as prescribed, 1 hr after administering PTU. *Caution*: If given before PTU, sodium iodide can exacerbate symptoms in susceptible persons.

- Administer small doses of insulin as prescribed to control hyperglycemia. Hyperglycemia can occur as an effect of thyroid storm because of the hypermetabolic state.

- Because O_2 demands are increased as the metabolism increases, administer prescribed **supplemental O_2** as necessary.

Meeting the Needs of Older Adults

Δ Symptoms in older adult clients are often more subtle than those in younger people and the classic signs may be absent.

Δ Occasionally an older adult client with hyperthyroidism demonstrates apathy or withdrawal instead of the more typical hypermetabolic state.

Δ Older adult clients with hyperthyroidism often present with heart failure and atrial fibrillation.

Primary Reference:

Ignatavicius, D. D., & Workman, M. L. (2006). *Medical-surgical nursing* (5th ed.). St. Louis, MO: Saunders.

Additional Resources:

NANDA International (2004). *NANDA nursing diagnoses: Definitions and classification 2005-2006.* Philadelphia: NANDA.

For more information, visit the EndocrineWeb.com at: *www.endocrineweb.com.*

Chapter 52: Hyperthyroidism and Thyroid Storm

Application Exercises

Scenario: A 46-year-old client visits the outpatient clinic for new symptoms of insomnia, anxiety, and feeling as though his heart is "racing." The client has lost 4.5 kg (10 lb) over the past 2 weeks without dieting. Based on his symptoms, thyroid studies are performed and reveal a decreased thyroid-stimulating hormone (TSH) and increased T_3 and T_4 levels. The client is diagnosed with hyperthyroidism and is scheduled to see an endocrinologist for further evaluation and treatment. In the meantime, the client is placed on metoprolol (Lopressor) 50 mg a day.

1. What is the usual treatment for hyperthyroidism?

2. Why did the primary care provider place the client on metoprolol?

3. A potential complication of hyperthyroidism is thyroid storm. What signs and symptoms correspond with thyroid storm and what would the nursing management include?

4. Identify which symptoms correspond with hyperthyroidism (>) and which ones correspond with hypothyroidism (<).

    _____   Dry skin

    _____   Heat intolerance

    _____   Constipation

    _____   Exophthalmos

    _____   Palpitations

    _____   Weight loss

    _____   Weight gain

    _____   Cold intolerance

    _____   Excess perspiration

    _____   Low blood pressure

    _____   Insomnia

    _____   Bradycardia

    _____   Increased blood pressure

Chapter 52: Hyperthyroidism and Thyroid Storm

Application Exercises Answer Key

Scenario: A 46-year-old client visits the outpatient clinic for new symptoms of insomnia, anxiety, and feeling as though his heart is "racing." The client has lost 4.5 kg (10 lb) over the past 2 weeks without dieting. Based on his symptoms, thyroid studies are performed and reveal a decreased thyroid-stimulating hormone (TSH) and increased T_3 and T_4 levels. The client is diagnosed with hyperthyroidism and is scheduled to see an endocrinologist for further evaluation and treatment. In the meantime, the client is placed on metoprolol (Lopressor) 50 mg a day.

1. What is the usual treatment for hyperthyroidism?

Treatment falls under one of three categories: surgery, antithyroid medications, or radioactive iodine. Surgery, once considered the gold standard, has fallen out of favor mainly due to the potential complications of hemorrhage, hypoparathyroidism, and vocal cord paralysis. The current gold standard is radioactive iodine. Treatment goals may be to make the client euthyroid or to totally ablate the gland, leaving the client hypothyroid. Desired results may take 4 to 12 weeks to reach. Side effects are minimal, but thyroiditis, inflammation of the thyroid gland with release of thyroid hormone, can occur. Treatment for hyperthyroidism may be accomplished with antithyroid medications. Antithyroid medications include methimazole (Tapazole) and propylthiouracil (PTU). These medications induce remission of the disease, but are not curative. Antithyroid medications can be used safely during pregnancy and may be the treatment option of choice for older adults or cardiac clients before initiating radioactive iodine. They may cause agranulocytosis.

2. Why did the primary care provider place the client on metoprolol?

The use of beta-blockers is part of the stabilization process that should be carried out as soon as possible. Stabilization is done to decrease the potential untoward cardiac effects, such as tachycardia and atrial fibrillation that may accompany hyperthyroidism. For a client with a history of asthma metoprolol (Lopressor) is a good choice as it is cardioselective and will not have effects on the respiratory tract.

3. A potential complication of hyperthyroidism is thyroid storm. What signs and symptoms correspond with thyroid storm and what would the nursing management include?

Thyroid storm, also called thyroid crisis or thyrotoxicosis, usually occurs with Graves' disease. The condition develops rapidly and can be life-threatening. Thyroid storm is precipitated often by trauma or infection. The rapid increase in metabolic rate leads to hypertension, nausea, diaphoresis, fever, and tachycardia. Priority nursing management includes:

Maintain a patent airway.

Offer a cooling blanket for hyperthermia.

Administer antipyretic as prescribed.

Administer supplementary oxygen therapy as prescribed.

Administer pharmacological interventions as ordered, such as PTU, methimazole, sodium iodide solution, propranolol, and glucocorticoids.

4. Identify which symptoms correspond with hyperthyroidism (>) and which ones correspond with hypothyroidism (<).

<	Dry skin
>	Heat intolerance
<	Constipation
>	Exophthalmos
>	Palpitations
>	Weight loss
<	Weight gain
<	Cold intolerance
>	Excess perspiration
<	Low blood pressure
>	Insomnia
<	Bradycardia
>	Increased blood pressure

Unit 6   Nursing Care of Clients with Endocrine Disorders

Section: Nursing Care of Clients with Thyroid Disorders

Chapter 53:	Thyroidectomy
	Contributor: Faith Darilek, MSN, RN

⟳ NCLEX-PN® Connections:

Learning Objective: Review and apply knowledge within "**Thyroidectomy**" in readiness for performance of the following nursing activities as outlined by the NCLEX-PN® test plan:

Δ   Perform/assist with relevant laboratory, diagnostic, and therapeutic procedures within the nursing role, including:

- Preparation of the client for the procedure.

- Reinforcement of client teaching (before and following the procedure).

- Accurate collection of specimens.

- Monitoring procedure results (compare to norms) and appropriate notification of the primary care provider.

- Monitoring the client's response (expected, unexpected adverse response, comparison to baseline) to the procedure.

- Monitoring and taking actions, including reinforcing client teaching, to prevent or minimize the risk of complications.

- Recognizing signs of potential complications and reporting to the primary care provider.

- Recommending changes in the test/procedure as needed based on client findings.

Δ   Recognize the client's recovery from anesthesia.

Δ   Monitor therapeutic devices (drainage/irrigating devices, chest tubes), if inserted, for proper functioning.

Key Points

△ Thyroidectomy is the **surgical removal** of part or all of the thyroid gland.

△ Thyroidectomy may be performed for the treatment of hyperthyroidism when **drug therapy fails** or radiation therapy is contraindicated. It may also be used to **correct diffuse goiter** and **thyroid cancer**. After surgery, the remaining thyroid tissue usually supplies enough thyroid hormone for normal function.

△ **Total thyroidectomy** may be performed for certain types of thyroid cancers. After total thyroidectomy, the client requires **lifelong thyroid hormone replacement therapy**.

△ The client will probably receive either propylthiouracil (PTU) or methimazole (Tapazole), usually starting 4 to 6 weeks before surgery. Expect the client to receive iodine as well for 10 to 14 days before surgery to reduce the gland's vascularity and thus prevent excess bleeding. The client may also be receiving propranolol (Inderal) to block adrenergic effects.

Diagnostic and Therapeutic Procedures and Nursing Interventions

△ Collect samples for serum thyroid hormones determination to check for euthyroidism preoperatively.

△ Arrange for an electrocardiogram preoperatively to evaluate cardiac status.

△ Surgical procedure – after the client is anesthetized, the surgeon:

- Extends the neck fully and determines the incision line by measuring bilaterally from each clavicle.

- Cuts through the skin, fascia, and muscle and raises skin flaps from the strap muscles.

- Separates these muscles midline, revealing the thyroid's isthmus, and ligates the thyroid artery and veins to help prevent bleeding.

- Locates and visualizes the laryngeal nerves and parathyroid glands and then begins dissection and removal of thyroid tissue, trying not to injure these nearby structures.

- Possibly inserts a Penrose drain or a closed-wound drainage device, such as a Hemovac drain.

- Sutures the incision.

Postoperative Assessments

Δ   Observe for signs of **respiratory distress**. Tracheal collapse, tracheal mucus accumulation, laryngeal edema, and vocal cord paralysis can all cause respiratory obstruction, with sudden stridor and restlessness. Keep a **tracheotomy tray** and suctioning equipment at the client's **bedside for 24 hr** after surgery and be prepared to assist with emergency tracheotomy, if necessary. Also provide air humidification.

Δ   Assess for **signs of hemorrhage**, which may cause shock, tracheal compression, and respiratory distress. Check the client's dressing and palpate the back of the neck, where drainage tends to flow. **Expect** about **50 mL** of drainage in the **first 24 hr**. If you find no drainage, check for drain kinking or the need to reestablish suction. Expect only scant drainage after 24 hr.

Δ   Watch for **hypocalcemia**, which may occur when the parathyroid glands are damaged. Test for Chvostek's and Trousseau's signs, which are indicators of neuromuscular irritability from hypocalcemia. Keep **calcium gluconate** available for **emergency IV** administration.

Δ   Be alert for signs of thyroid storm (For more information, refer to Chapter 52, Hyperthyroidism and Thyroid Storm).

NANDA Nursing Diagnoses

Δ   Risk for injury

Δ   Ineffective airway clearance

Δ   Knowledge deficit

Nursing Interventions

Δ   **Before the Procedure**

- Explain to the client the purpose of the thyroidectomy. Tell her that he will have an incision in his neck, a dressing, and possibly a drain in place. Tell him that he may experience some hoarseness and a sore throat from intubation and anesthesia.

- If the thyroidectomy is being performed to treat hyperthyroidism, ensure that the client has followed his preoperative medication regimen, which will render the gland euthyroid to prevent thyroid storm during surgery. Notify the surgeon immediately if the client has failed to follow his medication regimen.

Δ   **After the Procedure**

- Keep the client in a **high-Fowler's position** to **promote venous return** from the head and neck and to decrease oozing into the incision. **Check** for **laryngeal nerve damage** by asking the client **to speak** as soon as she awakens from anesthesia.

- As ordered, administer a mild analgesic to relieve a sore neck or throat. Reassure the client that her discomfort will resolve within a few days.

- If the client doesn't have a drain in place, prepare her for discharge the day following surgery, as indicated. However, if a drain is in place, the primary care provider will usually remove it, along with half of the surgical clips, on the second day after surgery. The remaining clips are removed the following day before discharge.

Complications and Nursing Implications

Δ   **Hemorrhage**

- The surgical dressing and incision need to be assessed for excessive drainage or bleeding during the postoperative period. Inspect the surgical dressing for bleeding, especially at the back of the neck, and change the dressing as directed.

- To avoid pressure on the suture line, encourage the client to **avoid neck flexion or extension.**

- **Support** the head and neck **with pillows or sandbags.** If the client needs to be transferred from stretcher to bed, support the head and neck in good body alignment.

Δ   **Thyroid Storm**

- Monitor for signs of thyrotoxicosis (tachycardia, diaphoreses, increased blood pressures, anxiety).

Δ   **Airway Obstruction** (because of edema)

- A tracheostomy tray should be kept near the client at all times during the immediate recovery period.

- Maintain the bed in a high-Fowler's position to decrease edema and swelling of the neck.

- If the client reports that the dressing feels tight, the surgeon needs to be alerted immediately.

Δ **Hypocalcemia and tetany** (due to damage of parathyroid glands)

- Monitor for signs of hypocalcemia (**tingling** of the **fingers** and **toes**, carpopedal spasms, and convulsions).

- Have **calcium gluconate** available.

- Maintain **seizure precautions**.

Δ **Nerve damage**

- Nerve damage can lead to vocal cord paralysis and vocal disturbances.

- Teach the client that she will be able to speak only rarely and will need to rest the voice for several days and should expect to be hoarse.

- After the procedure, monitor the client's ability to speak with each measurement of vital signs.

- Assess the client's voice tone and quality and compare it to the preoperative voice.

Primary Reference:

Ignatavicius, D. D., & Workman, M. L. (2006). *Medical-surgical nursing* (5th ed.). St. Louis, MO: Saunders.

Additional Resources:

Kumrow, D., & Dahlen, R. (2002). Thyroidectomy: Understanding the potential for complications. *MedSurg Nursing*, 11 (5), 228-235.

NANDA International (2004). *NANDA nursing diagnoses: Definitions and classification 2005-2006*. Philadelphia: NANDA.

Chapter 53: Thyroidectomy

Application Exercises

Scenario: A 25-year-old female client is being admitted to the postanesthesia care unit (PACU) following a thyroidectomy for hyperthyroidism. The client underwent 3 months of preoperative treatment with antithyroid medications and iodine preparations to establish a euthyroid status prior to her surgery. At the client's bedside, the nurse has placed a tracheostomy set, an endotracheal tube, a laryngoscope, and suction equipment. There are ampules of calcium gluconate on hand. The nurse places the client in a semi-Fowler's position and is supporting her head and neck with pillows and sandbags. The nurse frequently checks the client's vital signs and assesses her suture line for strain or bleeding. Once the immediate postoperative period has passed, the client will be transferred to the surgical floor where she will recuperate and learn about lifelong thyroid replacement therapy.

1. Why is it important for the client to be euthyroid prior to thyroidectomy?

2. Why is it mandatory to have emergency equipment and ampules of calcium gluconate on hand following thyroidectomy?

3. Why is it important to support the client's head and neck with sandbags and pillows?

4. Which of the following client interventions, following a thyroidectomy, could the registered nurse delegate to an assistive personnel team member?

      A. Assess client's pain level.

      B. Monitor and document vital signs.

      C. Check incision for evidence of bleeding and replace dressing as needed.

      D. Administer calcium gluconate, if tetany develops.

Chapter 53: Thyroidectomy

Application Exercises Answer Key

Scenario: A 25-year-old female client is being admitted to the postanesthesia care unit (PACU) following a thyroidectomy for hyperthyroidism. The client underwent 3 months of preoperative treatment with antithyroid medications and iodine preparations to establish a euthyroid status prior to her surgery. At the client's bedside, the nurse has placed a tracheostomy set, an endotracheal tube, a laryngoscope, and suction equipment. There are ampules of calcium gluconate on hand. The nurse places the client in a semi-Fowler's position and is supporting her head and neck with pillows and sandbags. The nurse frequently checks the client's vital signs and assesses her suture line for strain or bleeding. Once the immediate postoperative period has passed, the client will be transferred to the surgical floor where she will recuperate and learn about lifelong thyroid replacement therapy.

1. Why is it important for the client to be euthyroid prior to thyroidectomy?

> **The client needs to be euthyroid prior to thyroidectomy in order to decrease the risk of thyroid storm, which is a crisis state that can be precipitated by surgery, infection, or trauma. Thyroid storm is manifested by a high fever, tachycardia, dehydration, and extreme restlessness. Thyroid storm is potentially fatal, and thus every effort should be made to ensure that the preoperative client with hyperthyroidism is euthyroid.**

2. Why is it mandatory to have emergency equipment and ampules of calcium gluconate on hand following thyroidectomy?

> **It is mandatory to have a tracheostomy set, an endotracheal tube, a laryngoscope, and suction equipment on hand because the client may suddenly develop an airway obstruction due to edema of the glottis, bilateral laryngeal nerve damage, or tracheal compression due to bleeding. Ampules of IV calcium gluconate should also be on hand in case tetany develops (in the instance that one of the parathyroid glands has been damaged).**

3. Why is it important to support the client's head and neck with sandbags and pillows?

> **Sandbags and pillows are used to immobilize the client's head and neck in order to prevent flexion and hyperextension of the neck, which could strain the suture line and cause disruption of the sutures and hemorrhage.**

4. Which of the following client interventions, following a thyroidectomy, could the registered nurse delegate to an assistive personnel team member?

    A. Assess client's pain level.

    B. Monitor and document vital signs.

    C. Check incision for evidence of bleeding and replace dressing as needed.

    D. Administer calcium gluconate, if tetany develops.

Assessments, dressing changes, and administration of emergency medications are not within the role parameters of assistive personnel. With parameters regarding when to report findings and assurance of proper technique, assistive personnel can be very helpful in monitoring and documenting routine vital signs.

Unit 6   Nursing Care of Clients with Endocrine Disorders
Section: Nursing Care of Clients with Pituitary Disorders

Chapter 54:   Diabetes Insipidus
Contributor: Faith Darilek, MSN, RN

⟳ NCLEX-PN® Connections:

Learning Objective: Review and apply knowledge within "**Diabetes Insipidus**" in readiness for performance of the following nursing activities as outlined by the NCLEX-PN® test plan:

Δ   Assist with relevant laboratory, diagnostic, and therapeutic procedures within the nursing role, including:

- Preparation of the client for the procedure.
- Accurate collection of specimens.
- Monitoring client status during and after the procedure.
- Reinforcing client teaching (before and following the procedure).
- Recognizing the client's response (expected, unexpected adverse response) to the procedure.
- Monitoring results.
- Monitoring and taking actions to prevent or minimize the risk of complications.
- Notifying the primary care provider of signs of complications.

Δ   Recognize signs and symptoms of the client's problem – diabetes insipidus – and complete the proper documentation.

Δ   Provide and document care based on the client's health alteration – diabetes insipidus.

Δ   Monitor and document vital signs changes.

Δ   Interpret data that need to be reported immediately.

Δ   Reinforce client education on managing the client's health problem – diabetes insipidus.

Δ   Recognize and respond to emergency situations, including notification of the primary care provider.

Δ   Review the client's response to emergency interventions and complete the proper documentation.

Δ   Provide care that meets the age-related needs of clients 65 years of age or older, including recognizing expected physiological changes.

📖 Key Points

Δ   Diabetes insipidus results from a **deficiency of antidiuretic hormone (ADH)**, also known as **vasopressin**, secreted by the posterior lobe of the pituitary gland (neurohypophysis).

Key Factors

Δ   Decreased ADH reduces the ability of distal and collecting renal tubules in the kidneys to concentrate urine, resulting in **excessive diluted urination**, excessive thirst, and excessive fluid intake.

Δ   Types of diabetes insipidus include:

- **Neurogenic** (also known as central or primary) – caused by a defect in the hypothalamus or pituitary gland as in trauma, irradiation, or cranial surgery.

- **Nephrogenic** – inherited, renal tubules do not respond to ADH.

- **Drug-induced**.

Diagnostic Procedures and Nursing Interventions

Δ   **Urine** chemistry – think **DILUTE**.

- Decreased urine specific gravity (less than 1.005)

- Decreased urine osmolality (50 to 200 mOsm/kg)

- Decreased urine pH

- Decreased urine sodium

- Decreased urine potassium

- **As urine volume increases, urine osmolality decreases.**

Δ   **Serum** chemistry – think **CONCENTRATED**.

- Increased serum osmolality

- Increased serum sodium

- Increased serum potassium

- **As serum volume decreases, the serum osmolality increases.**

Δ   Radioimmunoassay – **decreased ADH**.

Δ   Water deprivation test (simplest and most reliable diagnostic test) – inability of kidneys to concentrate urine despite increased plasma osmolality and low plasma vasopressin level.

Δ   Vasopressin test – subcutaneous injection of vasopressin produces urine output with increased specific gravity if the client has central diabetes insipidus. This helps differentiate central from nephrogenic diabetes insipidus.

Assessments

Δ   Monitor for signs and symptoms of diabetes insipidus including:

- Polyuria (abrupt onset of excessive urination, **urinary output of 5 to 20 L/day** of dilute urine).

- Polydipsia (excessive thirst, consumption of 4 to 30 L/day).

- Nocturia.

- Fatigue.

- **Dehydration** as evidenced by extreme thirst, weight loss, muscle weakness, headache, tachycardia, hypotension, poor skin turgor, dry mucous membranes, constipation, and dizziness.

NANDA Nursing Diagnoses

Δ   Impaired urine elimination related to polyuria

Δ   Fluid volume deficit

Δ   Disturbed sleep pattern

Δ   Impaired oral mucous membrane

Nursing Interventions

Δ   Monitor vital signs, urinary output, central venous pressure, intake and output, specific gravity, and laboratory studies (potassium, sodium, BUN, creatinine, specific gravity, and osmolality).

Δ   Weigh the client daily.

Δ   Promote prescribed diet (regular diet with restriction of foods that exert a diuretic effect, such as caffeine).

Δ   **IV therapy:** hydration (intake and output must be matched to prevent dehydration), electrolyte replacement.

Δ   **Promote safety:** Keep bedside rails up and provide assistance with walking if the client is dizzy or has muscle weakness. Make sure the client has easy access to the bathroom or bedpan and answer the call lights promptly.

Δ   Add bulk foods and fruit juices to the diet if constipation develops. The client may require a mild laxative.

Δ   Assess skin turgor and mucous membranes.

Δ   Provide meticulous skin and mouth care and apply a lubricant to cracked or sore lips. Use a soft toothbrush and mild mouthwash to avoid trauma to the oral mucosa. Use alcohol-free skin care products and apply emollient lotion after baths.

Δ   Encourage the client to **drink fluids in response to thirst**.

Δ   Administer medications as prescribed:

- ADH *replacement* agents such as **desmopressin** acetate (DDAVP) or aqueous vasopressin (Pitressin) administered intranasally, orally, or parenterally.

- ADH *stimulants* such as carbamazepine (Tegretol).

- Give vasopressin (Pitressin) cautiously to clients with coronary artery disease because the medication may cause vasoconstriction.

- Educate the client regarding **lifelong vasopressin** therapy, daily weights, and the importance of reporting weight gain, polyuria, and polydipsia to the primary care provider.

Complications and Nursing Implications

Δ   **Untreated** diabetes insipidus can produce hypovolemia, hyperosmolality, circulatory collapse, unconsciousness, and central nervous system damage.

Meeting the Needs of Older Adults

Δ   Older adult clients are at higher risk for dehydration. The body content is 60% water compared to 70% in younger people; thirst response is lowered; kidneys do not concentrate urine as well; many older adult clients may be taking diuretics for other conditions; and some older adults may have swallowing difficulties or poor food intake.

Primary Reference:

Ignatavicius, D. D., & Workman, M. L. (2006). *Medical-surgical nursing* (5th ed.). St. Louis, MO: Saunders.

Additional Resources:

NANDA International (2004). *NANDA nursing diagnoses: Definitions and classification 2005-2006*. Philadelphia: NANDA.

For more information, visit the Diabetes Insipidus Foundation at: *www.diabetesinsipidus.org*.

Chapter 54: Diabetes Insipidus

Application Exercises

Scenario: A 78-year-old female client is admitted to a medical-surgical floor from the emergency department because of weakness and confusion. She is currently receiving radiation therapy for a brain tumor.

1. Why does radiation for a brain tumor place this client at risk for diabetes insipidus?

2. What symptoms do diabetes insipidus and diabetes mellitus have in common?

3. Should the nurse expect the client's urine specific gravity to be high or low? Why?

4. Should the nurse expect the client's serum osmolality to be high or low? Why?

5. What fluid-related nursing diagnosis is this client at risk for?

6. Upon admission to the medical-surgical floor, the following findings are reported by the emergency department nurse: blood pressure 100/60 mm Hg, pulse 96 beats/min, respiratory rate 16/min. The client reports thirst; her skin is tenting and flushed; urine output is 300 mL/hr with a specific gravity of 1.005; and she has flaccid muscle tone. What additional priority assessments need to be made at this time?

7. Based on a suspicion of fluid volume deficit related to inadequate release of ADH, what priority interventions should be taken?

8. Admitting orders include: serum osmolality, urine osmolality, and electrolytes. The laboratory reports: urine osmolality 95 mOsm/kg, serum osmolality 312 mOsm/kg, and sodium level 148 mEq/L. What is the significance of each finding?

9. Replacement therapy for diabetes insipidus includes administration of aqueous vasopressin (Pitressin). How should the nurse evaluate the effectiveness of the medication and fluid therapy?

10. The client begins treatment with desmopressin acetate (DDAVP). What signs of overdose should she be instructed to observe for?

Chapter 54: Diabetes Insipidus

Application Exercises Answer Key

Scenario: A 78-year-old female client is admitted to a medical-surgical floor from the emergency department because of weakness and confusion. She is currently receiving radiation therapy for a brain tumor.

1. Why does radiation for a brain tumor place this client at risk for diabetes insipidus?

   Any injury can directly or indirectly damage the pituitary gland, placing the client at risk for reduced ADH secretion and, consequently, diabetes insipidus.

2. What symptoms do diabetes insipidus and diabetes mellitus have in common?

   Polyuria and polydipsia are symptoms of both diabetes insipidus and diabetes mellitus.

3. Should the nurse expect the client's urine specific gravity to be high or low? Why?

   The client's specific gravity should be low because she is excreting too much water.

4. Should the nurse expect the client's serum osmolality to be high or low? Why?

   Her serum osmolality should be high because she is losing water and is becoming dehydrated.

5. What fluid-related nursing diagnosis is this client at risk for?

   Fluid volume deficit

6. Upon admission to the medical-surgical floor, the following findings are reported by the emergency department nurse: blood pressure 100/60 mm Hg, pulse 96 beats/min, respiratory rate 16/min. The client reports thirst; her skin is tenting and flushed; urine output is 300 mL/hr with a specific gravity of 1.005; and she has flaccid muscle tone. What additional priority assessments need to be made at this time?

Temperature (may be elevated in dehydration or infection)

Neurologic status: Note signs/symptoms of dehydration (hyperosmolality), such as restlessness and irritability.

Hydration status: Look especially for hypovolemia (dry and sticky mucous membranes, output greater than intake, dry skin with poor turgor).

7. Based on a suspicion of fluid volume deficit related to inadequate release of ADH, what priority interventions should be taken?

Calculate intake and output for net gain or loss.

Document any change in appearance and specific gravity of urine.

Ensure safety precautions.

Monitor neurologic status.

Observe for signs of hypernatremia.

8. Admitting orders include: serum osmolality, urine osmolality, and electrolytes. The laboratory reports: urine osmolality 95 mOsm/kg, serum osmolality 312 mOsm/kg, and sodium level 148 mEq/L. What is the significance of each finding?

Insufficient ADH secretion from the posterior pituitary causes immediate excretion of a large volume of dilute urine, leading to increased serum osmolality. Dehydration develops rapidly without ongoing fluid replacement.

The serum osmolality and sodium are only slightly elevated, indicating that the fluid replacement is adequate (intake matches output).

9. Replacement therapy for diabetes insipidus includes administration of aqueous vasopressin (Pitressin). How should the nurse evaluate the effectiveness of the medication and fluid therapy?

Stable vital signs, intake and output balance, electrolytes within normal limits, moist mucous membranes, good skin turgor, no report of thirst.

10. The client begins treatment with desmopressin acetate (DDAVP). What signs of overdose should she be instructed to observe for?

She should watch for signs of fluid overload, such as increasing weight and concentrated urine.

Unit 6 — Nursing Care of Clients with Endocrine Disorders

Section: Nursing Care of Clients with Pituitary Disorders

Chapter 55: Syndrome of Inappropriate Antidiuretic Hormone (SIADH)

Contributor: Faith Darilek, MSN, RN

NCLEX-PN® Connections:

Learning Objective: Review and apply knowledge within "**Syndrome of Inappropriate Antidiuretic Hormone (SIADH)**" in readiness for performance of the following nursing activities as outlined by the NCLEX-PN® test plan:

Δ   Assist with relevant laboratory, diagnostic, and therapeutic procedures within the nursing role, including:

- Preparation of the client for the procedure.

- Accurate collection of specimens.

- Monitoring client status during and after the procedure.

- Reinforcing client teaching (before and following the procedure).

- Recognizing the client's response (expected, unexpected adverse response) to the procedure.

- Monitoring results.

- Monitoring and taking actions to prevent or minimize the risk of complications.

- Notifying the primary care provider of signs of complications.

Δ   Recognize signs and symptoms of the client's problem and complete the proper documentation.

Δ   Provide and document care based on the client's health alteration.

Δ   Monitor and document vital signs changes.

Δ   Interpret data that need to be reported immediately.

Δ   Reinforce client education on managing the client's health problem.

Δ   Recognize and respond to emergency situations, including notification of the primary care provider.

Δ   Review the client's response to emergency interventions and complete the proper documentation.

Δ   Provide care that meets the age-related needs of clients 65 years of age or older, including recognizing expected physiological changes.

Key Points

Δ Syndrome of inappropriate antidiuretic hormone (SIADH) is an **excessive release of antidiuretic hormone** (ADH), also known as vasopressin, secreted by the posterior lobe of the pituitary gland (neurohypophysis).

Key Factors

Δ **Excess ADH** leads to renal reabsorption of water and suppression of renin-angiotensin mechanism, causing renal excretion of sodium leading to water intoxication, cellular edema, and dilutional hyponatremia. Fluid shifts within compartments cause **decreased serum osmolality**.

Δ **Conditions that stimulate the hypothalamus to hypersecrete ADH** include malignant tumors (most common cause is oat-cell lung cancer), increasing intrathoracic pressure (such as with positive pressure ventilation), head injury, meningitis, cardiovascular accident, medications (alcohol, lithium carbonate, phenytoin), trauma, pain, and stress.

Diagnostic Procedures and Nursing Interventions

Δ **Urine** Chemistry – Think **CONCENTRATED**.

- Increased urine sodium

- Increased urine osmolality

- As **urine volume decreases**, the **urine osmolality increases**.

Δ **Blood** chemistry – Think **DILUTE**.

- Decreased serum sodium (for example, 110 mEq/L)

- Decreased serum osmolality (less than 270 mEq/L)

- As the **serum volume increases**, the **serum osmolality decreases**.

- Radioimmunoassay – **increased ADH**.

Assessments

Δ **Early symptoms** of SIADH include **headache**, weakness, anorexia, **muscle cramps**, and weight gain (without edema because water, not sodium, is retained).

Δ As the serum sodium level decreases, the client experiences **personality changes**, hostility, sluggish deep tendon reflexes, nausea, vomiting, diarrhea, and **oliguria**.

Δ **Confusion**, lethargy, and Cheyne-Stokes respirations herald impending crisis. When the serum sodium level drops further, **seizures**, **coma**, and death may occur.

Δ Manifestations of **fluid volume excess** include: **tachycardia**, possibly hypertension, **crackles** in lungs, distended neck veins, and taut skin. Intake is greater than output.

NANDA Nursing Diagnoses

Δ Fluid volume excess

Δ Disturbed thought processes

Δ Risk for injury

Nursing Interventions

Δ **Restrict oral fluids** to 500 to 1,000 mL/day to prevent further hemodilution (first priority). During fluid restriction, provide comfort measure for thirst, including ice chips, mouth care, lozenges, and staggered water intake.

Δ Flush all enteral and gastric tubes with normal saline instead of water to replace sodium and prevent further hemodilution.

Δ Monitor **intake and output** accurately. Report decreased urine output.

Δ Monitor vital signs for increased blood pressure, tachycardia, and hypothermia.

Δ Monitor for decreased serum sodium/osmolality and elevated urine sodium/osmolality.

Δ **Weigh daily**; a weight gain of 0.9 kg (2 lb) indicates a gain of 1 L of fluid.

Δ Report altered mental status (headache, confusion, lethargy, seizures, coma).

Δ Reduce unnecessary environmental stimuli and orient the client, as needed.

Δ Provide a safe environment for the client with an altered level of consciousness. Take **seizure precautions.**

Δ Medications: **demeclocycline** (Declomycin) or lithium (lithium carbonate) to block the renal response to ADH.

Δ In severe hyponatremia/water intoxication, administration of 200 to 300 mL of hypertonic IV fluid (3 to 5% NaCl). The goal of hypertonic normal saline therapy is to elevate the sodium level enough to alleviate signs of neurologic compromise – not to raise the level to normal.

Δ   Observe for signs and symptoms of heart failure, that may occur due to fluid overload. Use of a loop diuretic may be indicated.

Δ   Supplement sodium intake orally or by hypertonic saline IV infusion.

Complications and Nursing Implications

Δ   Without prompt treatment, SIADH may lead to water intoxication, **cerebral edema**, and severe hyponatremia, with resultant coma and death.

Δ   Treatment for SIADH may result in central pontine myelinolysis (CPM) – a condition characterized by nerve damage caused by the destruction of the myelin sheath in the brainstem (pons). The most common cause is a rapid, drastic change in sodium levels in the body. This most commonly occurs when someone is being treated for hyponatremia and the levels rise too fast. During treatment with hypertonic saline or loop diuretics, plasma osmolality and serum sodium are monitored every 2 to 4 hr. Any deterioration in neurological status should be reported immediately.

Meeting the Needs of Older Adults

Δ   Diuretics are sometimes used to treat conditions such as congestive heart failure. Sodium losses due to diuretic use can further contribute to the problems caused by SIADH. A careful client history and medication review may help alert nurses to the possibility of SIADH.

Primary Reference:

Ignatavicius, D. D., & Workman, M. L. (2006). *Medical-surgical nursing* (5th ed.). St. Louis, MO: Saunders.

Additional Resources:

NANDA International (2004). *NANDA nursing diagnoses: Definitions and classification 2005-2006*. Philadelphia: NANDA.

Chapter 55: Syndrome of Inappropriate Antidiuretic Hormone (SIADH)

Application Exercises

Scenario: A nurse is assigned to care for a male client with the primary diagnosis of SIADH. His secondary diagnosis is lung cancer. He is being treated for symptoms of SIADH.

1. While planning care for this client, the nurse reviews his nursing diagnoses. Which priority fluid-related nursing diagnosis should the nurse expect?

2. Identifying the priority problem, how should the nurse monitor the client's fluid balance?

3. Why is the client at risk for seizures?

4. How can the nurse reduce this client's risk for injury from seizures?

5. What should the nurse expect the client's urine to look like?

6. What change in urine appearance should the nurse expect after treatment begins?

7. The client's wife states that she knows her husband is on a fluid restriction, but that he is complaining of extreme thirst. What strategies can you offer her?

8. Two days later, the client is vomiting, disoriented to time and place, and reporting a severe headache. What should the nurse do first?

9. The provider transfers the client to an ICU and prescribes the following: Start an IV of 3% normal saline and infuse 100 mL over 1 hr followed by stat serum sodium, chloride, bicarbonate, and osmolality levels and stat urine osmolality. Administer furosemide (Lasix) 40 mg IV push. Discuss the possible consequences of too rapid an infusion of the saline solution.

10. In relation to the order for infusion of 3% normal saline, when should the furosemide (Lasix) be given and why?

Chapter 55: Syndrome of Inappropriate Antidiuretic Hormone (SIADH)

Application Exercises Answer Key

Scenario: A nurse is assigned to care for a male client with the primary diagnosis of SIADH. His secondary diagnosis is lung cancer. He is being treated for symptoms of SIADH.

1. While planning care for this client, the nurse reviews his nursing diagnoses. Which priority fluid-related nursing diagnosis should the nurse expect?

   Because the client has too much ADH, he will be retaining water. A priority nursing diagnosis is fluid volume excess.

2. Identifying the priority problem, how should the nurse monitor the client's fluid balance?

   The best way to monitor fluid balance is by daily weights, at the same time each day, on the same scale, and in about the same clothes. In addition to daily weights, intake and output, vital signs, urine specific gravity, lung sounds, and skin turgor should be monitored.

3. Why is the client at risk for seizures?

   The client will retain water, which will reduce serum osmolality. This can cause cerebral edema, increased intracranial pressure, and seizures.

4. How can the nurse reduce this client's risk for injury from seizures?

   Side rails should be padded. If a seizure occurs, the client should be protected from harming himself through measures such as maintaining a patent airway.

5. What should the nurse expect the client's urine to look like?

   The nurse should expect the client's urine to be very concentrated because the client is not excreting much water.

6. What change in urine appearance should the nurse expect after treatment begins?

With effective treatment, the client's urine will look more dilute secondary to more excretion of water.

7. The client's wife states that she knows her husband is on a fluid restriction, but that he is complaining of extreme thirst. What strategies can you offer her?

Encourage ice chips, flavored popsicles, or hard candy to relieve the sensation of thirst.

Provide cold water on a "swish and spit" basis to relieve dry mouth without increasing fluid intake.

Provide/encourage frequent oral hygiene.

Space fluids throughout a 24-hr period.

8. Two days later, the client is vomiting, disoriented to time and place, and reporting a severe headache. What should the nurse do first?

Immediately notify the client's primary care provider. The client is exhibiting clinical manifestations of severe hyponatremia and is at high risk for seizures and coma.

9. The provider transfers the client to an ICU and prescribes the following: Start an IV of 3% normal saline and infuse 100 mL over 1 hr followed by stat serum sodium, chloride, bicarbonate, and osmolality levels and stat urine osmolality. Administer furosemide (Lasix) 40 mg IV push. Discuss the possible consequences of too rapid an infusion of the saline solution.

Infusion of 3% normal saline solution can induce severe volume overload and pulmonary edema. The client should be closely observed for signs of neurologic deterioration, congestive heart failure, and pulmonary edema.

10. In relation to the order for infusion of 3% normal saline, when should the furosemide (Lasix) be given and why?

Furosemide should be given concurrently with the normal saline infusion. Furosemide is administered to prevent circulatory overload as fluid shifts from the intracellular to the intravascular compartments.

Unit 6
Section:

Nursing Care of Clients with Endocrine Disorders
Nursing Care of Clients with Adrenal Disorders

Chapter 56:	Cushing's Disease/Syndrome

Contributor: Dana Bartlett, MSN, RN, CSPI

C NCLEX-PN® Connections:

Learning Objective: Review and apply knowledge within **"Cushing's Disease/ Syndrome"** in readiness for performance of the following nursing activities as outlined by the NCLEX-PN® test plan:

Δ   Assist with relevant laboratory, diagnostic, and therapeutic procedures within the nursing role, including:

- Preparation of the client for the procedure.
- Accurate collection of specimens.
- Monitoring client status during and after the procedure.
- Reinforcing client teaching (before and following the procedure).
- Recognizing the client's response (expected, unexpected adverse response) to the procedure.
- Monitoring results.
- Monitoring and taking actions to prevent or minimize the risk of complications.
- Notifying the primary care provider of signs of complications.

Δ   Recognize signs and symptoms of the client's problem and complete the proper documentation.

Δ   Provide and document care based on the client's health alteration.

Δ   Monitor and document vital signs changes.

Δ   Interpret data that need to be reported immediately.

Δ   Reinforce client education on managing the client's health problem.

Δ   Recognize and respond to emergency situations, including notification of the primary care provider.

Δ   Review the client's response to emergency interventions and complete the proper documentation.

Δ   Provide care that meets the age-related needs of clients 65 years of age or older, including recognizing expected physiological changes.

📖 Key Points

Δ **Cushing's disease and Cushing's syndrome** are characterized by adrenal glands **hyperfunctioning** and an **excess** production of the glucocorticoid **cortisol.**

Δ High levels of cortisol reduce lymphocyte activity which creates **immunosuppression.**

Key Factors

Δ **Endogenous causes** (excess production of cortisol) of **Cushing's disease** include:

- Adrenal hyperplasia.

- Adrenocortical neoplasm.

- Pituitary neoplasm that secretes adrenocorticotropic hormone (ACTH).

- Carcinomas of the lung, gastrointestinal tract, or pancreas (these tumors can secrete ACTH).

  ◊ Cushing's disease as a result of these disorders usually occurs in women between 25 and 40 years old.

Δ **Exogenous** causes (cortisol treatment of another disorder) of **Cushing's syndrome** include the therapeutic **use of glucocorticoids** for:

- Asthma.

- Autoimmune disorders.

- Organ transplantation.

- Cancer chemotherapy.

- Allergies.

- Chronic fibrosis.

Diagnostic and Therapeutic Procedures and Nursing Interventions

Δ **Diagnostic procedures** include:

- Plasma **cortisol** levels (draw at same time each day): **Elevated levels** in the absence of acute illness or stress are diagnostic for Cushing's disease/ syndrome.

- Urine cortisol levels (24-hr urine collection): Elevated levels of free cortisol

- Plasma ACTH levels vary based on the cause of the hypercortisolism: **Decreased** (except in ectopic causes)

- Serum **glucose** level: **Increased**

- Serum **potassium** and **calcium** levels: **Decreased**

- Serum **sodium** level: **Increased**

- **Dexamethasone suppression** tests: Vary in length and amount of dexamethasone administered. 24-hr urine collections reveal suppression of cortisol excretion in clients without Cushing's. **Nonsuppression of cortisol excretion is indicative** of Cushing's. Medications are withheld and stress is reduced prior to and during testing.

Δ **Therapeutic procedures** for endogenous hypercortisolism include:

- Surgical removal of the pituitary or adrenal gland (depending on cause).

  ◊ Hypophysectomy: Intervene for risks associated with cranial surgery.

  ◊ Adrenalectomy: Intervene for risks associated with flank or abdominal surgery. Provide glucocorticoid replacement as needed.

- Chemotherapy with cytotoxic agents: Monitor for adverse effects (for example, thrombocytopenia).

- Radiation therapy: Intervene for skin and alopecia effects.

Assessments

Δ Neurologic, cardiovascular, dermal, and endocrine system assessments are indicated.

Δ **Signs and symptoms** of Cushing's disease/syndrome include:

- Evidence of decreased immune function and decreased inflammatory response.

- **Hypertension** (sodium and water retention).

- **Changes in fat distribution**, including the characteristic fat distribution of moon face, truncal obesity, and fat collection on the back of the neck (buffalo hump).

- Emotional lability.

- Fractures (osteoporosis).

- Impaired glucose tolerance.

- Hirsutism.

- Bruising and petechiae (fragile blood vessels).

- **Muscle wasting.**

NANDA Nursing Diagnoses

Δ Disturbed body image

Δ Fatigue

Δ Excess fluid volume

Δ Risk for infection

Nursing Interventions

Δ Compensatory dietary alterations: Decreased sodium intake and increased intake of potassium, protein, and calcium.

Δ Take daily weights.

Δ Monitor intake and output.

Δ Maintain a safe environment to minimize the risk of pathological fractures and skin trauma.

Δ Prevent infection through strict handwashing techniques.

Δ Encourage physical activity within the client's limitations.

Δ Provide meticulous skin care. Monitor for and protect against skin breakdown.

Complications and Nursing Implications

Δ Perforated viscera/ulceration: Monitor **for evidence of gastrointestinal bleeding.** Administer **anti-ulcer** medications as prescribed.

Δ Risk for infection due to **immunosuppression:** Monitor for subtle signs of infection. Instruct the client in measures to minimize exposure to infectious organisms (avoiding ill persons and crowds, good handwashing).

Δ Risk for **adrenal crisis** (also know as **acute adrenal insufficiency) with abrupt withdrawal** of steroid medication. Signs include hypotension, hyperkalemia, abdominal pain, weakness, and weight loss. Instruct the client to **taper medication gradually**. Treatment of acute adrenal insufficiency is the administration of glucocorticoids. During times of stress, additional glucocorticoids may be needed to prevent adrenal crisis.

Primary Reference:

Ignatavicius, D. D., & Workman, M. L. (2006). *Medical-surgical nursing* (5th ed.). St. Louis, MO: Saunders.

Additional Resources:

NANDA International (2004). *NANDA nursing diagnoses: Definitions and classification 2005-2006*. Philadelphia: NANDA.

Chapter 56: Cushing's Disease/Syndrome

Application Exercises

Scenario: A nurse is caring for a client with Cushing's disease.

1. What is the basic cause of Cushing's disease?

2. What hormone is produced in excess in Cushing's disease?

3. Name two complications of Cushing's disease?

4. Will a client with Cushing's disease have hyperglycemia or hypoglycemia?

5. Will a client with Cushing's disease gain or lose weight?

6. Why is it important to monitor this client for infection?

7. The provider has ordered a chest x-ray and a CT of the thorax. Why?

Scenario: A nurse is caring for a female client who has just been diagnosed with Cushing's disease.

8. The client is reporting abdominal pain. Is this a serious sign? Why or why not?

9. The provider has ordered that the client's blood pressure be checked every 4 hr. Why?

10. The client's medication history indicates prolonged use of prednisone. What is the relationship between the use of this steroid and the client's physical appearance?

11. Why should the nurse caution the client not to stop taking her oral steroid medication without consulting her primary care provider first?

12. The nurse observes the nursing diagnosis "Risk for injury: fractures" on the client's nursing care plan. Why is the client at risk for fractures?

Chapter 56: Cushing's Disease/Syndrome

Application Exercises Answer Key

Scenario: A nurse is caring for a client with Cushing's disease.

1. What is the basic cause of Cushing's disease?

   An adrenal gland is hyperfunctioning.

2. What hormone is produced in excess in Cushing's disease?

   Cortisol

3. Name two complications of Cushing's disease?

   Perforated viscera/ulceration, infection, adrenal crisis with abrupt withdrawal

4. Will a client with Cushing's disease have hyperglycemia or hypoglycemia?

   Hyperglycemia

5. Will a client with Cushing's disease gain or lose weight?

   Weight gain

6. Why is it important to monitor this client for infection?

   People with Cushing's disease have a decreased immune response and decreased inflammatory response.

7. The provider has ordered a chest x-ray and a CT of the thorax. Why?

There can be tumors in the lungs that secrete ACTH.

Scenario: A nurse is caring for a female client who has just been diagnosed with Cushing's disease.

8. The client is reporting abdominal pain. Is this a serious sign? Why or why not?

It is serious because it can be a sign of a visceral perforation.

9. The provider has ordered that the client's blood pressure be checked every 4 hr. Why?

Cushing's disease can cause hypertension.

10. The client's medication history indicates prolonged use of prednisone. What is the relationship between the use of this steroid and the client's physical appearance?

Prolonged or excess cortisol intake alters the metabolism of fats, proteins, and carbohydrates, fluid and electrolyte balance, immune response, and other metabolic functions. Altered fat metabolism causes an abnormal accumulation of fat on the back and face, producing buffalo hump, moon face, and/or truncal obesity. Altered protein metabolism produces protein breakdown and subsequent muscle wasting, which results in thin arms and legs. Cortisol also causes veins to become fragile and skin to lose elasticity, resulting in thin skin that bruises easily.

11. Why should the nurse caution the client not to stop taking her oral steroid medication without consulting her primary care provider first?

When taken for a long period of time, exogenous steroids (prednisone) suppress the adrenal gland causing it to become non-functioning (known as "negative feedback" mechanism). When the medication is withdrawn, the adrenal gland cannot produce enough cortisol for bodily needs, and the client will develop adrenal crisis and could possibly die.

12. The nurse observes the nursing diagnosis "Risk for injury: fractures" on the client's nursing care plan. Why is the client at risk for fractures?

Excessive cortisol destroys bone proteins and alters calcium metabolism, which predisposes the person to back pain, compression fractures of the vertebrae, and rib fractures.

Unit 6

Section:

Nursing Care of Clients with Endocrine Disorders

Nursing Care of Clients with Adrenal Disorders

Chapter 57:   **Addison's Disease and Adrenal Crisis**

Contributor: Dana Bartlett, MSN, RN, CSPI

⟳ NCLEX-PN® Connections:

Learning Objective: Review and apply knowledge within **"Addison's Disease and Adrenal Crisis"** in readiness for performance of the following nursing activities as outlined by the NCLEX-PN® test plan:

Δ   Assist with relevant laboratory, diagnostic, and therapeutic procedures within the nursing role, including:

  • Preparation of the client for the procedure.

  • Accurate collection of specimens.

  • Monitoring client status during and after the procedure.

  • Reinforcing client teaching (before and following the procedure).

  • Recognizing the client's response (expected, unexpected adverse response) to the procedure.

  • Monitoring results.

  • Monitoring and taking actions to prevent or minimize the risk of complications.

  • Notifying the primary care provider of signs of complications.

Δ   Recognize signs and symptoms of the client's problem and complete the proper documentation.

Δ   Provide and document care based on the client's health alteration.

Δ   Monitor and document vital signs changes.

Δ   Interpret data that need to be reported immediately.

Δ   Reinforce client education on managing the client's health problem.

Δ   Recognize and respond to emergency situations, including notification of the primary care provider.

Δ   Review the client's response to emergency interventions and complete the proper documentation.

Δ   Provide care that meets the age-related needs of clients 65 years of age or older, including recognizing expected physiological changes.

Key Points

Δ   **Addison's disease** is an **adrenocortical insufficiency.** It is caused by damage or dysfunction of the adrenal cortex. The adrenal cortex produces:

- **Mineralocorticoids: Aldosterone** (increases sodium absorption, causes potassium excretion in the kidney)

- **Glucocorticoids: Cortisol** (affects glucose, protein, and fat metabolism, the body's response to stress, and the body's immune function)

- **Sex hormones:** Androgens and estrogens

Δ   With **Addison's disease**, the production of mineralocorticoids and glucocorticoids is diminished, resulting in **decreased aldosterone and cortisol.**

Δ   **Adrenal crisis**, also known as **acute adrenal insufficiency**, has a rapid onset. It is a medical emergency. If it is not quickly diagnosed and properly treated, the prognosis is poor.

Key Factors

Δ   The majority of cases of chronic Addison's disease are:

- Caused by an **idiopathic autoimmune dysfunction.**

- Associated with **tuberculosis.**

Δ   An adrenal crisis is caused by an acute exacerbation of chronic insufficiency due to:

- Sepsis.

- Trauma.

- **Stress.**

- Adrenal hemorrhage.

- **Steroid withdrawal.**

Δ   It's important to remember that **stress** can include myocardial infarction, surgery, anesthesia, hypothermia, volume loss, and hypoglycemia

Diagnostic Procedures and Nursing Interventions

Δ   **Diagnostic procedures** and **expected findings** include:

- Serum electrolytes: increased K+, decreased Na+, increased calcium

- BUN, creatinine: Increased

- ECG: Dysrhythmias

- **Serum glucose: Decreased**
- Serum cortisol: Decreased
- Adrenocorticotropic hormone (**ACTH**) **stimulation** test: ACTH is infused, and the cortisol response is measured. **Plasma cortisol levels do not rise.**

Assessments

Δ   Signs and symptoms of chronic **Addison's** disease **develop slowly.**

Δ   Signs and symptoms of **Adrenal Crisis develop rapidly.**

Δ   Signs and symptoms include:

- Hyperpigmentation.
- Weakness and fatigue.
- Nausea and vomiting.
- Dizziness with orthostatic hypotension.
- **Dehydration.**
- **Hyponatremia.**
- **Hyperkalemia.**
- **Hypoglycemia.**
- Hypercalcemia.

NANDA Nursing diagnoses

Δ   Risk for injury

Δ   Risk for injury

Δ   Fatigue

Nursing Interventions

Δ   To prevent adrenal crises, instruct clients with Addison's disease to increase corticosteroid doses during times of stress.

Δ   Monitor clients for fluid deficits and hyponatremia. Administer **saline infusions** to **restore fluid volume.** Observe for signs and symptoms of dehydration; take orthostatic vital signs.

Δ   Administer prescribed **hydrocortisone** boluses and a continuous infusion or periodic boluses.

Δ   Monitor for and **treat hyperkalemia**: Obtain a serum potassium and ECG. Administer sodium polystyrene sulfonate (Kayexalate), insulin, calcium, glucose, and sodium bicarbonate as prescribed.

Δ   Monitor for and **treat hypoglycemia**: Perform frequent checks of the client's neurologic status, monitor for signs and symptoms of hypoglycemia, and check serum glucose. Administer food and/or supplemental glucose.

Δ   Maintain a safe environment

Meeting the Needs of Older Adults

Δ   Older adult clients are less able to tolerate the complications of Addison's disease and adrenal crisis and will need more frequent monitoring.

Primary Reference:

Ignatavicius, D. D., & Workman, M. L. (2006). *Medical-surgical nursing* (5th ed.). St. Louis, MO: Saunders.

Additional Resources:

Kirkland, L. (2005, July 19). Adrenal Crisis. *eMedicine*, Topic 65. Retrieved May 17, 2006, from http://www.emedicine.com/med/topic65.htm.

NANDA International (2004). *NANDA nursing diagnoses: Definitions and classification 2005-2006*. Philadelphia: NANDA.

Odeke, S., & Nagelberg, S. B. (2006, March 17). Addison Disease. *eMedicine*, Topic 42. Retrieved May 17, 2006, from http://www.emedicine.com/med/topic42.htm.

Chapter 57: Addison's Disease and Adrenal Crisis

Application Exercises

Scenario: A nurse is caring for a client with Addison's disease.

1. Name two causes of Addison's disease.

2. Why is it important to ensure that the environment is safe for this client?

3. Why might this client be lethargic and confused?

4. The provider orders continuous cardiac monitoring. Why?

5. How should the nurse monitor this client for dehydration?

Scenario: A nurse is caring for a client who is in adrenal crisis.

6. Name three precipitating causes of adrenal crisis.

7. The nurse should question the rationale for which of the following interventions?

      A. Infusion of high volumes of normal saline to restore fluid volume

      B. Administration of insulin to treat acute hypokalemia

      C. Administration of glucose to treat hypoglycemia

      D. Administration of hydrocortisone to meet cortisol deficits

Chapter 57: Addison's Disease and Adrenal Crisis

Application Exercises Answer Key

Scenario: A nurse is caring for a client with Addison's disease.

1. Name two causes of Addison's disease.

   Autoimmune dysfunction and tuberculosis are the most common causes.

2. Why is it important to ensure that the environment is safe for this client?

   Dehydration and electrolyte abnormalities make the client weak and confused.

3. Why might this client be lethargic and confused?

   The client could be lethargic and confused due to hypoglycemia and hyponatremia associated with Addison's disease.

4. The provider orders continuous cardiac monitoring. Why?

   Hyperkalemia can cause dysrhythmias.

5. How should the nurse monitor this client for dehydration?

   Check orthostatic vital signs.

Scenario: A nurse is caring for a client who is in adrenal crisis.

6. Name three precipitating causes of adrenal crisis.

Stress, trauma, sepsis, adrenal hemorrhage, and steroid withdrawal are all possibilities.

7. The nurse should question the rationale for which of the following interventions?

      A. Infusion of high volumes of normal saline to restore fluid volume

      B. Administration of insulin to treat acute hypokalemia

      C. Administration of glucose to treat hypoglycemia

      D. Administration of hydrocortisone to meet cortisol deficits

Adrenal crises are characterized by hyperkalemia, hypovolemia, hypoglycemia, and cortisol deficits. Insulin promotes the movement of potassium into cells which can temporarily reduce life-threatening hyperkalemia.

Unit 6
Section:

Nursing Care of Clients with Endocrine Disorders
Nursing Care of Clients with Adrenal Disorders

Chapter 58:   **Pheochromocytoma**
Contributor: Dana Bartlett, MSN, RN, CSPI

↻ **NCLEX-PN® Connections:**

> **Learning Objective:** Review and apply knowledge within "**Pheochromocytoma**" in readiness for performance of the following nursing activities as outlined by the NCLEX-PN® test plan:
>
> Δ   Assist with relevant laboratory, diagnostic, and therapeutic procedures within the nursing role, including:
>
> - Preparation of the client for the procedure.
> - Accurate collection of specimens.
> - Monitoring client status during and after the procedure.
> - Reinforcing client teaching (before and following the procedure).
> - Recognizing the client's response (expected, unexpected adverse response) to the procedure.
> - Monitoring results.
> - Monitoring and taking actions to prevent or minimize the risk of complications.
>   - Notifying the primary care provider of signs of complications.
>
> Δ   Recognize signs and symptoms of the client's problem – pheochromocytoma – and complete the proper documentation.
>
> Δ   Provide and document care based on the client's health alteration – pheochromocytoma.
>
> Δ   Monitor and document vital signs changes.
>
> Δ   Interpret data that need to be reported immediately.
>
> Δ   Reinforce client education on managing the client's health problem – pheochromocytoma.
>
> Δ   Recognize and respond to emergency situations, including notification of the primary care provider.
>
> Δ   Review the client's response to emergency interventions and complete the proper documentation.
>
> Δ   Provide care that meets the age-related needs of clients 65 years of age or older, including recognizing expected physiological changes.

📖 Key Points

Δ   A **pheochromocytoma** is a tumor of the adrenal gland. It is a rare tumor, and only about 10% of pheochromocytomas are malignant.

Δ   Pheochromocytomas produce and store **catecholamines,** such as **epinephrine** and **norepinephrine.** The excess epinephrine and norepinephrine produce sympathetic nervous system effects.

Key Factors

Δ   The cause of pheochromocytomas is not known.

Δ   **Precipitating causes** of a catecholamine surge by a pheochromocytoma in a client may be:

- Anesthesia.

- Opiates and opiate antagonists (for example, naloxone).

- Dopamine antagonists (droperidol, phenothiazines).

- Drugs that inhibit catecholamine reuptake (tricyclic antidepressants).

- Childbirth.

- Radiographic contrast media.

- Foods high in tyramine (wine, aged cheese).

Δ   If the catecholamine surge of a pheochromocytoma is recognized promptly and treated appropriately, it is potentially curable. If the diagnosis is missed, the client could suffer severe cardiac and neurologic damage.

Δ   Increases in intra-abdominal pressure (for example, abdominal palpation) can cause a hypertensive episode.

Diagnostic and Therapeutic Procedures and Nursing Interventions

Δ   **Diagnostic tests** for pheochromocytoma include:

- Vanillylmandelic acid (VMA) testing: **24-hr urine collection** for catecholamines, metanephrine, and VMA (a breakdown product of catecholamines). Normal is 2 to 7 mg/24 hr. **High levels at rest** indicate pheochromocytoma. Nursing implications include:

    ◊   VMA (caffeine, vanilla, licorice) is restricted for 2 to 3 days before the test.

    ◊   Possibly hold aspirin and antihypertensive medications.

◊ Instruct the client to maintain a moderate level of activity.

◊ Monitor/instruct the client regarding 24-hr urine collection. Urine is collected for 24 hr (in a container with a preservative) beginning with an empty bladder.

- **Clonidine suppression test:** If a client does not have a pheochromocytoma, clonidine (Catapres) suppresses catecholamine release and decreases the serum level of catecholamines (decreased blood pressure). If the client does have a pheochromocytoma, the clonidine has no effect (no decreased blood pressure).

- A rapid decrease in systolic blood pressure of ≥ 35 mm Hg and diastolic blood pressure of ≥ 25 mm Hg with the administration of phentolamine (Regitine), an alpha blocker, is diagnostic.

Δ **Unilateral or bilateral adrenalectomy surgery** is the preferred **therapeutic procedure.**

- Blood pressure must be carefully controlled preoperatively and postoperatively. Preoperatively, alpha blockers initially and then also beta blockers are used to control hypertension. Postoperatively, the nurse must monitor for hypotension and hypovolemia due to the sudden decrease in catecholamines.

- After a **bilateral** adrenalectomy, **lifelong glucocorticoid** and mineralocorticoid **replacement** is required.

- After a unilateral adrenalectomy, glucocorticoid supplementation may be needed until the one gland is able to produce enough.

Assessments

Δ The **intermittent** signs and symptoms of pheochromocytoma include:

- Pain in chest/abdomen accompanied by nausea and vomiting.

- **Hypertension.**

- Headache.

- **Palpitations.**

- Diaphoresis.

- Heat intolerance.

- Tremor.

- Apprehension.

Δ **Assessments** should include frequent checks of pulse and blood pressure and frequent neurologic checks.

Nursing Interventions

Δ   Administer postoperative medication, monitor its effects, and observe for side effects.

Δ   The nurse should also provide the client with knowledge about the disease state, the reasons for the diagnostic tests, the need for yearly testing of metanephrine, and the need to monitor blood pressure and the symptoms of high blood pressure.

Complications and Nursing Implications

Δ   **Hypertensive crisis** is the most significant complication of a pheochromocytoma.

•   The nurse must closely monitor the client's blood pressure and observe for any signs or symptoms that may indicate a hypertensive crisis.

•   **Nursing response**: Administer **alpha blockers** as ordered (for example, phentolamine IV or phenoxybenzamine).

Meeting the Needs of Older Adults

Δ   Older adult clients may already have hypertension.

Δ   Older adult clients may be less able to tolerate an elevation in blood pressure caused by a pheochromocytoma.

Δ   Older adult clients are less able to tolerate intraoperative and postoperative stress.

Primary Reference:

Ignatavicius, D. D., & Workman, M. L. (2006). *Medical-surgical nursing* (5th ed.). St. Louis, MO: Saunders.

Additional Resources:

NANDA International (2004). *NANDA nursing diagnoses: Definitions and classification 2005-2006*. Philadelphia: NANDA.

Chapter 58: Pheochromocytoma

Application Exercises

Scenario: A nurse is caring for a client who has a pheochromocytoma and is scheduled to have surgery in several days.

1. The nurse knows that pheochromocytoma produces catecholamines that stimulate adrenergic receptors. Why has the primary care provider prescribed phenoxybenzamine only and not phenoxybenzamine and a beta-blocker?

2. Why is the clonidine suppression test used as a diagnostic test to detect pheochromocytoma?

3. Why would amitriptyline (Elavil), a tricyclic antidepressant, be contraindicated for this client?

4. Why is this client at risk for developing hypertension?

5. Why are neurologic checks important in this situation?

6. Why might this client be tachycardic and diaphoretic?

7. Which of the following are possible precipitating causes of a catecholamine surge? (Check all that apply.)

_____ General anesthesia

_____ Local anesthesia

_____ Morphine administration

_____ Naloxone (Narcan) administration

_____ Levodopa with carbidopa (Sinemet)

_____ Haloperidol (Haldol)

_____ Licorice ingestion

_____ Red wine consumption

_____ Coffee consumption

Chapter 58: Pheochromocytoma

Application Exercises Answer Key

Scenario: A nurse is caring for a client who has a pheochromocytoma and is scheduled to have surgery in several days.

1. The nurse knows that pheochromocytoma produces catecholamines that stimulate adrenergic receptors. Why has the primary care provider prescribed phenoxybenzamine only and not phenoxybenzamine and a beta-blocker?

   Phenoxybenzamine is an alpha-adrenergic blocker. If a beta-blocker is administered before alpha blockade is complete, there will be unopposed stimulation of the alpha receptors.

2. Why is the clonidine suppression test used as a diagnostic test to detect pheochromocytoma?

   Clonidine normally decreases sympathetic outflow and lowers heart rate and blood pressure by decreasing catecholamine release. If the client has a pheochromocytoma, there will be higher than normal levels of catecholamines and these vital sign changes will not occur with clonidine administration.

3. Why would amitriptyline (Elavil), a tricyclic antidepressant, be contraindicated for this client?

   Amitriptyline inhibits the reuptake of catecholamines. This would result in sustained high levels of epinephrine and sympathetic stimulation.

4. Why is this client at risk for developing hypertension?

   Pheochromocytomas secrete catecholamines. These catecholamines directly stimulate the alpha receptors, which causes vasoconstriction.

5. Why are neurologic checks important in this situation?

An elevated blood pressure can cause neurologic effects.

6. Why might this client be tachycardic and diaphoretic?

Catecholamines stimulate beta receptors in the heart and they cause an increase in gastric secretions.

7. Which of the following are possible precipitating causes of a catecholamine surge? (Check all that apply.)

__x__	General anesthesia
_____	Local anesthesia
__x__	Morphine administration
__x__	Naloxone (Narcan) administration
_____	Levodopa with carbidopa (Sinemet)
__x__	Haloperidol (Haldol)
__x__	Licorice ingestion
__x__	Red wine consumption
__x__	Coffee consumption

General anesthesia, opioids (for example, morphine), opioid antagonists (for example, naloxone), dopamine antagonists (for example, haloperidol), foods/beverages high in tyramine (red wine) and/or in VMA (licorice, coffee) can precipitate a catecholamine surge.

Unit 6   Nursing Care of Clients with Endocrine Disorders

Section: Nursing Care of Clients with Diabetes Mellitus

Chapter 59:   Diabetes Management

Contributor: Donna Funk, PhD, RN, ONC

⟳ NCLEX-PN® Connections:

Learning Objective: Review and apply knowledge within **"Diabetes Management"** in readiness for performance of the following nursing activities as outlined by the NCLEX-PN® test plan:

Δ   Assist with relevant laboratory, diagnostic, and therapeutic procedures within the nursing role, including:

  • Preparation of the client for the procedure.

  • Accurate collection of specimens.

  • Monitoring client status during and after the procedure.

  • Reinforcing client teaching (before and following the procedure).

  • Recognizing the client's response (expected, unexpected adverse response) to the procedure.

  • Monitoring results.

  • Monitoring and taking actions to prevent or minimize the risk of complications.

  • Notifying the primary care provider of signs of complications.

Δ   Recognize signs and symptoms of the client's problem – diabetes management – and complete the proper documentation.

Δ   Provide and document care based on the client's health alteration – diabetes management.

Δ   Monitor and document vital signs changes.

Δ   Interpret data that need to be reported immediately.

Δ   Reinforce client education on managing the client's health problem – diabetes management.

Δ   Recognize and respond to emergency situations, including notification of the primary care provider.

Δ   Review the client's response to emergency interventions and complete the proper documentation.

Δ   Provide care that meets the age-related needs of clients 65 years of age or older, including recognizing expected physiological changes.

Key Points

△ Diabetes mellitus is characterized by **chronic hyperglycemia** due to **problems with insulin secretion** and/or the effectiveness of endogenous insulin (for example, **insulin resistance**).

△ Diabetes mellitus is a contributing factor to **cardiovascular disease, hypertension, renal failure**, blindness, and **stroke** due to its impact on large and small blood vessels **(resulting in decreased tissue perfusion)**.

△ **Hallmark symptoms** associated with diabetes mellitus are the **3 P's: polyuria, polydipsia, and polyphagia**.

△ **Consistent** management of blood glucose levels within the **normal range** (70-120 mg/dL) is the **goal** of treatment.

Key Factors

△ **Type 1** diabetes mellitus is an **autoimmune** disorder characterized by **beta cell destruction**. It occurs in **genetically susceptible** individuals (islet cell antibodies), and typical onset is **before the age of 30**.

△ **Type 2** diabetes mellitus is often due to the development of **resistance to endogenous insulin** and frequently occurs in individuals with a **family disposition** who are **obese** and **over the age of 40**.

△ **Obesity, physical inactivity, high triglycerides** (> 250 mg/dL), and **hypertension** are the **hallmark risk factors** for the development of insulin resistance.

△ Secondary causes include pancreatitis and Cushing's syndrome.

△ Iatrogenic causes include glucocorticoid usage (transient).

Diagnostic Procedures and Nursing Interventions

△ **Diagnostic criteria** for diabetes mellitus include two findings (separate days) of one of the following:

• Symptoms of diabetes plus casual plasma glucose concentration of greater than 200 mg/dL (without regard to time since last meal).

• Fasting blood glucose greater than 126 mg/dL (8 hr fasting).

• Two-hour glucose greater than 200 mg/dL with an oral glucose tolerance test (10 to 12 hr fasting).

Δ   **Diagnostic Procedures and Nursing Interventions**

- **Fasting blood glucose**

  ◊ Ensure that client has fasted (no food or drink other than water) for the 8 hr prior to the blood draw. Antidiabetic medications should be postponed until after the level is drawn.

- **Oral glucose tolerance test**

  ◊ Instruct the client to consume a balanced diet for the 3 days prior to the test. Then instruct the client to fast for the 10 to 12 hr prior to the test. A fasting blood glucose level is drawn at start of the test. The client is then instructed to consume a specified amount of glucose. Blood glucose levels are drawn every 30 min for 2 hr. Clients must be assessed for hypoglycemia throughout the procedure.

- **Glycosylated hemoglobin** (HbA1c)

  ◊ The target is 4 to 6%. HbA1c is the best indicator of average blood glucose level for past 120 days. Assists in evaluating treatment effectiveness and compliance.

- **Pre-meal glucose**

  ◊ The target is 90 to 130 mg/dL. Follow or ensure that the client follows the proper procedure for blood sample collection and use of glucose meter. Supplemental short-acting insulin may be prescribed for elevated pre-meal glucose levels.

Assessments

Signs and Symptoms by Type of Diabetes	
Type 1:	**Type 2:**
Polyuria, polydipsia, polyphagia	Polyuria, polydipsia, polyphagia
Weight loss	**Obesity**
Fatigue	Fatigue
Increased frequency of infections	Increased frequency of infections
Rapid onset	**Gradual onset**
Controlled by exogenous insulin	**Controlled by oral antidiabetic medications and insulin**

Signs and Symptoms by Glucose Alteration	
Hypoglycemia (≤ 50 mg/dL)	**Hyperglycemia** (> 250 mg/dL)
Cool, clammy skin	Hot, dry skin
Diaphoresis	**Absence of diaphoresis**
Anxiety, **irritability**, confusion, **blurred vision**	Alert to coma (varies)
Hunger	Nausea and vomiting, abdominal pain (with ketoacidosis)
General weakness, seizures (severe hypoglycemia)	**Rapid deep respirations** (acetone/fruity odor due to ketones)

Δ   **Additional appropriate assessments** include:

- Blood glucose levels and factors affecting levels (for example, other medications).

- Intake and output, weight.

- Skin integrity and healing status of any wounds.

- Sensory alterations (tingling, numbness).

- Condition of feet and foot care practices.

- Dietary practices.

- Exercise patterns.

- Client's self monitoring blood glucose skill proficiency.

- Client's self medication administration proficiency.

- Pain levels.

NANDA Nursing Diagnoses

Δ   Risk for injury

Δ   Imbalanced nutrition: More than body requirements

Δ   Risk for impaired skin integrity

Δ   Deficient knowledge

Δ   Self-care deficit

Nursing Interventions

Δ **Refer the client to a diabetes educator** for comprehensive education in diabetes management.

Δ Provide information regarding the **importance of foot care** and provide instructions for foot care, including:

- Inspect feet daily. Wash feet daily with mild soap and *warm* water.

- Pat feet dry gently, especially between the toes.

- Use mild foot powder (powder with cornstarch) on sweaty feet.

- Do not use commercial remedies to remove calluses or corns.

- Consult a podiatrist.

- Cut toenails even with rounded contour of toes. Do not cut down corners.

- The best time to cut nails is after a bath/shower.

- Separate overlapping toes with cotton or lamb's wool.

- Avoid open-toe, open-heel shoes. Leather shoes are preferred to plastic ones. Wear slippers with soles. Do not go barefoot. Shake out shoes before putting them on.

- Wear clean, absorbent (cotton or wool) socks or stockings that have not been mended.

- Do not use hot water bottles or heating pads to warm feet. Wear socks for warmth.

- Avoid prolonged sitting, standing, and crossing of legs.

Δ Encourage the client to take measures to **reduce risk of injury** (wearing shoes, adequate lighting). Once the first line of defense has been compromised (skin), the ability to heal is prolonged for a person with diabetes mellitus. Teach clients to cleanse cuts with *warm* water and mild soap, gently dry and apply a dry dressing. Instruct clients to monitor healing and to seek intervention promptly.

Δ **Refer clients to dieticians** for nutritional management of diabetes. Support and reinforce nutrition instruction. Some guidelines to encourage are:

- Count grams of carbohydrates consumed. Dosage of insulin is determined by carbohydrate consumption (1 unit/15 g of carbohydrate).

- Restrict calories and increase physical activity as appropriate to facilitate weight loss for clients who are obese or to prevent obesity.

- Include fiber in the diet to increase carbohydrate metabolism and to help control cholesterol levels.

- Use artificial sweeteners.

- Use fat replacers within guidelines (may increase carbohydrate content of foods).

Δ   Teach the client **guidelines** to follow **when sick:**

- Monitor blood glucose every 4 hr.

- **Continue to take insulin or oral antidiabetic agents.**

- Consume 8 oz of sugar-free non-caffeinated liquid every hour to **prevent dehydration.**

- Meet carbohydrate needs through solid food if possible. If not, consume liquids equal to usual carbohydrate content.

- Test urine for ketones and report if abnormal (should be negative to small).

- Rest.

- **Call the primary care provider if:**

  ◊   Blood glucose is higher than 250 mg/dL.

  ◊   Ketones are moderate or large.

  ◊   Fever higher than 38.9° C (102° F), fever that does not respond to acetaminophen, or fever that lasts more than 12 hr.

  ◊   Feeling groggy or confused.

  ◊   Experiencing rapid breathing.

  ◊   Vomited more than once.

  ◊   Diarrhea occurs more than five times or for longer than 24 hr.

  ◊   Unable to keep down liquids.

  ◊   Illness lasts longer than 2 days.

Δ   Teach the client measures to take **in response to hypoglycemia symptoms:**

- **Check blood glucose level.**

- Follow guidelines outlined by the primary care provider/diabetes educator. Guidelines may include:

  ◊   Treat with 15 g carbohydrates.

  ◊   Recheck blood glucose in 15 min.

  ◊   If still low, give 15 g more of carbohydrates.

  ◊   Recheck blood glucose in 15 min.

  ◊   If blood glucose is within normal limits, take 7 g protein (if the next meal is more than an hour away).

- 15 g of carbohydrates examples: 4 oz orange juice, 2 oz grape juice, 8 oz milk, glucose tablets per manufacturer's suggestion to equal 15 g.

- 7 g protein: 1 oz of cheese (1 string cheese).

- **Fluid** is **more readily absorbed** (juice, non-diet soft drink, skim milk).

- Absorption of commercial products (glucose tablets, gel) is more predictable.

- If the client is **unconscious** or unable to swallow, administer **glucagon** SC or IM (repeat in 10 min if still unconscious) and notify the primary care provider.

Δ Teach the client measures to take **in response to hyperglycemia**:

- Encourage oral **fluid intake**.

- Administer insulin as prescribed.

- Restrict exercise when blood glucose levels are > 250 mg/dL.

- Test urine for ketones and report if abnormal.

- Consult the primary care provider if symptoms progress.

Δ Know the **onset, peak,** and **duration** of administered insulin, **plan for administration** of prescribed insulin, and **monitor** client for **signs of hypoglycemia** accordingly:

Rapid-acting: (Humalog, Lispro)	Long-acting: Lente
Onset: less than 15 min	Onset: 3-4 hr
Peak: 0.5-1.5 hr	Peak: 4-12 hr
Duration: 2-6 hr	Duration: 12-20 hr
Administer: **5-15 min ac**	
Short-acting: (Humulin R, Regular)	**Long-acting: Ultralente**
Onset: 30-60 min	Onset: 6-10 hr
Peak: 2-3 hr	Peak: 8-20 hr
Duration: 3-10 hr	Duration: 18-24 hr
Administer: **30 min ac**	
Intermediate-acting: (Humulin N, NPH, 70/30, 75/25)	**Long-acting: Lantus**
Onset: 2-4 hr	
Peak: 4-10 hr	Peak: None
Duration: 10-18 hr	Duration: 24-hr acting

Δ   Provide information regarding self administration of insulin, following guidelines including:

- **Rotation of injection sites** (prevent lipohypertrophy) within one anatomic site (prevent day-to-day changes in absorption rates).

- Inject at a **90° angle** (45° if thin). Aspiration for blood is not necessary.

- When mixing rapid- or short-acting insulin with a longer-acting insulin, **draw up the shorter-acting insulin into the syringe first and then the longer-acting insulin** (reduces risk of introducing longer-acting insulin into the shorter-acting insulin vial).

Δ   Observe the client perform self-administration and offer additional instruction as indicated.

Δ   Provide information regarding **oral antidiabetic** medications:

- Administer as prescribed (for example, 30 min before first main meal for most oral blood glucose lowering agents or with the first bite of each main meal for alpha-glucosidase inhibitors).

- **Avoid alcohol with sulfonylurea agents** (disulfiram-like reaction).

- Monitor renal function (biguanides).

- Monitor **liver function** (thiazolidinediones and alpha-glucosidase inhibitors).

- Advise women of childbearing age taking thiazolidinediones that additional contraception methods may be needed since these drugs reduce the blood levels of some oral contraceptives.

Complications and Nursing Implications

Δ   **Consistent** management of blood glucose levels within the **normal range** (70 to 120 mg/dL) is the best protection against the complications of diabetes mellitus.

Complication	Nursing Implication
Heart and blood vessel disease: The leading cause of death with diabetes. Three out of four diabetes-related deaths are caused by heart and blood vessels disease. People with diabetes are 2 to 4 times more likely to have heart disease than persons without diabetes. Clients with type 2 diabetes mellitus who do not have heart disease have an increased risk of having a heart attack. People with diabetes have risk factors for heart disease including high blood pressure and atherosclerosis.	1. Encourage yearly checks of cholesterol (HDL, LDL, triglycerides); every 3 month check of blood pressure, A1c 2. Follow blood pressure medication regimen prescribe by provider. 3. Exercise (10,000 steps/day). 4. Diet: Low-fat meals; high in fruits, vegetables, and whole grain foods. 5. Teach to report shortness of breath, headaches (persistent and transient), numbness in distal extremities, swelling of feet, infrequent urination, problems with vision. 6. Encourage dietary consult.

Complication	Nursing Implication
<u>Blindness</u>: Caused by diabetic retinopathy.	1. Encourage yearly eye exams to ensure the health of the eye and protect vision. 2. Encourage management of blood glucose levels. 3. Diet: Low in fats; high in fruits, vegetables, and whole grain foods. 4. Encourage dietary consult.
<u>Kidney Failure</u>: High blood glucose levels can damage the kidneys. Even when medications and diet are able to manage diabetes, the disease can lead to kidney disease (diabetic nephropathy) and kidney failure.	1. Encourage yearly urine analysis, BUN, and creatinine clearance. 2. If hospitalized, monitor strict intake and output. 3. Encourage management of blood glucose levels. 4. Diet: Low in fats; high in fruits, vegetables, and whole grain foods. 5. Encourage dietary consult. 6. Avoid soda pop, alcohol, and toxic levels of acetaminophen. 7. Drink an adequate amount of water when antibiotics are needed for infections. 8. If dialysis is needed for kidney failure, maintain dialysis diet and fistula health. 9. Encourage diabetic educator consult. 10. Encourage dietary consult.
<u>Foot Ulcers</u>: Adults with diabetes need to take special care of their feet. People with diabetes are at risk for foot injuries related to numbness caused by nerve damage (diabetic neuropathy) and low blood flow to the legs and feet. Clients with foot ulcers should use wound dressings, skin substitutes, or other treatments to protect and heal their skin.	1. Foot inspection daily. 2. Refer to above section for foot care. 3. Diet management. 4. Daily exercise (10,000 steps/day). 5. Medication regimen management. 6. ABC management (A1c less than 7%, blood pressure less than 130/80 mm Hg, cholesterol: LDL below 100 mg/dL, HDL above 40 mg/dL (men), above 50 mg/dL (women), triglycerides below 150 mg/dL). 7. Two pairs of shoes. 8. Yearly podiatrist checkup and as needed.

Δ   See chapter 60 for discussion of the nursing management of diabetic ketoacidosis (DKA) and hyperosmolar-hyperglycemic nonketotic syndrome (HHNS).

Meeting the Needs of Older Adults

Δ   Because of the aging deterioration of the function of all organs, the aging population is at risk for:

- Kidney and liver dysfunction leading to altered urinary output and altered metabolism of medications.

- Increased risk for injury related to vision alterations (yellowing of lens, decreased ability of depth perception, cataracts) as well as eye changes that may be related to diabetic retinopathy.

Δ   Vision and hearing deficits may interfere with the understanding of teaching, reading of materials, and the preparation of medications.

Δ   Self-care deficit related to tissue deterioration secondary to aging may impact food preparation, hygiene and other activities of daily living, foot/wound care, and glucose monitoring.

Δ   Fixed income can mean that there are limited funds to buy diabetic supplies, wound care supplies, insulin, and medications.

Δ   Older adult clients may not be able to drive to the primary care provider's office, grocery store, or drug store. Assess support systems available for the older adult client.

Primary Source:

Ignatavicius, D. D., & Workman, M. L. (2006). *Medical-surgical nursing* (5th ed.). St. Louis, MO: Saunders.

Additional Resources:

Gifford, R., & Childs, B. P. (2005, February). Diabetes care when you're sick. *Diabetes Forecast, 58*(2), 44-50.

NANDA International (2004). *NANDA nursing diagnoses: Definitions and classification 2005-2006*. Philadelphia: NANDA.

For more information, visit the American Diabetes Association at *www.diabetes.org.*

Chapter 59: Diabetes Management

Application Exercises

1. A client's blood glucose is 49 mg/dL. The client is lethargic but arousable. What are the priority nursing actions?

2. A medication record reads: Lispro insulin 10 units SC 0800. What are important nursing considerations?

3. A blood glucose taken at 0800 is 257 mg/dL, and the primary care provider's order for sliding scale insulin for this blood glucose result is 6 units SC Regular insulin. This client also receives 12 units of Lantus insulin SC every morning. How should the nurse draw up and administer the insulin?

4. A 50-year-old client with diabetes mellitus is transferred from the emergency department to a nurse's unit. The client's blood glucose level is 388 mg/dL. The emergency department nurse reports that insulin was given, but the chart does not include the time or dose. The receiving nurse's initial assessment reveals the following: temperature 37.7° C (99.8° F), pulse 88 beats/min and regular, respirations 22/min, and blood pressure 148/78 mm Hg. The client is alert to person only, which the daughter states is unusual for him. His skin is warm and dry, and he is requesting a drink. His face is flushed, and he is moving around in bed continuously and pulling at the covers. He verbalizes an inability to eat this morning. Orders include:

   18 units Humulin R and 38 units Humulin N insulin are to be given SC every morning before breakfast.

   Rocephin, 1 g intravenous piggyback every 24 hr.

   Ativan, 1 mg intramuscularly every 8 hr as needed.

   Dressing change on foot ulcerations as needed.

   Culture and sensitivity tests on open wounds in right foot.

   Insulin to sliding scale per protocol.

   What actions should the nurse take initially?

5. An adult client with type 1 diabetes mellitus is admitted to the hospital for circulatory impairment to the lower extremity and an open draining wound on the right foot. The client manages her own blood glucose monitoring and insulin injections at home. Her orders include blood glucose monitoring before meals and at bedtime. It is 0800. In what order should the nurse perform the following interventions?

_____ Complete the AM assessment.

_____ Teach client about complications of diabetes and circulation.

_____ Perform morning care and grooming.

_____ Administer morning insulin injection.

_____ Take vital signs.

_____ Perform finger stick for blood glucose monitoring.

_____ Assist with breakfast tray.

Chapter 59: Diabetes Management

Application Exercises Answer Key

1. A client's blood glucose is 49 mg/dL. The client is lethargic but arousable. What are the priority nursing actions?

   Give 15 g carbohydrates and re-check blood glucose in 15 min. If blood glucose remains below 70 mg/dL, give 15 g more carbohydrates. Re-check blood glucose in 15 min. Repeat until blood glucose is above 70 mg/dL. Follow with 7 g of protein. Report findings to the client's primary care provider and document actions.

2. A medication record reads: Lispro insulin 10 units SC 0800. What are important nursing considerations?

   This is rapid-acting insulin; wait until the breakfast tray arrives.

3. A blood glucose taken at 0800 is 257 mg/dL, and the primary care provider's order for sliding scale insulin for this blood glucose result is 6 units SC Regular insulin. This client also receives 12 units of Lantus insulin SC every morning. How should the nurse draw up and administer the insulin?

   In one insulin syringe, draw up 6 units of Regular insulin. In a separate insulin syringe, draw up 12 units of Lantus insulin and give two separate SC injections. Lantus and Regular insulin are not compatible.

4. A 50-year-old client with diabetes mellitus is transferred from the emergency department to a nurse's unit. The client's blood glucose level is 388 mg/dL. The emergency department nurse reports that insulin was given, but the chart does not include the time or dose. The receiving nurse's initial assessment reveals the following: temperature 37.7° C (99.8° F), pulse 88 beats/min and regular, respirations 22/min, and blood pressure 148/78 mm Hg. The client is alert to person only, which the daughter states is unusual for him. His skin is warm and dry, and he is requesting a drink. His face is flushed, and he is moving around in bed continuously and pulling at the covers. He verbalizes an inability to eat this morning. Orders include:

> 18 units Humulin R and 38 units Humulin N insulin are to be given SC every morning before breakfast.
>
> Rocephin, 1 g intravenous piggyback every 24 hr.
>
> Ativan, 1 mg intramuscularly every 8 hr as needed.
>
> Dressing change on foot ulcerations as needed.
>
> Culture and sensitivity tests on open wounds in right foot.
>
> Insulin to sliding scale per protocol.

What actions should the nurse take initially?

Determine whether the client took his morning dose of insulin.

Call the emergency department and determine whether insulin was given and the dosage.

Recheck the blood glucose.

Call the primary care provider.

5. An adult client with type 1 diabetes mellitus is admitted to the hospital for circulatory impairment to the lower extremity and an open draining wound on the right foot. The client manages her own blood glucose monitoring and insulin injections at home. Her orders include blood glucose monitoring before meals and at bedtime. It is 0800. In what order should the nurse perform the following interventions?

4	Complete the AM assessment.
7	Teach client about complications of diabetes and circulation.
6	Perform morning care and grooming.
3	Administer morning insulin injection.
1	Take vital signs.
2	Perform finger stick for blood glucose monitoring.
5	Assist with breakfast tray.

Unit 6

Section:

Nursing Care of Clients with Endocrine Disorders

Nursing Care of Clients with Diabetes Mellitus

Chapter 60:   Diabetic Ketoacidosis (DKA) and Hyperglycemic-Hyperosmolar Nonketotic Syndrome (HHNS)

Contributor: Andrea Rothman Mann, MSN, RN

⟳ NCLEX-PN® Connections:

Learning Objective: Review and apply knowledge within **"Diabetic Ketoacidosis (DKA) and Hyperglycemic-Hyperosmolar Nonketotic Syndrome (HHNS)"** in readiness for performance of the following nursing activities as outlined by the NCLEX-PN® test plan:

Δ   Assist with relevant laboratory, diagnostic, and therapeutic procedures within the nursing role, including:

- Preparation of the client for the procedure.

- Accurate collection of specimens.

- Monitoring client status during and after the procedure.

- Reinforcing client teaching (before and following the procedure).

- Recognizing the client's response (expected, unexpected adverse response) to the procedure.

- Monitoring results.

- Monitoring and taking actions to prevent or minimize the risk of complications.

- Notifying the primary care provider of signs of complications.

Δ   Recognize signs and symptoms of the client's problem and complete the proper documentation.

Δ   Provide and document care based on the client's health alteration.

Δ   Monitor and document vital signs changes.

Δ   Interpret data that need to be reported immediately.

Δ   Reinforce client education on managing the client's health problem.

Δ   Recognize and respond to emergency situations, including notification of the primary care provider.

Δ   Review the client's response to emergency interventions and complete the proper documentation.

Δ   Provide care that meets the age-related needs of clients 65 years of age or older, including recognizing expected physiological changes.

📖 **Key Points**

△ Diabetic ketoacidosis (**DKA**) is an acute, life-threatening condition **characterized by hyperglycemia (> 300 mg/dL)** resulting in breakdown of body fat for energy and an accumulation of ketones in the blood and urine. The onset is rapid, and the mortality rate of DKA is 1 to 10%.

△ Hyperglycemic-hyperosmolar nonketotic syndrome (**HHNS**) is an acute, life-threatening condition **characterized by profound hyperglycemia (> 600 mg/dL)**, dehydration, and an absence of ketosis. The onset is generally over several days, and the mortality rate of HHNS is up to 15% or more.

△ **Priority interventions** for both conditions include the administration of **fluids** and **insulin**.

Key Factors

△ Both conditions result in severe **hyperglycemia from**:

- A **lack of sufficient insulin** (new onset diabetes, lack of compliance with diabetes treatment plan).

- An **increased need for insulin** (stress, illness, infection, surgery, trauma).

△ DKA is more common in individuals with type 1 diabetes mellitus.

△ HHNS is more common in older adult clients and in individuals with untreated or undiagnosed type 2 diabetes mellitus.

Diagnostic Procedures and Nursing Interventions

△ Therapeutic management is guided by serial laboratory analysis.

Diagnostic Procedure	DKA	HHNS
Serum glucose levels	> 300 mg/dL	> 600 mg/dL
Serum Electrolytes • Sodium • Potassium	Na⁺ increased due to water loss K⁺ initially low due to diuresis, may increase due to acidosis	Na⁺ increased due to water loss K⁺ initially low due to diuresis
Serum Renal Studies • BUN • Creatinine	Increased secondary to dehydration	Increased secondary to dehydration
Ketone Levels • Serum • Urine	Present Present	Absent Absent
Serum Osmolarity	High	Very high
Serum pH (ABG)	Metabolic acidosis with respiratory compensation (Kussmaul respirations)	Absence of acidosis

Assessments

Δ   Monitor for **signs and symptoms.**

- Polyuria, polydipsia, polyphagia (early signs)

- **Change in mental status**

- Signs of **dehydration** (dry mucous membranes, weight loss, sunken eyeballs resulting from fluid loss such as polyuria)

- Kussmaul respiration pattern, rapid and deep respirations, "fruity" breath (DKA/metabolic acidosis)

- Nausea, vomiting, and/or abdominal pain (DKA/metabolic acidosis)

- Generalized seizures and reversible paralysis (HHNS)

NANDA Nursing Diagnoses

Δ   Deficient fluid volume

Δ   Deficient knowledge

Nursing Interventions

Δ   **Always treat the underlying cause** (for example, infectious process).

Δ   **Priority is isotonic fluid replacement.** Often large quantities are required to replace losses. Monitor the client for evidence of fluid volume excess.

Δ   Administer **IV regular insulin** to affect a 75 to 150 mg/dL/hr decrease in serum glucose level. Monitor glucose levels hourly.

Δ   When serum glucose levels approach 250 mg/dL, add glucose to IV fluids to minimize the risk of cerebral edema associated with drastic changes in serum osmolality.

Δ   **Monitor serum potassium levels.** With insulin therapy, potassium will shift into cells and the client will need to be monitored for hypokalemia. Provide potassium replacement therapy as indicated. Make sure urinary output is adequate before administering potassium.

Δ   Administer sodium bicarbonate by slow IV infusion for severe acidosis (pH < 7.0). Monitor potassium levels because too quick a correction of acidosis can lead to hypokalemia.

Δ   Provide client education to prevent reoccurrence:

- Take measures to decrease the risk of dehydration.

- Monitor glucose every 4 hr when ill and continue to take insulin.

- Consume liquids with carbohydrates and electrolytes (for example, sports drinks) when unable to eat solid food.

- Notify the primary care provider if illness lasts more than a day.

Complications and Nursing Implications

Δ **Rapid onset of hypoglycemia** due to an excessively rapid decrease in blood glucose (too much insulin too fast) can lead to:

- Electrolyte shifts (for example, hypokalemia).

- Cerebral edema (signs include seizures and change in level of consciousness).

- Fluid volume excess (signs include crackles, dyspnea, and weight gain).

Δ **Renal Failure**

- Signs include hourly output < 30 mL/hr.

- Monitor hydration and renal function (intake and output, creatinine levels).

Δ **Thromboembolism** (secondary to dehydration)

Meeting the Needs of Older Adults

Δ Encourage older adult clients to wear medical alert bracelets.

Δ Teach the older adult client to monitor blood glucose every 1 to 4 hr when ill.

Δ Emphasize the importance of not skipping insulin when ill.

Δ Maintain hydration, because older adult clients may have diminished thirst sensation.

Δ Changes in mental status may keep older adult clients from seeking treatment.

Δ Physiological changes in cardiac and pulmonary function may place the older adult client at greater risk for fluid overload (for example, precipitate congestive heart failure exacerbation) from fluid replacement therapy.

Primary Reference:

Ignatavicius, D. D., & Workman, M. L. (2006). *Medical-surgical nursing* (5th ed.). St. Louis, MO: Saunders.

Additional Resources:

Baird, M. S., Hicks Keen, J., Swearingen, P. L. (2005). *Manual of critical care nursing: Nursing interventions and collaborative management* (5th ed.). St. Louis, MO: Mosby.

NANDA International (2004). *NANDA nursing diagnoses: Definitions and classification 2005-2006*. Philadelphia: NANDA.

Chapter 60: Diabetic Ketoacidosis (DKA) and Hyperglycemic-Hyperosmolar Nonketotic Syndrome (HHNS)

Application Exercises

1. Which of the following is an appropriate client instruction regarding DKA prevention?

   A. "Check your blood glucose four times daily and have regular glycosylated hemoglobin tests."

   B. "If ill, take your insulin and drink clear liquids with carbohydrate."

   C. "Call 911 for emergency assistance if your blood glucose is over 300 mg/dL."

   D. "Use a dipstick to assess for ketones in your urine daily."

2. Which of the following signs and symptoms is **least likely** in HHNS?

   A. Abdominal pain

   B. Confusion

   C. Polyuria

   D. Polydipsia

3. Describe three priority interventions for the client with DKA. Identify the rationale for each intervention.

4. What type of acid-base imbalance is likely in a client with DKA? How would the nurse recognize compensation for this acid-base disorder?

5. A client with HHNS has an insulin infusion at 4 units/hr. What signs and symptoms should the nurse recognize as indications that the client has developed hypoglycemia?

6. When caring for a client with DKA, which of the following nursing diagnoses take priority?

   A. Knowledge deficit

   B. Imbalanced nutrition: Less than body requirements

   C. Fluid volume deficit

   D. Risk for injury

7. What is the relationship between stress and blood glucose levels in a client with diabetes?

8. What are precipitating factors for DKA?

9. Calculate the hourly infusion rate (mL/hr) for the following order: insulin infusion 5 units per hour (standard infusion of 50 units of insulin in 250 mL normal saline).

10. Describe the type of IV fluids used in treatment of DKA initially and as blood glucose decreases.

11. Why is it essential to monitor a client's serum potassium levels throughout DKA treatment?

Chapter 60: Diabetic Ketoacidosis (DKA) and Hyperglycemic-Hyperosmolar Nonketotic Syndrome (HHNS)

Application Exercises Answer Key

1. Which of the following is an appropriate client instruction regarding DKA prevention?

> A. "Check your blood glucose four times daily and have regular glycosylated hemoglobin tests."
>
> **B. "If ill, take your insulin and drink clear liquids with carbohydrate."**
>
> C. "Call 911 for emergency assistance if your blood glucose is over 300 mg/dL."
>
> D. "Use a dipstick to assess for ketones in your urine daily."

The client must be familiar with "sick day" management. He should take his insulin, check his blood glucose every 1 to 4 hr, and if unable to eat solid food, take in small frequent amounts of fluids and glucose-containing beverages.

2. Which of the following signs and symptoms is **least likely** in HHNS?

> **A. Abdominal pain**
>
> B. Confusion
>
> C. Polyuria
>
> D. Polydipsia

The client with HHNS would not have abdominal pain, a symptom of acidosis. Confusion from dehydration would be present, as would thirst and frequent urination.

3. Describe three priority interventions for the client with DKA. Identify the rationale for each intervention.

Correct responses include:

Administer fluids to replace those lost from hyperglycemia and osmotic diuresis.

Administer regular insulin as ordered to put glucose back in cells and control serum glucose levels.

Monitor intake and output and renal function tests for prompt detection of acute renal failure secondary to fluid volume deficit and osmotic diuresis.

Monitor for hypokalemia secondary to diuresis and insulin therapy or hyperkalemia if renal failure is present.

4. What type of acid-base imbalance is likely in a client with DKA? How would the nurse recognize compensation for this acid-base disorder?

Metabolic acidosis secondary to breakdown of fats for energy manifested by ketosis is most likely. Rapid, deep respirations (Kussmaul's respirations) will show compensation for the acidosis as the body "blows off" carbon dioxide, a respiratory acid.

5. A client with HHNS has an insulin infusion at 4 units/hr. What signs and symptoms should the nurse recognize as indications that the client has developed hypoglycemia?

Tachycardia, pallor, tremors, changes in mental status

6. When caring for a client with DKA, which of the following nursing diagnoses take priority?

    A. Knowledge deficit
    B. Imbalanced nutrition: Less than body requirements
    C. Fluid volume deficit
    D. Risk for injury

If the fluid volume deficit is untreated, it will lead to renal failure and death.

7. What is the relationship between stress and blood glucose levels in a client with diabetes?

Physical and/or psychological stress stimulates the sympathetic nervous system's fight or flight response. This results in an increased production of catecholamines (epinephrine and norepinephrine), which stimulate the release of cortisol. This results in glycolysis, the breakdown of glycogen into glucose.

8. What are precipitating factors for DKA?

Stress, illness such as myocardial infarction, infection, surgery, trauma, lack of insulin

9. Calculate the hourly infusion rate (mL/hr) for the following order: insulin infusion 5 units per hour (standard infusion of 50 units of insulin in 250 mL normal saline).

$$\frac{50 \text{ units}}{250 \text{ mL}} = \frac{5 \text{ units}}{x \text{ mL}}$$

Multiply the means and extremes. Therefore, 50x = 1,250.

Solve for x by dividing both sides by 50.

x = 25 mL/hr.

10. Describe the type of IV fluids used in treatment of DKA initially and as blood glucose decreases.

Initially 0.9% normal saline solution is infused to expand blood volume. Insulin is administered and as blood glucose decreases, the nurse anticipates adding a dextrose-containing solution to prevent hypoglycemia.

11. Why is it essential to monitor a client's serum potassium levels throughout DKA treatment?

DKA produces an intracellular to extracellular shift in potassium. Acidosis causes serum potassium to rise. As insulin is administered, glucose and potassium will move back into the cells, which may precipitate hypokalemia.

Unit 7   Nursing Care of Clients with Gastrointestinal Disorders

Section: Diagnostic and Therapeutic Procedures: Gastrointestinal

Chapter 61:   **Scope Procedures**

Contributor: Margaret C. Davis, MSN, RN

NCLEX-PN® Connections:

Learning Objective: Review and apply knowledge within "**Scope Procedures**" in readiness for performance of the following nursing activities as outlined by the NCLEX-PN® test plan:

Δ Perform/assist with relevant laboratory, diagnostic, and therapeutic procedures within the nursing role, including:

- Preparation of the client for the procedure.

- Reinforcement of client teaching (before and following the procedure).

- Accurate collection of specimens.

- Monitoring procedure results (compare to norms) and appropriate notification of the primary care provider.

- Monitoring the client's response (expected, unexpected adverse response, comparison to baseline) to the procedure.

- Monitoring and taking actions, including reinforcing client teaching, to prevent or minimize the risk of complications.

- Recognizing signs of potential complications and reporting to the primary care provider.

- Recommending changes in the test/procedure as needed based on client findings.

Δ Recognize the client's recovery from anesthesia, if used.

Δ Monitor therapeutic devices (drainage/irrigating devices, chest tubes), if inserted, for proper functioning.

📖 Key Points

- △ **Endoscopic procedures** allow direct visualization of body cavities, tissues, and organs. They are performed for diagnostic and therapeutic purposes.

- △ During some endoscopic procedures, a contrast medium is injected to allow visualization of structures beyond the capabilities of the scope.

- △ **Scope procedures** involve the use of a flexible tube that is inserted into a body cavity or orifice to allow visualization, biopsy, removal of abnormal tissue, and minor surgery.

- △ **The primary types of scope procedures** are:

  - **Arthroscopy** – allows visualization of a joint.

  - **Bronchoscopy** – allows visualization of the larynx, trachea, bronchi, and alveoli.

  - **Colonoscopy** – allows visualization of the anus, rectum, and colon.

  - **Cystoscopy** – allows visualization of the urethra, bladder, prostate, and ureters.

  - **Esophagogastroduodenoscopy (EGD)** – allows visualization of the oropharynx, esophagus, stomach, and duodenum.

  - **Endoscopic retrograde cholangiopancreatography (ERCP)** – allows visualization of the liver, gallbladder, and bile ducts.

  - **Sigmoidoscopy** – allows visualization of the anus, rectum, and sigmoid colon.

Key Factors

- △ **Age** can influence the client's ability to understand the procedures, tolerance of the positioning required for some of the procedures, and compliance with any pre-test preparation required for the procedure.

- △ **Recent food or fluid** intake: The presence of food or fluid in the gastrointestinal tract may affect the provider's ability to visualize key structures and increase the client's risk for complications (for example, aspiration).

- △ **Medications:** Some medications may place the client at greater risks for complications. For example, anticoagulant therapy = increased risk for bleeding.

- △ **Previous radiographic examinations:** Any recent radiographic examinations using barium may affect the provider's ability to view key structures.

Δ **Inadequate bowel preparation** prior to a lower gastrointestinal endoscopic examination can result in cancellation and delays in completing this diagnostic examination. This situation can also lead to the client experiencing extended periods of being NPO, leading to poor nutrition.

Δ **Electrolyte and fluid imbalances** may affect the client's ability to tolerate any bowel preparation orders.

Diagnostic Procedures and Nursing Interventions

Δ Endoscopic procedures can be performed in **outpatient diagnostic centers, provider offices, and acute care settings**. Endoscopic procedures are primarily performed for diagnostic purposes. However, during an endoscopic procedure, the provider can perform biopsies, remove abnormal tissue, and perform minor surgery such as cauterizing a bleeding ulcer.

Δ Several **nursing interventions** are common to all endoscopy procedures.

- Evaluate the client's understanding of the procedure.
- Verify that a consent form has been signed for the specific procedure.
- Assess vital signs before, during, and after the procedure.
- Verify client allergies.
- Evaluate baseline laboratory tests and report unexpected or abnormal findings to the provider. Laboratory tests may include CBC, electrolyte panel, BUN, creatinine, PT, aPTT, and liver function studies. A chest x-ray and electrocardiogram may also be ordered pre-procedure. Arterial blood gases may be measured before and after the procedure to assess oxygenation.
- Evaluate if the client's medical history increases the risk for complications.
- Position the client correctly for the procedure.
- Assess the client for evidence of complications during and after the procedure.
- Determine if barium was used in prior diagnostic studies.
- Ensure the client is NPO for at least 6 hr prior to most endoscopic examinations.

Type of Procedure	Anesthesia	Positioning	Preparation	Post-procedure
Arthroscopy	Local anesthetic, may be performed under general anesthesia	Affected joint elevated, may be wrapped, knee at 45° angle	NPO after midnight; shave hair above and below joint	Keep joint elevated; apply ice packs; monitor for s/s of infection; use crutches as ordered

Type of Procedure	Anesthesia	Positioning	Preparation	Post-procedure
Bronchoscopy	Topical anesthetic, conscious sedation – midazolam (Versed)	Sitting or supine with head elevated	NPO at least 6 hr; instruct on good oral hygiene; evaluate vital signs and respiratory status; remove dentures; administer atropine to reduce oral secretions if ordered	Keep NPO until gag reflex returns; assess vital signs and respiratory status; monitor for hemoptysis
Colonoscopy	Conscious sedation, diazepam (Valium) for anxiety	Left side with knees to chest	Bowel prep which may include laxatives such as Dulcolax® and GoLYTELY®; clear liquid diet; NPO after midnight; instruct client to avoid medications per provider's order	Monitor for rectal bleeding; resume normal diet if ordered; encourage plenty of fluids; monitor vital signs and respiratory status; instruct the client that there may be increased flatulence due to air instillation during procedure
Cystoscopy	Local anesthetic, conscious sedation	Lithotomy position	Void prior to procedure; may have clear liquids or light meal	Monitor vital signs and respiratory status; monitor urine for blood; notify provider of s/s of urinary tract infection

Type of Procedure	Anesthesia	Positioning	Preparation	Post-procedure
EGD	Topical anesthetic, conscious sedation	Sitting or supine with head elevated	NPO at least 6 hr; remove dentures prior to procedure	Monitor vital signs and respiratory status: notify provider of bleeding, abdominal or chest pain, and any evidence of infection
ERCP	Topical anesthetic, conscious sedation	Sitting or supine with head elevated	NPO at least 6 hr; remove dentures prior to procedure	Monitor vital signs and respiratory status; notify provider of bleeding, abdominal or chest pain, and any evidence of infection
Sigmoidoscopy	None required	Knee-chest position	Bowel prep which may include laxatives such as Dulcolax® and GoLYTELY®; clear liquid diet; NPO after midnight; instruct client to avoid medications per the primary care provider's order	Monitor for rectal bleeding; resume normal diet if ordered; encourage plenty of fluids; monitor vital signs and respiratory status; instruct client that there may be increased flatulence due to air instillation during procedure

Complications and Nursing Implications

Δ   Oversedation

- Any endoscopic procedure using conscious sedation places the client at risk for oversedation. Symptoms of oversedation include:

◊   Difficulty arousing the client.

◊   Poor respiratory effort.

◊   Evidence of hypoxemia.

◊   Tachycardia.

◊   Elevated or low blood pressure.

- The nurse should be prepared to administer antidotes to the sedatives administered prior to and during the procedure, maintain an open airway, administer oxygen, and monitor vital signs.

- If evidence of oversedation occurs, the provider should be informed immediately.

Δ   **Hemorrhage**

- Bleeding can occur after any endoscopic procedure. The nurse should monitor the client for evidence of bleeding after these procedures. Symptoms of hemorrhage include:

◊   Bleeding.

◊   Cool clammy skin.

◊   Hypotension.

◊   Tachycardia.

◊   Dizziness.

◊   Tachypnea.

- After an arthroscopy, the symptoms may include significant swelling of the joint and hematoma formation as well as the other symptoms previously mentioned.

- The nurse should monitor the client's vital signs after the procedure, monitor diagnostic test results (particularly hemoglobin and hematocrit), and assess for evidence of bleeding from the site.

- The primary care provider should be notified immediately if these symptoms occur.

Δ   **Aspiration**

- Aspiration may occur after any procedure using conscious sedation or any procedure using topical anesthesia that affects the gag reflex. The client should remain NPO until the gag reflex returns. The nurse should ensure that the client is awake and alert prior to the client consuming any food or fluid. In addition, the nurse should encourage deep breathing and coughing to keep the airway open. Symptoms of aspiration include:

◊   Dyspnea.

◊   Tachypnea.

◊   Adventitious breath sounds.

◊   Tachycardia.

◊   Fever.

- The provider should be notified if these symptoms occur.

Δ   **Perforation**

- Perforation of the gastrointestinal tract can occur with many of these endoscopic procedures. Symptoms include:

    ◊   Chest or abdominal pain.

    ◊   Fever.

    ◊   Nausea.

    ◊   Vomiting.

    ◊   Abdominal distention.

- The nurse should monitor diagnostic tests for evidence of infection, including elevated white blood cell counts.

- The provider should be notified if these symptoms occur.

Meeting the Needs of Older Adults

Δ   **Current Health Status** – Evaluate the older adult client's medical history for conditions and medications that can affect the older adult client's tolerance for and recovery from the procedure.

Δ   **Cognitive Status** – Assess the older adult client's understanding of the procedure.

Δ   **Support System** – Evaluate the older adult client's support system to determine if a support person will assist the client after the procedure.

Primary Reference:

Ignatavicius, D. D., & Workman, M. L. (2006). *Medical-surgical nursing* (5th ed.). St. Louis, MO: Saunders.

Additional Resources:

NANDA International (2004). *NANDA nursing diagnoses: Definitions and classification 2005-2006*. Philadelphia: NANDA.

Smith, S. F., Duell, D. J., & Martin, B. C. (2004). *Clinical Nursing Skills* (6th ed.). Upper Saddle River, NJ: Prentice Hall.

For more information, visit the American Society for Gastrointestinal Endoscopy at *www.asge.org*.

Chapter 61: Scope Procedures

Application Exercises

1. Describe the education required prior to any endoscopic procedure.

2. Describe the priority nursing assessments that should be performed prior to any endoscopic procedure.

3. Explain potential complications and their symptoms that can occur after an endoscopic procedure.

4. Describe the appropriate nursing interventions after an endoscopic procedure involving the upper gastrointestinal tract.

5. Describe the significance of laboratory testing prior to any endoscopic procedure.

6. A client is scheduled for a colonoscopy this morning. The nurse notes the client is continuing to have stool in the last output after an enema. The appropriate action for the nurse to take is to

    A. continue to administer enemas until return is clear.
    B. cancel the procedure.
    C. notify the primary care provider.
    D. document the findings.

7. After a scope procedure, the client is difficult to arouse. An important nursing action for the nurse to perform at this time is to

    A. open the client's airway.
    B. allow the client to sleep.
    C. continue to monitor the client closely.
    D. evaluate pre-procedure laboratory tests for abnormalities.

8. A client is scheduled for a cystoscopy. The nurse recognizes that the client understands the procedure if the client states,

    A. "The physician will inject a dye to see if I'm having any problems with my colon."

    B. "I can't eat or drink anything before this procedure."

    C. "The physician will insert a tube into my bladder so she can see what's causing this bleeding."

    D. "This procedure should correct the problems I'm having with kidney stones."

9. A client is scheduled for a colonoscopy. The provider has ordered a bowel prep using GoLYTELY®. The nurse should include which of the following in the instructions to the client?

    A. Avoid taking any medications with this prep as they will not be absorbed.

    B. Drink plenty of fluids with this prep to help clear out your bowels.

    C. This solution will usually not begin acting until morning.

    D. You should consume at least half of this solution to get the best results.

Chapter 61: Scope Procedures

Application Exercises Answer Key

1. Describe the education required prior to any endoscopic procedure.

   Client education should include the purpose of the procedure, what to expect during the procedure, any preparation required prior to the procedure.

2. Describe the priority nursing assessments that should be performed prior to any endoscopic procedure.

   Priority nursing assessments should include: Verify the provider's order, NPO maintained prior to the procedure, and compliance and results of preparation; verify any allergies, medications, and conditions affecting the procedure; evaluate diagnostic tests; determine if there were any radiologic procedures performed with barium in the week before the procedure; evaluate the client's knowledge of the procedure; and verify that there is a signed consent form.

3. Explain potential complications and their symptoms that can occur after an endoscopic procedure.

   Potential complications include aspiration, perforation, oversedation, and hemorrhage. The symptoms are listed in the chapter.

4. Describe the appropriate nursing interventions after an endoscopic procedure involving the upper gastrointestinal tract.

   Appropriate nursing interventions include assessment of the airway, vital signs, evidence of bleeding or other complications, and return of the gag reflex and instruction on symptoms to report to the provider.

5. Describe the significance of laboratory testing prior to any endoscopic procedure.

CBC detects the presence of anemia and infection. Electrolyte panel, BUN, and creatinine provide information regarding fluid volume status, renal function, and any electrolyte imbalances. PT and aPTT can indicate a risk for bleeding. Liver function studies can indicate the presence of liver disease, which can impact clotting.

6. A client is scheduled for a colonoscopy this morning. The nurse notes the client is continuing to have stool in the last output after an enema. The appropriate action for the nurse to take is to

    A. continue to administer enemas until return is clear.

    B. cancel the procedure.

    C. notify the primary care provider.

    D. document the findings.

Stool will impede visualization. Additional interventions may be necessary, including delay or cancellation of the procedure.

7. After a scope procedure, the client is difficult to arouse. An important nursing action for the nurse to perform at this time is to

    A. open the client's airway.

    B. allow the client to sleep.

    C. continue to monitor the client closely.

    D. evaluate pre-procedure laboratory tests for abnormalities.

A priority intervention is airway maintenance.

8. A client is scheduled for a cystoscopy. The nurse recognizes that the client understands the procedure if the client states,

> A. "The physician will inject a dye to see if I'm having any problems with my colon."
>
> B. "I can't eat or drink anything before this procedure."
>
> **C. "The physician will insert a tube into my bladder so she can see what's causing this bleeding."**
>
> D. "This procedure should correct the problems I'm having with kidney stones."

A cystoscopy allows visualization of the urethra, bladder, prostate, and ureters and does not involve the injection of dye.

9. A client is scheduled for a colonoscopy. The provider has ordered a bowel prep using GoLYTELY®. The nurse should include which of the following in the instructions to the client?

> **A. Avoid taking any medications with this prep as they will not be absorbed.**
>
> B. Drink plenty of fluids with this prep to help clear out your bowels.
>
> C. This solution will usually not begin acting until morning.
>
> D. You should consume at least half of this solution to get the best results.

The client will need to consume the full prescribed amount of GoLYTELY®. Its effects are immediate. Motility will be increased with the effects of the GoLYTELY®, which would greatly reduce the likelihood of medication absorption.

Unit 7
Section:

Nursing Care of Clients with Gastrointestinal Disorders
Diagnostic and Therapeutic Procedures: Gastrointestinal

Chapter 62:   Ostomies
Contributor: Margaret C. Davis, MSN, RN

⟳ **NCLEX-PN® Connections:**

Learning Objective: Review and apply knowledge within "**Ostomies**" in readiness for performance of the following nursing activities as outlined by the NCLEX-PN® test plan:

Δ   Support the client with altered bowel elimination.

Δ   Provide skin care to the client with altered bowel elimination.

Δ   Assist/evaluate the client with bowel retraining and restoration/maintenance of altered bowel elimination.

Δ   Perform/assist with relevant laboratory, diagnostic, and therapeutic procedures within the nursing role, including:

- Preparation of the client for the procedure.

- Reinforcement of client teaching (before and following the procedure).

- Accurate collection of specimens.

- Monitoring procedure results (compare to norms) and appropriate notification of the primary care provider.

- Monitoring the client's response (expected, unexpected adverse response, comparison to baseline) to the procedure.

- Monitoring and taking actions, including reinforcing client teaching, to prevent or minimize the risk of complications.

- Recognizing signs of potential complications and reporting to the primary care provider.

- Recommending changes in the test/procedure as needed based on client findings.

Δ   Monitor therapeutic devices (drainage/irrigating devices, chest tubes), if inserted, for proper functioning.

Key Points

Δ   An **ostomy** is surgery to create an opening from the inside of the body to the outside. Ostomies may be permanent or temporary.

Δ   A **stoma** is an artificial opening from the inside of the body to the outside created during the ostomy surgery.

Δ   Peristomal skin is the skin surrounding the stoma.

Δ   The three main types of ostomies are:

•   An **ileostomy** is a surgical opening into the ileum to drain stool.

•   A **colostomy** is a surgical opening into the large intestine to drain stool.

•   A **urostomy** is a surgical opening to drain urine.

Key Factors

Δ   **Age** can influence the client's ability to manage an ostomy. In addition, the age of the client can influence the psychosocial impact of the ostomy.

Δ   **General health** can impact the client's recovery from and management of an ostomy.

Δ   **Culture** can influence a client's acceptance of the ostomy as well as all other aspects of care.

Δ   **Past experiences** can create unwillingness to comply with the treatment plan or lack of motivation to learn new information.

Δ   **Environmental conditions** can influence the client's ability to focus on education regarding care and management of the ostomy. In addition, the client may feel embarrassed or unwilling to expose the ostomy if adequate privacy and quiet is not provided.

Δ   **Support system**: A support system is critical to ensuring a client's success with ostomy management. The client's primary support person (parent, guardian, spouse, friend, or any other person identified by the client) should be educated on management of the ostomy.

Therapeutic Procedures and Nursing Interventions

	Ileostomy	Transverse Colostomy	Sigmoid Colostomy	Urostomy
Normal postoperative output	Less than 1,000 mL/day. May be bile-colored and liquid.	Small **semi-liquid** with some **mucus** 2-3 days after surgery. Blood may be present in the first few days after surgery.	Small to moderate amount of **mucus** with semi-formed stool 4-5 days after surgery.	Depending on the type of urostomy, normal urine output with some **mucus** and blood. If an artificial bladder was formed using a portion of the large intestine, some of the water may be reabsorbed from the urine, resulting in a lower output.
Postoperative changes in output	After several days to weeks, the output will decrease to approximately 500 to 1,000 mL/day. Becomes more paste-like as the small intestine assumes the absorptive function of the large intestine.	After several days to weeks, output will become more stool-like, semi-formed, or formed.	After several days to weeks, output will resemble semi-formed stool.	After several days, the urine output should continue to be normal amounts (minimum of 30 mL/hr) with some mucus possible. No blood should be noted in the output.
Pattern of output	**Continuous** output	Resumes a pattern similar to the **preoperative pattern.**	Resumes a pattern similar to the **preoperative pattern.**	**Continuous** output

Δ Evaluate output from the stoma. The **higher** up an ostomy is placed in the small intestine, the **more liquid** and **acidic** the output will be from the ostomy. Therefore, the nurse should assess the peristomal skin for erosion and ulceration due to proteolytic enzymes contained in the output. Any leakage on the skin should be removed as soon as possible to prevent erosion and ulceration.

Δ Assess the type and fit of the ostomy appliance. Monitor for leakage (risk to skin integrity). The nurse should fit the ostomy appliance based on several factors including the:

- Type of ostomy.

- Location of the ostomy.

- Visual acuity and manual dexterity of the client.

Δ Assess peristomal skin integrity and the appearance of stoma. The stoma should appear pink and moist.

Δ Apply skin barriers and creams such as stoma adhesive paste when applying wafers to protect the peristomal skin. Let skin sealants dry before applying new appliance.

Δ Assess for fluid and electrolyte imbalances, particularly with a new ileostomy.

Δ Monitor diagnostic test results including hemoglobin, hematocrit, potassium, sodium, chloride, BUN, and creatinine. Notify the primary care provider of any abnormal or unexpected findings.

Δ Educate the client regarding lifestyle changes that may be necessary as a result of the ostomy. For example, the client will need to understand how frequently the ostomy bag will need to be emptied (in general, when bag is ¼ to ½ full).

Δ Educate the client regarding dietary changes and ostomy appliances that can help manage flatus and odor.

- Foods that can cause **odor** include fish, eggs, asparagus, garlic, beans, and dark green leafy vegetables.

- Foods that can cause **gas** include dark green leafy vegetables, beer, carbonated beverages, dairy products, and corn.

- After an ostomy is placed involving the small intestine, the client should be instructed to **avoid high fiber** foods for the **first 2 months** after surgery, chew food well, **drink plenty of fluids**, and evaluate for any evidence of blockage when slowly adding high-fiber foods.

Δ Provide opportunities for the client to discuss feelings about the ostomy and concerns about its impact on the client's life. In particular, use the PLISSIT or another model to encourage the client to discuss any concerns related to sexuality. The **PLISSIT model**:

- **Permission** – Give the client permission to discuss sexual concerns.

- **Limited information** – Provide the client with information regarding the impact of the ostomy on sexuality. Be careful not to overwhelm the client.

- **Specific suggestion** – Give the client specific suggestions to address concerns.

- **Intensive therapy** – Refer the client to a qualified therapist or practitioner for serious problems.

Δ   Refer the client to a local support group like the United Ostomy Society.

Δ   Encourage the client to look at and touch the stoma.

Complications and Nursing Implications

Δ   **Stomal ischemia/necrosis**

- **The stomal appearance should normally be pink or red and moist.** The nurse should note any changes in the appearance of the stoma indicating ischemia or necrosis. Signs of stomal **ischemia** are **pale pink** or **bluish/ purple** in color and dry in appearance. If the stoma appears **black** or purple in color, this indicates a **serious impairment of blood flow** and requires immediate intervention. In this situation, nurses need to obtain vital signs, pulse oximetry, and current laboratory results. This information will assist the provider in determining possible causes for the ischemia. The provider or surgeon should be notified immediately because the client may require additional surgical intervention.

Δ   **Intestinal obstruction**

- Obstruction can occur for a variety of reasons. The nurse should monitor and record output from the stoma to evaluate for this potential complication. The nurse should also **assess** the client for other **symptoms of obstruction** including abdominal pain, hypoactive or **absent bowel sounds**, distention, nausea, and vomiting. If these symptoms appear, the nurse should notify the surgeon.

Meeting the Needs of Older Adults

Δ   Assess the client's visual acuity in order to determine if the client is able to recognize problems with peristomal skin and evidence of complications.

Δ   Assess manual dexterity to determine if the client is able to manipulate ostomy appliances.

Δ   Assess the client's cognitive status to determine the client's ability to understand the care and management of the ostomy.

Δ   Evaluate the client's support system to determine if adequate support is available and accessible to assist the client with management of the ostomy if needed.

Δ   Instruct the client and support person regarding care and management of an ostomy before surgery (if possible) and after surgery (always).

Primary Reference:

Ignatavicius, D. D., & Workman, M. L. (2006). *Medical-surgical nursing* (5th ed.). St. Louis, MO: Saunders.

Additional Resources:

Hampton, B. G., & Bryant, R. A. (1992). *Ostomies and continent diversions: Nursing management*. St. Louis, MO: Mosby.

NANDA International (2004). *NANDA nursing diagnoses: Definitions and classification 2005-2006*. Philadelphia: NANDA.

Chapter 62: Ostomies

Application Exercises

1. Discuss the educational needs of a client who is scheduled for an ostomy.

2. What nursing considerations are important when evaluating an older adult client prior to an ostomy?

3. Two days after an ileostomy, the nurse notes the following: temperature 37.7° C (99.8° F), blood pressure 102/60 mm Hg, pulse 98 beats/min, respiratory rate 20/min, and urine output less than 10 mL/hr. The client's skin appears dry. What additional assessment data should be collected regarding this client? What nursing interventions are appropriate for this client?

4. A client with an ileostomy reports that he is experiencing abdominal pain and no output for the past 24 hr. What additional information should be obtained from the client? Describe appropriate nursing interventions that should be taken at this time.

5. A client with a sigmoid colostomy states, "I just feel so unattractive. I'm afraid to let my boyfriend touch me now." Using the PLISSIT model, describe nursing interventions to assist this client with her concerns.

6. A nurse is assessing a client in the immediate postoperative period after an ostomy. The nurse notes that the stoma appears red and moist. The appropriate action by the nurse at this time is to

   A. notify the primary care provider immediately.

   B. check the client's oxygenation.

   C. document the findings.

   D. encourage the client to cough and deep breathe.

7. A client had a sigmoid colostomy placed several months ago. The client reports that he is having problems with odor and flatulence. Which of the following dietary changes should the nurse recommend?

    A. Avoid fruits and vegetables.

    B. Limit the amount of dairy products and dark green leafy vegetables.

    C. Increase the amount of dark green leafy vegetables.

    D. Drink plenty of carbonated beverages.

8. A nurse notes that a client with a sigmoid colostomy has not had any output from her ostomy 3 days after surgery. The nurse recognizes that

    A. the client has an obstruction and needs immediate intervention.

    B. this finding is expected at this point in the postoperative period.

    C. the client needs to increase activity and fluid intake.

    D. the client should not eat or drink at this point.

Chapter 62: Ostomies

Application Exercises Answer Key

1. Discuss the educational needs of a client who is scheduled for an ostomy.

   Education should include the type of ostomy planned, appliances available, and lifestyle changes that may be necessary.

2. What nursing considerations are important when evaluating an older adult client prior to an ostomy?

   Nursing considerations should include evaluation of visual acuity, manual dexterity, chronic diseases which can affect management of ostomy, and the client's support system.

3. Two days after an ileostomy, the nurse notes the following: temperature 37.7° C (99.8° F), blood pressure 102/60 mm Hg, pulse 98 beats/min, respiratory rate 20/min, and urine output less than 10 mL/hr. The client's skin appears dry. What additional assessment data should be collected regarding this client? What nursing interventions are appropriate for this client?

   Assessment data should include the ileostomy output, vital signs, and laboratory tests results. The nurse should contact the primary care provider to discuss clinical symptoms and anticipate that the provider may order fluid and electrolyte replacement.

4. A client with an ileostomy reports that he is experiencing abdominal pain and no output for the past 24 hr. What additional information should be obtained from the client? Describe appropriate nursing interventions that should be taken at this time.

   Additional information should include current diet and any associated symptoms, such as fever, nausea, vomiting, and abdominal distention. The nurse should encourage the client to notify his primary care provider.

5. A client with a sigmoid colostomy states, "I just feel so unattractive. I'm afraid to let my boyfriend touch me now." Using the PLISSIT model, describe nursing interventions to assist this client with her concerns.

Encourage the client to discuss her concerns; provide information regarding the client's concerns; provide specific suggestions that may alleviate concerns (such as covers for ostomy appliances and emptying the bag prior to any sexual activity); and, if the problems appear serious, then refer the client to counseling.

6. A nurse is assessing a client in the immediate postoperative period after an ostomy. The nurse notes that the stoma appears red and moist. The appropriate action by the nurse at this time is to

    A. notify the primary care provider immediately.

    B. check the client's oxygenation.

    C. document the findings.

    D. encourage the client to cough and deep breathe.

These are expected findings for a healthy stoma.

7. A client had a sigmoid colostomy placed several months ago. The client reports that he is having problems with odor and flatulence. Which of the following dietary changes should the nurse recommend?

    A. Avoid fruits and vegetables.

    B. Limit the amount of dairy products and dark green leafy vegetables.

    C. Increase the amount of dark green leafy vegetables.

    D. Drink plenty of carbonated beverages.

Foods that can cause gas include dark green leafy vegetables, beer, carbonated beverages, dairy products, and corn.

8. A nurse notes that a client with a sigmoid colostomy has not had any output from her ostomy 3 days after surgery. The nurse recognizes that

    A. the client has an obstruction and needs immediate intervention.

    B. this finding is expected at this point in the postoperative period.

    C. the client needs to increase activity and fluid intake.

    D. the client should not eat or drink at this point.

Expected postoperative output is a small to moderate amount of mucus with semi-formed stool 4 to 5 days after surgery.

Chapter 63:   **Paracentesis**
Contributor: Margaret C. Davis, MSN, RN

NCLEX-PN® Connections:

Learning Objective: Review and apply knowledge within "**Paracentesis**" in readiness for performance of the following nursing activities as outlined by the NCLEX-PN® test plan:

Δ   Perform/assist with relevant laboratory, diagnostic, and therapeutic procedures within the nursing role, including:

- Preparation of the client for the procedure.

- Reinforcement of client teaching (before and following the procedure).

- Accurate collection of specimens.

- Monitoring procedure results (compare to norms) and appropriate notification of the primary care provider.

- Monitoring the client's response (expected, unexpected adverse response, comparison to baseline) to the procedure.

- Monitoring and taking actions, including reinforcing client teaching, to prevent or minimize the risk of complications.

- Recognizing signs of potential complications and reporting to the primary care provider.

- Recommending changes in the test/procedure as needed based on client findings.

Δ   Recognize the client's recovery from anesthesia, if used.

Δ   Monitor therapeutic devices (drainage/irrigating devices, chest tubes), if inserted, for proper functioning.

📖 Key Points

Δ **Ascites** is an abnormal accumulation of protein-rich fluid in the abdominal cavity most often caused by cirrhosis of the liver.

Δ A **paracentesis** is performed by inserting a needle or trocar through the abdominal wall into the peritoneal cavity and withdrawing ascitic fluid for **diagnostic purposes.** Therapeutically, a larger quantity of ascitic fluid (up to 1 L) can be withdrawn in order to **relieve abdominal pressure** from ascites buildup.

Δ Ascitic fluid samples collected by a paracentesis can be used to **diagnose** a variety of medical conditions, including **intra-abdominal bleeding, infection,** and **pancreatitis.** Various cell counts and cultures can be performed on collected fluid.

Δ A paracentesis can be performed in a physician's office, an outpatient center, or in an acute care setting.

Δ The paracentesis may be performed at the bedside or in the radiology department **using an ultrasound** to ensure correct placement of the needle.

Key Factors

Δ **Respiratory distress** is the overall determining **factor** in the use of a paracentesis in the treatment of ascites, and in the evaluation of treatment effectiveness.

Δ **Fluid volume balance** is maintained in part by the amount of protein in the vascular space. When a large amount of protein-rich fluid is removed, fluid will shift between the intravascular space and the interstitial tissue causing **hypovolemia.** This fluid shift is a **major factor in determining the rate** at which ascitic fluid can be safely removed.

Δ The age of the client will affect his ability to tolerate this procedure, particularly if the procedure is being performed for the treatment of ascites.

Δ The presence of additional chronic and acute diseases can influence the ability of the client to tolerate this procedure and may require adaptation in positioning.

Nursing Interventions

Δ Several nursing interventions are critical when caring for a client undergoing a paracentesis (refer to the chart on the next page).

Before the Procedure	During the Procedure	After the Procedure
1. Explain the procedure and its purpose. 2. Assess the client's knowledge of the procedure. 3. Take baseline vital signs, record **weight, and measure abdominal girth**. 4. Gather equipment for the procedure. 5. Verify that the consent form has been signed. 6. Position the client as tolerated. 7. Have the client **void prior** to the procedure, or insert a Foley catheter. 8. Instruct the client that local anesthetics will be used at the needle-insertion site. 9. Administer any sedation prescribed by the primary care provider.	1. Explain that the client may experience pressure or pain with needle insertion. 2. Continue to monitor vital signs during the procedure. 3. Adhere to standard precautions. 4. Label any laboratory specimens and send to the laboratory.	1. Maintain **pressure at the needle-insertion site for several minutes.** Apply dressing to site. 2. Take vital signs, record weight, and measure abdominal girth post procedure. **Compare them to pre-procedure measurements.** 3. Continue to monitor vital signs and needle insertion site per agency protocol. 4. Monitor temperature every 4 hr for a minimum of 48 hr. 5. Assess intake and output every 4 hr. 6. Administer IV fluids or albumin as ordered by the primary care provider. 7. Place the client **on the unaffected side for 1-2 hr after** the procedure. 8. **Document color, odor, consistency, and amount** of fluid removed, location of needle insertion, any **evidence of leakage** at the needle insertion site, **signs and symptoms of hypovolemia**, and changes in mental status. Also, document vital signs, temperature, intake and output, weight, and abdominal girth.

△ The client needs to **void prior to the paracentesis** in order to reduce the risk of puncturing the bladder during needle insertion. If the client is unable to void, a Foley catheter may be inserted if the primary care provider's order is obtained.

△ The client may be **sitting up** or supine during the procedure, depending on his tolerance. If the client has ascites, he may find it difficult to lie flat during the procedure. Therefore, the client may find it more comfortable to sit up with his legs dangling off the side of the bed and arms resting on a bedside table.

Δ   If the needle-insertion site **continues to leak after holding pressure** for several minutes, **dry sterile gauze dressings** should be applied and changed as often as necessary.

Δ   In general, 1 L of fluid is the maximum withdrawn in a relatively short period of time. Some providers may choose to attach a catheter to the trocar to allow for **slow drainage** of more than 1 L of peritoneal fluid over several hours. The nurse is responsible for monitoring the amount of drainage and notifying the primary care provider of any evidence of complications.

Δ   **Albumin levels can drop dangerously low** as a result of a paracentesis because the peritoneal fluid removed contains a large amount of protein. The removal of this protein-rich fluid can cause shifting of intravascular volume, resulting in **hypovolemia.**

Δ   The nurse may be responsible for **administering IV fluids or albumin, prior to or after a paracentesis, to restore fluid balance.**

Δ   **Diuretics** such as spironolactone (Aldactone) and furosemide (Lasix) may be prescribed to **control fluid volume**. Potassium supplements may be necessary as a result of these diuretics. Nurses should monitor serum electrolytes to assess for complications from these medications.

Δ   Removal of **1 L of fluid equals 1 kg (2.2 lb) in weight.**

Δ   Prior to and after a paracentesis, the following laboratory tests should be performed:

   •   **Albumin** – Normal range = 3.1 to 4.3 g/dL

   •   **Protein** – Normal range = 6.0 to 8.0 g/dL

   •   **Glucose** – Normal range = 80 to 120 mg/dL

   •   **Amylase** – Normal range = 53 to 123 units/L

   •   **BUN** – Normal range = 8 to 25 mg/dL

   •   **Creatinine** – Normal range = 0.6 to 1.5 mg/dL

Δ   Each of these laboratory tests are performed on a venous blood sample. The nurse should educate the client about the purpose of these tests. These tests are designed to measure some aspect of liver and renal function or vascular volume. Nurses should also monitor serum electrolytes and report abnormal or unexpected findings to the provider. **Low levels of protein and albumin** in the blood can **cause increased fluid retention leading to increased ascites and generalized edema.**

Complications and Nursing Implications

Δ   **Hypovolemia**

- **Preventive** measures include **slow** versus rapid **drainage** of fluid and the administration of plasma expanders, such as albumin, to counter albumin losses.

- Nurses should carefully monitor clients for evidence of hypovolemia after a paracentesis. The **symptoms include tachycardia, hypotension, pallor, diaphoresis, and dizziness.**

- Any abnormal symptoms should be reported to the provider.

- The nurse should also monitor the client's daily weight, intake and output, and vital signs after a paracentesis to recognize this condition early and intervene quickly.

Δ   **Bladder perforation**

- Bladder perforation is a rare but possible complication.

- **Symptoms** of bladder perforation **include hematuria, low or no urine output, suprapubic pain and/or distention, symptoms of cystitis, and fever.**

- If bladder perforation is suspected, the nurse should notify the provider immediately.

Δ   **Peritonitis**

- Peritonitis can occur as the result of injury to the intestines from the needle inserted for diagnostic or therapeutic paracentesis.

- **Symptoms** of peritonitis **include sharp, constant abdominal pain, fever, nausea, vomiting, and diminished or absent bowel sounds.**

- If the client exhibits symptoms of peritonitis, the nurse should notify the provider immediately.

Meeting the Needs of Older Adults

Δ   Monitor for positional discomfort due to physiological changes, such as osteoporosis arthritis.

Δ   Evaluate the older adult client's medical history for evidence of chronic or acute disease that could impact the older adult client's recovery from this procedure.

Δ   Evaluate the older adult client's cognitive function to determine his ability to understand the procedure.

Δ   Assess for evidence of dehydration, impaired renal function, or medications that could influence the older adult client's recovery from this procedure.

Primary Reference:

Ignatavicius, D. D., & Workman, M. L. (2006). *Medical-surgical nursing* (5th ed.). St. Louis, MO: Saunders.

Additional Resources:

Corbett, J. V. (2004). *Laboratory tests and diagnostic procedures with nursing diagnoses* (6th ed.). Upper Saddle River, NJ: Prentice Hall Health.

Daniels, R. (2002). *Delmar's guide to laboratory and diagnostic tests.* Albany, NY: Delmar Thomson Learning.

NANDA International (2004). *NANDA nursing diagnoses: Definitions and classification 2005-2006.* Philadelphia: NANDA.

Chapter 63: Paracentesis

Application Exercises

1. A 57-year-old male client had a paracentesis performed 15 min ago with removal of 750 mL of pale, straw-colored liquid due to ascites. Prior to the procedure, his vital signs were: blood pressure 136/88 mm Hg, heart rate 96 beats/min, respirations 24/min, and temperature 37.2° C (99.0° F). The client's weight is 100.4 kg (221 lb), and his abdominal girth is 121.9 cm (48 in). Currently, his vital signs are: blood pressure 100/60 mm Hg, heart rate 124 beats/min, respirations 24/min, and temperature 37.1° C (98.8° F). His weight is now 99.8 kg (219.5 lb), and his abdominal girth is 109.2 cm (43 in). What are the implications of this assessment data? What nursing interventions should be taken at this time?

2. A client complains of feeling "lots of pressure" when the primary care provider is inserting the trocar for a paracentesis. What is the appropriate response by the nurse?

3. What are the signs and symptoms a client may exhibit if the bowel is perforated during a paracentesis?

4. The nurse is providing care to a client 1 day after a paracentesis. The nurse notes that a clear, pale yellow fluid is leaking out of the needle puncture site. Identify the appropriate nursing interventions based on the information provided.

5. Two days after a paracentesis, a client reports abdominal tenderness. His temperature is 38.6° C (101.5° F). What action should the nurse take at this time?

6. What education should the nurse expect to provide to a client undergoing a paracentesis?

7. An 80-year-old client is scheduled for a paracentesis in the morning. What are special considerations required when preparing this client for this procedure?

8. Which of the following nursing interventions would be the most effective in assessing for hypovolemia after a paracentesis?

A. Taking vital signs every 4 hr

B. Measuring intake and output during every shift

C. Performing daily weights

D. Measuring abdominal girth during every shift

9. A client weighing 90.9 kg (200 lb) prior to a paracentesis had 1,000 mL of fluid removed. How much weight should the nurse anticipate the client lost based on this fluid removal?

A. 1 kg (2.2 lb)

B. 3.6 kg (8 lb)

C. 0.91 kg (2 lb)

D. 0.64 kg (1.4 lb)

10. A client's laboratory results are albumin 2.3 g/dL, BUN 36 mg/dL, and creatinine 1.8 mg/dL prior to a scheduled paracentesis. The appropriate action for the nurse to take is to

A. prepare the client for the paracentesis.

B. document these findings.

C. notify the provider or the charge nurse.

D. cancel the procedure.

11. Prior to a client's discharge from the outpatient diagnostic center, the nurse evaluates the client's understanding of potential complications and symptoms to report. Which of the following statements indicates that the client understands what symptoms to report to the provider?

A. "I will notify the doctor if this leakage continues from the needle insertion site."

B. "The doctor should be called if I develop a fever or have abdominal pain."

C. "If my abdomen does not continue to decrease in size, I should call my doctor."

D. "I will call the doctor if I notice any weight change over the next several days."

Chapter 63: Paracentesis

Application Exercises Answer Key

1. A 57-year-old male client had a paracentesis performed 15 min ago with removal of 750 mL of pale, straw-colored liquid due to ascites. Prior to the procedure, his vital signs were: blood pressure 136/88 mm Hg, heart rate 96 beats/min, respirations 24/min, and temperature 37.2° C (99.0° F). The client's weight is 100.4 kg (221 lb), and his abdominal girth is 121.9 cm (48 in). Currently, his vital signs are: blood pressure 100/60 mm Hg, heart rate 124 beats/min, respirations 24/min, and temperature 37.1° C (98.8° F). His weight is now 99.8 kg (219.5 lb), and his abdominal girth is 109.2 cm (43 in). What are the implications of this assessment data? What nursing interventions should be taken at this time?

   The client is exhibiting symptoms of hypovolemia. The response should include notifying the provider of the symptoms, preparing for interventions such as the administration of IV fluids or albumin, and laboratory tests. Maintain the client in a position of comfort with the head of the bed elevated. Instruct the client on the purpose of the interventions being performed, and document all of the client's symptoms and all nursing interventions.

2. A client complains of feeling "lots of pressure" when the primary care provider is inserting the trocar for a paracentesis. What is the appropriate response by the nurse?

   The nurse should instruct the client that during the procedure, the feeling of pressure is normal when the provider is inserting the needle. Explain that this pressure should resolve within a few minutes.

3. What are the signs and symptoms a client may exhibit if the bowel is perforated during a paracentesis?

   Symptoms include abdominal pain and rigidity, low or diminished bowel sounds, fever, nausea, vomiting, anorexia, and rebound tenderness in the abdomen.

4. The nurse is providing care to a client 1 day after a paracentesis. The nurse notes that a clear, pale yellow fluid is leaking out of the needle puncture site. Identify the appropriate nursing interventions based on the information provided.

Apply a dry, sterile gauze dressing, and change it as necessary. Assess site during dressing changes for evidence of infection. Notify the provider of any changes of the color, odor, amount, or consistency of the drainage.

5. Two days after a paracentesis, a client reports abdominal tenderness. His temperature is 38.6° C (101.5° F). What action should the nurse take at this time?

The nurse should obtain vital signs and notify the provider or charge nurse of the client's symptoms.

6. What education should the nurse expect to provide to a client undergoing a paracentesis?

The nurse should explain the purpose of the procedure, what to expect during the procedure, and signs and symptoms that the client should report to the provider.

7. An 80-year-old client is scheduled for a paracentesis in the morning. What are special considerations required when preparing this client for this procedure?

The nurse should evaluate the client's ability to tolerate the position desired for the procedure, the level of the client's understanding of the procedure, and the potential risks associated with the procedure for this client based on his prior medical history and current physical status. In addition, the nurse should evaluate the client's ability to provide care to the puncture site and to recognize and report any complications.

8. Which of the following nursing interventions would be the most effective in assessing for hypovolemia after a paracentesis?

    A. Taking vital signs every 4 hr

    B. Measuring intake and output during every shift

    C. Performing daily weights

    D. Measuring abdominal girth during every shift

Assessment of vital signs will reveal tachycardia and hypotension, which are signs of hypovolemia.

9. A client weighing 90.9 kg (200 lb) prior to a paracentesis had 1,000 mL of fluid removed. How much weight should the nurse anticipate the client lost based on this fluid removal?

    A. 1 kg (2.2 lb)

    B. 3.6 kg (8 lb)

    C. 0.91 kg (2 lb)

    D. 0.64 kg (1.4 lb)

1 L of fluid is equal to 1 kg (2.2 lb) of weight.

10. A client's laboratory results are albumin 2.3 g/dL, BUN 36 mg/dL, and creatinine 1.8 mg/dL prior to a scheduled paracentesis. The appropriate action for the nurse to take is to

    A. prepare the client for the paracentesis.

    B. document these findings.

    C. notify the provider or the charge nurse.

    D. cancel the procedure.

These are significantly abnormal laboratory values. The albumin level is low (normal range = 3.1 to 4.3 g/dL); the BUN is high (normal range = 10 to 20 mg/dL), and the creatinine level is high (normal range = 0.6 to 1.5 mg/dL).

11. Prior to a client's discharge from the outpatient diagnostic center, the nurse evaluates the client's understanding of potential complications and symptoms to report. Which of the following statements indicates that the client understands what symptoms to report to the provider?

    A. "I will notify the doctor if this leakage continues from the needle insertion site."

    B. "The doctor should be called if I develop a fever or have abdominal pain."

    C. "If my abdomen does not continue to decrease in size, I should call my doctor."

    D. "I will call the doctor if I notice any weight change over the next several days."

Fever and abdominal pain are signs of peritonitis and should be reported.

Unit 7   Nursing Care of Clients with Gastrointestinal Disorders
Section: Nursing Care of Clients with Esophageal Disorders

Chapter 64:   Gastroesophageal Reflux Disease
Contributor: Polly Gerber Zimmermann, MSN, MBA, RN, CEN

NCLEX-PN® Connections:

Learning Objective: Review and apply knowledge within "**Gastroesophageal Reflux Disease**" in readiness for performance of the following nursing activities as outlined by the NCLEX-PN® test plan:

Δ   Assist with relevant laboratory, diagnostic, and therapeutic procedures within the nursing role, including:

- Preparation of the client for the procedure.

- Accurate collection of specimens.

- Monitoring client status during and after the procedure.

- Reinforcing client teaching (before and following the procedure).

- Recognizing the client's response (expected, unexpected adverse response) to the procedure.

- Monitoring results.

- Monitoring and taking actions to prevent or minimize the risk of complications.

- Notifying the primary care provider of signs of complications.

Δ   Recognize signs and symptoms of the client's problem and complete the proper documentation.

Δ   Provide and document care based on the client's health alteration.

Δ   Monitor and document vital signs changes.

Δ   Interpret data that need to be reported immediately.

Δ   Reinforce client education on managing the client's health problem.

Δ   Recognize and respond to emergency situations, including notification of the primary care provider.

Δ   Review the client's response to emergency interventions and complete the proper documentation.

Δ   Provide care that meets the age-related needs of clients 65 years of age or older, including recognizing expected physiological changes.

📖 Key Points

Δ **Gastroesophageal reflux disease**, or GERD, is a common condition characterized by gastric content and enzyme leakage **into the esophagus**. These **corrosive** fluids irritate the esophageal tissue and limit its ability to clear the esophagus.

Δ Causes are related to the weakness or inappropriate prolonged or frequent transient **relaxation** of the **lower esophageal sphincter (LES)** at the base of the esophagus, **or delayed gastric emptying**.

Δ GERD is a common occurrence; it affects more than 14% of Americans.

Δ **The chief symptom** of GERD is frequent and prolonged **retrosternal heartburn** (dyspepsia) and **regurgitation** (acid reflux) in relationship to eating or activities. Other symptoms can include chronic cough, dysphagia, belching (eructation), flatulence (gas), atypical chest pain, and asthma exacerbations.

Δ **Untreated GERD** leads to **inflammation**, **breakdown**, and long-term complications.

Δ **The primary treatment** of GERD is **diet and lifestyle changes**, advancing into **medication use** (antacids, H_2 antagonists, and proton pump inhibitors).

Key Factors

Δ Etiology includes:

• Any factor that **relaxes the LES**, such as **smoking, caffeine, alcohol**, or drugs.

• Any factor that **increases** the **abdominal pressure**, such as **obesity**, tight clothing at the waist, ascites, or pregnancy.

• Older age and/or a debilitating condition that **weakens the LES tone**.

Δ **Contributing factors**

• Diet: Excessive ingestion of **foods that relax the LES** include:

◊ **Fatty** and fried foods.

◊ Chocolate.

◊ Caffeinated beverages such as coffee.

◊ Peppermint.

◊ Spicy foods.

◊ Tomatoes.

◊ Citrus fruits.

◊ **Alcohol.**

- Distended abdomen from overeating or delayed emptying

- **Increased abdominal pressure** resulting from obesity, pregnancy, bending at the waist, ascites or tight clothing at the waist

- **Drugs that relax the LES**, such as theophylline, nitrates, calcium channel blockers, anticholinergics, and diazepam (Valium)

- Drugs, such as NSAIDs, or events (stress) that increase gastric acid

- Debilitation or age-related conditions resulting in weakened LES tone

- Hiatal hernia (LES displacement into the thorax with delayed esophageal clearance)

- Lying flat

Diagnostic Procedures and Nursing Interventions

Δ History: Symptoms **4 to 5 times per week** on a **consistent** basis

Δ **Improvement after a 6-week course** of proton pump inhibitors (PPI)

Δ Diagnostic interventions taken to differentiate GERD from gastritis (temporary occasional irritation of gastric mucosa that 35 to 50% of the population experiences) and from gastric/peptic ulcer (ulceration of gastric mucosa)

- Barium Upper GI: Prepare the client for the procedure. Post procedure: Assess for bowel sounds and potential constipation.

- **Endoscopy** is used while the client is under conscious sedation to observe for tissue damage (in 60% of clients with GERD) and possibly to dilate structures. Post procedure: Verify gag response prior to providing oral fluids or food.

- Esophageal manometry is used to measure muscle tone of LES and pH monitoring.

Therapeutic Procedures and Nursing Interventions

Δ **Surgery (fundoplication) may be indicated for clients who fail to** respond. The surgeon wraps the fundus of the stomach around and behind the esophagus through laparoscopy to create a physical barrier.

Δ **New option: Stretta procedure** uses radiofrequency energy, applied by laparoscopy, to the LES muscle. This causes the tissue to contract and tighten.

Assessments

Δ Monitor for **signs and symptoms.**

- **Classic symptoms: Dyspepsia**, especially **after eating** an offending food/fluid, and regurgitation.

- **Other symptoms:** Symptoms from throat irritation (chronic cough, laryngitis), hypersalivation, eructation, flatulence, or **atypical chest pain from esophageal spasm.** Chronic GERD can lead to dysphagia (difficulty swallowing).

Δ **Assess the client's:**

- Dietary intake patterns, paying particular attention to foods containing caffeine and fat.

- Smoking history.

- Alcohol use.

- Weight.

NANDA Nursing Diagnoses

Δ Acute pain

Δ Deficient knowledge

Nursing Interventions

Δ **Educate the client regarding:**

- **Diet**

  ◊ Avoid offending foods.

  ◊ Avoid large meals.

  ◊ Remain upright after eating.

  ◊ Avoid eating before going to bed.

- **Lifestyle**

  ◊ Avoid tight-fitting clothing around the middle.

  ◊ Lose weight, if applicable.

  ◊ Elevate the head of the bed 15.2 to 20.3 cm (6 to 8 in) with blocks. The use of pillows is not recommended, as this rounds the back, bringing the stomach contents up closer to the chest.

Δ   **Medications**

- Encourage consistent appropriate use of prescribed medications:

    ◊   **Antacids**, such as aluminum hydroxide (Mylanta), neutralize excess acid. Antacids should be administered when the acid secretion is highest (1 to 3 hr after eating and at bedtime). Antacids should be separated from other medications by at least 1 hr.

    ◊   **Histamine₂ receptor antagonists**, such as ranitidine (Zantac), famotidine (Pepcid), nizatidine (Axid), and cimetidine (Tagamet), reduce the secretion of acid. The onset is longer than antacids, but the effect has a longer duration.

    ◊   **Proton pump inhibitors (PPI)**, such as pantoprazole (Protonix), omeprazole (Prilosec), esomeprazole (Nexium), and lansoprazole (Prevacid) reduce gastric acid by inhibiting the cellular pump necessary to secrete it. Studies show that PPI are more effective than H_2 antagonists.

    ◊   Medications such as metoclopramide hydrochloride (Reglan), increase the motility of the esophagus and stomach.

Δ   Teach the client not to interchange prescription medications with over-the-counter medications.

Δ   Assess the client's response to medications.

Complications and Nursing Implications

Δ   Risks associated with **aspiration** include:

- Asthma exacerbations from inhaled aerosolized acid.

- Frequent upper respiratory, sinus, or ear infections.

- Aspiration pneumonia.

- Formation of esophageal strictures (scarring).

- Erosive esophagitis, ulceration, and hemorrhage.

- Barrett's epithelium (premalignant) and esophageal adenocarcinoma.

Meeting the Needs of Older Adults

Δ   Incidence of GERD increases with age. The first indications may include esophageal bleeding or respiratory complications (for example, aspiration pneumonia).

Δ   Symptoms may come from expected physiological changes (delayed gastric emptying) related to aging.

Δ   Cimetidine (Tagamet) is no longer first-line because it has a higher risk profile in older adult clients and interacts with more than 60 other medications.

Primary Reference:

Ignatavicius, D. D., & Workman, M. L. (2006). *Medical-surgical nursing* (5th ed.). St. Louis, MO: Saunders.

Additional Resources:

Karlowicz, D. J. (2003, December). An endoscopic approach to GERD? *RN, 66* (12): 56-62.

NANDA International (2004). *NANDA nursing diagnoses: Definitions and classification 2005-2006*. Philadelphia: NANDA.

For more information, visit the Digestive Disease National Coalition at *www.ddnc.org*, the American Gastroenterological Association at *www.gastro.org*, the National Digestive Diseases Information Clearinghouse at *www.niddk.nih.gov/health/digest/nddic.htm*, or the National Heartburn Alliance at *www.heartburnalliance.org*.

Chapter 64: Gastroesophageal Reflux Disease

Application Exercises

Scenario: A 25-year-old woman has been diagnosed with gastroesophageal reflux disease (GERD). The client, who is overweight, has been experiencing dyspepsia, belching, bloating after meals, dysphagia, and chest pain.

1. What pathophysiologic problem is causing this client to experience chest pain?

2. What client education should be provided?

3. What classifications of medications will help to relieve the symptoms of GERD that result from the reflux of gastrointestinal contents containing acid?

4. Identify which of the following factors contribute to decreased lower esophageal sphincter (LES) and the occurrence of GERD. (Check all that apply.)

    _____   Cigarette smoking

    _____   Decaffeinated coffee

    _____   Ice cream with chocolate sauce

    _____   Candy cane

    _____   Diltiazem (Cardizem)

    _____   Cheeseburger and french fries

    _____   Low-fat milk

    _____   Tomato salsa

    _____   Alcohol

    _____   Exercise

    _____   Weight loss

Chapter 64: Gastroesophageal Reflux Disease

Application Exercises Answer Key

Scenario: A 25-year-old woman has been diagnosed with gastroesophageal reflux disease (GERD). The client, who is overweight, has been experiencing dyspepsia, belching, bloating after meals, dysphagia, and chest pain.

1. What pathophysiologic problem is causing this client to experience chest pain?

   Chest pain in clients with GERD is caused by spasms of the esophagus as a result of the reflux of acidic stomach contents and inflammatory response.

2. What client education should be provided?

   The nurse should instruct the client to eat small frequent meals; chew foods thoroughly; avoid evening snacks, fatty foods, chocolate, alcohol, coffee, and tea; and start a weight-loss program. The client should elevate the head of the bed on blocks, and she should avoid elevating her head with pillows. She should also keep a food diary to see what foods trigger symptoms. If the client smokes, she should seek assistance quitting.

3. What classifications of medications will help to relieve the symptoms of GERD that result from the reflux of gastrointestinal contents containing acid?

   Antacids, histamine$_2$ receptor antagonists, and proton pump inhibitors

4. Identify which of the following factors contribute to decreased lower esophageal sphincter (LES) and the occurrence of GERD. (Check all that apply.)

__X__	Cigarette smoking
_____	Decaffeinated coffee
__X__	Ice cream with chocolate sauce
__X__	Candy cane
__X__	Diltiazem (Cardizem)
__X__	Cheeseburger and french fries
_____	Low-fat milk
__X__	Tomato salsa
__X__	Alcohol
_____	Exercise
_____	Weight loss

Unit 7 Nursing Care of Clients with Gastrointestinal Disorders

Section: Nursing Care of Clients with Esophageal Disorders

Chapter 65:   Esophageal Varices

Contributor: Dana Bartlett, MSN, RN, CSPI

⟲ NCLEX-PN® Connections:

Learning Objective: Review and apply knowledge within **"Esophageal Varices"** in readiness for performance of the following nursing activities as outlined by the NCLEX-PN® test plan:

Δ   Assist with relevant laboratory, diagnostic, and therapeutic procedures within the nursing role, including:

   • Preparation of the client for the procedure.

   • Accurate collection of specimens.

   • Monitoring client status during and after the procedure.

   • Reinforcing client teaching (before and following the procedure).

   • Recognizing the client's response (expected, unexpected adverse response) to the procedure.

   • Monitoring results.

   • Monitoring and taking actions to prevent or minimize the risk of complications.

   • Notifying the primary care provider of signs of complications.

Δ   Recognize signs and symptoms of the client's problem and complete the proper documentation.

Δ   Provide and document care based on the client's health alteration.

Δ   Monitor and document vital signs changes.

Δ   Interpret data that need to be reported immediately.

Δ   Reinforce client education on managing the client's health problem.

Δ   Recognize and respond to emergency situations, including notification of the primary care provider.

Δ   Review the client's response to emergency interventions and complete the proper documentation.

Δ   Provide care that meets the age-related needs of clients 65 years of age or older, including recognizing expected physiological changes.

Key Points

Δ   Esophageal varices are **swollen, fragile blood vessels in the esophagus.** Because of **liver damage**, blood flow through the liver is restricted, and it is diverted to other vessels, such as the vessels of the esophagus. The increased blood flow (**portal hypertension**) causes swelling, and varices result.

Δ   Esophageal varices are **often a medical emergency** and are associated with a high mortality rate. Reoccurrence of esophageal bleeding is common.

Δ   **Complications** of esophageal varices include **hypovolemic shock** and complications of anemia.

Key Factors

Δ   **Portal hypertension** is the **primary risk factor** for the development of esophageal varices. Portal hypertension conditions include:

- **Alcoholic cirrhosis.**

- Viral hepatitis.

Therapeutic Procedures and Nursing Interventions

Δ   Treatment of esophageal varices is complex. Several **therapeutic procedures** can be employed, including:

- **Endoscopic** evaluation as the first step. **Ligating bands** can be placed, and/or **injection sclerotherapy** can be performed through an endoscopic procedure. After the procedure, monitor the client's client's vital signs and take measures to prevent aspiration.

- Transjugular intrahepatic **portal-systemic shunt** (TIPS): The client is sedated and a balloon is used to enlarge the portal vein, and a metal stent is used to keep it open.

- Esophagogastric **balloon tamponade**: An esophagogastric tube with balloons is used to **compress blood vessels.** Traction is applied and then gradually released when bleeding is stopped. Check balloons for leaks prior to insertion.

- Gastric **lavage with saline** is performed through a large-bore NG tube. Position the client in a side-lying position. Up to 200 mL of NS is instilled and then suctioned, causing vasoconstriction. The procedure is continued until return is clear.

Assessments

Δ   Monitor for **signs and symptoms** (bleeding esophageal varices).

- **Hematemesis**

- Melena

- **Hypotension**
- Tachycardia

NANDA Nursing Diagnoses

Δ   Risk for deficient fluid volume

Δ   Ineffective tissue perfusion

Nursing Interventions

Δ   Administer a nonselective **beta-blocker**, such as propanolol (Inderal), as prescribed to decrease heart rate and consequently reduce hepatic venous pressure.

Δ   Administer **vasoconstrictors**, such as vasopressin (Desmopressin) and octreotide (Sandostatin), as prescribed to decrease portal inflow.

Δ   If the client is bleeding, establish IV access, monitor vital signs and hematocrit, type and crossmatch for **possible blood transfusions**, and monitor for overt and occult bleeding.

Complications and Nursing Implications

Δ   **Hemorrhage** and **hypovolemic shock** are serious complications of esophageal varices. Observe the client carefully for signs of hemorrhage and shock.

- Monitor vital signs, hemoglobin, and hematocrit.
- Replace losses and employ therapeutic procedures, such as gastric lavage, shunts, and sclerotherapy, to stop/control bleeding.

Meeting the Needs of Older Adults

Δ   Older adult clients frequently have depressed immune function, decreased liver function, and cardiac disorders that make them especially vulnerable to bleeding.

Primary Reference:

Ignatavicius, D. D., & Workman, M. L. (2006). *Medical-surgical nursing* (5th ed.). St. Louis, MO: Saunders.

Additional Resources:

Azer, S. A. (2006, April 12). Esophageal varices. *eMedicine*, Topic 745. Retrieved May 23, 2006, from http://www.emedicine.com/med/topic745.htm.

NANDA International (2004). *NANDA nursing diagnoses: Definitions and classification 2005-2006*. Philadelphia: NANDA.

Chapter 65: Esophageal Varices

Application Exercises

Scenario: A nurse is caring for a client with esophageal varices. The client is hypotensive and confused as to time, place, and person.

1. Why is this client confused?

2. Why is this client hypotensive?

3. What dietary restriction should be ordered for this client and why?

4. Which of the following nursing interventions should be given the highest priority?

> A. Observe the client for signs of hematemesis and melena.
>
> B. Monitor vital signs and hematocrit levels.
>
> C. Administer IV fluids and vasoconstrictors as prescribed.
>
> D. Provide a high-calorie, protein-restricted diet.

Chapter 65: Esophageal Varices

Application Exercises Answer Key

Scenario: A nurse is caring for a client with esophageal varices. The client is hypotensive and confused as to time, place, and person.

1. Why is this client confused?

   Esophageal varices are caused by liver damage. This results in decreased ammonia clearance, which causes confusion.

2. Why is this client hypotensive?

   The hypotension is due to bleeding.

3. What dietary restriction should be ordered for this client and why?

   Ammonia is a breakdown product of protein; therefore, the client should be on a protein-restricted diet.

4. Which of the following nursing interventions should be given the highest priority?

   A. Observe the client for signs of hematemesis and melena.
   B. Monitor vital signs and hematocrit levels.
   C. Administer IV fluids and vasoconstrictors as prescribed.
   D. Provide a high-calorie, protein-restricted diet.

   This client is at risk for hypovolemic shock. Administration of replacement fluids and medications to decrease variceal bleeding are life-saving priorities over ongoing client assessments and nutritional interventions.

Unit 7   **Nursing Care of Clients with Gastrointestinal Disorders**
Section: Nursing Care of Clients with Stomach Disorders

Chapter 66:   Peptic Ulcer Disease

Contributor: Dana Bartlett, MSN, RN, CSPI

◯ NCLEX-PN® Connections:

Learning Objective: Review and apply knowledge within "**Peptic Ulcer Disease**" in readiness for performance of the following nursing activities as outlined by the NCLEX-PN® test plan:

Δ   Assist with relevant laboratory, diagnostic, and therapeutic procedures within the nursing role, including:

- Preparation of the client for the procedure.
- Accurate collection of specimens.
- Monitoring client status during and after the procedure.
- Reinforcing client teaching (before and following the procedure).
- Recognizing the client's response (expected, unexpected adverse response) to the procedure.
- Monitoring results.
- Monitoring and taking actions to prevent or minimize the risk of complications.
- Notifying the primary care provider of signs of complications.

Δ   Recognize signs and symptoms of the client's problem and complete the proper documentation.

Δ   Provide and document care based on the client's health alteration.

Δ   Monitor and document vital signs changes.

Δ   Interpret data that need to be reported immediately.

Δ   Reinforce client education on managing the client's health problem.

Δ   Recognize and respond to emergency situations, including notification of the primary care provider.

Δ   Review the client's response to emergency interventions and complete the proper documentation.

Δ   Provide care that meets the age-related needs of clients 65 years of age or older, including recognizing expected physiological changes.

Key Points

Δ   A **peptic ulcer** is an erosion of the mucosal lining of the stomach or duodenum. **Peptic ulcer disease** (PUD) occurs when the mucosa is eroded to the point at which the epithelium is exposed to gastric acid and pepsin.

Δ   There are **gastric ulcers, duodenal ulcers,** and **stress ulcers** (these occur after major stress or trauma).

Key Factors

Δ   Causes of peptic ulcers include:

- *Helicobacter pylori* **infection.**

- Nonsteroidal anti-inflammatory drug (**NSAID)** use.

- Severe stress.

- Hypersecretory states.

Diagnostic Procedures and Nursing Interventions

Δ   *Helicobacter pylori* testing:

- **Gastric samples** are collected via an endoscopy to test for *Helicobacter pylori*. Several medications (bismuth, misoprostol, sucralfate, histamine$_2$ antagonists) can interfere with testing for *Helicobacter pylori (*false negatives). Therefore, a complete medication history should be collected prior to testing.

- **Urea breath testing** is when the client exhales into a collection container (baseline), drinks carbon-enriched urea solution, and is asked to exhale once again into a collection container. The client should take nothing by mouth prior to the test. If *Helicobacter pylori* is present, the solution will break down and carbon dioxide will be released. The two collections are compared to confirm the presence of *Helicobacter pylori*.

- **IgG serologic testing** documents the presence of *Helicobacter pylori* based on antibody assays.

- **Stool sample** tests for the presence of the *Helicobacter pylori* antigen.

Δ   **Esophagogastroduodenoscopy (EGD)** is the most definitive for diagnosis of peptic ulcers and may be repeated to evaluate treatment effectiveness. Prepare the client for the endoscopic procedure (remove dentures, nothing by mouth), including witnessing the client's signature on the informed consent form. Monitor the client during the procedure. After the procedure, maintain the client's safety and assess return of the client's gag reflex prior to providing fluid/food.

Δ   **Stool sample** for occult blood (risk of PUD).

Assessments

Δ Monitor for **signs and symptoms** of a peptic ulcer.

- **Dyspepsia** – heartburn, bloating, and nausea. May be perceived as uncomfortable fullness or hunger.

- **Pain**

Gastric ulcer	Duodenal ulcer
30 to 60 min after a meal	1.5 to 3 hr after a meal
Rarely occurs at night	Often occurs at night
Pain worsens with food ingestion	Pain relieved by food ingestion

Δ Assess/monitor the client for:

- **Orthostatic changes** in vital signs (20 mm Hg drop in systolic, 10 mm Hg drop in diastolic, and/or tachycardia; these findings are suggestive of gastrointestinal bleeding).

NANDA Nursing Diagnoses

Δ Acute pain or chronic pain

Δ Risk for deficient fluid volume

Δ Disturbed sleep pattern

Nursing Interventions

Δ Administer prescribed medications.

- Most commonly used is **"triple therapy."** This includes:

  ◊ **Bismuth or a Hyposecretory medication** (proton pump inhibitors, histamine$_2$ antagonists, and prostaglandin analogues).

  ◊ Two antibiotics to combat *Helicobacter pylori*: **metronidazole (Flagyl)** along with either **tetracycline, clarithromycin,** or **amoxicillin.**

  ◊ **Antacids** are given 1 to 3 hr after meals to **neutralize gastric acid,** which occurs with food ingestion and at bedtime. Give 1 hr apart from other medications to avoid reducing the absorption of other medications.

  ◊ **Sucralfate (Carafate)** is given 1 hr before meals and at bedtime. Protects healing ulcers. Monitor for side effects of constipation.

△ Assist the client with understanding/compliance with recommended dietary changes:

- Avoiding/limiting substances that increase gastric acid secretion (caffeine, alcohol, and tobacco).

- Avoiding foods that cause discomfort.

- Smaller meals.

Complications and Nursing Implications

△ The nurse should perform periodic assessments of the client's pain and vital signs to detect subtle changes that may indicate perforation or bleeding.

- **Perforation** is severe epigastric pain spreading across the abdomen. The abdomen is rigid, board-like, hyperactive to diminished bowel sounds, and has rebound tenderness.

- **Perforation** is a surgical emergency.

- **Gastrointestinal bleeding** consists of hematemesis, melena, hypotension, tachycardia, dizziness, confusion, and decreased hemoglobin.

△ The nurse should report findings, prepare the client for endoscopic or surgical intervention, replace fluid and blood losses, insert nasogastric tube, provide saline lavages, and maintain the client's blood pressure.

Meeting the Needs of Older Adult Clients

△ Older adult clients may have chronic illnesses and depend on NSAIDs.

△ Older adult clients are less able to compensate for the complications of peptic ulcer disease.

Primary Reference:

Ignatavicius, D. D., & Workman, M. L. (2006). *Medical-surgical nursing* (5th ed.). St. Louis, MO: Saunders.

Additional Resources:

Fantry, G. T. (2005, May 6). Peptic ulcer disease. *eMedicine*, Topic 1776. Retrieved May 22, 2006, from http://www.emedicine.com/med/topic1776.htm.

NANDA International (2004). *NANDA nursing diagnoses: Definitions and classification 2005-2006*. Philadelphia: NANDA.

Chapter 66: Peptic Ulcer Disease

Application Exercises

1. List the two most common causes of peptic ulcer disease.

2. List two signs and/or symptoms of peptic ulcer disease.

3. List two tests that can be performed to check for *Helicobacter pylori*.

4. List two antibiotics that can be used to treat peptic ulcer disease.

5. List two complications of peptic ulcer disease.

6. List two differences in the pattern of pain between a gastric ulcer and a duodenal ulcer.

7. How would a nurse determine whether or not a client has gastrointestinal bleeding?

8. How would a nurse determine whether or not a client has suffered a perforation?

9. A nurse is caring for a client diagnosed with a duodenal ulcer. Why are antibiotics prescribed for this client?

10. What is the rationale behind the "triple therapy" approach to the treatment of peptic ulcer disease?

Chapter 66: Peptic Ulcer Disease

Application Exercises Answer Key

1. List the two most common causes of peptic ulcer disease.

   Helicobacter pylori **infection and nonsteroidal anti-inflammatory medication use**

2. List two signs and/or symptoms of peptic ulcer disease.

   Abdominal pain, dyspepsia, nausea, vomiting, heartburn, guaiac positive stool, and melena

3. List two tests that can be performed to check for *Helicobacter pylori*.

   Gastric samples, urea breath testing, and IgG serologic testing

4. List two antibiotics that can be used to treat peptic ulcer disease.

   Metronidazole (Flagyl), clarithromycin, tetracycline, and amoxicillin

5. List two complications of peptic ulcer disease.

   Perforation, gastrointestinal bleeding, pyloric obstruction, and intractable disease

6. List two differences in the pattern of pain between a gastric ulcer and a duodenal ulcer.

   The pain of a gastric ulcer begins 30 to 60 min after a meal and does not occur at night. The pain of a duodenal ulcer begins 90 min to 3 hr after a meal and often occurs at night.

7. How would a nurse determine whether or not a client has gastrointestinal bleeding?

Assess the character, location, and severity of the client's pain. Also, monitor the client's orthostatic vital signs and collect a stool for testing.

8. How would a nurse determine whether or not a client has suffered a perforation?

Carefully assess the pain to determine if it differs in character and severity from the pain the client normally experiences. Check the client's temperature and orthostatic vital signs.

9. A nurse is caring for a client diagnosed with a duodenal ulcer. Why are antibiotics prescribed for this client?

Infection with the bacteria *Helicobacter pylori* is the most common cause of peptic ulcer disease.

10. What is the rationale behind the "triple therapy" approach to the treatment of peptic ulcer disease?

The "triple therapy" approach directly protects the gastric mucosa from acid (antacids), decreases the secretion of acids, (histamine$_2$ antagonists, prostaglandin analogues, and proton pump inhibitors) and kills the bacteria that causes peptic ulcer disease (antibiotics).

Unit 7
Section:

Nursing Care of Clients with Gastrointestinal Disorders
Nursing Care of Clients with Stomach Disorders

Chapter 67:   Gastric Surgery and Dumping Syndrome
Contributor: Jeanne Wissmann, PhD, RN, CNE

↻ NCLEX-PN® Connections:

Learning Objective: Review and apply knowledge within "**Gastric Surgery and Dumping Syndrome**" in readiness for performance of the following nursing activities as outlined by the NCLEX-PN® test plan:

Δ   Assist with relevant laboratory, diagnostic, and therapeutic procedures within the nursing role, including:

- Preparation of the client for the procedure.
- Accurate collection of specimens.
- Monitoring client status during and after the procedure.
- Reinforcing client teaching (before and following the procedure).
- Recognizing the client's response (expected, unexpected adverse response) to the procedure.
- Monitoring results.
- Monitoring and taking actions to prevent or minimize the risk of complications.
- Notifying the primary care provider of signs of complications.

Δ   Recognize signs and symptoms of the client's problem and complete the proper documentation.

Δ   Provide and document care based on the client's health alteration.

Δ   Monitor and document vital signs changes.

Δ   Interpret data that need to be reported immediately.

Δ   Reinforce client education on managing the client's health problem.

Δ   Recognize and respond to emergency situations, including notification of the primary care provider.

Δ   Review the client's response to emergency interventions and complete the proper documentation.

Δ   Provide care that meets the age-related needs of clients 65 years of age or older, including recognizing expected physiological changes.

Gastric Surgery

 Key Points

Δ   Gastric surgeries, include:

- **Gastrectomy** – All or part of the stomach is removed. This surgery may be performed with laparoscopy or open surgery.

- **Antrectomy** – An antrum portion of the stomach is removed.

- **Gastrojejunostomy (Billroth II procedure)** – The lower portion of the stomach is excised and the remaining stomach is anastomosed to the jejunum and the remaining duodenum is surgically closed.

- **Vagotomy** – The branches of the vagus nerve that supply the stomach are cut to disrupt acid production.

- **Pyloroplasty** – The opening between the stomach and small intestine is enlarged to increase the rate of gastric emptying.

Key Factors

Δ   **Indications** for gastric surgery include:

- Ineffective management of **peptic ulcer disease.**

- Emergency surgical intervention for **perforation** and hemorrhage.

- Surgical removal/reduction of **gastric cancer.**

Diagnostic Procedures and Nursing Interventions

Δ   To **biopsy** and/or to **visualize the location** of cancer or ulceration preoperatively:

- **Endoscopy** or **laparoscopy:**

  ◊   Prepare the client for the procedure (for example, nothing by mouth).

  ◊   Maintain client safety following the procedure (for example, assess the client's gag reflex).

  ◊   Gas pains may occur with laparoscopy and are improved with ambulation.

- **Computerized tomography (CT) scans:**

  ◊   Assess the client's allergies to iodine.

  ◊   Prepare the client for the procedure (for example, nothing by mouth).

  ◊   Monitor elimination following the procedure.

Assessments

Δ   Postoperatively, assess:

- Vital signs.

- **Respiratory status** – breath sounds and chest movement.

- **Bowel sounds** – diminished or absent with surgery and anesthesia. Monitor for return (3 to 5 per quadrant/min).

- Intake and output.

- Pain levels.

- If a **nasogastric tube** is present:

  ◊   **Patency** of nasogastric tube (avoid abdominal distention).

  ◊   **Nasogastric secretions** (a scant amount of blood is expected in first 12 to 24 hr).

NANDA Nursing Diagnoses

Δ   Acute pain

Δ   Imbalanced nutrition: Less than body requirements

Δ   Risk for infection

Nursing Interventions

Δ   Place the client in a **semi-Fowler's** position to facilitate respiratory movements.

Δ   Encourage the client to **turn, cough, deep breathe**, and to use an incentive spirometer.

Δ   Monitor the client's nasogastric output as appropriate and intervene to avoid **abdominal distention**. Notify the surgeon before repositioning or irrigating the nasogastric tube (disruption of sutures).

Δ   Follow guidelines for reintroduction of fluids and foods. Healing of sutures is enhanced by nothing by mouth status. Generally, resumption of enteral intake begins with clear liquids and the client's diet is advanced as tolerated. Abdominal distention is avoided.

Δ   Effectively treat the client's pain.

Δ   Educate the client regarding the need for vitamin and mineral supplementation after a gastrectomy, including vitamin B_{12}, vitamin D, calcium, iron, and folate.

Complications and Nursing Implications

Δ **Pernicious anemia** is due to deficiency of intrinsic factor normally secreted by the gastric mucosa.

- Symptoms include:
    - ◊ Pallor.
    - ◊ Glossitis.
    - ◊ Fatigue.
    - ◊ Paresthesias.
- Routine lifelong vitamin B_{12} injections will prevent this complication.

Δ **Dumping Syndrome** *(see next section)*

Dumping Syndrome

Key Points

Δ Dumping syndrome consists of **vasomotor** symptoms that occur in response to food ingestion.

Δ Symptoms result from the **rapid emptying** of gastric contents into the small intestine. In response to the sudden influx of a hypertonic fluid, the small intestine pulls fluid from the extracellular space to convert the hypertonic fluid to an isotonic fluid. This fluid shift causes a **decrease in circulating volume**, resulting in vasomotor symptoms.

Key Factors

Δ **Gastric surgery**, especially **gastrojejunostomy (Billroth II)**, poses the greatest risk for dumping syndrome. Following gastric surgery, the reduced stomach has less ability to control the amount and rate of chyme that enters the small intestine after a meal.

Assessments

Δ Monitor for **vasomotor** symptoms:

	Early symptoms	Late symptoms
Onset	Within 30 min after eating	90 min to 3 hr after eating
Cause	Rapid emptying	Excessive insulin release
Symptoms	• Vertigo, syncope, pallor • Diaphoresis • Tachycardia • Palpitations	• Abdominal distention and cramping, borborygmi, nausea • Dizziness, diaphoresis, confusion

NANDA Nursing Diagnoses

Δ   Imbalanced nutrition: Less than body requirements

Δ   Risk for injury

Nursing Interventions

Δ   Instruct the client that **lying down after a meal** will slow the movement of food within the intestines.

Δ   Assist/instruct the client to lie down when vasomotor symptoms occur.

Δ   Provide client education.

- Limit the amount of fluid ingested at one time.

- **Eliminate liquids with meals** and for 1 hr prior to and following a meal.

- Consume a high-protein, high-fat, and a low- to moderate-carbohydrate diet.

- **Avoid milk, sweets, or sugars** (for example, fruit juice, sweetened fruit, milk shakes, honey, syrup, jelly).

- Small, frequent meals rather than large meals.

Δ   Administer medications as prescribed:

- Administration of powered pectin or octreotide (Sandostatin) subcutaneously may be prescribed if symptoms are severe and not effectively controlled with dietary measures. Pectin slows the absorption of carbohydrates. Octreotide blocks gastric and pancreatic hormones, which factor into dumping syndrome symptoms.

- **Antispasmodic medications**, such as dicyclomine (Bentyl).

Complications and Nursing Implications

Δ   Malnutrition and fluid electrolyte imbalances can occur due to altered absorption. Monitor intake and output, laboratory values, and the client's weight.

Δ   **Postprandial hypoglycemia** can occur due to excessive insulin release. Monitor for signs of hypoglycemia (shakiness, tachycardia, anxiousness, diaphoresis, hunger). Provide the client with a carbohydrate source.

Primary Reference:

Ignatavicius, D. D., & Workman, M. L. (2006). *Medical-surgical nursing* (5th ed.). St. Louis, MO: Saunders.

Additional Resources:

NANDA International (2004). *NANDA nursing diagnoses: Definitions and classification 2005-2006*. Philadelphia: NANDA.

Chapter 67: Gastric Surgery and Dumping Syndrome

Application Exercises

Scenario: A 44-year-old female client is first-day postoperative after a subtotal gastrectomy for stomach cancer. Her vital signs are stable and she has been up to the side of the bed one time. She has a nasogastric tube in place, which is connected to low intermittent suction.

1. What assessments should the nurse make when evaluating the client's nasogastric suction?

2. What potential problem is the client at risk for when she begins to consume food and fluids? What can be done to prevent it?

3. The client is ready to be discharged home. What problems or symptoms will the nurse teach the client to recognize and report?

Scenario: A 45-year-old client with peptic ulcer disease has undergone a Billroth II surgical procedure. After being discharged home, the client develops dumping syndrome. During her first postoperative visit to the clinic the client, reports that she experiences weakness, diaphoresis, tachycardia, faintness, and abdominal distention 15 to 30 min after every meal. The client also mentions that 2 or 3 hr after eating she experiences symptoms of a hypoglycemic reaction: sweating, mental confusion, anxiety, weakness, and tachycardia. The nurse provides the client with a teaching guide that lists dietary regulations and restrictions for people diagnosed with dumping syndrome. The nurse also advises the client to lie down following meals.

4. What causes the early manifestations of dumping syndrome?

5. How does the client benefit from eating a high-fat, high-protein, low-carbohydrate diet?

6. Why is it suggested that clients diagnosed with dumping syndrome lie down after a meal?

7. Why does post prandial hypoglycemia occur 2 to 3 hr after eating in clients with dumping syndrome?

8. Identify which of the following should be avoided by clients with dumping syndrome. (Check all that apply.)

_____ Soup
_____ Cinnamon roll with icing
_____ Sweetened orange juice
_____ Pancakes and syrup
_____ White bread and diet jelly
_____ Cooked carrots with butter sauce
_____ Toasted cheese sandwich
_____ Cup of coffee
_____ Glass of water

Chapter 67: Gastric Surgery and Dumping Syndrome

Application Exercises Answer Key

Scenario: A 44-year-old female client is first-day postoperative after a subtotal gastrectomy for stomach cancer. Her vital signs are stable and she has been up to the side of the bed one time. She has a nasogastric tube in place, which is connected to low intermittent suction.

1. What assessments should the nurse make when evaluating the client's nasogastric suction?

   Check the client's nasogastric tube for patency and proper functioning of the suction apparatus. The amount of suction should be verified to make certain that too much suction is not being exerted on the gastric suture line internally.

   Assess the character and amount of drainage postoperatively. It may contain some blood for the first 12 to 24 hr but should otherwise be a greenish-yellow color.

   The client's nares should be assessed for signs of ischemia.

   Assess the client for increased abdominal distention or discomfort and report any abnormal assessment findings to the primary care provider.

2. What potential problem is the client at risk for when she begins to consume food and fluids? What can be done to prevent it?

   The client is at risk for dumping syndrome, a condition of weakness and sweating following eating related to rapid emptying of the stomach. Dumping syndrome may be relieved by eating small, frequent meals without fluids and by lying down after eating to slow the movement of food through the alimentary canal.

3. The client is ready to be discharged home. What problems or symptoms will the nurse teach the client to recognize and report?

   Instruct the client to report:

   An increase in abdominal pain or abdominal distention.

   Any signs of incisional site infection (redness, swelling, warmth, tenderness, purulent drainage, fever).

   Nausea or vomiting.

   Any symptoms related to dumping syndrome (sensations of fullness, weakness, faintness, dizziness, palpitations, diaphoresis, cramping pains, excessive diarrhea).

Scenario: A 45-year-old client with peptic ulcer disease has undergone a Billroth II surgical procedure. After being discharged home, the client develops dumping syndrome. During her first postoperative visit to the clinic, the client reports that she experiences weakness, diaphoresis, tachycardia, faintness, and abdominal distention 15 to 30 min after every meal. The client also mentions that 2 or 3 hr after eating she experiences symptoms of a hypoglycemic reaction: sweating, mental confusion, anxiety, weakness, and tachycardia. The nurse provides the client with a teaching guide that lists dietary regulations and restrictions for people diagnosed with dumping syndrome. The nurse also advises the client to lie down following meals.

4. What causes the early manifestations of dumping syndrome?

Early manifestations of dumping syndrome are caused by the decreased capacity of the stomach to control the amount of gastric chyme that enters the small intestine after a meal. The smaller stomach capacity allows an abnormally large bolus of hypertonic fluid to rapidly enter the intestine. As a result, the intestine pulls fluid from the extracellular space to convert the hypertonic fluid to an isotonic fluid. This fluid shift causes a decrease in circulating blood volume, manifested by weakness and faintness. Abdominal distention results from distention of the jejunum with food and fluid.

5. How does the client benefit from eating a high-fat, high-protein, low-carbohydrate diet?

A high-fat, high-protein, low-carbohydrate diet is beneficial because proteins and fats help to rebuild body tissues and meet energy needs. Concentrated carbohydrates such as honey, jelly, and jam cause dizziness, diarrhea, and abdominal distention. Carbohydrates also empty sooner, possibly increasing the symptoms of dumping syndrome. Thus, a low- to moderate-carbohydrate diet will reduce the likelihood of dumping syndrome symptoms.

6. Why is it suggested that clients diagnosed with dumping syndrome lie down after a meal?

Lying down after eating slows the movement of food through the gastrointestinal tract, which decreases symptoms.

7. Why does post prandial hypoglycemia occur 2 to 3 hr after eating in clients with dumping syndrome?

Post prandial hypoglycemia occurs 2 to 3 hr after eating in clients with dumping syndrome because the sudden entry of a bolus of high-carbohydrate fluid into the small intestine causes the release of large amounts of insulin into the circulation. This insulin lowers blood glucose, leading to hypoglycemia.

8. Identify which of the following should be avoided by clients with dumping syndrome. (Check all that apply.)

X	Soup
X	Cinnamon roll with icing
X	Sweetened orange juice
X	Pancakes and syrup
___	White bread and diet jelly
___	Cooked carrots with butter sauce
___	Toasted cheese sandwich
X	Cup of coffee
X	Glass of water

The client should avoid soup, because liquids should not be consumed with meals. Coffee and water can be consumed, but not with meals and not 1 hr prior to or following a meal. A cinnamon roll, sweetened orange juice, and pancakes with syrup are all sweets and should be avoided.

Unit 7   Nursing Care of Clients with Gastrointestinal Disorders

Section: Nursing Care of Clients with Intestinal Disorders

Chapter 68:   **Constipation and Diarrhea**
               Contributor: Dana Bartlett, MSN, RN, CSPI

↻ **NCLEX-PN® Connections:**

> **Learning Objective:** Review and apply knowledge within **"Constipation and Diarrhea"** in readiness for performance of the following nursing activities as outlined by the NCLEX-PN® test plan:
>
> Δ   Assist with relevant laboratory, diagnostic, and therapeutic procedures within the nursing role, including:
>
> - Preparation of the client for the procedure.
> - Accurate collection of specimens.
> - Monitoring client status during and after the procedure.
> - Reinforcing client teaching (before and following the procedure).
> - Recognizing the client's response (expected, unexpected adverse response) to the procedure.
> - Monitoring results.
> - Monitoring and taking actions to prevent or minimize the risk of complications.
> - Notifying the primary care provider of signs of complications.
>
> Δ   Recognize signs and symptoms of the client's problem and complete the proper documentation.
>
> Δ   Provide and document care based on the client's health alteration.
>
> Δ   Monitor and document vital signs changes.
>
> Δ   Interpret data that need to be reported immediately.
>
> Δ   Reinforce client education on managing the client's health problem.
>
> Δ   Recognize and respond to emergency situations, including notification of the primary care provider.
>
> Δ   Review the client's response to emergency interventions and complete the proper documentation.
>
> Δ   Provide care that meets the age-related needs of clients 65 years of age or older, including recognizing expected physiological changes.

Key Points

- Δ **Constipation** is defined as bowel movements that are infrequent, hard or dry, and difficult to pass.

- Δ **Diarrhea** is defined as an increased number of loose, liquid stools.

- Δ There are objective ways to assess for the presence of constipation or diarrhea, but **individual bowel patterns vary greatly**.

- Δ For healthy clients, constipation and diarrhea are not serious. But for older adult clients or clients with pre-existing health problems, constipation or diarrhea can be serious.

Key Factors

- Δ **Causes of constipation** include:
  - Frequent use of laxatives.
  - Advanced age.
  - Inadequate fluid intake.
  - Inadequate fiber intake.
  - Immobilization due to injury.
  - A sedentary lifestyle.

- Δ **Causes of diarrhea** include:
  - Viral gastroenteritis.
  - Overuse of laxatives.
  - Use of certain antibiotics.
  - Inflammatory bowel disease.
  - Irritable bowel syndrome.
  - Food-borne pathogens.

Diagnostic Procedures and Nursing Interventions

- Δ **Fecal occult blood test** – a fecal sample is obtained using a medical aseptic technique and wearing disposable gloves. Perform a Hemoccult® slide test and record results. Certain foods (red meat, raw vegetables) and medications (aspirin, NSAIDs) can cause false positives. Bleeding can be a sign of cancer, which can be a contributing factor to constipation.

Δ **Digital rectal exam** checks for **impaction**. The client should be positioned on the left side with knees flexed. A lubricated index finger should be gently inserted into the rectal wall. During the procedure the client's vital signs and response should be monitored.

Δ Obtaining **stool cultures** is done by obtaining a fecal sample using a medical aseptic technique and wearing disposable gloves. The specimen should be labeled and promptly sent to the laboratory. Intestinal bacteria can be a contributing factor to diarrhea.

Assessments

Δ Monitor for **signs and symptoms** of constipation.

- Abdominal bloating

- Abdominal cramping

- Straining at defecation

Δ Monitor for **signs and symptoms** of diarrhea.

- Signs and symptoms of dehydration

- Frequent loose stools

- Abdominal cramping

Δ **Nursing assessments** should include:

- A physical examination of the abdomen (bowel sounds and tenderness).

- Assessment for signs and symptoms of fluid deficit.

- Assessment of the skin integrity around the anal area.

- Collection of a detailed history of the client's diet, exercise, and bowel habits.

NANDA Nursing Diagnoses

Δ Constipation

Δ Diarrhea

Δ Fluid volume deficit

Δ Impaired skin integrity

Nursing Interventions

- Δ Closely monitor the client's fluid status. Maintain a strict record of intake and output.

- Δ Monitor the client for signs and symptoms of dehydration (for example, postural hypotension, dizziness when changing positions).

- Δ Closely monitor the client's elimination pattern.

- Δ Observe and document the character of the client's bowel movements.

- Δ Carefully check for blood or pus. If the client is experiencing diarrhea, measure the volume of the stools.

- Δ Perform an abdominal assessment daily and as needed.

- Δ Administer laxatives and/or enemas as prescribed.

- Δ Encourage the client to engage in adequate fluid intake (especially water intake), adequate fiber intake, and exercise within reason.

- Δ Monitor the client's skin integrity.

- Δ Suggest that clients who are taking antibiotics eat yogurt to help re-establish an intestinal balance of beneficial bacteria.

Complications and Nursing Implications

- Δ Complications of **constipation** include:

  - • Fecal impaction.

  - • Development of hemorrhoids or rectal fissure.

  - • Bradycardia, hypotension, and syncope associated with the Valsalva maneuver (occurs with straining/bearing down).

  - • Monitoring constipation carefully. Instruct clients not to strain to have bowel movements. Take measures to effectively treat and prevent constipation.

  - • Removing a fecal impaction entails positioning the client on the left side with knees flexed, gently inserting a lubricated gloved index finger slowly along the inside of the rectal wall. Break apart the impact and remove small amounts slowly. Monitor the client's vital signs and response. Removing the impaction is frequently preceded by administration of a glycerin or bisacodyl (Dulcolax).

Δ   Complications of **diarrhea** include:

- Signs and symptoms of dehydration and fluid and electrolyte disturbances (for example, metabolic acidosis caused by excessive loss of bicarbonate).

- Skin breakdown around the anal area.

- Replace losses as prescribed. Monitor the client's skin breakdown carefully and follow skin care protocols.

Meeting the Needs of Older Adults

Δ   Older adult clients are more susceptible to developing constipation as bowel tone decreases with age, and they are more at risk for developing fecal impaction.

Δ   Adequate fluid and fiber intake and exercise are very important.

Δ   Older adult clients are less able to compensate for fluid lost due to diarrhea.

Primary Reference:

Ignatavicius, D. D., & Workman, M. L. (2006). *Medical-surgical nursing* (5th ed.). St. Louis, MO: Saunders.

Additional Resources:

Basson, M. D. (2006). Constipation. *eMedicine*, Topic 2833. Retrieved May 22, 2006, from http://www.emedicine.com/med/topic2833.htm.

NANDA International (2004). *NANDA nursing diagnoses: Definitions and classification 2005-2006*. Philadelphia: NANDA.

Chapter 68: Constipation and Diarrhea

Application Exercises

Scenario: A nurse is caring for a client who is chronically constipated.

1. What are three causes of constipation?

2. What are some therapeutic interventions for constipation?

3. What client teaching should be done by the nurse?

Scenario: A nurse is caring for a client who is having profuse diarrhea.

4. What are three causes of diarrhea?

5. What are clinical signs of dehydration that may be observed in a client with diarrhea?

6. What nursing interventions are appropriate for this situation?

7. What client teaching is appropriate for this situation?

8. Identify which of the following food choices are appropriate for a client instructed to increase dietary fiber. (Check all that apply.)

_____ Bran cereal

_____ Fresh pear

_____ Chicken

_____ Frozen spinach

_____ Yogurt

_____ Orange

_____ White toast

_____ Baked potato

Chapter 68: Constipation and Diarrhea

Application Exercises Answer Key

Scenario: A nurse is caring for a client who is chronically constipated.

1. What are three causes of constipation?

    Causes of constipation include age, overuse of laxatives, a diet low in fiber and fluids, immobilization, and sedentary lifestyle.

2. What are some therapeutic interventions for constipation?

    Therapeutic interventions could include increasing fluid and fiber intake, enemas, and laxatives.

3. What client teaching should be done by the nurse?

    Nurses should instruct/encourage the client to exercise, increase fluid and fiber intake, and avoid straining when defecating.

Scenario: A nurse is caring for a client who is having profuse diarrhea.

4. What are three causes of diarrhea?

    Diarrhea can be caused by viral gastroenteritis, food-borne pathogens, inflammatory bowel disease, irritable bowel syndrome, and the overuse of laxatives.

5. What are clinical signs of dehydration that may be observed in a client with diarrhea?

Clinical signs include: Orthostatic vital sign changes (tachycardia and hypotension), weight loss, lethargy, decreased urine output, poor skin turgor, and fever.

6. What nursing interventions are appropriate for this situation?

Nursing interventions include: maintaining a strict record of intake and output, monitoring for signs and symptoms of dehydration, and maintaining the skin integrity of the perineal area.

7. What client teaching is appropriate for this situation?

The client should be instructed to maintain an adequate fluid intake, observe for any blood or pus in bowel movements, and report signs and symptoms of dehydration.

8. Identify which of the following food choices are appropriate for a client instructed to increase dietary fiber. (Check all that apply.)

__X__	Bran cereal
__X__	Fresh pear
_____	Chicken
__X__	Frozen spinach
_____	Yogurt
__X__	Orange
_____	White toast
__X__	Baked potato

Unit 7

Section:

Nursing Care of Clients with Gastrointestinal Disorders

Nursing Care of Clients with Intestinal Disorders

Chapter 69:   **Intestinal Obstruction**

Contributor: Polly Gerber Zimmermann, MSN, MBA, RN, CEN

NCLEX-PN® Connections:

Learning Objective: Review and apply knowledge within "**Intestinal Obstruction**" in readiness for performance of the following nursing activities as outlined by the NCLEX-PN® test plan:

Δ   Assist with relevant laboratory, diagnostic, and therapeutic procedures within the nursing role, including:

- Preparation of the client for the procedure.

- Accurate collection of specimens.

- Monitoring client status during and after the procedure.

- Reinforcing client teaching (before and following the procedure).

- Recognizing the client's response (expected, unexpected adverse response) to the procedure.

- Monitoring results.

- Monitoring and taking actions to prevent or minimize the risk of complications.

- Notifying the primary care provider of signs of complications.

Δ   Recognize signs and symptoms of the client's problem and complete the proper documentation.

Δ   Provide and document care based on the client's health alteration.

Δ   Monitor and document vital signs changes.

Δ   Interpret data that need to be reported immediately.

Δ   Reinforce client education on managing the client's health problem.

Δ   Recognize and respond to emergency situations, including notification of the primary care provider.

Δ   Review the client's response to emergency interventions and complete the proper documentation.

Δ   Provide care that meets the age-related needs of clients 65 years of age or older, including recognizing expected physiological changes.

📖 Key Points

Δ   Intestinal obstruction can result from mechanical or nonmechanical causes. Mechanical obstruction usually requires surgery.

Δ   Symptoms vary according to location.

- **Higher-level obstructions** have colicky, intermittent pain and profuse vomiting.

- **Lower-level obstructions** tend to have vague, diffused, constant pain and significant abdominal distention.

Δ   **Bowel sounds** will be hyperactive above obstruction and hypoactive below.

Δ   Obstructions of the small intestine are the most common.

Δ   **Treatment** focuses on fluid and electrolyte balance, decompressing the bowel, and relief/removal of the obstruction.

Key Factors

Δ   **Mechanical obstructions** (90% of all obstructions) are the result of:

- Encirclement or compression of intestine by adhesions, tumors, fibrosis (for example, endometriosis), or strictures (for example, Crohn's disease, radiation).

- Twisting (**volvulus**) or telescoping (**intussusception**) of bowel segments.

- Fecal impactions.

Δ   Post-surgical adhesions are the most common cause of small bowel obstructions.

Δ   Carcinomas are the most common cause of large intestine obstructions.

Δ   **Nonmechanical obstructions** (**paralytic ileus**) are the result of **decreased peristalsis** from:

- Neurogenic disorders (for example, manipulation of bowel during major surgery and spinal fracture).

- Vascular disorders (for example, vascular insufficiency and mesenteric emboli).

- Electrolyte imbalances (for example, hypokalemia).

- Inflammatory responses (for example, peritonitis or sepsis).

Diagnostic Procedures and Nursing Interventions

Δ   Complete blood count may reveal signs of dehydration (for example, elevated hemoglobin and hematocrit) and elevated white blood cell count with bowel strangulation.

Δ   Acid-base balance assessment: Metabolic alkalosis with high obstruction of the small bowel and metabolic acidosis with low obstruction of the large intestine.

Δ   Electrolytes: Hypokalemia related to losses.

Δ   X-ray: Flat plate and upright abdominal x-rays looking for free air and gas patterns.

Δ   Endoscopy or barium enema: Investigates cause of obstruction. Prepare the client for the procedure and monitor the client's safety following the procedure (for example, assess the client's gag reflex, monitor for the excretion of barium).

Δ   Computed tomography scan: Identifies the cause and exact location of the obstruction.

Assessments

Δ   Symptoms vary depending on the location of the obstruction.

Small bowel and large intestine obstructions	Small bowel obstructions	Large intestine obstructions
Obstipation – the inability to pass a stool and/or flatus for more than 8 hr despite feeling the need to defecate	Pain is spasmodic and colicky.	Pain is diffuse and constant.
Abdominal distension	Visible peristaltic waves	Significant abdominal distension
High-pitched bowel sounds before site of obstruction with hypoactive bowel sounds after, or overall hypoactive; absent bowel sounds later in process	Profuse, (projectile) sudden vomiting with feculent odor; vomiting relieves pain	Infrequent vomiting; the client can have diarrhea around an impaction.

Nursing Interventions

Δ   **Nonmechanical**

• Nothing by mouth with bowel rest

• Nasogastric tube to decompress the bowel

◊ Possibly a nasointestinal (mercury-weighted tip) tube (for example, Cantor or Miller-Abbott) for a small bowel obstruction

◊   Maintain tube patency with irrigation.

◊   Maintain good mouth care.

- Intravenous fluid and electrolyte replacement (particularly potassium)

  ◊   Gastric output is considered part of the client's total output.

- Pain management once diagnosis is made

- Ambulation

Δ   **Mechanical**

- Prepare the client for surgery and provide postoperative nursing care.

- Withhold intake until peristalsis resumes.

Complications and Nursing Implications

Δ   Dehydration (potential hypotension; small bowel obstruction)

- Assess the client's hydration through hematocrit, BUN, orthostatic vital signs, rising pulse, skin turgor/mucous membranes, urine output, and specific gravity.

Δ   Electrolyte Imbalance (small bowel obstruction)

- Monitor the client's potassium levels.

Δ   Perforation

- Monitor the client for pain that is localized, relieved, and then diffused; shoulder tip pain; signs and symptoms of acute infection; and abdomen tender with rebound tenderness.

Δ   Ischemic or Strangulated Bowel

- Monitor the client for compromised blood flow to bowel.

Δ   Peritonitis

- Monitor the client for signs and symptoms of infection, rigid abdomen, and rebound tenderness.

Δ   Shock (hypovolemic from third-spacing and septic)

- Monitor the client for rising pulse and lower blood pressure.

Δ   Metabolic Alkalosis (from higher level obstruction from loss of gastric hydrochloride and vomiting)

- Monitor the client for hypoventilation from compensatory action by the lungs, confusion, tingling of fingers and toes, and obtain arterial blood gas.

Δ   Metabolic Acidosis (from lower level obstruction as alkaline fluids not reabsorbed)

- Monitor the client for deep, rapid respirations (compensatory action by the lungs), confusion, hypotension, and flushed skin.

- Obtain ABG.

Meeting the Needs of Older Adults

Δ   Diverticulitis and tumors are common causes of obstruction in older adult clients.

Δ   Older adult clients are at greater risk for fecal impactions. Bowel regimens can be effective in preventing impactions.

Primary Reference:

Ignatavicius, D. D., & Workman, M. L. (2006). *Medical-surgical nursing* (5th ed.). St. Louis, MO: Saunders.

Additional Resources:

Lewis, S., Heitkemper, M., & Dirksen, S. (2004). *Medical-surgical nursing: Assessment and management of clinical problems* (6th ed.). St. Louis, MO: Mosby.

NANDA International (2004). *NANDA nursing diagnoses: Definitions and classification 2005-2006*. Philadelphia: NANDA.

For more information about intestinal obstruction, visit the American Gastroenterological Association at *www.gastro.org*, or the American Society for Gastrointestinal Endoscopy (ASGE) at *www.asge.org*.

Chapter 69: Intestinal Obstruction

Application Exercises

1. A client admitted to the hospital is diagnosed with a small bowel obstruction. The nurse should validate that the primary care provider is aware of which of the following findings? (Check all that apply.)

_____ The client reports spasms of abdominal pain rated at a "7."

_____ The client has a profuse emesis prior to insertion of the nasogastric tube.

_____ The client's urine specific gravity reading is 1.040, and hematocrit is 60%.

_____ The client's serum potassium level is 3.0 mEq/L.

_____ The client's oral temperature is 38.5° C (99.5° F) and white blood cell count is 10,000 mm³.

2. Which of the following findings are not expected for a client with a tumor obstruction in the descending colon? (Check all that apply.)

_____ Deep, rapid respirations.

_____ Pain that occurs in waves and is rated at "8."

_____ Hyperactive bowel sounds on the right side of the abdomen and hypoactive on the left.

_____ Abdominal distention with tympany upon percussion.

_____ Small amounts of liquid stool.

3. A client is admitted for a small bowel obstruction, and a nasogastric tube (NGT) is inserted as part of the treatment plan. Which of the following are appropriate actions for the nurse to take in managing this client's care? (Check all that apply.)

_____ Include the NGT drainage amount as part of the client's output.

_____ Irrigate the NGT with 20 cc normal saline every 2 hr.

_____ Assess the client's bowel sounds.

_____ Provide the client with oral care.

_____ Clamp the NGT while the client ambulates to the bathroom.

4. A client is admitted with a large intestine toxic megacolon. Which of the following client findings is most important for the nurse to follow up on first?

> A. The client reports shoulder tip pain and abdominal pain that was intense but is now relieved without an analgesic.
>
> B. No bowel sounds are auscultated and the client has obstipation.
>
> C. The client's morning laboratory results are: potassium 3.5 mEq/L, sodium 135 mg/dL, and BUN 20 mg/dL.
>
> D. The client's vital signs are: lying – blood pressure 128/88 mm Hg, pulse 100 beats/min; standing – blood pressure 120/80 mm Hg, pulse 110 beats/min.

5. A client is admitted with a small bowel obstruction from adhesions. Which of the following is **NOT** an expected client assessment with this diagnosis?

> A. The vomitus is more than 500 cc and has a fecal odor.
>
> B. The client's abdominal pain is persistent and colicky.
>
> C. The client states the pain is improved after vomiting.
>
> D. The client's abdomen is firm, rigid, and has positive rebound tenderness.

6. An 80-year-old client is a long-term resident in a nursing home. Which of the following would be most important for the nurse to consider in determining if the client has a stool impaction causing a large intestine obstruction?

> A. The client states he had a bowel movement yesterday.
>
> B. The client has small amounts of liquid stool.
>
> C. The client has a slightly distended abdomen and is flatulent.
>
> D. The client indicates he vomited once this morning.

Chapter 69: Intestinal Obstruction

Application Exercises Answer Key

1. A client admitted to the hospital is diagnosed with a small bowel obstruction. The nurse should validate that the primary care provider is aware of which of the following findings? (Check all that apply.)

_____ The client reports spasms of abdominal pain rated at a "7."

_____ The client has a profuse emesis prior to insertion of the nasogastric tube.

__x__ The client's urine specific gravity reading is 1.040, and hematocrit is 60%.

__x__ The client's serum potassium level is 3.0 mEq/L.

_____ The client's oral temperature is 38.5° C (99.5° F) and white blood cell count is 10,000 mm³.

The client's results indicate significant dehydration and a need for aggressive treatment. The client is hypokalemic and needs an intravenous potassium replacement. Choices one and two are normal expectations for this diagnosis. The last choice mentions the client's temperature and white blood cell count being within normal range. Any mild elevation could be a result of stress and is not indicative of an acute infection.

2. Which of the following findings are not expected for a client with a tumor obstruction in the descending colon? (Check all that apply.)

__x__ Deep, rapid respirations.

_____ Pain that occurs in waves and is rated at "8."

_____ Hyperactive bowel sounds on the right side of the abdomen and hypoactive on the left.

_____ Abdominal distention with tympany upon percussion.

_____ Small amounts of liquid stool.

Kussmaul respirations indicate acidosis, which is a possible complication of lower intestine obstruction since the alkaline fluids are not reabsorbed. Constant vague significant pain, hyperactive bowel sounds before the obstruction and hypoactive after the obstruction, and abdominal distention from flatus is expected. Liquid stool can pass around a solid obstruction.

3. A client is admitted for a small bowel obstruction, and a nasogastric tube (NGT) is inserted as part of the treatment plan. Which of the following are appropriate actions for the nurse to take in managing this client's care? (Check all that apply.)

__x__	Include the NGT drainage amount as part of the client's output.
__x__	Irrigate the NGT with 20 cc normal saline every 2 hr.
__x__	Assess the client's bowel sounds.
__x__	Provide the client with oral care.
__x__	Clamp the NGT while the client ambulates to the bathroom.

Nasogastric drainage, particularly in a small intestine obstruction, can be significant and is considered part of the output when planning fluid replacement. The NGT is typically irrigated to maintain patency. Auscultating bowel sounds is part of the ongoing client assessment with an obstruction. An NGT promotes mouth breathing and frequent oral care is needed. Clients can tolerate short-term clamping of the tube after the initial decompression. In fact, the client may be placed on a scheduled clamping before the tube is removed.

4. A client is admitted with a large intestine toxic megacolon. Which of the following client findings is most important for the nurse to follow up on first?

    A. The client reports shoulder tip pain and abdominal pain that was intense but is now relieved without an analgesic.

    B. No bowel sounds are auscultated and the client has obstipation.

    C. The client's morning laboratory results are: potassium 3.5 mEq/L, sodium 135 mg/dL, and BUN 20 mg/dL.

    D. The client's vital signs are: lying – blood pressure 128/88 mm Hg, pulse 100 beats/min; standing – blood pressure 120/80 mm Hg, pulse 110 beats/min.

The client findings in option A are classic signs of perforation, with free air irritating the phrenic nerve in the diaphragm. This is an emergent condition. The findings in B are expected. The laboratory results are "borderline," but still within normal limits. The client is exhibiting possible borderline vital signs for dehydration, but these vitals are not clearly orthostatic and would not be as important as perforation.

5. A client is admitted with a small bowel obstruction from adhesions. Which of the following is NOT an expected client assessment with this diagnosis?

     A. The vomitus is more than 500 cc and has a fecal odor.

     B. The client's abdominal pain is persistent and colicky.

     C. The client states the pain is improved after vomiting.

     D. The client's abdomen is firm, rigid, and has positive rebound tenderness.

These are classic signs of peritonitis and warrant further assessment. A small bowel obstruction has profuse (projectile) vomiting of feculent material that relieves pressure.

6. An 80-year-old client is a long-term resident in a nursing home. Which of the following would be most important for the nurse to consider in determining if the client has a stool impaction causing a large intestine obstruction?

     A. The client states he had a bowel movement yesterday.

     B. The client has small amounts of liquid stool.

     C. The client has a slightly distended abdomen and is flatulent.

     D. The client indicates he vomited once this morning.

Liquid stool can, and frequently does, go around an impaction. Having a bowel movement yesterday does not preclude having an impaction. Having flatus resulting is mild distention is not a classic sign of large intestine obstruction. Vomiting once can be from various causes and does not necessarily indicate an impaction. Vomiting is a late sign in large bowel obstructions.

Unit 7   Nursing Care of Clients with Gastrointestinal Disorders
Section: Nursing Care of Clients with Intestinal Disorders

Chapter 70:   Appendicitis
Contributor: Annette M. Peacock-Johnson, MSN, RN

⟳ NCLEX-PN® Connections:

Learning Objective: Review and apply knowledge within "**Appendicitis**" in readiness for performance of the following nursing activities as outlined by the NCLEX-PN® test plan:

Δ   Assist with relevant laboratory, diagnostic, and therapeutic procedures within the nursing role, including:

- Preparation of the client for the procedure.
- Accurate collection of specimens.
- Monitoring client status during and after the procedure.
- Reinforcing client teaching (before and following the procedure).
- Recognizing the client's response (expected, unexpected adverse response) to the procedure.
- Monitoring results.
- Monitoring and taking actions to prevent or minimize the risk of complications.
- Notifying the primary care provider of signs of complications.

Δ   Recognize signs and symptoms of the client's problem and complete the proper documentation.

Δ   Provide and document care based on the client's health alteration.

Δ   Monitor and document vital signs changes.

Δ   Interpret data that need to be reported immediately.

Δ   Reinforce client education on managing the client's health problem.

Δ   Recognize and respond to emergency situations, including notification of the primary care provider.

Δ   Review the client's response to emergency interventions and complete the proper documentation.

Δ   Provide care that meets the age-related needs of clients 65 years of age or older, including recognizing expected physiological changes.

📖 Key Points

Δ   Appendicitis results from **obstruction, inflammation, and infection of the appendix.** Obstruction leads to hypoxia, which can result in **gangrene and/or perforation** of the appendix. Perforation can result in the formation of an **abscess and/or peritonitis.**

Δ   Appendicitis is the most common cause of right lower quadrant inflammation and the most common indication for emergency abdominal surgery.

Δ   Appendicitis is not preventable, therefore early detection is important.

Key Factors

Δ   Peak incidence is among adolescent males and individuals between ages 20 and 30 years old.

Diagnostic Procedures and Nursing Interventions

Δ   **White blood cell (WBC)** count and differential: Mild to moderate **elevation of 10,000 to 18,000/mm³ with left shift** is consistent with appendicitis; greater than 20,000/mm³ may indicate peritonitis.

Δ   Ultrasound of the abdomen may show an enlarged appendix.

Δ   Abdominal computed tomography (CT) may be diagnostic if symptoms are recurrent or prolonged. Check allergies and renal function if contrast dye is used.

Therapeutic Procedures and Nursing Interventions

Δ   Surgical management includes an **appendectomy,** which can be done using a laparoscope (using several small incisions and an endoscope) or an open approach (requiring a larger abdominal incision).

Assessments

Δ   Monitor for **signs and symptoms.**

- Mild or cramping, epigastric or periumbilical pain (initial)

- Constant, intense **right lower quadrant pain** (later)

- Nausea, vomiting, anorexia

- **Rebound tenderness** (pain after deep pressure is applied and released) over **McBurney's point** (located halfway between the umbilicus and anterior iliac spine)

- Pain that decreases with a decrease in right hip flexion or increases with coughing and movement may indicate perforation with peritonitis.

- Muscle rigidity, tense positioning, guarding may indicate perforation with peritonitis.
- Normal to low-grade temperature (higher suggests peritonitis)

NANDA Nursing Diagnoses

Δ Acute pain

Δ Risk for infection

Δ Risk for deficient fluid volume

Δ Deficient knowledge

Δ Anxiety

Nursing Interventions

Δ **Preoperative**

- Upon admission, maintain NPO status due to the possibility of emergency surgery.
- Administer IV fluids as prescribed.
- Encourage semi-Fowler's position to contain abdominal drainage in the lower abdomen.
- Avoid laxatives/enemas or application of heat to the abdomen, which could cause perforation.

Δ **Postoperative**

- Administer opioid analgesia (usually morphine sulfate) as ordered.
- Administer IV antibiotics as ordered (surgical prophylaxis, perforation).
- For peritonitis, monitor nasogastric (NG) tube drainage.
- For perforation or abscess, monitor surgical drains.

Complications and Nursing Implications

Δ **Peritonitis due to perforation** – Perforation is a life-threatening emergency.

- The risk of perforation is greatest 48 hr following the onset of appendicitis pain.
- Carefully assess the client for:
    ◊ **Fever of 38.2° C (101° F) or higher.**
    ◊ Acutely ill appearance.
    ◊ Board-like abdomen.

◊ Decreased urinary output.

◊ Septicemia.

• Treatment includes administration of broad spectrum IV antibiotics.

Meeting the Needs of Older Adults

Δ Appendicitis is rare in older adult clients.

Δ The symptoms of appendicitis are less pronounced; as a result, older adult clients may delay seeking treatment. The risk for perforation is increased due to delays in diagnosis and treatment.

Primary Reference:

Ignatavicius, D. D., & Workman, M. L. (2006). *Medical-surgical nursing* (5th ed.). St. Louis, MO: Saunders.

Additional Resources:

Black, J. M., & Hawks, J. H. (2005). *Medical-surgical nursing: Clinical management for positive outcomes* (7th ed.). St. Louis, MO: Saunders.

NANDA International (2004). *NANDA nursing diagnoses: Definitions and classification 2005-2006*. Philadelphia: NANDA.

Chapter 70: Appendicitis

Application Exercises

Scenario: A young adult client is admitted to the emergency department with reports of abdominal pain. A diagnosis of acute appendicitis is suspected.

1. What additional nursing assessments are indicated?

2. Which of the following assessment findings suggests early appendicitis?

      A. Nausea and vomiting

      B. Periumbilical pain

      C. Tense positioning

      D. Abdominal rigidity

3. On the following diagram, place an "X" to indicate the location for McBurney's point. Describe the significance of McBurney's point.

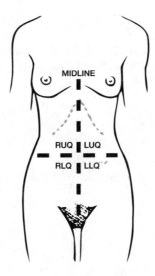

4. The client is scheduled for a CT of the abdomen to rule out acute appendicitis. What client teaching should the nurse provide regarding this procedure? What preparation is required for the CT?

5. In preparing the client for surgery, the nurse should anticipate which of the following interventions? (Check all that apply.)

_____   Administer enema.

_____   Maintain NPO status.

_____   Deliver IV fluids.

_____   Apply heat to abdomen.

_____   Obtain surgical consent.

6. Which of the following statements by the client indicates correct understanding of the procedure and/or postoperative care?

A. "Bedrest will be necessary to minimize the pain."

B. "Pain medication should be avoided to prevent constipation."

C. "I will have drains to help with healing."

D. "I will have several small incisions or punctures."

7. Identify priority nursing diagnoses.

8. The client returns to the nursing unit following surgery for a ruptured appendix. The client has an NG tube connected to low suction. An IV of 0.9% normal saline is infusing at 100 cc/hr. In providing postoperative care, the nurse should anticipate assisting with which of the following interventions? (Check all that apply.)

_____   Monitoring of the abdominal incision

_____   Administration of a full-liquid diet

_____   Administration of opioid analgesics

_____   Measurement of intake and output

_____   Maintenance of bedrest with frequent repositioning

Chapter 70: Appendicitis

Application Exercises Answer Key

Scenario: A young adult client is admitted to the emergency department with reports of abdominal pain. A diagnosis of acute appendicitis is suspected.

1. What additional nursing assessments are indicated?

> **Assessment should include a history of the client's pain status (onset, duration, intensity, location, aggravating/alleviating factors) and gastrointestinal disturbances (nausea, vomiting, anorexia). The nurse should complete an abdominal assessment, noting the presence of muscle rigidity, tenderness, and guarding. Assessment of the vital signs may indicate a low-grade fever and tachycardia.**

2. Which of the following assessment findings suggests early appendicitis?

> A. Nausea and vomiting
> **B. Periumbilical pain**
> C. Tense positioning
> D. Abdominal rigidity

> **Periumbilical pain is the initial symptom, followed by nausea and vomiting. Tense positioning and abdominal rigidity are late signs associated with perforation.**

3. On the following diagram, place an "X" to indicate the location for McBurney's point. Describe the significance of McBurney's point.

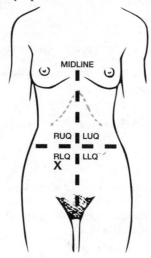

An "X" should be made halfway between the anterior iliac crest and the umbilicus in the right lower quadrant. This is the classic location for localized pain during the later stages of appendicitis.

4. The client is scheduled for a CT of the abdomen to rule out acute appendicitis. What client teaching should the nurse provide regarding this procedure? What preparation is required for the CT?

Teach the client that the procedure is not associated with pain and sedation is not necessary. If an IV contrast dye is used, the nurse should assess the client for allergies to the dye and ability to excrete the dye.

5. In preparing the client for surgery, the nurse should anticipate which of the following interventions? (Check all that apply.)

_____	Administer enema.
__x__	Maintain NPO status.
__x__	Deliver IV fluids.
_____	Apply heat to abdomen.
__x__	Obtain surgical consent.

Enemas and heat to the abdomen are contraindicated because they can increase the risk of perforation.

6. Which of the following statements by the client indicates correct understanding of the procedure and/or postoperative care?

> A. "Bedrest will be necessary to minimize the pain."
>
> B. "Pain medication should be avoided to prevent constipation."
>
> C. "I will have drains to help with healing."
>
> **D. "I will have several small incisions or punctures."**

Several small incisions are made during an exploratory laparoscopy for insertion of the endoscope and surgical instruments. Early ambulation is required to facilitate postoperative recovery and minimize complications associated with immobility. Pain medication should be encouraged as ordered to facilitate participation in postoperative activities including ambulation. If the appendix ruptures, a large incision is made with placement of drains.

7. Identify priority nursing diagnoses.

Priority nursing diagnoses include:

Acute pain related to inflammation.

Deficient knowledge related to disease process, surgical experience.

Risk for infection related to rupture of appendix.

8. The client returns to the nursing unit following surgery for a ruptured appendix. The client has an NG tube connected to low suction. An IV of 0.9% normal saline is infusing at 100 cc/hr. In providing postoperative care, the nurse should anticipate assisting with which of the following interventions? (Check all that apply.)

> __x__ Monitoring of the abdominal incision
>
> _____ Administration of a full-liquid diet
>
> __x__ Administration of opioid analgesics
>
> __x__ Measurement of intake and output
>
> _____ Maintenance of bedrest with frequent repositioning

Routine postoperative care includes: monitoring of the abdominal incision for drainage and signs of infection, administering opioid analgesics as ordered for pain, and the measurement of intake and output for clients with an NG tube and IV infusion. A full-liquid diet is contraindicated for a client with an NG tube connected to suction. Progressive activity with ambulation is encouraged to facilitate peristalsis, promote postoperative recovery, and minimize the effects of immobility.

Unit 7   Nursing Care of Clients with Gastrointestinal Disorders

Section: Nursing Care of Clients with Intestinal Disorders

Chapter 71:   **Ulcerative Colitis, Crohn's Disease, and Diverticulitis**

Contributor: Polly Gerber Zimmermann, MSN, MBA, RN, CEN

NCLEX-PN® Connections:

Learning Objective: Review and apply knowledge within "**Ulcerative Colitis, Crohn's Disease, and Diverticulitis**" in readiness for performance of the following nursing activities as outlined by the NCLEX-PN® test plan:

Δ   Assist with relevant laboratory, diagnostic, and therapeutic procedures within the nursing role, including:

- Preparation of the client for the procedure.

- Accurate collection of specimens.

- Monitoring client status during and after the procedure.

- Reinforcing client teaching (before and following the procedure).

- Recognizing the client's response (expected, unexpected adverse response) to the procedure.

- Monitoring results.

- Monitoring and taking actions to prevent or minimize the risk of complications.

- Notifying the primary care provider of signs of complications.

Δ   Recognize signs and symptoms of the client's problem and complete the proper documentation.

Δ   Provide and document care based on the client's health alteration.

Δ   Monitor and document vital signs changes.

Δ   Interpret data that need to be reported immediately.

Δ   Reinforce client education on managing the client's health problem.

Δ   Recognize and respond to emergency situations, including notification of the primary care provider.

Δ   Review the client's response to emergency interventions and complete the proper documentation.

Δ   Provide care that meets the age-related needs of clients 65 years of age or older, including recognizing expected physiological changes.

📖 Key Points

Δ **Inflammatory bowel disease** (IBD) is an umbrella term that includes the chronic inflammatory GI diseases ulcerative colitis and Crohn's disease. IBD is characterized by **diarrhea** (up to 20 stools during acute exacerbation), **crampy abdominal pain**, and **exacerbations** ("flare-ups")/**remissions**.

- **Ulcerative colitis**: edematous, inflamed mucosa with multiple abscesses beginning in the rectum and moving upward through the large intestine. Changes from its chronic nature increase cancer risk.

- **Crohn's disease**: intermittent involvement throughout the entire GI tract, most commonly in the small intestine and the terminal ileum. Typically, the disease eventually extends through all layers of the bowel.

Δ **Diverticulitis** is an acute inflammation of the diverticulum. Most frequently, diverticulitis occurs in the abdominal lower left quadrant, where stool is a solid consistency. It involves deep, longitudinal discontinuous ulcerations that involve all layers of the bowel wall.

Δ Acute treatment for all disorders involves **fluids and bowel rest**, medications, and potential surgery. Long-term treatment for **IBD involves low-fiber (low-residue) diet** and medication. Long-term treatment for **diverticulitis involves a high-fiber diet.**

Δ **Differentiate from irritable bowel syndrome (IBS)**, which is intermittent constipation/diarrhea patterns from abnormal intestinal motility and increased sensitivity. There is no inflammation.

- IBS is a disorder of function that affects up to 20% of Americans.

- Diagnosed by ruling out other more serious illnesses. It does not evolve into any life-threatening health problem.

- Some theorize IBS symptoms in adults may be undiagnosed nontropical sprue (celiac) disease.

- Clients with IBS should **avoid/limit gas-forming foods.**

Key Factors

Δ The etiology of IBD is uncertain; evidence indicates there may be a genetic predisposition, possibly an autoimmune or immunoregulation disorder.

Δ Ulcerative colitis primarily affects younger people (age 15 to 25) and is more common in females. Crohn's disease primarily affects individuals between 15 and 40 years. Diverticulitis primarily occurs in individuals older than 50.

Diagnostic Procedures and Nursing Interventions

Δ   White Blood Cell Count (infection), Hemoglobin (blood loss), Electrolytes (gastrointestinal losses), Erythrocyte Sedimentation Rate (inflammation)

Δ   Antibody Testing

- pANCA (perinuclear antineutrophil cytoplasmic antibody): Elevated in clients with ulcerative colitis

- Antiglycan antibody: Elevated in clients with Crohn's disease

Δ   **A definitive diagnosis is usually made by colonoscopy.**

- Ulcerative colitis shows chronic inflammatory changes but not granulomas (little tumors).

- Crohn's disease shows intermittent inflammation, granulomas, and classic cobblestone appearance.

- Diverticulum will be seen on colonoscopy; signs of acute infection are present with diverticulitis.

- Client preparation: Clear liquids for 24 hr pre-procedure; GoLYTELY® or similar cathartic; monitor client response, including vital signs and fluid and electrolyte values.

Δ   Barium enema: Assist client with bowel preparation. Post procedure monitor for elimination of barium.

Therapeutic Procedures and Nursing Interventions

Δ   **Colectomy and Colostomy Surgery**

- Cure for ulcerative colitis (50% of clients eventually need, usually colostomy)

- Only palliative for Crohn's disease (70 to 80% of clients eventually need) as it reoccurs in healthy intestines

Assessments

Δ   Monitor for **signs and symptoms.**

- **Ulcerative colitis:** Bloody diarrhea with mucus and cramping, abdominal pain

- **Crohn's disease:** Non-bloody diarrhea, crampy abdominal pain, insidious onset of weight loss, fatigue, low-grade fever

- **Diverticulitis:** Localized pain, fever, elevated WBCs

Nursing Interventions

Δ   For an **acute exacerbation**, the nurse should:

- Keep the client **NPO with an IV** and promote **bowel rest** (decrease intestinal motility).

- Correct malnutrition (for example, TPN).

- Pain control focuses on controlling inflammation.

Δ   Administer prescribed **medications**.

- **5-aminosalicylic acid drugs**, such as **sulfasalazine (Azulfidine)** or mesalamine (Asacol) for extended periods of time for anti-inflammatory effects – encourage fluids because sulfa will crystallize in the kidney if the client is dehydrated.

- **Corticosteroids** (immunosuppression precautions), such as prednisone

- **Immunosuppressant agents**, such as azathioprine (Imuran) and 6-mercaptopurine (Purinethol) – watch for signs and symptoms of bone marrow toxicity.

- Biologic therapy (for refractory disease) such as infliximab (Remicade) to block TNFa, a cytokine that intensifies inflammation

- Antibiotics and antidiarrheal drugs if applicable

Δ   Assess bowel sounds, fluid and electrolyte balance, and signs and symptoms of infection.

Δ   Provide **high-calorie, high-protein, low-fat, and low-fiber (low-residue) diet** adjusted to the client's food sensitivities. Provide dietary instruction.

Δ   Provide **nutritional supplements** (vitamin B_{12} injections for Crohn's disease because the small intestine can't absorb it).

Complications and Nursing Implications

Δ   **IBD**

- Fluid and electrolyte imbalance/malnutrition

  ◊   Monitor laboratory values and provide replacement therapy.

  ◊   Monitor weight.

- Strictures, bowel obstruction, pseudopolyps (from healed abscesses that thicken and shorten colon)

- **Perforation** (erosion of the wall of the intestine) results in lower **gastrointestinal bleeding** and **peritonitis.**

  ◊   Monitor hemoglobin and hematocrit and stools for evidence of bleeding.

  ◊   Replace losses.

◊   Support the client during and following the surgical intervention.

◊   Administer antibiotics as prescribed.

Δ   **Ulcerative Colitis**

- **Toxic megacolon**: Dilation and paralysis of colon; risk for perforation

- Increased risk for colon cancer, especially after having the disease for 10 years

Δ   **Crohn's Disease**

- **Fistulas** (one-third of clients will develop) to other organs of abdomen (bladder, anal fissures, perianal abscesses, perilabial)

- Massive or repeated bowel resections resulting in short-bowel syndrome and permanent dependence on total parenteral nutrition (TPN)

- Risk for cholelithiasis (poor absorption of bile salts in terminal ileum)

- Risk for pancreatitis (from treating drugs or impaired pancreatic drainage)

Meeting the Needs of Older Adults

Δ   IBD is primarily a disease of younger people; diverticulitis is primarily a disease of older adults.

Δ   Fifty percent of Americans have diverticulosis (asymptomatic outpouching of smooth muscles in intestinal wall) by age 80, related to effects of aging and low dietary fiber. The diverticulum become inflamed from stool retention, bacteria, or inflammation in 15% of clients with diverticulosis.

Δ   Cancer risk (ulcerative colitis) increases with age.

Δ   Fluid and electrolyte imbalance from gastrointestinal prep is more likely in the older adult client.

Δ   Difficulty manipulating ileostomy/colostomy apparatus with age.

Primary Reference:

Ignatavicius, D. D., & Workman, M. L. (2006). *Medical-surgical nursing* (5th ed.). St. Louis, MO: Saunders.

Additional Resources:

NANDA International (2004). *NANDA nursing diagnoses: Definitions and classification 2005-2006*. Philadelphia: NANDA.

Veronesi, J. F. (2003, May). Inflammatory bowel disease. *RN*, 66(5): 36-46.

For more information, visit the Crohn's and Colitis Foundation of America at *www.ccfa.org* or the National Institute of Diabetes & Digestive & Kidney Diseases at *www.niddk.nih.gov*.

Chapter 71: Ulcerative Colitis, Crohn's Disease, and Diverticulitis

Application Exercises

1. A client is admitted for an exacerbation of IBD. Which of the following are appropriate nursing actions? (Check all that apply.)

_____ Monitor the client's blood pressure and pulse lying and sitting.

_____ Encourage intake of fresh raw fruits and vegetables.

_____ Inform the client that the sulfasalazine (Azulfidine) can be weaned after the symptoms stop.

_____ Obtain a stool culture to determine the causative organism for the client's diarrhea.

_____ Teach the client on prednisone not to discontinue the medication abruptly.

2. A client is on prednisone following an exacerbation of IBD. Which of the following client findings is the greatest concern?

A. The client indicates the scratch on his arm is taking longer to heal.

B. The client's morning glucose is 140 mg/dL.

C. The client reports having the "flu," and his temperature is 38° C (100.4° F).

D. The client indicates he has gained some weight.

3. A client is on sulfasalazine (Azulfidine) for ulcerative colitis. Which of the following laboratory results indicates a need for follow-up?

A. Potassium 3.5 mEq/L, sodium 135 mEq/L

B. White blood cell count 10,500/mm^3, creatinine 1.2 mg/dL

C. Glucose 130 mg/dL, hemoglobin 11 g/dL

D. Hematocrit 50%, BUN 50 mg/dL.

4. A female client is admitted to the hospital with the diagnosis of Crohn's disease exacerbation. Which of the following assessment findings is most important for the nurse to follow up?

A. The client had 15 diarrhea stools yesterday.

B. The client indicates cramping abdominal pain rated at "7."

C. The client reports new brownish vaginal discharge.

D. The client's BUN is 20 mg/dL and WBC is 10,000/mm^3.

5. A 60-year-old client presents to the emergency department with severe left lower quadrant pain. Rebound tenderness is present. Which of the following is most important for the nurse to do initially?

> A. Obtain an order for an analgesic.
>
> B. Make the client NPO.
>
> C. Determine the time of the last bowel movement.
>
> D. Auscultate bowel sounds.

6. Which of the following is most important to do in caring for a client prior to and following a diagnostic colonoscopy?

> A. Administer GoLYTELY® the night before.
>
> B. Teach the client to increase fiber in the diet.
>
> C. Notify the provider if the hemoglobin is less than 12 g/dL.
>
> D. Check for a gag reflex after the procedure.

Chapter 71: Ulcerative Colitis, Crohn's Disease, and Diverticulitis

Application Exercises Answer Key

1. A client is admitted for an exacerbation of IBD. Which of the following are appropriate nursing actions? (Check all that apply.)

   __x__   Monitor the client's blood pressure and pulse lying and sitting.

   _____   Encourage intake of fresh raw fruits and vegetables.

   _____   Inform the client that the sulfasalazine (Azulfidine) can be weaned after the symptoms stop.

   _____   Obtain a stool culture to determine the causative organism for the client's diarrhea.

   __x__   Teach the client on prednisone not to discontinue the medication abruptly.

   Long-term treatment of IBD involves a low-residue diet, so encouraging fresh raw fruits and vegetables is incorrect.

   Salicylate medications are usually continued for a year or more.

   The exacerbation of IBD is related to the intestine's inflammation and ulceration, not a gastrointestinal organism.

2. A client is on prednisone following an exacerbation of IBD. Which of the following client findings is the greatest concern?

   A. The client indicates the scratch on his arm is taking longer to heal.

   B. The client's morning glucose is 140 mg/dL.

   C. **The client reports having the "flu," and his temperature is 38°C (100.4° F).**

   D. The client indicates he has gained some weight.

   Clients on steroids are immunosuppressed and have a blunted response to infection. A new low-grade fever requires further investigation. The other options are expected side-effects of the medication, not complications.

3. A client is on sulfasalazine (Azulfidine) for ulcerative colitis. Which of the following laboratory results indicates a need for follow-up?

        A. Potassium 3.5 mEq/L, sodium 135 mEq/L

        B. White blood cell count 10,500/mm³, creatinine 1.2 mg/dL

        C. Glucose 130 mg/dL, hemoglobin 11 g/dL

        D. Hematocrit 50%, BUN 50 mg/dL.

The client is dehydrated. Sulfa drugs crystallize in the kidney if there is not adequate hydration. The other findings are expected related to the condition; none are specific to this medication.

4. A female client is admitted to the hospital with the diagnosis of Crohn's disease exacerbation. Which of the following assessment findings is most important for the nurse to follow up?

        A. The client had 15 diarrhea stools yesterday.

        B. The client indicates cramping abdominal pain rated at "7."

        C. The client reports new brownish vaginal discharge.

        D. The client's BUN is 20 mg/dL and WBC is 10,000/mm³.

This could signal a new tract has developed and further investigation is needed. The rest are expected findings for the condition.

5. A 60-year-old client presents to the emergency department with severe left lower quadrant pain. Rebound tenderness is present. Which of the following is most important for the nurse to do initially?

        A. Obtain an order for an analgesic.

        B. Make the client NPO.

        C. Determine the time of the last bowel movement.

        D. Auscultate bowel sounds.

The client has an acute abdomen; the presentation indicates possible diverticulitis. It is important to keep the client NPO while further assessments are made in case surgery for perforation is needed. The other actions can be done later.

6. Which of the following is most important to do in caring for a client prior to and following a diagnostic colonoscopy?

> **A. Administer GoLYTELY® the night before.**
>
> B. Teach the client to increase fiber in the diet.
>
> C. Notify the provider if the hemoglobin is less than 12 g/dL.
>
> D. Check for a gag reflex after the procedure.

Clients are on clear liquids 24 hr prior to the procedure. A hemoglobin value of 10 g/dL or higher is required for general anesthesia. Colonoscopies are usually done under conscious sedation. There is no need to check for a gag reflex; that is a requirement for a gastroscopy.

Unit 7   Nursing Care of Clients with Gastrointestinal Disorders

Section: Nursing Care of Clients with Intestinal Disorders

Chapter 72:   Colorectal Cancer
            Contributor: Dana Bartlett, MSN, RN, CSPI

NCLEX-PN® Connections:

Learning Objective: Review and apply knowledge within "**Colorectal Cancer**" in readiness for performance of the following nursing activities as outlined by the NCLEX-PN® test plan:

Δ   Assist with relevant laboratory, diagnostic, and therapeutic procedures within the nursing role, including:

  • Preparation of the client for the procedure.

  • Accurate collection of specimens.

  • Monitoring client status during and after the procedure.

  • Reinforcing client teaching (before and following the procedure).

  • Recognizing the client's response (expected, unexpected adverse response) to the procedure.

  • Monitoring results.

  • Monitoring and taking actions to prevent or minimize the risk of complications.

  • Notifying the primary care provider of signs of complications.

Δ   Recognize signs and symptoms of the client's problem and complete the proper documentation.

Δ   Provide and document care based on the client's health alteration.

Δ   Monitor and document vital signs changes.

Δ   Interpret data that need to be reported immediately.

Δ   Reinforce client education on managing the client's health problem.

Δ   Recognize and respond to emergency situations, including notification of the primary care provider.

Δ   Review the client's response to emergency interventions and complete the proper documentation.

Δ   Provide care that meets the age-related needs of clients 65 years of age or older, including recognizing expected physiological changes.

📖 Key Points

Δ **Colorectal cancer** (CRC) is the second most common cancer and the second leading cause of death by cancer in Western countries.

Δ Most CRCs are **adenocarcinomas** (colon epithelium).

Δ Colorectal cancer grows slowly. Many times, the client is asymptomatic, but occult blood is discovered in the stool during a rectal exam.

Δ Colorectal cancer can metastasize (through blood or lymph) to the liver (most common), lungs, brain, or bones. Spread can also occur as a result of peritoneal seeding (for example, during surgical resection of tumor).

Δ Colorectal cancer can be cured with **early detection**. Regular colorectal **screening is recommended for individuals older than 50** years of age or with a family history of colorectal cancer.

Key Factors

Δ Colon cancer is more common in women; rectal cancer is more common in men.

Δ **Risk Factors**

- Adenomatous colon polyps

- **Family history** of colorectal cancer

- Inflammatory Bowel Disease (ulcerative colitis, Crohn's disease)

- **High-fat, low-fiber diet**

- **Older than 50** years of age

Δ The most common location of CRC is the rectosigmoidal region.

Diagnostic Procedures and Nursing Interventions

Δ **Fecal Occult Blood Test** (FOBT) – two stool samples within 3 consecutive days. False-positive results can occur with ingestion of some foods or drugs. In general, meat, NSAIDs, and vitamin C are avoided for the 48 hr prior to testing.

Δ **Carcinoembryonic Antigen (CEA)** serum test – CEA levels are elevated in most individuals with CRC.

Δ **Sigmoidoscopy/Colonoscopy** provides a **definitive diagnosis** of CRC. This scope procedure permits visualization of tumors, removal of polyps, and tissue biopsy. Bowel is cleansed prior to procedure with GoLYTELY or other cathartic.

Δ Barium enemas; CT scans of the abdomen, pelvis, lungs, and liver; chest x-rays; and liver scans may be done to further identify the specific location of cancer and to identify sites of metastases.

Therapeutic Procedures and Nursing Interventions

Δ Colon resection, colectomy, colostomy, and abdominoperineal (AP) resection surgeries may be performed to remove all or portions of CRC. Preoperatively, the client is on clear liquids for a couple of days prior to surgery, bowel prep with cathartics (GoLYTELY) is performed, and antibiotics, such as neomycin and metronidazole (Flagyl), are administered to eradicate intestinal flora.

Δ Chemotherapy (monitor for myelosuppression and pancytopenia) and radiation (monitor fatigue and diarrhea) are possible adjuvant therapies.

Assessments

Δ Monitor for **signs and symptoms.**

- Fatigue due to occult blood loss

- **Change in bowel habits**

- Visible blood in the stool

- Mass on digital rectal exam (DRE)

- Signs and symptoms due to metastases – partial bowel obstruction (high pitched tingling bowel sounds), complete bowel obstruction (no bowel sounds in 5 min)

Δ Postoperatively, if the client has a stoma, assess the color and integrity of the **stoma** (should be **reddish pink, moist**, and may have a small amount of visible blood immediately postoperative; report any evidence of stoma ischemia or necrosis).

NANDA Nursing Diagnoses

Δ Constipation

Δ Diarrhea

Δ Imbalanced nutrition: Less than body requirements

Δ Deficient fluid volume

Δ Acute/chronic pain

Δ Disturbed body image

Nursing Interventions

Δ Advise clients with a strong history of colorectal cancer to **reduce intake of fats and meat proteins**.

Δ Explain the need for, and side effects of, chemotherapy, surgery, and radiation therapy.

Δ Closely monitor intake and output and the client's elimination pattern.

Δ Closely observe for visible or occult signs of bleeding.

Δ **Postoperative Care**

- Maintain nasogastric suction (decompression).

- Provide pain management, generally with patient-controlled analgesia.

- Monitor output from drain(s).

- Provide wound care.

- Promote measures to reduce risk of respiratory complications (turn, cough, deep breathe, ambulate, splint).

- Promote measures to reduce risk of embolic complications (compression stockings, low level anticoagulation).

- Slowly progress diet, monitoring client response.

- Provide client education regarding activity limits (no lifting, use of stool softeners to avoid straining).

- Provide ostomy teaching (signs of ischemia to report, expected output, appliance management), if applicable.

- Support the client with disturbed body image.

Complications and Nursing Implications

Δ **Bowel Obstruction**

- Monitor for high-pitched bowel sounds before site of obstruction with hypoactive bowel sounds after, or overall hypoactive bowel sounds.

- Decompression and/or surgical intervention.

Δ **Perforation** (erosion of the wall of the intestine) resulting in lower **gastrointestinal bleeding** and **peritonitis**

- Monitor hemoglobin, hematocrit, and stools for evidence of bleeding.

- Replace losses.

- Support the client during and following surgical intervention.

- Administer antibiotics as prescribed.

Δ **Abscess/Fistula**

- Prepare the client for incisional/surgical drainage.

- Provide antibiotics as prescribed.

Meeting the Needs of Older Adults

Δ Older adult clients may have a more difficult postoperative course and are at a greater risk for intraoperative complications.

Δ Older adult clients may be less able to handle fluid volume deficits.

Δ Management of a colostomy may be more difficult with older adult clients due to impaired vision and the need for fine motor skills.

Primary Reference:

Ignatavicius, D. D., & Workman, M. L. (2006). *Medical-surgical nursing* (5th ed.). St. Louis, MO: Saunders.

Additional Resources:

NANDA International (2004). *NANDA nursing diagnoses: Definitions and classification 2005-2006.* Philadelphia: NANDA.

Chapter 72: Colorectal Cancer

Application Exercises

Scenario: A nurse is caring for an older adult client with colon cancer. The client has a new colostomy.

1. What are three nursing diagnoses that are appropriate for this situation?

2. What are some specific areas of ostomy care that should be addressed in this situation?

3. What ongoing assessment, visually and by laboratory exam, should be carried out in this situation?

4. What are three complications of colon cancer? How should the nurse monitor for these complications?

5. What is one area of emotional and intellectual support in which this client might need assistance?

6. Postoperative care of the client following colon resection for colorectal cancer includes which of the following? (Check all that apply.)

   _____ Discourage the client from turning, coughing, and deep breathing.
   _____ Monitor and treat pain; evaluate pain-relief measures.
   _____ Start full liquid diet upon return to medical unit.
   _____ Provide wound care using surgical aseptic technique.
   _____ Advise the client to use stool softeners to prevent straining.

Chapter 72: Colorectal Cancer

Application Exercises Answer Key

Scenario: A nurse is caring for an older adult client with colon cancer. The client has a new colostomy.

1. What are three nursing diagnoses that are appropriate for this situation?

   Appropriate nursing diagnoses include:

   Disturbed body image

   Deficient fluid volume

   Imbalance nutrition: Less than body requirements

   Acute/chronic Pain

2. What are some specific areas of ostomy care that should be addressed in this situation?

   Impaired vision and decreased fine motor control may interfere with the older adult client's ability to perform ostomy care. Discharge planning should include ensuring adequate help is available to the client.

3. What ongoing assessment, visually and by laboratory exam, should be carried out in this situation?

   The nurse should continue to check for blood in the stools and monitor laboratory values.

4. What are three complications of colon cancer? How should the nurse monitor for these complications?

   Complications of colon cancer include metastases, bleeding, and infection. The client should be monitored for signs and symptoms of bleeding, metastases, and infection by orthostatic vitals sign checks, hemoccult examination of the stool, pain and/or swelling in new areas, and temperature checks.

5. What is one area of emotional and intellectual support in which this client might need assistance?

In this situation, the emotional and intellectual challenges of having a colostomy can be very intimidating and support from the nurse is vital.

6. Postoperative care of the client following colon resection for colorectal cancer includes which of the following? (Check all that apply.)

_____	Discourage the client from turning, coughing, and deep breathing.
_x_	Monitor and treat pain; evaluate pain-relief measures.
_____	Start full liquid diet upon return to medical unit.
_x_	Provide wound care using surgical aseptic technique.
_x_	Advise the client to use stool softeners to prevent straining.

Pain should be routinely monitored, treated, and evaluated for treatment efficacy. Use surgical aseptic technique for wound care to prevent infection. Straining at stool can put undue stress on the surgical incision and lead to wound dehiscence. Clients should be encouraged to turn, cough, and deep breathe to reduce the risk of respiratory complications. Oral intake should start with ice chips, then clear liquids, and then advance as tolerated.

Nursing Care of Clients with Gastrointestinal Disorders
Nursing Care of Clients with Gallbladder and Pancreas Disorders

Chapter 73:   Cholecystitis and Cholecystectomy
Contributor: Dana Bartlett, MSN, RN, CSPI

🔄 NCLEX-PN® Connections:

Learning Objective: Review and apply knowledge within **"Cholecystitis and Cholecystectomy"** in readiness for performance of the following nursing activities as outlined by the NCLEX-PN® test plan:

Δ Assist with relevant laboratory, diagnostic, and therapeutic procedures within the nursing role, including:

   • Preparation of the client for the procedure.

   • Accurate collection of specimens.

   • Monitoring client status during and after the procedure.

   • Reinforcing client teaching (before and following the procedure).

   • Recognizing the client's response (expected, unexpected adverse response) to the procedure.

   • Monitoring results.

   • Monitoring and taking actions to prevent or minimize the risk of complications.

   • Notifying the primary care provider of signs of complications.

Δ Recognize signs and symptoms of the client's problem and complete the proper documentation.

Δ Provide and document care based on the client's health alteration.

Δ Monitor and document vital signs changes.

Δ Interpret data that need to be reported immediately.

Δ Reinforce client education on managing the client's health problem.

Δ Recognize and respond to emergency situations, including notification of the primary care provider.

Δ Review the client's response to emergency interventions and complete the proper documentation.

Δ Provide care that meets the age-related needs of clients 65 years of age or older, including recognizing expected physiological changes.

📖 Key Points

Δ **Cholecystitis is an inflammation of the gallbladder wall.** The "attack" usually subsides in 2 to 3 days.

Δ Cholecystitis is most often caused by gallstones (**cholelithiasis**) obstructing the cystic and/or common bile ducts (bile flow from gallbladder to duodenum); cholecystitis without gallstones is rare and serious.

Δ Bile is used for the digestion of fats. It is produced in the liver and stored in the gall bladder.

Δ Cholecystitis can be acute or chronic, and it can also obstruct the pancreatic duct.

Key Factors

Δ **Risk Factors**

- More common in females
- **High-fat** diet
- Obesity (impaired fat metabolism, high cholesterol levels)
- Genetic predisposition
- Older than 60 years of age (more likely to develop gallstones)
- Individuals with type 1 diabetes mellitus (high triglycerides)
- Low-calorie, liquid protein diets
- Rapid weight loss (increases cholesterol)

Δ **Triggering Factors**

- Trauma
- Surgery
- Coronary events
- Diabetes
- Fasting
- Immobility
- Hormone replacement therapy (HRT)
- Pregnancy

Diagnostic Procedures and Nursing Interventions

Δ **Right upper quadrant (RUQ) ultrasound** is the most diagnostic. Visualizes gallbladder edema.

Δ Abdominal x-ray (may visualize calcified gallstones)

Δ White blood cell count (elevations with left shift indicate inflammation)

Δ Direct (normal is 0.1 to 0.3 mg/dL), indirect (0.2 to 0.8 mg/dL), and total (0.1 to 1.0 mg/dL) serum bilirubin levels (elevated if obstruction)

Δ Aspartate aminotransferase (AST) and lactate dehydrogenase (LDH) (elevated if liver dysfunction)

Δ Serum cholesterol (elevated above 200 mg/dL)

Δ Hepatobiliary scan (assesses patency of biliary duct system)

Therapeutic Procedures and Nursing Interventions

Δ **Cholecystectomy** – removal of the gallbladder with a laparoscopic or an open approach (when exploration of biliary ducts is indicated).

- Postoperatively, clients may experience free air pain following laparoscopic surgery.

- Ambulation is helpful.

- Following an open approach, nursing care includes monitoring drainage from inserted Jackson-Pratt (JP) drains and T-tube.

Assessments

Δ An attack of cholecystitis (also known as a "gallbladder attack") is characterized by:

- **Sharp pain in the right upper quadrant** of the abdomen, often radiating to the right shoulder.

- **Pain with deep inspiration** during right subcostal palpation (**Murphy's sign**).

- Intense pain (increased heart rate, pallor, diaphoresis) after ingestion of a large quantity of high-fat food.

- Rebound tenderness.

- Nausea, anorexia, and vomiting.

- Dyspepsia, eructation (belching), and flatulence.

- Fever.

Δ   Jaundice, clay-colored stools, dark urine, steatorrhea (fatty stools), and pruritus (accumulation of bile salts in the skin) may be seen in clients with chronic cholecystitis (due to biliary obstruction).

NANDA Nursing Diagnoses

Δ   Acute pain

Δ   Impaired gas exchange

Δ   Risk for infection

Δ   Deficient knowledge

Nursing Interventions

Δ   **Dietary Counseling**

- Encourage a **low-fat diet** (reduced dairy; avoid fried foods, chocolate, nuts, and gravies).

- Promote weight reduction.

- **Fat-soluble vitamins and bile salts** may be prescribed if obstruction is present to enhance absorption and aid digestion.

- **Avoid gas-forming foods** (beans, cabbage, cauliflower, broccoli).

- Smaller, more frequent meals may be tolerated better.

Δ   Administer **analgesics** as needed and prescribed.

- **Meperidine (Demerol) is generally preferred** over morphine, because morphine may increase biliary spasms.

- Antispasmodics and anticholinergics

- Antiemetics

Δ   **Postoperative Care**

- Support pain management.

- Encourage splinting to reduce pain.

- Encourage measures to reduce risk of respiratory complications (turn, cough, deep breathe, ambulate).

- Monitor wound incision(s) and provide wound care.

  ◊ **Monitor and record T-tube drainage** (initially bloody, then green-brown bile).

  ◊ Initially, may drain > 400 mL/day and then gradually decreases in amount.

◊ Report sudden increases in drainage or amounts exceeding 1,000 mL/day.

◊ Inspect surrounding skin.

◊ Maintain flow by gravity.

◊ **Clamp 1 to 2 hr ac and pc.**

◊ **Monitor and document the client's response to food.**

- **Client Education**

◊ Activity precautions 4 to 6 weeks

◊ Care of T-tube (up to 6 weeks postoperatively) – Report sudden increase in drainage or foul odor; Clamp 1 to 2 hr before and after meals.

◊ Stool color should return to brown color in about a week.

◊ Encourage a low-fat diet.

Complications and Nursing Implications

Δ **Obstruction of the bile duct** can cause ischemia and a rupture of the gallbladder wall is possible. Rupture of the gallbladder wall can cause a local **abscess** or **peritonitis** (rigid, board-like abdomen, guarding), which requires surgical intervention and administration of broad spectrum antibiotics.

Meeting the Needs of Older Adults

Δ Older adult clients may have diabetes mellitus and have atypical presentations of cholecystitis (for example, absence of pain or fever).

Δ The postoperative period is always more risky for the older adult clients.

Δ Older adult clients may have difficulty taking care of a T-tube at home and may have difficulty changing lifelong dietary patterns.

Primary Reference:

Ignatavicius, D. D., & Workman, M. L. (2006). *Medical-surgical nursing* (5th ed.). St. Louis, MO: Saunders.

Additional Resources:

NANDA International (2004). *NANDA nursing diagnoses: Definitions and classification 2005-2006*. Philadelphia: NANDA.

Chapter 73: Cholecystitis and Cholecystectomy

Application Exercises

Scenario: A client is admitted with severe upper abdominal pain following a family dinner celebration. She reports frequent belching. She is febrile.

1. What could be a possible cause for the fever and the pain?

2. What should the nurse suspect regarding the quantity and type of food consumed at the dinner celebration by this client?

3. What medication(s) should the nurse anticipate being prescribed for this client at this point?

4. Which of the following food choices might trigger a cholecystitis attack? (Check all that apply.)

_____	Ice cream	_____	Broccoli with cheese sauce
_____	Brownie with nuts	_____	Biscuits and gravy
_____	Pasta with marinara sauce	_____	Sweetened strawberries
_____	Turkey sandwich	_____	Fried eggs and bacon

5. Which of the following client findings indicates biliary obstruction? (Check all that apply.)

_____ Conjugated (direct) serum bilirubin 0.6 mg/dL

_____ Serum cholesterol 278 mg/dL

_____ Unconjugated (indirect) serum bilirubin 0.4 mg/dL

_____ Total serum bilirubin 1 mg/dL

_____ Yellow sclera

_____ Light colored bowel movements

_____ Steatorrhea (fatty stools)

_____ Dilute yellow urine

_____ Calcifications noted on abdominal x-ray

6. Which of the following instructions is/are appropriate for a client going home with a T-tube drain? (Check all that apply. For instructions deemed inappropriate, identify why.)

_____ Take baths rather than showers.

_____ Clamp T-tube for 1 to 2 hr before and after meals.

_____ Keep the drainage system above the level of the gallbladder.

_____ Avoid heavy lifting and strenuous activity.

_____ Empty drainage bag at the same time each day.

Chapter 73: Cholecystitis and Cholecystectomy

Application Exercises Answer Key

Scenario: A client is admitted with severe upper abdominal pain following a family dinner celebration. She reports frequent belching. She is febrile.

1. What could be a possible cause for the fever and the pain?

   The client's gallbladder has likely ruptured.

2. What should the nurse suspect regarding the quantity and type of food consumed at the dinner celebration by this client?

   Large quantity, high in fat content

3. What medication(s) should the nurse anticipate being prescribed for this client at this point?

   Antispasmodics and/or meperidine (Demerol); probably not morphine because of its possible increase of biliary spasms

4. Which of the following food choices might trigger a cholecystitis attack? (Check all that apply.)

_X_	Ice cream	_X_	Broccoli with cheese sauce
_X_	Brownie with nuts	_X_	Biscuits and gravy
___	Pasta with marinara sauce	___	Sweetened strawberries
___	Turkey sandwich	_X_	Fried eggs and bacon

5. Which of the following client findings indicates biliary obstruction? (Check all that apply.)

__x__	Conjugated (direct) serum bilirubin 0.6 mg/dL
__x__	Serum cholesterol 278 mg/dL
_____	Unconjugated (indirect) serum bilirubin 0.4 mg/dL
_____	Total serum bilirubin 1 mg/dL
__x__	Yellow sclera
__x__	Light colored bowel movements
__x__	Steatorrhea (fatty stools)
_____	Dilute yellow urine
__x__	Calcifications noted on abdominal x-ray

6. Which of the following instructions is/are appropriate for a client going home with a T-tube drain? (Check all that apply. For instructions deemed inappropriate, identify why.)

_____	Take baths rather than showers.
__x__	Clamp T-tube for 1 to 2 hr before and after meals.
_____	Keep the drainage system above the level of the gallbladder.
__x__	Avoid heavy lifting and strenuous activity.
__x__	Empty drainage bag at the same time each day.

Soaking in bath water increases risk for introduction of organisms and consequently infection.

The drainage system needs to be kept below the level of the abdomen in order to allow drainage by gravity and to prevent reflux.

Unit 7 Nursing Care of Clients with Gastrointestinal Disorders

Section: Nursing Care of Clients with Gallbladder and Pancreas Disorders

Chapter 74: Pancreatitis and Pancreatic Cancer

Contributor: Polly Gerber Zimmermann, MSN, MBA, RN, CEN

⟳ NCLEX-PN® Connections:

Learning Objective: Review and apply knowledge within "**Pancreatitis and Pancreatic Cancer**" in readiness for performance of the following nursing activities as outlined by the NCLEX-PN® test plan:

Δ Assist with relevant laboratory, diagnostic, and therapeutic procedures within the nursing role, including:

- Preparation of the client for the procedure.
- Accurate collection of specimens.
- Monitoring client status during and after the procedure.
- Reinforcing client teaching (before and following the procedure).
- Recognizing the client's response (expected, unexpected adverse response) to the procedure.
- Monitoring results.
- Monitoring and taking actions to prevent or minimize the risk of complications.
- Notifying the primary care provider of signs of complications.

Δ Recognize signs and symptoms of the client's problem and complete the proper documentation.

Δ Provide and document care based on the client's health alteration.

Δ Monitor and document vital signs changes.

Δ Interpret data that need to be reported immediately.

Δ Reinforce client education on managing the client's health problem.

Δ Recognize and respond to emergency situations, including notification of the primary care provider.

Δ Review the client's response to emergency interventions and complete the proper documentation.

Δ Provide care that meets the age-related needs of clients 65 years of age or older, including recognizing expected physiological changes.

Pancreatitis

 Key Points

Δ   The pancreas' islets of Langerhans secrete insulin and glucagon. The pancreatic exocrine tissues secret digestive enzymes that break down carbohydrates, proteins, and fats.

Δ   Pancreatitis is an **autodigestion** of the pancreas from a premature activation (before reaching the intestines) of the pancreatic digestive enzymes (exact mechanism unknown). It can result in **inflammation, necrosis,** and **hemorrhage.**

Δ   Classic signs and symptoms of an acute attack include **severe, constant, knife-like pain** (right upper quadrant, gastric, and/or radiating to the back) that is unrelieved by nausea and vomiting.

Δ   **Acute pancreatitis** is an inflammation of the pancreas resulting from activated pancreatic enzymes autodigesting the pancreas. Severity varies, but overall mortality is 10 to 20%.

Δ   **Chronic pancreatitis** is a progressive **destruction of the pancreas** with development of calcification and **necrosis**, possibly resulting in hemorrhagic pancreatitis. Mortality can be as high as 50%.

Key Factors

Δ   **Two primary causes** of pancreatitis are **alcoholism and biliary tract disease** (gallstones can cause blockage where the common bile duct and pancreatic duct meet).

Δ   Pancreatitis is also a possible complication of **endoscopic retrograde cholangiopancreatography (ERCP).**

Δ   **Triggering factors** include intake of large amounts of fat and/or **alcohol.**

Diagnostic Procedures and Nursing Interventions

Δ   **Serum amylase** (rises within 12 hr, lasts 4 days) and **serum lipase** (rises slower but lasts up to 2 weeks).

-   Urine amylase also remains elevated for up to 2 weeks.

-   Rises in these enzymes indicate pancreatic cell injury.

-   **Memory aid: In pancreatitis, the "ases" (aces) are high.**

-   To be considered positive, the enzyme rise must be significant (2 to 3 times the normal value for amylase and 3 to 5 times the normal value for lipase). The degree of enzyme elevation does not directly correlate with the severity of disease.

Δ   **Serum calcium and magnesium levels: Decreased** due to fat necrosis with pancreatitis)

Δ   **Serum liver enzymes and bilirubin levels: Elevated** with associated biliary dysfunction)

Δ   **White blood cell count: Elevated** due to infection and inflammation

Δ   Computed tomography (CT) scan with contrast: Reliably diagnostic of acute pancreatitis

Therapeutic Procedures and Nursing Interventions

Δ   Endoscopic retrograde cholangiopancreatography (**ERCP**) to create an opening in the sphincter of Oddi and/or an **open cholecystectomy** are possibly effective treatments if the pancreatitis is a result of gallstones.

Assessments

Δ   Monitor for **signs and symptoms.**

- Sudden onset of severe, boring pain
  - ◊ Epigastric, radiating to back, left flank, or left shoulder
  - ◊ Worse when lying down or with eating
  - ◊ Not relieved with vomiting
  - ◊ Some relief in fetal position
- Nausea and vomiting
- Weight loss
- Signs and symptoms of inflammation or peritonitis
- Seepage of blood-stained exudates into tissue
  - ◊ Ecchymoses on the flanks (Turner's sign)
  - ◊ Bluish periumbilical discoloration (Cullen's sign)
- Generalized jaundice
- Paralytic ileus
- Hyperglycemia

Δ   **Assess/Monitor**

- Pain level
- Nutritional status
- Bowel function

- Blood glucose levels
- Diet and alcohol intake history
- Fluid and electrolyte status

NANDA Nursing Diagnoses

Δ   Acute pain

Δ   Imbalanced nutrition: Less than body requirements

Nursing Interventions

Δ   **Rest the pancreas.**

- **NPO – no food until pain free**
- Nasogastric tube – gastric decompression
- Total parenteral nutrition (TPN)
- When diet is resumed: bland, low-fat diet with no stimulants (caffeine); small, frequent meals rather than large meals
- No alcohol
- No smoking
- Limit stress

Δ   **Pain Management**

- Administer **opioids** as prescribed. Often large doses of intravenous narcotics are needed for pain management. Traditionally, meperidine (Demerol) has been preferred, because pain is acute and morphine sulfate can cause spasms in the sphincter of Oddi.
- **Position for comfort** (fetal, side-lying, with the head of the bed elevated or sitting up/leaning forward).

Δ   Administer other **medications** as prescribed.

- Anticholinergics
- Antibiotics
- Vitamin supplements
- Pancreatic enzymes such as pancreatin (Donnazyme), pancrelipase (Viokase); take with meals and snacks to aid with digestion of fats and proteins.

Δ   Monitor blood glucose levels and provide insulin as needed (potential for hyperglycemia).

Δ   Monitor hydration levels (orthostatic blood pressure, intake and output, laboratory values).

Δ   Monitor for hypocalcemia.

Δ   Tetany

Δ   Trousseau's sign (hand spasm when blood pressure cuff is inflated on that arm)

Δ   Chvostek's sign (facial twitching when facial nerve is tapped)

Complications and Nursing Implications

Δ   **Hypovolemia** (up to 6 L can be third-spaced, retroperitoneal loss of protein-rich fluid from proteolytic digestion): Monitor vital signs, provide IV fluid and electrolyte replacement.

Δ   Chronic pancreatitis: Avoid alcohol intake, participate in alcoholic support groups.

Δ   **Hypocalcemia**

Δ   Pancreatic Infection: Pseudocyst (outside pancreas); abscess (inside pancreas)

Δ   Type 1 diabetes mellitus: Total destruction of the pancreas

Δ   Left lung effusion and atelectasis: Monitor for hypoxia, provide ventilatory support.

Δ   Organ failure (for example, renal failure): Monitor laboratory values, provide organ support.

Δ   Coagulation defects (for example, disseminated intravascular coagulopathy): Monitor bleeding times.

Meeting the Needs of Older Adults

Δ   The primary cause of chronic pancreatitis is chronic alcoholism. The older adult client can become dependent on alcohol to cope with life changes. Explore alcohol intake. Age-related changes reduce the older adult's ability to physiologically handle alcohol.

Pancreatic Cancer

 Key Points

Δ **Pancreatic carcinoma** has vague symptoms and is usually diagnosed in late stages after liver or gallbladder involvement.

Δ It has a **high mortality rate** (less than 20% live longer than 1 year after diagnosis).

Key Factors

Δ The cause is unknown, but there is a possible inherited risk.

Δ The highest incidence occurs:

• For people between 60 and 80 years of age.

• Among smokers.

Diagnostic Procedures and Nursing Interventions

Δ Serum amylase and lipase: Elevated

Δ Serum alkaline phosphatase and bilirubin levels: Elevated

Δ Carcinoembryonic antigen (CEA): Elevated

Δ Computed tomography (CT): Visualization of tumor

Δ ERCP: Most definitive; allows for placement of drain or stent for biliary drainage

Δ Abdominal paracentesis: Test for malignant cells

Therapeutic Procedures and Nursing Interventions

Δ **Whipple procedure** – removal of the head of the pancreas, duodenum, parts of the jejunum and stomach, gallbladder, and possibly the spleen. The pancreatic duct is connected to the common bile duct. The stomach is connected to the jejunum.

Δ Chemotherapy (monitor for myelosuppression and pancytopenia) and radiation (monitor fatigue and diarrhea) are possible therapies to shrink tumor size.

Assessments

Δ   Monitor for **signs and symptoms.**

- Vague abdominal pain

- Anorexia and weight loss

- Fatigue

- Signs of obstruction: Jaundice (late sign), clay colored stools, dark urine

NANDA Nursing Diagnoses

Δ   Acute pain

Δ   Imbalanced nutrition: Less than body requirements

Nursing Interventions

Δ   **Pain management is the priority intervention.** Generally, large doses of opioids (for example, morphine) are given.

Δ   Provide postoperative care as appropriate.

- Monitor NG and surgical drainage (serosanguineous initially). Protect sites of anastomosis.

- Place the client in semi-Fowler's position to facilitate lung expansion and to prevent stress on suture line.

- Provide IV replacement of fluid and blood losses as appropriate.

- Assess breath sounds and respirations and facilitate deep breathing. Encourage use of incentive spirometer and administer oxygen as needed.

Δ   Monitor glucose levels and administer insulin as prescribed.

Δ   Provide nutritional support (for example, enteral supplements).

Complications and Nursing Interventions

Δ   **Venous thromboembolism**

- The most common complication of pancreatic cancer.

- Monitor pulses and for areas of warmth and tenderness.

- Administer anticoagulants as prescribed.

Δ   **Fistulas**

- Possible complication of Whipple procedure due to breakdown of a site of anastomosis.

Δ   **Peritonitis**

- Internal leakage of corrosive pancreatic fluid.

- Monitor for signs and symptoms of peritonitis such as elevated fever, WBC, abdominal pain, abdominal tenderness/rebound tenderness, alteration in bowel sounds, and shoulder tip pain.

- Provide antibiotics as prescribed.

Primary Source

Ignatavicius, D. D., & Workman, M. L. (2006). *Medical-surgical nursing* (5th ed.). St. Louis, MO: Saunders.

Additional Resources

NANDA International (2004). *NANDA nursing diagnoses: Definitions and classification 2005-2006*. Philadelphia: NANDA.

For more information, visit the Pancreatitis Association International at *www.pancassociation.org* or the National Digestive Diseases Information Clearinghouse at *digestive.niddk.nih.gov/ddiseases/pubs/pancreatitis.*

Chapter 74: Pancreatitis and Pancreatic Cancer

Application Exercises

1. Which of the following nursing interventions are appropriate for a client diagnosed with acute pancreatitis? (Check all that apply.)

   _____ Drink plenty of fluids.

   _____ Avoid alcohol.

   _____ Avoid smoking.

   _____ Encourage relaxation.

   _____ Place the client in a rescuer position for maximum comfort.

   _____ Practice pursed-lip breathing.

2. A client is admitted to the hospital with a diagnosis of an acute pancreatitis attack. Which of the following client assessments is most important for the nurse to follow up on first?

   A. History of cholelithiasis

   B. Serum amylase levels are three times the normal value

   C. Reports severe pain radiating to the back, rated at "8"

   D. Hand spasm present when the nurse is taking the blood pressure

3. The client has arrived from the emergency department with the diagnosis of acute pancreatitis. Which of the following client assessment findings is most important for the nurse to deal with first?

   A. Client has bluish discoloration around the periumbilical area.

   B. Lying: BP 120/80 mm Hg, HR 80 beats/min; standing: BP 94/70 mm Hg, HR 110 beats/min.

   C. Serum amylase and lipase levels are five times the normal values.

   D. Client reports vomiting two times in the last hour.

4. Which of the following is most important for a nurse to teach a client who is hospitalized with acute pancreatitis?

   A. Technique regarding how to give home injections of insulin

   B. Importance of monitoring amylase and lipase levels

   C. Avoidance of alcohol use for 1 year

   D. Use of aspirin instead of acetaminophen (Tylenol) as an OTC medication

5. A client had a Whipple procedure 3 days ago for pancreatic cancer. Which of the following client assessments is most important for the nurse to follow up?

      A. Bowel sounds are auscultated 10/min

      B. Wound edges are slightly edematous, reddish, and soft

      C. Client reports abdominal pain radiating to shoulder and has a fever

      D. WBC 9,000/mm^3

6. Discuss some possible complications following a Whipple procedure for a client with pancreatic cancer. For each identify an appropriate nursing intervention.

Chapter 74: Pancreatitis and Pancreatic Cancer

Application Exercises Answer Key

1. Which of the following nursing interventions are appropriate for a client diagnosed with acute pancreatitis? (Check all that apply.)

_____	Drink plenty of fluids.
__x__	Avoid alcohol.
__x__	Avoid smoking.
__x__	Encourage relaxation.
_____	Place the client in a rescuer position for maximum comfort.
_____	Practice pursed-lip breathing.

The client is initially NPO. Fluids are needed, but by IV route. Clients are more comfortable with the head of the bed elevated or sitting, leaning forward. The rescuer position is flat, side-lying. Pursed-lip breathing is used to extend the exhalation for air trapping with COPD clients. Clients with pancreatitis are encouraged to deep breathe.

2. A client is admitted to the hospital with a diagnosis of an acute pancreatitis attack. Which of the following client assessments is most important for the nurse to follow up on first?

A. History of cholelithiasis

B. Serum amylase levels are three times the normal value

C. Reports severe pain radiating to the back, rated at "8"

D. Hand spasm present when the nurse is taking the blood pressure

Trousseau's sign indicates hypocalcemia, a systemic complication that can have cardiac effects. This must be dealt with first. Biliary tract disease is one of the two leading causes of acute pancreatitis and probably explains why the client has this problem. Elevated serum amylase and lipase levels are how the diagnosis is made. Pain is not desirable and should be treated with meperidine (Demerol), but the systemic hypocalcemia is the priority.

3. The client has arrived from the emergency department with the diagnosis of acute pancreatitis. Which of the following client assessment findings is most important for the nurse to deal with first?

   A. Client has bluish discoloration around the periumbilical area.

   B. Lying: BP 120/80 mm Hg, HR 80 beats/min; standing: BP 94/70 mm Hg, HR 110 beats/min.

   C. Serum amylase and lipase levels are five times the normal values.

   D. Client reports vomiting two times in the last hour.

The client is experiencing orthostatic changes and needs fluid replacement. Cullen's sign (bluish periumbilical discoloration) and vomiting are expected findings. Elevated enzyme levels are how the diagnosis is made, but the level of rise does not necessarily correlate with the seriousness of the disease episode.

4. Which of the following is most important for a nurse to teach a client who is hospitalized with acute pancreatitis?

   A. Technique regarding how to give home injections of insulin

   B. Importance of monitoring amylase and lipase levels

   C. Avoidance of alcohol use for 1 year

   D. Use of aspirin instead of acetaminophen (Tylenol) as an OTC medication

Chronic alcohol consumption can cause chronic pancreatitis. Clients may need insulin initially for hyperglycemia, but generally not as healing occurs. Amylase and lipase levels are used for diagnostic purposes (released from the injured cells) and are usually close to normal around 2 weeks. Tylenol does not need to be avoided in pancreatitis; it is avoided in hepatitis.

5. A client had a Whipple procedure 3 days ago for pancreatic cancer. Which of the following client assessments is most important for the nurse to follow up?

   A. Bowel sounds are auscultated 10/min

   B. Wound edges are slightly edematous, reddish, and soft

   C. Client reports abdominal pain radiating to shoulder and has a fever

   D. WBC 9,000/mm³

These are classic signs and symptoms of peritonitis and require further investigation. The bowel sounds are within normal range (5 to 35/min) and would be anticipated to be hypoactive 3 days postoperative. Wound edges should show minor inflammation. Slight elevation of WBC is expected after surgery due to inflammation.

6. Discuss some possible complications following a Whipple procedure for a client with pancreatic cancer. For each identify an appropriate nursing intervention.

Fistula (most serious and most common). Monitor for signs and symptoms of peritonitis such as elevated fever, WBC, abdominal pain, abdominal tenderness/rebound tenderness, alteration in bowel sounds, pain radiating to shoulder.

Hyperglycemia/diabetes mellitus. Monitor blood glucose.

Wound infection. Monitor temperature and wound site.

Bowel obstruction. Monitor bowel sounds, stool.

Intra-abdominal abscess. Monitor temperature, pancreatitis-like severe pain.

Pulmonary complications. Monitor breath sounds, pulse oximetry, and respirations.

Unit 7   Nursing Care of Clients with Gastrointestinal Disorders

Section: Nursing Care of Clients with Liver Disorders

Chapter 75:   **Hepatitis**

Contributor: Vicky Simbro, BSN, RN

NCLEX-PN® Connections:

Learning Objective: Review and apply knowledge within **"Hepatitis"** in readiness for performance of the following nursing activities as outlined by the NCLEX-PN® test plan:

Δ   Assist with relevant laboratory, diagnostic, and therapeutic procedures within the nursing role, including:

- Preparation of the client for the procedure.
- Accurate collection of specimens.
- Monitoring client status during and after the procedure.
- Reinforcing client teaching (before and following the procedure).
- Recognizing the client's response (expected, unexpected adverse response) to the procedure.
- Monitoring results.
- Monitoring and taking actions to prevent or minimize the risk of complications.
- Notifying the primary care provider of signs of complications.

Δ   Recognize signs and symptoms of the client's problem and complete the proper documentation.

Δ   Provide and document care based on the client's health alteration.

Δ   Monitor and document vital signs changes.

Δ   Interpret data that need to be reported immediately.

Δ   Reinforce client education on managing the client's health problem.

Δ   Recognize and respond to emergency situations, including notification of the primary care provider.

Δ   Review the client's response to emergency interventions and complete the proper documentation.

Δ   Provide care that meets the age-related needs of clients 65 years of age or older, including recognizing expected physiological changes.

Key Points

Δ   Hepatitis is an **inflammation of the liver**. Viral hepatitis can be acute or chronic.

Δ   There are **five major categories** of viral hepatitis (hepatitis F and G have been identified but are uncommon).

- Hepatitis A virus (HAV)

- Hepatitis B virus (HBV)

- Hepatitis C virus (HCV)

- Hepatitis D virus (HDV)

- Hepatitis E virus (HEV)

Δ   All these viruses can cause an acute or short-term illness and may become a chronic debilitating disease with increasing severity in symptoms over a long period of time.

Δ   Each year 250,000 people in the United States become infected with hepatitis, but only a portion of these cases are reported. Persons with hepatitis are carriers and can spread the disease without showing any symptoms of the disease.

Δ   People with hepatitis should **never** donate blood, body organs, or other body tissue. Every healthcare worker should take the series of hepatitis B vaccines.

Δ   It is required to **report all cases of hepatitis** to the health department.

Key Factors

Δ   **Risk Factors by Type of Hepatitis**

Type	Route of Transmission	Risk Factors
Hepatitis **A** (HAV)	Oral-fecal route	Ingestion of contaminated food/water
Hepatitis **B** (HBV)	**B**lood	Drug abuse Sexual contact Healthcare work
Hepatitis C (HCV)	Blood	Drug abuse Sexual contact
Hepatitis D (HDV)	Co-infection with HBV	Drug abuse
Hepatitis **E** (HEV)	Oral-fecal route	Ingestion of contaminated water

Δ **High Risk Behaviors**

- **Failure to follow Universal Precautions**

- Percutaneous exposure (dirty needles, sharp instruments, body piercing, tattooing, use of another person's drug paraphernalia or personal hygiene tools)

- Unprotected sexual intercourse with a hepatitis-infected person; sex with multiple partners and/or anal sex

- Unscreened blood transfusions (prior to 1992)

- Hemodialysis

- Ingestion of food prepared by a hepatitis-infected person who fails to take proper sanitation precautions

- Travel/residence in underdeveloped country (using tap water to clean food products and drinking contaminated water)

- Eating and/or living in crowded environments (correctional facilities, dormitories, universities, long-term care facilities, military base housing)

Diagnostic Assessments and Nursing Interventions

Δ **Serum liver enzymes: Elevated**

- Alanine aminotransferase (ALT): Elevated (normal – 8 to 20 units/L; 3 to 35 IU/L); most definitive for **assessment of liver tissue damage.**

- Aspartate aminotransferase (AST): Elevated (normal – 5 to 40 units/L)

- Alkaline phosphatase (ALP): Elevated (normal – 42 to 128 units/L; 30 to 85 IU/L)

Δ **Serum bilirubin: Elevated**

- Bilirubin – direct (conjugated): Elevated (normal – 0.1 to 0.3 mg/dL)

- Bilirubin – indirect (unconjugated): Elevated (normal – 0.2 to 0.8 mg/dL)

- Bilirubin – total: Elevated (normal – 0.1 to 1.0 mg/dL)

- Albumin: Decreased (normal – 3 to 5 g/dL)

Δ Serologic Markers: Identify **presence of virus** (HAV, HBsAg and Anti HBc IgM, HCV, HDV, HEV). **Serum presence of HBsAg for longer than 6 months indicates chronic hepatitis and/or hepatitis carrier status.**

Δ **Hepatitis antibody serum testing:** Identify exposure to anti-HAV, HBsAb, anti-HCV, anti-HDV, anti-HEV. **Serum presence of HBsAb indicates immunity to HBV either following recovery from hepatitis B or successful vaccination.**

Δ Abdominal films to visualize possible hepatomegaly, ascites, spleen enlargement.

Δ **Liver biopsy: Most definitive**. Identifies intensity of infection and degree of tissue damage. Nursing interventions include:

- Obtain consent for liver biopsy.

- Review/explain to client the biopsy procedure and what is expected following the procedure.

- Require the client to **lie on affected surgical side for short period of time after biopsy** has been taken.

Assessments

Δ Monitor for **signs and symptoms.**

- Influenza symptoms (headache, fatigue, low grade fever, right upper quadrant abdominal pain, nausea and vomiting).

- HBV presents with additional symptoms: hepatomegaly, signs of obstruction (light colored stools, dark urine, jaundice, elevated bilirubin and liver enzyme levels).

Δ **Assess for alterations in physical assessment related to hepatitis:**

- Inspect overall color of skin, eyes, and mucus membranes for presence of jaundice and skin irritations probably due to pruritus.

- Pain in muscles, joints, and abdomen.

- Fever, malaise, increased fatigue, and nausea and vomiting.

- Change in color of stool (clay colored) or dark urine.

- Palpate right upper abdomen for swelling and complaints of tenderness. Have the client take deep breath to feel border of liver under ribs and measure/record abdominal distention.

Δ **Pertinent Client History**

- Take an inventory of recent travel, work history, and onset and intensity of symptoms.

- Identify measures the client has already taken such as pain medicine, fluids, and diet changes.

- Identify exposure agents.

- When interviewing the client, use a nonjudgmental manner. Behaviors that may have caused this disease occurred years before the present illness and can be embarrassing to the client to express comfortably.

NANDA Nursing Diagnoses

Δ Fatigue

Δ Nausea

Nursing Interventions

Δ Implement **contact isolation precautions** (universal precautions, private room, gloves, gown, dedicated equipment).

Δ **Limit client activity** (for example, bedrest) in order to promote hepatic healing.

Δ Provide dietary education regarding a high-carbohydrate, high-calorie, low- to moderate-fat, and **low- to moderate-protein diet** and small, frequent meals to promote nutrition and healing.

Δ Medications are used sparingly for **hepatic rest** and regeneration of tissue.

Δ Administer **interferon** as prescribed for HBV and HCV. Monitor clients receiving interferon for side effects of flu-like symptoms, alopecia, and bone marrow suppression. Monitor CBC and administer antiemetics as needed during interferon therapy.

Δ Educate the client and family regarding **measures to prevent transmission** of disease with others at home (for example, avoid sexual intercourse until hepatitis antibody testing is negative).

Δ Provide **comfort measures**.

Δ **Encourage hepatitis prevention activities:**

- Community health educational interventions on transmission and exposure.

- Hepatitis B vaccination prophylaxis for all healthcare workers.

- Proper use of Universal Precautions.

- Use of a needleless system when delivering medications and parental solutions.

- Frequent handwashing (before eating and after using the toilet) and use of personal protective equipment appropriate to type of exposure (gown, gloves, goggles).

- If traveling in underdeveloped countries, drink bottled water, and limit sharing of bed linens and eating utensils.

- Report hepatitis outbreaks to health authorities.

- Instruct clients to avoid excess alcohol and all drugs not prescribed by the primary care provider.

- Consider administration of immunoglobin (Ig) to clients exposed to hepatitis A or hepatitis B. Hepatitis B immune globulin (HBIG) and/or the hepatitis B vaccine series may be administered prophylactically following exposure to blood of a client with known HBsAg.

Complications and Nursing Implications

Δ **Chronic hepatitis** – results from hepatitis B, C, or D. Increases the client's risk for liver cancer.

Δ **Fulminating hepatitis** – this fatal form of hepatitis is due to the inability of the liver cells to regenerate with increased progression of the necrotic process. This disease results in hepatic encephalopathy and death. Monitor the client for neurological changes, manage fluid and electrolytes, and provide comfort measures.

Δ **Cirrhosis of the liver** – continued episodes of chronic hepatitis result in scarring and permanent injury to the liver and also is a risk factor for liver cancer. (*For information, refer to chapter 76, Cirrhosis.*)

Δ **Liver cancer** – chief report is abdominal discomfort. Diagnosis is made by ultrasound, computerized tomography (CT), elevated liver enzymes, and liver biopsy for confirmation of cancer. (*For information, refer to chapter 77, Liver Cancer.*)

Δ **Liver failure** – chronic hepatitis, liver abscesses, and fatty liver infiltration all result in changes within the healthy liver and cause irreversible damage.

Meeting the Needs of Older Adults

Δ Older adult clients with HBV and HCV have significant impairment of their liver function and are acutely ill and require more nursing interventions.

Δ Care for older adult clients is more involved and requires a lot of supportive care to maintain nutrition, push fluids, and plan rest periods with limited activity to encourage hepatic regeneration and healing.

Primary Reference:

Ignatavicius, D. D., & Workman, M. L. (2006). *Medical-surgical nursing* (5th ed.). St. Louis, MO: Saunders.

Additional Resources:

NANDA International (2004). *NANDA nursing diagnoses: Definitions and classification 2005-2006*. Philadelphia: NANDA.

Porth, C. M. (2004). *Essentials of pathophysiology: Concepts of altered health states*. Philadelphia: Lippincott Williams & Wilkins.

Chapter 75: Hepatitis

Application Exercises

1. A client has an elevated temperature, is very anxious, and reports diarrhea for the past 2 weeks unrelieved by antidiarrheal medicine. She works at a daycare center with children. Which of the following types of hepatitis would be the most likely cause of these symptoms?

   A. Hepatitis A

   B. Hepatitis B

   C. Hepatitis C

   D. Hepatitis E

2. Assessing which of the following is an observational method to determine the initial level of involvement of hepatitis?

   A. Weight

   B. Vital signs

   C. Skin color

   D. Temperature

3. Diet intervention for the client with hepatitis should include which of the following? (Check all that apply.)

   _____ Foods high in protein

   _____ Foods high in carbohydrates

   _____ Alcohol

   _____ Whole grain foods

   _____ Foods low in fat

4. Which of the following interventions are appropriate for clients with hepatitis? (Check all that apply.)

   _____ Bedrest with limited physical activity

   _____ Avoid alcohol.

   _____ Administer acetaminophen every 3 to 4 hr around the clock for comfort.

   _____ Implement isolation precautions.

   _____ Administer supplemental vitamins.

5. Which of the following laboratory findings is supportive of a diagnosis of hepatitis?

      A. ALT 45 units/L
      B. WBC 7,800/mm³
      C. Total bilirubin 1.0 mg/dL
      D. Albumin 4.9 g/dL

6. Which of the following precautions are appropriate to prevent the transmission of viral hepatitis? (Check all that apply.)

     _____   Wear gloves when emptying a bedpan containing feces.
     _____   Administer immunoglobin following exposure.
     _____   Discourage tattoos and body piercings.
     _____   Instruct food handlers to carefully wash hands prior to food preparation.
     _____   Use universal precautions with all clients.

Chapter 75: Hepatitis

Application Exercises Answer Key

1. A client has an elevated temperature, is very anxious, and reports diarrhea for the past 2 weeks unrelieved by antidiarrheal medicine. She works at a daycare center with children. Which of the following types of hepatitis would be the most likely cause of these symptoms?

> **A. Hepatitis A**
> B. Hepatitis B
> C. Hepatitis C
> D. Hepatitis E

Because the client works in a daycare, it's most likely she has hepatitis A. HAV usually resolves on its own.

2. Assessing which of the following is an observational method to determine the initial level of involvement of hepatitis?

> A. Weight
> B. Vital signs
> **C. Skin color**
> D. Temperature

All of these observations should be part of the assessment; however, skin color is a way to assess the level of hepatic involvement. If jaundice is present, it immediately indicates that some hepatic infection dysfunction is present.

3. Diet intervention for the client with hepatitis should include which of the following? (Check all that apply.)

> _____   Foods high in protein
> __x__   Foods high in carbohydrates
> _____   Alcohol
> _____   Whole grain foods
> __x__   Foods low in fat

Initially, the nurse should encourage frequent small meals with a diet high in carbohydrates and low in fat. This diet is less taxing on the liver, whereas protein and alcohol tax the liver. In general, hepatic rest is indicated so as to promote hepatic regeneration.

4. Which of the following interventions are appropriate for clients with hepatitis? (Check all that apply.)

    x   Bedrest with limited physical activity

    x   Avoid alcohol.

               Administer acetaminophen every 3 to 4 hr around the clock for comfort.

    x   Implement isolation precautions.

    x   Administer supplemental vitamins.

Bedrest is necessary for the healing of hepatocellular tissue. Alcohol and drugs tax the liver. Additionally, acetaminophen can also contribute to hepatotoxicity. Most hepatitis clients do need to be isolated. Isolation and hygiene precautions are necessary in the hospital during the infection, and precautions are necessary at home to prevent transmission of the disease. The liver plays a significant role in meeting vitamin needs. Supplementation of vitamins during periods of liver stress is appropriate.

5. Which of the following laboratory findings is supportive of a diagnosis of hepatitis?

A. ALT 45 units/L

B. WBC 7,800/mm³

C. Total bilirubin 1.0 mg/dL

D. Albumin 4.9 g/dL

A normal ALT range is 8 to 20 units/L. An ALT (Alanine aminotransferase) level is a definitive serum test for detecting liver damage. Infection usually results in elevations in WBC above 10,000/mm³. A total bilirubin level of 1.0 mg/dL and an albumin level of 4.9 g/dL are within normal ranges.

6. Which of the following precautions are appropriate to prevent the transmission of viral hepatitis? (Check all that apply.)

    x   Wear gloves when emptying a bedpan containing feces.

    x   Administer immunoglobin following exposure.

    x   Discourage tattoos and body piercings.

    x   Instruct food handlers to carefully wash hands prior to food preparation.

    x   Use universal precautions with all clients.

Unit 7   Nursing Care of Clients with Gastrointestinal Disorders
Section: Nursing Care of Clients with Liver Disorders

Chapter 76:   Cirrhosis
Contributor: Vicky Simbro, BSN, RN

⟳ NCLEX-PN® Connections:

Learning Objective: Review and apply knowledge within "**Cirrhosis**" in readiness for performance of the following nursing activities as outlined by the NCLEX-PN® test plan:

Δ   Assist with relevant laboratory, diagnostic, and therapeutic procedures within the nursing role, including:

  •   Preparation of the client for the procedure.

  •   Accurate collection of specimens.

  •   Monitoring client status during and after the procedure.

  •   Reinforcing client teaching (before and following the procedure).

  •   Recognizing the client's response (expected, unexpected adverse response) to the procedure.

  •   Monitoring results.

  •   Monitoring and taking actions to prevent or minimize the risk of complications.

    •   Notifying the primary care provider of signs of complications.

Δ   Recognize signs and symptoms of the client's problem and complete the proper documentation.

Δ   Provide and document care based on the client's health alteration.

Δ   Monitor and document vital signs changes.

Δ   Interpret data that need to be reported immediately.

Δ   Reinforce client education on managing the client's health problem.

Δ   Recognize and respond to emergency situations, including notification of the primary care provider.

Δ   Review the client's response to emergency interventions and complete the proper documentation.

Δ   Provide care that meets the age-related needs of clients 65 years of age or older, including recognizing expected physiological changes.

📖 Key Points

Δ Cirrhosis refers to extensive **scarring of the liver** caused by necrotic injury or a **chronic reaction to inflammation** over a prolonged period of time.

Δ Cirrhosis can be life-threatening, but can be controlled if discovered early.

Key Factors

Δ **Causes**

- Alcohol abuse

- Chronic viral hepatitis (hepatitis B, C, or D)

- Autoimmune hepatitis (destruction of the liver cells by the immune system)

- Steatohepatitis (fatty liver disease causing chronic inflammation)

- Damage to the liver by drugs, toxins, and other infections

- Chronic biliary cirrhosis (bile duct obstruction, bile stasis, and hepatic fibrosis)

Δ **Cardiac cirrhosis** is a result of severe right heart failure inducing necrosis and fibrosis due to lack of blood flow.

Diagnostic Procedures and Nursing Interventions

Δ **Serum liver enzymes: Elevated initially**

- Alanine aminotransferase (ALT): normal – 8 to 20 units/L; 3 to 35 IU/L

- Aspartate aminotransferase (AST): normal – 5 to 40 units/L

- Alkaline phosphatase (ALP): normal – 42 to 128 units/L; 30 to 85 IU/L

- ALT and AST are elevated initially due to hepatic inflammation and then normal when liver cells are no longer able to create an inflammatory response. ALP increases in cirrhosis due to intrahepatic biliary obstruction.

Δ **Serum bilirubin: Elevated**

- Bilirubin – direct (conjugated): Elevated (normal – 0.1 to 0.3 mg/dL)

- Bilirubin – indirect (unconjugated): Elevated (normal – 0.2 to 0.8 mg/dL)

- Bilirubin – total: Elevated (normal – 0.1 to 1.0 mg/dL)

- Bilirubin levels are elevated in cirrhosis due to the inability of the liver to excrete bilirubin.

Δ Serum proteins and serum albumin (normal 3 to 5 g/dL) are lowered due to the **lack of hepatic synthesis.**

Δ Hematological tests: CBC, WBC, and platelets all are decreased **secondary to anemia.**

Δ **PT/INR** are prolonged due to decreased synthesis of prothrombin.

Δ **Ammonia levels (normal 15 to 110 mg/dL) rise when hepatocellular injury (cirrhosis) prevents the conversion of ammonia to urea for excretion.**

Δ Serum creatinine levels (normal 0.6 to 1.2 mg/dL) may increase due to deteriorating kidney function which may occur as a result of advanced liver disease.

Δ Abdominal films and ultrasonography are used to visualize possible hepatomegaly, ascites, and spleen enlargement.

Δ **Liver biopsy (most definitive)** – identifies progression and extent of cirrhosis.

- To minimize the risks, an interventional radiologist performs the biopsy through the jugular vein, which is then threaded to the hepatic vein to obtain tissue for a microscopic evaluation.

- This is done under fluoroscopy for safety because this procedure can be problematic for cirrhosis clients due to an increased risk for bleeding complications.

- Nursing interventions include:

  ◊ Obtain consent for a liver biopsy.

  ◊ Review/explain to the client the biopsy procedure and what is expected following the procedure.

  ◊ Requiring the client to **lie on affected surgical side for short period of time after biopsy** has been taken.

Δ Esophagogastroduodenoscopy (EGD) under conscious sedation is used to detect the presence of esophageal varices.

Therapeutic Procedures and Nursing Interventions

Δ **Paracentesis** (*For information, refer to chapter 63, Paracentesis.*) is used to relieve ascites. Avoid rapid removal of the ascitic fluid.

Δ **Injection sclerotherapy** – varices are sclerosed endoscopically.

Δ **Transjugular intrahepatic portosystemic shunt (TIPS) procedure is used to control ascites and variceal bleeding.** The client is given moderate sedation, or general anesthesia. The shunt is guided through the liver into the portal vein, the vein is ballooned opened, and the shunt is placed. A doppler study is performed to measure the blood flow through the shunt. Clients are discharged 2 to 4 days post procedure and monitored with ultrasound exams during the first year. In certain circumstances, reballooning of the shunt is necessary during that year.

Δ **Surgical bypass shunting procedures** are interventions considered as a last resort for clients with portal hypertension and esophageal varices. For example, peritoneovenous and portacaval shunts. **Ascites is shunted from the abdominal cavity to the superior vena cava.**

Δ **Liver transplantation** – cirrhosis is the most common reason for transplantation. To avoid organ rejection, medications like steroids and other immunosuppressants are used to weaken the ability of the body to reject the new liver. Changes in behavior are necessary to prevent the return of the problems that initially caused the reason for the transplantation in the first place.

Assessments

Δ Monitor for **signs and symptoms.**

- **Fatigue**

- Weight loss, abdominal pain, and distention

- **Pruritus** (severe itching of skin)

- Confusion or difficulty thinking (due to the build-up of waste products in the blood and brain that the liver is unable to get rid of).

- Gastrointestinal bleeding (enlarged veins [**varices**] develop and burst, causing vomiting and passing of blood in bowel movements)

- **Ascites** (bloating or swelling due to fluid build-up in abdomen and legs)

- **Jaundice** (yellowing of skin) and icterus (yellowing of the eyes)

- **Petechiae** (round, pinpoint, and red-purple lesions), ecchymosis (large yellow and purple blue bruises), nose bleeds, hematemesis, melena (decreased synthesis of prothrombin and deteriorating hepatic function)

- Palmar erythema (redness and warmth of the palms of the hands)

- Spider angiomas (red lesions vascular in nature with branches radiating on the nose, cheeks, upper thorax, and shoulders)

- Dependent peripheral edema of extremities and sacrum

- Personality and mentation changes, emotional lability, euphoria, and sometimes depression

- **Asterixis** (liver flapping tremor) is a coarse tremor characterized by rapid, nonrhythmic extension and flexion of the wrists and fingers

- Fetor hepaticus (liver breath) is a fruity or musty odor

Δ **Assess/Monitor**

- Respiratory status
- Skin integrity
- Vital signs
- Neurological status
- Nutritional status

NANDA Nursing Diagnoses

Δ Excess fluid volume

Δ Ineffective breathing pattern

Δ Risk for impaired skin integrity

Δ Risk for infection

Δ Chronic pain

Δ Risk for imbalanced nutrition: Less than body requirements

Nursing Interventions

Δ Provide **comfort measures** by positioning the client to ease respiratory effort. Have the client sit in a chair or elevate the head of the bed to 30°.

Δ Observe the client for **potential bleeding complications**. Give blood transfusions (packed red blood cells and fresh frozen plasma) to replace blood volume and clotting factors as ordered by primary care provider. Monitor the trends in hemoglobin and hematocrit levels and note coagulation studies (aPTT, PT/INR).

Δ Follow diet guidelines:

- High-calorie, moderate-fat diet.
- Low-sodium diet (if the client has excessive fluid in the abdomen).
- Low-protein (if encephalopathy, elevated ammonia).
- Small, frequent, well-balanced nutritional meals.
- Supplemental vitamin enriched liquids (Ensure, Boost).
- Replace and administer vitamins due to inability of the liver to store them.
- If serum sodium is low, fluid intake may be restricted.

- **Encourage the client to not drink alcohol.**
  - ◊ Helps prevent further scarring and fibrosis of liver.
  - ◊ Allows healing and regeneration of liver tissue.
  - ◊ Prevents irritation of the stomach and esophagus lining.
  - ◊ Helps decrease the risk of bleeding.
  - ◊ Helps to prevent other life-threatening complications.
- Δ Initiate appropriate referrals (social services, Alcoholics Anonymous and Al-Anon).
- Δ Provide **medications** as prescribed:
  - As the metabolism of most medications is dependent upon a functioning liver, general medications are administered sparingly, especially opioids, sedatives, and barbiturates.
  - Diuretics – monitor for hypokalemia and hypotension.
  - H$_2$ receptor antagonist – stress ulcer.
  - Lactulose – promote excretion ammonia via the stool.
  - Neomycin and metronidazole (Flagyl) – removes intestinal bacteria which produces ammonia.

Complications and Nursing Implications

- Δ **Portal systemic encephalopathy (PSE)** – clients who have a poorly functioning liver are unable to convert ammonia and other waste products to a less toxic form. These products are carried to the brain and cause neurological symptoms. These clients are treated with medications to reduce the ammonia levels in the body. Medications include lactulose, neomycin sulfate, and metronidazole. Reductions in dietary protein are indicated as ammonia is formed when protein is broken down by intestinal flora.

- Δ **Esophageal varices** – assist with saline lavage (vasoconstriction), esophagogastric balloon tamponade, blood transfusions, ligation and sclerotherapy, and shunts are used to stop bleeding and reduce the risk for hypovolemic shock. Monitor the client's hemoglobin level and vital signs.

Primary Reference:

Ignatavicius, D. D., & Workman, M. L. (2006). *Medical-surgical nursing* (5th ed.). St. Louis, MO: Saunders.

Additional Resources:

NANDA International (2004). *NANDA nursing diagnoses: Definitions and classification 2005-2006*. Philadelphia: NANDA.

For more information about liver health and liver disease prevention, visit the American Liver Foundation at *www.liverfoundation.org*.

Chapter 76: Cirrhosis

Application Exercises

Scenario: A client with a history of chronic biliary disease is admitted to the acute care facility with reports of anorexia, vomiting, chronic indigestion, and abdominal pain. Her liver is swollen and her abdomen is enlarged and protruding. The client's liver enzymes are elevated. Based on her history, physical examination, and laboratory studies, the client is diagnosed with cirrhosis of the liver.

1. What is the significance and cause of the client's enlarged and protruding abdomen?

2. Why is the client at an increased risk for development of ineffective breathing?

3. What client findings (physical and laboratory) would suggest the development of hepatic encephalopathy? (Check all that apply.)

    _____   Delirium

    _____   Serum ammonia 220 mg/dL

    _____   Asterixis

    _____   Serum sodium of 138 mEq/dL

    _____   Fruity breath odor

4. With signs of hepatic encephalopathy, what dietary alteration is indicated?

Chapter 76: Cirrhosis

Application Exercises Answer Key

Scenario: A client with a history of chronic biliary disease is admitted to the acute care facility with reports of anorexia, vomiting, chronic indigestion, and abdominal pain. Her liver is swollen and her abdomen is enlarged and protruding. The client's liver enzymes are elevated. Based on her history, physical examination, and laboratory studies, the client is diagnosed with cirrhosis of the liver.

1. What is the significance and cause of the client's enlarged and protruding abdomen?

    Her large, protruding abdomen is consistent with the ascites that is commonly associated with cirrhosis. Ascites is due to portal hypertension, decreased synthesis of albumin, and obstruction of hepatic lymph flow.

2. Why is the client at an increased risk for development of ineffective breathing?

    The client's ascites, if not relieved by paracentesis, will place pressure on her lungs and internal organs, placing her at risk for ineffective breathing.

3. What client findings (physical and laboratory) would suggest the development of hepatic encephalopathy? (Check all that apply.)

x	Delirium
x	Serum ammonia 220 mg/dL
x	Asterixis
	Serum sodium of 138 mEq/dL
x	Fruity breath odor

    Changes in LOC, coarse tremors (for example, asterixis), fetor hepaticus (fruity breath odor), and elevated ammonia levels are signs of hepatic encephalopathy. A normal serum sodium level is 135 to 145 mEq/L.

4. With signs of hepatic encephalopathy, what dietary alteration is indicated?

    Reductions in dietary protein are indicated as ammonia is formed when protein is broken down by intestinal flora.

Unit 7   Nursing Care of Clients with Gastrointestinal Disorders
Section: Nursing Care of Clients with Liver Disorders

Chapter 77:   Liver Cancer
                   Contributor: Vicky Simbro, BSN, RN

NCLEX-PN® Connections:

Learning Objective: Review and apply knowledge within "**Liver Cancer**" in readiness for performance of the following nursing activities as outlined by the NCLEX-PN® test plan:

Δ   Assist with relevant laboratory, diagnostic, and therapeutic procedures within the nursing role, including:

- Preparation of the client for the procedure.
- Accurate collection of specimens.
- Monitoring client status during and after the procedure.
- Reinforcing client teaching (before and following the procedure).
- Recognizing the client's response (expected, unexpected adverse response) to the procedure.
- Monitoring results.
- Monitoring and taking actions to prevent or minimize the risk of complications.
- Notifying the primary care provider of signs of complications.

Δ   Recognize signs and symptoms of the client's problem and complete the proper documentation.

Δ   Provide and document care based on the client's health alteration.

Δ   Monitor and document vital signs changes.

Δ   Interpret data that need to be reported immediately.

Δ   Reinforce client education on managing the client's health problem.

Δ   Recognize and respond to emergency situations, including notification of the primary care provider.

Δ   Review the client's response to emergency interventions and complete the proper documentation.

Δ   Provide care that meets the age-related needs of clients 65 years of age or older, including recognizing expected physiological changes.

Key Points

Δ The most common liver tumor in the world is hepatocellular carcinoma (HCC).

Δ Most liver tumors are unresectable.

Δ The 5-year survival rate is less than 9%.

Key Factors

Δ **Risk Factors**

- **Cirrhosis**
  ◊ Chronic HBV infection
  ◊ Chronic HCV infection
  ◊ Alcoholic Liver Disease
- **Metastasis from another site**

Diagnostic Procedures and Nursing Interventions

Δ **Alpha-fetoprotein** (AFP), a tumor marker, is **elevated** in liver cancer.

Δ The serum liver enzyme **alkaline phosphatase** (ALP) is **elevated** (normal – 42 to 128 units/L; 30 to 85 IU/L).

Δ Ultrasound and computerized tomography can be used to visualize a tumor.

Δ **A liver biopsy is the most definitive diagnostic procedure.**

- To minimize the risks, an interventional radiologist performs the biopsy through the jugular vein to the hepatic vein to obtain tissue for microscopic evaluation.
- This is done under fluoroscopy.
- Nursing interventions include:
  ◊ Obtain consent for the liver biopsy.
  ◊ Review/explain to the client the biopsy procedure and what is expected following the procedure.
  ◊ The client will be required to **lie on the affected surgical side for a short period of time after the biopsy** has been taken.

Therapeutic Procedures and Nursing Interventions

Δ **Chemotherapy is given through surgically implanted controlled infusion pumps** so that the chemotherapeutic medications are deposited directly into the liver tumor.

Δ **Liver transplantation**: Portions of healthy livers from trauma victims or living donors may be used for transplant.

- The transplanted liver portion will regenerate and grow in size based on the needs of the body.

- Clients with severe cardiac and respiratory disease, metastatic malignant liver cancer, and a history of alcohol/substance abuse are not candidates for liver transplantation.

- Transplantation takes about 12 hr.

- Nursing interventions include:

  ◊ Administer immunosuppressant therapy, as ordered, to prevent organ rejection.

  ◊ Protect the client from infection.

  ◊ Monitor the client for symptoms of organ rejection.

Δ **Surgical resection**: If liver cancer is secluded to one lobe, surgical removal may be indicated. Liver-lobe resection can result in successful survival rates of up to 5 years.

Δ Radiation is not generally used because liver tissue does not tolerate high doses of radiation.

Δ **Chemoembolization**: A chemotherapeutic drug like doxorubicin (Rubex) is delivered through a catheter, along with tiny particles. The particles block blood vessels leading into the tumor. This keeps the chemotherapeutic drug within the liver for an extended period of time.

Assessments

Δ Monitor for **signs and symptoms.**

- Abdominal discomfort

- Anorexia

- Weight loss

- Signs of biliary obstruction, such as jaundice

- Symptoms of cirrhosis (*For information, refer to chapter 76, Cirrhosis.*)

Δ **Assess/Monitor**

- Pain

- Fluid and electrolyte status

- Hepatic function

- Nutritional status

NANDA Nursing Diagnoses

Δ Acute/chronic pain

Δ Imbalanced nutrition: Less than body requirements

Nursing Interventions

Δ Observe the client for **potential bleeding complications**, and give blood transfusions (packed red blood cells and fresh frozen plasma) to replace blood volume and clotting factors as ordered by the provider. Monitor trends in hemoglobin and hematocrit levels, and note coagulation studies (aPTT, PT/INR).

Δ Encourage the client to follow **diet guidelines**.

- High-calorie, moderate fat diet

- Low-sodium diet (if the client has excessive fluid in the abdomen)

- Low-protein diet (if there is encephalopathy, elevated ammonia)

- Small, frequent, well-balanced nutritional meals

- Supplemental vitamin-enriched liquids (Ensure, Boost)

- Replacement and administration of vitamins due to the inability of the liver to store them

- Restriction of fluid intake (if serum sodium is low)

Δ Encourage the client to **avoid drinking alcohol** because this will:

- Help prevent further scarring and fibrosis of liver.

- Allow healing and regeneration of liver tissue.

- Prevent irritation of stomach and esophagus lining.

- Help decrease the risk of bleeding.

- Help to prevent other life-threatening complications.

Δ Initiate appropriate **referrals**, such as social services, hospice, Alcoholics Anonymous.

Δ   Provide medications as prescribed.

- As the metabolism of most drugs is dependent upon a functioning liver, medications generally are administered sparingly (especially opioids, sedatives, and barbiturates).

Complications and Nursing Implications

Δ   **Acute graft rejection post liver transplantation** can occur between 4 and 10 days after surgery.

- Symptoms of rejection include:

◊   Tachycardia.

◊   Upper right flank pain.

◊   Jaundice.

◊   Laboratory results indicative of liver failure.

- Prevention interventions include the administration of immunosuppressants, such as cyclosporine (Sandimmune).

- Administration of increased doses of immunosuppressants is an appropriate response to rejection symptoms.

Primary Reference:

Ignatavicius, D. D., & Workman, M. L. (2006). *Medical-surgical nursing* (5th ed.). St. Louis, MO: Saunders.

Additional Resources:

NANDA International (2004). *NANDA nursing diagnoses: Definitions and classification 2005-2006*. Philadelphia: NANDA.

Chapter 77: Liver Cancer

Application Exercises

Scenario: A 65-year-old male client is being evaluated for possible primary hepatocellular carcinoma. The client is slightly jaundiced, and he has been experiencing nausea, anorexia, and abdominal pain. His provider has also discovered a small abdominal mass in the right upper quadrant. The client's serum sodium level is 140 mEq/L. His ammonia level is 100 mg/dL. There is no evidence of hepatic encephalopathy or ascites at this time.

1. Which of the following laboratory findings are expected? (Check all that apply.)

   _____ Elevated alpha-fetoprotein (AFP)

   _____ Alkaline phosphatase (ALP) 189 units/L

   _____ Hemoglobin 14 g/dL

   _____ Serum total bilirubin 1.0 mg/dL

2. What are the dietary implications for this client? (Check all that apply.)

   _____ High-calorie, moderate fat diet

   _____ Low-sodium diet

   _____ Low-protein diet

   _____ Small, frequent, well-balanced nutritional meals

   _____ Supplemental vitamin-enriched liquids

   _____ Replacement and administration of vitamins due to inability of the liver to store them

   _____ Fluid restriction

3. Identify some of the factors that will determine the client's placement and status on a liver-transplant candidate list. For each factor, identify if it is positive (in favor of transplant candidacy) or negative (not in favor of transplant candidacy).

Factors in Favor of Liver Transplant Candidacy	Factors Against Liver Transplant Candidacy

Chapter 77: Liver Cancer

Application Exercises Answer Key

Scenario: A 65-year-old male client is being evaluated for possible primary hepatocellular carcinoma. The client is slightly jaundiced, and he has been experiencing nausea, anorexia, and abdominal pain. His provider has also discovered a small abdominal mass in the right upper quadrant. The client's serum sodium level is 140 mEq/L. His ammonia level is 100 mg/dL. There is no evidence of hepatic encephalopathy or ascites at this time.

1. Which of the following laboratory findings are expected? (Check all that apply.)

   __X__   Elevated alpha-fetoprotein (AFP)

   __X__   Alkaline phosphatase (ALP) 189 units/L

   _____   Hemoglobin 14 g/dL

   _____   Serum total bilirubin 1.0 mg/dL

   Both AFP and ALP are elevated in liver cancer. The hemoglobin and serum total bilirubin levels are within normal limits.

2. What are the dietary implications for this client? (Check all that apply.)

   __X__   High-calorie, moderate fat diet

   _____   Low-sodium diet

   _____   Low-protein diet

   __X__   Small, frequent, well-balanced nutritional meals

   __X__   Supplemental vitamin-enriched liquids

   __X__   Replacement and administration of vitamins due to inability of the liver to store them

   _____   Fluid restriction

   The client's sodium level is within normal limits, and there is no evidence of ascites at this time, so a low-sodium diet and fluid restriction are not necessary. The client's ammonia level is normal, and there is no evidence of hepatic encephalopathy, so a low-protein diet is not indicated.

3. Identify some of the factors that will determine the client's placement and status on a liver-transplant candidate list. For each factor, identify if it is positive (in favor of transplant candidacy) or negative (not in favor of transplant candidacy).

Factors in Favor of Liver Transplant Candidacy	Factors Against Liver Transplant Candidacy
Primary tumor	Secondary tumor due to metastasis
Tumor limited to one lobe	Heart failure
Early detection	Respiratory failure
Liver without cirrhosis	Alcohol/substance abuse

Unit 8 Nursing Care of Clients with Neurosensory Disorders
Section: Diagnostic and Therapeutic Procedures: Neurosensory

Chapter 78: Monitoring Intracranial Pressure
Contributor: Faith Darilek, MSN, RN

NCLEX-PN® Connections:

Learning Objective: Review and apply knowledge within **"Monitoring Intracranial Pressure"** in readiness for performance of the following nursing activities as outlined by the NCLEX-PN® test plan:

Δ   Monitor the client's neurological status and report changes.

Δ   Provide care for the client with increased intracranial pressure.

Δ   Perform/assist with relevant laboratory, diagnostic, and therapeutic procedures within the nursing role, including:

  •   Preparation of the client for the procedure.

  •   Reinforcement of client teaching (before and following the procedure).

  •   Accurate collection of specimens.

  •   Monitoring procedure results (compare to norms) and appropriate notification of the primary care provider.

  •   Monitoring the client's response (expected, unexpected adverse response, comparison to baseline) to the procedure.

  •   Monitoring and taking actions, including reinforcing client teaching, to prevent or minimize the risk of complications.

  •   Recognizing signs of potential complications and reporting to the primary care provider.

  •   Recommending changes in the test/procedure as needed based on client findings.

Δ   Monitor therapeutic devices (drainage/irrigating devices, chest tubes), if inserted, for proper functioning.

📖 **Key Points**

Δ   Death following head trauma is usually related to increased intracranial pressure (ICP) within the rigid, nonexpandable skull.

Δ   **Normal ICP is 10 to 15 mm Hg.**

Δ   **Symptoms** suggesting increased ICP include:

- Severe headache.

- **Deteriorating level of consciousness**, restlessness, irritability.

- Dilated or pinpoint pupils, slow to react/nonreactive.

- Alteration in breathing pattern (Cheyne-Stokes respirations, central neurogenic hyperventilation, apnea).

- Deterioration in motor function, abnormal posturing (decerebrate, decorticate, or flaccidity).

- **Cushing reflex** is a late sign characterized by severe hypertension with widening pulse pressure (systolic – diastolic) and bradycardia.

Δ   Monitoring intracranial pressure facilitates continual assessment and is more precise than vague clinical manifestations.

- In ICP **electronic monitoring**, pressure exerted by the brain, blood, and cerebral spinal fluid (CSF) against the inside of the skull is measured by an inserted monitoring device.

- The procedure requires drilling a small hole into the skull and inserting the monitor device into the subarachnoid space, the ventricles, or into the brain itself.

- The device is then connected to a monitor that shows a picture of the pressure waveforms on the monitor screen.

- The insertion procedure is not painful to the client since the brain and skull have no pain receptors.

- The insertion procedure is always performed by a neurosurgeon in the operating room, emergency department, or critical care unit.

Δ   Insertion and care of any ICP monitoring device **requires surgical aseptic technique to reduce the risk for central nervous system (CNS) infection.**

Key Factors

Δ   The criteria for ICP monitoring depend on the client, but in general, clients who are **comatose** and have a **Glasgow coma score (GCS) of 8 or less** should be monitored.

Δ   ICP is increased by:

- Hypercarbia leading to cerebral vasodilation.

- Endotracheal or oral tracheal suctioning.

- Coughing.

- Blowing nose forcefully.

- Extreme neck or hip flexion/extension.

- Head of the bed less than 30°.

- Increased intra-abdominal pressure (restrictive clothing, Valsalva)

Diagnostic Procedures and Nursing Interventions

Δ   **Lumbar puncture is contraindicated with increased intracranial pressure.**

Δ   **Four Basic Types of ICP Monitoring Systems**

- **Intraventricular Catheter** (also called a **ventriculostomy**)

    ◊   A fluid-filled catheter is inserted into the anterior horn of the lateral ventricles (most often on the right side) through a burr hole. The catheter is connected to a sterile drainage system with a three-way stopcock that allows simultaneous monitoring of pressures by a transducer connected to a bedside monitor and drainage of CSF.

- **Subarachnoid Screw or Bolt**

    ◊   A special hollow, threaded screw or bolt is placed into the subarachnoid space through a twist-drill burr hole in the front of the skull, behind the hairline. The bolt is connected by fluid-filled tubing to a transducer leveled at the approximate location of the lateral ventricles.

- **Epidural or Subdural Sensor**

    ◊   A fiber-optic sensor is inserted into the epidural space through a burr hole. The fiber-optic device measures changes in the amount of light reflected from a pressure-sensitive diaphragm in the catheter tip. The cable is connected to a pre-calibrated monitor that displays the numerical value of ICP. This method of monitoring is non-invasive because the device does not penetrate the dura.

- **Intraparenchymal Monitoring**

    ◊   A thin, pressure-sensitive catheter is inserted through a small subarachnoid bolt and, after punctuating the dura, advanced a few centimeters into the brain's white matter. It is used to detect pressure changes.

Nursing Interventions

Δ   **Caring for clients undergoing ICP monitoring**

- Before the insertion procedure, medication may be given to help the client relax. The head is shaved around the insertion site. The site is then scrubbed with an antibacterial solution. Local anesthetic is applied to numb the area.

- After the insertion procedure, the nurse observes ICP waveforms, noting the pattern of waveforms and monitoring **for increased intracranial pressure (a sustained elevation of pressure above 15 mm Hg)**.

- Assess the client's clinical status and monitor routine and neurologic vital signs every hour as needed.

- Calculate cerebral perfusion pressure (CPP) hourly. To calculate CPP, subtract ICP from mean arterial pressure (MAP).

- Keep the **system closed** at all times. There is a serious risk of infection.

- **Inspect the insertion site** at least every 24 hr for redness, swelling, and drainage. Change the **sterile dressing covering the access site** per facility protocol.

- ICP monitoring equipment must be balanced and recalibrated as per facility protocols.

Δ   **Caring for clients with or at risk for increased ICP**

- Monitoring and **maintaining airway patency is the PRIORITY** intervention for clients with increased ICP and deteriorating neurological status.

- When suctioning a client with increased ICP, **hyperoxygenate with 100% oxygen prior to each suctioning attempt**.

- Keep the partial pressure of arterial carbon dioxide **(PaCO$_2$) around 35 mm Hg** and maintain a normal oxygen level by adjusting the rate of mechanical ventilation (for example, hyperventilating to blow off CO$_2$). Hypercarbia leads to cerebral vasodilation, which increases ICP.

- **Maintain head in midline neutral position and keep the head of the bed at greater than 30° to promote venous drainage.** Prevent neck flexion or extension. Log roll client when turning.

- Avoid clustering nursing activities.

- Avoid overstimulation of the client:

  ◊   Keep the client's room dark and quiet.

  ◊   Discuss visiting limitations.

  ◊   Speak softly and limit conversations to light and pleasant discussions.

Complications and Nursing Implications

Δ   **Infection and Bleeding**

- Follow strict surgical aseptic technique.

- Perform sterile dressing changes per facility protocol.

- Keep drainage systems closed.

- Limit monitoring to 3 to 5 days.

- Irrigate the system only as needed to maintain patency.

Δ   **Occlusion of the Catheter** – brain herniation

Δ   **Overdrainage and Collapse of the Ventricles**

Meeting the Needs of Older Adults

Δ   Older adult clients often have impaired immune defenses, which may predispose them to infection.

Primary Reference:

Ignatavicius, D. D., & Workman, M. L. (2006). *Medical-surgical nursing* (5th ed.). St. Louis, MO: Saunders.

Additional Resources:

Arbour, R. (2004). Intracranial hypertension: Monitoring and nursing assessment. *Critical Care Nurse, 24,*19-32.

NANDA International (2004). *NANDA nursing diagnoses: Definitions and classification 2005-2006.* Philadelphia: NANDA.

Chapter 78: Monitoring Intracranial Pressure

Application Exercises

Scenario: A 68-year-old male client is admitted following a motor vehicle crash. He is exhibiting symptoms of increasing intracranial pressure from a suspected closed head injury. He is admitted to the ICU for a ventriculostomy (intraventricular ICP monitoring).

1. The client is taken to surgery for a ventriculostomy. His wife is afraid and asks the nurse what is going to happen in surgery. How should the nurse respond?

2. Which "at-risk" nursing diagnosis has a priority for this client when he returns from surgery?

3. What nursing interventions should be included in this client's plan of care to decrease chances of this complication occurring?

4. Which of the following client behaviors suggest an increase in ICP? (Check all that apply.)

_____ Severe headache
_____ Motor, verbal, and eye opening responses to deep pain only
_____ Pupils equal at 5 mm and reactive to bright light
_____ Arms flexed with internal rotation and plantar flexion of legs
_____ Glasgow coma scale score of 3
_____ DTR 2+ BL lower extremities
_____ Blood pressure 168/58 mm Hg, heart rate 48/min
_____ Shallow breaths followed by a period of apnea then deep breaths

Chapter 78: Monitoring Intracranial Pressure

Application Exercises Answer Key

Scenario: A 68-year-old male client is admitted following a motor vehicle crash. He is exhibiting symptoms of increasing intracranial pressure from a suspected closed head injury. He is admitted to the ICU for a ventriculostomy (intraventricular ICP monitoring).

1. The client is taken to surgery for a ventriculostomy. His wife is afraid and asks the nurse what is going to happen in surgery. How should the nurse respond?

   The nurse should explain that he will be given medication to help him relax. A small area of the scalp will be shaved and then numbed. The primary care provider will create a hole in the skull through which a tube will be inserted to monitor the pressures inside the skull. Her husband should not feel discomfort because there are no pain receptors in the brain or skull.

2. Which "at-risk" nursing diagnosis has a priority for this client when he returns from surgery?

   Risk for infection

3. What nursing interventions should be included in this client's plan of care to decrease chances of this complication occurring?

   Follow strict surgical aseptic technique.

   Perform sterile dressing changes per facility protocol.

   Keep drainage systems closed.

   Limit monitoring to 3 to 5 days.

   Irrigate the system only as needed to maintain patency.

4. Which of the following client behaviors suggest an increase in ICP? (Check all that apply.)

__x__	Severe headache
__x__	Motor, verbal, and eye opening responses to deep pain only
_____	Pupils equal at 5 mm and reactive to bright light
__x__	Arms flexed with internal rotation and plantar flexion of legs
__x__	Glasgow coma scale score of 3
_____	DTR 2+ BL lower extremities
__x__	Blood pressure 168/58 mm Hg, heart rate 48/min
__x__	Shallow breaths followed by a period of apnea then deep breaths

A severe headache, deteriorating level of consciousness, abnormal posturing (decorticate in this case), Cushing reflex/triad of hypertension, bradycardia, and widened pulse pressure (110 mm Hg in this case), and alterations in respiratory pattern (Cheyne-Stokes respirations in this case) are signs of increased ICP. Normal pupil findings include 3 to 5 mm size with reactivity to light. DTR 2+ BL lower extremities is a normal neurological finding.

Unit 8
Section:

Nursing Care of Clients with Neurosensory Disorders
Diagnostic and Therapeutic Procedures: Neurosensory

Chapter 79:   **Pain Management**

Contributor: Lora McGuire, MS, RN

⟳ NCLEX-PN® Connections:

Learning Objective: Review and apply knowledge within "**Pain Management**" in readiness for performance of the following nursing activities as outlined by the NCLEX-PN® test plan:

Δ   Monitor the client's need for pain medication and provide care to meet the client's need for pain intervention.

Δ   Monitor the effectiveness of pain intervention and advocate for the client's needs as indicated.

Δ   Reinforce client instruction regarding the purposes and possible effects of pain medications.

Δ   Provide comfort interventions to clients with pain.

Δ   Recognize and document signs and symptoms associated with the client's problem – acute/chronic pain.

Δ   Reinforce client teaching regarding management of the client's health problem – acute/chronic pain

Δ   Recognize and respond to emergency situations, including notification of the primary care provider.

Δ   Review and the client's response to emergency interventions and complete the proper documentation.

Δ   Provide care that meets the age-related needs of clients 65 years of age or older, including recognizing expected physiological changes.

✒ Key Points

Δ   Pain is whatever the client says it is and it exists whenever the client says it does. **Self-report of pain is the single most reliable indicator of pain.**

Δ   Clients have a right to adequate assessment and management of pain. Nurses are accountable for the assessment of pain. The nurse's role is that of an **advocate and educator** for proper pain management.

Δ   Undertreatment of pain is a serious healthcare problem in the U.S. Consequences of undertreatment of pain include physiological and psychological components.

   •   Acute/chronic pain can cause anxiety/fear and depression.

   •   Poorly managed acute pain may lead to chronic pain syndrome.

Δ   Assessment challenges may occur with clients who are cognitively impaired and ventilator-dependent.

Δ   Proper pain management includes the use of pharmacological and nonpharmacological pain management therapies. Invasive therapies such as nerve ablation may be appropriate for intractable cancer-related pain.

Key Factors

Δ   **Risk factors** for undertreatment of pain include:

   •   Cultural and societal attitudes.

   •   Lack of knowledge.

   •   Fear of addiction.

   •   Exaggerated fear of respiratory depression.

Δ   **Populations at risk** for undertreatment of pain include:

   •   Infants.

   •   Children.

   •   Older Adults.

   •   Clients with substance abuse problems.

Δ   **Causes of acute and chronic pain** include:

   •   Trauma.

   •   Surgery.

   •   Cancer (for example, tumor invasion, nerve compression, and bone metastases).

- Arthritis.

- Fibromyalgia.

- Neuropathy.

- Treatment procedure (for example, injection, intubation, and radiation).

Diagnostic Procedures and Nursing Interventions

Δ   The **client's report of pain** is the most reliable diagnostic measure of pain.

Δ   **Visual analog scales** (for example, description scale, number rating scale) can be used to:

- Measure pain.

- Monitor pain.

- Evaluate effectiveness of interventions.

Δ   **Pain questionnaire** (for example, McGill-Melzack) can be used to gather information regarding:

- Location of pain.

- Character and quality of pain.

- Duration of pain.

- Precipitating factors.

- Aggravating/relieving factors.

Assessments

Δ   Monitor for **signs and symptoms.**

- **Acute pain**

  ◊   Hypertension

  ◊   **Tachycardia**

  ◊   **Anxiety**

  ◊   Dilated pupils

  ◊   Diaphoresis

- **Chronic pain**

  ◊   No alteration in vital signs

  ◊   **Depression**

  ◊   **Fatigue**

  ◊   Decreased level of functioning

Δ   **Routinely Assess**

-    **PQRST** of pain
    ◊   **P**rovokes: What causes pain?
    ◊   **Q**uality: What does it feel like?
    ◊   **R**adiates: Where does the pain radiate?
    ◊   **S**everity: How severe is the pain.
    ◊   **T**ime: When did the pain start?
-    Perceived impact of intervention on pain relief/management

NANDA Nursing Diagnoses

Δ   Acute pain

Δ   Chronic pain

Δ   Ineffective coping

Δ   Constipation

Nursing Interventions

Δ   **Pharmacological Interventions**

-    **Analgesics** are the mainstay for relieving pain. The three classes of analgesics are: **non-opioids, opioids, and adjuvants.**

-    **Guidelines for the administration of non-opioids include:**
    ◊   Appropriate for the treatment of **mild to moderate pain.**
    ◊   Awareness of the hepatotoxic effects of acetaminophen. **No more than 4 g/day should be given to a client with a healthy liver.**
    ◊   Monitoring for salicylism (tinnitus, vertigo, and decreased hearing acuity).
    ◊   Monitoring and intervening with the administration of non-steroidal **anti-inflammatory** drugs (NSAIDs). For example, aspirin and ibuprofen.
    ◊   **Prevention of gastric upset** by taking with food or antacids.
    ◊   Monitoring output and skin, and practicing caution with long-term NSAID use to **prevent bleeding.**

- **Guidelines for the administration of opioids include:**

  ◊ Appropriate for the treatment of **severe and/or chronic pain.**

  ◊ Becoming familiar with an equianalgesic chart for opioids.

  ◊ Recognizing that meperidine can have toxic side effects such as seizures, and it should never be given for longer than 48 hr.

  ◊ **Giving intravenous push opioids slowly over several minutes to prevent harm (for example, hypotension, respiratory depression).**

  ◊ Knowing PCA opioids commonly used are morphine, hydromorphone, and fentanyl.

  ◊ Understanding the client is the only person who should push the PCA button to prevent inadvertent overdosing.

  ◊ **Using epidural analgesia** (fentanyl and bupivacaine) often for postoperative pain. The client should be assessed for epidural side effects such as **sedation, nausea, pruritus, lower extremity sensory effects, urinary retention, and respiratory depression.** To prevent catheter displacement, ensure all catheter line connections are secure, and maintain an occlusive sterile dressing over the catheter site.

  ◊ Administering opioids orally for chronic pain. The oral route is the preferred route for opioid administration.

- **Monitor and intervene for adverse effects of opioid use.**

  ◊ Constipation – preventative approach (for example, monitor bowel movements, fluids, fiber intake, exercise, stool softeners, stimulant laxatives, and enemas).

  ◊ Urinary retention – Monitor the client's intake and output, assess for distention, administer bethanechol (Urecholine), and catheterize as needed.

  ◊ Nausea/vomiting – Administer antiemetics, such as prochlorperazine (Compazine), metoclopramide (Reglan), or ondansetron (Zofran); lie still, and/or move slowly during the first hours after initiation.

  ◊ Sedation – Monitor the client's level of consciousness and take safety precautions.

  ◊ Respiratory depression – Monitor the client's respiratory rate prior to and following administration of opioids (especially in opioid naïve clients); preceded by sedation, monitor sedation; initial treatment of respiratory depression and sedation is generally a reduction in opioid dose; if necessary, slowly administer diluted naloxone (Narcan) to reverse opioid effects.

  ◊ Pruritus – may be treated with a small dose of naloxone (Narcan).

- **Guidelines for the administration of adjuvant analgesics include:**

  ◊ For **neuropathic pain**, consider adjuvant use of:

    ° **Antiepileptic medications** such as carbamazepine (Tegretol) – Monitor for agranulocytosis; or gabapentin (Neurontin) – Monitor for hyponatremia.

    ° **Tricyclic antidepressants** such as amitriptyline (Elavil)

    ° Topical lidocaine

  ◊ Antianxiety medications such as benzodiazepines – Monitor for sedation, hypotension, confusion.

Δ **Nonpharmacological Interventions**

- Cutaneous (skin) stimulation – transcutaneous electrical nerve stimulation (TENS), heat, cold, therapeutic touch, and massage

  ◊ Acute/chronic pain

  ◊ **Interrupt pain pathways**

  ◊ Cold for inflammation

  ◊ Heat to increase blood flow and to reduce stiffness

- Distraction

  ◊ Acute pain

  ◊ May include ambulation, deep breathing, visitors, television, and music

- Imagery

  ◊ Chronic pain

  ◊ Focus on a pleasant thought to divert focus

  ◊ Requires an ability to concentrate

- Acupuncture – vibration or electrical stimulation via tiny needles inserted into the skin and subcutaneous tissues at specific points.

Δ **Invasive Interventions**

- Nerve blocks – local anesthetic into a nerve root. Generally used for intractable cancer-related pain. Monitor the client's sensation and bowel/bladder dysfunction.

- Nerve root ablation – radiofrequency (heat) or cryoanalgesia (cold).

Complications and Nursing Implications

△ **Undertreatment of pain** is a serious complication and may lead to increased anxiety with acute pain and depression with chronic pain.

△ **Overdosing** of opioid analgesics can lead to respiratory depression and even death. However, this is rare when opioids are administered orally. Sedation always precedes respiratory depression. Problems with sedation are more common at the beginning of opioid treatment when doses have increased or with renal insufficiency. Also, if rapid IV administration of opioids is given and/or concurrent use of other central nervous system depressant medications are given. Special attention should be given to opioid naïve clients. Oversedation and respiratory depression can be prevented by:

- Identifying risks, titrating doses carefully, and monitoring the client.

- Stopping the opioid and giving the antagonist naloxone if the client's respirations are less than 8/min and shallow and the client is difficult to arouse. Naloxone must be diluted in normal saline (0.4 mg/10 mL) and given by IV slowly. After administration of naloxone, the client should be reassessed.

- Assessing the cause of sedation and monitoring the client's level of arousal and respiratory rate and depth for one full minute.

- Using a sedation scale in addition to a pain rating scale to assess a client's pain, especially when administering opioids.

Meeting the Needs of Older Adult Clients

△ Recognize that pain is often undertreated in this population.

△ Older adult clients may under-report pain due to expectations of pain as just a result of aging.

△ Remember the physiological and psychological consequences of unrelieved pain.

△ Pain is a common condition due to arthritis, cancer, osteoporosis, diabetes, post-herpetic neuralgia (shingles), fractures, and post CVA.

△ When assessing a client's pain, avoid the word "pain" and use words such as ache, sore, or hurt.

△ Use a standard scale and ask about present pain only.

△ In cognitively impaired clients, observe for nonverbal indicators of pain (facial expressions, grimacing, body movements, and behavioral changes).

△ Assume pain is present with diseases and conditions commonly associated with pain, and consider a trial of around-the-clock analgesics.

Δ   Start low and go slow when using opioids for pain due to changes in the body's metabolism of medications. Monitor the client carefully for oversedation and toxicity.

Δ   Use NSAIDs with caution due to the potential risk of gastrointestinal bleeding and renal toxicities.

Δ   Do not use meperidine, codeine, or propoxyphene in this population due to the toxic side effects of these medications.

Primary Reference:

Ignatavicius, D. D., & Workman, M. L. (2006). *Medical-surgical nursing* (5th ed.). St. Louis, MO: Saunders.

Additional Resources

American Pain Society. (2003). *Principles of analgesic use in the treatment of acute pain and cancer pain* (5th ed.). Glenview, IL: American Pain Society.

NANDA International (2004). *NANDA nursing diagnoses: Definitions and classification 2005-2006*. Philadelphia: NANDA.

St. Marie, B. (Ed.) (2002). *Core curriculum for pain management nursing*. Philadelphia: Saunders.

Chapter 79: Pain Management

Application Exercises

1. What are the most important assessment parameters for any client receiving opioids?

2. Caution should be exercised in administration of opioids in which of the following situations? (Check all that apply.)

_____ Sedated client with respiratory rate of 8/min

_____ Client in intractable pain

_____ Client taking multiple opioids

_____ Client with increased intracranial pressure

_____ Client with urinary retention

3. Which of the following is the best indication of a client's need for pharmacological pain intervention?

A. Blood pressure 140/80 mm Hg and pulse rate 95 beats/min

B. Pain rating of 9 on a pain numeric rating scale of 0 to 10

C. Stage IV decubitus ulceration on coccyx

D. Bone metastasis

4. A client is taking carbamazepine (Tegretol) for neuralgic pain. Which of the following indicates that the client is experiencing an adverse effect?

A. White blood cell count of 3,500/mm^3

B. Serum creatinine of 1.1 mg/dL

C. Sodium 140 mEq/L

D. Hemoglobin 13 g/dL

5. A client is taking acetaminophen (Tylenol) on a consistent basis. Which of the following client findings indicates possible acetaminophen toxicity?

A. White blood cell count of 5,500/mm^3

B. Platelet count of 350,000/mm^3

C. Direct bilirubin 2.0 mg/dL

D. Aspartate aminotransferase of 30 units/L

Chapter 79: Pain Management

Application Exercises Answer Key

1. What are the most important assessment parameters for any client receiving opioids?

   Constipation

   Urinary retention

   Nausea/vomiting

   Sedation

   Respiratory depression

   Pruritus

2. Caution should be exercised in administration of opioids in which of the following situations? (Check all that apply.)

__x__	Sedated client with respiratory rate of 8/min
_____	Client in intractable pain
__x__	Client taking multiple opioids
__x__	Client with increased intracranial pressure
__x__	Client with urinary retention

   Sedation precedes respiratory depression. A respiratory rate of 8/min is effective for maintaining adequate tissue oxygenation. Use of multiple opioids could lead to additive central nervous system depression. The use of opioids in clients with increased intracranial pressure is generally avoided due to the risk of masking the signs of neurological deterioration. Urinary retention is a side effect of opioids, and opioids can exacerbate this problem.

3. Which of the following is the best indication of a client's need for pharmacological pain intervention?

        A. Blood pressure 140/80 mm Hg and pulse rate 95 beats/min

        B. Pain rating of 9 on a pain numeric rating scale of 0 to 10

        C. Stage IV decubitus ulceration on coccyx

        D. Bone metastasis

The most accurate indicator/measurement of pain is a client's self-report regarding pain.

4. A client is taking carbamazepine (Tegretol) for neuralgic pain. Which of the following indicates that the client is experiencing an adverse effect?

        A. White blood cell count of 3,500/mm³

        B. Serum creatinine of 1.1 mg/dL

        C. Sodium 140 mEq/L

        D. Hemoglobin 13 g/dL

Agranulocytosis (WBC < 5,000/mm³) is a possible adverse effect of carbamazepine (Tegretol).

5. A client is taking acetaminophen (Tylenol) on a consistent basis. Which of the following client findings indicates possible acetaminophen toxicity?

        A. White blood cell count of 5,500/mm³

        B. Platelet count of 350,000/mm³

        C. Direct bilirubin 2.0 mg/dL

        D. Aspartate aminotransferase of 30 units/L

A direct bilirubin of 2 mg/dL (normal 0.1 to 0.3 mg/dL) indicates possible liver dysfunction. The laboratory values for options A, B, and D are within normal limits.

Unit 8   Nursing Care of Clients with Neurosensory Disorders

Section: Nursing Care of Clients with Brain Disorders

Chapter 80:   Seizures and Epilepsy

Contributor: Lynn C. Parsons, DSN, RN, CNA-BC

NCLEX-PN® Connections:

Learning Objective: Review and apply knowledge within "**Seizures and Epilepsy**" in readiness for performance of the following nursing activities as outlined by the NCLEX-PN® test plan:

Δ   Monitor the client's neurological status and report changes.

Δ   Assist with relevant laboratory, diagnostic, and therapeutic procedures within the nursing role, including:

- Preparation of the client for the procedure.

- Accurate collection of specimens.

- Monitoring client status during and after the procedure.

- Reinforcing client teaching (before and following the procedure).

- Recognizing the client's response (expected, unexpected adverse response) to the procedure.

- Monitoring results.

- Monitoring and taking actions to prevent or minimize the risk of complications.

- Notifying the primary care provider of signs of complications.

Δ   Protect the client from injury.

Δ   Recognize signs and symptoms of the client's problem and complete the proper documentation.

Δ   Provide and document care based on the client's health alteration.

Δ   Monitor and document vital signs changes.

Δ   Interpret data that need to be reported immediately.

Δ   Reinforce client education on managing the client's health problem.

Δ   Recognize and respond to emergency situations, including notification of the primary care provider.

Δ   Review the client's response to emergency interventions and complete the proper documentation.

Δ   Provide care that meets the age-related needs of clients 65 years of age or older, including recognizing expected physiological changes.

📖 **Key Points**

Δ   Seizures are **abrupt, uncontrolled electrical brain discharges** that cause **alterations in level of consciousness** and changes in motor and sensory behavior.

Δ   **Epilepsy** is a group of syndromes characterized by **recurring seizures**.

   •   Epilepsy can be idiopathic (unknown cause) or secondary caused by conditions (such as brain tumor, acute alcohol withdrawal, electrolyte imbalance).

   •   It is not associated with alterations in intellectual capabilities.

Δ   Seizures are classified as **neurologic emergencies** in all triage systems. **Sustained untreated seizures can result in hypoxia, cardiac dysrhythmias, and lactic acidosis.**

Key Factors

Δ   **Risk Factors/Contributing Factors**

   •   Genetic predisposition

   •   Acute febrile state

   •   Head trauma

   •   Cerebral edema

   •   **Abrupt cessation of antiepileptic drugs** (AEDs)

   •   Infection

   •   Metabolic disorder (for example, hypoglycemia)

   •   Exposure to toxins

   •   Brain tumor

   •   Hypoxia

   •   Acute drug and alcohol withdrawal

   •   Fluid and electrolyte imbalances

Δ   **Triggering factors may include:**

   •   Increased physical activity.

   •   Stress.

   •   Fatigue.

   •   Alcohol.

   •   Caffeine.

   •   Some chemicals.

Diagnostic Procedures and Nursing Interventions

Δ **Electroencephalogram** (EEG) records electrical activity and identifies the origin of seizure activity. **Client instruction** includes:

- **No caffeine**.

- Wash hair before the procedure (no oils, sprays) and after the procedure (remove electrode glue).

- May be asked to take deep breaths and/or be exposed to flashes of a strobe light during test.

- Sleep may be withheld prior to test and possibly induced during test.

Δ Blood and urine tests, magnetic resonance imaging (MRI), computed tomography imaging (CT)/computed axial tomography (CAT) scan, positron emission tomography (PET) scan, cerebrospinal fluid (CSF) analysis, skull x-ray, electrolyte profile and drug screen may all be used to identify or rule out potential causes of seizures.

Assessments

Δ **Assess/Monitor**

- Airway patency

- Aspiration

- Injury post seizure

- If client experienced an **aura** (warning sensation); possible indication of the origin of seizure

- Possible trigger factors (for example, fatigue)

NANDA Nursing Diagnoses

Δ Risk for injury

Δ Risk for impaired spontaneous ventilation

Δ Risk for ineffective tissue perfusion (cerebral)

Nursing Interventions

Δ Protect the client from injury (for example, move furniture away).

Δ Maintain a patent airway.

Δ Be prepared to suction.

Δ Turn the client to the side (decrease risk of aspiration).

Δ   Loosen clothing.

Δ   Do not attempt to restrain the client.

Δ   Do not attempt to open jaw during seizure activity (may damage teeth, lips, and tongue). **Do not use padded tongue blades**.

Δ   Administer oxygen as prescribed.

Δ   Administer prescribed medications (for example, anticonvulsant and sedative medications to prevent or decrease seizure activity).

Δ   Document onset and duration of seizure and client findings/observations prior to, during, and following the seizure (level of consciousness, apnea, cyanosis, motor activity, incontinence).

Δ   **Post Seizure**

   •   Maintain the client in a side-lying position to prevent aspiration and to facilitate drainage of oral secretions.

   •   Check vital signs.

   •   Perform neurological checks.

   •   Reorient and calm the client (may be agitated).

   •   Institute seizure precautions.

Δ   Provide **client education** regarding seizure management:

   •   The importance of **monitoring AED levels and maintaining therapeutic medication levels**.

   •   Possible drug interactions (for example, decreased effectiveness of oral contraceptives).

   •   Encourage the client to wear a medical alert bracelet (necklace) at all times.

Δ   **Seizure Precautions**

   •   Standby oxygen, airway, and suctioning equipment

   •   **IV access** (medication administration during seizure)

   •   **Side rails in up position** and **bed in lowest** position

Complications and Nursing Implications

Δ   **Aspiration**

- Turn the client to side, suction as needed.

Δ   **Status Epilepticus**

- Potential complication of all seizure disorders.

- Establish airway, provide oxygen, ensure IV access, perform EKG monitoring, and monitor ABG results.

- As prescribed, administer diazepam (Valium) or lorazepam (Ativan) and a loading dose following by a continuous infusion of phenytoin (Dilantin).

Meeting the Needs of Older Adults

Δ   Increased seizure incidence is associated with cerebrovascular diseases.

Δ   Other prescription medications can interact with seizure control medications.

Δ   Absorption, distribution, metabolism, and excretion of medications can become altered due to age-related changes in renal and liver function.

Δ   Cost associated with antiseizure medication can lead to poor adherence for older adult clients on a fixed income.

Primary Reference:

Ignatavicius, D. D., & Workman, M. L. (2006). *Medical-surgical nursing* (5th ed.). St. Louis, MO: Saunders.

Additional Resources:

Gerber Zimmerman, P., & Herr, R. D. (2006). *Triage nursing secrets*. St. Louis, MO: Mosby.

NANDA International (2004). *NANDA nursing diagnoses: Definitions and classification 2005-2006*. Philadelphia: NANDA.

Smeltzer, S. C., & Bare, B. G. (2004). *Brunner and Suddarth's textbook of medical-surgical nursing* (10th ed.). Philadelphia: Lippincott Williams & Wilkins.

For more information, visit the National Institute of Neurological Disorders and Stroke at *www.ninds.nih.gov/disorders/epilepsy/epilepsy.htm.*

Chapter 80: Seizures and Epilepsy

Application Exercises

Scenario: A client is admitted for a routine hernia repair. The client has a history of a seizure disorder, and he states that he thinks he is about to have a seizure.

1. How does the client know he is going to have a seizure?

2. What is the priority nursing diagnosis?

3. Which of the following nursing interventions are appropriate during a seizure? (Check all that apply.)

_____ Provide privacy.
_____ Ease the client to the floor if standing.
_____ Make the immediate environment safe; move furniture away from the client.
_____ Loosen the client's clothing.
_____ Insert an oral airway.
_____ Protect the head with padding.
_____ Restrain the client to protect from injury.

4. What are priority interventions following a generalized seizure?

Chapter 80: Seizures and Epilepsy

Application Exercises Answer Key

Scenario: A client is admitted for a routine hernia repair. The client has a history of a seizure disorder, and he states that he thinks he is about to have a seizure.

1. How does the client know he is going to have a seizure?

   Many clients experience an aura (visual, olfactory, or auditory) prior to a seizure. This information can give clues to the origin of the seizure within the brain.

2. What is the priority nursing diagnosis?

   Risk for injury related to seizure activity

3. Which of the following nursing interventions are appropriate during a seizure? (Check all that apply.)

_X_	Provide privacy.
_X_	Ease the client to the floor if standing.
_X_	Make the immediate environment safe; move furniture away from the client.
_X_	Loosen the client's clothing.
_____	Insert an oral airway.
_X_	Protect the head with padding.
_____	Restrain the client to protect from injury.

4. What are priority interventions following a generalized seizure?

   Keep the client in a side-lying position to prevent aspiration.
   Ensure patent airway.
   Reorient client to the environment.
   Reassure a client who is agitated postictal (post seizure).

Unit 8   Nursing Care of Clients with Neurosensory Disorders
Section: Nursing Care of Clients with Brain Disorders

Chapter 81:   Alzheimer's Disease and Dementia
Contributor: Lynn C. Parsons, DSN, RN, CNA-BC

NCLEX-PN® Connections:

Learning Objective: Review and apply knowledge within "**Alzheimer's Disease and Dementia**" in readiness for performance of the following nursing activities as outlined by the NCLEX-PN® test plan:

Δ   Monitor the client's neurological status and report changes.

Δ   Assist with relevant laboratory, diagnostic, and therapeutic procedures within the nursing role, including:

- Preparation of the client for the procedure.

- Accurate collection of specimens.

- Monitoring client status during and after the procedure.

- Reinforcing client teaching (before and following the procedure).

- Recognizing the client's response (expected, unexpected adverse response) to the procedure.

- Monitoring results.

- Monitoring and taking actions to prevent or minimize the risk of complications.

- Notifying the primary care provider of signs of complications.

Δ   Protect the client from injury.

Δ   Recognize signs and symptoms of the client's problem and complete the proper documentation.

Δ   Provide and document care based on the client's health alteration.

Δ   Monitor and document vital signs changes.

Δ   Interpret data that need to be reported immediately.

Δ   Reinforce client education on managing the client's health problem.

Δ   Recognize and respond to emergency situations, including notification of the primary care provider.

Δ   Review the client's response to emergency interventions and complete the proper documentation.

Δ   Provide care that meets the age-related needs of clients 65 years of age or older, including recognizing expected physiological changes.

📖 Key Points

Δ   Alzheimer's disease (AD) is a non-reversible dementia that progressively develops through three stages over many years.

Δ   AD is characterized by memory loss, problems with judgment, and changes in personality.

Δ   Severe physical decline occurs along with deteriorating **cognitive** functions.

Key Factors

Δ   **Risk Factors/Contributing Factors**

•   Older age

•   Genetic predisposition

•   Environmental agents (herpes virus, metal, or toxic waste)

•   Previous head injury

Diagnostic Procedures and Nursing Interventions

Δ   There is no definitive diagnostic procedure except brain tissue examination upon death.

Δ   Magnetic resonance imaging (MRI), computed tomography (CT) imaging/computed axial tomography (CAT) scan, positron emission tomography (PET) scan, and electroencephalogram (EEG) may be performed to rule out other possible causes of symptoms.

Δ   Genetic testing for the presence of apolipoprotein A.

Assessments

Δ   Monitor for **signs and symptoms.**

- **Stage 1: Lasts 1 to 3 years**
  - ◊   Short-term memory loss
  - ◊   Decreased attention span
  - ◊   Subtle personality changes
  - ◊   Mild cognitive deficits
  - ◊   Difficulty with money, numbers, and bills
  - ◊   Difficulty with depth perception

- **Stage 2: Lasts 2 to 10 years**
  - ◊   Obvious memory loss (recent and remote)
  - ◊   Confusion about time and place worsen
  - ◊   Wandering behavior
  - ◊   Confabulation
  - ◊   "Sundowning" (confused at dusk)
  - ◊   Irritability and agitation
  - ◊   Decreased spatial orientation
  - ◊   Impaired motor skills
  - ◊   Impaired judgment
  - ◊   Impaired self-care skills

- **Stage 3: Lasts 8 to 10 years**
  - ◊   Absent and/or severe impairment of all cognitive abilities. For example, aphasia (inability to speak or understand); apraxia (inability to use objects appropriately); anomia (inability to find words); and agnosia (loss of sensory comprehension).
  - ◊   Disoriented to time and place
  - ◊   Disturbed sleep patterns, with increased sleep time
  - ◊   Impaired or absent motor skills and communication
  - ◊   Bowel and bladder incontinence
  - ◊   Inability to recognize family and friends

Δ   **Assess/Monitor**

- Cognitive status, memory, judgment, and personality changes.
- Bowel and bladder function.
- Client and family coping.
- Environmental safety.
- Sleep pattern.
- Ability to communicate.
- Nutritional status.
- Skin integrity.

NANDA Nursing Diagnoses

Δ   Risk for injury

Δ   Self-care deficit

Δ   Ineffective coping

Δ   Chronic confusion

Δ   Risk for caregiver role strain

Δ   Imbalanced nutrition: Less than body requirements

Δ   Total urinary and bowel incontinence

Δ   Risk for impaired tissue integrity

Nursing Interventions

Δ   **Cognitive Stimulation**

- Offer varied environmental stimulation.
- Introduce change gradually.
- Use a calendar to assist with orientation.
- Use short directions.
- Use repetition.
- Use therapeutic touch.

Δ **Memory Training**

- Reminisce with the client about past.

- Use memory techniques (e.g., making lists and rehearsing).

- Stimulate memory by repeating client's last statement.

Δ Avoid overstimulation (keep noise and clutter to a minimum and avoid crowds).

Δ Promote **consistency** (routine place for routine objects and routine schedule).

Δ **Reality Orientation** (early stages)

- Easily viewed clock and single day calendar

- Pictures of family

- Frequent reorientation to time, place, and person

Δ **Validation Therapy** (later stages)

- Acknowledge the client's feelings.

- Don't argue with the client, but don't reinforce.

Δ Promote self care as long as possible. Assist the client with activities of daily living as appropriate.

Δ Speak directly to the client in short, concise sentences.

Δ Maintain a safe environment (no throw rugs or wide spaces).

Δ Reduce agitation (use calm, redirecting statements; provide a diversion).

Δ Provide a routine toileting schedule.

Δ Administer prescribed medications (for example, cholinesterase inhibitors slow disease progression), antidepressants, and antipsychotic and neuroleptic medications (treat hallucinations and delirium). Use of chemical restraints for agitation and combativeness should be a last resort.

Δ Refer to social services and case managers (long term/home management, respite care, durable medical equipment needs, and support groups).

Complications and Nursing Implications

Δ **Wandering**

- Wandering is a common complication.

- Have the client wear identification, including contact information for primary caregiver.

- Place stop signs on exit doors.

- Install alarm systems and lock exit doors.

- Enroll clients in Safe Return Program (Alzheimer's Association).

- Have primary care provider keep an up-to-date picture of client.

- Have client walk frequently with supervision.

- Plan structured, supervised activities.

- Play soft background music.

- Apply physical restraints only as a last resort.

Meeting the Needs of Older Adults

Δ Increased risk of severe dementia related to Alzheimer's disease is common among clients over age 65.

Δ Increased risk for falls and injury is related to decreased cognitive function.

Δ Older adult clients with decreased cognitive function are at an increased risk for pneumonia, dehydration, or malnutrition.

Primary Reference:

Ignatavicius, D. D., & Workman, M. L. (2006). *Medical-surgical nursing* (5th ed.). St. Louis, MO: Saunders.

Additional Resources

NANDA International (2004). *NANDA nursing diagnoses: Definitions and classification 2005-2006.* Philadelphia: NANDA.

Smeltzer, S. C., & Bare, B. G. (2004). *Brunner and Suddarth's textbook of medical- surgical nursing* (10th ed.). Philadelphia: Lippincott Williams & Wilkins.

Stanley, M., Blair, K. A., & Gauntlett Beare, P. (Eds.).(2005). *Gerontological nursing: Promoting successful aging with older adults.* Philadelphia: F. A. Davis.

For information about Alzheimer's disease, visit the Alzheimer's Association at *www.alz.org.*

Chapter 81: Alzheimer's Disease and Dementia

Application Exercises

Scenario: A 72-year-old man was reluctantly placed by his children in a long-term care Alzheimer's facility after he wandered away from home late at night and was lost for several days. He is in very good physical health, but has suffered progressive memory loss and inability to sleep over the past 8 to 10 years. None of the client's children are physically or financially able to care for their father on a full-time basis. An extensive evaluation of the client indicates he is in stage 2 of the disease process.

1. What data best supports that the client is in stage 2 of the disease process?

2. Did the children make the right decision regarding placing their father in a long-term care Alzheimer's facility?

3. How can the nurse best intervene to address the client's risk for injury? Sleep pattern disturbance?

4. How can the nurse offer emotional support to the client's children?

5. Identify the stage (stage 1, stage 2, or stage 3) of Alzheimer's disease that corresponds to each of the following signs and symptoms of the disease.

    _____ Confusion about time and place worsen
    _____ Subtle personality changes
    _____ Decreased spatial orientation
    _____ Disturbed sleep patterns with increased sleep time
    _____ Inability to recognize family and friends
    _____ Difficulty with money, numbers, and bills
    _____ Bowel and bladder incontinence

Chapter 81: Alzheimer's Disease and Dementia

Application Exercises Answer Key

Scenario: A 72-year-old man was reluctantly placed by his children in a long-term care Alzheimer's facility after he wandered away from home late at night and was lost for several days. He is in very good physical health, but has suffered progressive memory loss and inability to sleep over the past 8 to 10 years. None of the client's children are physically or financially able to care for their father on a full-time basis. An extensive evaluation of the client indicates he is in stage 2 of the disease process.

1. What data best supports that the client is in stage 2 of the disease process?

   Obvious memory loss; wandering behavior; confusion (he became lost); and impaired judgment.

2. Did the children make the right decision regarding placing their father in a long-term care Alzheimer's facility?

   From the data provided, it seems that the family made the correct decision. If family members are unavailable to care for the client 24 hr a day every day, then the client should be placed where his safety will be protected. Additionally, health care workers who care for clients with Alzheimer's disease are generally well prepared to address the client's physical and emotional problems.

3. How can the nurse best intervene to address the client's risk for injury? Sleep pattern disturbance?

   Risk for injury: maintain a safe environment where wandering away from the building is not possible (but without the use of physical or medication restraints); provide constant supervision; keep routines consistent; attach labels to room contents and belongings to reduce confusion; and put stop signs on exit doors and keep them locked.

4. How can the nurse offer emotional support to the client's children?

Refer the children to community resources and social services in their area; encourage the children to visit a support group; provide information about the disease, especially as it relates to their father; keep the children informed of their father's condition, adjustment to the facility, and progress; reassure the children that they made the right decision regarding their father's care; encourage the children to spend time with their father and allow them to participate in his care and care planning.

5. Identify the stage (stage 1, stage 2, or stage 3) of Alzheimer's disease that corresponds to each of the following signs and symptoms of the disease.

2	Confusion about time and place worsen
1	Subtle personality changes
2	Decreased spatial orientation
3	Disturbed sleep patterns with increased sleep time
3	Inability to recognize family and friends
3	Difficulty with money, numbers, and bills
3	Bowel and bladder incontinence

Unit 8
Section:

Nursing Care of Clients with Neurosensory Disorders
Nursing Care of Clients with Brain Disorders

Chapter 82:   Parkinson's Disease
Contributor: Lynn C. Parsons, DSN, RN, CNA-BC

⟳ **NCLEX-PN® Connections:**

Learning Objective: Review and apply knowledge within **"Parkinson's Disease"** in readiness for performance of the following nursing activities as outlined by the NCLEX-PN® test plan:

Δ   Monitor the client's neurological status and report changes.

Δ   Assist with relevant laboratory, diagnostic, and therapeutic procedures within the nursing role, including:

•   Preparation of the client for the procedure.

•   Accurate collection of specimens.

•   Monitoring client status during and after the procedure.

•   Reinforcing client teaching (before and following the procedure).

•   Recognizing the client's response (expected, unexpected adverse response) to the procedure.

•   Monitoring results.

•   Monitoring and taking actions to prevent or minimize the risk of complications.

•   Notifying the primary care provider of signs of complications.

Δ   Recognize signs and symptoms of the client's problem and complete the proper documentation.

Δ   Provide and document care based on the client's health alteration.

Δ   Monitor and document vital signs changes.

Δ   Interpret data that need to be reported immediately.

Δ   Reinforce client education on managing the client's health problem.

Δ   Recognize and respond to emergency situations, including notification of the primary care provider.

Δ   Review the client's response to emergency interventions and complete the proper documentation.

Δ   Provide care that meets the age-related needs of clients 65 years of age or older, including recognizing expected physiological changes.

Key Points

Δ Parkinson's disease (PD) is a **progressively debilitating** disease that grossly affects motor function. It is characterized by four cardinal symptoms: **tremor, rigidity, akinesia (slow movement), and postural instability.**

Δ Pervasive **degeneration** of substantia nigra results in **decreased dopamine** and consequently an **inability to control voluntary movements.**

Key Factors

Δ The etiology of Parkinson's disease is unknown.

Δ Risk Factors/Contributing Factors

- Onset of symptoms at age 40 to 70

- More common in men

- Genetic predisposition

- Exposure to environmental toxins

Diagnostic Procedures and Nursing Interventions

Δ There is no definitive diagnostic procedure.

Δ Magnetic resonance imaging (MRI), computed tomography (CT)/computed axial tomography (CAT) scan, positron emission tomography (PET) scan, and/or electroencephalogram (EEG) to rule out other neurological diseases.

Δ Cerebrospinal fluid analysis may reveal a decrease in dopamine levels.

Therapeutic Procedures and Nursing Interventions

Δ **Stereotactic Pallidotomy**

- With a CT scan or MRI.

- Mild electrical stimulation through a burr hole to a target area.

- Assess the client for decreases in tremor and muscle rigidity.

- A lesion is formed when the ideal location is found.

Δ **Deep Brain Stimulation**

- Electrode to thalamus.

- Currently delivered through an implanted pacemaker generator.

Δ   **Fetal Tissue Substantia Nigra Transplantation**

- Human/pig

- Use of human tissue is controversial.

Assessments

Δ   Monitor for **signs and symptoms.**

- Stooped posture

- Slow, shuffling, and propulsive gait

- Tremor

- Muscle rigidity

- Bradykinesia

- Autonomic symptoms (e.g., orthostatic hypotension, flushing, and diaphoresis)

- Difficulty chewing and swallowing

- Progressive difficulty with activities of daily living (ADL)

- Mood swings

- Cognitive impairment (e.g., dementia)

NANDA Nursing Diagnoses

Δ   Impaired physical mobility

Δ   Risk for falls

Δ   Self-care deficit

Δ   Impaired verbal communication

Δ   Chronic confusion

Δ   Risk for imbalanced nutrition: Less than body requirements

Nursing Interventions

Δ **Assess/Monitor** the client's:

- Medication effectiveness.
- Swallowing difficulties.
- Nutrition and hydration status.
- Cognitive status.
- Depression.
- Family coping.

Δ Administer the client's prescribed medications.

- May take several weeks of use before symptom improvement is seen.
- Maintain therapeutic medication levels.
- **Dopamine replacements** such as levodopa (Dopar). Monitor for "wearing off" phenomenon and dyskinesias (problems with movement). Addition of carbidopa can greatly increase effectiveness.
- **Dopamine agonists** such as bromocriptine (Parlodel) and pramipexole (Mirapex). Monitor for orthostatic hypotension and hallucinations.
- **Anticholinergics** such as benztropine (Cogentin) and trihexyphenidyl (Artane) to control tremors and rigidity. Monitor for anticholinergic effects (dry mouth, constipation, urinary retention).

Δ Maintain adequate **nutrition and hydration** for the client.

- Consult the client's dietician.
- Monitor the client's weight.
- Keep a diet intake log.
- Encourage fluids.
- Provide smaller, more frequent meals.
- Add commercial powder to thicken food.
- Provide supplements as prescribed.
- Consult speech and language therapist (SLT) to assess swallowing.

Δ Maintain **client mobility** for as long as possible.

- Encourage nontraditional forms of exercise such as yoga (may improve mental status as well).
- Encourage use of assistive devices as disease progresses.
- Encourage range-of-motion (ROM) exercises.

- Teach the client to stop occasionally when walking to slow down speed and reduce risk of injury.

- Promote sleep and rest.

- Pace activity.

Δ Promote **client communication** for as long as possible.

- Teach the client muscle strengthening exercises.

- Encourage the client to speak slowly and to pause frequently.

- Use alternate forms of communication as appropriate.

- Refer client to a speech-language pathologist.

Δ Provide a **safe environment** (for example, no throw rugs and encourage the use of a safety razor).

Δ Establish an effective communication system for the client and family.

Δ Assist the client with **activities of daily living** (ADLs) as needed (hygiene, dressing).

Δ Provide a list of **community resources** (for example, support groups) to the client and the client's family.

Δ Refer the client to a social worker or case manager (financial issues, long term/ home care, and respite care).

Complications and Nursing Implications

Δ **Aspiration Pneumonia**

- Use interventions to decrease the risk of aspiration.

- Have suction on standby.

Δ **Altered Cognition** (for example, dementia)

- Slow onset.

- Not reversible.

- Reorientation strategies may be effective in early stages.

- Acknowledge the client's feelings without arguing.

- Provide for a safe environment.

- Treat symptoms (for example, agitation).

Meeting the Needs of Older Adults

Δ   There is a higher incidence of the disease among older adult clients, especially in older men.

Δ   PD is the most common neurodegenerative disease that affects the motor system of older adult clients.

Δ   Signs and symptoms of PD may be mistaken for normal age-related changes.

Δ   Increased risk for falls occurs with normal aging.

Primary Reference:

Ignatavicius, D. D., & Workman, M. L. (2006). *Medical-surgical nursing* (5th ed.). St. Louis, MO: Saunders.

Additional Resources:

NANDA International (2004). *NANDA nursing diagnoses: Definitions and classification 2005-2006.* Philadelphia: NANDA.

Smeltzer, S. C., & Bare, B. G. (2004). *Brunner and Suddarth's textbook of medical- surgical nursing* (10th ed.). Philadelphia: Lippincott Williams & Wilkins.

Stanley, M., Blair, K. A., & Gauntlett Beare, P. (Eds.).(2005). *Gerontological nursing: Promoting successful aging with older adults.* Philadelphia: F.A. Davis.

For information about Parkinson's disease, visit Parkinson's Disease Information at *www.parkinsons.org*.

Chapter 82: Parkinson's Disease

Application Exercises

Scenario: A 79-year-old man was diagnosed with Parkinson's disease 2 years ago. In spite of his condition, he is able to live independently with his partner of 59 years. He takes levodopa (Dopar) with carbidopa (Sinemet) (dopamine agonists) to control his disease. The couple has two adult children who live nearby and offer assistance when needed. Due to a recent episode of pneumonia, the client is receiving home health visits.

1. If the client has classic Parkinson's disease, what four cardinal signs and symptoms can the nurse expect the client to exhibit?

2. Why is the client at an increased risk for the development of pneumonia?

3. What is the advantage, if any, of administering the medications levodopa and carbidopa at the same time?

4. What clinical findings support the "wearing off" phenomenon (loss of response) associated with use of dopamine replacers such as levodopa with carbidopa?

5. A client is to start taking bromocriptine (Parlodel) for management of Parkinson's disease. Which of the following instructions should the client be given to manage common side effects?

        A. Rise slowly when standing up

        B. Increase dietary fiber and fluid intake

        C. Chew sugarless gum

        D. Wear sunscreen when outdoors

Chapter 82: Parkinson's Disease

Application Exercises Answer Key

Scenario: A 79-year-old man was diagnosed with Parkinson's disease 2 years ago. In spite of his condition, he is able to live independently with his partner of 59 years. He takes levodopa (Dopar) with carbidopa (Sinemet) (dopamine agonists) to control his disease. The couple has two adult children who live nearby and offer assistance when needed. Due to a recent episode of pneumonia, the client is receiving home health visits.

1. If the client has classic Parkinson's disease, what four cardinal signs and symptoms can the nurse expect the client to exhibit?

The nurse can expect to observe the classic symptoms associated with Parkinson's disease: muscle rigidity, akinesia, tremors, and postural instability.

2. Why is the client at an increased risk for the development of pneumonia?

Individuals with Parkinson's disease experience muscle weakness, which can affect their ability to swallow. Therefore, individuals with Parkinson's disease are at an increased risk for aspiration pneumonia.

3. What is the advantage, if any, of administering the medications levodopa and carbidopa at the same time?

Levodopa converts to dopamine, an essential neurotransmitter. Since dopamine stores are lost from degeneration, administration of levodopa relieves symptoms of Parkinson's disease. Carbidopa prevents the peripheral metabolism of levodopa. The advantage of administering these medications at the same time is that less levodopa is needed and the client experiences fewer side effects.

4. What clinical findings support the "wearing off" phenomenon (loss of response) associated with use of dopamine replacers such as levodopa with carbidopa?

Variance in mobility – periods of good mobility alternating with periods of poor mobility. May be impacted by ingestion of food with medication. Adjustments in dosage and/or frequency of dosing are indicated.

5. A client is to start taking bromocriptine (Parlodel) for management of Parkinson's disease. Which of the following instructions should the client be given to manage common side effects?

A. Rise slowly when standing up
B. Increase dietary fiber and fluid intake
C. Chew sugarless gum
D. Wear sunscreen when outdoors

Orthostatic hypotension is a common side effect of bromocriptine. Rising slowly will decrease the risk of dizziness and lightheadedness. Bromocriptine does not have anticholinergic effects so it is not necessary to instruct the client to increase dietary fiber and fluid intake and chew sugarless gum. Wearing sunscreen when outdoors is good health promotion but does not relate to side effects of bromocriptine.

Unit 8

Section:

Nursing Care of Clients with Neurosensory Disorders

Nursing Care of Clients with Brain Disorders

Chapter 83:   Brain Tumor

Contributor: Lynn C. Parsons, DSN, RN, CNA-BC

⟳ NCLEX-PN® Connections:

Learning Objective: Review and apply knowledge within **"Brain Tumor"** in readiness for performance of the following nursing activities as outlined by the NCLEX-PN® test plan:

Δ   Monitor the client's neurological status and report changes.

Δ   Assist with relevant laboratory, diagnostic, and therapeutic procedures within the nursing role, including:

- Preparation of the client for the procedure.

- Accurate collection of specimens.

- Monitoring client status during and after the procedure.

- Reinforcing client teaching (before and following the procedure).

- Recognizing the client's response (expected, unexpected adverse response) to the procedure.

- Monitoring results.

- Monitoring and taking actions to prevent or minimize the risk of complications.

- Notifying the primary care provider of signs of complications.

Δ   Recognize signs and symptoms of the client's problem and complete the proper documentation.

Δ   Provide and document care based on the client's health alteration.

Δ   Monitor and document vital signs changes.

Δ   Interpret data that need to be reported immediately.

Δ   Reinforce client education on managing the client's health problem.

Δ   Recognize and respond to emergency situations, including notification of the primary care provider.

Δ   Review the client's response to emergency interventions and complete the proper documentation.

Δ   Provide care that meets the age-related needs of clients 65 years of age or older, including recognizing expected physiological changes.

Key Points

Δ   Brain tumors can develop anywhere in the brain and are named according to the **cell or tissue of origin**. For example: malignant gliomas (neuroglial cells), benign meningiomas (meninges), pituitary tumors, acoustic neuromas (acoustic cranial nerve).

Δ   **Primary brain tumors originate from the central nervous system (CNS) and** rarely metastasize. **Secondary brain tumors result from metastases** from other areas (lung, breast, kidney, gastrointestinal tract).

Δ   Brain tumors that occur in the **cerebral hemispheres** above the tentorium cerebelli are classified as **supratentorial tumors**. Those below the tentorium cerebelli, such as tumors of the **brainstem and cerebellum,** are classified as **infratentorial tumors.**

Δ   Brain tumors **compress and displace** brain tissue, resulting in **cerebral edema, increased intracranial pressure, neurologic deficits, and pituitary problems.**

Δ   Brain tumors have a high overall mortality rate.

Key Factors

Δ   The cause is unknown, but possible factors include:

- Genetic risk.

- Exposure to ionizing radiation.

- Exposure to electromagnetic fields.

- Previous head injury.

Diagnostic Procedures and Nursing Interventions

Δ   Computed tomography (CT) imaging scan, magnetic resonance imaging (MRI), brain scan, and position emission tomography (PET) scan are all used to **determine the size, location, and extent of the tumor.**

Δ   Cerebral angiography – to assess vascular supply to the brain

Δ   Biopsy – to identify cellular pathology

Therapeutic Procedures and Nursing Interventions

Δ **Craniotomy** for complete or partial resection of brain tumor. Postoperative care includes:

- Monitor for increased intracranial pressure (ICP).
- Keep the head of the bed at 30° to promote venous drainage from head.
- Have the client avoid lying on operative side to avoid displacement.
- Maintain head in neutral position and avoid neck flexion.
- Avoid hip/knee flexion.

Δ **Stereotactic radiosurgery** with implantation of isotope seeds (brachytherapy) is able to reach locations not reachable by craniotomy.

Δ Systemic, intra-arterial, or intrathecal **chemotherapy** (monitor for myelosuppression and pancytopenia) and **radiation** (monitor fatigue and diarrhea) are possible adjuvant therapies to reduce tumor size.

Assessments

Δ Monitor for signs of supratentorial brain tumor.

- Severe headache (upon awakening)
- Visual symptoms
- Seizures
- Paralysis
- Change in mentation (memory loss, language impairment)
- Change in personality
- Optic disk swelling (papilledema)

Δ Monitor for signs of infratentorial brain tumor.

- Hearing loss
- Nystagmus
- Autonomic nervous system (ANS) dysfunction
- Ataxia

NANDA Nursing Diagnoses

- Δ Decreased intracranial adaptive capacity
- Δ Impaired memory
- Δ Impaired physical mobility
- Δ Risk for falls

Nursing Interventions

- Δ Maintain airway—Monitor oxygen levels, administer oxygen as needed, monitor lung sounds.
- Δ Monitor neurological status, in particular assessing for changes in level of consciousness and occurrence of seizures.
- Δ Monitor ICP (goal is to maintain at ≤ 15 to 20 mm Hg).
- Δ Maintain client safety (avoid scatter rugs, provide assistive devices).
- Δ Initiate appropriate referrals (social services, support groups, physical and occupational therapy, adaptive equipment).
- Δ Take seizure precautions.
- Δ Administer medications as prescribed.
- Δ Analgesics to treat headache
  - Dexamethasone (Decadron) to reduce cerebral edema
  - Phenytoin (Dilantin) to prevent or treat seizures
  - H_2-antagonist to reduce risk of stress ulcer
  - Antiemetics

Complications and Nursing Implications

- Δ **Post Craniotomy**
  - **Syndrome of Inappropriate Antidiuretic Hormone** (SIADH): Fluid restriction and treatment of hyponatremia
  - **Diabetes Insipidus** (DI): Fluid replacement and desmopressin
  - **Increased ICP**: Hyperventilating mechanically ventilated client to keep CO_2 at about 35 mm Hg may be an effective strategy to reduce ICP.

Meeting the Needs of Older Adults

Δ   Brain tumors can produce personality changes, confusion, speech dysfunction, and/or gait disturbances. In older adult clients, signs and symptoms of intracranial tumors can be mistaken for normal age-related changes.

Primary Reference:

Ignatavicius, D. D., & Workman, M. L. (2006). *Medical-surgical nursing* (5th ed.). St. Louis, MO: Saunders.

Additional Resources:

Armstrong, T., & Gilbert, M. R. (2000). Metastatic brain tumors: Diagnosis, treatment, and nursing interventions. *Clinical Journal of Oncology Nursing, 4 (5), 217-225.*

NANDA International (2004). *NANDA nursing diagnoses: Definitions and classification 2005-2006.* Philadelphia: NANDA.

Rude, M. (2002). Selected neurological complications in the patient with cancer. *Critical Care Nursing Clinics of North America, 12 (3), 269-278.*

Smeltzer, S. C., & Bare, B. G. (2004). *Brunner and Suddarth's textbook of medical-surgical nursing* (10th ed.). Philadelphia: Lippincott Williams & Wilkins.

For more information, visit the American Brain Tumor Association at *hope.abta.org* or the National Brain Tumor Foundation at *braintumor.org*.

Chapter 83: Brain Tumor

Application Exercises

Scenario: A 52-year-old female client is having surgery for removal of an encapsulated acoustic tumor.

1. What potential complications should the nurse anticipate postoperatively?

2. What are two possible priority nursing diagnoses?

3. Which of the following assessment findings indicate increased intracranial pressure? (Check all that apply.)

> _____ Disoriented to time and place
> _____ Restlessness and irritability
> _____ $PaCO_2$ 55 mm Hg
> _____ ICP 25 mm Hg
> _____ Headache

4. A client with a brain tumor is prescribed dexamethasone (Decadron). Which of the following are true regarding steroid therapy? (Check all that apply.)

> _____ Prescribed to reduce cerebral swelling
> _____ Hypoglycemia is an expected adverse effect
> _____ Can result in bone loss
> _____ Has a diuretic effect
> _____ Can cause fluid retention

Chapter 83: Brain Tumor

Application Exercises Answer Key

Scenario: A 52-year-old female client is having surgery for removal of an encapsulated acoustic tumor.

1. What potential complications should the nurse anticipate postoperatively?

> **Potential complications include:**
>
> > **Increased (ICP)**
> >
> > **Hematoma**
> >
> > **Hypovolemic shock**
> >
> > **Hydrocephalus**
> >
> > **Respiratory complications**
> >
> > **Infection**
> >
> > **Meningitis**
> >
> > **Fluid and electrolyte imbalances**
> >
> > **Seizure potential**
> >
> > **CSF leak**
> >
> > **Cerebral edema**

2. What are two possible priority nursing diagnoses?

> **Decreased intracranial adaptive capacity**
>
> **Impaired memory**

3. Which of the following assessment findings indicate increased intracranial pressure? (Check all that apply.)

__x__	Disoriented to time and place
__x__	Restlessness and irritability
__x__	PaCO$_2$ 55 mm Hg
__x__	ICP 25 mm Hg
_____	Headache

Changes in level of consciousness are a possible indicator of increased ICP. Increase ICP can cause behavior changesHypercarbia causes cerebral vasodilation, which increases ICP. Normal ICP is ≤ 15 to 20 mm Hg. Headache is a symptom of increased ICP.

4. A client with a brain tumor is prescribed dexamethasone (Decadron). Which of the following are true regarding steroid therapy? (Check all that apply.)

__x__	Prescribed to reduce cerebral swelling
_____	Hypoglycemia is an expected adverse effect
__x__	Can result in bone loss
_____	Has a diuretic effect
__x__	Can cause fluid retention

Dexamethasone is a common steroid prescribed to reduce cerebral edema through its anti-inflammatory effects. Hyperglycemia, osteoporosis, fluid retention, and weight gain are adverse effects of dexamethasone.

Unit 8   Nursing Care of Clients with Neurosensory Disorders
Section: Nursing Care of Clients with Peripheral Nervous System Disorders

Chapter 84:   Myasthenia Gravis
                  Contributor: Lynn C. Parsons, DSN, RN, CNA-BC

⟳ NCLEX-PN® Connections:

Learning Objective: Review and apply knowledge within "**Myasthenia Gravis**" in readiness for performance of the following nursing activities as outlined by the NCLEX-PN® test plan:

Δ   Monitor the client's neurological status and report changes.

Δ   Assist with relevant laboratory, diagnostic, and therapeutic procedures within the nursing role, including:

- Preparation of the client for the procedure.
- Accurate collection of specimens.
- Monitoring client status during and after the procedure.
- Reinforcing client teaching (before and following the procedure).
- Recognizing the client's response (expected, unexpected adverse response) to the procedure.
- Monitoring results.
- Monitoring and taking actions to prevent or minimize the risk of complications.
- Notifying the primary care provider of signs of complications.

Δ   Recognize signs and symptoms of the client's problem and complete the proper documentation.

Δ   Provide and document care based on the client's health alteration.

Δ   Monitor and document vital signs changes.

Δ   Interpret data that need to be reported immediately.

Δ   Reinforce client education on managing the client's health problem.

Δ   Recognize and respond to emergency situations, including notification of the primary care provider.

Δ   Review the client's response to emergency interventions and complete the proper documentation.

Δ   Provide care that meets the age-related needs of clients 65 years of age or older, including recognizing expected physiological changes.

📖 Key Points

Δ   Myasthenia gravis is a **progressive autoimmune disease** that produces **severe muscular weakness**. It is characterized by periods of exacerbation and remission.

Key Factors

Δ   Causes

- Co-existing autoimmune disorder
- Strong association with hyperthyroidism
- Hyperplasia of the thymus gland

Δ   Exacerbation Trigger Factors

- Infection
- Stress
- Fatigue
- Cathartics
- Heat (sauna, hot tubs, sunbathing)

Diagnostic Procedures and Nursing Interventions

Δ   Tensilon Testing

- Baseline assessment of cranial muscle strength.
- Administration of small IV dose of Tensilon.
- Marked improvement in muscle strength that lasts for 5 min is positive.
- Positive results if given to a client experiencing a myasthenic crisis (undermedication).

Δ   Electromyography – shows the neuromuscular transmission characteristics of myasthenia gravis.

Therapeutic Procedures and Nursing Interventions

Δ   Plasmapheresis – removal of circulating antibodies.

Δ   Thymectomy – removal of the thymus gland.

Assessments

Δ   Monitor for **signs and symptoms.**

- **Progressive muscle weakness**
- Poor posture
- Ptosis (drooping eyelids)
- Dysphagia (difficulty swallowing)
- Diplopia (double vision)
- Respiratory compromise
- Bowel and bladder dysfunction
- Fatigue

Δ   **Assess/Monitor**

- **Respiratory status**
- Swallowing ability/risk for aspiration
- Muscle strength
- Medication history

NANDA Nursing Diagnoses

Δ   Ineffective airway clearance

Δ   Ineffective breathing pattern

Δ   Self-care deficit

Δ   Impaired physical mobility

Δ   Imbalanced nutrition: Less than body requirements

Δ   Constipation

Δ   Impaired verbal communication

Δ   Risk for impaired spontaneous ventilation

Nursing Interventions

Δ   Assess and intervene as needed to maintain a patent airway (muscle weakness of diaphragm, respiratory, and intercostal muscles).

Δ   Assess swallowing to prevent aspiration. Keep O_2 administration, endotracheal intubation, suctioning equipment, and Ambu bag available at the bedside.

Δ   Utilize energy conservation measures. Allow for rest periods.

Δ   Consult physical therapy (PT) for durable medical equipment (DME) needs.

Δ   Consult occupational therapy for assistive devices to facilitate activities of daily living (ADLs).

Δ   Monitor intake and output, serum albumin levels, and daily weights. Provide small, frequent high-calorie meals

Δ   Consult with speech and language therapist if weakening of facial muscles impacts communication.

Δ   Encourage the client to wear a medical alert bracelet (necklace) at all times.

Δ   Administer **medications** as prescribed.

- Immunosuppressants such as azathioprine (Imuran) and prednisone (Deltasone).
  - ◊ Monitor for risk for infection.
  - ◊ Taper use gradually.
- IV immunoglobulins (IVIg) – acute management
- **Cholinesterase inhibitor** medications are the first line therapy.
  - ◊ Pyridostigmine (Mestinon)
  - ◊ Take with food to address gastrointestinal side effects.
  - ◊ **Eat within 45 min** of taking medication to **strengthen chewing and reduce aspiration risk**.
  - ◊ Stress the **importance of maintaining therapeutic levels** and taking the medication at the same time each day.

Complications and Nursing Implications

Myasthenic Crisis Undermedication	Cholinergic Crisis Overmedication
Respiratory muscle weakness – mechanical ventilation	Muscle twitching to the point of respiratory muscle weakness – mechanical ventilation
Myasthenic symptoms – weakness, incontinence, fatigue	Cholinergic symptoms – hypersecretions (nausea, diarrhea, respiratory secretions), hypermotility (abdominal cramps)
Hypertension	Hypotension
Temporary improvement of symptoms with administration of Tensilon	Tensilon has no positive effect on symptoms, may worsen (more anticholinesterase – more cholinergic symptoms)
	Symptoms improve with administration of anticholinergic medication (for example, atropine)

Primary Reference:

Ignatavicius, D. D., & Workman, M. L. (2006). *Medical-surgical nursing* (5th ed.). St. Louis, MO: Saunders.

Additional Resources:

NANDA International (2004). *NANDA nursing diagnoses: Definitions and classification 2005-2006*. Philadelphia: NANDA.

Smeltzer, S. C., & Bare, B. G. (2004). *Brunner and Suddarth's textbook of medical-surgical nursing* (10th ed.). Philadelphia: Lippincott Williams & Wilkins.

For more information, visit the Myasthenia Gravis Foundation of America at *www.myasthenia.org*.

Chapter 84: Myasthenia Gravis

Application Exercises

Scenario: A client is recovering from a myasthenic crisis during which time he suffered respiratory distress requiring mechanical ventilation for several days. The primary care provider believes an earlier episode of gastroenteritis triggered the crisis.

1. What is myasthenic crisis and what symptoms most likely prompted the client to seek medical attention?

2. Why is the client's earlier episode with gastroenteritis suspected to be the trigger for his crisis?

3. Why is it necessary to teach the client to recognize cholinergic crisis?

4. A nurse has instructed a client with myasthenia gravis regarding risk factors for myasthenia gravis exacerbations. Which of the following client statements indicates a need for further instruction?

    A. "I should take my medication 45 min ahead of breakfast, lunch, and dinner."

    B. "I have suction equipment at home in case I get really choked."

    C. "It will be really relaxing to take a long soak in the hot tub when I get home."

    D. "I have ordered a medical alert bracelet and I will wear it every day."

Chapter 84: Myasthenia Gravis

Application Exercises Answer Key

Scenario: A client is recovering from a myasthenic crisis during which time he suffered respiratory distress requiring mechanical ventilation for several days. The primary care provider believes an earlier episode of gastroenteritis triggered the crisis.

1. What is myasthenic crisis and what symptoms most likely prompted the client to seek medical attention?

   Myasthenic crisis is the sudden onset of muscular weakness that may be related to a stress response, undermedication, systemic infection, surgery, or trauma. Symptoms are the same as with the primary disease, only more severe (weakness, fatigue, dysphagia, dysarthria, choking, respiratory distress).

2. Why is the client's earlier episode with gastroenteritis suspected to be the trigger for his crisis?

   Gastroenteritis is an infectious disease. It places stress on the body and causes vomiting and diarrhea, which may have resulted in the client undermedicating himself.

3. Why is it necessary to teach the client to recognize cholinergic crisis?

   Cholinergic crisis is caused by too much medication. It must be differentiated in order to select the correct treatment. Cholinergic crisis produces gastrointestinal symptoms, which differ from those of myasthenic crisis but may be confused with acute gastroenteritis.

4. A nurse has instructed a client with myasthenia gravis regarding risk factors for myasthenia gravis exacerbations. Which of the following client statements indicates a need for further instruction?

      A. "I should take my medication 45 min ahead of breakfast, lunch, and dinner."

      B. "I have suction equipment at home in case I get really choked."

      C. "It will be really relaxing to take a long soak in the hot tub when I get home."

      D. "I have ordered a medical alert bracelet and I will wear it every day."

Heat can be a trigger for the development of myasthenic symptoms. The client should be instructed to avoid soaking in a hot tub. The nurse can suggest other forms of relaxation such as listening to music.

Unit 8   Nursing Care of Clients with Neurosensory Disorders
Section: Nursing Care of Clients with Peripheral Nervous System Disorders

Chapter 85:	Guillain-Barré Syndrome

Contributor: Lynn C. Parsons, DSN, RN, CNA-BC

NCLEX-PN® Connections:

Learning Objective: Review and apply knowledge within **"Guillain-Barré Syndrome"** in readiness for performance of the following nursing activities as outlined by the NCLEX-PN® test plan:

Δ   Monitor the client's neurological status and report changes.

Δ   Assist with relevant laboratory, diagnostic, and therapeutic procedures within the nursing role, including:

  •   Preparation of the client for the procedure.

  •   Accurate collection of specimens.

  •   Monitoring client status during and after the procedure.

  •   Reinforcing client teaching (before and following the procedure).

  •   Recognizing the client's response (expected, unexpected adverse response) to the procedure.

  •   Monitoring results.

  •   Monitoring and taking actions to prevent or minimize the risk of complications.

  •   Notifying the primary care provider of signs of complications.

Δ   Recognize signs and symptoms of the client's problem and complete the proper documentation.

Δ   Provide and document care based on the client's health alteration.

Δ   Monitor and document vital signs changes.

Δ   Interpret data that need to be reported immediately.

Δ   Reinforce client education on managing the client's health problem.

Δ   Recognize and respond to emergency situations, including notification of the primary care provider.

Δ   Review the client's response to emergency interventions and complete the proper documentation.

Δ   Provide care that meets the age-related needs of clients 65 years of age or older, including recognizing expected physiological changes.

📖 Key Points

Δ   Guillain-Barré syndrome (GBS) is an **acute destruction of myelin sheaths** due to an **autoimmune** disorder that results in varying degrees of **muscle weakness and paralysis.**

Δ   Cranial and motor nerves are affected more often, resulting in altered sensory perception. These inappropriate sensory signals create pain and tingling sensations, and the client may report "crawling skin."

Δ   Aggregates of lymphocytes can cause secondary damage, which can delay recovery or result in permanent deficits.

Δ   Chronic inflammatory demyelinating polyneuropathy (CIDP) is a different type of GBS that progresses over a very long period, and recovery is rare.

Δ   Three stages characterize the course of GBS:

   •   Initial period – 1 to 4 weeks; onset of symptoms until no further deterioration is noted.

   •   Plateau period – several days to 2 weeks; no deterioration, no improvement.

   •   Recovery period – 4 to 6 months and up to 2 years; demyelination and return of muscle strength.

Key Factors

Δ   Etiology unknown – evidence indicates a cell-mediated immunologic reaction.

Δ   **Risk Factors**

   •   Recent (within 1 to 3 weeks) history of:

      ◊   **Acute illness** (upper respiratory infection, gastrointestinal illness).

      ◊   Viruses such as cytomegalovirus (CMV) or Epstein Barr virus (EBV).

      ◊   Vaccination.

      ◊   Surgery.

Diagnostic Procedures and Nursing Interventions

Δ   Electromyography (EMG) and nerve conduction velocity (NCV) show evidence of denervation after 4+ weeks.

   •   Prepare the client for temporary discomfort.

   •   Monitor needle sites for hematoma formation.

   •   Apply ice to prevent hematoma formation.

Δ   White cell count: Shows leukocytosis.

Δ   Lumbar puncture (LP): Shows the **distinguishing characteristic** GBS finding of **an increase in protein within the** CSF without an increase in cell count.

Therapeutic Procedures and Nursing Interventions

Δ   **Plasmapheresis**—removes circulating antibodies from plasma.

- Maintain shunt patency.

- Monitor for the possible complications of hypovolemia, hypokalemia, and hypocalcemia.

Assessments

Δ   Monitor for **signs and symptoms.**

- Acute progressing muscle **weakness** to muscle **flaccidity** without muscle atrophy

   ◊   Ascending (bilateral lower extremity muscles initially then progresses upward)

   ◊   Descending (face muscles initially then progresses downward)

- Decreased/absent deep tendon reflexes

- Signs of respiratory compromise

- Paresthesias – creeping/crawling sensations across skin

- Cranial nerve symptoms (facial weakness, dysphagia, diplopia, dysarthria)

- Autonomic manifestations (fluctuating blood pressure, dysrhythmias)

Δ   **Assess/Monitor**

- **Airway patency**

- **Respiratory status**

- Vital signs

- Heart rhythm

- Cranial nerve function

- Pain level

- Skin integrity

NANDA Nursing Diagnoses

Δ   Ineffective breathing pattern

Δ   Ineffective airway clearance

Δ   Impaired gas exchange

Δ   Acute pain

Δ   Impaired physical mobility

Δ   Risk for impaired skin integrity

Nursing Interventions

Δ   Maintain a patent airway; suction and/or intubate as needed.

Δ   Monitor ABGs; administer oxygen or mechanical ventilation as needed.

Δ   Keep the head of the bed at 45°; turn, cough, deep breathe every 2 hr; conduct incentive spirometry/chest physiotherapy.

Δ   Monitor blood pressure and respond to fluctuations as needed (beta-blocker administration for hypertension, IV fluids for hypotension).

Δ   Continuously monitor heart rhythm and intervene as indicated (for example, atropine for bradycardia).

Δ   Provide comfort measures (frequent repositioning, ice, heat, massage, distraction).

Δ   Monitor cranial nerve function and intervene to maintain safety accordingly (e.g., risk of aspiration, risk for injury).

Δ   Facilitate effective communication (for example, use of a communication board to help clients with dysarthria).

Δ   Initiate appropriate referrals (social service, physical therapy, occupational therapy).

Δ   Assess coping and depression.

Δ   Administer medications as prescribed.

- Analgesia (for example, PCA morphine) – Monitor for respiratory depression and constipation.

- IV Immunoglobulin (IVIg) – Monitor for side effects such as chills, fever, and myalgia, and for possible complications including anaphylaxis or renal failure.

Complications and Nursing Implications

Δ   **Respiratory compromise** – Recognize progressing paralysis and be prepared to intervene promptly.

- Intubate and mechanically ventilate as needed.

- Provide assistance in mobilization and removal of secretions.

- Monitor oxygen status and administer oxygen as needed.

Primary Reference:

Ignatavicius, D. D., & Workman, M. L. (2006). *Medical-surgical nursing* (5th ed.). St. Louis, MO: Saunders.

Additional Resources:

NANDA International (2004). *NANDA nursing diagnoses: Definitions and classification 2005-2006*. Philadelphia: NANDA.

Smeltzer, S. C., & Bare, B. G. (2004). *Brunner and Suddarth's textbook of medical-surgical nursing* (10th ed.). Philadelphia: Lippincott Williams & Wilkins.

For more information, visit the GBS/CIDP Foundation International at *www.guillain-barre.com*.

Chapter 85: Guillain-Barré Syndrome

Application Exercises

Scenario: A client is admitted with ascending Guillain-Barré syndrome (GBS).

1. Which of the following is the client most likely to report during the admission interview?

      A. Spinal cord injury

      B. Head injury

      C. Upper respiratory infection

      D. Bacterial meningitis

2. What equipment should the nurse place at the client's bedside?

3. Which of the following client findings should the nurse anticipate? (Check all that apply.)

    _____   Muscle weakness

    _____   Muscle atrophy

    _____   Incontinence

    _____   Ineffective cough

    _____   Hyperreflexia

4. Rank in order the expected client findings for ascending GBS. Assign 1 to the first expected client finding.

    _____   Tingling of toes

    _____   Difficulty speaking

    _____   Respiratory compromise

    _____   Incontinence

    _____   Inability to walk

    _____   Ophthalmoplegia

Chapter 85: Guillain-Barré Syndrome

Application Exercises Answer Key

Scenario: A client is admitted with ascending Guillain-Barré syndrome (GBS).

1. Which of the following is the client most likely to report during the admission interview?

        A. Spinal cord injury

        B. Head injury

        C. Upper respiratory infection

        D. Bacterial meningitis

A history of an upper respiratory or gastrointestinal infection, stress such as surgery/ trauma, or recent vaccination within the last 1 to 3 weeks is a common history finding in clients with GBS.

2. What equipment should the nurse place at the client's bedside?

Endotracheal intubation, Ambu bag, nasotracheal suctioning equipment, heart rhythm monitoring system

3. Which of the following client findings should the nurse anticipate? (Check all that apply.)

      __x__   Muscle weakness

      _____   Muscle atrophy

      __x__   Incontinence

      __x__   Ineffective cough

      _____   Hyperreflexia

A characteristic of GBS is muscle weakness without atrophy. Ineffective cough and incontinence are likely due to muscle weakness. Reflexes are decreased or absent.

4. Rank in order the expected client findings for ascending GBS. Assign 1 to the first expected client finding.

1	Tingling of toes
5	Difficulty speaking
4	Respiratory compromise
3	Incontinence
2	Inability to walk
6	Ophthalmoplegia

With ascending GBS, paresthesia and muscle weakness symptoms begin in the lower extremities and proceed upward.

Unit 8 Nursing Care of Clients with Neurosensory Disorders

Section: Nursing Care of Clients with Spinal Cord Disorders

Chapter 86: Multiple Sclerosis

Contributor: Lynn C. Parsons, DSN, RN, CNA-BC

⟲ NCLEX-PN® Connections:

Learning Objective: Review and apply knowledge within "**Multiple Sclerosis**" in readiness for performance of the following nursing activities as outlined by the NCLEX-PN® test plan:

Δ Assist with relevant laboratory, diagnostic, and therapeutic procedures within the nursing role, including:

- Preparation of the client for the procedure.

- Accurate collection of specimens.

- Monitoring client status during and after the procedure.

- Reinforcing client teaching (before and following the procedure).

- Recognizing the client's response (expected, unexpected adverse response) to the procedure.

- Monitoring results.

- Monitoring and taking actions to prevent or minimize the risk of complications.

- Notifying the primary care provider of signs of complications.

Δ Recognize signs and symptoms of the client's problem and complete the proper documentation.

Δ Provide and document care based on the client's health alteration.

Δ Monitor and document vital signs changes.

Δ Interpret data that need to be reported immediately.

Δ Reinforce client education on managing the client's health problem.

Δ Recognize and respond to emergency situations, including notification of the primary care provider.

Δ Review the client's response to emergency interventions and complete the proper documentation.

Δ Provide care that meets the age-related needs of clients 65 years of age or older, including recognizing expected physiological changes.

Key Points

Δ   Multiple sclerosis (MS) is an autoimmune disorder characterized by **development of plaque** in the white matter of the central nervous system (CNS). This plaque damages the myelin sheath and **blocks impulse transmission** between the CNS system and the body.

Δ   The disease follows two major courses: (1) relapsing and remitting, and (2) chronic and progressive.

Δ   There is **no cure** for the disease.

Key Factors

Δ   The onset of MS typically occurs between 20 and 40 years of age and twice as often in women. The etiology of MS is unknown. There is a family history (first-degree relative) of MS in 15% of cases.

Δ   **Trigger Factors**

• Virus and infectious agent

• Living in cold climate

• Physical injury

• Emotional stress

• Pregnancy

• Fatigue

• Overexertion

• Temperature extremes

• Hot shower/bath

Diagnostic Procedures and Nursing Interventions

Δ   **Magnetic resonance imaging** (MRI) of brain and spine: Plaques (**most diagnostic**)

Δ   Cerebrospinal fluid (CSF) analysis: Elevated protein level and a slight increase in white blood cells

Assessments

Δ   Monitor for **signs and symptoms.**

• Vague and nonspecific

• Muscle weakness

- **Muscle spasticity**

- **Fatigue** (especially of the lower extremities)

- Paresthesia

- Ataxia

- Dysarthria, dysphagia

- Diplopia, nystagmus, changes in peripheral vision, decreased visual acuity

- **Uhthoff's sign** (a temporary worsening of vision and other neurological functions commonly seen in clients with MS, or clients predisposed to MS, just after exertion or in situations where they are exposed to heat)

- Tinnitus, vertigo, decreased hearing acuity

- Bowel dysfunction (constipation, fecal incontinence)

- Bladder dysfunction (areflexia, urgency, nocturia)

- Cognitive changes (memory loss, impaired judgment)

Δ **Assess/Monitor**

- Activity tolerance

- Speech patterns (for example, fatigue with talking)

- Visual acuity

- Skin integrity

NANDA Nursing Diagnoses

Δ Fatigue

Δ Activity intolerance

Δ Disturbed sensory perception (visual)

Δ Impaired physical mobility

Δ Impaired urinary elimination

Δ Chronic pain

Δ Imbalanced nutrition: Less than body requirements

Nursing Interventions

Δ Encourage fluid intake and other measures to **decrease risk of developing a UTI.** Assist the client with bladder elimination (intermittent self-catheterization, bladder pacemaker, Credé).

Δ Monitor **cognitive changes** and take interventions to maintain function (reorient client, place routine objects in routine places).

Δ   Facilitate effective **communication** (dysarthria) with, for example, use of a communication board or a speech language therapist referral.

Δ   Apply alternating eye patches to treat **diplopia**. Teach scanning techniques.

Δ   Utilize energy conservation measures.

Δ   Promote and maintain **safe home and hospital environment** to reduce the risk of injury. Consider referral to occupational and physical therapy for home environment assessment to determine safety and ease of mobility. Adaptive devices to assist with activities of daily living.

Δ   Plan for disease progression. Provide community resources and respite services for the client and family.

Δ   Provide **medications** as prescribed.

- Immunosuppressive agents (azathioprine, cyclosporine) reduce the frequency of relapses. Monitor for long-term effects.

- Corticosteroids (prednisone) – reduce inflammation in acute exacerbations. Monitor for increased risk of infection, hypervolemia, hypernatremia, hypokalemia, hyperglycemia, gastrointestinal bleeding, and personality changes.

- Antispasmodic therapy such as dantrolene (Dantrium), possibly intrathecally.

- Interferon (Betaseron)

- Anticonvulsants such as carbamazepine (Tegretol) – paresthesia

- Stool softeners such as docusate sodium (Colace) – constipation

- Anticholinergics such as propantheline (Pro-Banthine) – bladder dysfunction

- Beta-blockers, primidone, clonazepam – tremors

Complications and Nursing Implications

Δ   **Spasticity – range-of-motion (ROM) exercises** to maintain function. Administer **antispasmodic** medications (baclofen, dantrolene) to relieve spasm. Spinal injections and surgery to cut tendons are possible options.

Δ   **Neurogenic bladder** – The nerve communication between brain and bladder is faulty. Control fluid intake. Provide interventions to regulate elimination such as intermittent self-catheterization.

Primary Reference:

Ignatavicius, D. D., & Workman, M. L. (2006). *Medical-surgical nursing* (5th ed.). St. Louis, MO: Saunders.

Additional Resources:

NANDA International (2004). *NANDA nursing diagnoses: Definitions and classification 2005-2006*. Philadelphia: NANDA.

Smeltzer, S. C., & Bare, B. G. (2004). *Brunner and Suddarth's textbook of medical-surgical nursing* (10th ed.). Philadelphia: Lippincott Williams & Wilkins.

For more information, visit the National Multiple Sclerosis Society at *www.nmss.org* or MS ActiveSource at *www.msactivesource.com.*

Chapter 86: Multiple Sclerosis

Application Exercises

Scenario: A home health care nurse is interviewing a 24-year-old client with newly diagnosed multiple sclerosis (MS). The client is upset over her increasing loss of mobility, decreased visual acuity, and the severe fatigue that worsens as the day progresses. In addition, the client states she is experiencing mood swings she cannot control. As the client has a decreased libido, she is also worried about her relationship with her husband. The client tells the nurse she and her husband had planned a pregnancy, but now they have been forced to put their lives on hold.

1. What initial assessments should the home health care nurse make in regard to the client's MS?

2. What actions should the nurse take to help the client increase mobility and lessen fatigue?

3. Which of the following client history findings might have triggered this MS exacerbation?

    _____   Recent bout of flu
    _____   LT use of NSAIDs
    _____   Large meal intake
    _____   Recent insomnia
    _____   Stress
    _____   Snow ski trip

4. How is MS definitively diagnosed?

Chapter 86: Multiple Sclerosis

Application Exercises Answer Key

Scenario: A home health care nurse is interviewing a 24-year-old client with newly diagnosed multiple sclerosis (MS). The client is upset over her increasing loss of mobility, decreased visual acuity, and the severe fatigue that worsens as the day progresses. In addition, the client states she is experiencing mood swings she cannot control. As the client has a decreased libido, she is also worried about her relationship with her husband. The client tells the nurse she and her husband had planned a pregnancy, but now they have been forced to put their lives on hold.

1. What initial assessments should the home health care nurse make in regard to the client's MS?

The nurse should assess the client's: (a) motor dysfunction (weakness, paralysis, spasticity, abnormal gait); (b) cognitive dysfunction (changes in short-term memory, short-attention span); (c) emotional lability; (d) sensory dysfunction (paresthesias, decreased temperature perception and proprioception, and blurred vision); (e) cerebellar dysfunction (tremor, ataxia, vertigo); (f) bowel and bladder dysfunction (constipation, incontinence, spastic bladder); (g) sexual dysfunction; (h) fatigue; and (i) the ability to perform the activities of daily living (ADLs).

2. What actions should the nurse take to help the client increase mobility and lessen fatigue?

It is important to encourage the client to conserve her energy and increase mobility by using assistive devices such as canes, walkers, and wheelchairs. In addition, for safety, the client should wear non-slip, flat, tie shoes. The nurse should check the home environment to make certain that lighting is adequate, and that cords and throw rugs that could trip the client have been removed. The client can schedule major activities in the morning and then plan rest periods during the afternoon. The nurse should arrange with physical therapy and occupational therapy departments for periodic home visits if able and insurance allows.

3. Which of the following client history findings might have triggered this MS exacerbation?

__x__	Recent bout of flu
_____	LT use of NSAIDs
_____	Large meal intake
__x__	Recent insomnia
__x__	Stress
__x__	Snow ski trip

4. How is MS definitively diagnosed?

Magnetic resonance imaging (MRI) of brain and spine: Plaques (most diagnostic) Cerebrospinal fluid (CSF) analysis: Elevated protein level and a slight increase in white blood cells. Ruling out other neurologic diseases

Unit 8

Nursing Care of Clients with Neurosensory Disorders

Section: Nursing Care of Clients with Spinal Cord Disorders

Chapter 87:   Amyotrophic Lateral Sclerosis (ALS)

Contributor: Lynn C. Parsons, DSN, RN, CNA-BC

⟳ NCLEX-PN® Connections:

Learning Objective: Review and apply knowledge within "**Amyotrophic Lateral Sclerosis (ALS)**" in readiness for performance of the following nursing activities as outlined by the NCLEX-PN® test plan:

Δ   Assist with relevant laboratory, diagnostic, and therapeutic procedures within the nursing role, including:

- Preparation of the client for the procedure.

- Accurate collection of specimens.

- Monitoring client status during and after the procedure.

- Reinforcing client teaching (before and following the procedure).

- Recognizing the client's response (expected, unexpected adverse response) to the procedure.

- Monitoring results.

- Monitoring and taking actions to prevent or minimize the risk of complications.

- Notifying the primary care provider of signs of complications.

Δ   Recognize signs and symptoms of the client's problem and complete the proper documentation.

Δ   Provide and document care based on the client's health alteration.

Δ   Monitor and document vital signs changes.

Δ   Interpret data that need to be reported immediately.

Δ   Reinforce client education on managing the client's health problem.

Δ   Recognize and respond to emergency situations, including notification of the primary care provider.

Δ   Review the client's response to emergency interventions and complete the proper documentation.

Δ   Provide care that meets the age-related needs of clients 65 years of age or older, including recognizing expected physiological changes.

📖 **Key Points**

Δ   Amyotrophic lateral sclerosis (ALS) is a **deteriorating disease of the motor system** characterized by muscle weakness progressing to muscle atrophy and eventually paralysis and death. ALS does not involve autonomic changes, sensory alterations, or cognitive changes.

Δ   ALS is also known as Lou Gehrig's disease for the professional baseball player who died of the disease in 1941.

Δ   There is no cure. Death typically occurs within 2 to 5 years after the onset of symptoms, and death is attributed to respiratory failure (upward progression of paralysis affecting the respiratory muscles and causing respiratory compromise, pneumonia, and death).

Key Factors

Δ   ALS affects more men than women, often developing in the 5th and 6th decades of life.

Diagnostic Procedures and Nursing Interventions

Δ   Creatine kinase (CK) level: Increased

Δ   Electromyogram (EMG): Muscle fasciculations

Δ   Muscle biopsy: Muscle atrophy

Δ   Serial muscle testing: Loss of muscle strength

Assessments

Δ   Monitor for **signs and symptoms.**

•   Muscle weakness, especially of hands and arms

•   Fatigue

•   Dysphagia (swallowing difficulties)

•   Dysarthria (speech difficulties)

Δ   **Assess/Monitor**

•   Airway patency

•   Respiratory status

•   Ability to swallow

•   Speech patterns (for example, fatigue with talking)

•   Skin integrity

NANDA Nursing Diagnoses

- Δ Impaired spontaneous ventilation
- Δ Risk for aspiration
- Δ Ineffective airway clearance
- Δ Impaired physical mobility
- Δ Risk for falls
- Δ Impaired verbal communication
- Δ Risk for activity intolerance
- Δ Fatigue
- Δ Risk for impaired skin integrity
- Δ Deficient knowledge

Nursing Interventions

- Δ Maintain a **patent airway** and suction and/or intubate as needed.
- Δ Monitor arterial blood gases (ABGs) and administer oxygen, intermittent positive pressure ventilation, bilevel positive airway pressure, or mechanical ventilation as needed.
- Δ Keep the head of the bed at 45°; turn, cough, deep breathe every 2 hr; conduct incentive spirometry/chest physiotherapy.
- Δ Facilitate effective **communication** (dysarthria) with, for example, use of a communication board or a speech language therapist referral.
- Δ Initiate appropriate referrals (dietician, social service, physical therapy, occupational therapy, clinical psychologist).
- Δ Assess coping and depression.
- Δ Assess swallow reflex and ensure safety with oral intake.
- Δ Meet **nutritional needs** for calories, fiber, and fluids. Provide enteral nutrition as prescribed (for example, when no longer able to swallow).
- Δ Utilize energy conservation measures.
- Δ Consider referral to speech pathologist. Plan for when speech is no longer possible (progressive muscle weakness).

Δ   Consider hospice referral to provide support to the client and family coping with terminal illness.

Δ   Address the client's interest in establishment of advance directives/living wills.

Δ   Provide **medications** as prescribed.

- Riluzole (Rilutek): Unknown mechanism of action, extends survival time, hepatoxic risk (monitor liver function tests).

- Antispasmodics – baclofen (Lioresal), dantrolene sodium (Dantrium), diazepam (Valium)

Complications and Nursing Implications

Δ   **Pneumonia** due to respiratory muscle paralysis. Assess respiratory status routinely and provide antimicrobial therapy as indicated.

Δ   **Respiratory failure** necessitating mechanical ventilation. Assess respiratory status and be prepared to provide ventilatory support as needed per the client's directives.

Primary Reference:

Ignatavicius, D. D., & Workman, M. L. (2006). *Medical-surgical nursing* (5th ed.). St. Louis, MO: Saunders.

Additional Resources:

NANDA International (2004). *NANDA nursing diagnoses: Definitions and classification 2005-2006*. Philadelphia: NANDA.

Rowland, L. P., & Shneider, N. A. (2001). Medical progress: Amyotrophic lateral sclerosis. *New England Journal of Medicine, 344 (22)*, 205-217.

Smeltzer, S. C., & Bare, B. G. (2004). *Brunner and Suddarth's textbook of medical-surgical nursing* (10th ed.). Philadelphia: Lippincott Williams & Wilkins.

For more information, visit the ALS Association at *www.alsa.org*.

Chapter 87: Amyotrophic Lateral Sclerosis (ALS)

Application Exercises

Scenario: A nurse is caring for a client admitted to the hospital with respiratory difficulty after being diagnosed with ALS approximately 1 year ago.

1. What equipment should the nurse place at the client's bedside?

2. Which of the following client findings should the nurse anticipate? (Check all that apply.)

_____ Muscle weakness

_____ Gradual loss of sensation

_____ Fluctuations in blood pressure

_____ Muscle atrophy

_____ Incontinence

_____ Ineffective cough

_____ Loss of cognitive function

3. What types of self-care deficits should the nurse anticipate?

4. The client's muscle weakness worsens and mechanical ventilation is necessary. What are the long-term implications of a mechanical ventilation decision?

Chapter 87: Amyotrophic Lateral Sclerosis (ALS)

Application Exercises Answer Key

Scenario: A nurse is caring for a client admitted to the hospital with respiratory difficulty after being diagnosed with ALS approximately 1 year ago.

1. What equipment should the nurse place at the client's bedside?

Endotracheal intubation, Ambu bag, nasotracheal suctioning equipment, heart rhythm monitoring system

2. Which of the following client findings should the nurse anticipate? (Check all that apply.)

   <u> x </u>   Muscle weakness
   <u>   </u>   Gradual loss of sensation
   <u>   </u>   Fluctuations in blood pressure
   <u> x </u>   Muscle atrophy
   <u> x </u>   Incontinence
   <u> x </u>   Ineffective cough
   <u>   </u>   Loss of cognitive function

ALS is a deteriorating disease of the motor system characterized by muscle weakness progressing to muscle atrophy and eventually paralysis and death. ALS does not involve autonomic changes, sensory alterations, or cognitive changes.

3. What types of self-care deficits should the nurse anticipate?

Bathing
Grooming
Ambulating
Eating (especially after the disease progresses)

4. The client's muscle weakness worsens and mechanical ventilation is necessary. What are the long-term implications of a mechanical ventilation decision?

ALS is a deteriorating disease with death from respiratory failure a certainty. Mechanical ventilation will prolong survival but will not change the outcome since the muscle weakness is not reversible or treatable. Many clients with ALS elect not to be ventilated.

Unit 8   Nursing Care of Clients with Neurosensory Disorders
Section: Medical Emergencies: Neurological

Chapter 88:   Head Injury
                Contributor: Lynn C. Parsons, DSN, RN, CNA-BC

NCLEX-PN® Connections:

Learning Objective: Review and apply knowledge within **"Head Injury"** in readiness for performance of the following nursing activities as outlined by the NCLEX-PN® test plan:

Δ   Monitor the client's neurological status and report changes.

Δ   Assist with relevant laboratory, diagnostic, and therapeutic procedures within the nursing role, including:

- Preparation of the client for the procedure.

- Accurate collection of specimens.

- Monitoring client status during and after the procedure.

- Reinforcing client teaching (before and following the procedure).

- Recognizing the client's response (expected, unexpected adverse response) to the procedure.

- Monitoring results.

- Monitoring and taking actions to prevent or minimize the risk of complications.

- Notifying the primary care provider of signs of complications.

Δ   Recognize signs and symptoms of the client's problem and complete the proper documentation.

Δ   Provide and document care based on the client's health alteration.

Δ   Monitor and document vital signs changes.

Δ   Interpret data that need to be reported immediately.

Δ   Reinforce client education on managing the client's health problem.

Δ   Recognize and respond to emergency situations, including notification of the primary care provider.

Δ   Review the client's response to emergency interventions and complete the proper documentation.

Δ   Provide care that meets the age-related needs of clients 65 years of age or older, including recognizing expected physiological changes.

📖 **Key Points**

Δ Head injuries can be classified as **open** (skull integrity is lost – penetrating trauma) or **closed** (skull integrity is maintained – blunt trauma). Head injuries are also classified as mild, moderate, or severe, depending upon **Glasgow coma scale** (GCS) ratings and length of loss of consciousness.

Δ Open head injuries pose a high risk for **infection**.

Δ Skull fractures are often associated with **brain injury**. Damage to the brain tissue occurs when the supply of oxygen and/or glucose to the brain is negatively affected.

Δ Head injuries may or may not be associated with **hemorrhage** (epidural, subdural, and intracerebral). Cerebrospinal fluid leakage is also possible. Any collections occupy space within the confines of the skull and consequently pose dangers for cerebral edema, cerebral hypoxia, and brain herniation.

Δ Cervical **spine injury** should always be suspected when head injury occurs.

Key Factors

Δ **Risk Factors**

- Young males

- Motor vehicle or motorcycle crashes

- Drug and alcohol use

- Sports injuries

- Assault

- Gunshot wounds

- Falls

Diagnostic and Therapeutic Procedures and Nursing Interventions

Δ Arterial blood gases (ABGs) are used to assess oxygen status.

Δ Computed tomography (CT)/computed axial tomography (CAT) scan are used to assess the location (epidural, subdural) and extent of the head injury.

Δ Intracranial pressure monitoring (ICP) – intraventricular, subarachnoid, epidural, and/or subdural. Elevated ICP poses a risk of infection. Normal ICP level is 10 to 15 mm Hg.

Δ Craniotomy – removal of nonvital brain tissue to allow for expansion and/or removal of epidural or subdural hematomas. This involves drilling a burr hole or creating a small or large bone flap to permit access to the affected area. Intracranial hemorrhages require surgical evacuation.

Assessments

Δ   **Assess/Monitor**

- **Respiratory status** – the **PRIORITY** assessment

- **Changes in level of consciousness** – the **EARLIEST** indication of neurological deterioration

- Alcohol or drug use at time of injury (can mask increased ICP)

- Amnesia (loss of memory) before or after injury

- Loss of consciousness and length

- **Cushing reflex** (severe hypertension with a widened pulse pressure and bradycardia) – late sign of increased ICP

- Posturing (decorticate, decerebrate, flaccid)

- Cranial nerve function

- Pupillary changes (PERRLA, pinpoint, fixed/nonresponsive, dilated)

- Signs of infection (nuchal rigidity with meningitis)

- Cerebrospinal fluid leakage from nose and ears ("halo" sign – yellow stain surrounded by blood; test positive for glucose)

- **GCS rating (15 normal; 3 = deep coma)**

Glasgow Coma Scale			
Eye Opening Response (E)	**Verbal response (V)**	**Motor Response (M)**	
4 = Spontaneous	5 = Normal conversation	6 = Normal	
3 = To Voice	4 = Disoriented conversation	5 = Localizes to pain	
2 = To Pain	3 = Words, but not coherent	4 = Withdraws to pain	
1 = None	2 = No words, only sounds	3 = Decorticate posture	
	1 = None	2 = Decerebrate	
		1 = None	
E Score	V Score	M Score	E + V + M = Total score

NANDA Nursing Diagnoses

Δ   Ineffective tissue perfusion (cerebral)

Δ   Decreased intracranial adaptive capacity

Δ   Ineffective breathing pattern

Δ   Ineffective airway clearance

Nursing Interventions

Δ   **Maintain a patent airway**. Provide mechanical ventilation as indicated.

Δ   Maintain c-spine stability until cleared by x-ray.

Δ   **Elevate head to reduce intracranial pressure** and to promote venous drainage. Avoid extreme flexion or extension, maintain head in midline neutral position, keep the head of the bed elevated 30°.

Δ   Instruct the client to avoid coughing and blowing nose (increases ICP).

Δ   Report presence of cerebrospinal fluid (CSF) from nose or ears to the primary care provider.

Δ   Provide a calm, restful environment (limit visitors, minimize noise).

Δ   Use energy conservation measures; alternate activities with rest periods.

Δ   Implement seizure precautions.

Δ   Implement measures to prevent complications of immobility (turn every 2 hr, footboard and splints).

Δ   Monitor the client's vital signs, level of consciousness, pupils, motor activity, sensory perception, and verbal responses at frequent intervals.

Δ   Monitor fluid and electrolyte values and osmolarity to detect changes in sodium regulation, the onset of diabetes insipidus, or severe hypovolemia.

Δ   Provide adequate fluids to maintain cerebral perfusion. When a large amount of IV fluids is ordered, monitor the client carefully for excess fluid volume.

Δ   Maintain client safety (side rails up, padded side rails).

Δ   Administer medications as prescribed:

•   Pain medications as prescribed in the absence of increased ICP (avoid opioids such as morphine sulfate because they produce respiratory depression, pupillary changes, nausea, and CNS clouding).

•   Dexamethasone (Decadron), methylprednisolone (Solu-Medrol) to reduce cerebral edema.

- Mannitol (Osmitrol) – osmotic diuresis to treat cerebral edema.

- Neuromuscular blocking agents, sedatives, and opioids to manage agitation (be cautious as they can mask changes in level of consciousness).

- Pentobarbital (Nembutal), sodium thiopental to induce a barbiturate coma in order to decrease cerebral metabolic demands.

- Phenytoin (Dilantin) to prevent/treat seizures.

Δ Provide nutritional support (for example, enteral nutrition)

Δ Health Promotion/Prevention

- Wear helmets.

- Wear seat belts when driving.

- Avoid dangerous activities (speeding, drinking and driving).

Complications and Nursing Implications

Δ **Brain herniation** – downward shift of brain tissue. Signs include fixed dilated pupils, deteriorating level of consciousness, Cheyne Stoke respirations, hemodynamic instability, and abnormal posturing.

Meeting the Needs of Older Adults

Δ Head injury is the 5th leading cause of death in older adult clients.

Δ The 65 to 75 age group has the 2nd highest incidence of head injury of all age groups.

Primary Reference:

Ignatavicius, D. D., & Workman, M. L. (2006). *Medical-surgical nursing* (5th ed.). St. Louis, MO: Saunders.

Additional Resources:

Hickey, J. V. (2003). *The clinical practice of neurological and neurosurgical nursing* (5th ed.). Philadelphia: Lippincott Williams & Wilkins.

NANDA International (2004). *NANDA nursing diagnoses: Definitions and classification 2005-2006.* Philadelphia: NANDA.

Smeltzer, S. C., & Bare, B. G. (2004). *Brunner and Suddarth's textbook of medical-surgical nursing* (10th ed.). Philadelphia: Lippincott Williams & Wilkins.

For more information, visit the Brain Injury Resource Center at *www.headinjury.com.*

Chapter 88: Head Injury

Application Exercises

Scenario: A 31-year-old woman received a closed head injury during a motor vehicle crash approximately 6 hr ago. Her CT scan indicates she has sustained a frontal contrecoup contusion of moderate severity to the left side of her brain. She is unresponsive to verbal commands, opens her eyes only to pain, withdraws to pain stimulus, and only occasionally makes sounds, which are incomprehensible. Her blood pressure is 150/68 mm Hg, heart rate 72 beats/min, and respirations are 28/min and mildly labored.

1. What is the priority nursing diagnosis and corresponding interventions for this client?

2. What is the significance of the client's vital signs in relation to her head injury?

3. Cite three desired outcomes of nursing care for this client.

4. Calculate the client's GCS score.

   Eye Opening Response =

   Verbal Response =

   Motor Response =

   Total =

Chapter 88: Head Injury

Application Exercises Answer Key

Scenario: A 31-year-old woman received a closed head injury during a motor vehicle crash approximately 6 hr ago. Her CT scan indicates she has sustained a frontal contrecoup contusion of moderate severity to the left side of her brain. She is unresponsive to verbal commands, opens her eyes only to pain, withdraws to pain stimulus, and only occasionally makes sounds, which are incomprehensible. Her blood pressure is 150/68 mm Hg, heart rate 72 beats/min, and respirations are 28/min and mildly labored.

1. What is the priority nursing diagnosis and corresponding interventions for this client?

   Diagnosis: High risk for ineffective airway clearance related to hypoxia secondary to brain contusion. Related to coma and possible labored breathing.

   Interventions: Establish and maintain a patent airway; position to facilitate respirations; elevate head of bed 30° to reduce intracranial pressure; suction if needed (can increase ICP); implement seizure precautions; prepare to place the client on mechanical ventilation if needed; monitor for signs of increased ICP; monitor ABGs; and determine GCS.

2. What is the significance of the client's vital signs in relation to her head injury?

   Her vital signs are consistent with increased ICP, which includes slowing of the pulse rate and widening of pulse pressure with increasing systolic pressure.

3. Cite three desired outcomes of nursing care for this client.

   Maintain effective airway, ventilation, and oxygenation

   Regain normal acid-base and electrolyte balance

   Remain free of skin alterations

   Remain free of injury

   Maintain adequate nutritional status

4. Calculate the client's GCS score.

Eye Opening Response = **2 (eye opening to pain)**

Verbal Response = **2 (incomprehensible sounds)**

Motor Response = **4 (motor response to pain)**

Total = **8**

Unit 8   Nursing Care of Clients with Neurosensory Disorders
Section: Medical Emergencies: Neurological

Chapter 89:   Spinal Cord Injury
               Contributor: Lynn C. Parsons, DSN, RN, CNA-BC

⟲ NCLEX-PN® Connections:

Learning Objective: Review and apply knowledge within "**Spinal Cord Injury**" in readiness for performance of the following nursing activities as outlined by the NCLEX-PN® test plan:

Δ   Monitor the client's neurological status and report changes.

Δ   Assist with relevant laboratory, diagnostic, and therapeutic procedures within the nursing role, including:

   •   Preparation of the client for the procedure.

   •   Accurate collection of specimens.

   •   Monitoring client status during and after the procedure.

   •   Reinforcing client teaching (before and following the procedure).

   •   Recognizing the client's response (expected, unexpected adverse response) to the procedure.

   •   Monitoring results.

   •   Monitoring and taking actions to prevent or minimize the risk of complications.

   •   Notifying the primary care provider of signs of complications.

Δ   Recognize signs and symptoms of the client's problem and complete the proper documentation.

Δ   Provide and document care based on the client's health alteration.

Δ   Monitor and document vital signs changes.

Δ   Interpret data that need to be reported immediately.

Δ   Reinforce client education on managing the client's health problem.

Δ   Recognize and respond to emergency situations, including notification of the primary care provider.

Δ   Review the client's response to emergency interventions and complete the proper documentation.

Δ   Provide care that meets the age-related needs of clients 65 years of age or older, including recognizing expected physiological changes.

Key Points

Δ **Spinal cord injuries** (SCI) involve **losses of motor function, sensory function, reflexes, and control of elimination.**

Δ The level of cord involved dictates the consequences of spinal cord injury. For example, injury at C3 to C5 poses a great risk for impaired spontaneous ventilation because of proximity of the phrenic nerve.

Δ **Tetraplegia/paresis** = all 4 extremities. **Paraplegia/paresis** = 2 lower extremities.

Δ SCIs range from contusions to complete transection of the cord. **Complete SCI** = loss of all innervation below level of the injury. **Incomplete SCI** = some function below the level of the injury.

Key Factors

Δ **Causes**

- Trauma

  ◊ Hyperflexion forward (head-on collision, diving)

  ◊ Hyperextension backward (rear-end collision, fall on chin)

  ◊ Axial loading/vertical compression (land on head or feet)

  ◊ Rotation beyond normal range

  ◊ Penetrating injury (gunshot, knife wound)

Δ Risk Factors

- Single male, age 16 to 30

- High-risk activities

- Active in sports

- Alcohol and/or drug abuse

Diagnostic Procedures and Nursing Interventions

Δ X-rays, magnetic resonance imaging (MRI), and computed tomography (CT) imaging/computed axial tomography (CAT) scan can be used to assess the extent of the damage and location of blood or bone fragments.

Δ Laboratory tests (urinalysis, hemoglobin, ABGs) are used to monitor for bleeding and respiratory status.

Therapeutic Procedures and Nursing Interventions

Δ   **Spinal Stabilization Surgery** (for example, spinal fusion)

Δ   **Decompressive Laminectomy** – removal of bone fragments, penetrating objects, or hematomas that are compressing the spinal cord.

Δ   Application of **immobilization devices** and **traction**, which include:

- Halo fixation device, cervical tongs. The purpose is to **immobilize the spinal column.**

  ◊   Nursing Interventions

    °   Maintain body alignment.

    °   Monitor skin integrity and provide pin care as appropriate.

    °   Ensure weights hang freely.

Assessments

Δ   **Assess/Monitor** the client's:

- **Airway patency – This should be the first priority.**

- Respiratory status (lung sounds, respiratory pattern, and oxygen saturation levels).

- Tissue perfusion.

- Vital signs for bradycardia, hypotension, and hypothermia (possible loss of sympathetic input).

- Intake and output.

- Neurological status (hand grasp, toe, and foot movement).

- Muscle strength.

- Mobility (level).

- Sensory abilities by dermatome (light touch, pinprick) – complete loss, decreased, or increased sensation.

- Bowel and bladder function (distention, impaction).

- Gastrointestinal function (hemorrhage, distention, and ileus).

- Skin Integrity.

NANDA Nursing Diagnoses

Δ   Risk for ineffective tissue perfusion

Δ   Potential for autonomic dysreflexia

Δ Interrupted family processes

Δ Depression

Δ Ineffective airway clearance

Δ Impaired gas exchange

Δ Risk for constipation

Δ Impaired tissue integrity

Δ Impaired adjustment

Nursing Interventions

Δ Maintain a patent airway (immobilize neck and spine to prevent further injury).

Δ Provide the client with oxygen.

Δ Maintain mechanical ventilation as prescribed.

Δ Suction as needed.

Δ Turn the client every 2 hr and encourage deep breathing exercises ("cough assist").

Δ Monitor the client for signs of thrombophlebitis (swelling of extremity, absent/decreased pulses, and areas of warmth and/or tenderness).

Δ Teach the client urinary elimination methods (**Credé's method** prior to bladder elimination, intermittent self-catheterization) and the importance of following a schedule for routine urinary elimination.

Δ Teach the client a bowel retraining program (consistent time such as 30 min after meal; high fluid intake and fiber intake; rectal stimulation; stool softeners; use of Valsalva maneuver; massage abdomen along large intestine).

Δ Encourage active range-of-motion (ROM) exercises for the client and have the client perform passive ROM exercises as needed.

Δ Teach the client regarding alterations in sexual function and possible adaptive strategies.

Δ Facilitate the client's participation in physical therapy and occupational therapy.

Δ Mobilize the client using assistive devices as needed (wheelchair, tilt table).

Δ Maintain the client's skin integrity (assist with repositioning the client every 2 hr; use of padding devices).

Δ Maintain an adequate fluid intake for the client.

Δ   Referral to social services (financial interventions, rehabilitation, and home management).

Δ   Refer the client to an SCI support group.

Δ   Administer medications as prescribed:

- **Glucocorticoids** – adrenocortical steroids such as dexamethasone (Decadron) suppress the immune response. Monitor for increased risk for infection.

- **Vasopressors** – norepinephrine and dopamine to treat hypotension.

- **Plasma expanders** – such as dextran to treat shock.

- **Atropine** – to treat bradycardia.

- **Muscle relaxants**

- **Anti-spasmodics** – dantrolene sodium (Dantrium).

- **Analgesics** – opioids, non-opioids, and NSAIDs.

- **Antidepressants**

- **Histamine$_2$-receptor antagonists** – such as ranitidine hydrochloride (Zantac) to prevent gastric ulcer formation.

- **Anticoagulants** – heparin or low molecular weight heparins for DVT prophylaxis.

- **Stool softeners** – such as docusate sodium to prevent constipation.

- **Vasodilators** – hydralazine and nitroglycerin to treat hypertension (for example, autonomic dysreflexia).

- **Anti-seizure** – gabapentin, phenytoin.

Complications and Nursing Implications

Δ   **Orthostatic Hypotension**

- Occurs with changes in position.

- Due to interruption in autonomic innervation.

- **Change client positioning slowly** (possibly with a tilt table).

- Use elastic wraps to increase venous return.

Δ   **Neurogenic Shock** (spinal shock)

- Bradycardia, hypotension, flaccid paralysis, loss of reflex activity below level of injury, and paralytic ileus

- Risk is in first hour after injury due to loss of autonomic function.

- Monitor vital signs for **hypotension** and **bradycardia**.

- Treat symptoms (vasopressors, atropine).

Δ **Autonomic Dysreflexia**

- Hypertension, bradycardia, sudden **severe headache, flushing above** level of SCI (flushed face and neck), **pallor below** level of SCI, nasal stuffiness, dilated pupils, blurred vision, diaphoresis, and piloerection (goosebumps)

- Due to simultaneous sympathetic and parasympathetic stimulation

- Assess and **treat cause**.

  ◊ Distended bladder (for example, kinked urinary catheter)

  ◊ Fecal impaction

  ◊ Cold stress

  ◊ Tight clothing

- Monitor vital signs for **severe hypertension and bradycardia**.

- Administer antihypertensives (nitrates, hydralazine).

Primary Reference:

Ignatavicius, D. D., & Workman, M. L. (2006). *Medical-surgical nursing* (5th ed.). St. Louis, MO: Saunders.

Additional Resources:

NANDA International (2004). *NANDA nursing diagnoses: Definitions and classification 2005-2006*. Philadelphia: NANDA.

Smeltzer, S. C., & Bare, B. G. (2004). *Brunner and Suddarth's textbook of medical-surgical nursing* (10th ed.). Philadelphia: Lippincott Williams & Wilkins.

For more information about spinal cord injuries, visit the Spinal Cord Injury Recovery Center at *www.sci-recovery.org* or the National Spinal Cord Injury Association at *www.spinalcord.org*.

Chapter 89: Spinal Cord Injury

Application Exercises

Scenario: A 19-year-old college student suffered a 12th thoracic fracture with resulting paraplegia while playing football. He has no muscle control of his lower limbs, bowel, bladder, or genital area. He is a week postoperative from spinal stabilization surgery.

1. What are the primary goals of collaborative management during the acute phase following spinal cord injury?

2. The client received a high dose of glucocorticoid medication therapy when initially admitted to the neurosurgery unit. What effect do these medications have and what risks do they pose for the client?

3. What actions should the nurse take if the client develops autonomic dysreflexia?

4. If the client's SCI had been at C4, how would his emergency management have differed?

5. The nurse should question which of the following prescribed interventions?

   A. Administration of glucocorticoids to suppress the client's immune response

   B. Administration of vasopressors and plasma expanders to treat hypotension and shock

   C. Administration of H_2 antagonists to prevent stress ulcer formation

   D. Administration of atropine to treat tachycardia

Chapter 89: Spinal Cord Injury

Application Exercises Answer Key

Scenario: A 19-year-old college student suffered a 12th thoracic fracture with resulting paraplegia while playing football. He has no muscle control of his lower limbs, bowel, bladder, or genital area. He is a week postoperative from spinal stabilization surgery.

1. What are the primary goals of collaborative management during the acute phase following spinal cord injury?

   Maintain physiological stability, prevent further spinal cord injury, and prevent spinal shock.

2. The client received a high dose of glucocorticoid medication therapy when initially admitted to the neurosurgery unit. What effect do these medications have and what risks do they pose for the client?

   Steroids reduce inflammation by suppressing the immune response and subsequently reducing swelling of the injured spinal cord. Steroids can pose a risk by increasing the client's susceptibility to infections such as pulmonary, urinary tract, and wound infections.

3. What actions should the nurse take if the client develops autonomic dysreflexia?

   Prevent precipitating causes (noxious stimuli to the sympathetic nervous system); recognize occurrence early; remove of cause (if known); remain with the client if it occurs; raise the head of the bed to decrease the client's blood pressure; anticipate the administration of ganglionic blockers, adrenergic blockers, and/or vasodilators.

4. If the client's SCI had been at C4, how would his emergency management have differed?

   An SCI at the level of C4 poses a great risk for respiratory compromise. Maintenance of airway and provision of ventilatory support (as needed) would have been priority interventions.

5. The nurse should question which of the following prescribed interventions?

   A. Administration of glucocorticoids to suppress the client's immune response
   B. Administration of vasopressors and plasma expanders to treat hypotension and shock
   C. Administration of H_2 antagonists to prevent stress ulcer formation
   D. Administration of atropine to treat tachycardia

Atropine increases heart rate and is appropriate for treatment of bradycardia, which is a possible client finding during the spinal shock phase following spinal cord injury.

Unit 8
Section:

Nursing Care of Clients with Neurosensory Disorders
Medical Emergencies: Neurological

Chapter 90: Cerebrovascular Accident (Stroke)
Contributor: Lynn C. Parsons, DSN, RN, CNA-BC

↻ NCLEX-PN® Connections:

Learning Objective: Review and apply knowledge within "**Cerebrovascular Accident (Stroke)**" in readiness for performance of the following nursing activities as outlined by the NCLEX-PN® test plan:

Δ Monitor the client's neurological status and report changes.

Δ Assist with relevant laboratory, diagnostic, and therapeutic procedures within the nursing role, including:

  • Preparation of the client for the procedure.

  • Accurate collection of specimens.

  • Monitoring client status during and after the procedure.

  • Reinforcing client teaching (before and following the procedure).

  • Recognizing the client's response (expected, unexpected adverse response) to the procedure.

  • Monitoring results.

  • Monitoring and taking actions to prevent or minimize the risk of complications.

  • Notifying the primary care provider of signs of complications.

Δ Recognize signs and symptoms of the client's problem and complete the proper documentation.

Δ Provide and document care based on the client's health alteration.

Δ Monitor and document vital signs changes.

Δ Interpret data that need to be reported immediately.

Δ Reinforce client education on managing the client's health problem.

Δ Recognize and respond to emergency situations, including notification of the primary care provider.

Δ Review the client's response to emergency interventions and complete the proper documentation.

Δ Provide care that meets the age-related needs of clients 65 years of age or older, including recognizing expected physiological changes.

📖 Key Points

Δ   Cerebrovascular accidents (strokes) involve a **disruption in cerebral blood flow** related to ischemia, hemorrhage, or embolism.

Δ   Strokes are considered a medical emergency. Mortality and degree of disability from a stroke can be significantly decreased by rapid recognition and intervention.

Δ   Clients with a history of **uncontrolled hypertension** are at increased risk for a stroke.

Key Factors

Δ   **Risk Factors**

- **Hypertension**
- Atherosclerosis
- **Hyperlipidemia**
- **Diabetes mellitus**
- Cocaine use
- Atrial fibrillation
- Smoking
- Use of oral contraceptives
- Obesity
- Hypercoagulability
- Cerebral aneurysm
- Arteriovenous malformation (AV)

Diagnostic Procedures and Nursing Interventions

Δ   Magnetic resonance imaging (MRI) and/or computed tomography (CT) imaging/ computed axial tomography (CAT) scan are used to identify edema, ischemia, and necrosis.

Δ   Magnetic resonance angiography (MRA) or cerebral angiography is used to identify the presence of cerebral hemorrhage, abnormal vessel structures, vessel ruptures, and regional perfusion of blood flow in the brain.

Δ   Lumbar puncture is used to assess for presence of blood in the cerebrospinal fluid (CSF).

Therapeutic Procedures and Nursing Interventions

Δ Carotid endarterectomy is performed to open the artery by removing atherosclerotic plaque.

Δ Interventional radiology is performed to treat cerebral aneurysms.

Assessments

Δ Monitor for **signs and symptoms.**

- Symptoms will vary based on the area of the brain that is not adequately supplied with oxygenated blood.

◊ The left cerebral hemisphere is responsible for language, mathematic skills, and analytic thinking.

° Aphasia (language use or comprehension difficulty)

° Alexia (reading difficulty)

° Agraphia (writing difficulty)

° Right hemiplegia or hemiparesis

° Slow, cautious behavior

° Depression and quick frustration

° Visual changes, such as hemianopsia

◊ The right cerebral hemisphere is responsible for visual and spatial awareness and proprioception.

° Unawareness of deficits (neglect syndrome, overestimation of abilities)

° Loss of depth perception

° Disorientation

° Impulse-control difficulty

° Poor judgment

° Left hemiplegia or hemiparesis

° Visual changes, such as hemianopsia

Δ **Assess/Monitor**

- Airway patency

- Swallowing ability/aspiration risk

- Level of consciousness

- Neurological status

- Motor function
- Sensory function
- Cognitive function
- Glasgow Coma Scale score

NANDA Nursing Diagnoses

Δ   Ineffective tissue perfusion (cerebral)

Δ   Disturbed sensory perception

Δ   Impaired physical mobility

Δ   Unilateral neglect

Δ   Risk for injury

Δ   Self-care deficit

Δ   Impaired verbal communication

Δ   Impaired swallowing

Nursing Interventions

Δ   Maintain a patent airway.

Δ   Monitor for changes in the client's level of consciousness (increased intracranial pressure sign).

Δ   **Elevate the client's head to reduce intracranial pressure** (ICP) and to promote venous drainage. Avoid extreme flexion or extension, maintain the head in the midline neutral position, and elevate the head of the bed to 30°.

Δ   Institute seizure precautions.

Δ   Maintain a non-stimulating environment.

Δ   Assist with communication skills if the client's speech is impaired. Consult a speech and language therapist.

Δ   Assist with **safe feeding**.

- Assess swallowing reflexes: **swallowing, gag, and cough** before feeding.
- The client's liquids may need to be thickened to avoid aspiration.
- Have the client eat in an upright position and **swallow with the head and neck flexed slightly forward.**

- **Place food in the back of the mouth on the unaffected side.**

- Suction on standby.

- Maintain a distraction-free environment during meals.

Δ Maintain **skin integrity**.

- Reposition the client frequently and use padding.

- Monitor bony prominences, paying particular attention to the affected extremities.

Δ Encourage passive range of motion every 2 hr to the affected extremities and active range of motion every 2 hr to the unaffected extremities.

Δ Elevate the affected extremities to promote venous return and to reduce swelling.

Δ Maintain a safe environment to reduce the risk of falls.

Δ Instruct the client to use a scanning technique (turning head from side to side) when eating and ambulating to compensate for hemianopsia.

Δ Provide care to prevent deep-vein thrombosis (sequential compression stockings, frequent position changes, mobilization).

Δ Administer medications as prescribed.

- **Systemic or catheter-directed thrombolytic therapy** restores cerebral blood flow. It must be administered within hours of the onset of symptoms. It is contraindicated for treatment of hemorrhagic stroke and for clients with an increased risk of bleeding. Rule out hemorrhagic stroke with an MRI prior to initiation of thrombolytic therapy.

  ◊ Anticoagulants: Sodium heparin, warfarin (Coumadin)

  ◊ Antiplatelets: Ticlopidine (Ticlid), clopidogrel (Plavix)

  ◊ Antiepileptic medications: Phenytoin (Dilantin), gabapentin (Neurontin)

Δ Provide assistance with activities of daily living (ADLs) as needed. Prevent complications of immobility.

Δ Initiate referrals to social services (rehabilitation services) and Physical/Occupational Therapy (adaptive equipment needs in the home).

Complications and Nursing Implications

Δ Dysphagia and aspiration – Suction as needed. Preassess the client's swallowing abilities.

Δ Unilateral neglect – loss of awareness of the side affected by the CVA. This poses great risk for injury and inadequate self care. Instruct the client to dress the affected side first. Teach the client to care for both sides.

Meeting the Needs of Older Adults

Δ Arteriosclerosis among older adult clients contributes significantly to an increased incidence of stroke.

Δ Older adult clients who have neurologic deficits are at a high risk for falls related to impaired mobility.

Δ Risk for nutritional deficits related to impaired swallowing occurs in older adult clients with neurologic deficits.

Δ Increased risk for behavioral changes, such as emotional instability and depression, are common clinical manifestations.

Primary Reference:

Ignatavicius, D. D., & Workman, M. L. (2006). *Medical-surgical nursing* (5th ed.). St. Louis, MO: Saunders.

Additional Resources:

NANDA International (2004). *NANDA nursing diagnoses: Definitions and classification 2005-2006.* Philadelphia: NANDA.

Smeltzer, S. C., & Bare, B. G. (2004). *Brunner and Suddarth's textbook of medical-surgical nursing* (10th ed.). Philadelphia: Lippincott Williams & Wilkins.

Stanley, M., Blair, K. A., & Gauntlett Beare, P. (Eds.). (2005). *Gerontological nursing: Promoting successful aging with older adults.* Philadelphia: F.A. Davis.

For more information, visit the National Stroke Association at *www.stroke.org* or the American Stroke Association at *www.strokeassociation.org*.

Chapter 90: Cerebrovascular Accident (Stroke)

Application Exercises

Scenario: An older adult woman is admitted to the acute care facility after her family found her in an unconscious state early this morning. The admission assessment reveals no history of hypertension or other health problems. The client reported a headache on the day prior to admission. She has a Glasgow Coma Scale score of 5 and her vital signs are blood pressure 150/96 mm Hg, respirations 16/min, pulse 56 beats/min, and temperature 38.3° C (101° F). Her admitting medical diagnosis is a suspected stroke. The client's initial CT scan shows evidence of ischemia and infarction within the right cerebral hemisphere.

1. Is the client a candidate for thrombolytic therapy?

2. Based on the CT results, which of the following signs and symptoms should the nurse expect? (Check all that apply.)

_____ Aphasia (language use or comprehension difficulty)

_____ Right hemiplegia or hemiparesis

_____ Unawareness of deficits (neglect syndrome, overestimation of abilities)

_____ Impulse-control difficulty

_____ Slow, cautious behavior

_____ Left hemiplegia or hemiparesis

_____ Visual changes, such as hemianopsia

3. Should the nurse plan to place objects on the client's right or left side?

4. When the client resumes dietary intake, which of the following actions should the nurse take? (Check all that apply.)

_____ Give the client thin liquids.

_____ Encourage the client to converse while eating.

_____ Thicken liquids to the consistency of oatmeal.

_____ Place food on the unaffected side of the mouth.

_____ Allow plenty of time for chewing and swallowing.

_____ Teach the client to swallow with the head and neck flexed slightly forward.

_____ Monitor the client's swallow and gag reflexes prior to starting dietary intake.

5. A nurse is trying to converse with a client with a CVA and aphasia. Which of the following strategies is appropriate? (Check all that apply.)

_____ Speak to the client at a slower rate.

_____ Look directly at the client during speech.

_____ Allow plenty of time for the client to answer.

_____ Complete sentences that the client cannot finish.

_____ Break tasks into parts and give instructions one step at a time.

_____ Consult a speech and language therapist.

6. What strategies can be suggested for coping with the effects of hemianopsia?

Chapter 90: Cerebrovascular Accident (Stroke)

Application Exercises Answer Key

Scenario: An older adult woman is admitted to the acute care facility after her family found her in an unconscious state early this morning. The admission assessment reveals no history of hypertension or other health problems. The client reported a headache on the day prior to admission. She has a Glasgow Coma Scale score of 5 and her vital signs are blood pressure 150/96 mm Hg, respirations 16/min, pulse 56 beats/min, and temperature 38.3° C (101° F). Her admitting medical diagnosis is a suspected stroke. The client's initial CT scan shows evidence of ischemia and infarction within the right cerebral hemisphere.

1. Is the client a candidate for thrombolytic therapy?

   No. The CT results indicate that it has been several hours since the infarction occurred. Thrombolytic therapy should be given within 3 hr of the onset of symptoms.

2. Based on the CT results, which of the following signs and symptoms should the nurse expect? (Check all that apply.)

____	Aphasia (language use or comprehension difficulty)
____	Right hemiplegia or hemiparesis
__X__	Unawareness of deficits (neglect syndrome, overestimation of abilities)
__X__	Impulse-control difficulty
____	Slow, cautious behavior
__X__	Left hemiplegia or hemiparesis
__X__	Visual changes, such as hemianopsia

3. Should the nurse plan to place objects on the client's right or left side?

   The client will have motor effects of the left side; therefore, objects should be placed on the unaffected right side within the client's reach.

4. When the client resumes dietary intake, which of the following actions should the nurse take? (Check all that apply.)

_____	Give the client thin liquids.
_____	Encourage the client to converse while eating.
x	Thicken liquids to the consistency of oatmeal.
x	Place food on the unaffected side of the mouth.
x	Allow plenty of time for chewing and swallowing.
x	Teach the client to swallow with the head and neck flexed slightly forward.
x	Monitor the client's swallow and gag reflexes prior to starting dietary intake.

5. The nurse is trying to converse with a client with a CVA and aphasia. Which of the following strategies is appropriate? (Check all that apply.)

x	Speak to the client at a slower rate.
x	Look directly at the client during speech.
x	Allow plenty of time for the client to answer.
_____	Complete sentences that the client cannot finish.
x	Break tasks into parts and give instructions one step at a time.
x	Consult a speech and language therapist.

6. What strategies can be suggested for coping with the effects of hemianopsia?

Encourage the client to turn her head to scan the lost visual field.

Approach the client from the unimpaired field of vision.

Place objects in the client's unimpaired field of vision.

Unit 8   Nursing Care of Clients with Neurosensory Disorders
Section: Medical Emergencies: Neurological

Chapter 91:   Meningitis
              Contributor: Lynn C. Parsons, DSN, RN, CNA-BC

NCLEX-PN® Connections:

Learning Objective: Review and apply knowledge within "**Meningitis**" in readiness for performance of the following nursing activities as outlined by the NCLEX-PN® test plan:

Δ   Monitor the client's neurological status and report changes.

Δ   Assist with relevant laboratory, diagnostic, and therapeutic procedures within the nursing role, including:

  • Preparation of the client for the procedure.

  • Accurate collection of specimens.

  • Monitoring client status during and after the procedure.

  • Reinforcing client teaching (before and following the procedure).

  • Recognizing the client's response (expected, unexpected adverse response) to the procedure.

  • Monitoring results.

  • Monitoring and taking actions to prevent or minimize the risk of complications.

  • Notifying the primary care provider of signs of complications.

Δ   Recognize signs and symptoms of the client's problem and complete the proper documentation.

Δ   Provide and document care based on the client's health alteration.

Δ   Monitor and document vital signs changes.

Δ   Interpret data that need to be reported immediately.

Δ   Reinforce client education on managing the client's health problem.

Δ   Recognize and respond to emergency situations, including notification of the primary care provider.

Δ   Review the client's response to emergency interventions and complete the proper documentation.

Δ   Provide care that meets the age-related needs of clients 65 years of age or older, including recognizing expected physiological changes.

✏ Key Points

Δ   Meningitis is an inflammation of the **meninges**, which are the membranes that protect the brain and spinal cord.

Δ   **Viral**, or aseptic, **meningitis** is the most common form of meningitis and commonly resolves without treatment.

Δ   **Bacterial**, or septic, **meningitis** is a **contagious** infection with a high mortality rate. The prognosis depends on the supportive care given to the client.

Δ   A meningitis vaccine is available for high-risk populations, such as residential college students.

Key Factors

Δ   Risk Factors for Viral Meningitis

•   Viral illnesses such as the mumps, measles, and herpes

Δ   Risk Factors for Bacterial Meningitis

•   Bacterial infections (*Neisseria meningitidis, Streptococcus pneumoniae, Haemophilus influenzae*), such as **upper respiratory infections** (otitis media, pneumonia, sinusitis)

•   Immunosuppression

•   Invasive procedures, skull fracture, or penetrating head wound (direct access to cerebrospinal fluid)

•   **Overcrowded living conditions**

Diagnostic Procedures and Nursing Interventions

Δ   **Cerebrospinal Fluid** (CSF) analysis is the **most definitive** diagnostic procedure.

•   Collect CSF with a lumbar puncture (performed by the primary care provider, usually a physician).

◊   Have the client empty his or her bladder.

◊   Place the client in the fetal position and assist in maintaining proper positioning.

◊   The skin is cleaned and a local anesthetic is injected.

◊   A spinal needle is inserted into the subarachnoid space.

◊   Instruct the client to report any shooting pain or tingling.

◊ Pressure readings are taken, followed by the collection of three to five test tubes of CSF.

◊ The needle is removed, pressure is applied, and the injection site is covered with dressing.

◊ Appropriately label specimens and deliver them to the laboratory.

- The client should remain in bed for 4 to 8 hr in a flat position to prevent leakage and a resulting spinal headache.

- Monitor the site for hematoma or infection.

- Results indicative of meningitis:

  ◊ Appearance of CSF: Cloudy (bacterial) or clear (viral)

  ◊ Elevated WBC

  ◊ Elevated protein

  ◊ Decreased glucose (bacterial)

  ◊ Elevated CSF pressure

Δ Perform blood culture and sensitivity to identify an appropriate broad-spectrum antibiotic.

Δ A CT scan or an MRI may be performed to identify increased ICP and/or an abscess.

Assessments

Δ Monitor for **signs and symptoms.**

- Excruciating, unrelenting **headache**

- Fever and chills

- Photophobia

- Nausea and vomiting

- Altered level of consciousness

- **Nuchal rigidity**

- Positive Kernig's sign (resistance to extension of the client's leg from a flexed position)

- Positive Brudzinski's sign (flexion of extremities occurring with deliberate flexion of the client's neck)

- Tachycardia

- Seizures

- Red macular rash (meningococcal meningitis)

Δ   Frequently assess/monitor:

- Airway, breathing, and circulation.

- Vital signs (Monitor for signs of shock).

- Neurological checks.

- Cranial nerve function.

- Intake and output.

- Signs of increased intracranial pressure (change in level of consciousness, widening of pulse pressure, pupil changes).

NANDA Nursing Diagnoses

Δ   Ineffective airway clearance

Δ   Impaired spontaneous ventilation

Δ   Risk for injury

Δ   Acute confusion

Δ   Deficient fluid volume

Δ   Ineffective thermoregulation

Nursing Interventions

Δ   Maintain **isolation precautions** per hospital policy (for example, until antibiotics have been administered for 24 hr).

Δ   Implement fever-reduction measures, such as a cooling blanket, if necessary.

Δ   Report meningococcal infections to the public health department.

Δ   **Decrease environmental stimuli.**

- Provide a quiet environment.

- Minimize exposure to bright light (natural and electric).

Δ   Maintain bedrest with the head of the bed elevated to 30°.

Δ   Maintain client safety, such as seizure precautions.

Δ   Administer medications as prescribed.

- **Antibiotics** (bacterial infections) – such as ceftriaxone (Rocephin) or cefotaxime (Claforan) until culture and sensitivity results are available

- Anticonvulsants – phenytoin (Dilantin)

- Antipyretics – acetaminophen (Tylenol)

- Analgesics – non-opioid to avoid masking changes in the level of consciousness
- Fluid and electrolyte replacement as indicated by laboratory values
- Prophylactic antibiotics to individuals in close contact with the client

Complications and Nursing Implications

Δ **Increased ICP** (possibly to the point of brain herniation)

- Monitor for signs of increasing ICP, such as decreased level of consciousness, pupillary changes, and widening pulse pressure. (*For information, refer to chapter 78, Monitoring Intracranial Pressure.*)
- Provide interventions to reduce ICP, such as positioning and avoidance of coughing and straining.

Δ **Syndrome of Inappropriate Antidiuretic Hormone** (SIADH)

- Monitor for signs and symptoms (dilute blood, concentrated urine).
- Provide interventions, such as the administration of demeclocycline (Declomycin) and restriction of fluid.

Δ **Septic Emboli** (leading to disseminated intravascular coagulation or cardiovascular accident)

- Monitor circulatory status.
- Monitor coagulation.

Meeting the Needs of Older Adults

Δ Older adult clients are more prone to severe infections and complications.

Δ Older adult clients are at an increased risk for secondary complications, such as pneumonia.

Primary Reference:

Ignatavicius, D. D., & Workman, M. L. (2006). *Medical-surgical nursing* (5th ed.). St. Louis, MO: Saunders.

Additional Resources:

NANDA International (2004). *NANDA nursing diagnoses: Definitions and classification 2005-2006.* Philadelphia: NANDA.

Smeltzer, S. C., & Bare, B. G. (2004). *Brunner and Suddarth's textbook of medical-surgical nursing* (10th ed.). Philadelphia: Lippincott Williams & Wilkins.

For more information, visit the Meningitis Foundation of America at *www.musa.org* or the Directors of Health Promotion and Education at *www.astdhpphe.org/infect/Bacmeningitis. html*.

Chapter 91: Meningitis

Application Exercises

Scenario: A 21-year-old college student is taken to the emergency department after her roommate found her lying with her right thigh flexed up toward her abdomen. The client is reporting a severe headache and a stiff neck. Initial assessment by the nurse reveals a positive Kernig's sign and a positive Brudzinski's sign. Bacterial meningitis is suspected.

1. What is the significance of the positive Kernig's and Brudzinski's signs?

2. For what other signs should the nurse assess in order to confirm the presence of bacterial meningitis?

3. Which of the following are appropriate interventions for a client with meningitis at risk for increased ICP? (Check all that apply.)

    _____   Implement seizure precautions.

    _____   Perform neurological checks once each day.

    _____   Administer morphine for the report of neck and generalized pain.

    _____   Turn off room lights and television.

    _____   Administer prescribed broad-spectrum antibiotics after blood cultures are obtained.

    _____   Instruct the client to maintain bedrest in a flat position for several hours following lumbar puncture.

    _____   Encourage the client to cough and breathe deeply frequently.

4. How does the clinical presentation of septic (bacterial) meningitis differ from aseptic (viral) meningitis?

Chapter 91: Meningitis

Application Exercises Answer Key

Scenario: A 21-year-old college student is taken to the emergency department after her roommate found her lying with her right thigh flexed up toward her abdomen. The client is reporting a severe headache and a stiff neck. Initial assessment by the nurse reveals a positive Kernig's sign and a positive Brudzinski's sign. Bacterial meningitis is suspected.

1. What is the significance of the positive Kernig's and Brudzinski's signs?

   Both signs are indications of the meningeal irritation that may occur as a result of septic or bacterial meningitis.

2. For what other signs should the nurse assess in order to confirm the presence of bacterial meningitis?

   The nurse should monitor for an altered level of consciousness, fever and chills, photophobia, and seizures.

3. Which of the following are appropriate interventions for a client with meningitis at risk for increased ICP? (Check all that apply.)

__x__	Implement seizure precautions.
_____	Perform neurological checks once each day.
_____	Administer morphine for the report of neck and generalized pain.
__x__	Turn off room lights and television.
__x__	Administer prescribed broad-spectrum antibiotics after blood cultures are obtained.
__x__	Instruct the client to maintain bedrest in a flat position for several hours following lumbar puncture.
_____	Encourage the client to cough and breathe deeply frequently.

   Neurological checks need to be performed more frequently. Opioids mask the changes in the level of consciousness associated with increasing ICP. Coughing increases ICP.

4. How does the clinical presentation of septic (bacterial) meningitis differ from aseptic (viral) meningitis?

Aseptic meningitis is a less severe form of meningitis than septic meningitis. The client presents with mild, flu-like symptoms, headache, nausea/vomiting, drowsiness, and nuchal rigidity, but fever is usually low-grade rather than high.

Unit 8   Nursing Care of Clients with Neurosensory Disorders
Section: Nursing Care of Clients with Sensory Disorders

Chapter 92:   Sensory Alteration: Reduced Vision

Contributor: Jeanne Wissmann, PhD, RN, CNE

NCLEX-PN® Connections:

Learning Objective: Review and apply knowledge within "**Sensory Alteration: Reduced Vision**" in readiness for performance of the following nursing activities as outlined by the NCLEX-PN® test plan:

Δ   Identify the needs of the client with reduced visual acuity.

Δ   Provide assistance to the client with reduced visual acuity.

Δ   Assist with relevant laboratory, diagnostic, and therapeutic procedures within the nursing role, including:

•   Preparation of the client for the procedure.

•   Accurate collection of specimens.

•   Monitoring client status during and after the procedure.

•   Reinforcing client teaching (before and following the procedure).

•   Recognizing the client's response (expected, unexpected adverse response) to the procedure.

•   Monitoring results.

•   Monitoring and taking actions to prevent or minimize the risk of complications.

•   Notifying the primary care provider of signs of complications.

Δ   Recognize signs and symptoms of the client's problem and complete the proper documentation.

Δ   Provide and document care based on the client's health alteration.

Δ   Monitor and document vital signs changes.

Δ   Interpret data that need to be reported immediately.

Δ   Reinforce client education on managing the client's health problem.

Δ   Recognize and respond to emergency situations, including notification of the primary care provider.

Δ   Review the client's response to emergency interventions and complete the proper documentation.

Δ   Provide care that meets the age-related needs of clients 65 years of age or older, including recognizing expected physiological changes.

Key Points

- Δ Visual acuity of **20/200 or less** with corrective lenses constitutes **legal blindness**.

- Δ Reduced visual acuity can be **unilateral (one eye) or bilateral (both eyes)**.

Key Factors

- Δ Causes

  - Presbyopia (age-related loss of the eye's ability to focus on close objects)

  - Cataracts (opacity of lens)

  - Glaucoma (loss of peripheral vision)

  - Diabetic retinopathy (microaneurysms)

  - Macular degeneration (loss of central vision)

  - Eye infection, inflammation, or injury

  - Brain tumor

Diagnostic Procedures and Nursing Interventions

- Δ **Tonometry** is used to measure intraocular pressure (IOP). IOP (normal is 10 to 21 mm Hg) is elevated with glaucoma, especially angle-closure.

- Δ **Gonioscopy** is used to determine the drainage angle of the anterior chamber of the eyes.

Therapeutic Procedures and Nursing Interventions

- Δ Surgery such as cataract removal releases aqueous humor. Postoperative care generally includes avoiding activities that increase IOP.

Assessments

- Δ Monitor for **signs and symptoms.**

  - Frequent headaches

  - Frequent eyestrain

  - Blurred vision

  - Poor judgment of depth

  - Tendency to close or favor one eye

  - Diplopia

  - Poor eye-hand coordination

Δ **Assess/Monitor**

- Visual acuity (Snellen, Rosenbaum)
- External and internal eye structures (ophthalmoscope)
- Functional ability

NANDA Nursing Diagnoses

Δ Disturbed sensory perception (visual)

Δ Risk for injury

Nursing Interventions

Δ Assist the client in **adapting environment to maintain safety**.

- Increase the amount of light in a room.
- Arrange the home to remove hazards (for example, eliminate throw rugs).
- Provide phones with large numbers and/or auto dial.

Δ Assist the client with adaptation to reduced vision.

- Provide magnifying lens and large print books/newspapers.
- Provide talking devices such as clocks.

Δ Health promotion to prevent eye and vision problems:

- Wear sunglasses to protect eyes.
- Wear eye protection when performing tasks with an airborne risk.
- Wash hands before and after touching eyes.
- Don't smoke.
- Limit alcohol intake.
- Keep blood pressure and cholesterol under control.
- Clients with diabetes mellitus should keep blood glucose under control.
- Eat foods rich in antioxidants such as green leafy vegetables.

Δ Administer medications as prescribed.

- **Anticholinergics** such as atropine (Isopto Atropine)
  - ◊ Intraocular exam/surgery
  - ◊ **Mydriasis** (dilation of the pupil); **cycloplegia** (ciliary paralysis)
  - ◊ Adverse effects include reduced accommodation, blurred vision, and photophobia. With systemic absorption, there could be anticholinergic effects (tachycardia, decreased secretions).

- **Cholinergic agonists** such as pilocarpine (Isopto Carpine)

  ◊ Angle-closure glaucoma

  ◊ **Miosis** (constriction of the pupil)

  ◊ Adverse effects include decreased visual acuity. With systemic absorption, there could be cholinergic effects (bradycardia, bronchospasm, hypotension, and excess secretions).

- **Beta-blockers** such as timolol (Timoptic)

  ◊ Open-angle glaucoma

  ◊ Decrease in aqueous humor production

  ◊ Adverse effects include transient ocular stinging. With systemic absorption, there could be bronchoconstriction, bradycardia, and atrioventricular (AV) block.

Δ Initiate referrals as appropriate to social services, support groups, and low vision resources.

Δ Encourage **adults 40 or older to have an annual examination** including a measurement of intraocular pressure.

Complications and Nursing Implications

Δ **Risk for injury** – Monitor for safety risks (for example, ability to drive safely) and intervene to reduce risks. Encourage annual eye examinations and good eye health.

Meeting the Needs of Older Adults

Δ Age is the most significant risk for visual sensory alterations. Disturbed visual sensory perception is a well-known risk factor for injury, disease, and mortality in older adults.

Primary Reference:

Ignatavicius, D. D., & Workman, M. L. (2006). *Medical-surgical nursing* (5th ed.). St. Louis, MO: Saunders.

Additional Resources:

NANDA International (2004). *NANDA nursing diagnoses: Definitions and classification 2005-2006.* Philadelphia: NANDA.

Chapter 92: Sensory Alteration: Reduced Vision

Application Exercises

Scenario: A 70-year-old client with diabetes mellitus has reduced vision.

1. What are some possible causes of the client's reduced vision?

2. If the client's vision alteration is presbyopia (age-related loss of the eye's ability to focus on close objects), what client findings should be expected?

3. The client is diagnosed with macular degeneration. What client findings are expected?

4. Which of the following interventions are appropriate to help the client cope with macular degeneration?

   _____ Provide talking watches and clocks.

   _____ Provide large print books/newspapers/menus.

   _____ Teach the client to place self-care objects in the center of tables.

   _____ Instruct the client to remove area rugs from the home.

   _____ Suggest that the client put important telephone numbers on auto dial.

5. The client is admitted to an unfamiliar hospital setting. How should the nurse orient the client to his environment?

Chapter 92: Sensory Alteration: Reduced Vision

Application Exercises Answer Key

Scenario: A 70-year-old client with diabetes mellitus has reduced vision.

1. What are some possible causes of the client's reduced vision?

   Correct responses include:

   > **Presbyopia.**

   > **Macular degeneration.**

   > **Cataracts.**

   > **Glaucoma.**

   > **Diabetic retinopathy.**

2. If the client's vision alteration is presbyopia (age-related loss of the eye's ability to focus on close objects), what client findings should be expected?

   The client will have an inability to focus on objects up close such as print in a newspaper. Often, the client will report a headache and eye fatigue with close work. Instruct the client to hold reading materials at arm's length.

3. The client is diagnosed with macular degeneration. What client findings are expected?

   The client will experience loss of central vision and will only be able to see peripherally.

4. Which of the following interventions are appropriate to help the client cope with macular degeneration?

__x__	Provide talking watches and clocks.
__x__	Provide large print books/newspapers/menus.
_____	Teach the client to place self-care objects in the center of tables.
__x__	Instruct the client to remove area rugs from the home.
__x__	Suggest that the client put important telephone numbers on auto dial.

Providing talking watches and large print text and setting auto dial for important telephone numbers will help the client cope with the vision deficits associated with macular degeneration. Removing area rugs in the home will help prevent injury. A client with macular degeneration has loss of central vision and will only be able to see peripherally. Therefore, the client should be taught to place self-care items in the peripheral line of sight.

5. The client is admitted to an unfamiliar hospital setting. How should the nurse orient the client to his environment?

Use one object as a focal point and orient the client in relation to that point (to the right of the bed is a closet with two doors, in the 2 o'clock position are green beans).

Show the client the way to the bathroom.

Let the client establish a fixed location for items such as a call bell or phone.

Don't leave the client alone until the client is familiar with the room.

Assist the client with ambulation by allowing the client to grasp the guide's arm at the elbow.

Identify oneself when entering the client's room.

Unit 8   Nursing Care of Clients with Neurosensory Disorders
Section: Nursing Care of Clients with Sensory Disorders

Chapter 93:   **Retinal Detachment**
               Contributor: Jeanne Wissmann, PhD, RN, CNE

NCLEX-PN® Connections:

Learning Objective: Review and apply knowledge within **"Retinal Detachment"** in readiness for performance of the following nursing activities as outlined by the NCLEX-PN® test plan:

Δ   Identify the needs of the client with reduced visual acuity.

Δ   Provide assistance to the client with reduced visual acuity.

Δ   Assist with relevant laboratory, diagnostic, and therapeutic procedures within the nursing role, including:

   • Preparation of the client for the procedure.

   • Accurate collection of specimens.

   • Monitoring client status during and after the procedure.

   • Reinforcing client teaching (before and following the procedure).

   • Recognizing the client's response (expected, unexpected adverse response) to the procedure.

   • Monitoring results.

   • Monitoring and taking actions to prevent or minimize the risk of complications.

   • Notifying the primary care provider of signs of complications.

Δ   Recognize signs and symptoms of the client's problem and complete the proper documentation.

Δ   Provide and document care based on the client's health alteration.

Δ   Monitor and document vital signs changes.

Δ   Interpret data that need to be reported immediately.

Δ   Reinforce client education on managing the client's health problem.

Δ   Recognize and respond to emergency situations, including notification of the primary care provider.

Δ   Review the client's response to emergency interventions and complete the proper documentation.

Δ   Provide care that meets the age-related needs of clients 65 years of age or older, including recognizing expected physiological changes.

📖 **Key Points**

- △ Retinal detachment is a painless separation of the retina from the epithelium, resulting in the **loss of vision in fields** surrounding separation.

- △ **The onset is abrupt**.

- △ Retinal detachment is a **medical emergency** and the assistance of a primary care provider should be sought immediately.

Key Factors

- △ **Risk Factors**

  - Nearsightedness

  - Family history

  - Previous cataract surgery

  - Eye injury

- △ **Causes**

  - Retinal tear (for example, trauma)

  - Fibrous vitreous tissue (pulls retina)

  - Exudate (form under retina)

Therapeutic Procedures and Nursing Interventions

- △ The application of freezing probes, laser beams, or high frequency current is used to create an inflammatory response for the purpose of rebinding the retina.

- △ **Scleral Buckling**

  - "Eye rest" prior to the procedure.

  - It involves general anesthesia for the insertion of silicone and an encircling band to promote attachment and infiltration of gas to push the retina back against the wall of the eye.

  - An eye patch and shield are applied and the client will lie with affected eye up.

  - Avoid activities that cause rapid eye movement (reading, writing) for a specified period of time.

Assessments

Δ   Monitor for **signs and symptoms.**

- Bright flashes of light

- Floating dark spots – "floaters"

- Partial: "Curtain drawing over visual field" sensation

- Loss of vision

NANDA Nursing Diagnoses

- Disturbed sensory perception (visual)

- Risk for injury

Nursing Interventions

Δ   Restrict activity to prevent additional detachment.

Δ   Cover the affected eye with an eye patch.

Δ   Monitor for drainage.

Δ   Administer **medications** as prescribed.

- Mydriatics (dilating) – prevent pupil constriction and reduce accommodation

- Antiemetics

- Analgesics

Δ   Instruct the client to **avoid activities that increase intraocular pressure (IOP),** such as:

- Bending over at the waist.

- Sneezing.

- Coughing.

- Straining.

- Vomiting.

- Head hyperflexion.

- Wearing restrictive clothing (for example, tight shirt collars).

Complications and Nursing Interventions

Δ **Loss of vision** – the final visual result is not always known for several months postoperatively. More than one attempt at repair may be required. The greatest risk for permanent progressive loss of vision is when the detachment is not treated prior to extension to the macula. Therefore, it is important for clients to know and recognize signs of detachment and to seek professional help immediately.

Primary Reference:

Ignatavicius, D. D., & Workman, M. L. (2006). *Medical-surgical nursing* (5th ed.). St. Louis, MO: Saunders.

Additional Resources:

NANDA International (2004). *NANDA nursing diagnoses: Definitions and classification 2005-2006*. Philadelphia: NANDA.

Chapter 93: Retinal Detachment

Application Exercises

1. A nurse is caring for a client with a detached left retina. Which of the following client findings indicates an acute bleed has occurred as a result of detachment?

        A. Severe left eye pain

        B. Left palpebral edema

        C. Bilateral loss of vision

        D. Reporting a burst of black spots

2. Which of the following client findings is a risk factor for retinal detachment?

        A. BL vision 20/100

        B. Blood pressure 165/85 mm Hg

        C. Fingerstick glucose 254

        D. History of migraines

3. What immediate action should be taken for a client with evidence of a retinal detachment?

4. Which of the following activities/client conditions increase intraocular pressure? (Check all that apply.)

    _____   Wearing a neck scarf

    _____   Seasonal allergies

    _____   Swimming

    _____   Leaning over a side rail

    _____   Constipation

    _____   Intestinal flu

    _____   Tying shoes

Chapter 93: Retinal Detachment

Application Exercises Answer Key

1. A nurse is caring for a client with a detached left retina. Which of the following client findings indicates an acute bleed has occurred as a result of detachment?

        A. Severe left eye pain

        B. Left palpebral edema

        C. Bilateral loss of vision

        D. Reporting a burst of black spots

A sudden onset of flashes of bright light or dark floating spots ("floaters") in the affected eye is a classic sign of detachment. There are no pain fibers within the retina so no pain is generally experienced.

2. Which of the following client findings is a risk factor for retinal detachment?

        A. BL vision 20/100

        B. Blood pressure 165/85 mm Hg

        C. Fingerstick glucose 254

        D. History of migraines

Nearsightedness (myopia) is a risk factor for retinal trauma and consequently retinal detachment.

3. What immediate action should be taken for a client with evidence of a retinal detachment?

Retinal detachment is a medical emergency and the assistance of a primary care provider should be sought immediately. Restrict activity to prevent additional detachment. Cover the affected eye with an eye patch. Avoid activities that cause rapid eye movement (reading, writing).

4. Which of the following activities/client conditions increase intraocular pressure? (Check all that apply.)

__x__	Wearing a neck scarf
__x__	Seasonal allergies
____	Swimming
__x__	Leaning over a side rail
__x__	Constipation
__x__	Intestinal flu
__x__	Tying shoes

Activities that increase IOP include:

Bending over at the waist.

Sneezing.

Coughing.

Straining.

Vomiting.

Head hyperflexion.

Restrictive clothing (tight shirt collars).

Unit 8
Section:

Nursing Care of Clients with Neurosensory Disorders
Nursing Care of Clients with Sensory Disorders

Chapter 94:	Cataracts

Contributor: Dana Bartlett, MSN, RN, CSPI

NCLEX-PN® Connections:

Learning Objective: Review and apply knowledge within **"Cataracts"** in readiness for performance of the following nursing activities as outlined by the NCLEX-PN® test plan:

Δ   Identify the needs of the client with reduced visual acuity.

Δ   Provide assistance to the client with reduced visual acuity.

Δ   Assist with relevant laboratory, diagnostic, and therapeutic procedures within the nursing role, including:

- Preparation of the client for the procedure.

- Accurate collection of specimens.

- Monitoring client status during and after the procedure.

- Reinforcing client teaching (before and following the procedure).

- Recognizing the client's response (expected, unexpected adverse response) to the procedure.

- Monitoring results.

- Monitoring and taking actions to prevent or minimize the risk of complications.

- Notifying the primary care provider of signs of complications.

Δ   Recognize signs and symptoms of the client's problem and complete the proper documentation.

Δ   Provide and document care based on the client's health alteration.

Δ   Monitor and document vital signs changes.

Δ   Interpret data that need to be reported immediately.

Δ   Reinforce client education on managing the client's health problem.

Δ   Recognize and respond to emergency situations, including notification of the primary care provider.

Δ   Review the client's response to emergency interventions and complete the proper documentation.

Δ   Provide care that meets the age-related needs of clients 65 years of age or older, including recognizing expected physiological changes.

Key Points

Δ   A **cataract** is an **opacity in the lens of an eye** that impairs vision.

Δ   Cataract surgery is the most common surgery for people 65 years and older. Cataract surgery is 95% successful.

Key Factors

Δ   **Probable Causes**

- **Advanced age**

- Diabetes

- Heredity

- Trauma

- Excessive exposure to the sun

- Chronic steroid use

Therapeutic Procedures and Nursing Interventions

Δ   **Surgical Removal of the Lens**

- Medications such as acetazolamide (Diamox) are administered preoperatively to reduce intraocular pressure, to dilate pupils, and to create eye paralysis to prevent lens movement.

- A small incision is made and the lens is removed, but the posterior capsule is retained.

- A replacement lens is inserted. Replacement lenses can correct refractive errors, resulting in improved distant vision.

- Postoperative care should be focused on:

   ◊   Preventing infection.

   ◊   Administering ophthalmic medications.

   ◊   Pain relief.

   ◊   Client teaching for self-care at home.

Assessments

Δ   Monitor for **signs and symptoms.**

- **Progressive and painless loss of vision**
- Decreased visual acuity (prescription changes, reduced night vision)
- Glare and light sensitivity
- Blurred vision
- Visible opacity
- Absent red reflex
- Diplopia

Δ   **Assess/Monitor**

- Client's history of visual problems
- Visual acuity

NANDA Nursing Diagnoses

Δ   Risk for injury

Δ   Disturbed sensory perception (visual)

Nursing Interventions

Δ   **Postoperative Client Education**

- Wear **dark glasses** in bright light.
- Report signs of infection such as yellow or green drainage.

Δ   **Instruct the client to avoid activities that increase intraocular pressure (IOP).**

- Bending over at the waist
- Sneezing
- Coughing
- Straining
- Vomiting
- Head hyperflexion
- Restrictive clothing (for example, tight shirt collars)
- Sexual intercourse

Δ   Administer postoperative medications as prescribed.

- **Antibiotic steroid eye drops** – tobramycin combined with dexamethasone (TobraDex). Instruct the client or the client's caregiver on proper instillation technique.

- Analgesics for discomfort

Δ   **Limit activities.**

- Tilting head back to wash hair

- Only cooking and light housekeeping

- No rapid jerky movements (for example, vacuuming)

- Avoid driving and operating machinery

- Avoid sports

Δ   **Report pain with nausea/vomiting** – indications of increased intraocular pressure or hemorrhage.

Δ   **Final best vision is not expected until 4 to 6 weeks postoperative.**

Complications and Nursing Implications

Δ   **Infection** – in addition to reporting yellow or green drainage, instruct the client to report increased redness, reduction in visual acuity, increased tear production, and/or photophobia as these may be signs of infection.

Δ   **Bleeding** – a potential risk several days after surgery. Clients should immediately report any sudden change in visual acuity.

Primary Reference:

Ignatavicius, D. D., & Workman, M. L. (2006). *Medical-surgical nursing* (5th ed.). St. Louis, MO: Saunders.

Additional Resources:

NANDA International (2004). *NANDA nursing diagnoses: Definitions and classification 2005-2006*. Philadelphia: NANDA.

Chapter 94: Cataracts

Application Exercises

Scenario: A nurse is caring for a client who has just been diagnosed with bilateral cataracts.

1. Which of the following client findings should the nurse anticipate? (Check all that apply.)

_____ Eye pain

_____ Floating spots

_____ Blurred vision

_____ White pupils

_____ Bilateral red reflexes

_____ Reduced visual acuity

2. The client is scheduled for surgical removal of the lens. Identify the purpose of the following preoperative medications.

Medication	Purpose
Atropine (Isopto Atropine)	
Phenylephrine	
Acetazolamide (Diamox)	

3. Postoperative cataract surgery, the client reports nausea and severe eye pain. Which of the following actions should be taken?

    A. Notify the surgeon.

    B. Administer an analgesic.

    C. Administer an antiemetic.

    D. Turn the client onto operative side.

Chapter 94: Cataracts

Application Exercises Answer Key

Scenario: A nurse is caring for a client who has just been diagnosed with bilateral cataracts.

1. Which of the following client findings should the nurse anticipate? (Check all that apply.)

_____	Eye pain
_____	Floating spots
__x__	Blurred vision
__x__	White pupils
_____	Bilateral red reflexes
__x__	Reduced visual acuity

Cataracts are generally not painful. Floating spots are a characteristic of retinal detachment. Red reflexes are generally absent.

2. The client is scheduled for surgical removal of the lens. Identify the purpose of the following preoperative medications.

Medication	Purpose
Atropine (Isopto Atropine)	**Dilation (mydriasis)** **Cycloplegia (paralysis of ciliary muscle)**
Phenylephrine	**Dilation (mydriasis)**
Acetazolamide (Diamox)	**Decrease intraocular pressure**

3. Postoperative cataract surgery, the client reports nausea and severe eye pain. Which of the following actions should be taken?

   A. Notify the surgeon.
   B. Administer an analgesic.
   C. Administer an antiemetic.
   D. Turn the client onto operative side.

These are signs of increased intraocular pressure or hemorrhage. The surgeon should be notified immediately.

Unit 8
Section:

Nursing Care of Clients with Neurosensory Disorders
Nursing Care of Clients with Sensory Disorders

Chapter 95:   Glaucoma
Contributor: Dana Bartlett, MSN, RN, CSPI

NCLEX-PN® Connections:

Learning Objective: Review and apply knowledge within "**Glaucoma**" in readiness for performance of the following nursing activities as outlined by the NCLEX-PN® test plan:

Δ   Identify the needs of the client with reduced visual acuity.

Δ   Provide assistance to the client with reduced visual acuity.

Δ   Assist with relevant laboratory, diagnostic, and therapeutic procedures within the nursing role, including:

- Preparation of the client for the procedure.

- Accurate collection of specimens.

- Monitoring client status during and after the procedure.

- Reinforcing client teaching (before and following the procedure).

- Recognizing the client's response (expected, unexpected adverse response) to the procedure.

- Monitoring results.

- Monitoring and taking actions to prevent or minimize the risk of complications.

- Notifying the primary care provider of signs of complications.

Δ   Recognize signs and symptoms of the client's problem and complete the proper documentation.

Δ   Provide and document care based on the client's health alteration.

Δ   Monitor and document vital signs changes.

Δ   Interpret data that need to be reported immediately.

Δ   Reinforce client education on managing the client's health problem.

Δ   Recognize and respond to emergency situations, including notification of the primary care provider.

Δ   Review the client's response to emergency interventions and complete the proper documentation.

Δ   Provide care that meets the age-related needs of clients 65 years of age or older, including recognizing expected physiological changes.

📖 **Key Points**

Δ **Glaucoma** is a disturbance of the functional or structural integrity of the optic nerve. **Decreased fluid drainage or increased fluid secretion** increases intraocular pressure (IOP) and can cause atrophic changes and visual defects.

Δ Glaucoma is a leading cause of blindness. **Early diagnosis** and treatment is essential in **preventing vision loss** from glaucoma.

Δ There are two primary types of glaucoma:

- **Open-angle glaucoma** – most common form of glaucoma. Open-angle refers to the angle between the iris and sclera; it is normal.

- **Angle-closure glaucoma** – less common form of glaucoma. IOP rises suddenly. In angle-closure glaucoma, the angle between the iris and the sclera is decreased.

Δ The goal of therapy is to lower IOP and control the progression of the disease. The objectives of nursing care include helping the client understand the disease and cope with limitations it places on their activities.

Key Factors

Δ **Risk Factors**

- Age
- Infection
- Tumors
- Diabetes mellitus
- Genetic predisposition

Diagnostic Procedures and Nursing Interventions

Δ **Tonometry** is used to measure IOP. IOP (normal is 10 to 21 mm Hg) is elevated with glaucoma, especially angle-closure.

Δ **Gonioscopy** determines the drainage angle of the anterior chamber of the eyes.

Therapeutic Procedures and Nursing Interventions

Δ **Laser surgery or conventional surgery** – both procedures are aimed at improving the flow of the aqueous humor.

- IOP is checked 1 to 2 hr postoperatively by the surgeon.
- The postoperative eye is covered with a patch and protective shield.
- The client is instructed not to lie on the operative side and to report severe pain or nausea (possible hemorrhage).

Assessments

Δ Monitor for **signs and symptoms: Open-angle Glaucoma**

- **Loss of peripheral vision**
- Decreased accommodation
- Elevated IOP (> 21 mm Hg)

Δ Monitor for **signs and symptoms: Angle-closure Glaucoma**

- **Rapid onset of elevated IOP**
- Decreased or blurred vision
- Seeing **halos** around lights
- Pupils are nonreactive to light
- **Severe pain**
- Photophobia

Δ Assessments include a visual assessment and an assessment of the ability of the client to cope with changes in vision.

NANDA Nursing Diagnoses

Δ Disturbed sensory perception (visual)

Δ Risk for injury

Nursing Interventions

Δ Administer medications as prescribed.

- **Miotics** – pilocarpine (Isopto Carpine) constricts the pupil and allows for better circulation of aqueous humor. Miotics can cause blurred vision.

- **Beta-blockers** – timolol (Timoptic) and **carbonic anhydrase inhibitors such as acetazolamide (Diamox)** decrease IOP by reducing aqueous humor production.

- **IV mannitol** – emergency treatment for angle-closure glaucoma to quickly decrease IOP

- **Ocular steroid** – prednisolone acetate (Ocu-Pred).

Complications and Nursing Implications

Δ   **Blindness** – consequence of undiagnosed and untreated glaucoma.

- Early detection
  ◊   Encourage **adults 40 or older to have an annual examination** including a measurement of intraocular pressure.

Primary Reference:

Ignatavicius, D. D., & Workman, M. L. (2006). *Medical-surgical nursing* (5th ed.). St. Louis, MO: Saunders.

Additional Resources:

NANDA International (2004). *NANDA nursing diagnoses: Definitions and classification 2005-2006*. Philadelphia: NANDA.

Pascotto, A., Soreca, E., & Saccà, S. C. (2005, March 17). Glaucoma, complications and management of glaucoma filtering. *eMedicine*, Topic 720. Retrieved June 7, 2006, from http://www.emedicine.com/oph/topic720.htm.

Chapter 95: Glaucoma

Application Exercises

Scenario: A nurse is caring for a client diagnosed with angle-closure glaucoma.

1. The nurse should anticipate which of the following medications in the management of glaucoma? (Check all that apply. For any medications not selected, identify why not.)

   _____ Pilocarpine (Isopto Carpine, Pilocar)

   _____ Timolol maleate (Timoptic)

   _____ Epinephrine (Epifrin)

   _____ Carteolol (Ocupress)

   _____ Acetazolamide (Diamox)

2. The client asks how long she will need to take medications for her glaucoma. How should the nurse respond?

3. A nurse performs a Snellen chart test on a client with a diagnosis of legal blindness. How far from the Snellen chart should the nurse ask the client to stand?

4. What vision result should the nurse anticipate?

Chapter 95: Glaucoma

Application Exercises Answer Key

Scenario: A nurse is caring for a client diagnosed with angle-closure glaucoma.

1. The nurse should anticipate which of the following medications in the management of glaucoma? (Check all that apply. For any medications not selected, identify why not.)

   __x__   Pilocarpine (Isopto Carpine, Pilocar)

   __x__   Timolol maleate (Timoptic)

   _____   Epinephrine (Epifrin)

   __x__   Carteolol (Ocupress)

   __x__   Acetazolamide (Diamox)

   Epinephrine does reduce aqueous humor production; however, it dilates pupils. Mydriasis reduces aqueous humor outflow, which is dangerous for clients with angle-closure glaucoma.

2. The client asks how long she will need to take medications for her glaucoma. How should the nurse respond?

   Glaucoma is a chronic disease. It is not curable and its consequences are irreversible. Therefore, the nurse should help the client realize the importance of lifelong compliance with glaucoma medication therapy.

3. A nurse performs a Snellen chart test on a client with a diagnosis of legal blindness. How far from the Snellen chart should the nurse ask the client to stand?

   20 ft

4. What vision result should the nurse anticipate?

   20/200 vision or less even with correction

Chapter 96: Sensory Alteration: Hearing Loss

Contributor: Jeanne Wissmann, PhD, RN, CNE

NCLEX-PN® Connections:

Learning Objective: Review and apply knowledge within **"Sensory Alteration: Hearing Loss"** in readiness for performance of the following nursing activities as outlined by the NCLEX-PN® test plan:

Δ   Identify the needs of the client with altered hearing and provide assistance accordingly.

Δ   Assist the client with alternative methods of communication to compensate for altered hearing as appropriate.

Δ   Assist with relevant laboratory, diagnostic, and therapeutic procedures within the nursing role, including:

- Preparation of the client for the procedure.

- Accurate collection of specimens.

- Monitoring client status during and after the procedure.

- Reinforcing client teaching (before and following the procedure).

- Recognizing the client's response (expected, unexpected adverse response) to the procedure.

- Monitoring results.

- Monitoring and taking actions to prevent or minimize the risk of complications.

- Notifying the primary care provider of signs of complications.

Δ   Recognize signs and symptoms of the client's problem and complete the proper documentation.

Δ   Interpret data that need to be reported immediately.

Δ   Reinforce client education on managing the client's health problem.

Δ   Recognize and respond to emergency situations, including notification of the primary care provider.

Δ   Review the client's response to emergency interventions and complete the proper documentation.

Δ   Provide care that meets the age-related needs of clients 65 years of age or older, including recognizing expected physiological changes.

Key Points

- Δ **Conductive hearing loss** occurs when sound waves are blocked before reaching the inner ear.

- Δ **Sensorineural hearing loss** occurs with cranial nerve VIII and/or cochlear damage.

Key Factors

- Δ **Causes of conductive hearing loss** include:

  - Obstruction (cerumen, foreign object).

  - Tympanic membrane perforation.

  - Ear infections.

  - Otosclerosis.

- Δ **Causes of sensorineural hearing loss** include:

  - Exposure to loud noises.

  - Ototoxic medications (for example, aminoglycosides).

  - Aging (presbycusis).

  - Acoustic neuroma (benign tumor CNVIII).

Diagnostic Procedures and Nursing Interventions

- Δ Audiometry – an audiogram **identifies if hearing loss is sensorineural and/or conductive.**

Therapeutic Procedures and Nursing Interventions

- Δ **Conductive Hearing Loss**

  - **Hearing aid** – lowest setting that allows hearing without feedback noise. To clean the ear mold, use mild soap and water. The hearing aid should be turned off and the battery removed when not in use. Also, extra batteries should be kept on hand.

  - **Tympanoplasty** (middle ear)/**myringoplasty** (eardrum) – ear packing, sterile dressing. Position the client flat with operative ear up for 12 hr.

  - **Stapedectomy** – ear packing. Assess the client for facial nerve damage. Intervene for vertigo, nausea, and vomiting (common). Hearing is initially worse.

Δ **Sensorineural Hearing Loss**

- **Cochlear implant** – electrodes are placed in the inner ear and a computer is attached to the external ear. Electronic impulses stimulate the nerve fibers.

Δ **Client education following ear surgery** should include instructing the client to avoid straining, coughing, sneezing with mouth closed, air travel, hair washing, rapid head movements, and people with infections.

Assessments

Δ Monitor for **signs and symptoms.**

- **Conductive** hearing loss

  ◊ Obstruction

  ◊ Abnormal tympanic membrane findings

  ◊ Soft spoken

  ◊ Hears well in a noisy environment

  ◊ AC > BC

  ◊ Lateralization to affected ear

- **Sensorineural** hearing loss

  ◊ Tinnitus

  ◊ Dizziness

  ◊ Loud spoken

  ◊ Hears poorly in a noisy environment

  ◊ AC < BC

  ◊ Lateralization to unaffected ear

Δ **Assess/Monitor**

- Hearing acuity (whisper test, **Weber test, Rinne test**)

- Tympanic membrane and bone structures (otoscope)

- Functional ability

NANDA Nursing Diagnoses

Δ Disturbed sensory perception (auditory)

Δ Impaired verbal communication

Δ Social isolation

Δ Impaired physical mobility

Nursing Interventions

Δ   Communication

- Get the **client's attention** before speaking.

- Stand/sit **facing the client** in a well-lit, quiet room without distractions.

- Speak **clearly and slowly** to the client without shouting and without hands or other objects covering the mouth.

- Arrange for communication assistance (sign language interpreter, closed-caption, phone amplifiers, TTY capabilities) as needed.

Δ   Health promotion

- **No sharp objects** should be placed in the ear.

- **Ear protection** should be worn for exposure to high-intensity noise and/or risk for ear trauma.

- External ear and canal should be washed daily.

- Nose should be blown gently and with both nostrils unoccluded.

- When wearing head receivers, **volume should be kept as low** as possible.

Δ   Administer medications as prescribed.

- Vertigo – meclizine hydrochloride (Antivert)

- Antiemetics – droperidol (Inapsine)

Δ   Check the hearing of clients receiving **ototoxic medications for more than 5 days.** Ototoxic medications include:

- Multiple antibiotics – gentamicin, amikacin, or metronidazole.

- Diuretics – furosemide (Lasix).

- NSAIDs – aspirin or ibuprofen.

- Chemotherapeutic agents – cisplatin.

Complications and Nursing Interventions

Δ   **Injury due to vertigo** – teach the client to move head and to change positions slowly. Assist the client as needed with ambulation.

Meeting the Needs of Older Adults

Δ   Risk for and degree of hearing loss progressively advances with aging.

Δ   Reduced renal function that occurs with aging increases the risk for ototoxicity.

Primary Reference:

Ignatavicius, D. D., & Workman, M. L. (2006). *Medical-surgical nursing* (5th ed.). St. Louis, MO: Saunders.

Additional Resources:

NANDA International (2004). *NANDA nursing diagnoses: Definitions and classification 2005-2006*. Philadelphia: NANDA.

Chapter 96: Sensory Alteration: Hearing Loss

Application Exercises

Scenario: A nurse is caring for a client with possible hearing loss.

1. How should the nurse assess for lateralization of sound?

2. When performing the otoscopic examination, how should the nurse position the pinna prior to insertion of the otoscope?

3. Which of the following client findings are possible causative factors for the client's hearing loss? (Check all that apply.)

    _____ Daily use of warfarin (Coumadin)

    _____ Age 85

    _____ Antibiotic therapy with reduced renal function

    _____ Employed as a ground crew member at a large airport

    _____ Presbyopia

    _____ Presbycusis

    _____ High doses of IV furosemide (Lasix) for congestive heart failure exacerbation

    _____ Chronic use of NSAIDs for rheumatoid arthritis management

4. The client reports ringing in her ears and difficulty hearing in loud environments. The Weber test reveals lateralization to the unaffected ear. The nurse should expect the audiogram to reveal which type of hearing loss?

    A. Sensorineural

    B. Conductive

Scenario: A nurse is caring for a client who uses sign language to communicate. The nurse does not know sign language.

5. What is the nurse's responsibility?

6. What is the interpreter's responsibility?

Chapter 96: Sensory Alteration: Hearing Loss

Application Exercises Answer Key

Scenario: A nurse is caring for a client with possible hearing loss.

1. How should the nurse assess for lateralization of sound?

   Place a vibrating tuning fork on the midline center of the client's head. Instruct the client to state in which ear the sound is the loudest. A normal finding is no lateralization or equal sound in both ears. Lateralization to the affected ear is consistent with conductive hearing loss, whereas lateralization to the unaffected ear is consistent with sensorineural hearing loss.

2. When performing the otoscopic examination, how should the nurse position the pinna prior to insertion of the otoscope?

   The nurse should pull the pinna up and back with the nondominant hand.

3. Which of the following client findings are possible causative factors for the client's hearing loss? (Check all that apply.)

_____	Daily use of warfarin (Coumadin)
__X__	Age 85
__X__	Antibiotic therapy with reduced renal function
__X__	Employed as a ground crew member at a large airport
_____	Presbyopia
__X__	Presbycusis
__X__	High doses of IV furosemide (Lasix) for congestive heart failure exacerbation
__X__	Chronic use of NSAIDs for rheumatoid arthritis management

4. The client reports ringing in her ears and difficulty hearing in loud environments. The Weber test reveals lateralization to the unaffected ear. The nurse should expect the audiogram to reveal which type of hearing loss?

   A. Sensorineural

   B. Conductive

Background noise reduces ability to filter and process communication. Lateralization to the unaffected side is a sign of sensorineural hearing loss.

Scenario: A nurse is caring for a client who uses sign language to communicate. The nurse does not know sign language.

5. What is the nurse's responsibility?

Assess the client's level of functioning and arrange for a sign interpreter as needed.

6. What is the interpreter's responsibility?

Δ   Code of Ethics for Interpreters in Health Care*

- The interpreter treats as confidential, within the treating team, all information learned in the performance of his or her professional duties, while observing relevant requirements regarding disclosure.

- The interpreter strives to render the message accurately, conveying the content and spirit of the original message, taking into consideration its cultural context.

Δ   The interpreter strives to maintain impartiality and refrains from counseling, advising or projecting personal biases or beliefs.

Δ   The interpreter maintains the boundaries of the professional role, refraining from personal involvement.

*Source: http://www.ncihc.org/NCIHC_PDF/NationalCodeofEthicsforInterpretersinHealthCare.pdf

Nursing Care of Clients with Neurosensory Disorders

Nursing Care of Clients with Sensory Disorders

Chapter 97:   Inner Ear Problems

Contributor: Jeanne Wissmann, PhD, RN, CNE

⟳ NCLEX-PN® Connections:

Learning Objective: Review and apply knowledge within "**Inner Ear Problems**" in readiness for performance of the following nursing activities as outlined by the NCLEX-PN® test plan:

Δ   Identify the needs of the client with altered hearing and provide assistance accordingly.

Δ   Assist the client with alternative methods of communication to compensate for altered hearing as appropriate.

Δ   Assist with relevant laboratory, diagnostic, and therapeutic procedures within the nursing role, including:

- Preparation of the client for the procedure.

- Accurate collection of specimens.

- Monitoring client status during and after the procedure.

- Reinforcing client teaching (before and following the procedure).

- Recognizing the client's response (expected, unexpected adverse response) to the procedure.

- Monitoring results.

- Monitoring and taking actions to prevent or minimize the risk of complications.

- Notifying the primary care provider of signs of complications.

Δ   Recognize signs and symptoms of the client's problem and complete the proper documentation.

Δ   Interpret data that need to be reported immediately.

Δ   Reinforce client education on managing the client's health problem.

Δ   Recognize and respond to emergency situations, including notification of the primary care provider.

Δ   Review the client's response to emergency interventions and complete the proper documentation.

Δ   Provide care that meets the age-related needs of clients 65 years of age or older, including recognizing expected physiological changes.

📖 Key Points

Δ   **Inner ear problems** are characterized by **tinnitus** (continuous ringing in ear), **vertigo** (whirling sensation), and **dizziness**.

- Labyrinthitis and Ménière's disease are inner ear problems.

- **Labyrinthitis** is an infection of the labyrinth, usually secondary to otitis media.

- **Ménière's disease** is a **vestibular** disease characterized by tinnitus, unilateral sensorineural hearing loss, and vertigo.

Δ   Visual, vestibular, and proprioceptive systems provide the brain with input regarding balance. Problems within any of these systems **pose a risk for loss of balance**.

Key Factors

Δ   **Causes: Tinnitus**

- Presbycusis

- Otosclerosis

- Ménière's disease

- Ototoxic medications

- Exposure to loud noise

Δ   **Causes: Vertigo**

- Peripheral vestibular disorder

- Ototoxic medications

- Alcohol

Δ   **Causes: Dizziness**

- Central vestibular disorder (bradycardia, tachycardia, migraine, head injury, acoustic neuroma, orthostatic hypotension)

Diagnostic Procedures and Nursing Interventions

Δ   **Electronystagmography** (ENG) – used to detect peripheral and central diseases of the vestibular system. Client preparation includes fasting and caffeine restriction. Various procedures are performed in an effort to detect nystagmus (involuntary rapid eye movement).

Δ   **Caloric testing** – water (warmer or cooler than body temperature) is instilled in the ear in an effort to induce vertigo.

Therapeutic Procedures and Nursing Interventions

Δ **Labyrinthectomy** – transcanal surgery to remove labyrinth. Usually results in hearing loss in affected ear.

Assessments

Δ Monitor for **signs and symptoms: Tinnitus**

- **Mild ringing** to loud roaring in ear
- Reduced attention span

Δ Monitor for **signs and symptoms: Vertigo**

- **Nausea and vomiting**
- Falls
- Nystagmus
- Hearing Loss
- Tinnitus

Δ **Assess/Monitor**

- Hearing acuity (whisper test, Weber or Rinne test)
- Balance
- Functional ability

NANDA Nursing Diagnoses

Δ Risk for injury

Δ Activity intolerance

Δ Risk for deficient fluid volume

Δ Impaired physical mobility

Nursing Interventions

Δ Encourage the client to rest in a quiet, darkened environment when symptoms are severe.

Δ Encourage the client to participate in gait training/physical therapy and assistive devices (cane, walker) to assist with balance.

Δ Encourage the client to maintain a safe environment (for example, free of clutter).

Δ   Administer **medications** as prescribed.

- Diphenhydramine (Benadryl)

- Diphenhydrinate (Dramamine)

- Meclizine hydrochloride (Antivert)

- Diazepam (Valium)

- Scopolamine (Transderm Scop)

- Antiemetics, such as droperidol (Inapsine)

- Antibiotics, such as ampicillin (Omnipen)

Δ   Check the hearing of clients receiving **ototoxic medications for more than 5 days.** Ototoxic medications include:

- Multiple antibiotics, such as gentamicin, amikacin, and metronidazole.

- Diuretics, such as furosemide (Lasix).

- NSAIDs, such as aspirin, ibuprofen.

- Chemotherapeutic agents, such as cisplatin.

Complications and Nursing Interventions

Δ   **Injury due to vertigo** – instruct the client to move his or her head and to change positions slowly. Assist as needed with ambulation.

Meeting the Needs of Older Adults

Δ   Reduced renal function that occurs with aging increases the risk for ototoxicity.

Primary Reference:

Ignatavicius, D. D., & Workman, M. L. (2006). *Medical-surgical nursing* (5th ed.). St. Louis, MO: Saunders.

Additional Resources:

NANDA International (2004). *NANDA nursing diagnoses: Definitions and classification 2005-2006.* Philadelphia: NANDA.

Chapter 97: Inner Ear Problems

Application Exercises

Scenario: A nurse is caring for a client with Ménière's disease who is experiencing severe vertigo.

1. Which instruction(s) should the nurse give the client to assist in controlling the vertigo? (Check all that apply.)

    _____ Increase fluid intake to 3,000 mL/day.
    _____ Avoid sudden head movements.
    _____ Move slowly.
    _____ Increase dietary sodium.
    _____ Stop smoking.

2. In addition to vertigo, what is the most common client symptom associated with inner ear disorders?

3. A client who is hospitalized has developed tinnitus. In reviewing the client's medication record, developing toxicity of which of the following prescribed medications might be the causative factor? (Check all that apply.)

    _____ Propanolol (Inderal)
    _____ Diphenhydramine (Benadryl)
    _____ Acetylsalicylic acid (ASA)
    _____ Indomethacin (Indocin)
    _____ Furosemide (Lasix)
    _____ Tobramycin (Tobrex)

4. What actions should the nurse anticipate with regard to these medications?

Chapter 97: Inner Ear Problems

Application Exercises Answer Key

Scenario: A nurse is caring for a client with Ménière's disease who is experiencing severe vertigo.

1. Which instruction(s) should the nurse give the client to assist in controlling the vertigo? (Check all that apply.)

	Increase fluid intake to 3,000 mL/day.
x	Avoid sudden head movements.
x	Move slowly.
	Increase dietary sodium.
x	Stop smoking.

Fluid and sodium restrictions are sometimes prescribed to reduce the amount of endolymphatic fluid. Vasoconstriction occurs with smoking. Slow, cautious movements can lessen the vertigo sensations.

2. In addition to vertigo, what is the most common client symptom associated with inner ear disorders?

Tinnitus (continuous ringing in ears)

3. A client who is hospitalized has developed tinnitus. In reviewing the client's medication record, developing toxicity of which of the following prescribed medications might be the causative factor? (Check all that apply.)

_____	Propanolol (Inderal)
_____	Diphenhydramine (Benadryl)
__x__	Acetylsalicylic acid (ASA)
__x__	Indomethacin (Indocin)
__x__	Furosemide (Lasix)
__x__	Tobramycin (Tobrex)

NSAIDs like aspirin and indomethacin are ototoxic. Loop diuretics, such as furosemide (Lasix), and aminoglycosides, such as tobramycin (Tobrex) and gentamicin (Garamycin), are also ototoxic.

4. What actions should the nurse anticipate with regard to these medications?

Discontinuation and/or reduction in the dosage amount. Aminoglycoside levels are routinely drawn to monitor for developing toxicity.

Unit 9   Nursing Care of Clients with Musculoskeletal Disorders
Section: Diagnostic and Therapeutic Procedures: Musculoskeletal

Chapter 98:   Immobilizing Interventions: Casts, Splints, and Traction
Contributor: Janey A. Roach, MSN, RN, ONC

↻ NCLEX-PN® Connections:

> **Learning Objective:** Review and apply knowledge within "**Immobilizing Interventions: Casts, Splints, and Traction**" in readiness for performance of the following nursing activities as outlined by the NCLEX-PN® test plan:
>
> Δ   Provide care for the client with an orthopedic device.
>
> Δ   Perform/assist with relevant laboratory, diagnostic, and therapeutic procedures within the nursing role, including:
>
> - Preparation of the client for the procedure.
> - Reinforcement of client teaching (before and following the procedure).
> - Accurate collection of specimens.
> - Monitoring procedure results (compare to norms) and appropriate notification of the primary care provider.
> - Monitoring the client's response (expected, unexpected adverse response, comparison to baseline) to the procedure.
> - Monitoring and taking actions, including reinforcing client teaching, to prevent or minimize the risk of complications.
> - Recognizing signs of potential complications and reporting to the primary care provider.
> - Recommending changes in the test/procedure as needed based on client findings.
>
> Δ   Protect the client from injury.
>
> Δ   Monitor therapeutic devices (drainage/irrigating devices, chest tubes), if inserted, for proper functioning.

Key Points

Δ   Immobilization secures the injured extremity in order to:

  •   Prevent further injury.

  •   Promote healing/circulation.

  •   Reduce pain.

  •   Correct a deformity.

Δ   Types of immobilization devices include:

  •   Casts.

  •   Splints/immobilizers.

  •   Traction.

  •   External fixation.

Δ   **Closed reduction** is when a pulling force (traction) is applied manually to realign the displaced fractured bone fragments. Once the fracture is reduced, immobilization is used to allow the bone to heal.

Diagnostic Procedures and Nursing Interventions

Δ   **Radiographs** are used to verify fracture alignment and are repeated during recovery to ensure alignment and healing.

Therapeutic Procedures and Nursing Interventions

Δ   **Casts**

  •   Casts are more effective than splints or immobilizers because they cannot be removed by the client.

  •   Types of casts include:

    ◊   Short and long arm casts.

    ◊   Short and long leg casts.

    ◊   Spica cast, which refers to a portion of the trunk and one or two extremities.

    ◊   Body cast, which encircles the trunk of the body.

  •   Casting materials

    ◊   Plaster of Paris casts are heavy, not water resistant, and can take 24 to 48 hr to dry.

    ◊   Synthetic fiberglass casts are light, water resistant, and dry very quickly (in 30 min).

- Prior to casting, the area is cleaned and dried. Tubular cotton web roll is placed over the affected area to maintain skin integrity. The casting material is then applied.

- Casts, as circumferential immobilizers, are **applied once the swelling has subsided** (to avoid compartment syndrome). If the swelling continues after cast application and causes unrelieved pain, the cast can be split on one side (univalved) or on both sides (bi-valved).

- After cast application, position the client so that warm, dry air circulates around and under the cast (support the casted area without pressure under or directly on the cast) for faster drying and to prevent pressure from changing the shape of the cast. Use gloves to touch the cast until the cast is completely dry.

- **Elevate cast above the level of the heart** during the first 24 to 48 hr to prevent swelling.

- A window can be placed in an area of the cast to allow for skin inspection (if, for example, the client has a wound under the cast).

- If any drainage is seen on the cast, it should be outlined, dated, and timed so it can be monitored for any additional drainage.

- Moleskin is used over any rough area of the cast that may rub against the client's skin.

- Clients are instructed **not to place any foreign objects** under the cast to avoid trauma to the skin.

- Plastic coverings over the cast can be used to avoid soiling from urine or feces.

Δ **Splints and Immobilizers**

- Splints are removable and allow for monitoring of skin swelling or integrity.

- Splints can be used to **support fractured/injured areas** or used for post-paralysis injuries to **avoid joint contracture**.

- Immobilizers are prefabricated and are fastened with Velcro straps.

Δ **Traction**

- Traction uses a **pulling force** to promote and maintain alignment to the injured area. In straight or running traction, the countertraction is provided by the client's body. In balanced suspension traction, the countertraction is produced by devices such as slings or splints.

- **Goals** of traction include:

  ◊ **Realignment of bone fragments**.

  ◊ Decreasing muscle spasms and pain.

  ◊ Correcting or preventing further deformities.

- Traction prescriptions should include the type of traction, amount of weight, and whether traction can be removed for nursing care.

- Types of Traction

  ◊ **Manual**: A pulling force is applied by the hands of the provider for temporary immobilization, usually with sedation or anesthesia, in conjunction with the application of an immobilizing device.

  ◊ **Skin**: Used **intermittently**. The pulling force is applied by weights that are attached by rope to the client with tape, straps, boots, or cuffs. Examples include: Chin halter straps, Bryant's traction (congenital hip dislocation in children), and Buck's traction (used for hip fractures preoperatively for immobilization in adults).

  ◊ **Skeletal**: Used **continuously**. The pulling force is applied **directly to the bone** by weights attached by rope directly to a rod/screw placed through the bone. Examples include skeletal tongs (Gardner-Wells) or halo traction (used for cervical fractures).

  ◊ **Halo Traction**:

    ° Screws are placed through the bone and are attached to rods that are secured to a **non-removable vest** worn by the client.

    ° A wrench used to release the rods from the vest is taped to the front of the vest in the event of need for emergency CPR.

    ° The **client is moved as a unit** without pressure applied to the rods attached to the vest and halo ring. This is done to avoid loosening of the pins.

- Traction Guidelines

  ◊ **Maintain body alignment** and realign if the client seems uncomfortable or reports pain.

  ◊ **Avoid lifting or removing weights**.

  ◊ Assure that **weights hang freely**.

  ◊ If the weights are accidentally displaced, replace the weights. If the problem is not corrected, notify the primary care provider.

  ◊ Assure that pulley ropes are free of knots.

  ◊ Notify the primary care provider if the client experiences severe pain from muscle spasms unrelieved with medications and/or repositioning.

  ◊ **Routinely monitor skin integrity** and document.

Δ   **External Fixation**

- External fixation involves fracture immobilization (*For information, refer to chapter 100, Fractures.*) using **percutaneous pins and wires that are attached to a rigid external frame**.

- Used to treat:

  ◊   Comminuted fracture with extensive soft tissue.

  ◊   Leg length discrepancies from congenital defects.

  ◊   Bone loss related to tumors or osteomyelitis.

- Advantages include:

  ◊   Immediate fracture stabilization.

  ◊   Allows three plane correction of the injury.

  ◊   Minimal blood loss occurs in comparison with internal fixation.

  ◊   Allows for early mobilization and ambulation.

  ◊   Maintains alignment of closed fractures that could not be maintained in cast or splint.

  ◊   Permits wound care with open fractures.

- Disadvantages include:

  ◊   **Risk of pin tract infection**.

  ◊   Potential overwhelming appearance to client.

  ◊   Noncompliance issues.

Assessments and Interventions

Δ   **Range of motion (ROM) exercises are done at least once every shift** to those joints on the affected side that are not connected to the fracture.

Δ   **Neurovascular assessment is essential throughout immobilization.** Assessments are done frequently following initial trauma to prevent neurovascular compromise related to edema and/or immobilization device. Neurovascular assessment includes assessment of the following:

- Pain

- Paresthesia

- Pallor

- Polar

- Paralysis

- Pulses

Neurovascular Components	Early or Late Sign	Assessment Parameters	Client Teaching/Symptoms to Report
Pain	Early	Assess area involved using 0 to 10 rating scale: 0 = no pain 10 = worst pain imaginable	Increasing **pain not relieved** with elevation or pain medication
Paresthesia	Early	Assess for numbness/ tingling, pins or needles sensation: Should be absent.	**Numbness or tingling**, pins or needles sensation
Pallor	Early	Assess capillary refill. Brisk is < 3 seconds	**Increased capillary refill time > 3 seconds**, blue fingers or toes
Polar	Late	Assess skin temperature by touch: Warm Cool	**Cool/cold** fingers or toes
Paralysis	Late	Assess mobility: Moves fingers or toes Able to plantar dorsiflex the ankle area not involved or restricted by cast	**Unable to move** fingers or toes
Pulses	Late	Assess pulse(s) distal to injury: Pulse is palpable and strong	**Weak** palpable pulses, **unable to palpate** pulses, pulse detected only with Doppler

Δ   **Pin Site Care**

- Pin care is done frequently throughout immobilization (skeletal traction and external fixation methods) to prevent and to monitor for signs of infection including:

    ◊   Drainage (color, amount, odor).

    ◊   Loosening of pins.

    ◊   Tenting of skin at pin site (skin rising up pin).

- **Pin care protocols** (use of hydrogen peroxide, povidone iodine) are based on provider preference and institution policy. A primary concept of pin care is that **one cotton-tip swab** is used **per pin to avoid cross-contamination**. Every 8 hr is a common parameter for pin care schedule.

Δ   **Prophylactic** antibiotics are used to prevent infection when fracture immobilization is achieved using metal screws or wires. Typically, a **broad spectrum intravenous antibiotic** such as cefazolin (Ancef) is administered for 24 to 48 hr post injury.

Complications and Nursing Implications

Δ **Acute compartment syndrome** – a buildup of pressure within muscle compartment(s) that can cause serious circulatory obstruction resulting in tissue ischemia and possibly necrosis. Compartment syndrome is evidenced by **unrelieved pain or pain out of proportion to the injury**. Initial sensory alterations are paresthesias, pallor, and then diminished pulses. Notify the primary care provider immediately. Interventions to relieve pressure include loosening constricting bulky dressings and cutting (bivalving) cast.

Δ **Osteomyelitis** – inflammation within the bone secondary to penetration of organisms (trauma, surgery). It is characterized by **bone pain that is worse with movement**. Initially, erythema, edema, and fever may occur. Definitive diagnosis is with a bone biopsy. Cultures performed for detection of possible aerobic and anaerobic organisms. Treatment includes a **long course** (for example, 3 months) **of IV and oral antibiotic therapy**. Surgical debridement may also be indicated. Unsuccessful treatment can result in amputation.

Meeting the Needs of Older Adults

Δ External fixation is used for radius or ulnar fractures in older adult clients due to poor vascularity of bone or fragile bone structure (osteoporosis).

Δ Older adult clients have an increased risk for impaired skin integrity due to the loss of elasticity of the skin and decreased sensation (co-morbidities).

Primary Reference:

Ignatavicius, D. D., & Workman, M. L. (2006). *Medical-surgical nursing* (5th ed.). St. Louis, MO: Saunders.

Additional Resources:

Maher, A. B., Salmond, S. W., & Pellino, T. A. (2002). *Orthopaedic nursing* (3rd ed.). Philadelphia: Saunders.

NANDA International (2004). *NANDA nursing diagnoses: Definitions and classification 2005-2006*. Philadelphia: NANDA.

Chapter 98: Immobilizing Interventions: Casts, Splints, and Traction

Application Exercises

1. Which of the following client statements indicates understanding of how to safely manage an external fixation device applied to his distal radius and ulna? (Check all that apply.)

    _____ "I will continue to clean the pins three times a day."

    _____ "I will use one cotton swab per pin."

    _____ "I will let the skin grow up the pin to prevent infection."

    _____ "I will lift my arm by the middle of the device to reposition it."

2. Identify information that should be included in client education regarding pin care.

3. An 82-year-old client is admitted to the nursing unit with a diagnosis of right hip fracture. The client's surgery is scheduled for the following morning. What type of immobilization device and setup should the nurse anticipate will be used for this client preoperatively?

4. What are the nursing considerations for this client while awaiting surgery?

5. Match the terms below with the definitions provided.

    _____ Buck's traction

    _____ Bivalve

    _____ Halo traction

    _____ Closed reduction

    _____ Cast

    A. Splitting a cast along both sides to relieve pressure

    B. A type of skin traction used after a hip injury

    C. Using manual traction to realign fractured bones

    D. Skeletal traction used to immobilize the cervical spine

    E. A circumferential immobilization device that cannot be removed by the client

6. List the six components of the neurovascular assessment and indicate which are early signs and which are late signs.

7. A client had a cast applied 2 hr ago for a fractured left femur. Which of the following findings indicate the possibility of compartment syndrome? (Check all that apply.)

_____ Toes cool to touch bilaterally.

_____ Left toes are slightly edematous compared to right.

_____ Diminished left pedal pulses.

_____ Pain is unrelieved by second dose of oral narcotic.

_____ Inability to move toes on the left.

Chapter 98: Immobilizing Interventions: Casts, Splints, and Traction

Application Exercises Answer Key

1. Which of the following client statements indicates understanding of how to safely manage an external fixation device applied to his distal radius and ulna? (Check all that apply.)

   __x__   "I will continue to clean the pins three times a day."

   __x__   "I will use one cotton swab per pin."

   _____   "I will let the skin grow up the pin to prevent infection."

   _____   "I will lift my arm by the middle of the device to reposition it."

Pin care protocols are based on provider preference and institution policy. A primary concept of pin care is that one cotton-tip swab is used per pin to avoid cross contamination. Every 8 hr is a common parameter for pin care schedule.

2. Identify information that should be included in client education regarding pin care.

Client education regarding pin care should include:

Method of cleansing and proper technique.

Application of dressing, if to be used.

Frequency of pin care.

Signs/symptoms that indicate immediate notification of the primary care provider (for example, infection and neurovascular compromise).

3. An 82-year-old client is admitted to the nursing unit with a diagnosis of right hip fracture. The client's surgery is scheduled for the following morning. What type of immobilization device and setup should the nurse anticipate will be used for this client preoperatively?

The nurse should anticipate the use of a Buck's traction, which is a boot applied to the lower part of the affected extremity. The boot is attached by rope to freely hanging weights. The nurse should also expect that there are orders regarding the type of traction, amount of weight, and whether or not traction can be removed for nursing care.

4. What are the nursing considerations for this client while awaiting surgery?

In general, the affected limb is kept elevated and ice is applied. Protruding bone is covered with a sterile dressing. The nurse should ensure that neurovascular and skin assessments are completed and documented per orders. Abnormal findings should be reported.

5. Match the terms below with the definitions provided.

__B__	Buck's traction	A. Splitting a cast along both sides to relieve pressure
__A__	Bivalve	B. A type of skin traction used after a hip injury
__D__	Halo traction	C. Using manual traction to realign fractured bones
__C__	Closed reduction	D. Skeletal traction used to immobilize the cervical spine
__E__	Cast	E. A circumferential immobilization device that cannot be removed by the client

6. List the six components of the neurovascular assessment and indicate which are early signs and which are late signs.

   Pain, Pallor, Paresthesia (Early)

   Pulselessness, Paralysis, Polar (Late)

7. A client had a cast applied 2 hr ago for a fractured left femur. Which of the following findings indicate the possibility of compartment syndrome? (Check all that apply.)

   _____ Toes cool to touch bilaterally.

   _____ Left toes are slightly edematous compared to right.

   __x__ Diminished left pedal pulses.

   __x__ Pain is unrelieved by second dose of oral narcotic.

   __x__ Inability to move toes on the left.

   Pain: Pain unrelieved by second dose of oral narcotic

   Paralysis: inability to move toes on the left

   Pulses: diminished left pedal pulses

Nursing Care of Clients with Musculoskeletal Disorders
Diagnostic and Therapeutic Procedures: Musculoskeletal

Chapter 99:   Joint Replacements
Contributor: Janey A. Roach, MSN, RN, ONC

↻ NCLEX-PN® Connections:

Learning Objective: Review and apply knowledge within "**Joint Replacements**" in readiness for performance of the following nursing activities as outlined by the NCLEX-PN® test plan:

Δ   Perform/assist with relevant laboratory, diagnostic, and therapeutic procedures within the nursing role, including:

- Preparation of the client for the procedure.

- Reinforcement of client teaching (before and following the procedure).

- Accurate collection of specimens.

- Monitoring procedure results (compare to norms) and appropriate notification of the primary care provider.

- Monitoring the client's response (expected, unexpected adverse response, comparison to baseline) to the procedure.

- Monitoring and taking actions, including reinforcing client teaching, to prevent or minimize the risk of complications.

- Recognizing signs of potential complications and reporting to the primary care provider.

- Recommending changes in the test/procedure as needed based on client findings.

Δ   Protect the client from injury.

Δ   Recognize the client's recovery from anesthesia, if used.

Δ   Monitor therapeutic devices (drainage/irrigating devices, chest tubes), if inserted, for proper functioning.

Key Points

Δ   **Arthroplasty** refers to the surgical removal of a diseased joint and replacement with prosthetics or artificial components made of metal and plastic.

Δ   The joints most commonly replaced include the hip and the knee.

Δ   The goal of joint replacement surgery is to eliminate pain, restore joint motions, and improve the client's functional status and quality of life.

Key Factors

Δ   **Risk Factors**

•   Degenerative disease (osteoarthritis, rheumatoid arthritis)

Δ   **Contraindications** of total joint arthroplasty include:

•   Recent or active infection.

•   Arterial impairment to the affected extremity.

•   The client's inability to follow the post-surgery regimen.

•   A co-morbid condition (for example, unstable cardiac or respiratory conditions).

Δ   The client's risk for **venous thromboembolism** should also be considered prior to joint replacement surgery (previous history, obesity, advanced age, use of medications that increase risk such as hormone replacement therapy, NSAIDs).

Diagnostic Procedures and Nursing Interventions

Δ   Preoperative

•   Complete blood count (CBC), urinalysis, electrolytes, BUN, creatinine: Assess "surgical readiness", baseline, and to rule out anemia, infection, or organ failure.

•   Chest x-ray: Rule out pulmonary surgical contraindications (infection, tumor).

•   EKG: Gather a baseline rhythm and to identify cardiovascular surgical contraindications (for example, dysrhythmia).

Therapeutic Procedures and Nursing Interventions

Δ   **Hip Joint Replacement**

•   Total hip arthroplasty involves the replacement of the acetabular cup, the femoral head, and the femoral stem.

- **Hemiarthroplasty** refers to half of a joint replacement. Fractures of the femoral neck can be treated with the replacement of the femoral component only.

- Provide preoperative **client education** regarding:

  ◊ Postoperative care (incentive spirometry, autotransfusion, surgical drains, dressing, pain control, transfer, exercises, activity limits).

  ◊ Autologous blood donation.

- Monitor for **bleeding**.

  ◊ Check the dressing site frequently, noting any evidence of bleeding. Monitor and record drainage from surgical drains (usually maintained for 48 hr post surgery).

  ◊ Postoperative salvage may be used during period of excess drainage (first 24 hr).

  ◊ Monitor daily laboratory values, including hemoglobin and hematocrit levels.

  ◊ Provide blood transfusions as prescribed (relatively common 1 to 2 days postoperatively for hemoglobin levels < 9 g/dL). Epoetin alfa (Procrit) is a preventive measure taken to reduce the need for postoperative blood transfusions.

  ◊ Monitor blood pressure and pulse for hypotension and loss of blood volume. Report alterations.

- Monitor **intake and output**. Report urinary output less than 30 mL/hr. A Foley catheter is usually inserted intraoperatively.

- Take actions to prevent and monitor for **infection**.

  ◊ Monitor vital signs (for example, temperature).

  ◊ Encourage turn, cough, deep breathe, and use of incentive spirometry. Turning sometimes is only permitted to one side.

  ◊ Monitor lung sounds.

  ◊ Monitor CBC results for evidence of infection (for example, elevation in WBC count).

  ◊ Monitor the wound site and perform surgical aseptic dressing changes (the surgeon usually performs initial dressing change).

- Provide **medications** as prescribed.

  ◊ Analgesics: Opioids (Epidural, PCA, IV, oral), NSAIDs

  ◊ IV antibiotic therapy: Prophylaxis preoperatively and for 48 hr post surgery

  ◊ Deep vein thrombosis (DVT) prophylaxis: Aspirin; low molecular weight heparin such as enoxaparin (Lovenox); warfarin (Coumadin)

- Early Ambulation

  ◊ **Transfer out of bed from unaffected side.**

  ◊ Weight-bearing status is determined by the orthopedic surgeon and by choice of cemented (usually partial/full weight-bearing as tolerated) versus non-cemented prostheses (usually only partial weight-bearing until after a few weeks of bone growth).

  ◊ Use of assistive devices (for example, walker).

- **Monitor for and intervene to prevent DVT.**

  ◊ Sequential compression devices (SCDs), thigh high stocking hose

  ◊ Leg exercises and early mobilization

  ◊ Monitor lower extremities for unilateral areas of erythema, warmth, tenderness, and/or edema.

  ◊ Avoid knee gatch.

  ◊ Do not massage legs.

- Use total hip precautions **to prevent dislocation.**

Do	Don't
Use elevated seating/raised toilet set.	Avoid flexion of hip > 90°.
Use straight chairs with arms.	Avoid low chairs.
Use an abduction pillow between legs while in bed (and with turning).	Do not cross legs.
Externally rotate toes.	Do not internally rotate toes.

  ◊ Client position: Supine with head slightly elevated with affected leg in neutral position and a pillow or abduction device between legs to prevent abduction (movement toward midline), which could cause hip dislocation.

  ◊ Arrange for raised toilet seats, extended handle items (shoehorn, dressing sticks).

- NANDA Nursing Diagnoses

  ◊ Ineffective peripheral tissue perfusion

  ◊ Acute pain

  ◊ Risk for infection

  ◊ Impaired mobility

  ◊ Risk for injury (hip dislocation)

  ◊ Deficient fluid volume

Δ **Knee Replacement Surgery**

- Total knee arthroplasty involves the replacement of the distal femoral component, the tibia plate, and the patellar button. Total knee arthroplasty is a surgical option when conservative measures fail. Dislocation is not common following total knee arthroplasty.

- Uni-condylar knee replacements are done when the client's joint may be diseased in one compartment of the joint.

- Bilateral total knee arthroplasty is done when the client suffers from severe osteoarthritis of both knees.

- **Positions of flexion of the knee are limited to avoid flexion contractures.** Avoid knee gatch and pillows placed behind the knee. Knee immobilizer may be used while in bed. The goal is for the client to be able to straight leg raise.

- Kneeling and deep knee bends are limited indefinitely.

- **Continuous passive motion (CPM)** is used to promote motion in the knee and prevent scar tissue formation.

Complications and Nursing Implications

Δ **Deep Vein Thrombosis resulting in Pulmonary Embolism** – Symptoms of pulmonary embolism include acute onset of dyspnea, tachycardia, and pleuritic chest pain. DVT prophylaxis includes pharmacological management, the use of anti-embolic stockings and sequential compression devices, ankle exercises while in bed, and early mobilization with physical and occupational therapy.

Δ **Hip Dislocation/Subluxation** (following total hip arthroplasty) – Symptoms include acute onset of pain, client's report of hearing "a pop", internal rotation of affected extremity, and shortened affected extremity. Since the muscle surrounding the hip joint has been cut to expose and replace the diseased joint, the client is at risk for hip dislocation. Abduction of affected leg and positions of extreme flexion are avoided to prevent hip dislocation.

Meeting the Needs of Older Adults

Δ The typical client population requiring total joint arthroplasty is over 65 years old.

Δ The older adult client is at a higher risk for medical complications related to chronic conditions including hypertension, diabetes, coronary artery disease, and obstructive pulmonary disease.

Δ Due to the age and potential inability to follow weight-bearing restrictions, cemented prostheses are used.

Δ Monitor pressure points for skin breakdown due to fragile skin.

Δ Monitor for orthostatic hypotension.

Δ   Reinforce coughing and deep breathing and incentive spirometer due to increased risk of pneumonia.

Δ   Anticipate pain as the older adult client may be unable to verbalize or fears addiction.

Primary Reference:

Ignatavicius, D. D., & Workman, M. L. (2006). *Medical-surgical nursing* (5th ed.). St. Louis, MO: Saunders.

Additional Resources:

Maher, A. B., Salmond, S. W., & Pellino, T. A. (2002). *Orthopaedic nursing* (3rd ed.). Philadelphia: Saunders.

NANDA International (2004). *NANDA nursing diagnoses: Definitions and classification 2005-2006*. Philadelphia: NANDA.

Chapter 99: Joint Replacements

Application Exercises

Scenario: A 55-year-old client is undergoing a total hip arthroplasty.

1. What are the potential complications of this surgery for this client?

2. The client is aware that there will be activity restrictions after the surgery. Which of the following should be included in the teaching plan? (Check all that apply.)

    _____   Avoid hip flexion greater than 90°

    _____   Sit in low chairs

    _____   Avoid external rotation of toes

    _____   Use an abduction pillow while in bed

    _____   Continue isometric exercises

3. Which of the following is a contraindication for total joint replacement surgery?

A. Age greater than 70 years

B. History of cancer

C. Previous joint replacement surgery

D. Recent infection

4. Upon arrival to the orthopedic unit from the postanesthesia care unit, which of the following are the priority nursing interventions for a client who had a total hip arthroplasty? (Check all that apply.)

    _____   Vital signs

    _____   Postoperative dressing and drain assessment

    _____   Pain management

    _____   Removal of Foley catheter

    _____   Removal of thigh high stockings

    _____   Initiate continuous passive motion (CPM) machine

5. Outline a discharge teaching plan for a client going home after having total hip replacement surgery.

Chapter 99: Joint Replacements

Application Exercises Answer Key

Scenario: A 55-year-old client is undergoing a total hip arthroplasty.

1. What are the potential complications of this surgery for this client?

   DVT – the leading complication of total joint replacement surgery

   Infection – due to metal implant

   Hip dislocation – due to muscle incised and moved to replace the diseased joint

   Joint revision – due to the loosening of the cement or potential infection

   Hypotension – due to blood loss from surgery and being NPO

2. The client is aware that there will be activity restrictions after the surgery. Which of the following should be included in the teaching plan? (Check all that apply.)

__x__	Avoid hip flexion greater than 90°
_____	Sit in low chairs
_____	Avoid external rotation of toes
__x__	Use an abduction pillow while in bed
_____	Continue isometric exercises

   Total hip precautions will need to be addressed with the client. The client will need to avoid hip flexion greater than 90°. This could cause hip dislocation. The client needs to avoid low chairs (which will flex the hip more than 90°), sit in higher chairs with arms, and use an elevated toilet seat. The client should be instructed not to cross his legs or internally rotate the affected hip. While in bed, the client should use an abduction pillow. The client should continue to use the abduction pillow while in bed to avoid crossing his legs while sleeping.

3. Which of the following is a contraindication for total joint replacement surgery?

> A. Age greater than 70 years
> B. History of cancer
> C. Previous joint replacement surgery
> **D. Recent infection**

Recent infection, inability to follow postoperative regimen, and arterial impairment to the involved extremity are all contraindications for total joint replacement surgery.

4. Upon arrival to the orthopedic unit from the postanesthesia care unit, which of the following are the priority nursing interventions for a client who had a total hip arthroplasty? (Check all that apply.)

> __x__   Vital signs
> __x__   Postoperative dressing and drain assessment
> __x__   Pain management
> _____   Removal of Foley catheter
> _____   Removal of thigh high stockings
> _____   Initiate continuous passive motion (CPM) machine

Monitoring for evidence of bleeding and hypotension is essential, as is effective pain management (epidural, PCA opioids). A Foley catheter is appropriate for assessing output, renal function, and to reduce the risk of hip dislocation. Thigh high stockings are used to prevent DVT (high risk following hip surgery). CPM is used postoperatively for knee replacement surgery.

5. Outline a discharge teaching plan for a client going home after having total hip replacement surgery.

The client should continue to wear thigh high stockings until the follow-up visit with surgeon. The client should continue to take medications (for example, an anticoagulant) as prescribed by the provider. Monitor for unexpected bleeding. Early and regular ambulation is needed. Teach the client and family the signs/symptoms of DVT, including redness, pain, induration, and warmth in the calf. Notify the provider if symptoms should occur.

Unit 9

Nursing Care of Clients with Musculoskeletal Disorders

Section:

Nursing Care of Clients with Select Musculoskeletal Disorders

Chapter 100:   Fractures

Contributor: Janey A. Roach, MSN, RN, ONC

NCLEX-PN® Connections:

Learning Objective: Review and apply knowledge within "**Fractures**" in readiness for performance of the following nursing activities as outlined by the NCLEX-PN® test plan:

Δ   Assist with relevant laboratory, diagnostic, and therapeutic procedures within the nursing role, including:

   • Preparation of the client for the procedure.

   • Accurate collection of specimens.

   • Monitoring client status during and after the procedure.

   • Reinforcing client teaching (before and following the procedure).

   • Recognizing the client's response (expected, unexpected adverse response) to the procedure.

   • Monitoring results.

   • Monitoring and taking actions to prevent or minimize the risk of complications.

   • Notifying the primary care provider of signs of complications.

Δ   Protect the client from injury.

Δ   Recognize signs and symptoms of the client's problem and complete the proper documentation.

Δ   Provide and document care based on the client's health alteration.

Δ   Monitor and document vital signs changes.

Δ   Interpret data that need to be reported immediately.

Δ   Reinforce client education on managing the client's health problem.

Δ   Recognize and respond to emergency situations, including notification of the primary care provider.

Δ   Review the client's response to emergency interventions and complete the proper documentation.

Δ   Provide care that meets the age-related needs of clients 65 years of age or older, including recognizing expected physiological changes.

📖 **Key Points**

Δ   A fracture is **a break or disruption in the continuity of a bone.**

Δ   A **closed, or simple, fracture** does not break through the skin surface. An **open, or compound, fracture** disrupts the skin integrity, causing an open wound with a risk of infection.

Δ   Open fractures are graded based upon the extent of tissue injury.

- **Grade I** – minimal skin damage

- **Grade II** – damage includes skin and muscles contusions

- **Grade III** – damage to skin, muscles, nerves, and blood vessels

Δ   A **complete fracture** goes through the entire bone dividing it into two parts. An **incomplete fracture** goes through part of the bone.

Δ   **Common Fractures Sites**

- Upper Extremity: Clavicle, scapula, humerus, olecranon, radius, ulna, wrist, hand

- Lower Extremity: Intracapsular (within the joint) hip fracture, extracapsular (outside the joint) hip fracture, femur, patella, tibia, fibula, ankle, foot

- Trunk: Spine (compression), rib, sternum, pelvis

Δ   **Common Types of Fractures**

- Displaced: Bone fragments are not in alignment

- Non-displaced: Bone fragments remain in alignment

- Comminuted: Bone is fragmented

- Oblique: Fracture occurs at oblique angle

- Spiral: Fracture occurs from twisting motion (common with physical abuse)

- Impacted: Fractured bone is wedged inside opposite fractured fragment

- Greenstick: Fracture in only one cortex of bone

- Pathological: Fracture resulting from a tumor or lesion that has weakened the bone

- Segmented: Fracture resulting in two or more bone pieces (segments)

Key Factors

Δ   **Risk Factors**

- Osteoporosis

- Falls

- Motor vehicle crashes

- Substance abuse

- Diseases (bone cancer, Paget's disease)

- Contact sports and hazardous recreational activities (football, skiing)

- Physical abuse

Diagnostic Procedures and Nursing Interventions

Δ   Use x-ray, computed tomography (CT) imaging scan, and/or magnetic resonance imagery (MRI).

Δ   Identify type of fracture and location.

Δ   Indicate pathological fracture resulting from tumor or mass.

Δ   Determine soft tissue damage.

Δ   Bone scan is used to determine fracture complications/delayed healing.

Therapeutic Procedures and Nursing Interventions

Δ   **Immobilization** with cast, splint, or traction. (*For information, refer to chapter 98, Immobilizing Interventions: Casts, Splints, and Traction.*)

Δ   **Operative Procedures**

- Open Reduction Internal Fixation (ORIF)

◊   Method used to reduce and immobilize fracture.

◊   Open reduction refers to direct visualization of the fracture site and realignment of the bone.

◊   Internal fixation refers to the use of metal pins, screws, rods, plates, or prostheses to immobilize the fracture during healing.

◊   After the bone heals, the hardware may be removed depending on the location and type of hardware.

- External Fixation (*For information, refer to chapter 98, Immobilizing Interventions: Casts, Splints, and Traction.*)

- Bone Grafting

◊   Involves utilizing chips of bone taken from the client's iliac crest bone graft (or other site) and then packing or wiring the chips to the bone ends to facilitate bone growth. Bone allografts from a cadaver may be used.

Assessments

Δ   Monitor for **signs and symptoms.**

- Crepitus: A grating sound created by the rubbing of bone fragments

- Deformity: May observe internal rotation of extremity, shortened extremity, visible bone with open fracture

- Muscle spasms: Occur from the pulling forces of the bone when not aligned

- Edema: Swelling from trauma

- Ecchymosis: Bleeding into underlying soft tissues from trauma

Δ **Assess/Monitor**

- History of trauma, metabolic bone disorders, chronic conditions (using steroid therapy)

- Neurovascular assessment:

Neurovascular Components	Early or Late Sign	Assessment Parameters	Client Teaching / Symptoms to Report
Pain	Early	Assess area involved using 0 to 10 rating scale: 0 = no pain 10 = worse pain imaginable	Increasing **pain not relieved** with elevation or pain medication
Paresthesia	Early	Assess for numbness/tingling, pins and needles sensation: Should be absent.	**Numbness or tingling**, pins and needles sensation
Pallor	Early	Assess capillary refill. Brisk = less than 3 seconds	**Increased capillary refill time > 3 seconds**, blue fingers or toes
Polar	Late	Assess skin temperature by touch: Warm Cool	**Cool/cold** fingers or toes
Paralysis	Late	Assess mobility: Moves fingers or toes Able to plantar dorsiflex the ankle area not involved or restricted by cast	**Unable to move** fingers or toes
Pulses	Late	Assess pulse(s) distal to injury: Pulse is palpable and strong	**Weak** palpable pulses, **unable to palpate** pulses, pulse detected only with Doppler

NANDA Nursing Diagnoses

Δ Risk for peripheral neurovascular dysfunction

Δ Acute pain

Δ Risk for infection

Δ Impaired physical mobility

Nursing Interventions

Δ **Preoperative Nursing Care**

- First address life-threatening complications of injury.
  - ◊ Maintain ABCs.
  - ◊ Monitor vital signs.
  - ◊ Monitor neurological status.
  - ◊ Digital pressure to proximal artery nearest to fracture.
  - ◊ Position the client in supine position.
  - ◊ Keep the client warm.

- Risk for impaired skin integrity (pressure points if in traction)
  - ◊ Monitor pressure points (sacrum, heels, ankles, back).
  - ◊ Perform range of motion (ROM) to unaffected joints to prevent contracture (fracture to hip requires ROM to ankles/toes).

- Risk for hypovolemic shock
  - ◊ Assess organs near fracture site (pelvic fracture – assess abdomen, bladder for bleeding).
  - ◊ Monitor vital signs.
  - ◊ Monitor intake and output.
  - ◊ Promote hydration (IV therapy).
  - ◊ Keep the client in supine position.

- Stabilization of injured area (*For information, refer to chapter 98, Immobilizing Interventions: Casts, Splints, and Traction.*)

- Risk of peripheral vascular dysfunction
  - ◊ Perform neurovascular assessment.

- Risk for compartment syndrome
  - ◊ Perform neurovascular assessment.
  - ◊ Assess pain on passive stretch.
  - ◊ Do not elevate extremity further to avoid further ischemia.
  - ◊ Loosen bandage or immobilizer/bivalve cast.

- Pain
  - ◊ Assess on scale of 0 to 10.
  - ◊ Provide analgesics and assess relief.
  - ◊ Position for comfort.

- Impaired skin integrity (open fractures or fracture blisters)
  ◊ Monitor vital signs.
  ◊ Monitor laboratory values – white blood cell (WBC) count, erythrocyte sedimentation rate (ESR).
  ◊ Provide aseptic wound care.

Δ **Postoperative Nursing Care**

- Risk for peripheral vascular compromise
  ◊ Perform neurovascular assessment.

- Acute pain
  ◊ Assess on scale of 0 to 10.
  ◊ Provide analgesics and/or antispasmodics and assess relief.
  ◊ Position for comfort.

- Risk for infection
  ◊ Monitor vital signs.
  ◊ Monitor laboratory values (WBC, ESR).
  ◊ Provide surgical aseptic wound care.

- Impaired physical mobility
  ◊ Consult physical and occupational therapy for ambulation and activities of daily living (ADLs).
  ◊ Monitor orthostatic blood pressure when getting out of bed for the first time.
  ◊ Turn and position every 2 hr.
  ◊ Get out of bed from the unaffected side.
  ◊ Position for comfort (within restrictions).

- Imbalanced nutrition
  ◊ Encourage increased calorie intake.
  ◊ Ensure use of calcium supplements.
  ◊ Encourage small, frequent meals with snacks.
  ◊ Monitor for constipation.

Complications and Nursing Implications

Δ **Compartment syndrome** occurs when pressure within one or more of the muscle compartments of the extremity compromises circulation resulting in an ischemia–edema cycle. Capillaries dilate in an attempt to pull oxygen into the tissue. Increased capillary permeability from the release of histamine leads to edema from plasma proteins leaking into the interstitial fluid space. Increased edema causes pressure on the nerve endings resulting in pain. Blood flow is further reduced and ischemia persists resulting in compromised neurovascular status.

- Pressure can result from **external sources**, such as a tight cast or a constrictive bulky dressing.

- **Internal sources**, such as an accumulation of blood or fluid within the muscle compartment, can cause pressure as well.

- **Symptoms** include:

  ◊ Increased **pain unrelieved with elevation**, intense pain on passive stretch.

  ◊ Paresthesia.

  ◊ Color of tissue pales (pallor).

- If untreated, tissue **necrosis** can result. Neuromuscular damage occurs within 4 to 6 hr.

- **Prevention** includes:

  ◊ Cutting the cast on one side (univalve) or both sides (bivalve). (*For information, refer to chapter 98, Immobilizing Interventions: Casts, Splints, and Traction.*)

  ◊ Loosening the constrictive dressing or cutting the bandage or tape.

- Compartment pressure is monitored with a handheld device or with a catheter connected to a transducer. **Normal compartmental pressure is 0 to 8 mm Hg.** Clinical manifestations (evolving neurovascular compromise) and compartmental pressure readings greater than 8 mm Hg are used to indicate an emergent need for a fasciotomy.

- Surgical treatment is a **fasciotomy**.

  ◊ A surgical incision is made through the subcutaneous tissue and fascia of the affected compartment to relieve the pressure and restore circulation.

  ◊ After the fasciotomy, the open wounds require sterile packings and dressings until secondary closure occurs. Skin grafts may be necessary.

- **Complications** of compartment syndrome include infection from tissue necrosis, persistent motor weakness or contracture from injured nerves, and myoglobinuric renal failure from muscle tissue breakdown (rhabdomyolysis). Injured muscle tissue releases myoglobin, which can occlude the distal tubules resulting in acute renal failure.

Δ **Shock** can occur as bone trauma may lead to hemorrhage.

Δ **Fat embolism** can occur, usually within 48 hr following long bone fractures. Fat globules from the bone marrow are released into the vasculature and travel to the small blood vessels including those in the lungs resulting in acute respiratory insufficiency. Careful diagnosis should differentiate between fat embolism and pulmonary embolism.

- Clinical manifestations include:

  ◊ **Altered mental status** related to low arterial oxygen level (earliest sign).

  ◊ Respiratory distress.

  ◊ Tachycardia.

  ◊ Tachypnea.

  ◊ Fever.

  ◊ Cutaneous petechiae – flat red marks that occur on the neck, chest, upper arms, and abdomen (from the blockage of the capillaries by the fat globules).

- Treatment includes adequate splinting following fracture, bedrest and hydration to avoid hypovolemic shock, analgesia, oxygenation, and blood transfusion.

Δ **Deep vein thrombosis** is the most common complication following trauma, surgery, or disability related to immobility.

Δ **Osteomyelitis** – inflammation within the bone secondary to penetration of organisms (trauma, surgery).

- Signs and symptoms

  ◊ **Bone pain that is worse with movement.**

  ◊ Initially, erythema, edema, and fever may occur.

- Diagnostic procedures

  ◊ Definitive diagnosis is with a bone biopsy.

  ◊ Cultures performed for detection of possible aerobic and anaerobic organisms.

- Treatment

  ◊ **Long course (for example, 3 months) of IV and oral antibiotic therapy.**

  ◊ Surgical debridement may also be indicated.

  ◊ Unsuccessful treatment can result in amputation.

Δ **Avascular necrosis** results from the circulatory compromise that occurs after a fracture. Blood flow is disrupted to the fracture site and the resulting ischemia leads to tissue (bone) necrosis.

Δ **Failure of Fracture to Heal**

- **Delayed Union**: Fracture that has not healed within 6 months of injury (treatment is to find and correct the cause)

- **Nonunion**: Fracture that never heals (electrical bone stimulation and bone grafting can be used to treat nonunion)

- **Malunion**: Fracture heals incorrectly

Meeting the Needs of Older Adults

Δ Bone healing is affected by age.

Δ Postmenopausal women who lose estrogen are unable to form strong new bone.

Δ Chronic conditions such as peripheral vascular disease (arterial insufficiency) or poor nutrition affect the client's ability to form new bone. Adequate amounts of calcium, phosphorous, protein, and vitamin D are essential in the production of new bone.

Δ Surgical repair of hip fractures is becoming the most common surgical procedure for clients over the age of 85.

Primary Reference:

Ignatavicius, D. D., & Workman, M. L. (2006). *Medical-surgical nursing* (5th ed.). St. Louis, MO: Saunders.

Additional Resources:

NANDA International (2004). *NANDA nursing diagnoses: Definitions and classification 2005-2006*. Philadelphia: NANDA.

Maher, A. B., Salmond, S. W., & Pellino, T. A. (2002). *Orthopaedic nursing* (3rd ed.). Philadelphia: Saunders.

Chapter 100: Fractures

Application Exercises

Scenario: A pedestrian is struck by a car and sustains a leg injury.

1. What is the initial action that should be taken by the witnesses?

2. Upon admission to the emergency department, it is observed that the injured leg is painful, swollen, ecchymotic, and is shorter than the other leg. Are these findings consistent with a fracture? Explain why or why not.

3. The client reports continued and increasing pain not relieved with pain medication or elevation following the application of a long leg cast. What complication may be occurring with this client?

4. What is the priority nursing intervention?

5. Why was the pain not relieved with elevation?

6. The nurse should monitor for which client findings suggestive of the possibility of a fat embolism?

7. If the client develops a fat embolism, the nurse should plan to assist with which of the following therapies? (Check all that apply.)

    _____   Administration of antihypertensives

    _____   Administration of glucocorticosteroids

    _____   Intubation

    _____   Mechanical ventilation with positive end expiratory pressure (PEEP)

    _____   Administration of anticoagulants

Chapter 100: Fractures

Application Exercises Answer Key

Scenario: A pedestrian is struck by a car and sustains a leg injury.

1. What is the initial action that should be taken by the witnesses?

   Call for help and immobilize the leg prior to moving the client.

2. Upon admission to the emergency department, it is observed that the injured leg is painful, swollen, ecchymotic, and is shorter than the other leg. Are these findings consistent with a fracture? Explain why or why not.

   These findings are consistent with fracture, particularly the shortened extremity.

3. The client reports continued and increasing pain not relieved with pain medication or elevation following the application of a long leg cast. What complication may be occurring with this client?

   Compartment syndrome

4. What is the priority nursing intervention?

   Notify the primary care provider.

5. Why was the pain not relieved with elevation?

   Pain is not relieved because elevation causes further ischemia (lack or oxygen to the tissues).

6. The nurse should monitor for which client findings suggestive of the possibility of a fat embolism?

Petechiae, altered mental status, respiratory distress including tachypnea, tachycardia

7. If the client develops a fat embolism, the nurse should plan to assist with which of the following therapies? (Check all that apply.)

_____	Administration of antihypertensives
__X__	Administration of glucocorticosteroids
__X__	Intubation
__X__	Mechanical ventilation with positive end expiratory pressure (PEEP)
_____	Administration of anticoagulants

Fat embolism poses a risk for hypotension. Fat embolisms are not composed of blood clots; therefore, anticoagulants are not indicated. Respiratory failure secondary to fat embolism is a serious risk; therefore, intubation and mechanical ventilation are likely. Corticosteroids can treat the inflammatory reactions within the lung.

Unit 9   Nursing Care of Clients with Musculoskeletal Disorders

Section: Nursing Care of Clients with Select Musculoskeletal Disorders

Chapter 101:   Amputation

Contributor: Janey A. Roach, MSN, RN, ONC

⟳ NCLEX-PN® Connections:

Learning Objective: Review and apply knowledge within "**Amputation**" in readiness for performance of the following nursing activities as outlined by the NCLEX-PN® test plan:

Δ   Assist with relevant laboratory, diagnostic, and therapeutic procedures within the nursing role, including:

- Preparation of the client for the procedure.
- Accurate collection of specimens.
- Monitoring client status during and after the procedure.
- Reinforcing client teaching (before and following the procedure).
- Recognizing the client's response (expected, unexpected adverse response) to the procedure.
- Monitoring results.
- Monitoring and taking actions to prevent or minimize the risk of complications.
- Notifying the primary care provider of signs of complications.

Δ   Protect the client from injury.

Δ   Recognize signs and symptoms of the client's problem and complete the proper documentation.

Δ   Provide and document care based on the client's health alteration.

Δ   Monitor and document vital signs changes.

Δ   Interpret data that need to be reported immediately.

Δ   Reinforce client education on managing the client's health problem.

Δ   Recognize and respond to emergency situations, including notification of the primary care provider.

Δ   Review the client's response to emergency interventions and complete the proper documentation.

Δ   Provide care that meets the age-related needs of clients 65 years of age or older, including recognizing expected physiological changes.

Key Points

Δ   Amputation has both **physical and psychological nursing implications** related to the loss of a body part, most commonly an extremity.

Δ   **Disarticulation** is an amputation through the joint.

Δ   **Upper extremity amputations** include:

- Above the elbow amputation.

- Below the elbow amputation.

- Wrist disarticulation.

- Shoulder disarticulation.

- Finger amputation.

Δ   **Lower extremity amputations** include:

- Hip disarticulation.

- Above the knee amputation.

- Knee disarticulation.

- Below the knee amputation.

- Syme amputation (removal of the foot).

- Transmetatarsal amputation.

- Toe amputation.

- Ray amputation (removal of the toe and metatarsal).

Key Factors

Δ   **Indications** include:

- **Acute disease process**
  - ◊   Traumatic injury
  - ◊   Thermal injury (frostbite, electrocution, burns)
  - ◊   Peripheral vascular disease
  - ◊   Trauma
  - ◊   Malignancy

- **Chronic disease process**
  - ◊   Peripheral vascular disease resulting in ischemia/gangrene
  - ◊   Diabetes mellitus resulting in peripheral neuropathy leading to pressure ulcers

◊ Infection (osteomyelitis)

◊ Metabolic disorders

Diagnostic Procedures and Nursing Interventions

Δ **Testing Circulation: Invasive**

- **Angiography** – dye is injected into arteries for visualization of vessels. Does not provide a reliable prediction of healing after surgery.

Δ **Testing Circulation: Noninvasive**

- **Ankle-brachial index** – measuring the ratio of the ankle systolic blood pressure (SBP) to the brachial SBP. In a healthy client, the ankle SBP should be the same or slightly higher than the brachial SBP.

- **Doppler ultrasound** – using ultrasound to verify venous blood flow.

- **Transcutaneous oxygen pressure** – measuring oxygen pressure, which indicates blood flow to the limb.

Therapeutic Procedures and Nursing Interventions

Δ **Surgical Amputation Techniques**

- **Closed amputation** – the most common technique, allowing the skin flap to close the site.

- **Open amputation** – used with active infection, allowing the skin to be closed at a later date.

- Reconstructive/plastic surgery may be necessary.

Assessments

Δ **Assess/Monitor**

- Tissue perfusion (pink in light-skinned individuals, not discolored in dark-skinned individuals)

- Pain (phantom limb versus stump)

- Mobility

- Signs of infection

- Client's perception and feelings regarding amputation of body part

- Coping

- Prosthesis fit

Δ   Neurovascular Assessment

Neurovascular Components	Early or Late Sign	Assessment Parameters	Client Teaching / Symptoms to Report
Pain	Early	Assess area involved using 0 to 10 rating scale: 0 = no pain 10 = worst pain imaginable	Increasing **pain not relieved** with elevation or pain medication
Paresthesia	Early	Assess for numbness/tingling, pins and needles sensation: Should be absent.	**Numbness or tingling,** pins and needles sensation
Pallor	Early	Assess capillary refill. Brisk = Less than 3 seconds	**Increased capillary refill time > 3 seconds,** blue fingers or toes
Polar	Late	Assess skin temperature by touch: Warm Cool	**Cool/cold** fingers or toes
Paralysis	Late	Assess mobility: Moves fingers or toes Able to plantar dorsiflex the ankle area not involved or restricted by cast	**Unable to move** fingers or toes
Pulses	Late	Assess pulse(s) distal to injury: Pulse is palpable and strong	**Weak** palpable pulses, **unable to palpate** pulses, pulse detected only with Doppler

NANDA Nursing Diagnoses

Δ   Impaired physical mobility

Δ   Acute pain

Δ   Ineffective peripheral tissue perfusion

Δ   Impaired skin integrity

Δ   Disturbed body image

Δ   Ineffective coping

Δ   Anticipatory grieving

Nursing Interventions

Δ Assess **pain** characteristics on a scale of 0 to 10. Administer analgesics.

Δ Position the affected extremity in dependent position to promote blood flow/oxygenation.

Δ Consult a certified prosthetic orthotist for assessment and planning for prosthetic training.

Δ Consult physical therapy for upper extremity strengthening.

Δ Shape and shrink the residual limb in preparation for prosthetic training.

  - Stump shrinkage is done to decrease edema and to protect and shape the stump.

  - **Shrinkage interventions** include:

    ◊ Wrap the stump, using ace bandages (figure eight wrap) to prevent restriction of blood flow.

    ◊ Utilize a stump shrinker sock (easier for the client to apply).

    ◊ Use an air splint (plastic inflatable device) inflated to 20 to 22 mm Hg for 22 of 24 hr/day.

Δ Inspect area for signs and symptoms of infection. Administer antimicrobials.

Δ Record characteristics of drainage.

Δ Allow for the client/family to grieve for the loss of the body part and the potential loss of self-care activities.

Complications and Nursing Implications

Δ **Phantom Limb Pain** – the sensation of pain from the affected extremity following the amputation. This is related to severed nerve pathways and is a frequent complication in clients who experience chronic limb pain prior to the amputation. Phantom limb pain occurs less frequently following traumatic amputation. The nurse should recognize the pain is real and manage it accordingly. It may be described as deep and burning, cramping, shooting, or aching. Symptoms may be managed with various medications (opioids, antispasmodics, antiepileptics, beta blockers).

Δ **Flexion Contractures** – can occur in the hip or knee joint following amputation due to improper positioning. Prevention includes range-of-motion (ROM) exercises and proper positioning (avoid elevating the stump on a pillow after the first 24 hr, have client lie prone).

Δ **Hemorrhage** – acute trauma can lead to the severing of major blood vessels.

Δ   **Inadequate Circulation** – monitor the distal end of the residual limb to ensure proper healing of the incision without further breakdown. Monitor the client's neurovascular status.

Meeting the Needs of Older Adults

Δ   The older adult client has a higher risk of peripheral vascular disease and diabetes mellitus resulting in ischemia and peripheral neuropathy. Both conditions place the older adult client at risk for lower extremity amputation. These clients also have visual, cardiac, and kidney problems.

Δ   Older adult clients are poor candidates for prosthetic training due to the amount of energy required for ambulation.

Primary Reference:

Ignatavicius, D. D., & Workman, M. L. (2006). *Medical-surgical nursing* (5th ed.). St. Louis, MO: Saunders.

Additional Resources:

NANDA International (2004). *NANDA nursing diagnoses: Definitions and classification 2005-2006*. Philadelphia: NANDA.

Maher, A. B., Salmond, S. W., & Pellino, T. A. (2002). *Orthopaedic nursing* (3rd ed.). Philadelphia: Saunders.

Chapter 101: Amputation

Application Exercises

Scenario: A 24-year-old man is 12 hr postoperative below-the-knee amputation of his right leg as treatment for osteogenic sarcoma. The gauze and elastic dressings are dry and intact. His vital signs are stable and he is controlling his pain by self-administration of morphine sulfate through a patient-controlled analgesic pump.

1. Should the nurse elevate the client's stump on a pillow? Explain.

2. What postoperative measures should be provided to avoid hip or knee flexion contractures?

3. What postoperative assessments does the nurse need to make on a regular basis for the next few days?

4. The client reports that he is experiencing pain in the foot that is no longer there. How can the nurse best explain this phenomenon to the client?

5. The client is withdrawn and refuses to look at his stump when the dressings are being changed. What can the nurse do to support the client's grief process?

Chapter 101: Amputation

Application Exercises Answer Key

Scenario: A 24-year-old man is 12 hr postoperative below-the-knee amputation of his right leg as treatment for osteogenic sarcoma. The gauze and elastic dressings are dry and intact. His vital signs are stable and he is controlling his pain by self-administration of morphine sulfate through a patient-controlled analgesic pump.

1. Should the nurse elevate the client's stump on a pillow? Explain.

   Elevation of the stump prevents fluid accumulation in the stump, relieving pain due to swelling and facilitating healing of the stump incision and underlying structures. Elevation in the first 24 hr is generally accepted. However, to prevent flexion contractures, elevation on pillows after the first 24 hr is not encouraged.

2. What postoperative measures should be provided to avoid hip or knee flexion contractures?

   Encourage range-of-motion exercises and instruct the client to lie in a prone position.

3. What postoperative assessments does the nurse need to make on a regular basis for the next few days?

   Presence and amount of drainage (especially bloody drainage); indications of infection (foul odor, purulent drainage, increased pain, fever); presence of stump swelling; pain and response to pain measures; the client's ability and willingness to participate in self care; and indications of situational depression or ineffective individual coping.

4. The client reports that he is experiencing pain in the foot that is no longer there. How can the nurse best explain this phenomenon to the client?

   Explain that he is experiencing phantom pain related to severed nerve pathways. The pain often mimics preoperative pain in the limb and usually subsides with time. Phantom pain may be described as deep and burning, cramping, shooting, or aching. The nurse should encourage the client to use his pain medication to relieve phantom pain.

5. The client is withdrawn and refuses to look at his stump when the dressings are being changed. What can the nurse do to support the client's grief process?

Encourage the client to verbalize his fears, concerns, and possible lifestyle changes; demonstrate acceptance; offer emotional support; explain all procedures using simple explanations that are easily understood; encourage him to examine his strengths; encourage him to participate in his own care when he demonstrates interest.

Unit 9   Nursing Care of Clients with Musculoskeletal Disorders
Section: Nursing Care of Clients with Select Musculoskeletal Disorders

Chapter 102:   Osteoporosis
Contributor: Janey A. Roach, MSN, RN, ONC

NCLEX-PN® Connections:

Learning Objective: Review and apply knowledge within "**Osteoporosis**" in readiness for performance of the following nursing activities as outlined by the NCLEX-PN® test plan:

Δ   Assist with relevant laboratory, diagnostic, and therapeutic procedures within the nursing role, including:

- Preparation of the client for the procedure.
- Accurate collection of specimens.
- Monitoring client status during and after the procedure.
- Reinforcing client teaching (before and following the procedure).
- Recognizing the client's response (expected, unexpected adverse response) to the procedure.
- Monitoring results.
- Monitoring and taking actions to prevent or minimize the risk of complications.
  - Notifying the primary care provider of signs of complications.

Δ   Recognize signs and symptoms of the client's problem and complete the proper documentation.

Δ   Provide and document care based on the client's health alteration.

Δ   Monitor and document vital signs changes.

Δ   Interpret data that need to be reported immediately.

Δ   Reinforce client education on managing the client's health problem.

Δ   Recognize and respond to emergency situations, including notification of the primary care provider.

Δ   Review the client's response to emergency interventions and complete the proper documentation.

Δ   Provide care that meets the age-related needs of clients 65 years of age or older, including recognizing expected physiological changes.

Key Points

Δ Osteoporosis is the **most common metabolic bone disorder resulting in low bone density**. Osteoporosis occurs when the rate of bone resorption (osteoclast cells) exceeds the rate of bone formation (osteoblast cells) resulting in fragile bone tissue and subsequent fractures.

Δ **Osteopenia**, the precursor to osteoporosis, refers to low bone mineral density for what is expected for the person's age and sex.

Δ Peak bone mineral density occurs between the ages of 30 to 35 years. After peak years, **bone density decreases, rapidly in postmenopausal women due to estrogen loss.**

Δ Fragile, thin bone tissue is **susceptible to fracture**.

Key Factors

Δ **Risk Factors**

- Age over 60
- Postmenopausal estrogen deficiency
- Family history
- Thin, lean body build
- History of low calcium intake with suboptimal levels of vitamin D
- History of smoking
- History of high alcohol intake
- Lack of physical activity/prolonged immobility

Δ **Secondary osteoporosis** results from medical conditions including:

- Hyperparathyroidism.
- Long-term **corticosteroid use** (for example, asthma).
- Long-term immobility (for example, spinal cord injury).

Diagnostic Procedures and Nursing Interventions

Δ **Radiographs** of the spine and long bones reveal low bone density and fractures.

Δ **Dual energy x-ray absorptiometry (DEXA)** is used to screen for early changes in bone density. This painless test measures bone mineral density in the wrist, hip, and vertebral column.

Δ Serum calcium, vitamin D, phosphorus, and alkaline phosphatase levels are drawn to rule out other metabolic bone diseases (Paget's disease or osteomalacia).

Assessments

Δ Monitor for **signs and symptoms**.

- Thoracic kyphosis
- Reduced height (postmenopausal)
- Acute back pain after lifting or bending (worse with activity, relieved by rest)
- Restricted movement
- **Fractures**
- Fear of falling

NANDA Nursing Diagnoses

Δ Impaired mobility

Δ Imbalanced nutrition: Less than body requirement

Δ Risk for falls

Δ Ineffective health maintenance

Nursing Interventions

Δ   Administer medications as prescribed.

Classification	Medication	Nursing Considerations
Estrogen Hormone Supplement	Premarin, Prempro	Instruct on potential complications including breast and endometrial cancers and deep vein thrombosis (DVT). Reinforce monthly self breast exam.
Selective Estrogen Receptor Modulators	Evista	Avoid for clients with a history of DVT.
Calcium Supplement	Os-Cal, Caltrate-600, Citracal	Give with food in divided doses with 6 to 8 oz of water. May cause GI upset. Monitor for kidney stones.
Bisphosphonates (inhibit bone resorption)	Fosamax, Boniva, Actonel	Risk for esophagitis. Take in the early morning before eating with 8 oz water; remain upright for 30 min.
Thyroid Hormone	Calcitonin	Can be taken IM/SC or nasally; alternate nostrils.

Δ   Instruct the client and family regarding dietary calcium food sources.

Δ   Provide information regarding calcium supplementation (take with food).

Δ   Instruct the client of the need for adequate amounts of protein, magnesium, vitamin K, and other trace minerals needed for bone formation.

Δ   Reinforce the need for exposure to vitamin D (sunlight, fortified milk).

Δ   Assess the home environment for safety (remove throw rugs, adequate lighting, clear walkways).

Δ   Reinforce the use of safety equipment and assistive devices.

Δ   Instruct the client to avoid inclement weather (ice or slippery surfaces).

Δ   Clearly mark thresholds, doorways, and steps.

Δ   Prevention

•   Teach the importance of regular, weight-bearing exercises.

•   Introduce the importance of calcium intake to children to improve peak bone mass. Strong adult skeletons are built during childhood.

Complications and Nursing Implications

Δ   **Fractures** are the leading complication of osteoporosis. Early recognition and treatment is essential. The nurse should review risk factors for osteoporosis and falls, assess the client's dietary intake of calcium, reinforce daily exercise including weight-bearing activities, and ensure proper screening with a DEXA scan.

Meeting the Needs of Older Adults

Δ   Primary osteoporosis most frequently occurs in postmenopausal women.

Δ   The older adult client has an increased risk of falls related to decreased mobility, generalized weakness, and impaired vision and hearing. Orthostatic hypotension, urinary frequency, or confusion – which are common side effects of long-term medications used to treat chronic health conditions – can increase the client's risks for falls.

Primary Reference:

Ignatavicius, D. D., & Workman, M. L. (2006). *Medical-surgical nursing* (5th ed.). St. Louis, MO: Saunders.

Additional Resources:

NANDA International (2004). *NANDA nursing diagnoses: Definitions and classification 2005-2006*. Philadelphia: NANDA.

Maher, A. B., Salmond, S. W., & Pellino, T. A. (2002). *Orthopaedic nursing* (3rd ed.). Philadelphia: Saunders.

Chapter 102: Osteoporosis

Application Exercises

1. Which of the following clients is at the greatest risk for osteoporosis?

   A. 40-year-old man who has asthma

   B. 30-year-old female who jogs daily

   C. 65-year-old female who smokes cigarettes and is sedentary

   D. 65-year-old male who drinks alcohol excessively

2. In providing dietary instructions to a client to minimize the risk of osteoporosis, the nurse should recommend which of the following foods?

   A. Bread

   B. Yogurt

   C. Chicken

   D. Rice

Scenario: A 60-year-old client is admitted to the emergency department with a chief report of back pain. She is unable to recall any trauma or fall. She describes the pain becoming progressively worse to the point where she feels completely immobilized due to the pain, unable to ambulate even to the bathroom. The nurse suspects that the client has osteoporosis.

3. What questions should the nurse ask during the assessment process to confirm this diagnosis?

4. What physical findings are associated with osteoporosis?

5. A client is admitted to the orthopaedic unit with an admitting diagnosis of compression fracture of the lumbar spine (L 3-4, L 4-5). She has a history of osteoporosis and breast cancer. She is reporting intense pain in her lower back and weakness in her legs. The plan for this client is to treat her conservatively. What orders should the nurse expect to find as part of the treatment plan?

Chapter 102: Osteoporosis

Application Exercises Answer Key

1. Which of the following clients is at the greatest risk for osteoporosis?

> A. 40-year-old man who has asthma
> B. 30-year-old female who jogs daily
> **C. 65-year-old female who smokes cigarettes and is sedentary**
> D. 65-year-old male who drinks alcohol excessively

Age, female gender, cigarette smoking, and lack of weight-bearing exercise are all risk factors.

2. In providing dietary instructions to a client to minimize the risk of osteoporosis, the nurse should recommend which of the following foods?

> A. Bread
> **B. Yogurt**
> C. Chicken
> D. Rice

Dairy products are high in calcium.

Scenario: A 60-year-old client is admitted to the emergency department with a chief report of back pain. She is unable to recall any trauma or fall. She describes the pain becoming progressively worse to the point where she feels completely immobilized due to the pain, unable to ambulate even to the bathroom. The nurse suspects that the client has osteoporosis.

3. What questions should the nurse ask during the assessment process to confirm this diagnosis?

   Key information the nurse needs to ascertain includes:

   Δ   **Any loss of height?**

   Δ   **When did menopause start?**

   Δ   **What medications do you currently take? Do you take a calcium supplement? With vitamin D? Are you on estrogen replacement therapy?**

   Δ   **Do you smoke? Do you consume alcohol? If so, how much?**

   Δ   **Do you have any family history of osteoporosis?**

   Δ   **Do you exercise? If so, is it a weight-bearing exercise like walking?**

   Δ   **Any history of asthma or hyperparathyroidism?**

4. What physical findings are associated with osteoporosis?

   Physical findings include:

   Δ   **Loss of height over the past 20 years (3 to 5 inches)**

   Δ   **Small, thin body frame**

   Δ   **Hump back (dowager's hump) at upper thoracic spine**

5. A client is admitted to the orthopaedic unit with an admitting diagnosis of compression fracture of the lumbar spine (L 3-4, L 4-5). She has a history of osteoporosis and breast cancer. She is reporting intense pain in her lower back and weakness in her legs. The plan for this client is to treat her conservatively. What orders should the nurse expect to find as part of the treatment plan?

Neurovascular assessment

Bed rest initially

Back brace or corset for support

Physical therapy for strengthening and ROM, then progress to weight-bearing activities when allowed out of bed

Pain management including NSAIDs

Calcium with vitamin D supplement

Estrogen therapy with selective estrogen receptor modulator (Evista)

Unit 9   Nursing Care of Clients with Musculoskeletal Disorders
Section: Nursing Care of Clients with Select Musculoskeletal Disorders

Chapter 103:   Osteoarthritis
Contributor: Janey A. Roach, MSN, RN, ONC

⟳ NCLEX-PN® Connections:

> **Learning Objective**: Review and apply knowledge within "**Osteoarthritis**" in readiness
> for performance of the following nursing activities as outlined by the NCLEX-PN® test
> plan:
>
> Δ   Assist with relevant laboratory, diagnostic, and therapeutic procedures within the
>   nursing role, including:
>
>   •   Preparation of the client for the procedure.
>
>   •   Accurate collection of specimens.
>
>   •   Monitoring client status during and after the procedure.
>
>   •   Reinforcing client teaching (before and following the procedure).
>
>   •   Recognizing the client's response (expected, unexpected adverse response)
>   to the procedure.
>
>   •   Monitoring results.
>
>   •   Monitoring and taking actions to prevent or minimize the risk of
>   complications.
>
>   •   Notifying the primary care provider of signs of complications.
>
> Δ   Recognize signs and symptoms of the client's problem and complete the proper
>   documentation.
>
> Δ   Provide and document care based on the client's health alteration.
>
> Δ   Monitor and document vital signs changes.
>
> Δ   Interpret data that need to be reported immediately.
>
> Δ   Reinforce client education on managing the client's health problem.
>
> Δ   Recognize and respond to emergency situations, including notification of the
>   primary care provider.
>
> Δ   Review the client's response to emergency interventions and complete the proper
>   documentation.
>
> Δ   Provide care that meets the age-related needs of clients 65 years of age or older,
>   including recognizing expected physiological changes.

📖 Key Points

Δ   Osteoarthritis (OA) is a disorder characterized by **progressive deterioration of the articular cartilage**. It is a noninflammatory (unless localized), **nonsystemic** disease.

Δ   It is no longer thought to be a wear-and-tear disease associated with aging, but a process where new tissue is produced as a result of cartilage destruction within the joint. The destruction outweighs the production. The cartilage and bone beneath the cartilage erode and **osteophytes** (bone spurs) form, resulting in narrowed joint spaces. The changes within the joint lead to **pain, immobility, muscle spasms, and potential inflammation**.

Key Factors

Δ   **Risk Factors**

- Age

- Decreased muscle strength

- Obesity

- Possible genetic link

- Early in the disease process of OA, it may be difficult to distinguish from rheumatoid arthritis (RA).

Characteristic	Osteoarthritis	Rheumatoid Arthritis
Disease Process	Cartilage destruction with bone spur growth at joint ends; degenerative	Synovial membrane inflammation resulting in cartilage destruction and bone erosion; inflammatory
Symptoms	Pain with activity, improves at rest	Swelling, redness, warmth, pain at rest, after immobility (morning stiffness)
Effusions	Localized inflammatory response	All joints
Body Size	Usually overweight	Usually underweight
Nodes	Heberden and Bouchard's nodes	Swan-neck and Boutonniere deformities of hands
Systemic involvement	No, articular	Yes, lungs, heart, skin, extra-articular
Symmetrical	No	Yes
Diagnostic Tests	X-rays	X-rays, positive rheumatoid factor

Diagnostic Procedures and Nursing Interventions

Δ **Erythrocyte sedimentation rate (ESR) and high-sensitivity C-reactive protein** may be **slightly elevated** related to secondary synovitis.

Δ **Radiographs** can determine structural changes within the joint.

Δ **Computed tomography** (CT) imaging scan may be used to determine vertebral involvement.

Assessments

Δ Monitor for **signs and symptoms.**

- Joint pain and stiffness that resolves with rest or inactivity (chief report)
- Pain with joint palpation or range of motion (observe for muscle atrophy, loss of function, client limp when walking, and restricted activity due to pain)
- Crepitus in one or more of the affected joints
- Enlarged joint related to bone hypertrophy
- Heberden's nodes enlarged at the distal interphalangeal (DIP) joints
- Bouchard's nodes located at the proximal interphalangeal (PIP) joints (although OA is not a symmetrical disease, the nodes can occur bilaterally)
- Inflammation resulting from secondary synovitis, indicating advanced disease

Δ **Assess/Monitor**

- Pain: Level (0-10), location, characteristics, quality, and severity
- Degree of functional limitation
- Levels of pain and fatigue after activity
- Range of motion
- Proper functional/joint alignment
- Home barriers
- Ability to perform activities of daily living (ADLs)

NANDA Nursing Diagnoses

Δ Chronic pain

Δ Impaired physical mobility

Δ Activity intolerance

Δ Self care deficit

Δ Disturbed body image

Nursing Interventions

Δ   **Conservative therapy** includes:

- Balance rest with activity.

- Use bracing or splints.

- Apply thermal therapies (heat or cold).

- Analgesic therapy.

  ◊   Acetaminophen

  ◊   NSAIDS

  ◊   Topical salicylates

  ◊   Glucosamine (rebuilds cartilage)

  ◊   Intra-articular injections of glucocorticoids (treat localized inflammation)

Δ   When all other conservative measures fail, the client may choose to undergo **joint replacement surgery** to relieve the pain and improve mobility and quality of life. **Osteotomy** is done to remove damaged cartilage and correct the deformity.

Δ   Instruct the client on the use of analgesics and NSAIDS prior to activity and around the clock as needed.

Δ   **Balance rest with activity**.

Δ   Instruct the client on proper body mechanics.

Δ   Encourage the use of **thermal applications**: heat to alleviate pain, ice for acute inflammation.

Δ   Encourage the use of **complementary and alternative therapies**, including acupuncture, tai chi, hypnosis, magnets, and music therapy.

Δ   Encourage the use of **splinting** for joint protection and the use of larger joints.

Δ   Encourage the use of **assistive devices** to promote independence, including an elevated toilet seat, shower bench, and long-handled reacher and shoe horn.

Δ   Encourage the use of a daily schedule of activities that will promote independence (high-energy activities in the morning).

Δ   Encourage a well-balanced diet and ideal body weight. Consult a dietitian to provide meal-planning for balanced nutrition.

Meeting the Needs of Older Adults

Δ Large percentages (75%) of adults over the age of 55 have joint changes on x-ray. Reinforce to the client that OA is not a normal part of the aging process. Assess the client accurately and distinguish between OA and other causes for chronic pain and stiffness.

Primary Reference:

Ignatavicius, D. D., & Workman, M. L. (2006). *Medical-surgical nursing* (5th ed.). St. Louis, MO: Saunders.

Additional Resources:

NANDA International (2004). *NANDA nursing diagnoses: Definitions and classification 2005-2006*. Philadelphia: NANDA.

Maher, A. B., Salmond, S. W., & Pellino, T. A. (2002). *Orthopaedic nursing* (3rd ed.). Philadelphia: Saunders.

Chapter 103: Osteoarthritis

Application Exercises

1. A client comes to the office reporting right knee pain with ambulation. What are priority assessments?

2. What are the distinguishing characteristics of osteoarthritis?

3. What priority nursing diagnoses and interventions should be included in the plan of care to promote activity for a client with osteoporosis?

4. Identify whether each of the following characteristics is indicative of osteoarthritis (OA) or rheumatoid arthritis (RA).

   _____   Heberden's nodes
   _____   Systemic response
   _____   No clear laboratory test for diagnosis
   _____   Small body frame
   _____   Pain occurs with activity

Chapter 103: Osteoarthritis

Application Exercises Answer Key

1. A client comes to the office reporting right knee pain with ambulation. What are priority assessments?

  Δ   Pain (type, location, aggravating and alleviating factors)

  • Does it increase with activity and subside with rest?

  • Does it occur with weight-bearing activity?

  Δ   Joint swelling or inability to complete ADLs

  Δ   Family history of OA

  Δ   History of trauma

  Δ   Obesity

  Δ   Visible Bouchard or Heberden's nodes

2. What are the distinguishing characteristics of osteoarthritis?

Osteoarthritis involves cartilage destruction with bone spur formation at the joint ends. It is a degenerative disease where the client experiences pain with activity that improves with rest. If inflammation occurs, it is a localized inflammatory response. The client is usually overweight. The joints of the hands may develop Heberden and Bouchard's nodes. There is no definitive laboratory test for OA. Diagnoses are based on history and physical with x-rays.

3. What priority nursing diagnoses and interventions should be included in the plan of care to promote activity for a client with osteoporosis?

Δ   Acute/Chronic Pain

- Assess pain level (0-10) location, characteristics, quality, and severity.

- Instruct the client on use of analgesics and NSAIDS prior to activity and around the clock as needed.

- Assess for limited ROM and proper functional/joint alignment.

- Encourage use of splinting for joint protection.

- Instruct the client on proper body mechanics.

- Encourage use of thermal applications: heat to alleviate pain, ice for acute inflammation.

- Balance rest with activity.

- Encourage the use of complementary and alternative therapies, including acupuncture, tai chi, hypnosis, magnets, and music therapy.

- Instruct the client on the use of biologic agents such as glucosamine sulfate to rebuild cartilage.

Δ   Impaired Mobility

- Assess the degree of functional limitations related to pain, stiffness, and deformities.

- Encourage the use of orthotics and assistive devices.

- Support activities that can be stopped to promote rest and relief.

- Encourage joint protection and the use of larger joints.

- Encourage ideal body weight.

Δ   Self-Care Deficit

- Assess home barriers.

- Assess ability to perform ADLs.

- Encourage the use of assistive devices to promote independence, including an elevated toilet seat, shower bench, and long-handled reacher and shoe horn.

Δ   Activity Intolerance

- Assess pain and fatigue after activity.

- Encourage the use of daily schedule of activities that will promote independence (high-energy activities in the morning).

4. Identify whether each of the following characteristics is indicative of osteoarthritis (OA) or rheumatoid arthritis (RA).

<u> OA </u>   Heberden's nodes

<u> RA </u>   Systemic response

<u> OA </u>   No clear laboratory test for diagnosis

<u> RA </u>   Small body frame

<u> OA </u>   Pain occurs with activity

Unit 10 Nursing Care of Clients with Lymph, Immune, or Infectious Disorders

Section: Diagnostic and Therapeutic Procedures: Immune or Infectious

Chapter 104: Immunizations

Contributor: Dana Bartlett, MSN, RN, CSPI

NCLEX-PN® Connections:

Learning Objective: Review and apply knowledge within **"Immunizations"** in readiness for performance of the following nursing activities as outlined by the NCLEX-PN® test plan:

Δ Perform/assist with relevant laboratory, diagnostic, and therapeutic procedures within the nursing role, including:

- Preparation of the client for the procedure.

- Reinforcement of client teaching (before and following the procedure).

- Accurate collection of specimens.

- Monitoring procedure results (compare to norms) and appropriate notification of the primary care provider.

- Monitoring the client's response (expected, unexpected adverse response, comparison to baseline) to the procedure.

- Monitoring and taking actions, including reinforcing client teaching, to prevent or minimize the risk of complications.

- Recognizing signs of potential complications and reporting to the primary care provider.

- Recommending changes in the test/procedure as needed based on client findings.

Δ Monitor therapeutic devices (drainage/irrigating devices, chest tubes), if inserted, for proper functioning.

📖 Key Points

Δ **Immunity** is the body's protection against infectious disease. It is an organized series of actions by the body in response to a pathological organism, and it destroys or neutralizes the organism.

Δ The organs of the immune system include **bone marrow**, the **thymus gland, lymph nodes, the spleen, tonsils, and mucosal lymphatic tissue.**

Δ **Natural (innate)** immunity is inherited and involves the inflammatory response.

Δ **Acquired (adaptive)** immunity is achieved by either active or passive processes:

- **Active immunity** occurs when the body responds to:
  ◊ The presence of a pathologic organism and produces antibodies against that organism.
  ◊ A vaccine and produces antibodies against the pathological organism targeted by the immunization (vaccines, toxoids).

- **Passive immunity** is temporary and is achieved when antibodies are:
  ◊ Injected into an unprotected person – for example, antitoxins (diphtheria antitoxin), immunoglobulin (hepatitis B immune globulin).
  ◊ Passed from mother to fetus in utero.
  ◊ Transmitted to the infant through breast milk.

Δ **Humoral immunity** refers to the production of antibodies in response to the presence of a pathological organism.

Δ **Cell-mediated immunity** refers to the production of **sensitized T-lymphocytes** that neutralize or destroy pathologic organisms.

Δ For some pathogens, repeat vaccinations ("boosters") are needed. The immunity conferred by the vaccine will diminish over time.

Key Factors

Δ **Indications for adult vaccination** include those who:

- Are routinely exposed (providers, nurses) to infectious organisms.
- Travel.
- Are working on a regular basis with children.
- Are in contact with blood or body fluids.
- Are exposed to rabies or tetanus.

Δ   **Precautions/contraindications for adult vaccinations** include:

- Previous anaphylactic reaction.

- Immunocompromised state, such as cancer, leukemia, HIV, use of immunosuppressive drugs.

- Presence of a febrile illness.

- Recent receipt of an antibody-containing blood product (measles, mumps, and rubella vaccine).

- Allergy to eggs (influenza, pneumococcal, and meningococcal vaccines).

Δ   The use of **vaccines in women who are, or may soon become, pregnant requires special consideration.** The vaccines that should **not be given** are:

- Measles, mumps, and rubella (MMR).

- Hepatitis A.

- Hepatitis B.

- Varicella.

- Possibly pneumococcal and meningococcal.

Δ   The use of vaccines in women who are **breastfeeding requires special consideration**. The vaccines that **should not be given** are:

- Hepatitis A.

- Live, attenuated influenza vaccine.

- Pneumococcal (unlikely to be unsafe, but complete data is not available).

Therapeutic Procedures and Nursing Interventions

Δ   **Adult Immunizations**

- Tetanus and diphtheria (Td) vaccination: Booster dose every 10 years

- Influenza vaccine: Annually

- Pneumococcal vaccine: A dose with a one-time revaccination after 5 years

- Hepatitis B: Three doses (the first dose is followed by the second dose in 1 to 2 months and the third dose in 4 to 6 months) for individuals at risk, such as healthcare workers

- Varicella: Recommended for all individuals without evidence of immunity to varicella

Δ   **Assess** for:

- **Contraindications** to immunization.

- **Prior history** of reaction to the vaccine.

- **Allergies** to components of the vaccine.

Δ   **Educate the client** about the **possible side effects** (soreness at injection site, low-grade fever, myalgia, malaise for 1 to 2 days).

Δ   Monitor the client after the vaccine has been given for **localized or systemic reaction**.

Δ   **Report** and **document** any reaction to the vaccine.

Complications and Nursing Implications

Δ   **Anaphylactic reactions** are rare because the amount and strength of the organisms in vaccines is very low. Monitor for adverse reactions – such as dyspnea, stridor, and hypotension – and intervene as needed.

Meeting the Needs of Older Adults

Δ   Older adult clients may not be able to respond to vaccines as well as children and younger adults due to age-related changes in their immune systems.

Δ   Immunity conferred by vaccines may not be as strong.

Primary Reference:

Ignatavicius, D. D., & Workman, M. L. (2006). *Medical-surgical nursing* (5th ed.). St. Louis, MO: Saunders.

Additional Resources:

Lehne, R. A. (2004*). Pharmacology for nursing care* (5th ed.). St. Louis, MO: Saunders.

NANDA International (2004). *NANDA nursing diagnoses: Definitions and classification 2005-2006*. Philadelphia: NANDA.

For the most updated recommendations regarding immunizations and vaccines, visit the Centers for Disease Control and Prevention at *www.cdc.gov* and click on the Immunizations and Vaccines tab.

Chapter 104: Immunizations

Application Exercises

Scenario: A primary care provider has ordered hepatitis B and tetanus vaccinations for a client.

1. How should the nurse explain to the client how the vaccine works?

2. The client wants to know why his body's immune system is not sufficient in this case. What is the best answer to this question?

3. The nurse notes that the tetanus vaccine is supplied as tetanus toxoid and tetanus immune globulin. How do these products differ?

4. A client develops a mild fever of 37.8° C (100° F) orally after receiving an immunization. What should the client be told about this reaction?

Chapter 104: Immunizations

Application Exercises Answer Key

Scenario: A primary care provider has ordered hepatitis B and tetanus vaccinations for a client.

1. How should the nurse explain to the client how the vaccine works?

   Vaccines mimic the body's reaction to pathogens. Vaccines contain very tiny amounts of the pathogenic organism that have been altered so that it no longer causes disease. When given to the client, the client's immune system produces antibodies against the pathogen and stores it for future recognition. Upon the next exposure to the pathogen, the immune system is primed and ready to rid the body of the pathogen before it can produce the disease.

2. The client wants to know why his body's immune system is not sufficient in this case. What is the best answer to this question?

   Infection with the pathogen (or vaccination) is necessary in order for the body to produce an adequate number of antibodies to prevent future infections. Since the client has not been exposed to and infected with either of these diseases, immunity has not occurred. Tetanus and hepatitis B are serious diseases that can lead to death. The vaccine stimulates the client's body to produce antibodies so that the client will be protected from the disease without actually having had the disease.

3. The nurse notes that the tetanus vaccine is supplied as tetanus toxoid and tetanus immune globulin. How do these products differ?

   Tetanus toxoid is the bacterial toxin that has been weakened so that it does not produce disease, but it remains strong enough to cause the body to produce antibodies against it (active immunity). Tetanus immune globulin is an antibody (already produced) that is injected and has the ability to neutralize the tetanus toxin (passive immunity).

4. A client develops a mild fever of 37.8° C (100° F) orally after receiving an immunization. What should the client be told about this reaction?

Mild fever is not uncommon following immunization. The client should be told to contact the primary care provider if the fever persists for more than 3 days or exceeds 38.1° C (100.6° F) orally. If a child becomes lethargic or runs a high fever following vaccination, the child should be seen by the provider or taken to the emergency department for evaluation.

Unit 10
Section:

Nursing Care of Clients with Lymph, Immune, or Infectious Disorders
Diagnostic and Therapeutic Procedures: Immune or Infectious

Chapter 105: Definitive Diagnoses: Cultures and Biopsies
Contributor: Wendy Buenzli, MSN, RN

⟳ **NCLEX-PN® Connections**

Learning Objective: Review and apply knowledge within "**Definitive Diagnoses: Cultures and Biopsies**" in readiness for performance of the following nursing activities as outlined by the NCLEX-PN® test plan:

Δ   Perform/assist with relevant laboratory, diagnostic, and therapeutic procedures within the nursing role, including:

- Preparation of the client for the procedure.

- Reinforcement of client teaching (before and following the procedure).

- Accurate collection of specimens.

- Monitoring procedure results (compare to norms) and appropriate notification of the primary care provider.

- Monitoring the client's response (expected, unexpected adverse response, comparison to baseline) to the procedure.

- Monitoring and taking actions, including reinforcing client teaching, to prevent or minimize the risk of complications.

- Recognizing signs of potential complications and reporting to the primary care provider.

- Recommending changes in the test/procedure as needed based on client findings.

Δ   Recognize the client's recovery from anesthesia, if used.

Δ   Monitor therapeutic devices (drainage/irrigating devices, chest tubes), if inserted, for proper functioning.

Key Points

Δ   Effective **treatment** of infectious disease **begins with identification of the pathogenic microorganism.**

Δ   The most accurate and definitive way to identify microorganisms and cell characteristics is by examining blood, body fluids, and tissue samples under a microscope.

Δ   **Culture** refers to isolation of the pathogen on culture media.

Δ   **Sensitivity** refers to the effect that antimicrobials have on the microorganism.

•   If the microorganism is killed by the antimicrobial, the microbe is considered to be **sensitive** to that medication.

•   If tolerable levels of the medication are unable to kill the microbe, the microbe is considered to be **resistant** to that medication.

Δ   **Biopsy** is the removal of a sample of tissue by excision or needle aspiration for cytological (histological) examination.

Key Factors

Δ   Ideally, antimicrobial therapy should not begin until after the specimen for culture and sensitivity has been collected.

Δ   Nurses must understand the various tests in order to **accurately interpret test results and educate clients.**

Diagnostic Procedures and Nursing Interventions

Δ   **Culture and Sensitivity**

•   Use **standard precautions in collecting and handling** specimens, such as urine, sputum, blood, wound drainage, abscess fluid, and peritoneal fluid.

•   A sufficient quantity of a specimen should be collected and placed in a **sterile container**.

•   The specimen must be **properly labeled** and **delivered promptly** for appropriate storage and analysis.

•   Results of culture and sensitivity tests are usually available preliminarily within 24 to 48 hr with final results in 72 hr.

•   If culture and sensitivity results reveal that the cultured organism is not sensitive to prescribed antimicrobial agents, it is the nurse's responsibility to report the results to the provider before administering subsequent doses of an ineffective antimicrobial.

Δ   **Biopsy**

- A biopsy is the **extraction of a very small amount of tissue**, such as bone marrow, cervical, endometrial, brain, liver, lung, pleural, renal, skin, and lymph node tissue, to definitively diagnose cell type and to confirm or rule out malignancy.

- Biopsies can be performed with local anesthesia or conscious sedation in an ambulatory setting, intraoperatively, and/or during scope procedures.

- Teach the client about what to expect about the information provided by the test/procedure.

- Assist the provider with the test/procedure as needed.

- Monitor the client during and after the test/procedure.

    ◊   As appropriate, apply pressure to the biopsy site as needed to control bleeding.

    ◊   As appropriate, place a **sterile dressing over the biopsy site**.

    ◊   Monitor the client for evidence of **infection** (fever, increased WBC, pain) **and/or bleeding**.

    ◊   As appropriate, **monitor biopsy site**.

    ◊   Postbiopsy discomfort is usually relieved by mild **analgesics**.

- Teach the client to report excessive bleeding and/or signs of infection to the provider.

Meeting the Needs of Older Adults

Δ   Older adults are at greater risk for complications associated with sedation for biopsy procedures due to chronic illnesses.

Δ   An older adult's renal clearance also needs to be considered when using any analgesics for sedation.

Primary Reference:

Ignatavicius, D. D., & Workman, M. L. (2006). *Medical-surgical nursing* (5th ed.). St. Louis, MO: Saunders.

Additional Resources:

Chernecky, C. C., & Berger, B. J. (Eds.). (2004). *Laboratory tests and diagnostic procedures* (2nd ed.). St Louis, MO: Saunders.

Monahan, F. D., Sands, J. K., Neighbors, M., Marek, F. J., & Green, C. J. (Eds.). (2007). *Phipps' medical-surgical nursing: Health and illness perspectives* (8th ed.). St. Louis, MO: Mosby.

NANDA International (2004). *NANDA nursing diagnoses: Definitions and classification 2005-2006*. Philadelphia: NANDA.

Chapter 105: Definitive Diagnoses: Cultures and Biopsies

Application Exercises

Scenario: A client develops signs and symptoms of a urinary tract infection. A urine specimen is sent for culture and sensitivity. While awaiting culture and sensitivity results, the client is started on amikacin (Amikin) 15 mg/kg/day. She is allergic to sulfa medications. The results of the urine culture and sensitivity are as follows:

Urine Midstream Clean Catch

Final Report:

Colony Count: Greater than 100,000 colonies

Bacteria Type: *Escherichia coli* (heavy growth)

Sensitivity:

Medication	Susceptibility	
Trimethoprim-sulfamethoxazole	S 4+	
Amikacin	S 3+	
Gentamicin	R	
Tobramycin	S 1+	
Cephalosporin	S	
Ciprofloxacin	R	R = Resistant
Amoxicillin	S 2+	S = Sensitive to drug (levels 1-4)

1. Does the client definitively have a urinary tract infection? Why or why not?

2. Is the client on the most appropriate medication? Why or why not?

3. What laboratory test is indicated to rule out urosepsis?

4. A client presents with symptoms of hemoptysis, weight loss, and a 20-year history of smoking two packs of cigarettes per day. Chest x-ray reveals a cannonball lesion in the client's left lung. Does this client definitively have lung cancer? Why or why not?

Chapter 105: Definitive Diagnoses: Cultures and Biopsies

Application Exercises Answer Key

Scenario: A client develops signs and symptoms of a urinary tract infection. A urine specimen is sent for culture and sensitivity. While awaiting culture and sensitivity results, the client is started on amikacin (Amikin) 15 mg/kg/day. She is allergic to sulfa medications. The results of the urine culture and sensitivity are as follows:

Urine Midstream Clean Catch

Final Report:

Colony Count: Greater than 100,000 colonies

Bacteria Type: *Escherichia coli* (heavy growth)

Sensitivity:

Medication	Susceptibility	
Trimethoprim-sulfamethoxazole	S 4+	
Amikacin	S 3+	
Gentamicin	R	
Tobramycin	S 1+	
Cephalosporin	S	
Ciprofloxacin	R	R = Resistant
Amoxicillin	S 2+	S = Sensitive to drug (levels 1-4)

1. Does the client definitively have a urinary tract infection? Why or why not?

Heavy growth of greater than 100,000 colonies definitively diagnoses an infection. Negative results are less than 10,000 colonies. Indeterminate results are 10,000 to 100,000 colonies.

2. Is the client on the most appropriate medication? Why or why not?

The client is on the most appropriate medication. Appropriate medications are those with 3 to 4+ degrees of sensitivity. Based on these results, the most sensitive medication is trimethoprim-sulfamethoxazole (Bactrim); however, the client is allergic to sulfa.

3. What laboratory test is indicated to rule out urosepsis?

Blood cultures x 3 are indicated to rule out the presence of microorganisms within the blood stream. Urosepsis is definitively diagnosed by corresponding blood and urine cultures.

4. A client presents with symptoms of hemoptysis, weight loss, and a 20-year history of smoking two packs of cigarettes per day. Chest x-ray reveals a cannonball lesion in the client's left lung. Does this client definitively have lung cancer? Why or why not?

Although highly suggestive of lung cancer, these findings are not definitively diagnostic. A biopsy of lung tissue will need to be performed to definitively diagnose lung cancer and to determine the specific tumor cell.

Unit 10

Section:

Nursing Care of Clients with Lymph, Immune, or Infectious Disorders

Nursing Care of Clients with Infectious Disorders

Chapter 106:   Bacterial, Viral, and Fungal Infections: Prevention, Assessment, and Intervention

Contributor: Wendy Buenzli, MSN, RN

↻ NCLEX-PN® Connections:

Learning Objective: Review and apply knowledge within "**Bacterial, Viral, and Fungal Infections: Prevention, Assessment, and Intervention**" in readiness for performance of the following nursing activities as outlined by the NCLEX-PN® test plan:

Δ   Provide care for the client with an infection, including identifying signs and symptoms of infection and taking measures to prevent transmission.

Δ   Assist with relevant laboratory, diagnostic, and therapeutic procedures within the nursing role, including:

•   Preparation of the client for the procedure.

•   Accurate collection of specimens.

•   Monitoring client status during and after the procedure.

•   Reinforcing client teaching (before and following the procedure).

•   Recognizing the client's response (expected, unexpected adverse response) to the procedure.

•   Monitoring results.

•   Monitoring and taking actions to prevent or minimize the risk of complications.

•   Notifying the primary care provider of signs of complications.

Δ   Recognize signs and symptoms of the client's problem and complete the proper documentation.

Δ   Provide and document care based on the client's health alteration.

Δ   Monitor and document vital signs changes.

Δ   Interpret data that need to be reported immediately.

Δ   Reinforce client education on managing the client's health problem.

Δ   Recognize and respond to emergency situations, including notification of the primary care provider.

Δ   Review the client's response to emergency interventions and complete the proper documentation.

Δ   Provide care that meets the age-related needs of clients 65 years of age or older, including recognizing expected physiological changes.

Key Points

Δ   Infections and **infectious diseases are the leading cause of death worldwide.**

- Previously controlled infections are reemerging (malaria, tuberculosis, pertussis).

- Newer infections have emerged over the last several decades, including *Borrelia burgdorferi* (Lyme disease), human immunodeficiency virus (HIV), and coronavirus (SARS).

Δ   In the United States:

- Infectious diseases are of greater concern today than at any time over the past 50 years.

- The **resistance of microorganisms** may produce a level of concern similar to infections in the pre-antibiotic era (for example, vancomycin-resistant enterococcus [**VRE**], methicillin-resistant staphylococcus aureus [**MRSA**]).

Δ   **Bioterrorism is the latest threat** involving microorganisms (smallpox, tularemia, plague, anthrax).

Δ   Pathogens are the microorganisms that cause infections.

Δ   **Virulence** (low, high) is the ability of a pathogen to invade and injure the host.

Key Factors

Δ   **Risk Factors**

- **Environmental factors**

  ◊   Excessive alcohol consumption

  ◊   Smoking

  ◊   Malnutrition

- **Medication therapy** (immunosuppressive agents)

  ◊   Glucocorticosteroids

  ◊   Cancer chemotherapy

- **Chronic diseases**

  ◊   Diabetes mellitus

  ◊   Adrenal insufficiency

  ◊   Renal failure

  ◊   Hepatic failure

  ◊   Chronic lung disease

Δ   **Causes**

- **Bacteria** (*Staphylococcus aureus, Escherichia coli, Mycobacterium tuberculosis*)

- **Viruses** – pathogenic organisms that use the host's genetic machinery to reproduce (HIV, hepatitis, herpes simplex)

- **Fungi** – molds and yeasts (*Candida albicans, Aspergillus*)

- **Prions** – protein particles (for example, new variant Creutzfeldt-Jakob disease)

- **Parasites** – protozoa (malaria, toxoplasmosis) and helminths (worms, flukes)

Δ   The infection process (**chain of infection**) includes:

- **Causative agent** (bacteria, virus, fungus, prion, parasite).

- **Reservoir** (human, animal, water, soil, insects).

- **Portal of exit from the host** (means for leaving host).

  ◊ Respiratory tract (droplet, airborne)

    ° *Myobacterium tuberculosis, Streptococcus pneumoniae*

  ◊ Gastrointestinal tract

    ° Shigella, *Salmonella enteritidis, Salmonella typhi*, hepatitis A

  ◊ Genitourinary tract

    ° UTI is one of the most common infections.

    ° *Escherichia coli*, hepatitis A, herpes simplex virus (type I), HIV

  ◊ Skin/mucous membranes

    ° Herpes simplex virus, varicella

  ◊ Blood/body fluids

    ° Invasive devices (for example, intravenous catheters)

    ° HIV, hepatitis B and C

- **Mode of transmission.**

  ◊ Contact

    ° Direct physical contact – person to person

    ° Indirect contact with an inanimate object – object to person

    ° Fecal oral transmission (unwashed hands)

  ◊ Droplet

    ° Sneezing, coughing, talking

  ◊ Airborne

    ° Sneezing, coughing

◊ Vector borne

　　° Animals or insects as intermediaries (ticks transmit Lyme disease; mosquitoes transmit West Nile and malaria)

- **Portal of entry to the host.**

　　◊ May be the same as the portal of exit.

- **Susceptible host.**

　　◊ Compromised defense mechanisms leave the host more susceptible to infections.

Δ **Immune Defenses**

- **Nonspecific (innate) immune response**

　　◊ Provides temporary immunity.

　　◊ The skin, mucous membranes, secretions, enzymes, phagocytic cells, and protective proteins work in concert to prevent infections.

　　◊ **Intact skin is the body's first line of defense** against microbial invasion.

　　◊ **Inflammatory response:**

　　　° Provides immediate protection from the invading antigen (pathogen).

　　　° Phagocytic cells (neutrophils, monocytes), blood, complement, and interferon are involved.

　　　° Localizes the area of microbial invasion and prevents its spread.

- **Specific (adaptive) immunity**

　　◊ Provides permanent immunity.

　　◊ Involves B and T lymphocytes.

　　◊ Specific antibodies are produced against specific antigens.

Diagnostic Procedures and Nursing Interventions

Δ **White Blood Cell (WBC) Count with Differential**

- Provides information about the **type of infection** (bacterial, viral, parasitic, fungal) and the **body's response** to it.

- **Normal** values range between **5,000 to 10,000/mm^3**; a healthy older adult will have a range of 3,000 to 9,000/mm^3.

- A count **less than 4,300/mm^3** is called **leukopenia.** It may indicate a compromised inflammatory response or viral infection.

- A count **greater than 10,000/mm^3** indicates an **inflammatory response to a pathogen or a disease process.**

- The differential on the laboratory report is listed so the percentages of cells equal 100%. If the percent of one type of cell increases, the percents of other types decrease accordingly.

  ◊ **Neutrophils** are among the first cells to respond to a bacterial infection.

    ° A **70% increase** in neutrophils indicates a **bacterial infection**.

    ° This increase is often referred to as a **"shift to the left."**

  ◊ **Lymphocytes** are the second most commonly occurring WBCs. They primarily respond to viral infections but may also be elevated with some bacterial infections (mononucleosis, tuberculosis, or some tumors).

  ◊ **Eosinophils** are elevated with allergic reactions and parasitic infections.

Δ **Culture and Sensitivity**

- Use **standard precautions in collecting and handling** specimens (urine, sputum, blood, wound drainage, abscess fluid, peritoneal fluid).

- A sufficient quantity of a specimen should be collected and placed in a **sterile container**.

- The specimen must be **properly labeled and delivered promptly** for appropriate storage and analysis.

- Results of culture and sensitivity tests are usually available preliminarily within 24 to 48 hr, with final results ready in 72 hr.

- If culture and sensitivity reveal that the cultured organism is not sensitive to prescribed antimicrobial agents, it is the nurse's responsibility to report the results to the primary care provider before administering subsequent doses of an ineffective antimicrobial.

Δ **Erythrocyte Sedimentation Rate (ESR)** – the rate at which red blood cells settle out of plasma.

- A **normal** value for adults is between **15 to 20 mm/hr**.

- An **increase** indicates an **active inflammatory process or infection**.

Δ **Immunoglobulin Electrophoresis**

- Determines the **presence and quantity of specific immunoglobulins** (IgG, IgA, IgM)

- Used to detect hypersensitivity disorders, autoimmune disorders, chronic viral infections, immunodeficiency, multiple myeloma, and intrauterine infections.

Δ **Antibody Screening Tests**

- Detect the presence of **antibodies against specific causative agents** (bacteria, fungi, viruses, and parasites).

- A positive antibody test indicates that the client has been exposed to and developed antibodies to a specific pathogen, but does not provide information about whether or not the client is currently infected (for example, HIV antibodies).

Δ **Auto-antibody Screening Tests**

- Detects the **presence of antibodies against a person's own DNA** (self-cells).

- The presence of antibodies against self cells is associated with **autoimmune conditions** (systemic lupus erythematosus, rheumatoid arthritis).

Δ **Antigen Tests**

- Detects the **presence of a specific pathogen** (for example, HIV).

- Used to identify certain infections or disorders.

Δ **Gallium Scan**

- A **nuclear scan** that uses a radioactive substance to identify hot spots of **WBCs** within the client's body.

- Radioactive gallium citrate is injected intravenously and accumulates in areas where inflammation is present.

Δ X-rays, computed tomography (CT) scan, magnetic resonance imaging (MRI), and biopsies are used to determine the presence of infection, abscesses, and lesions.

Assessments

Δ **Signs and Symptoms** (depend on the type of infection and organs/tissues involved)

- Fever, chills
- Fatigue, malaise
- Enlarged lymph nodes
- Rash, skin lesions, purulent wound drainage, erythema
- Change in level of consciousness, nuchal rigidity, photophobia, headache
- Sore throat, odynophagia, dysphagia, hyperemia, enlarged tonsils
- Nausea, vomiting, anorexia, abdominal cramping, diarrhea
- Dyspnea, cough, purulent sputum, crackles
- Dysuria, urinary frequency, hematuria, pyuria

Δ   **Assess**

- Presence of **risk factors for infection**
- **Recent travel or exposure** to an infectious disease
- Behaviors that may put the client at **increased risk**

NANDA Nursing Diagnoses

Δ   Fatigue

Δ   Hyperthermia

Δ   Pain (mild to moderate)

Nursing Interventions

Δ   Administer **antipyretics** for fever and discomfort as prescribed.

Δ   Administer **antimicrobial therapy** as prescribed.

- Monitor for medication effectiveness (reduced fever, increased level of comfort, decreasing white blood cell count).
- Maintain medication schedule to assure consistent blood levels of antibiotic.

Δ   Encourage **increased fluid intake** or maintain **intravenous fluid replacement** to prevent dehydration.

Δ   Implement **infection control measures**.

- Use consistent handwashing to prevent transmission of infection to other clients.
- Maintain a clean environment.
- Use personal protective equipment/barriers (gloves, masks, gowns, goggles).
- Implement protective precautions as needed:
  - ◊   **Standard** (implemented for all clients).
  - ◊   **Airborne** (measles, varicella, tuberculosis).
  - ◊   **Droplet** (*Haemophilus influenzae* type B, pertussis, plague, streptococcal pneumonia).
  - ◊   **Contact** (*Clostridium difficile*, herpes simplex virus, impetigo).

Δ   Provide diversional activities if needed.

Δ   Teach the client regarding:

- Any infection control measures needed at home.

- Self administration of medication therapy.

- Complications that need to be reported immediately.

Complications and Nursing Implications

Δ   **Multi-drug-resistant infection** – obtain specimens for culture and sensitivity prior to initiation of antimicrobial therapy. Monitor antimicrobial levels and ensure therapeutic levels are maintained. Complete the full course of antimicrobial therapy. Avoid overuse of antimicrobials.

Δ   **Sepsis** – a systemic inflammatory response syndrome resulting from the body's response to a serious infection, usually bacterial (peritonitis, meningitis, pneumonia, wound infections, urinary tract infections). Risk factors for sepsis include very young, very old, weakened immune system, and severe injuries (trauma). Sepsis can lead to widespread inflammation, blood clotting, organ failure, and shock. Blood cultures definitively diagnose sepsis. Systemic antimicrobials are prescribed accordingly. Vasopressors and anticoagulants may be prescribed for shock and blood clotting symptoms. Mechanical ventilation, dialysis, and other interventions may be needed for treatment of specific organ failure.

Meeting the Needs of Older Adults

Δ   Older adults are at increased risk for infections due to:

- Slowed response to antibiotic therapy.

- Slowed immune response.

- Loss of subcutaneous tissue, thinning of skin.

- Decreased vascularity and slowed wound healing.

- Decreased cough and gag reflexes.

- Increased chronic illnesses (diabetes mellitus, COPD, neurological or musculoskeletal impairments).

- Decreased gastric acid production.

- Decreased mobility.

- Bowel/bladder incontinence.

- Dementia.

- Greater incidence of invasive devices (urinary catheter, tube feeding, tracheostomies, intravenous lines).

Primary Reference:

Ignatavicius, D. D., & Workman, M. L. (2006). *Medical-surgical nursing* (5th ed.). St. Louis, MO: Saunders.

Additional Resources:

Monahan, F. D., Sands, J. K., Neighbors, M., Marek, F. J., & Green, C. J. (Eds.). (2007). *Phipps' medical-surgical nursing: Health and illness perspectives* (8th ed.). St. Louis, MO: Mosby.

NANDA International (2004). *NANDA nursing diagnoses: Definitions and classification 2005-2006.* Philadelphia: NANDA.

Chapter 106: Bacterial, Viral, and Fungal Infections: Prevention, Assessment, and Intervention

Application Exercises

1. For the scenarios listed below, select the corresponding mode of transmission. Some modes may be used more than once.

   _____ A client's vomit lands on a nurse's uniform.

   _____ A nurse receives an accidental needle stick.

   _____ A mosquito bites a hiker while in the woods.

   _____ Someone with active TB sneezes while riding a bus.

   _____ A cook fails to wash his hands after using the bathroom.

   _____ A client sneezes into his hands and then touches a nurse's hand.

	Mode of Transmission
A	Airborne
B	Contact (Direct)
C	Contact (Indirect)
D	Vector
E	Fecal-oral

2. Which of the following factors increase a client's susceptibility to infection? (Check all that apply.)

_____	Alcohol consumption	_____	Smoking
_____	Exercise	_____	Chronic illness
_____	Older age	_____	Steroid use
_____	Asthma	_____	High-fiber diet

3. Place the following nursing actions in the correct sequence for a client with an infectious disease of the respiratory system.

   _____ Collect specimen for culture and sensitivity.

   _____ Implement droplet or airborne precautions.

   _____ Assess lung sounds and respiratory rate.

   _____ Teach the client about infection control at home.

   _____ Maintain intravenous antibiotic therapy.

4. Which of the following clients is at the greatest risk for infection? Explain.

      A. A 35-year-old who is pregnant

      B. A 45-year-old who is a vegetarian

      C. A 66-year-old who smokes a pack a day

      D. A 72-year-old who takes a daily walk

5. For each of the following client situations, identify the appropriate infection control measures. (Select all that apply for each client situation.)

A. Caring for a client with active TB

B. Irrigation of a wound with MRSA

C. Caring for a client with *Neisseria meningitidis*

D. Caring for a client with *Clostridium difficile* colitis

A	Standard precautions (handwashing, gloves)
B	Mask
C	Goggles
D	N95 Respirator
E	Gown
F	Private room
G	Negative airflow room
H	Dedicated equipment (blood pressure cuff, thermometer)

Chapter 106: Bacterial, Viral, and Fungal Infections: Prevention, Assessment, and Intervention

Application Exercises Answer Key

1. For the scenarios listed below, select the corresponding mode of transmission. Some modes may be used more than once.

   ___B___   A client's vomit lands on a nurse's uniform.

   ___C___   A nurse receives an accidental needle stick.

   ___D___   A mosquito bites a hiker while in the woods.

   ___A___   Someone with active TB sneezes while riding a bus.

   ___E___   A cook fails to wash his hands after using the bathroom.

   ___B___   A client sneezes into his hands and then touches a nurse's hand.

	Mode of Transmission
A	Airborne
B	Contact (Direct)
C	Contact (Indirect)
D	Vector
E	Fecal-oral

2. Which of the following factors increase a client's susceptibility to infection? (Check all that apply.)

__x__	Alcohol consumption	__x__	Smoking
_____	Exercise	__x__	Chronic illness
__x__	Older age	__x__	Steroid use
__x__	Asthma	_____	High-fiber diet

3. Place the following nursing actions in the correct sequence for a client with an infectious disease of the respiratory system.

   ___3___   Collect specimen for culture and sensitivity.

   ___1___   Implement droplet or airborne precautions.

   ___2___   Assess lung sounds and respiratory rate.

   ___5___   Teach the client about infection control at home.

   ___4___   Maintain intravenous antibiotic therapy.

   Nurses must prioritize initiation of infection control precautions to protect others from acquiring the infection. Specimens for culture and sensitivity should be drawn prior to initiating antibiotic therapy to accurately verify the presence of an infectious organism.

4. Which of the following clients is at the greatest risk for infection? Explain.

> A. A 35-year-old who is pregnant
>
> B. A 45-year-old who is a vegetarian
>
> **C. A 66-year-old who smokes a pack a day**
>
> D. A 72-year-old who takes a daily walk

The 66-year-old client has the greatest number of risk factors for infection: age greater than 65 years and smoking a pack per day. "A" and "D" both have one risk factor each (pregnancy, age). "B" has no risk factors for infection.

5. For each of the following client situations, identify the appropriate infection control measures. (Select all that apply for each client situation.)

A. Caring for a client with active TB

Airborne Precautions: A, D, G

B. Irrigation of a wound with MRSA

Contact Precautions: A, C, E, F, H. Goggles are indicated whenever an eye splash is possible.

C. Caring for a client with *Neisseria meningitidis*

Droplet Precautions: A, B, F

D. Caring for a client with *Clostridium difficile* colitis

Contact Precautions: A, E, F, H

A	Standard precautions (handwashing, gloves)
B	Mask
C	Goggles
D	N95 Respirator
E	Gown
F	Private room
G	Negative airflow room
H	Dedicated equipment (blood pressure cuff, thermometer)

Nursing Care of Clients with Lymph, Immune, or Infectious Disorders
Nursing Care of Clients with Infectious Disorders

Chapter 107: HIV/AIDS
Contributor: Wendy Buenzli, MSN, RN

⟳ NCLEX-PN® Connections:

> **Learning Objective**: Review and apply knowledge within "**HIV/AIDS**" in readiness for performance of the following nursing activities as outlined by the NCLEX-PN® test plan:
>
> Δ Protect the client who is immunocompromised.
>
> Δ Assist with relevant laboratory, diagnostic, and therapeutic procedures within the nursing role, including:
>
> - Preparation of the client for the procedure.
>
> - Accurate collection of specimens.
>
> - Monitoring client status during and after the procedure.
>
> - Reinforcing client teaching (before and following the procedure).
>
> - Recognizing the client's response (expected, unexpected adverse response) to the procedure.
>
> - Monitoring results.
>
> - Monitoring and taking actions to prevent or minimize the risk of complications.
>
> - Notifying the primary care provider of signs of complications.
>
> Δ Recognize signs and symptoms of the client's problem and complete the proper documentation.
>
> Δ Provide and document care based on the client's health alteration.
>
> Δ Monitor and document vital signs changes.
>
> Δ Interpret data that need to be reported immediately.
>
> Δ Reinforce client education on managing the client's health problem.
>
> Δ Recognize and respond to emergency situations, including notification of the primary care provider.
>
> Δ Review the client's response to emergency interventions and complete the proper documentation.
>
> Δ Provide care that meets the age-related needs of clients 65 years of age or older, including recognizing expected physiological changes.

📖 Key Points

Δ Human immunodeficiency virus (HIV) is a **retrovirus** that is **transmitted through blood and body fluids**.

Δ HIV targets **CD4+ lymphocytes**, also known as **T-cells** or T-lymphocytes.

- T-cells work in concert with B-lymphocytes; both are part of specific acquired (adaptive) immunity.

- HIV integrates its RNA into host cell DNA through reverse transcriptase, reshaping the host's immune system.

Δ HIV infection is one continuous disease process with **three stages**:

- **Primary HIV-1 infection**

  ◊ Manifestations occur within 2 to 4 weeks of infection.

  ◊ Symptoms are similar to the flu.

  ◊ Marked by rapid rise in HIV viral load, decreased CD4+ cells, and increased CD8 cells.

  ◊ Resolution of clinical manifestations coincides with decline in viral HIV copies.

  ◊ Lymphadenopathy persists throughout the disease process.

- **Chronic asymptomatic infection**

  ◊ May be **prolonged and clinically silent** (asymptomatic).

  ◊ Client may remain asymptomatic for 10 years or more.

  ◊ Anti-HIV antibodies are produced (HIV positive).

  ◊ Over time, the **virus begins active replication** using the host's genetic machinery.

    ° CD4+ cells are destroyed.

    ° Viral load increases.

    ° Dramatic loss of immunity begins.

- **AIDS**

  ◊ Characterized by **life-threatening opportunistic infections**.

  ◊ **End stage of HIV infection**.

  ◊ Without treatment, death occurs within 3 to 5 years.

  ◊ All persons with AIDS have HIV, but not all persons with HIV have AIDS.

Key Factors

Δ **Risk Factors**

- Unprotected sex (vaginal, anal, oral)

- Multiple sex partners

- Occupational exposure (healthcare workers)

- Perinatal exposure

- Blood transfusions (not a significant source of infection in the U.S.)

- Intravenous drug use with contaminated needle

Δ HIV is **transmitted through blood and body** fluids (semen, vaginal secretions).

Δ HIV is found in breast milk, amniotic fluid, urine, feces, saliva, tears, cerebrospinal fluid, lymph nodes, cervical cells, corneal tissue, and brain tissue, but epidemiologic studies indicate that these are unlikely sources of infection.

Diagnostic Procedures and Nursing Interventions

Δ **Antibody Assays: Positive** (within 3 weeks to 3 months following infection)

- Enzyme-linked immunosorbent assay (**ELISA**)

  ◊ Most common and least expensive.

- **Western blot**

  ◊ Confirms positive ELISA.

Δ **Plasma HIV-1 RNA Viral Load: Increased (> 1,500 copies)**

- Non-detectable to highly elevated levels (> 100,000 copies/mL).

- Viral load increases coincide with active viral replication.

Δ **CD4+ Cell Count: Decreased (750 cells/mm³)**

- Measures the extent of immune damage from HIV.

- Predicts disease progress.

- Clients with values below 200 cells/mm³ have an 85% likelihood of progressing to AIDS within 3 years.

Δ **Complete Blood Count (CBC) and Differential: Abnormal** (anemia, thrombocytopenia, leukopenia)

Δ **Platelet Count: Decreased**

Δ **Biochemical Profile** (for example, liver studies): **Altered** for clients receiving drug therapy

Δ **Brain or Lung MRI or CT Scan: Abnormal**

Assessments

Δ **Signs and Symptoms** (clinical findings depend on the stage of HIV infection and the presence of opportunistic infections)

- Chills, fever (may be low grade)

- Anorexia, nausea, weight loss

- Lymphadenopathy

- Weakness, fatigue

- Headache

- Night sweats

- Skin lesions

- Opportunistic infections

  ◊ **Fungal infection** (*Candida albicans*)

    ° Red, bleeding gums and oral mucous membranes

  ◊ Bacterial infections

    ° *Mycobacterium avium, Mycobacterium tuberculosis* (persistent high fever, night sweats, fatigue, anorexia, weight loss, abdominal pain, diarrhea, dry or productive cough, chest discomfort)

    ° *Cryptococcus neoformans* (dyspnea, cough, fever, headache, blurred vision, dizziness, nausea, vomiting, seizures)

  ◊ Protozoan infections

    ° *Pneumocystis carinii* (pneumonia, dyspnea, fever, tachypnea, non-productive cough, crackles, cyanosis)

    ° *Cryptosporidium* (fever, nausea, vomiting, abdominal pain, severe watery diarrhea, electrolyte imbalance)

    ° *Toxoplasmosis gondii* (headache, confusion, delirium, fever, vomiting, hemiparesis, seizures)

  ◊ **Viral infections**

    ° Cytomegalovirus (lung inflammation, colitis, blindness)

    ° Herpes simplex virus (painful vascular lesions, seizures, blindness, deafness)

  ◊ **Cancer**

    ° Kaposi's sarcoma (purplish or brown skin lesions)

    ° Non-Hodgkin's B-cell lymphomas (weight loss, fever, night sweats)

- **Wasting Syndrome**
  - ◊ Secondary to severe opportunistic infections
  - ◊ Weight loss from malnutrition

Δ **Assess/Monitor**

- Risk factors (sexual practices, IV drug use)
- Fluid intake/urinary output
- Weight
- Nutritional intake
- Electrolytes
- Skin integrity
- Pain status
- Vital signs (especially temperature)
- Lung sounds/respiratory status
- Neurological status

NANDA Nursing Diagnoses

Δ Risk for infection

Δ Imbalanced nutrition: Less than body requirements

Δ Fatigue/activity intolerance

Δ Fluid volume deficit

Δ Ineffective coping

Δ Ineffective therapeutic regimen management

Nursing Interventions

Δ Provide **client teaching** regarding:

- Transmission, infection control measures, safe sex practices.
- The need for maintaining a well-balanced diet.
- Self administration of prescribed medications and potential side effects.
- Signs/symptoms that need to be reported immediately (for example, infection).
- The need for frequent follow-up monitoring of CD4+ and viral load counts.

Δ   Identify **factors that may interfere with nutrition** and correct when possible (nausea, anorexia, mouth soreness).

Δ   Encourage activity alternated with **rest periods**.

Δ   Administer supplemental **oxygen** as needed.

Δ   Provide **analgesia** as needed.

Δ   Provide **skin care** as needed.

Δ   Emphasize the importance of carefully **complying with anti-retroviral dosing** schedules.

Δ   Encourage use of constructive **coping mechanisms**.

Δ   Assist the client with identifying **primary support systems**.

Δ   Refer the client to local **AIDS support groups** as appropriate.

Complications and Nursing Implications

Δ   **Opportunistic Infections**

- Implement and maintain **anti-retroviral drug therapy** as prescribed.
  ◊ Highly active antiretroviral therapy (HARRT)
    ° Protease inhibitors (indinavir, saquinavir)
    ° Nucleoside reverse transcriptase inhibitors (didanosine, zidovudine)
    ° Nonnucleoside reverse transcriptase inhibitors (nevirapine, delavirdine)
  ◊ Antineoplastic (interferon alpha-2a, interferon alpha-2b)
  ◊ Antibiotics (isoniazid, azithromycin, rifampin)
  ◊ Antifungals (amphotericin B, fluconazole)
  ◊ Antidiarrheals (diphenoxylate hydrochloride and atropine)
  ◊ Antidepressants (paroxetine, sertraline)
  ◊ Analgesics (opioids, NSAIDs)
  ◊ Appetite stimulants (to enhance nutrition)
  ◊ Antivirals (ganciclovir)
- Monitor for **skin breakdown**.
- Maintain **fluid intake**.
- Maintain **nutrition**.
- Teach the client to **report signs of infection immediately** to the primary care provider.

Δ **Wasting Syndrome**

- Maintain nutrition orally or by total parenteral nutrition (TPN) if indicated.

- Provide between-meal supplements/snacks.

- Serve at least six small feedings with high value protein.

Δ **Fluid/Electrolyte Imbalance**

- Monitor fluid/electrolyte status.

- Report abnormal laboratory data promptly.

- Maintain intravenous IV fluid replacement.

Δ **Seizures** (HIV encephalopathy)

- Maintain client safety.

- Implement seizure precautions.

Meeting the Needs of Older Adults

Δ HIV infection may go undiagnosed due to the similarity of its manifestations to other illnesses that are common in this age group.

Δ Older adults are more susceptible to fluid and electrolyte imbalances, malnutrition, skin alterations, and wasting syndrome than younger adults.

Δ Older women experience vaginal dryness and thinning of the vaginal wall, increasing their susceptibility to HIV infection.

Primary Reference:

Ignatavicius, D. D., & Workman, M. L. (2006). *Medical-surgical nursing* (5th ed.). St. Louis, MO: Saunders.

Additional Resources:

Monahan, F. D., Sands, J. K., Neighbors, M., Marek, F. J., & Green, C. J. (Eds.). (2007). *Phipps' medical-surgical nursing: Health and illness perspectives* (8th ed.). St. Louis, MO: Mosby.

NANDA International (2004). *NANDA nursing diagnoses: Definitions and classification 2005-2006*. Philadelphia: NANDA.

For more information on HIV/AIDS, visit the Centers for Disease Control and Prevention at *www.cdc.gov* or the World Health Organization at *www.who.int*.

Chapter 107: HIV/AIDS

Application Exercises

1. Which of the following clients is/are at the greatest risk for contracting HIV infection? Explain your answer.

    A. A 16-year-old who is in a monogamous relationship and uses condoms

    B. A married couple who are monogamous and use birth control

    C. A homosexual couple who are tested regularly and use condoms

    D. A non-exclusive couple in their mid-60s who occasionally use condoms

---

Scenario: A client visits an outpatient clinic and reports night sweats and fatigue. He states that he has a cough, has been nauseated, and is having abdominal pain and frequent diarrhea. His temperature is 38.1° C (100.6° F) orally. He states that he is afraid he has HIV.

---

2. Which of the following are priority nursing interventions for this client at this time? (Check all that apply.)

    _____   Perform a physical assessment.

    _____   Determine when current symptoms began.

    _____   Teach the client about disease transmission.

    _____   Draw blood for HIV testing.

    _____   Offer emotional support.

    _____   Initiate oxygen therapy.

    _____   Access an IV line for medications.

    _____   Obtain a sexual history.

3. If the client has HIV, which stage of infection is he experiencing? Provide a rationale for your answer.

4. Predict the changes that have occurred to the client's CD4+ cell count and HIV-RNA viral load count based on his presenting symptoms.

Chapter 107: HIV/AIDS

Application Exercises Answer Key

1. Which of the following clients is/are at the greatest risk for contracting HIV infection? Explain your answer.

        A. A 16-year-old who is in a monogamous relationship and uses condoms

        B. A married couple who are monogamous and use birth control

        C. A homosexual couple who are tested regularly and use condoms

        D. A non-exclusive couple in their mid-60s who occasionally use condoms

Couple "D" have the greatest number of risk factors for HIV infection. They are non-exclusive (multiple partners) and only occasionally use condoms. Because of vaginal dryness and thinning, the older adult female is at increased risk for HIV infection.

Scenario: A client visits an outpatient clinic and reports night sweats and fatigue. He states that he has a cough, has been nauseated, and is having abdominal pain and frequent diarrhea. His temperature is 38.1° C (100.6° F) orally. He states that he is afraid he has HIV.

---

2. Which of the following are priority nursing interventions for this client at this time? (Check all that apply.)

    __x__   Perform a physical assessment.

    __x__   Determine when current symptoms began.

    _____   Teach the client about disease transmission.

    _____   Draw blood for HIV testing.

    __x__   Offer emotional support.

    _____   Initiate oxygen therapy.

    _____   Access an IV line for medications.

    __x__   Obtain a sexual history.

3. If the client has HIV, which stage of infection is he experiencing? Provide a rationale for your answer.

The client has AIDS, which is the third and last stage of infection. The client is symptomatic (cough, fever, diarrhea), which indicates that his immune system is significantly deficient and he is no longer able to fight off opportunistic infections.

4. Predict the changes that have occurred to the client's CD4+ cell count and HIV-RNA viral load count based on his presenting symptoms.

His CD4+ cell count may be as low as 200 cells/mm^3 and his HIV-RNA viral load may be as high as 55,000 copies.

Unit 10   Nursing Care of Clients with Lymph, Immune, or Infectious Disorders

Section: Nursing Care of Clients with Immune and Lymph Disorders

Chapter 108:   Cancer and Oncological Emergencies

Contributor: Andrea Rothman Mann, MSN, RN

NCLEX-PN® Connections:

Learning Objective: Review and apply knowledge within **"Cancer and Oncological Emergencies"** in readiness for performance of the following nursing activities as outlined by the NCLEX-PN® test plan:

Δ   Observe the client for signs and symptoms of the adverse effects of radiation therapy.

Δ   Intervene to minimize or counter the adverse effects of radiation therapy.

Δ   Reinforce client teaching regarding the adverse effects of radiation therapy and strategies to minimize its impact.

Δ   Monitor the client's response to nursing care interventions for side effects of radiation therapy.

Δ   Intervene to protect the client who is immunocompromised.

Δ   Assist with relevant laboratory, diagnostic, and therapeutic procedures within the nursing role, including:

•   Preparation of the client for the procedure.

•   Accurate collection of specimens.

•   Monitoring client status during and after the procedure.

•   Recognizing the client's response (expected, unexpected adverse response) to the procedure.

•   Monitoring and taking actions to prevent or minimize the risk of complications.

•   Notifying the primary care provider of signs of complications.

Δ   Monitor and document vital signs changes.

Δ   Interpret data that need to be reported immediately.

Δ   Reinforce client education on managing the client's health problem.

Δ   Recognize and respond to emergency situations, including notification of the primary care provider, review of the client's response to emergency interventions, and completion of the proper documentation.

Δ   Provide care that meets the age-related needs of clients 65 years of age or older, including recognizing expected physiological changes.

📖 Key Points

△ Cancer is a **neoplastic disease process** that involves **abnormal cell growth and differentiation**.

△ The exact **cause of cancer is unknown,** but **viruses, physical and chemical agents, hormones, genetics, and diet** are thought to be factors that trigger abnormal cell growth.

△ Cancer cells **may invade surrounding tissues and/or spread to other areas** of the body through lymph and blood vessels (metastasis).

△ Cancers may arise from the **skin, bone, organs, or blood**.

• **Carcinomas** arise from epithelial tissue.

• **Adenocarcinomas** arise from glandular organs.

• **Sarcomas** arise from mesenchymal tissue.

• **Leukemias** are malignancies of the blood-forming cells.

• **Lymphomas** arise from the lymph tissue.

• **Multiple myeloma** arises from plasma cells and affects the bone.

△ **Screening and early diagnosis** are the most important aspects of care.

△ Many cancers are **curable when diagnosed early.**

Key Factors

△ **Risk Factors**

• Age

• Genetic predisposition

• Exposures to chemicals, viruses, tobacco, and alcohol

• Diet high in fat and red meat, low in fiber

• Sun, ultraviolet light, or radiation exposure (radon)

• Sexual lifestyles: Multiple sexual partners, STD, HIV/AIDS

• Other risk factors include poverty, obesity, and chronic GERD

Diagnostic Procedures and Nursing Interventions

△ **Tissue biopsy** – the definitive diagnosis of abnormal cancer cells.

△ **CBC and differential** – screenings for **leukemias**.

Δ Chest x-ray, computed tomography (CT) scan, magnetic resonance imaging (MRI), positron emission tomography (PET) scan, and single photon emission computed tomography (SPECT) scans are used to **visualize tumors, metastasis, or progression of cancer.**

Δ **Tumor marker assays** (CEA, CA 125, alpha fetoprotein) – screenings that screen for cancers of the colon, pancreas, liver, prostate, uterus, and ovaries. Elevated values are suggestive of cancer.

Therapeutic Procedures and Nursing Interventions

Δ **Radiation therapy** - ionizing radiation of tissues by the path of a radiation beam resulting in the death of cells. Side effects include skin changes, hair loss, and debilitating fatigue.

- Internal radiation therapy

  ☆ Client should be placed in a private room and bath.

  ☆ Appropriate signage should be placed on the door warning of the radiation source.

  ☆ Health care personnel should wear a dosimeter film badge that records the amount of radiation exposure.

  ☆ Visitors should be limited to 30-min visits and maintain a distance of 6 ft.

  ☆ Visitors and health care personnel who are pregnant or under the age of 16 should not come in contact with the client.

  ◊ A lead container should be kept in the client's room if the delivery method could allow spontaneous loss of radioactive material.

  ◊ Precautions listed above should be carried out at home if the client is discharged during therapy.

- External radiation therapy

  ☆ Wash skin over irradiated area gently, with mild soap and water, and dry thoroughly using patting motions.

  ☆ Do not remove radiation "tattoos" that are used to guide therapy.

  ☆ Do not apply powders, ointments, lotions, or perfumes to irradiated skin.

  ☆ Wear soft clothing over irradiated skin and avoid tight or constricting clothes.

  ☆ Do not expose irradiated skin to sun or a heat source.

Δ **Surgical excision** – diagnostic, curative, or palliative. Risk of "seeding."

Δ **Chemotherapy** – a certified provider administers systemic or local cytoxic medications to destroy rapid dividing cells. Often, combinations of anticancer medications are used. The most significant adverse effect is **immunosuppression** (bone marrow suppression). Measures must be employed to reduce risk, **especially at the medications' nadir.** Nausea and vomiting, alopecia, and mucositis are common side effects. Take measures to prevent extravasation of vesicants.

Assessments

Δ **Signs and Symptoms** (clinical findings depend on the type and location of cancer)

  ☆ Seven warning signs *(CAUTION)*
      Change in bowel or bladder habits
      A sore that doesn't heal
      Unusual bleeding or discharge
      Thickening or lump in the breast or elsewhere
      Indigestion or difficulty swallowing
      Obvious change in warts or moles
      Nagging cough or hoarseness

  ☆ Weight loss

  ☆ Fatigue/weakness

  ☆ Pain (may not occur until late in the disease process)

  ☆ Nausea/anorexia

Δ **Assess/Monitor**

  • For pain – evaluate PQRST (provokes, quality, radiates, severity, time) of pain (*For information, refer to chapter 79, Pain Management.*)

  • Sleep/rest patterns to determine the need for intervention

  • Oral cavity for ulcer/myositis related to immune suppression secondary to cancer treatment

  • Fatigue/shortness of breath

  • Vital signs, especially temperature to detect fever related to infection

  • WBC and platelet count

  • Intake and output

  • Serum electrolytes

  • Weight loss, cachexia, and wasting

  • Diarrhea

  • Skin alterations

  • Agitation and restlessness

  • Presence of support systems

NANDA Nursing Diagnoses

Δ   Anticipatory grieving

Δ   Risk for infection

Δ   Fear/anxiety

Δ   Imbalanced nutrition: Less than body requirements

Δ   Ineffective tissue perfusion

Nursing Interventions

Δ   **Encourage screenings** (Pap smear, mammogram, colonoscopy, stool for occult blood).

Δ   Implement **pain control measures** as prescribed.

- Use the World Health Organization (WHO) stepwise approach to pain.

- Provide pain medication before pain becomes severe.

- Serve small amounts of cool food if mouth pain is present.

- Provide frequent oral care, soft toothbrush or swab, local anesthetic mouth rinse (for example, "magic" mouthwash).

- Use distraction when appropriate (music therapy and imagery).

Δ   **Encourage/maintain nutrient intake.**

- Perform calorie counts to determine intake.

- Provide liquid supplements as needed.

- Perform mouth care prior to serving meals to enhance appetite.

- Premedicate with antiemetics such as ondansetron (Zofran).

- Administer megestrol (Megace) to increase appetite.

- Add protein powders to food or tube feedings.

Δ   Reduce risks of **neutropenia.**

- Protect the client from sources of possible infection.

  ◊   Use **hand hygiene.**

  ◊   Encourage the client/significant others to use hand hygiene.

  ◊   Encourage the client **to avoid crowds** while undergoing **chemotherapy.**

Δ   Administer **colony-stimulating factors** (Neupogen, Neulasta) as prescribed to stimulate white blood cell production.

Δ   Reduce risks of **anemia.**

- Administer oxygen as needed for fatigue.

- Encourage rest periods between periods of activity.

- Administer recombinant erythropoietin alpha as prescribed.

Δ   Reduce risks of **thrombocytopenia.**

- Avoid ASA/NSAIDs and IM injections if platelet count is decreased.

Δ   Administer antiemetics before treatments and meals.

Δ   Maintain **intravenous fluids** as prescribed.

Δ   Implement **post-radiation care,** if applicable:

- Interventions are based on site of radiation:

  ◊   Antidiarrheals for GI tract.

  ◊   Mouth care for head and neck.

  ◊   Octreotide (Sandostatin) if prescribed.

Δ   Encourage female clients to wear a hat or wig if undergoing radiation or chemotherapy that produces alopecia (hair loss).

Δ   **Listen to the client's concerns.**

Δ   Avoid false reassurance.

Δ   Provide prescribed **anxiolytics** if necessary.

Δ   Allow time for the client to **discuss feelings regarding loss and to grieve** (mastectomy, hysterectomy, limb, lack of options for further treatment).

Complications and Nursing Implications

Δ   **Oncologic Emergencies**

- **Syndrome of inappropriate antidiuretic hormone** (SIADH) – due to excessive intravascular volume to increased ADH (common in bronchogenic cancers). Monitor the client for hyponatremia and low serum osmolality. Administer furosemide (Lasix), IV normal saline, and/or hypertonic saline as prescribed for severe hyponatremia.

- **Spinal cord compression** – related to metastases. Assess the client's neurological status, including motor and/or sensory deficits. Administer corticosteroids as prescribed. Support the client during radiation therapy.

- **Hypercalcemia** – a common complication of leukemia; breast, lung, head, and neck cancers; lymphomas; multiple myelomas; and bony metastases of any cancer. Symptoms include anorexia, nausea, vomiting, shortened QT interval, kidney stones, bone pain, and changes in mental status. Administer isotonic saline, furosemide (Lasix), pamidronate, and phosphates as prescribed.

- **Superior vena cava syndrome** – results from obstruction (for example, metastases from breast or lung cancers) of venous return and engorgement of the vessels from the head and upper body. Symptoms include periorbital and facial edema, erythema of the upper body, dyspnea, and epistaxis. Initial response is to position the client in a high-Fowler's position to facilitate lung expansion. High dose radiation therapy may be used for emergency temporary relief.

- **Disseminated intravascular coagulation (DIC)** – a coagulation complication secondary to leukemia or adenocarcinomas. Observe the client for bleeding and apply pressure as needed. Avoid aspirin and NSAIDs.

Meeting the Needs of Older Adults

Δ   The **highest incidence of cancer occurs in older adults,** Older adult women most commonly develop colorectal, breast, lung, pancreatic, and ovarian cancers. Older adult men most commonly develop lung, colorectal, prostate, pancreatic, and gastric cancers.

Δ   Cancer chemotherapy and radiation therapy increase an older adult's risk for secondary infections and altered skin integrity.

Primary Reference:

Ignatavicius, D. D., & Workman, M. L. (2006). *Medical-surgical nursing* (5th ed.). St. Louis, MO: Saunders.

Additional Resources:

Held-Warmkessel, J. (2005, January). Managing three critical cancer complications. *Nursing, 35*(1), 58-64.

Monahan, F. D., Sands, J. K., Neighbors, M., Marek, F. J., & Green, C. J. (Eds.). (2007). *Phipps' medical-surgical nursing: Health and illness perspectives* (8th ed.). St. Louis, MO: Mosby.

NANDA International (2004). *NANDA nursing diagnoses: Definitions and classification 2005-2006.* Philadelphia: NANDA.

Otto, S. E. (2001). *Oncology Nursing.* (4th ed.). Philadelphia: Mosby.

For more information on cancer, visit the American Cancer Society at *www.cancer.org* and the World Health Organization at *www.who.int.*

Chapter 108: Cancer and Oncological Emergencies

Application Exercises

1. Which of the following client statements indicates the need for further teaching?

       A. "I see a dermatologist regularly for the mole on my thigh."

       B. "I take milk of magnesia for occasional constipation."

       C. "I look so much better when I have a good sun tan."

       D. "I used to smoke, but haven't done so for 3 years."

2. The intake of which of the following food/food groups may be beneficial in preventing certain cancers? (Check all that apply.)

       _____ Low saturated fats

       _____ Alcohol

       _____ Fruits

       _____ Fiber

       _____ Any red meats

       _____ Simple carbohydrates

       _____ Vegetables

       _____ Fish

3. A client with lung cancer is exhibiting signs of SIADH. Which of the following findings are essential to report to the primary care provider? (Check all that apply and support your answers.)

       _____ Behavioral changes

       _____ Headache

       _____ Urine output 40 mL/hr

       _____ Nausea/vomiting

       _____ Hyponatremia

       _____ High urine specific gravity

       _____ Lethargy

       _____ Seizures

4. A client is in hypercalcemic crisis. Which of the following orders should the nurse question?

        A. Restrict fluid intake to 1,000 mL/24 hr.

        B. Administer 40 mg furosemide (Lasix) intravenously.

        C. Administer prochlorperazine (Compazine) intramuscularly for nausea.

        D. Obtain an electrocardiogram today.

5. What actions should a nurse take if a client is suspected of having spinal cord compression secondary to breast cancer?

Chapter 108: Cancer and Oncological Emergencies

Application Exercises Answer Key

1. Which of the following client statements indicates the need for further teaching?

    A. "I see a dermatologist regularly for the mole on my thigh."

    B. "I take milk of magnesia for occasional constipation."

    C. "I look so much better when I have a good sun tan."

    D. "I used to smoke, but haven't done so for 3 years."

Exposure to radiation from excessive sun bathing is a common risk factor for skin cancer.

2. The intake of which of the following food/food groups may be beneficial in preventing certain cancers? (Check all that apply.)

__x__	Low saturated fats
_____	Alcohol
__x__	Fruits
__x__	Fiber
_____	Any red meats
_____	Simple carbohydrates
__x__	Vegetables
__x__	Fish

3. A client with lung cancer is exhibiting signs of SIADH. Which of the following findings are essential to report to the primary care provider? (Check all that apply and support your answers.)

__x__	Behavioral changes
__x__	Headache
_____	Urine output 40 mL/hr
__x__	Nausea/vomiting
__x__	Hyponatremia
_____	High urine specific gravity
__x__	Lethargy
__x__	Seizures

SIADH occurs when excessive levels of antidiuretic hormones are secreted secondary to cancer or other disease processes. The syndrome causes the body to retain water and certain levels of electrolytes in the blood to fall (e.g., sodium). As serum sodium falls, cellular swelling occurs. The brain is particularly susceptible to swelling and produces nausea, vomiting, behavioral changes, headache and seizures – all of which should be reported immediately.

4. A client is in hypercalcemic crisis. Which of the following orders should the nurse question?

A. Restrict fluid intake to 1,000 mL/24 hr.

B. Administer 40 mg furosemide (Lasix) intravenously.

C. Administer prochlorperazine (Compazine) intramuscularly for nausea.

D. Obtain an electrocardiogram today.

Treatment of hypercalcemia includes promoting calcium loss with loop diuretics and intravenous fluids. Therefore, the order for restricting fluids should be questioned. The other orders are appropriate: antiemetic for vomiting, which is a manifestation of hypercalcemia; furosemide, since it is a loop diuretic; and obtaining an ECG, since hypercalcemia may shorten the QT interval.

5. What actions should a nurse take if a client is suspected of having spinal cord compression secondary to breast cancer?

Report abnormal neurological assessment data to the primary care provider immediately. Prepare the client for interventions such as intravenous corticosteroids, radiation, or surgical intervention.

Unit 10 Nursing Care of Clients with Lymph, Immune, or Infectious Disorders

Section: Nursing Care of Clients with Immune and Lymph Disorders

Chapter 109: Rheumatoid Arthritis

Contributor: Dana Bartlett, MSN, RN, CSPI

⟳ NCLEX-PN® Connections:

Learning Objective: Review and apply knowledge within "**Rheumatoid Arthritis**" in readiness for performance of the following nursing activities as outlined by the NCLEX-PN® test plan:

Δ Protect the client who is immunocompromised.

Δ Assist with relevant laboratory, diagnostic, and therapeutic procedures within the nursing role, including:

- Preparation of the client for the procedure.

- Accurate collection of specimens.

- Monitoring client status during and after the procedure.

- Reinforcing client teaching (before and following the procedure).

- Recognizing the client's response (expected, unexpected adverse response) to the procedure.

- Monitoring results.

- Monitoring and taking actions to prevent or minimize the risk of complications.

- Notifying the primary care provider of signs of complications.

Δ Recognize signs and symptoms of the client's problem and complete the proper documentation.

Δ Provide and document care based on the client's health alteration.

Δ Monitor and document vital signs changes.

Δ Interpret data that need to be reported immediately.

Δ Reinforce client education on managing the client's health problem.

Δ Recognize and respond to emergency situations, including notification of the primary care provider.

Δ Review the client's response to emergency interventions and complete the proper documentation.

Δ Provide care that meets the age-related needs of clients 65 years of age or older, including recognizing expected physiological changes.

Key Points

Δ   Rheumatoid arthritis is a **chronic, systemic, progressive inflammatory disease** of the synovial tissue. It is a bilateral systemic inflammatory disease process involving **multiple joints**. In contrast, osteoarthritis is a unilateral degenerative disease process of a single joint.

Δ   It is classified as an **autoimmune process** in which **antibodies are formed against synovial tissues**, including:

- Synovial membrane.

- Articular cartilage.

- Joint capsule.

- Tendons and ligaments surrounding the joint.

- Involvement of the spine, particularly the cervical joints.

Δ   The natural course of the disease is one of **exacerbations and remissions**.

Δ   Inflammation and tissue damage can cause severe deformities that greatly restrict function.

Key Factors

Δ   **Risk Factors**

- Female gender

- Age 20 to 50 years

- Genetic predisposition

- Epstein Barr virus

- Stress

Diagnostic Procedures and Nursing Interventions

Δ   **Rheumatoid Factor (RF) antibody**

- Diagnostic for rheumatoid arthritis = 1:40 to 1:60 (normal ≤ 1:20).

- High titers correlate with severe disease.

Δ   **Antinuclear Antibody (ANA) Titer** (antibody produced against one's own DNA)

- A positive ANA titer is associated with RA (normal is negative ANA titer at 1:20 dilution).

Δ **Erythrocyte Sedimentation Rate (ESR): Elevated**

- 20 to 40 mm/hr = **mild** inflammation.

- 40 to 70 mm/hr = **moderate** inflammation.

- 70 to 150 mm/hr = **severe** inflammation

Δ **Arthrocentesis**

- Synovial fluid aspiration by needle

- With RA, **increased white blood cells (WBCs) and RF** are present.

Assessments

Δ **Signs and Symptoms** (clinical findings depend on the area affected by the disease process)

- **Pain** at rest and with movement

- Morning **stiffness**

- Joint **swelling**

- Joint **deformity**

- Anorexia/**weight loss**

- **Fever** (generally low grade)

- **Fatigue**

- **Muscle weakness**/atrophy

Δ **Assess/Monitor**

- **Pain** (character, intensity, effectiveness of relief measures)

- **Functional ability**

- Indications of **infection**

NANDA Nursing Diagnoses

Δ Fatigue

Δ Impaired physical mobility

Δ Chronic pain

Δ Disturbed body image

Δ Risk for injury

Nursing Interventions

Δ   Apply **heat or cold** to affected areas as indicated based on client response.

- Morning stiffness (hot shower)

- Pain (heated paraffin)

- Edema (cold therapy)

Δ   Assist with and **encourage physical activity** to maintain joint mobility (within the capabilities of the client).

Δ   **Teach** the client measures to:

- **Maximize functional activity.**

- **Minimize pain.**

- **Conserve energy** (pacing activities, rest periods).

Δ   Provide a **safe environment**.

- Facilitate the use of **assistive devices.**

- Remove unnecessary equipment/supplies.

Δ   Utilize **progressive muscle relaxation.**

Δ   Monitor the client for **signs/symptoms of fatigue.**

Δ   Refer the client to **support groups** as appropriate.

Δ   Administer medications as prescribed.

- **Analgesics**

- **Anti-inflammatories**

  ◊ **Nonsteroidal anti-inflammatory drugs (NSAIDs)**, such as hydroxychloroquine (Plaquenil), sulfasalazine (Azulfidine)

  ◊ **Steroids**, such as prednisone

  ◊ Monitor for fluid retention, hypertension, and renal dysfunction.

- **Immunosuppressants** (may slow the progression of disease)

  ◊ **Disease-modifying anti-rheumatic medications**, such as hydroxychloroquine, sulfasalazine, minocycline

  ◊ **Methotrexate** (Rheumatrex)

  ◊ Cyclophosphamide (**Cytoxan**)

  ◊ **Leflunomide** (for example, Arava)

  ◊ Monitor for toxic effects (bone marrow suppression, increased liver enzymes).

- **Biological response modifiers**: Inhibit the action of tumor necrosis factor (TNF)

    ◊ Examples include etanercept (Enbrel), **infliximab** (Remicade), **adalimumab** (Humira), and **anakinra** (Kineret).

    ◊ Do not administer if the client has a serious infection.

    ◊ Monitor for injection/infusion reactions.

    ◊ Monitor CBC and the client for signs of infection.

Δ Monitor for **medication effectiveness** (reduced pain, increased mobility).

Δ Teach the client regarding signs/symptoms that need to be reported immediately **(fever, infection)**.

Complications and Nursing Implications

Δ Sjögren's syndrome (dry eyes, dry mouth, dry vagina)

Δ Joint deformity (tendon rupture, secondary osteoporosis)

Δ Vasculitis (ischemic organs)

Δ Cervical subluxation (risk of quadriplegia and respiratory compromise)

Meeting the Needs of Older Adults

Δ Early signs of RA such as fatigue and joint discomfort are vague and may be attributed to other disorders in older adults.

Δ Large joints are generally affected in older adults, and the onset is acute.

Δ Joint pain and dysfunction may have a greater effect on older clients than on younger clients due to the presence of other chronic conditions.

Δ Older adults may be less able to overcome and/or cope with joint pain/deformity.

Primary Reference:

Ignatavicius, D. D., & Workman, M. L. (2006). *Medical-surgical nursing* (5th ed.). St. Louis, MO: Saunders.

Additional Resources:

Gupta, K., Nicholas, J. J., & Bhagia, S.M. (2006, March 22). Rheumatoid arthritis. *eMedicine*, Topic 124. Retrieved June 8, 2006, from http://www.emedicine.com/pmr/topic124.htm

Monahan, F. D., Sands, J. K., Neighbors, M., Marek, F. J., & Green, C. J. (Eds.). (2007). *Phipps' medical-surgical nursing: Health and illness perspectives* (8th ed.). St. Louis, MO: Mosby.

NANDA International (2004). *NANDA nursing diagnoses: Definitions and classification 2005-2006*. Philadelphia: NANDA.

Chapter 109: Rheumatoid Arthritis

Application Exercises

Scenario: A 47-year-old client visits the outpatient clinic due to an exacerbation of her rheumatoid arthritis (RA). She is experiencing increased joint tenderness and swelling. She has subcutaneous nodules in the metacarpophalangeal (MCP) and distal interphalangeal (DIP) joints of her hands bilaterally.

1. What further data is essential in order to plan care for this client? (Check all that apply.)

      _____ Exacerbating factors   _____ Date of original diagnosis

      _____ History of recent illness   _____ Temperature

      _____ Blood pressure   _____ Range of motion

      _____ Family members with disease   _____ Pain status

2. Which of the following laboratory tests are likely to be ordered for this client? (Check all that apply.)

      _____ Urinalysis   _____ ANA titer

      _____ ESR   _____ White blood cell count

      _____ Rheumatoid factor   _____ BUN

      _____ Arterial blood gases   _____ Platelet count

3. The client wants to know why the nurse is placing ice on her swollen joints. What is the best response to the client's question?

4. Prioritize nursing diagnoses for this client, using "1" as the first priority. Provide a rationale for your prioritization.

      _____ Disturbed body image

      _____ Risk for injury

      _____ Impaired physical mobility

      _____ Pain: Chronic

      _____ Deficient knowledge

Chapter 109: Rheumatoid Arthritis

Application Exercises Answer Key

Scenario: A 47-year-old client visits the outpatient clinic due to an exacerbation of her rheumatoid arthritis (RA). She is experiencing increased joint tenderness and swelling. She has subcutaneous nodules in the metacarpophalangeal (MCP) and distal interphalangeal (DIP) joints of her hands bilaterally.

1. What further data is essential in order to plan care for this client? (Check all that apply.)

_x_	Exacerbating factors	____	Date of original diagnosis
_x_	History of recent illness	_x_	Temperature
____	Blood pressure	_x_	Range of motion
____	Family members with disease	_x_	Pain status

> **RA symptoms include a low-grade fever. Identification of exacerbating factors, such as recent illness, is important to developing a comprehensive plan of care. Baselines regarding range of motion and pain status are needed for evaluation of intervention effectiveness.**

2. Which of the following laboratory tests are likely to be ordered for this client? (Check all that apply.)

____	Urinalysis	_x_	ANA titer
_x_	ESR	_x_	White blood cell count
_x_	Rheumatoid factor	____	BUN
____	Arterial blood gases	____	Platelet count

> **Elevations in ESR, RF, ANA titer, and WBC counts are consistent with an RA diagnosis.**

3. The client wants to know why the nurse is placing ice on her swollen joints. What is the best response to the client's question?

> **Ice decreases circulation to the area, which prevents swelling. Decreasing or controlling swelling often relieves pain.**

4. Prioritize nursing diagnoses for this client, using "1" as the first priority. Provide a rationale for your prioritization.

      __5__ Disturbed body image

      __2__ Risk for injury

      __3__ Impaired physical mobility

      __1__ Pain: Chronic

      __4__ Deficient knowledge

Of the diagnoses presented here, relief of pain is the most basic of the human needs (Maslow); therefore, it must be addressed first. The second human need is for safety; therefore, risk for injury is addressed next. Impaired physical mobility should be addressed next because it can result in injury. Knowledge deficiency is addressed before disturbed body image because body image may be less significant if the client knows how to control her disease.

Unit 10   Nursing Care of Clients with Lymph, Immune, or Infectious Disorders

Section: Nursing Care of Clients with Immune and Lymph Disorders

Chapter 110:   Systemic Lupus Erythematosus (SLE)

Contributor: Andrea Rothman Mann, MSN, RN

↻ NCLEX-PN® Connections:

Learning Objective: Review and apply knowledge within "**Systemic Lupus Erythematosus (SLE)**" in readiness for performance of the following nursing activities as outlined by the NCLEX-PN® test plan:

Δ   Protect the client who is immunocompromised.

Δ   Assist with relevant laboratory, diagnostic, and therapeutic procedures within the nursing role, including:

- Preparation of the client for the procedure.

- Accurate collection of specimens.

- Monitoring client status during and after the procedure.

- Reinforcing client teaching (before and following the procedure).

- Recognizing the client's response (expected, unexpected adverse response) to the procedure.

- Monitoring results.

- Monitoring and taking actions to prevent or minimize the risk of complications.

- Notifying the primary care provider of signs of complications.

Δ   Recognize signs and symptoms of the client's problem and complete the proper documentation.

Δ   Provide and document care based on the client's health alteration.

Δ   Monitor and document vital signs changes.

Δ   Interpret data that need to be reported immediately.

Δ   Reinforce client education on managing the client's health problem.

Δ   Recognize and respond to emergency situations, including notification of the primary care provider.

Δ   Review the client's response to emergency interventions and complete the proper documentation.

Δ   Provide care that meets the age-related needs of clients 65 years of age or older, including recognizing expected physiological changes.

📖 Key Points

Δ   Lupus is classified as discoid, systemic, or drug-induced.

- **Discoid**
  ◊   Primarily affects the **skin.**
  ◊   Characteristic **erythematosus butterfly rash over nose and cheeks.**
  ◊   Generally self-limiting.

- **Systemic**
  ◊   Affects the **connective tissues of multiple organ systems.**
  ◊   Can lead to **major organ failure.**

- **Drug-induced**
  ◊   Drugs: **Procainamide, hydralazine, isoniazid**
  ◊   Symptoms **resolve when the drug is discontinued.**
  ◊   **Does not cause renal or neurological disease.**

Δ   Systemic Lupus Erythematosus (SLE) is a **chronic, inflammatory autoimmune** disease.

- Varies in **severity and progression.**
- Generally characterized by **periods of exacerbations (flares) and remissions.**

Δ   Lupus may be **difficult to diagnose** because of the vagueness of early symptoms. The cause of lupus is **unknown.**

Δ   There is **no known cure** for discoid or systemic lupus.

Key Factors

Δ   **Risk Factors**

- Female gender between the ages of 15 and 40
- African American descent
- Asian descent
- Native American descent

Δ   The incidence of lupus drops in women following menopause but remains steady in men.

Diagnostic Procedures and Nursing Interventions

Δ **Antinuclear Antibody Titer** (antibody produced against one's own DNA)

- **Positive ANA titer** (normal is negative ANA titer at 1:20 dilution) in 90% of clients with lupus.

Δ **Lupus Antibodies**

- **Anti-Smith (anti-Sm)** – positive in 20% to 60% of clients

- **Anti-DNA** – positive in 20% to 60% of clients

- **Anti-RO** (SSA) – high titers

- **Anti-LA** (SSB) – positive titer

- **Anti-phospholipids** (AP) – positive titer

Δ **Serum complement** (C3, C4): **Decreased**

Δ **BUN, Serum Creatinine: Elevated** (with renal involvement)

Δ Urinalysis: **Positive for protein, RBCs** (renal involvement)

Δ CBC: **Pancytopenia**

Assessments

Δ Monitor for **signs and symptoms**.

- **Fatigue/malaise**

- Fever (also major symptom of exacerbation)

- Butterfly rash on face

- Alopecia

- Anorexia/weight loss

- Anemia

- Lymphadenopathy

- Depression

- Joint pain, swelling, tenderness

- Raynaud's phenomenon (arteriolar vasospasm in response to cold/stress)

Δ   Assess/Monitor

- **Pain, mobility, and fatigue**

- **Vital signs** (especially blood pressure)

- For **systemic manifestations:**

  ◊   Hypertension, edema (renal compromise)

  ◊   Urine output (renal compromise)

  ◊   Diminished breath sounds (pleural effusion)

  ◊   Tachycardia, sharp inspiratory chest pain (pericarditis)

  ◊   Rubor, pallor, cyanosis of hands/feet (vasculitis/vasospasm, Raynaud's phenomenon)

  ◊   Arthralgias, myalgias, polyarthritis (joint, connective tissue involvement)

  ◊   Changes in mental status that indicate neurologic involvement (psychoses, paresis, seizures)

  ◊   BUN, serum creatinine, urinary output for renal involvement

  ◊   Nutritional status

NANDA Nursing Diagnoses

Δ   Risk for infection

Δ   Acute pain, chronic pain

Δ   Deficient knowledge

Δ   Ineffective coping

Δ   Risk for altered tissue perfusion (cardiac, renal, peripheral)

Nursing Interventions

Δ   Teach the client regarding the need to:

- Avoid **UV and sun exposure.** Use sunscreen when outside and exposed to sunlight.

- Use **mild protein shampoo** and avoid harsh hair treatments.

- Use **steroid creams** for skin rash.

- Report **peripheral and periorbital edema** promptly.

- Report signs/symptoms of **infection** related to immunosuppression.

Δ   Prescribed **medications** include:

- **NSAIDs** to reduce inflammation.
  - ◊   Contraindicated for clients with renal compromise.
  - ◊   Monitor for NSAID-induced hepatitis.
- **Corticosteroids** for immunosuppression and to reduce inflammation.
  - ◊   Monitor for fluid retention, hypertension, and renal dysfunction.
  - ◊   Do not stop taking steroids abruptly.
- **Immunosuppressant agents**, such as methotrexate and azathioprine (Imuran), to suppress the immune response.
  - ◊   Monitor for toxic effects (bone marrow suppression, increased liver enzymes).
- **Antimalarial** (hydroxychloroquine) for suppression of synovitis, fever, and fatigue.
  - ◊   Encourage frequent eye examinations.

Δ   Provide **small, frequent meals if anorexia** is a problem. Offer between-meal supplements.

Δ   Encourage the client to **limit salt intake for fluid retention** secondary to steroid therapy.

Δ   Provide emotional support to the client and significant others. Refer to **support groups** as appropriate.

Complications and Nursing Implications

Δ   **Renal failure/glomerulonephritis** (major cause of death)

Δ   **Pericarditis, myocarditis** (instruct client to report chest pain)

Δ   **Vasculitis** (major organ ischemia)

Δ   **Osteonecrosis** (constriction of small blood vessels supplying hip joint) secondary to corticosteroids

Δ   Increased incidence of **miscarriage, stillbirth, premature birth**, and other pregnancy-related complications (sexual counseling regarding contraception)

Meeting the Needs of Older Adults

Δ   Diagnosis of SLE may be delayed in older adult clients because many of the clinical manifestations mimic other disorders or may be associated with reports common to the normal aging process.

Δ   Joint pain and swelling may significantly limit ADLs in older adult clients with co-morbidities.

Δ   Older adult clients are at increased risk for fractures.

Primary Reference:

Ignatavicius, D. D., & Workman, M. L. (2006). *Medical-surgical nursing* (5th ed.). St. Louis, MO: Saunders.

Additional Resources:

Monahan, F. D., Sands, J. K., Neighbors, M., Marek, F. J., & Green, C. J. (Eds.). (2007). *Phipps' medical-surgical nursing: Health and illness perspectives* (8th ed.). St. Louis, MO: Mosby.

NANDA International (2004). *NANDA nursing diagnoses: Definitions and classification 2005-2006*. Philadelphia: NANDA.

For more information, visit the Lupus Foundation of America at: *www.lupus.org*.

Chapter 110: Systemic Lupus Erythematosus (SLE)

Application Exercises

Scenario: A 32-year-old female client is experiencing an exacerbation of systemic lupus erythematosus (SLE). She reports fatigue, joint tenderness, and anorexia. Her knees are swollen, she has an oral temperature of 38.2° C (100.8° F), and her blood pressure is 152/90 mm Hg. Renal compromise is suspected.

1. Based on the client's data, which of the following abnormal laboratory findings should the nurse anticipate? (Check all that apply.)

   _____ Positive ANA   _____ Decreased white blood cell count

   _____ Elevated serum potassium   _____ Elevated BUN

   _____ 2+ urine protein   _____ Increased hematocrit

   _____ Increased hemoglobin   _____ Decreased serum complement

2. Which of the following nursing activities are indicated for the client's pain? (Check all that apply and identify the rationale for each selected activity.)

   _____ Massage her knees using a local analgesic.

   _____ Immobilize the affected joints.

   _____ Administer a prescribed NSAID.

   _____ Place a heating pad on her swollen knees.

3. What is the rationale for administering each of these medications to the client?

Medications	Rationale
Corticosteroids	
Anti-malarials	
Immune suppressant agents	

4. Why is the client at increased risk for renal damage?

5. The client will be discharged on the medication prednisone (Deltasone) until symptoms improve. The nurse should teach the client about which possible side effects from this medication? (Check all that apply.)

_____ Orthostatic hypotension   _____ Moon face

_____ Weight gain   _____ Abdominal striae

_____ Loss of appetite   _____ Hair loss

_____ Buffalo hump   _____ Elevated blood glucose

Chapter 110: Systemic Lupus Erythematosus (SLE)

Application Exercises Answer Key

Scenario: A 32-year-old female client is experiencing an exacerbation of systemic lupus erythematosus (SLE). She reports fatigue, joint tenderness, and anorexia. Her knees are swollen, she has an oral temperature of 38.2° C (100.8° F), and her blood pressure is 152/90 mm Hg. Renal compromise is suspected.

1. Based on the client's data, which of the following abnormal laboratory findings should the nurse anticipate? (Check all that apply.)

   __x__ Positive ANA   _____ Decreased white blood cell count

   _____ Elevated serum potassium   __x__ Elevated BUN

   __x__ 2+ urine protein   _____ Increased hematocrit

   _____ Increased hemoglobin   __x__ Decreased serum complement

   Positive ANA titers and decreased serum complement are expected findings with SLE. Elevated BUN and urine protein provide information regarding renal involvement.

2. Which of the following nursing activities are indicated for the client's pain? (Check all that apply and identify the rationale for each selected activity.)

   _____ Massage her knees using a local analgesic.

   __x__ Immobilize the affected joints.

   __x__ Administer a prescribed NSAID.

   _____ Place a heating pad on her swollen knees.

   The joints of clients with SLE may be temporarily immobilized until the swelling and pain decrease. Joint deformity is not common with SLE, so it is safe to immobilize joints. NSAIDS reduce inflammation and inhibit the immune response, both of which will control the client's pain. Massaging the client's knees will exacerbate her pain and should be avoided. Ice, rather than heat, slows circulation to the affected areas and prevents further swelling, which reduces pain.

3. What is the rationale for administering each of these medications to the client?

Medications	Rationale
Corticosteroids	Reduce inflammation and inhibit the immune response.
Anti-malarials	Help suppress synovitis, fever, and fatigue.
Immune suppressant agents	Inhibit the immune response and antibody production. Antibodies cause tissue injury.

4. Why is the client at increased risk for renal damage?

Immunoglobulins are produced against the client's own cells (autoimmune reaction) forming antigen-antibody complexes. These complexes enter the circulation and are filtered by the kidneys. The immune complexes collect in the glomerulus because they are too large to leave the glomerular pores. Consequently, they damage the glomerulus, causing renal compromise.

5. The client will be discharged on the medication prednisone (Deltasone) until symptoms improve. The nurse should teach the client about which possible side effects from this medication? (Check all that apply.)

        Orthostatic hypotension   _x_ Moon face

   _x_ Weight gain   _x_ Abdominal striae

        Loss of appetite   Hair loss

   _x_ Buffalo hump   _x_ Elevated blood glucose

These are findings associated with steroid use. Hypertension rather than hypotension is expected secondary to fluid retention. The client should also be taught to not stop taking this medication abruptly.

Unit 11   Nursing Care of Clients with Integumentary Disorders
Section: Nursing Care of Clients with Select Integumentary Disorders

Chapter 111:   Pressure Ulcers
Contributor: Linda Turchin, MSN, RN

⟳ NCLEX-PN® Connections:

Learning Objective: Review and apply knowledge within **"Pressure Ulcers"** in readiness for performance of the following nursing activities as outlined by the NCLEX-PN® test plan:

Δ   Plan and provide care to the client with a pressure ulcer that promotes wound healing and restoration and maintenance of skin integrity.

Δ   Assist with relevant laboratory, diagnostic, and therapeutic procedures within the nursing role, including:

- Preparation of the client for the procedure.
- Accurate collection of specimens.
- Monitoring client status during and after the procedure.
- Reinforcing client teaching (before and following the procedure).
- Recognizing the client's response (expected, unexpected adverse response) to the procedure.
- Monitoring results.
- Monitoring and taking actions to prevent or minimize the risk of complications.
- Notifying the primary care provider of signs of complications.

Δ   Recognize signs and symptoms of the client's problem and complete the proper documentation.

Δ   Provide and document care based on the client's health alteration.

Δ   Monitor and document vital signs changes.

Δ   Interpret data that need to be reported immediately.

Δ   Reinforce client education on managing the client's health problem.

Δ   Recognize and respond to emergency situations, including notification of the primary care provider.

Δ   Review the client's response to emergency interventions and complete the proper documentation.

Δ   Provide care that meets the age-related needs of clients 65 years of age or older, including recognizing expected physiological changes.

📖 Key Points

Δ   A pressure ulcer is a specific **tissue injury caused by external forces** that result in unrelieved **pressure that causes ischemia** and damage to the underlying tissue.

Δ   Pressure ulcers range from blanchable tissue redness to full-thickness skin loss with damage to underlying muscle and bone. They are categorized as Stage I, II, III, and IV.

Δ   Excellent nursing care is the primary factor in the prevention of pressure ulcers.

Δ   The primary focus of **prevention and treatment** is to **relieve the pressure** and provide for good nutrition and hydration.

Δ   All clients must be **assessed** regularly for skin integrity status and evaluated regularly for **risk factors** that contribute to the development of impaired skin integrity.

Key Factors

Δ   **Risk Factors**

• Skin changes related to aging

• Immobility

• Incontinence or excessive moisture

• Skin friction and shearing

• Vascular disorders

• Obesity

Δ   Factors that **contribute to development** of pressure ulcers include:

• Inadequate nutrition and/or hydration.

• Anemia.

• Fever.

• Impaired circulation.

• Edema.

• Sensory deficits.

• Low diastolic blood pressure.

• Impaired cognitive functioning.

• Neurological disorders.

- Chronic diseases (diabetes mellitus, chronic renal failure, congestive heart disease, chronic lung disease).

- Sedation that impairs spontaneous repositioning.

Diagnostic Procedures and Nursing Interventions

Δ **Wound Culture and Sensitivity** (swab cultures and/or wound biopsies): Definitively identify and quantify wound bacteria.

Δ **Complete Blood Count (CBC) with Differential**: Assess immune response.

Δ **Blood Cultures**: Rule out sepsis.

Δ **Serum Albumin** (normal > 3.5 g/dL) and **Prealbumin** (normal 17 to 40 mg/dL): Assess nutritional status (low levels indicate malnutrition).

Therapeutic Procedures and Nursing Interventions

Δ **Vacuum-assisted Wound Closure** – continuous low-level negative pressure is applied to a sponge-covered suction tube for several hours.

Δ **Hyperbaric Oxygen Therapy** – administration of high-pressurized 100% oxygen directly over the wound for 60 to 90 min.

Δ **Surgical Debridement and/or Wound Grafting** – surgical excision of nonviable tissue to promote wound healing and/or grafting of skin from donor sites to clean granulating or freshly excised wound bed.

Assessments

Δ Monitor for **signs and symptoms.**

Stage I	Stage II	Stage III	Stage IV
Intact	Partial-thickness (epidermis and dermis), for example, blister	Full-thickness (down to fascia)	Full-thickness (down to muscle and bone)
Does not blanch	Superficial	Shallow to deep	Deep

Δ **Some ulcers cannot be staged** because they are covered with **eschar** – dark, leathery scab (crust) made of necrotic tissue – and the wound bed cannot be visualized.

Δ **Assess/Monitor**

- Alterations in skin integrity

- Skin moisture status

- Incontinence

- Nutritional status

- Hydration status
- Problems with mobility

NANDA Nursing Diagnoses

Δ   Acute pain, chronic pain

Δ   Impaired skin integrity

Δ   Impaired tissue integrity

Δ   Ineffective peripheral tissue perfusion

Nursing Interventions

Δ   Assist with interventions, such as surgical debridement, to **remove eschar**.

Δ   **Stage I**

- Epidermal involvement only.
- Lightly pigmented skin: redness; darker skin tones: red, blue, or purple in tone.
- **Non blanchable** – color does not return within 20 seconds after pressure is removed.
- REVERSIBLE IF pressure is relieved.
- **Interventions**
  - ◊   Relieve pressure.
  - ◊   Frequent turning/repositioning.
  - ◊   Use pressure relieving devices, such as an air-fluidized bed.
  - ◊   Utilize pressure reduction surfaces (air mattress, foam mattress).
  - ◊   Keep the client dry, clean, and well-nourished and hydrated.

Δ   **Stage II**

- Partial-thickness skin loss involving epidermis and/or dermis.
- Lesion presents as an abrasion, shallow crater, or blister. `
- May appear swollen and may be painful.
- Takes several weeks to heal after pressure is relieved.
- **Interventions**
  - ◊   Maintain a moist healing environment (saline or occlusive dressing).
  - ◊   Promote natural healing while preventing formation of scar tissue.

◊ Provide nutritional supplements as needed.

◊ Administer analgesics as needed.

Δ **Stage III**

- Full-thickness skin loss, including subcutaneous tissue and underlying fascia.

- Lesion presents as a deep crater with or without **undermining** of adjacent tissue and may have foul smelling purulent drainage if locally infected.

- Yellow slough and/or necrotic tissue in wound bed.

- May require months to heal after pressure is relieved.

- **Interventions**

  ◊ Clean and/or debride:

    ° Wet-to-dry dressing.

    ° Surgical intervention.

    ° Proteolytic enzymes.

  ◊ Provide nutritional supplements as needed.

  ◊ Administer analgesics as needed.

  ◊ Administer antimicrobials (topical and/or systemic).

Δ **Stage IV**

- Extensive damage to underlying structures including tendons, muscles, and bones.

- Lesion may appear small on the surface but can have extensive **tunneling** out of sight beneath superficial tissue and usually includes foul smelling discharge.

- Local infection can easily spread causing sepsis (systemic infection).

- May take months or years to heal after pressure is relieved.

- **Interventions**

  ◊ Perform non-adherent dressing changes every 12 hr.

  ◊ May require skin grafts.

  ◊ Provide nutritional supplements as needed.

  ◊ Administer analgesics as needed.

  ◊ Administer antimicrobials (topical and/or systemic).

Δ   **Prevention of Pressure Ulcers**

- Maintain clean, dry skin and wrinkle-free linens.

    ◊   Appropriately use pressure-reducing surfaces and pressure-relieving devices.

    ◊   Inspect skin frequently and document risk (for example, Braden Scale) and findings.

    ◊   Clean and dry skin **immediately following urinary or stool incontinence**.

    ◊   **Apply moisture barrier** creams to the skin of incontinent clients.

    ◊   Use **tepid** water (not hot), minimal scrubbing, and **pat skin dry**.

- **Reposition** the client in bed **at least every 2 hr** and every 1 hr when sitting in a chair. Document position changes.

    ◊   Place **pillows strategically between bony surfaces**.

    ◊   Maintain the **head of the bed at or below 30°** angle (or flat), unless contraindicated, to relieve pressure on sacrum, buttocks, and heels.

    ◊   **Prevent the client from sliding down** in bed as this increases shearing forces that pull tissue layers apart and cause damage.

    ◊   **Lift rather than pull** a client up in bed or in a chair, because pulling creates friction that can damage the client's outer layer of skin (epidermis).

    ◊   Raise the client's **heels off of the bed** to prevent pressure on the heels.

    ◊   Ambulate the client as soon as possible and as often as possible.

    ◊   Implement active/passive exercises for immobile clients.

    ◊   **Do not massage** bony prominences.

- Provide **adequate hydration** (2,000 to 3,000 mL/day) and meet **protein** and calorie needs.

    ◊   Note if serum albumin levels are low (< 3.5 g/dL), because a lack of protein puts the client at greater risk for skin breakdown, slowed healing, and infection.

    ◊   Provide nutritional support as indicated, such as vitamin and mineral supplements, nutritional supplements, enteral nutrition, and parenteral nutrition.

Complications and Nursing Implications

Δ **Deterioration** to a higher stage ulceration and/or infection – monitor the ulcer frequently and report increases in the size or depth of the lesion; changes in granulation tissues (color, texture); and changes in exudates (color, quantity, odor).

Δ **Systemic Infection** – monitor for signs of sepsis (changes in level of consciousness, persistent recurrent fever, tachycardia, tachypnea, hypotension, oliguria, increased white blood cell count) and intervene accordingly.

Meeting the Needs of Older Adults

Δ Be mindful that the aging process produces the following physiological changes:

- Loss of lean body mass.

- Thinning of the epidermis.

- Changes in collagen fibers resulting in loss of strength and elasticity.

- Decreased oil production resulting in dry and scaly skin.

- Compromised peripheral circulation.

- Decreased pain perception.

- Possible cognitive functioning compromise.

- Slowing of cell regeneration.

- Presence of chronic disease(s) that compromise circulation, oxygenation, or healing.

- Potential for inadequate nutrition and fluid intake.

Primary Reference:

Ignatavicius, D. D., & Workman, M. L. (2006). *Medical-surgical nursing* (5th ed.). St. Louis, MO: Saunders.

Additional Resources:

Brown, P., & Phelps Maloy, J. (2005). *Quick Reference to Wound Care* (2nd ed.). Boston: Jones and Bartlett Publishers.

NANDA International (2004). *NANDA nursing diagnoses: Definitions and classification 2005-2006*. Philadelphia: NANDA.

Potter, P. A., & Perry, A. G. (2005). *Fundamentals of nursing* (6th ed.). St. Louis, MO: Mosby.

Wound Care Made Incredibly Easy (2nd ed.). (2003). Philadelphia: Lippincott Williams & Wilkins.

Chapter 111: Pressure Ulcers

Application Exercises

Scenario: A 75-year-old male client is admitted to an acute care facility with a report of pain in his right shoulder. The client has a history of a right hemisphere cardiovascular accident 3 years ago that has left him with severe weakness on the left side of his body. He continues to neglect his left side and requires frequent reminders to change position while in his wheelchair. The client requires assistance to transfer from the bed to a chair and was unable to use a walker even before his shoulder pain began. He is incontinent of bladder and bowels approximately 70% of the time. He eats 70 to 85% of all meals but requires frequent prompting to drink fluids.

1. Identify the client findings that pose the greatest risk to this client for the development of a pressure ulcer.

2. Identify several nursing interventions directed at minimizing the client's risk for developing a pressure ulcer.

3. Identify the appropriate wound stage based on each of the following wound descriptions.

Wound Descriptions	Stage I	Stage II	Stage III	Stage IV	Unable to Stage
Non blanching reddened area on right heel					
Deep crater with undermining of adjacent tissue					
Leathery scab					
Blister on left elbow					
Bone visible, purulent drainage					

4. Which of the following clients is at greatest risk of developing a pressure ulcer?

    A. 25-year-old client who has spina bifida and is wheelchair bound

    B. 75-year-old client who is bedfast with terminal COPD

    C. 82-year-old client post CVA with mild right hemiplegia

    D. 70-year-old client following a total hip arthroplasty

5. Which of the following diagnostic tests is most relevant for assessing the risk of developing a pressure ulcer for a 73-year-old client with no major health issues?

    A. Serum albumin

    B. White blood cells

    C. Red blood cells

    D. Serum potassium

6. Which of the following is an appropriate nursing intervention for a client at risk for developing a pressure ulcer?

    A. Massaging directly over reddened areas to help improve circulation

    B. Positioning the HOB at a 45° angle to improve tissue perfusion

    C. Using hot, soapy water to clean the client to remove fecal/urine incontinence

    D. Repositioning a bedfast client at least every 2 hr to minimize pressure

7. What is the one event that must occur before pressure ulcer healing can begin?

Chapter 111: Pressure Ulcers

Application Exercises Answer Key

Scenario: A 75-year-old male client is admitted to an acute care facility with a report of pain in his right shoulder. The client has a history of a right hemisphere cardiovascular accident 3 years ago that has left him with severe weakness on the left side of his body. He continues to neglect his left side and requires frequent reminders to change position while in his wheelchair. The client requires assistance to transfer from the bed to a chair and was unable to use a walker even before his shoulder pain began. He is incontinent of bladder and bowels approximately 70% of the time. He eats 70 to 85% of all meals but requires frequent prompting to drink fluids.

1. Identify the client findings that pose the greatest risk to this client for the development of a pressure ulcer.

   Altered sensory perception: Left hemiplegia and neglect

   Limited mobility: Requires assistance

   Moisture: Frequently incontinent

   Risk of dehydration: Requires prompting to drink fluids

2. Identify several nursing interventions directed at minimizing the client's risk for developing a pressure ulcer.

   Assess skin regularly for signs of breakdown.

   Maintain adequate food and fluid intake.

   Cleanse the skin immediately if the client is incontinent.

   Use pressure relief devices while in wheelchair.

   Encourage position change every 15 min while in wheelchair.

   Avoid leaving the client in the wheelchair for extended periods of time.

   Monitor serum albumin levels.

   Educate family/caregivers on preventive measures.

3. Identify the appropriate wound stage based on each of the following wound descriptions.

Wound Descriptions	Stage I	Stage II	Stage III	Stage IV	Unable to Stage
Non blanching reddened area on right heel	X				
Deep crater with undermining of adjacent tissue			X		
Leathery scab					X
Blister on left elbow		X			
Bone visible, purulent drainage				X	

4. Which of the following clients is at greatest risk of developing a pressure ulcer?

   A. 25-year-old client who has spina bifida and is wheelchair bound

   B. 75-year-old client who is bedfast with terminal COPD

   C. 82-year-old client post CVA with mild right hemiplegia

   D. 70-year-old client following a total hip arthroplasty

All the clients have some level of risk. Confinement to bed, hypoxemia, and the physiological changes that occur with a terminal illness pose serious risks for pressure ulcer development.

5. Which of the following diagnostic tests is most relevant for assessing the risk of developing a pressure ulcer for a 73-year-old client with no major health issues?

   A. Serum albumin

   B. White blood cells

   C. Red blood cells

   D. Serum potassium

Serum albumin levels provide information regarding the adequacy of protein intake. Inadequate protein poses a great risk for altered skin integrity and ineffective healing.

6. Which of the following is an appropriate nursing intervention for a client at risk for developing a pressure ulcer?

      A. Massaging directly over reddened areas to help improve circulation

      B. Positioning the HOB at a 45° angle to improve tissue perfusion

      C. Using hot, soapy water to clean the client to remove fecal/urine incontinence

      D. Repositioning a bedfast client at least every 2 hr to minimize pressure

Relief of pressure is the most effective preventive measure. Massage is contraindicated over bony prominences. HOB above 30° places pressure on the sacrum. Use tepid rather than hot water. Mild, heavily fatted soaps should be used and skin should be patted dry. Avoid scrubbing.

7. What is the one event that must occur before pressure ulcer healing can begin?

Pressure must be relieved.

Unit 11 Nursing Care of Clients with Integumentary Disorders
Section: Nursing Care of Clients with Select Integumentary Disorders

Chapter 112: Wound Management
Contributor: Linda Turchin, MSN, RN

NCLEX-PN® Connections:

Learning Objective: Review and apply knowledge within "**Wound Management**" in readiness for performance of the following nursing activities as outlined by the NCLEX-PN® test plan:

Δ Provide care that promotes wound healing and restoration and maintenance of skin integrity.

Δ Assist with relevant laboratory, diagnostic, and therapeutic procedures within the nursing role, including:

- Preparation of the client for the procedure.

- Accurate collection of specimens.

- Monitoring client status during and after the procedure.

- Reinforcing client teaching (before and following the procedure).

- Recognizing the client's response (expected, unexpected adverse response) to the procedure.

- Monitoring results.

- Monitoring and taking actions to prevent or minimize the risk of complications.

- Notifying the primary care provider of signs of complications.

Δ Recognize signs and symptoms of the client's problem and complete the proper documentation.

Δ Provide and document care based on the client's health alteration.

Δ Monitor and document vital signs changes.

Δ Interpret data that need to be reported immediately.

Δ Reinforce client education on managing the client's health problem.

Δ Recognize and respond to emergency situations, including notification of the primary care provider.

Δ Review the client's response to emergency interventions and complete the proper documentation.

Δ Provide care that meets the age-related needs of clients 65 years of age or older, including recognizing expected physiological changes.

Key Points

Δ A wound is a **disruption of the normal anatomical structure and function of the skin**. Wound depth is classified by the extent of tissue involvement:

- **Partial-thickness** – superficial wounds to epidermis and dermis. Heal by re-epithelialization.

- **Deep partial-thickness** – extend into the subcutaneous tissue.

- **Full-thickness** – extend beyond subcutaneous tissue into fascia, muscle, and bone.

Δ **Wound healing** is influenced by a variety of factors, and it is the nurse's responsibility to assess for risk factors and attempt to minimize their effects through appropriate nursing interventions.

- **Phases** of wound healing

  ◊ Inflammatory (clot formation, migration of white blood cells)

  ◊ Fibroblastic (fibroblast migration, collagen forms scar, granulation, and wound contraction)

  ◊ Maturation (collagen scar strengthens and thins and pales)

- **Categories** of wound healing

  ◊ By first intention (approximation of wounds without tissue loss)

  ◊ By second intention (inside out – gradual filling in of the dead space of wounds with tissue loss with connective tissue)

  ◊ By third intention (approximation is delayed until after inflammation has subsided)

Δ **Wound exudate** depends on the presence or absence of **infection**. Uninfected wounds have serosanguineous exudate. Infected wounds have purulent exudate, and the color varies among infective organisms (for example, yellow with staphylococcus, green with pseudomonas).

Δ **Wound care** is a nursing responsibility that has a high impact on wound healing. Principles of wound care include **assessment**, **cleansing**, and **protection**.

Key Factors

Δ **Wound healing** occurs most rapidly in tissue that is **hydrated, oxygenated, and contains few organisms**.

Δ **Factors that influence wound healing:**

- **Nutrition** – provides elements required for wound healing and energy requirements.

- **Tissue perfusion** – provides the circulation needed to deliver the required elements for tissue repair and infection control.

- **Immune system** – provides for the destruction of invading pathogens thus preventing wound infection.

- **Age** – individuals on either end of the age continuum may lack the necessary components for wound healing.

- **Obesity** – fatty tissue lacks blood supply.

- **Chronic diseases** – present additional stress on the body's healing mechanisms (for example, diabetes mellitus).

- **Chronic stress** – creates additional stressors that impede healing.

- **Medications** – affect the body's ability to heal or prevent infection (for example, immunosuppressants).

- **Smoking** – impairs oxygenation and clotting.

- **Wound stress** – stresses suture line and disrupts wound healing process (for example, vomiting, coughing).

Diagnostic Procedures and Nursing Interventions

Δ Wound Culture and Sensitivity (swab cultures and/or wound biopsies): **Definitively identify and quantify wound bacteria.**

Δ **Serum Albumin** (normal > 3.5 g/dL) and Prealbumin (normal 17 to 40 mg/dL): Assess nutritional status (low levels indicate malnutrition; wound healing is significantly delayed by malnutrition).

Δ **Hemoglobin A1c and Serum Glucose**: Assess glucose control for clients with diabetes mellitus (consistent blood glucose level below 200 mg/dL promotes wound healing).

Δ Complete Blood Count (CBC) with Differential: Assess immune response.

Δ Blood Cultures: Rule out sepsis.

Therapeutic Procedures and Nursing Interventions

Δ **Vacuum-Assisted Wound Closure** – continuous low-level negative pressure is applied to a sponge-covered suction tube for several hours.

Δ **Hyperbaric Oxygen Therapy** – administration of high-pressurized 100% oxygen directly over the wound for 60 to 90 min.

Δ **Surgical Debridement and/or Wound Grafting** – surgical excision of nonviable tissue to promote healing and/or grafting of skin from donor sites to clean granulating or freshly excised wound bed.

Assessments

Δ   Monitor for **signs and symptoms**.

- Wound healing
  - ◊ Approximation
  - ◊ Granulation
- Wound (localized) infection
  - ◊ Pain
  - ◊ Erythema
  - ◊ Edema
  - ◊ Warmth
  - ◊ Purulent drainage
- Systemic infection
  - ◊ Fever
  - ◊ Chills
  - ◊ Malaise
  - ◊ Elevated white blood cell count

Δ   **Assess/Monitor**

- Wound appearance: Location, size (length, width), color, extent of tissue involvement (depth)
- Wound drainage
- Fluid status
  - ◊ Intake and output
- Nutritional status
  - ◊ Food intake
  - ◊ Serum albumin and prealbumin
  - ◊ Weight
- Vital signs, especially temperature

NANDA Nursing Diagnoses

Δ   Acute pain

Δ   Risk for infection

Δ   Impaired skin integrity

Δ   Impaired tissue integrity

Δ   Risk for injury

Δ   Disturbed body image

Δ   Imbalanced nutrition: Less than body requirements

Δ   Fluid imbalance

Δ   Anxiety

Nursing Interventions

Δ   **Prevent complications:**

- Maintain asepsis.

- Use appropriate handwashing techniques.

- Implement Universal Precautions.

Δ   Provide **adequate hydration** and meet **protein** and calorie needs.

- Encourage intake of 2,000 to 3,000 mL of water per day, if not contraindicated (congestive heart failure, renal failure).

- Provide client education regarding **high sources of protein** (meat, fish, poultry, eggs, dairy products, beans, nuts, and whole grains).

- Note if serum albumin levels are low (< 3.5 g/dL), indicating malnutrition. A lack of protein puts the client at greater risk for delayed wound healing and infection.

- Provide nutritional support as indicated (vitamin and mineral supplements, nutritional supplements, enteral nutrition, parenteral nutrition).

Δ   Perform wound cleansing, wound dressing, and/or debridement as prescribed.

- Isotonic solution

- Absorbent/non-absorbent dressing (barrier to external environment)

- Wet-to-dry dressing, proteolytic enzymes, and/or surgical intervention

Δ   Administer analgesics as needed.

Δ   Administer antimicrobials (topical and/or systemic).

Complications and Nursing Implications

Δ **Wound dehiscence/evisceration** – partial to complete separation of wound layers with possible protrusion of organs. Obesity, diabetes, and/or steroid use are risk factors for wound dehiscence/evisceration. Often occurs on the fifth to 10th postoperative day with coughing, vomiting, straining, or movement. **Nursing response to this emergency** is to call for help, stay with the client, apply a sterile nonadherent or a saline-soaked gauze dressing to the wound. **Do not attempt to reinsert organs**; place the client in supine position with hips and knees bent; and **observe the client for signs of shock**.

Meeting the Needs of Older Adults

Δ In older adult clients, the following factors impede wound healing:

- Slower turnover rate in epidermal cells.

- Poorer oxygenation at the wound site due to:

  ◊ Increasingly fragile capillaries.

  ◊ Reduction in skin vascularization.

- Altered nutrition and fluid intake resulting from:

  ◊ Reduced saliva production.

  ◊ Declining sense of smell and taste.

  ◊ Decreased stomach motility.

  ◊ Troubling social/personal issues (ill fitting dentures, financial concerns, social isolation, depression, problems attaining or preparing food).

- Impaired function of the respiratory or immune systems.

- Chronic cardiovascular or renal disorders.

- Medication use.

- Altered sensitivity to pain, heat, and cold.

- Reduced dermal and subcutaneous mass leading to an increased risk of chronic pressure ulcers.

- In older adults, healed wounds may lack tensile strength and thus be prone to re-injury.

Primary Reference:

Ignatavicius, D. D., & Workman, M. L. (2006). *Medical-surgical nursing* (5th ed.). St. Louis, MO: Saunders.

Additional Resources:

Brown, P., & Phelps Maloy, J. (2005). *Quick Reference to Wound Care* (2nd ed.). Boston: Jones and Bartlett Publishers.

NANDA International (2004). *NANDA nursing diagnoses: Definitions and classification 2005-2006*. Philadelphia: NANDA.

Potter, P. A., & Perry, A. G. (2005). *Fundamentals of nursing* (6th ed.). St. Louis, MO: Mosby.

Wound Care Made Incredibly Easy (2nd ed.). (2003). Philadelphia: Lippincott Williams & Wilkins.

Chapter 112: Wound Management

Application Exercises

Scenario: An 82-year-old male client is seen in the emergency department for a fall that occurred at the grocery store. Examination reveals a frail, thin man with poor skin turgor and very dry skin. He is unkempt, stating, "Since my wife died, I'm not doing too well on my own." His assessment fails to uncover any significant findings except for skin tears to his arms bilaterally. The client has a history of mild congestive heart failure for which he is taking digoxin (Lanoxin) and furosemide (Lasix) daily.

1. Identify the specific client findings that could affect this client's wound healing.

2. What risk do the above client findings pose in terms of wound healing?

3. What client teaching is appropriate for this client?

4. Which nursing intervention is most important in helping to prevent the risk of infection in this client?

5. Which of the following terms describes wound drainage that is thick and yellow?

      A. Serous

      B. Sanguineous

      C. Serosanguineous

      D. Purulent

6. When should a surgical wound dressing first be changed?

      A. 2 hr after the client is discharged from post recovery

      B. When it becomes saturated with drainage

      C. Based on written orders for dressing change

      D. The first dressing change is done by the surgeon

7. Which of the following client findings may negatively impact wound healing? (Check all that apply.)

_____ Family history of pressure ulcers

_____ Type 2 diabetes mellitus

_____ Strict vegetarian

_____ Cigarette smoker

_____ Long-term use of glucocorticosteroids

8. Which of the following interventions is performed first when changing a dressing or giving wound care?

A. Put on gloves.

B. Wash hands thoroughly.

C. Remove the soiled dressing.

D. Observe for amount, type, and odor of drainage.

Chapter 112: Wound Management

Application Exercises Answer Key

Scenario: An 82-year-old male client is seen in the emergency department for a fall that occurred at the grocery store. Examination reveals a frail, thin man with poor skin turgor and very dry skin. He is unkempt, stating, "Since my wife died, I'm not doing too well on my own." His assessment fails to uncover any significant findings except for skin tears to his arms bilaterally. The client has a history of mild congestive heart failure for which he is taking digoxin (Lanoxin) and furosemide (Lasix) daily.

1. Identify the specific client findings that could affect this client's wound healing.

>   **Nutrition – frail, thin man with poor skin turgor and dry skin**
>   **Tissue perfusion – congestive heart failure**
>   **Age – decreased immune response**
>   **Chronic diseases – congestive heart failure**
>   **Medication – diuretic use poses risk for dehydration and hypokalemia**

2. What risk do the above client findings pose in terms of wound healing?

>   **Infection and poor wound healing**

3. What client teaching is appropriate for this client?

>   **The need for adequate protein, calories, vitamins, and potassium-rich foods**
>
>   **Examples of foods high in protein (meat, fish, poultry, eggs, dairy products, beans, nuts, and whole grains)**
>
>   **Importance of proper hydration and means to assure hydration**
>
>   **Wound care for skin tears**
>
>   **Safety issues related to environment**
>
>   **Available community resources (senior center, Meals on Wheels)**

4. Which nursing intervention is most important in helping to prevent the risk of infection in this client?

Adequate handwashing – especially important since he may be immunosuppressed.

5. Which of the following terms describes wound drainage that is thick and yellow?

    A. Serous

    B. Sanguineous

    C. Serosanguineous

    D. Purulent

Wound exudate depends on the presence or absence of infection. Uninfected wounds have serosanguineous exudate. Infected wounds have purulent exudate, and the color varies among infective organisms (for example, yellow with staphylococcus, green with pseudomonas).

6. When should a surgical wound dressing first be changed?

    A. 2 hr after the client is discharged from post recovery

    B. When it becomes saturated with drainage

    C. Based on written orders for dressing change

    D. The first dressing change is done by the surgeon

Generally, surgeons change the first dressing. Postoperatively, nurses should routinely inspect dressings for drainage and record findings (amount, color). Drawing an outline on the dressing around the drainage can be helpful in monitoring progression. Excessive drainage should be reported to the surgeon.

7. Which of the following client findings may negatively impact wound healing? (Check all that apply.)

_____	Family history of pressure ulcers
__x__	Type 2 diabetes mellitus
__x__	Strict vegetarian
__x__	Cigarette smoker
__x__	Long-term use of glucocorticosteroids

Diabetes negatively impacts the immune response. A strict vegetarian may not have adequate protein intake. Smoking impairs oxygenation. Use of glucocorticoids depresses the immune response.

8. Which of the following interventions is performed first when changing a dressing or giving wound care?

    A. Put on gloves.

    B. Wash hands thoroughly.

    C. Remove the soiled dressing.

    D. Observe for amount, type, and odor of drainage.

Handwashing is the most effective infection control measure.

Unit 11   Nursing Care of Clients with Integumentary Disorders
Section: Nursing Care of Clients with Select Integumentary Disorders

Chapter 113:   Skin Cancer
Contributor: Sharon Lytle, MS, RN, CNM

◯ NCLEX-PN® Connections:

Learning Objective: Review and apply knowledge within **"Skin Cancer"** in readiness for performance of the following nursing activities as outlined by the NCLEX-PN® test plan:

Δ   Assist with relevant laboratory, diagnostic, and therapeutic procedures within the nursing role, including:
- Preparation of the client for the procedure.
- Accurate collection of specimens.
- Monitoring client status during and after the procedure.
- Reinforcing client teaching (before and following the procedure).
- Recognizing the client's response (expected, unexpected adverse response) to the procedure.
- Monitoring results.
- Monitoring and taking actions to prevent or minimize the risk of complications.
- Notifying the primary care provider of signs of complications.

Δ   Recognize signs and symptoms of the client's problem and complete the proper documentation.

Δ   Provide and document care based on the client's health alteration.

Δ   Monitor and document vital signs changes.

Δ   Interpret data that need to be reported immediately.

Δ   Reinforce client education on managing the client's health problem.

Δ   Recognize and respond to emergency situations, including notification of the primary care provider.

Δ   Review the client's response to emergency interventions and complete the proper documentation.

Δ   Provide care that meets the age-related needs of clients 65 years of age or older, including recognizing expected physiological changes.

📖 Key Points

Δ   **Sunlight exposure** is the leading cause of skin cancer. The most effective strategy for prevention of skin cancer is avoidance or reduction of skin exposure to sunlight.

Δ   Precancerous skin lesions, called **actinic keratoses**, are common in people with chronically sun-damaged skin, such as older adults.

Δ   The three types of skin cancer are:

-   **Squamous cell carcinoma**, a cancer of the epidermis, which can invade locally and is potentially metastatic.

-   **Basal cell carcinoma**, a cancer of the basal cell layer of the epidermis, which can damage underlying tissues and progress to include vital structures. Not usually metastatic.

-   **Malignant melanoma**, a highly metastatic cancer originating in the melanin-producing cells of the epidermis.

Key Factors

Δ   **Risk Factors**

-   Exposure to ultraviolet light (such as natural light or tanning booths) over long periods of time

-   Chronic skin irritation

-   Fair complexion (blonde or red hair, fair skin, freckles, blue eyes) with a tendency to burn easily

-   Having several large or many small moles

-   Family history of unusual moles

-   Family or personal history of melanoma

Diagnostic and Therapeutic Procedures and Nursing Interventions

Δ **Biopsy** (of suspicious lesions): **Definitive**

	Instrument	Procedure
Punch	A 2 to 6 cm, circular instrument (punch)	Small circle of tissue removed to depth of subcutaneous fat. May be sutured.
Shave	Scalpel or razor blade	Skin elevated above the surrounding tissue by injection of local anesthetic is "shaved off". For superficial or raised lesions.
Excision	Scalpel	A deep incision is made and then sutured after the entire lesion is removed. For large or deep lesions.

- Prepare the client by offering a brief explanation of what to expect.

- Establish a sterile field and assemble supplies and instruments, including local anesthetic, specimen containers, and dressings.

- Provide wound care following excision.

- Schedule follow-up appointment and provide home care instructions.

Δ **Cryosurgery** – freeze tissue by application of liquid nitrogen (-200° C). Cleanse with hydrogen peroxide and apply topical antimicrobial until healed.

Assessments

Δ Monitor for **signs and symptoms.**

- The **ABCDs** of melanoma:

  ◊ Asymmetry – one side does not match the other.

  ◊ Borders – irregular, ragged, notched, or blurred edges.

  ◊ Color – lack of uniformity in pigmentation (shades of tan, brown, or black).

  ◊ Diameter – the width is greater than 6 mm (about the size of a pencil eraser).

Δ **Assess/Monitor**

- Risk factors

- Skin for presence of suspicious lesions

- Moles that change in color, size, shape, or sensation

- Oozing, bleeding, crusting, or scaling of a lesion

- Redness or swelling around a suspicious lesion

NANDA Nursing Diagnoses

  ∆   Impaired skin integrity

  ∆   Impaired tissue integrity

  ∆   Disturbed body image

Nursing Interventions

  ∆   Advise the client to:

- **Avoid sun exposure during peak hours** (1100 to 1500).
- Wear light-colored clothing, a hat, and sunglasses outside.
- Use sunscreens with appropriate **sun protection factor (SPF) of at least 15**. Reapply at least every 2 hr.
- Perform **monthly skin self-examinations**.
- **Report skin changes**, moles, or suspicious lesions to the provider immediately.

  ∆   Administer **medications** as prescribed.

- **Topical chemotherapy** with 5-flourouracil cream for treatment of actinic keratoses. Prepare the client for an unsightly appearance during therapy. Reassure the client that the appearance following treatment of lesions will be positive.
- **Interferon** for postoperative treatment of stage III or greater melanomas. Report and provide relief for side effects or toxic effects of chemotherapy. Encourage adequate nutrition and fluid intake.

Complications and Nursing Implications

  ∆   **Metastasis** – melanomas are highly metastatic. Survival requires early diagnosis and treatment.

Meeting the Needs of Older Adults

  ∆   Because of the cumulative effects of sun damage over the lifespan, screening for suspicious lesions is an essential part of the routine physical assessment of the older adult.

Primary Reference:

Ignatavicius, D. D., & Workman, M. L. (2006). *Medical-surgical nursing* (5th ed.). St. Louis, MO: Saunders.

Additional Resources:

Lewis, Heitkemper, and Dirksen (2004). *Medical-surgical nursing: Assessment and management of clinical problems* (6th ed.). St. Louis, MO: Mosby.

NANDA International (2004). *NANDA nursing diagnoses: Definitions and classification 2005-2006*. Philadelphia: NANDA.

For more information, visit the National Cancer Institute at: *www.cancer.gov/cancertopics/types/skin/*.

Chapter 113: Skin Cancer

Application Exercises

Scenario: A 58-year-old male construction worker presents to his primary care provider for removal of a large mole from his right shoulder. He reports that the mole has bothered him for a couple of weeks. Ever since he was scraped on the shoulder by a wooden pallet, the mole has been crusting and oozing.

1. List important questions to ask the client when conducting the initial interview.

2. What are characteristics of this client's mole that might suggest a malignancy?

3. To definitively determine the malignancy of the mole, what diagnostic procedure should be anticipated?

4. Following the skin biopsy, which of the following client statements indicates a need for further instruction?

      A. "I will call the doctor if I see any wound drainage."

      B. "I will return to the doctor in a few days to have the sutures removed."

      C. "I will put antibiotic ointment on it."

      D. "I will remove the dressing and wash it with tap water when I get home."

5. Which of the following skin lesions is suggestive of a malignant melanoma? (Check all that apply.)

     _____   Irregular shaped mole

     _____   A lesion with asymmetric borders and variegated colors

     _____   A rough, pink scaly patch

     _____   A uniformly colored papule

     _____   Diffuse vesicles

Chapter 113: Skin Cancer

Application Exercises Answer Key

Scenario: A 58-year-old male construction worker presents to his primary care provider for removal of a large mole from his right shoulder. He reports that the mole has bothered him for a couple of weeks. Ever since he was scraped on the shoulder by a wooden pallet, the mole has been crusting and oozing.

1. List important questions to ask the client when conducting the initial interview.

   Recent changes in size, color, or sensation of the lesion?

   Geographic location where client previously and currently resides?

   Occupational and recreational activities?

   Occupational exposure to carcinogens?

2. What are characteristics of this client's mole that might suggest a malignancy?

   Injury to a lesion located on a part of the body prone to chronic sun exposure and irritation

   Oozing, bleeding, and crusting of the lesion

3. To definitively determine the malignancy of the mole, what diagnostic procedure should be anticipated?

   Skin biopsy and possibly excision/cryosurgery

4. Following the skin biopsy, which of the following client statements indicates a need for further instruction?

   A. "I will call the doctor if I see any wound drainage."
   B. "I will return to the doctor in a few days to have the sutures removed."
   C. "I will put antibiotic ointment on it."
   D. "I will remove the dressing and wash it with tap water when I get home."

   In general, the dressing should be left on for several hours prior to cleansing.

5. Which of the following skin lesions is suggestive of a malignant melanoma? (Check all that apply.)

__x__	Irregular shaped mole
__x__	A lesion with asymmetric borders and variegated colors
_____	A rough, pink scaly patch
_____	A uniformly colored papule
_____	Diffuse vesicles

Irregular shaped moles and a lesion with asymmetric borders and variegated colors are suggestive of malignant melanoma. The other skin lesions are not.

Unit 11
Section:

Nursing Care of Clients with Integumentary Disorders
Nursing Care of Clients with Select Integumentary Disorders

Chapter 114:   Herpes Zoster (Shingles)
Contributor: Dana Bartlett, MSN, RN, CSPI

🗘 NCLEX-PN® Connections:

Learning Objective: Review and apply knowledge within "**Herpes Zoster (Shingles)**" in readiness for performance of the following nursing activities as outlined by the NCLEX-PN® test plan:

Δ   Assist with relevant laboratory, diagnostic, and therapeutic procedures within the nursing role, including:

  • Preparation of the client for the procedure.

  • Accurate collection of specimens.

  • Monitoring client status during and after the procedure.

  • Reinforcing client teaching (before and following the procedure).

  • Recognizing the client's response (expected, unexpected adverse response) to the procedure.

  • Monitoring results.

  • Monitoring and taking actions to prevent or minimize the risk of complications.

  • Notifying the primary care provider of signs of complications.

Δ   Recognize signs and symptoms of the client's problem and complete the proper documentation.

Δ   Provide and document care based on the client's health alteration.

Δ   Monitor and document vital signs changes.

Δ   Interpret data that need to be reported immediately.

Δ   Reinforce client education on managing the client's health problem.

Δ   Recognize and respond to emergency situations, including notification of the primary care provider.

Δ   Review the client's response to emergency interventions and complete the proper documentation.

Δ   Provide care that meets the age-related needs of clients 65 years of age or older, including recognizing expected physiological changes.

📖 Key Points

△ Herpes zoster is a **viral infection**. It initially produces chicken pox, and then the virus lies dormant in the dorsal root ganglia of the sensory cranial and spinal nerves. It is then reactivated as **shingles**.

△ An attack of shingles is usually preceded by a **prodromal period** of several days: pain, tingling, or burning along the involved dermatome.

△ An attack of shingles can be **very painful** and debilitating.

Key Factors

△ **Risk Factors**

- Adults older than 20 years

- Increasing age

- Concurrent illness

- **Stress**

- **Compromise to the immune system**

- Fatigue

- Poor nutritional status

△ Most individuals in the U.S. (95%) have antibodies to herpes zoster virus.

Diagnostic Procedures and Nursing Interventions

△ **Cultures**: Definitive diagnosis (but the virus grows so slow that cultures are often of minimal diagnostic use)

△ Occasionally, an **immunofluorescence assay** can be done.

Assessments

△ Monitor for **signs and symptoms.**

- Vesicular, **unilateral** rash (the rash and lesions occur on the skin area innervated by the infected nerve)

- Rash that is erythematous, vesicular, pustular, or crusting (depending on the stage)

- **Rash usually resolves in 14 to 21 days**

- Paresthesia

- Pain

- Low-grade fever

Δ **Assess/Monitor**

- Pain

- Condition of the lesions

- Presence of fever

- Neurologic complications

- Signs of infection

NANDA Nursing Diagnoses

Δ Acute pain

Δ Impaired skin integrity

Δ Risk for infection

Δ Risk for situational low self-esteem

Nursing Interventions

Δ Use an air mattress or bed cradle for pain prevention/control.

Δ **Isolate the client** until the vesicles are crusted.

Δ Maintain strict **wound care precautions**.

Δ Herpes zoster is **potentially transmissible** and caution should be exercised around infants, pregnant women who have not had chickenpox, and immunocompromised clients.

Δ Administer **medications** as prescribed.

- Analgesics (NSAIDs, narcotics)

- Anti-viral agents, such as acyclovir, valacyclovir, famciclovir (shorten the clinical course)

Δ Moisten dressings with cool tap water or 5% aluminum acetate (Burow's solution) and apply to the affected skin for 30 to 60 min four to six times per day as prescribed.

Δ Lotions (for example, Calamine) may help relieve discomfort.

Complications and Nursing Implications

Δ **Postherpetic neuralgia** is characterized by pain that persists for longer than 1 month following resolution of the vesicular rash. Tricyclic antidepressants may be prescribed.

Δ **Encephalitis** is a potential complication, especially in immunocompromised individuals.

Meeting the Needs of Older Adults

Δ The older client is more susceptible to herpes zoster infection. The older client's immune function may also be compromised; assess the older adult client carefully for local or systemic signs of infection.

Δ Postherpetic neuralgia is common in adults older than 60 years.

Primary Reference:

Ignatavicius, D. D., & Workman, M. L. (2006). *Medical-surgical nursing* (5th ed.). St. Louis, MO: Saunders.

Additional Resources:

NANDA International (2004). *NANDA nursing diagnoses: Definitions and classification 2005-2006*. Philadelphia: NANDA.

Chapter 114: Herpes Zoster (Shingles)

Application Exercises

1. Which of the following client findings is suggestive of herpes zoster?

> A. Generalized body rash
> B. Blue-white spots with a red base
> C. Red edematous rash on cheeks bilaterally
> D. Clusters of vesicles

2. Which diagnostic laboratory test might be ordered to definitively diagnose herpes zoster?

3. Which of the following nurses should avoid providing direct care to a client with herpes zoster? (Check all that apply.)

> _____ The nurse who never had mumps
> _____ The nurse who never had roseola
> _____ The nurse who never had chickenpox
> _____ The nurse who never had German measles
> _____ The nurse who is immunocompromised

4. How long does an attack of shingles usually last?

5. Name two classes of drugs that can be used to treat an attack of shingles.

6. What cluster of signs and symptoms might a client experience immediately prior to an outbreak of shingles?

7. Has every client who experiences herpes zoster previously had chickenpox?

Chapter 114: Herpes Zoster (Shingles)

Application Exercises Answer Key

1. Which of the following client findings is suggestive of herpes zoster?

       A. Generalized body rash

       B. Blue-white spots with a red base

       C. Red edematous rash on cheeks bilaterally

       D. Clusters of vesicles

Herpes zoster is characterized by vesicles. Classic presentation is along a dermatome. The vesicles present unilaterally.

2. Which diagnostic laboratory test might be ordered to definitively diagnose herpes zoster?

Cultures: Definitive diagnosis (but the virus grows so slow that cultures are often of minimal diagnostic use)

3. Which of the following nurses should avoid providing direct care to a client with herpes zoster? (Check all that apply.)

_____	The nurse who never had mumps
_____	The nurse who never had roseola
__X__	The nurse who never had chickenpox
_____	The nurse who never had German measles
__X__	The nurse who is immunocompromised

The nurse who never had the chickenpox is at risk for acquiring the virus and experiencing a varicella (chicken pox) infection. The immunocompromised nurse is at risk for acquiring the herpes zoster infection because of immunosuppression.

4. How long does an attack of shingles usually last?

The rash usually resolves in 14 to 21 days. Use of antiviral agents can shorten the course.

5. Name two classes of drugs that can be used to treat an attack of shingles.

Analgesics (NSAIDs, narcotics)

Anti-viral agents, such as acyclovir, valacyclovir, famciclovir (shorten the clinical course)

6. What cluster of signs and symptoms might a client experience immediately prior to an outbreak of shingles?

An attack of shingles is usually preceded by a prodromal period of several days: pain, tingling, or burning along the involved dermatome.

7. Has every client who experiences herpes zoster previously had chickenpox?

Yes. Herpes zoster is a reactivation of the dormant varicella-zoster virus. The virus is dormant from when the individual had the chickenpox.

Nursing Care of Clients with Integumentary Disorders
Medical Emergencies: Integumentary

Chapter 115: Burns
Contributor: Wendy Buenzli, MSN, RN

↻ NCLEX-PN® Connections:

Learning Objective: Review and apply knowledge within "**Burns**" in readiness for performance of the following nursing activities as outlined by the NCLEX-PN® test plan:

Δ   Provide care to the client with burns that promotes wound healing and restoration and maintenance of skin integrity.

Δ   Assist with relevant laboratory, diagnostic, and therapeutic procedures within the nursing role, including:

- Preparation of the client for the procedure.

- Accurate collection of specimens.

- Monitoring client status during and after the procedure.

- Reinforcing client teaching (before and following the procedure).

- Recognizing the client's response (expected, unexpected adverse response) to the procedure.

- Monitoring results.

- Monitoring and taking actions to prevent or minimize the risk of complications.

- Notifying the primary care provider of signs of complications.

Δ   Recognize signs and symptoms of the client's problem and complete the proper documentation.

Δ   Provide and document care based on the client's health alteration.

Δ   Monitor and document vital signs changes.

Δ   Interpret data that need to be reported immediately.

Δ   Reinforce client education on managing the client's health problem.

Δ   Recognize and respond to emergency situations, including notification of the primary care provider.

Δ   Review the client's response to emergency interventions and complete the proper documentation.

Δ   Provide care that meets the age-related needs of clients 65 years of age or older, including recognizing expected physiological changes.

Key Points

Δ Burns are the 6ᵗʰ leading cause of accidental death in the United States.

Δ Thermal, chemical, electrical, and radioactive agents can cause burns, which are a result of **cellular destruction of the skin layers** and subsequent depletion of fluid and electrolytes.

Δ Burns result in a **loss of temperature regulation** and sweat and sebaceous gland function. The protection of cells, tissues, and organs is compromised and there is a **loss of sensory function**.

Δ The skin is the largest sensory and excretory organ in the body. Burns are classified by how they damage the tissue layers of the skin. The **severity** depends on amount of **body surface area** burned and the **depth** of the burn. The more area and deeper the burn the more severe the injury.

Δ To evaluate the extent of damage when assessing burns, it is important to know:

- The type of burning agent (dry heat, moist heat, contact, chemical, electrical, ionizing radiation).

- The duration of contact.

- The site of injury.

Δ The areas most vulnerable to burns are: eyelids, ears, nose, genitalia, and the tops of the hands and feet (including fingers and toes).

Δ **Classification of Burns**

	Superficial	Partial-Thickness	Deep Partial-Thickness	Full-Thickness	Deep Full-Thickness
Tissue layer damaged	Epidermis	Entire epidermis to some of dermis	Extends to deeper layer of the dermis	Entire dermis	Entire dermis and subcutaneous fat. Skin can not heal on its own.
Color	Pink to red	Pink to red	Red to white	Black, brown, yellow	Black
Blisters	No	Yes	Rare	No	No
Edema	Mild	Mild to moderate	Moderate	Severe	Absent
Pain	Yes	Yes	Yes	Yes and No	Absent

	Superficial	Partial-Thickness	Deep Partial-Thickness	Full-Thickness	Deep Full-Thickness
Eschar	No	No	Yes, soft and dry	Yes, hard and inelastic	Yes, hard and elastic
Treatment	No emergency care needed	No emergency care needed	Depending on area burned, a local emergency department	Emergency care at the scene and transfer to burn center or hospital with expertise	Care and nearest emergency department and transfer to burn center
Healing	3 to 5 days	2 weeks	2 to 6 weeks	Weeks to months	Weeks to months

Key Factors

Δ **Risk for Death from Burns**

- Age > 60 years

- Burn involves > 40% total body surface area

- Inhalation injury

Diagnostic Procedures and Nursing Interventions

Δ Laboratory values that should be evaluated include: complete blood count (CBC), serum electrolytes, BUN, arterial blood gas (ABGs), fasting blood glucose, liver enzymes, urinalysis, and clotting studies.

- **Initial fluid shift** (first 24 hr after injury)

  ◊ Hemoglobin and hematocrit: Elevated due to loss of fluid volume and fluid shifts **into interstitial** (third spacing)

  ◊ Sodium: Decreased due to third spacing

  ◊ Potassium: Increased due to cell destruction

- **Fluid mobilization** (48 to 72 hr after injury)

  ◊ Hemoglobin and hematocrit: Decreased due to fluid shift from interstitial **into vascular**

  ◊ Sodium: Decreased due to renal and wound loss

  ◊ Potassium: Decreased due to renal loss and movement back into cells

- White blood cell (WBC) count: Initial increase then decrease with left shift

- Glucose: Elevated due to stress response

- ABGs: Slight hypoxemia, metabolic acidosis

- Total protein and albumin: Low due to loss via burns

Therapeutic Procedures and Nursing Interventions

Δ **Surgical debridement and/or wound grafting** – surgical excision of necrotic burned tissue (full-thickness and deep partial-thickness) down to bleeding tissue. Skin from donor sites, allograft (human cadaver), or xenograft (another species, such as pigs) is grafted to granulating or freshly excised bleeding wound bed.

Δ **Plastic/Reconstructive Surgery**

Assessments

Δ **Assess/Monitor**

- Head-to-toe assessment

- **Airway patency** (especially burns of the face that occur in closed spaces)

- Mouth, nose, and pharynx for singed hairs (evidence of inhalation injury)

- Oxygenation status

- Vital signs, heart rhythm (especially with electrical burns)

- Fluid status

- Circulatory status (hypovolemia, decreased cardiac output, edema, third spacing)

- Size and depth of burns – body surface area (BSA), rule of nines, Lund-Browder and Berkow methods

- Renal function (urine output decreased first 24 hr)

- Bowel sounds (commonly reduced/absent)

- Stool and emesis for evidence of bleeding (ulcer risk)

NANDA Nursing Diagnoses

Δ Ineffective breathing pattern

Δ Decreased cardiac output

Δ Deficient fluid volume

Δ Ineffective peripheral tissue perfusion

Δ Acute pain and chronic pain

Δ Impaired skin integrity

Δ Risk for infection

Δ Risk for ineffective thermoregulation

Δ   Imbalanced nutrition: Less than body requirements

Δ   Disturbed body image

Nursing Interventions

Δ   Ensure **airway patency** (intubation, tracheostomy) and provide oxygen as needed (for example, mechanical ventilation).

Δ   Maintain the client's thermodynamics (warm room, cover with blankets).

Δ   Monitor vital signs, pulses, capillary refill (particularly for evidence of shock and adequate tissue perfusion).

Δ   Administer fluids, inotropic agents, and osmotic diuretics as needed to maintain adequate cardiac output and tissue perfusion.

Δ   **Begin IV fluid and electrolyte replacement.** A central line may be indicated to accommodate the large volumes of fluid. Burn resuscitation formulas are used as guides. The minimum is the amount needed to ensure hourly urine output of 30 mL/hr. Insertion of hemodynamic monitoring devices may be necessary to monitor fluid status.

Δ   Keep the client NPO (reduced gastrointestinal blood flow, risk of ileus, Curling's stress ulcer). Administer H_2-antagonists.

Δ   Elevate the client's extremities (increase venous return).

Δ   Encourage the client to cough and deep breathe and to utilize incentive spirometry.

Δ   Administer tetanus prophylaxis per hospital protocol.

Δ   Prevent infection and implement infection control measures. Use aseptic technique. **Change gloves between caring for wounds on different areas** of the body and between handling old and new dressings. Apply topical antimicrobials, such as silver sulfadiazine (Silvadene), except to freshly grafted areas.

Δ   Wound care and dressing changes should be done with surgical aseptic technique as ordered; use pressure dressing to prevent scarring and edema.

Δ   Monitor and assess for pain. **Pain medication should be given prior to any treatment and especially before dressing changes.**

Δ   Provide nutrition support as ordered; **hyperalimentation may be necessary** if the client is intubated or has impaired digestion/peristalsis. A dietician consult is important for proper caloric and protein needs. **Nutritional requirements** for clients with extensive burns **can exceed 5,000 cal/day. A high-protein intake** is also needed for wound healing (hypermetabolic state).

Δ Encourage **range of motion** exercises to prevent immobility and the use of splints to maintain correct positioning. **Neutral positions with minimum flexion are best to prevent contractures.**

Δ Collaborative care is vital for these clients. Physical therapy, occupational therapy, dietary, pharmacy, social services, and other disciplines should be involved in the plan of care.

Δ Initiate referrals as appropriate (counseling, support groups).

Complications and Nursing Implications

Δ **Airway Injury**

- Symptoms include: progressive hoarseness, brassy cough, difficulty swallowing, drooling, and expiratory sounds that include audible wheezes, crowing and stridor.

- Airway injuries can progress to rapid obstruction in a short time and thus require immediate treatment.

- Carbon monoxide poisoning is the leading cause of death associated with fires.

- Thermal heat injuries, such as steam inhalation, aspiration of scalding liquid, and explosion while breathing, can damage the airway.

- Chemical inhalation can cause airway injuries.

Δ **Inadequate Tissue Perfusion**

- Especially with circumferential burns (extremity, thorax)

- Escharotomy and/or fasciotomy may be necessary to relieve compartmental pressure and/or to facilitate breathing.

Meeting the Needs of Older Adults

Δ Persons 75 and older are at the highest risk for burn injury.

Δ Older adults are at higher risk for injury because their skin is thinner.

Δ Older adults have a higher risk for complications from burns because of chronic illnesses (diabetes mellitus, cardiovascular disease).

Δ Older adults have increased risk for fluid and electrolyte imbalances and infection related to the normal physiological processes of aging.

Primary Reference:

Ignatavicius, D. D., & Workman, M. L. (2006). *Medical-surgical nursing* (5th ed.). St. Louis, MO: Saunders.

Additional Resources:

NANDA International (2004). *NANDA nursing diagnoses: Definitions and classification 2005-2006*. Philadelphia: NANDA.

Chapter 115: Burns

Application Exercises

1. A client went to the beach and was sunburned. Which of the following is the proper classification of this burn?

    A. Full-thickness

    B. Partial-thickness

    C. Superficial

    D. Deep-thickness

2. There is an explosion at the local chemical factory. Several people are burned and are being rushed to the emergency department. Which of the following clients should be seen first?

    A. 25-year-old man with a small burn on his left arm

    B. 65-year-old man with burns on his hands and face

    C. 42-year-old woman with burns on her left leg

    D. 33-year-old woman with burns to her right arm and shoulder

Scenario: A nurse is caring for a client who sustained burns to 35% of his total body surface area. Of the burns, 20% are full-thickness. The burns are on the client's arms, face, neck, and shoulders. The client's voice seems hoarse and he develops a brassy cough.

3. What might these clinical findings indicate?

4. What should be the next action taken?

5. Is this an urgent concern?

6. Each of the following body systems are altered during a burn injury. Describe the expected abnormal assessment findings for each system.

Cardiovascular	
Pulmonary	
Hepatic	
Gastrointestinal	
Genitourinary	
Integumentary	

Chapter 115: Burns

Application Exercises Answer Key

1. A client went to the beach and was sunburned. Which of the following is the proper classification of this burn?

> A. Full-thickness
>
> B. Partial-thickness
>
> **C. Superficial**
>
> D. Deep-thickness

A sunburn is a superficial burn.

2. There is an explosion at the local chemical factory. Several people are burned and are being rushed to the emergency department. Which of the following clients should be seen first?

> A. 25-year-old man with a small burn on his left arm
>
> **B. 65-year-old man with burns on his hands and face**
>
> C. 42-year-old woman with burns on her left leg
>
> C. 33-year-old woman with burns to her right arm and shoulder

Because the man is 65 and has burns to his face and hands, he is at higher risk for injury (inhalation, circumferential burns).

Scenario: A nurse is caring for a client who sustained burns to 35% of his total body surface area. Of the burns, 20% are full-thickness. The burns are on the client's arms, face, neck, and shoulders. The client's voice seems hoarse and he develops a brassy cough.

---

3. What might these clinical findings indicate?

The fact that the client is becoming progressively hoarse and has a brassy cough is a sign that the client may have a respiratory injury.

4. What should be the next action taken?

The next step would be to complete a respiratory assessment and provide pulmonary support as needed.

5. Is this an urgent concern?

This is urgent. Clients with inhalation injury can have rapid obstruction in a short time. This is something that should be a top nursing priority.

6. Each of the following body systems are altered during a burn injury. Describe the expected abnormal assessment findings for each system.

Cardiovascular	Slow capillary refill, increased heart rate
Pulmonary	Rapid respiratory rate
Hepatic	Release of glycogen stores and increased metabolism
Gastrointestinal	Blood in stool, decreased function, slow or no motility, decreased bowel sounds, abdominal distention, nausea and vomiting
Genitourinary	Decreased urine output, concentrated urine
Integumentary	Extremities pale and cool, edema, fluid retention

Unit 11   Nursing Care of Clients with Integumentary Disorders
Section: Medical Emergencies: Integumentary

Chapter 116:   Wound Dehiscence/Evisceration
Contributor: Linda Turchin, MSN, RN

⟳ NCLEX-PN® Connections:

Learning Objective: Review and apply knowledge within **"Wound Dehiscence/ Evisceration"** in readiness for performance of the following nursing activities as outlined by the NCLEX-PN® test plan:

Δ   Provide care that promotes wound healing and restoration and maintenance of skin integrity.

Δ   Respond quickly and appropriately to wound dehiscence/evisceration.

Δ   Assist with relevant laboratory, diagnostic, and therapeutic procedures within the nursing role, including:

- Preparation of the client for the procedure.

- Accurate collection of specimens.

- Monitoring client status during and after the procedure.

- Reinforcing client teaching (before and following the procedure).

- Recognizing the client's response (expected, unexpected adverse response) to the procedure.

- Monitoring results.

- Monitoring and taking actions to prevent or minimize the risk of complications.

- Notifying the primary care provider of signs of complications.

Δ   Recognize signs and symptoms of the client's problem and complete the proper documentation.

Δ   Provide and document care based on the client's health alteration.

Δ   Monitor and document vital signs changes.

Δ   Interpret data that need to be reported immediately.

Δ   Reinforce client education on managing the client's health problem.

Δ   Recognize and respond to emergency situations, including notification of the primary care provider.

Δ   Review the client's response to emergency interventions and complete the proper documentation.

Δ   Provide care that meets the age-related needs of clients 65 years of age or older, including recognizing expected physiological changes.

Key Points

Δ **Wound dehiscence** is the partial or complete separation of the wound edges at the incision line.

Δ **Wound evisceration** is the protrusion of loops of the bowel through the suture line.

Δ These are serious complications with mortality rates of up to 30%. They usually occur between the fifth and 10th postoperative day.

Key Factors

Δ **Risk Factors**

- Chronic disease
- Advanced age
- **Obesity**
- **Wound infection**
- Dehydration/malnutrition
- Ineffective suturing
- Weak abdominal tissue/muscles
- Invasive abdominal cancer
- **Diabetes mellitus**
- Immunocompromised condition
- Excessive postoperative gas or abdominal distention
- Severe vomiting or retching
- Obstructed nasogastric (NG) tube, Jackson-Pratt (JP) drain, or Hemovac drain
- Improper splinting of incision during coughing or vomiting

Diagnostic Procedures and Nursing Interventions

Δ Complete blood count

Δ Wound and tissue cultures

Δ Ultrasound to evaluate for pus and pockets of fluid

Δ Computed tomography (CT) imaging scan to evaluate for pus and pockets of fluid

Assessments

Δ   Monitor for **signs and symptoms.**

- Appreciable, sudden increase in the flow of serosanguineous fluid on the wound dressings

- Preceded by a sudden straining (coughing, sneezing, or vomiting)

- Client stating that, "something just popped in my stomach"

- May or may not be painful

Δ   **Assess/Monitor**

- Vital signs

- Drainage from wound (color, odor, amount)

- Wound dressing

- Approximation of the suture line as well as signs of infection

- Nausea and vomiting; excessive coughing

- Abdomen for distention; presence of bowel sounds

- Nasogastric tube for patency

- Drainage tubes for patency

NANDA Nursing Diagnoses

Δ   Impaired skin and/or tissue integrity

Δ   Risk of infection

Δ   Acute pain

Δ   Fear

Δ   Anxiety

Δ   Disturbed body image

Δ   Impaired organ/tissue perfusion

Nursing Interventions

Δ **Prevention**

- Instruct the client to splint the incision when coughing, vomiting, or with activity.

- Use meticulous surgical aseptic technique when dressing the wound to prevent infection and weakening of wound edges.

- Have clients who are obese wear an abdominal binder.

- Report severe coughing, retching, vomiting, or abdominal distention.

- Recognize and report signs of infection immediately and obtain a wound culture and complete blood count (CBC).

Δ **Emergency Treatment: Immediately**

- Call for help.

- Stay with the client.

- Cover the wound and any protruding organs with sterile towels or dressings that have been soaked in saline solution.

- **DO NOT ATTEMPT TO REINSERT ORGANS.**

- Place the client in a supine position with hips and knees bent.

- Notify the primary care provider.

- Assess vital signs every 5 min until the primary care provider arrives.

- Be prepared to:

  ◊ Start oxygen.

  ◊ Secure IV access and provide fluids.

  ◊ Prepare the client for surgery.

- Maintain a calm environment.

Complications and Nursing Implications

Δ **Shock** – monitor vital signs (tachycardia, hypotension). Administer fluids and plasma expanders as indicated. Emergency surgery and use of retention sutures may be indicated.

Meeting the Needs of Older Adults

Δ Age is a risk factor for both dehiscence and evisceration.

Δ Older adult clients may have decreased skin and tissue integrity as well as impaired circulation.

Primary Reference:

Ignatavicius, D. D., & Workman, M. L. (2006). *Medical-surgical nursing* (5th ed.). St. Louis, MO: Saunders.

Additional Resources:

NANDA International (2004). *NANDA nursing diagnoses: Definitions and classification 2005-2006*. Philadelphia: NANDA.

Potter, P. A., & Perry, A. G. (2005). *Fundamentals of nursing* (6th ed.). St. Louis, MO: Mosby.

Wound Care Made Incredibly Easy (2nd ed.). (2003). Philadelphia: Lippincott Williams & Wilkins.

Chapter 116: Wound Dehiscence/Evisceration

Application Exercises

Scenario: A 55-year-old female client who is obese had an exploratory abdominal surgery 6 days earlier. The client has developed an upper respiratory infection and has been sneezing and coughing for the last 24 hr. The client is coughing and suddenly feels "something give away." She immediately calls for help. The nurse quickly examines the wound and finds that the suture line is no longer intact, a large amount of pink serosanguineous fluid has escaped from the wound, and a loop of bowel is protruding from the wound.

1. What should be the nurse's next actions?

2. What are five signs of shock that the nurse should observe for and immediately report?

3. The client is taken back to the surgical suite to repair the wound. Following surgery, the client returns to the unit with retention sutures. What assessments should the nurse now make in regard to the client's wound?

4. What is an important nursing intervention that can help prevent dehiscence in this particular client?

5. Why did wound dehiscence and evisceration occur on the 6th day following the client's surgery?

6. In the event of wound dehiscence, why is it important to place the client in a semi-Fowler's position with knees bent?

7. Which of the following interventions is **inappropriate** for the treatment of a wound evisceration?

    A. Medicate the client for pain as ordered.

    B. Cover the protruding organs with sterile, moistened dressings.

    C. Orally hydrate the client to maintain blood pressure.

    D. Lower the head of the bed to no more than 30°.

8. Which of the following clients is at the greatest risk for a dehiscence?

    A. 35-year-old female who is obese and is having a hysterectomy

    B. 83-year-old client who is diabetic with an infected cholecystectomy incision

    C. 25-year-old client who is 2 days postoperative appendectomy

    D. 32-year-old client who has had a repeat C-section

9. A nurse should monitor a client at risk for evisceration for which of the following postoperative symptoms?

    A. Tachycardia with a weak thready pulse

    B. Hypotension with a decreased level of consciousness

    C. Shallow, rapid respiration and nausea

    D. Low-grade fever and increasing serosanguineous incisional drainage

10. Which of the following interventions will have the greatest impact on reducing the risk of dehiscence in an otherwise healthy postoperative client?

    A. Placing the client in a supine position with hips and knees bent

    B. Splinting the abdomen appropriately

    C. Medicating the client appropriately for pain

    D. Encouraging early ambulation

Chapter 116: Wound Dehiscence/Evisceration

Application Exercises Answer Key

Scenario: A 55-year-old female client who is obese had an exploratory abdominal surgery 6 days earlier. The client has developed an upper respiratory infection and has been sneezing and coughing for the last 24 hr. The client is coughing and suddenly feels "something give away." She immediately calls for help. The nurse quickly examines the wound and finds that the suture line is no longer intact, a large amount of pink serosanguineous fluid has escaped from the wound, and a loop of bowel is protruding from the wound.

1. What should be the nurse's next actions?

   The nurse should delegate another person to immediately notify the surgeon. The nurse should place the client in a supine position with hips and knees bent and cover the wound and loop of bowel with a sterile dressing moistened with warm normal saline solution. While waiting for the surgeon to arrive, the nurse should remain with the client and provide constant reassurance while carefully observing the client for signs of shock.

2. What are five signs of shock that the nurse should observe for and immediately report?

   Increased heart rate

   Increased respiratory rate

   Change in blood pressure (initially increases then decreases)

   Change in mentation, decreased level of consciousness

   Moist, clammy skin

3. The client is taken back to the surgical suite to repair the wound. Following surgery, the client returns to the unit with retention sutures. What assessments should the nurse now make in regard to the client's wound?

> The nurse needs to assess the wound for:
>
> > Signs of wound infection (erythema, edema, pain, drainage, and odor).
> >
> > Bleeding.
> >
> > Edema.
> >
> > Areas of indurated or hardened tissue.
> >
> > Approximation of the suture line.

4. What is an important nursing intervention that can help prevent dehiscence in this particular client?

> This client is obese and should wear an abdominal binder in order to support the wound, prevent disruption of the sutures, and keep the dressings in place. Splint the wound/abdomen when coughing, turning, getting out of bed, or performing other activities that could stress the wound.

5. Why did wound dehiscence and evisceration occur on the 6th day following the client's surgery?

> Wound dehiscence and evisceration occurred on the sixth day following the client's surgery because the wound was at its weakest at that time and the client's URI and coughing caused the already weakened incision to separate.

6. In the event of wound dehiscence, why is it important to place the client in a semi-Fowler's position with knees bent?

> Placing the client in a supine position with hips and knees bent following wound dehiscence may help to prevent further tearing of the incision and wound evisceration by lessening intra-abdominal pressure on the wound.

7. Which of the following interventions is **inappropriate** for the treatment of a wound evisceration?

> A. Medicate the client for pain as ordered.
>
> B. Cover the protruding organs with sterile, moistened dressings.
>
> **C. Orally hydrate the client to maintain blood pressure.**
>
> D. Lower the head of the bed to no more than 30°.

The client will need emergency surgery and should be NPO.

8. Which of the following clients is at the greatest risk for a dehiscence?

> A. 35-year-old female who is obese and is having a hysterectomy
>
> **B. 83-year-old client who is diabetic with an infected cholecystectomy incision**
>
> C. 25-year-old client who is 2 days postoperative appendectomy
>
> D. 32-year-old client who has had a repeat C-section

Chronic diseases, such as diabetes mellitus, pose risk. Hyperglycemia and infection delay healing.

9. A nurse should monitor a client at risk for evisceration for which of the following postoperative symptoms?

> A. Tachycardia with a weak thready pulse
>
> B. Hypotension with a decreased level of consciousness
>
> C. Shallow, rapid respiration and nausea
>
> **D. Low-grade fever and increasing serosanguineous incisional drainage**

Appreciable, sudden increase in the flow of serosanguineous fluid on the wound dressings and/or signs of wound infection are symptoms of dehiscence/evisceration.

10. Which of the following interventions will have the greatest impact on reducing the risk of dehiscence in an otherwise healthy postoperative client?

      A. Placing the client in a supine position with hips and knees bent

      B. Splinting the abdomen appropriately

      C. Medicating the client appropriately for pain

      D. Encouraging early ambulation

Prevention strategies include:

Instruct the client to splint the incision when coughing or with activity or vomiting.

Use meticulous surgical aseptic technique when dressing the wound to prevent infection and weakening of wound edge.

Have clients who are obese wear an abdominal binder.

Report severe coughing, retching, vomiting, or abdominal distention.

Recognize and report signs of infection immediately and obtain a wound culture and complete blood count (CBC).

Unit 12   Nursing Care of Clients with Reproductive Disorders
Section: Diagnostic and Therapeutic Procedures: Reproductive

Chapter 117:   Hormone Replacement Therapy
Contributor: Sharon Lytle, MS, RN, CNM

⟳ NCLEX-PN® Connections:

Learning Objective: Review and apply knowledge within "**Hormone Replacement Therapy**" in readiness for performance of the following nursing activities as outlined by the NCLEX-PN® test plan:

Δ   Perform/assist with relevant laboratory, diagnostic, and therapeutic procedures within the nursing role, including:

- Preparation of the client for the procedure.

- Reinforcement of client teaching (before and following the procedure).

- Accurate collection of specimens.

- Monitoring procedure results (compare to norms) and appropriate notification of the primary care provider.

- Monitoring the client's response (expected, unexpected adverse response, comparison to baseline) to the procedure.

- Monitoring and taking actions, including reinforcing client teaching, to prevent or minimize the risk of complications.

- Recognizing signs of potential complications and reporting to the primary care provider.

- Recommending changes in the test/procedure as needed based on client findings.

Key Points

Δ   Hormone replacement therapy (HRT) is prescribed to **help control symptoms associated with estrogen deficiency**. Estrogen deficiency symptoms occur naturally as part of the aging process during perimenopause and menopause. Menopause may also occur if the ovaries are surgically removed (oophorectomy).

Δ **Signs and symptoms of estrogen deficiency** include:

- Vasomotor symptoms: Hot flashes and irregular menses.

- Genitourinary: Atrophic vaginitis, vaginal dryness, and incontinence.

- Psychologic: Mood swings, changes in sleep patterns, and decreased REM sleep.

- Skeletal: Decreased bone density.

- Cardiovascular: Decreased HDL, increased LDL.

- Dermatologic: Decreased skin elasticity, breast tissue changes.

Δ Hormone replacement therapy includes estrogen for women without a uterus or estrogen combined with progesterone for women with a uterus.

Δ Many different preparations of HRT are available, including **oral, transdermal, intravaginal, and intramuscular.** HRT may be prescribed as a continuous, combined estrogen-progesterone therapy or a variety of cyclic patterns.

Δ Based on their individual risk factors and healthcare needs, women should discuss the risks and benefits of using HRT with their primary care provider.

Δ If a woman and her primary care provider believe that the use of HRT is required for management of menopausal symptoms, the best recommendation is to **use HRT on a short-term basis, generally less than 5 years.**

Δ HRT is not indicated for prophylaxis of heart disease and generally is not prescribed for women at high risk for heart disease.

Key Factors

Δ **Risk Factors** (contraindications for HRT)

- Pregnancy

- Heavy smoking

- Cancer

  ◊ Cancer of the breast

  ◊ Cancer of the uterus

  ◊ Undiagnosed abnormal vaginal bleeding

- Embolism

  ◊ Active thrombophlebitis

  ◊ Thromboembolic disorder

◊ Stroke

◊ Heart disease or high risk for heart disease (for example, hypertensive)

- Liver dysfunction

- Gallbladder disease

Diagnostic Procedures and Nursing Interventions (to guide HRT initiation/continuation)

Δ Rule out **cancer**.

- Pelvic examination with PAP smear

- Breast examination with mammogram

- Biopsy of uterine lining in cases of undiagnosed abnormal uterine bleeding in a woman over 40 years old or in whom menses has stopped for a year and bleeding begins again

Δ Follicle stimulating hormone (FSH), if needed to confirm menopause

Δ Blood, urine, saliva hormone levels (estrogens, progesterone, DHEA-S, testosterone)

Δ Bone mass measurements to confirm the presence of osteopenia/osteoporosis

Therapeutic Procedure: HRT

Δ **Assess/Monitor**

- Side effects from HRT

- Increased blood pressure

- Increased weight due to fluid retention

- Breast lumps or abnormalities

- Vaginal bleeding

- Venous thrombosis

- Symptoms of heart or cerebrovascular disease

Δ Monitor for **side effects of estrogen.**

- Nausea

- Fluid retention

- Breast enlargement

- Headache

Δ   Monitor for **side effects of progesterone.**

- Increased appetite

- Weight gain

- Irritability

- Depression

- Spotting

- Breast tenderness

Δ   **Client Education**

- Instruct the client in advantages and disadvantages of HRT.

- Instruct the client in self-administration of HRT.

- Advise the client to immediately quit smoking if applicable.

- Teach the client how to prevent and assess the development of venous thrombosis.

  ◊   Avoid wearing constricting socks.

  ◊   Avoid wearing knee-high stockings.

  ◊   Note and report symptoms of leg pain.

  ◊   Note and report unilateral leg edema.

  ◊   Note and report whether skin of affected extremity is warm, red, or tender.

  ◊   Avoid sitting for long periods of time.

  ◊   Take short walks throughout the day to promote circulation.

  ◊   Perform frequent ankle pumps and move and stretch legs.

- Schedule annual physicals, pelvic examinations, and mammograms.

- Schedule bone density tests when ordered.

- Instruct the client on atypical presentation of myocardial infarction signs and symptoms in women (abdominal pain, vague chest symptoms, arm pain, leg swelling) and to seek assistance immediately.

- If oral therapy causes nausea, taking pills with food may help.

- If using vaginal creams or suppositories of estrogen compounds, be sure to refrain from inserting prior to intercourse or partner may absorb some of the product.

Complications and Nursing Implications

Δ **Teratogenesis** (malformations of an embryo or fetus)

- Confirm menopause prior to initiation.
- Instruct the client to discontinue immediately if pregnancy is suspected.

Δ **Embolic Complications** (risk increased by concurrent smoking)

- Myocardial infarction, especially during the first year of therapy
- Stroke
- Venous thrombosis – thrombophlebitis, especially during the first year of therapy

Δ **Cancer**

- Long-term use of HRT increases the risk for breast cancer.
- Long-term use of estrogen-only HRT increases the risk for ovarian and endometrial cancer, but this risk is decreased with 12 or more days of progesterone per month.

Meeting the Needs of Older Adults

Δ HRT is beneficial in prevention of age-related problems:

- Osteoporosis
- Atrophic vaginitis, which is characterized by vaginal burning and bleeding, pruritus, and painful intercourse

Δ Older clients can also decrease the risk of osteoporosis by performing regular weight bearing exercises; increasing intake of high-protein and high-calcium foods; avoiding alcohol, caffeine, and tobacco; and taking calcium with vitamin D supplements.

Primary Reference:

Ignatavicius, D. D., & Workman, M. L. (2006). *Medical-surgical nursing* (5th ed.). St. Louis, MO: Saunders.

Additional Resources:

Lewis, Heitkemper, and Dirksen (2004). *Medical-surgical nursing: Assessment and management of clinical problems* (6th ed.). St. Louis, MO: Mosby.

NANDA International (2004). *NANDA nursing diagnoses: Definitions and classification 2005-2006*. Philadelphia: NANDA.

Chapter 117: Hormone Replacement Therapy

Application Exercises

Scenario: A 51-year-old nulliparous female presents to the women's health clinic with reports of hot flashes and absent menses. She has not had a period for 6 months now and states that she cannot sleep at night because the hot flashes awaken her. She is requesting hormone replacement therapy (HRT) for relief of menopausal symptoms. She stopped using oral contraceptive pills several years ago when her husband passed away. She has not been sexually active since his death. This is her first visit to a healthcare provider in 3 years.

1. What assumptions can the nurse make about the client's cessation of menstruation?

2. What diagnostic tests should the nurse anticipate this client will need prior to initiating HRT?

3. Identify priority nursing diagnoses for this client.

4. Identify nursing interventions for this client.

5. The client begins short-term hormone therapy. The client experiences an episode of breakthrough bleeding. What action should the client take?

Chapter 117: Hormone Replacement Therapy

Application Exercises Answer Key

Scenario: A 51-year-old nulliparous female presents to the women's health clinic with reports of hot flashes and absent menses. She has not had a period for 6 months now and states that she cannot sleep at night because the hot flashes awaken her. She is requesting hormone replacement therapy (HRT) for relief of menopausal symptoms. She stopped using oral contraceptive pills several years ago when her husband passed away. She has not been sexually active since his death. This is her first visit to a healthcare provider in 3 years.

1. What assumptions can the nurse make about the client's cessation of menstruation?

   The client is probably menopausal. She is not sexually active. She has not menstruated for 6 months and is experiencing the vasomotor symptoms and sleep disturbance commonly associated with menopause.

2. What diagnostic tests should the nurse anticipate this client will need prior to initiating HRT?

   Because she has not received medical care for 3 years, she will most likely need a complete physical exam including a clinical breast exam, mammogram, pelvic exam, and Pap smear. She will also need a complete blood count and cholesterol testing.

3. Identify priority nursing diagnoses for this client.

   Ineffective thermoregulation

   Disturbed sleep pattern

   Fatigue

4. Identify nursing interventions for this client.

Provide instructions related to safe use of HRT.

Provide instructions related to side effects and complications of HRT.

Educate the client about maintenance of a cool environment and reducing caffeine and alcohol intake to reduce heat production.

Instruct the client in relaxation techniques.

Advise the client to increase air circulation at night in the bedroom and avoid heavy bedding.

Advise the client to wear loose-fitting clothing.

Suggest vitamin E in doses up to 600 IU daily.

5. The client begins short-term hormone therapy. The client experiences an episode of breakthrough bleeding. What action should the client take?

The client should continue to take the prescribed HRT; however, she should be instructed to record the quantity and timing of bleeding for 3 months and to report to her provider. Persistent or recurrent vaginal bleeding can be a possible indication of endometrial cancer.

Unit 12
Section:

Nursing Care of Clients with Reproductive Disorders
Diagnostic and Therapeutic Procedures: Reproductive

Chapter 118:   Hysterectomy
Contributor: Dana Bartlett, MSN, RN, CSPI

↻ **NCLEX-PN® Connections:**

Learning Objective: Review and apply knowledge within "**Hysterectomy**" in readiness for performance of the following nursing activities as outlined by the NCLEX-PN® test plan:

Δ   Perform/assist with relevant laboratory, diagnostic, and therapeutic procedures within the nursing role, including:

- Preparation of the client for the procedure.

- Reinforcement of client teaching (before and following the procedure).

- Accurate collection of specimens.

- Monitoring procedure results (compare to norms) and appropriate notification of the primary care provider.

- Monitoring the client's response (expected, unexpected adverse response, comparison to baseline) to the procedure.

- Monitoring and taking actions, including reinforcing client teaching, to prevent or minimize the risk of complications.

- Recognizing signs of potential complications and reporting to the primary care provider.

- Recommending changes in the test/procedure as needed based on client findings.

Δ   Recognize the client's recovery from anesthesia, if used.

Δ   Monitor therapeutic devices (drainage/irrigating devices, chest tubes), if inserted, for proper functioning.

📖 **Key Points**

Δ   A hysterectomy is the **removal of the uterus** and, in some cases, removal of the ovaries and fallopian tubes.

Δ   A hysterectomy is a very common operation, being the most commonly performed surgery in women over the age of 50. But as with all operations, there are intraoperative and postoperative complications.

Key Factors

Δ   A hysterectomy is usually performed for the treatment of:

- **Uterine cancer.**

- Noncancerous conditions – such as **fibroids, endometriosis (inflammation of the endometrium), and genital prolapse** – that cause pain, bleeding, or emotional stress.

Δ   **Signs and symptoms** of these disorders include:

- Painful intercourse.

- Hypermenorrhea.

- Pelvic pressure.

- Urinary urgency or frequency.

- Constipation.

Therapeutic Procedures and Nursing Interventions: Hysterectomy

Δ   There are three methods of performing a hysterectomy:

- **Abdominal approach**, also known as a total abdominal hysterectomy (TAH).

- **Vaginal approach.**

- **Laparoscopy-assisted vaginal hysterectomy.**

Δ   Postoperatively, the nurse must **monitor for vaginal bleeding**. Excess is more than one saturated pad in 4 hr.

Δ   A Foley catheter is generally inserted intraoperatively and in place for first 24 hr postoperatively.

Δ Priority assessments and interventions following a **total abdominal hysterectomy** include:

- Monitor vital signs (fever, hypotension).

- Monitor breath sounds (risk of atelectasis; turn, cough, deep breathe; incentive spirometry; ambulation).

- Monitor bowel sounds (risk of paralytic ileus).

- Monitor urine output (call if less than 30 mL/hr).

- Provide IV fluid and electrolyte replacement (until bowel sounds return).

- Monitor the incision (infection, integrity, risk of dehiscence).

- Monitor for signs of thrombophlebitis (warmth, tenderness, edema).

- Take thromboembolism precautions (sequential compression devices, ambulation).

- Monitor blood loss (hemoglobin and hematocrit).

- Instruct the client on a well-balanced diet that is high in protein and vitamin C for wound healing and high in iron if the client is anemic.

- Instruct the client regarding activity restrictions (heavy lifting, strenuous activity, driving, stairs, sexual activity) for 4 to 6 weeks.

Complications and Nursing Implications

Δ **Hemorrhage/hypovolemic shock** due to blood loss. Monitor hemoglobin and hematocrit. Fluid replacement therapy and/or blood transfusions as indicated.

Δ **Psychological reactions** can occur months to years after surgery. Encourage discussion of positive aspects of life. Occasional sadness is normal. Persistent sadness or depression indicates a need for counseling assistance.

Meeting the Needs of Older Adults

Δ Older adults are more susceptible to intraoperative and postoperative complications.

Primary Reference:

Ignatavicius, D. D., & Workman, M. L. (2006). *Medical-surgical nursing* (5th ed.). St. Louis, MO: Saunders.

Additional Resources:

NANDA International (2004). *NANDA nursing diagnoses: Definitions and classification 2005-2006*. Philadelphia: NANDA.

Chapter 118: Hysterectomy

Application Exercises

Scenario: A 55-year-old female client reports hypermenorrhea and fatigue to her primary care provider.

1. What diagnostic interventions are indicated and why?

2. The client's hemoglobin is 9.4 g/dL. Cancer is ruled out. Medical management is the selected initial approach. What medications will most likely be prescribed?

3. The client is scheduled for a total abdominal hysterectomy. Which of the following preoperative client findings pose a surgical concern? (Check all that apply.)

   _____ WBC 9,500/mm³

   _____ Hemoglobin 7.8 g/dL

   _____ Creatinine 2.1 mg/dL

   _____ Serum osmolality 285 mOsm/L

   _____ Pulse oximetry 95%

4. Create a list of appropriate nursing assessments and interventions for a client who is postoperative TAH.

Chapter 118: Hysterectomy

Application Exercises Answer Key

Scenario: A 55-year-old female client reports hypermenorrhea and fatigue to her primary care provider.

1. What diagnostic interventions are indicated and why?

   Hemoglobin and hematocrit to assess blood loss.

   Pap smear, ultrasonography (abdominal/ transvaginal), laparoscopy, and biopsy to assess the presence of cancer cells.

2. The client's hemoglobin is 9.4 g/dL. Cancer is ruled out. Medical management is the selected initial approach. What medications will most likely be prescribed?

   Iron supplementation and hormone therapy

3. The client is scheduled for a total abdominal hysterectomy. Which of the following preoperative client findings pose a surgical concern? (Check all that apply.)

	WBC 9,500/mm³
x	Hemoglobin 7.8 g/dL
x	Creatinine 2.1 mg/dL
	Serum osmolality 285 mOsm/L
	Pulse oximetry 95%

   Anemia poses a surgical risk for bleeding as well as hypovolemic shock. A high creatinine level may indicate renal dysfunction, which poses a surgical risk. All other client findings are within normal ranges.

4. Create a list of appropriate nursing assessments and interventions for a client who is postoperative TAH.

Monitor vital signs (fever, hypotension).

Monitor breath sounds (risk of atelectasis; turn, cough, deep breathe; incentive spirometry; ambulation).

Monitor bowel sounds (risk of paralytic ileus).

Monitor urine output (call if less than 30 mL/hr).

Provide IV fluid and electrolyte replacement (until bowel sounds return).

Monitor the incision (infection, integrity, risk of dehiscence).

Monitor for signs of thrombophlebitis (warmth, tenderness, edema).

Take thromboembolism precautions (sequential compression devices, ambulation).

Monitor blood loss (hemoglobin and hematocrit).

Instruct the client on a well-balanced diet that is high in protein and vitamin C for wound healing and high in iron if the client is anemic.

Instruct the client regarding activity restrictions (heavy lifting, strenuous activity, driving, stairs, sexual activity) for 4 to 6 weeks.

Unit 12   Nursing Care of Clients with Reproductive Disorders
Section: Diagnostic and Therapeutic Procedures: Reproductive

Chapter 119:   Prostate Surgeries
                 Contributor: Dana Bartlett, MSN, RN, CSPI

NCLEX-PN® Connections:

Learning Objective: Review and apply knowledge within "**Prostate Surgeries**" in readiness for performance of the following nursing activities as outlined by the NCLEX-PN® test plan:

Δ   Perform/assist with relevant laboratory, diagnostic, and therapeutic procedures within the nursing role, including:

- Preparation of the client for the procedure.

- Reinforcement of client teaching (before and following the procedure).

- Accurate collection of specimens.

- Monitoring procedure results (compare to norms) and appropriate notification of the primary care provider.

- Monitoring the client's response (expected, unexpected adverse response, comparison to baseline) to the procedure.

- Monitoring and taking actions, including reinforcing client teaching, to prevent or minimize the risk of complications.

- Recognizing signs of potential complications and reporting to the primary care provider.

- Recommending changes in the test/procedure as needed based on client findings.

Δ   Recognize the client's recovery from anesthesia, if used.

Δ   Monitor therapeutic devices (drainage/irrigating devices, chest tubes), if inserted, for proper functioning.

📖 Key Points

Δ **Benign prostatic hypertrophy (BPH)** obstructs the bladder neck. A **transurethral resection of the prostate (TURP)** is a commonly performed procedure that can alleviate the signs and symptoms of BPH – **urinary frequency, nocturia, urinary hesitancy**, hematuria, bladder distention, and overflow incontinence.

Δ A **radical prostatectomy** is used for clients with prostate cancer. These clients have many of the same signs and symptoms as clients with BPH.

Key Factors

Δ **Indications for Prostate Surgery**

- BPH

- Prostate cancer

Diagnostic Procedures and Nursing Interventions (for clients with BPH and prostate cancer)

Δ **Digital rectal exam (DRE)** – a physical exam of the prostate for size and consistency. The client is in a side-lying fetal position or bends over a table during the examination.

- **BPH:** Enlarged, elastic

- **Prostate cancer:** Hard, palpable irregularities

Δ **Prostate-Specific Antigen (PSA)** serum levels: Elevated with BPH, prostatitis, and prostate cancer (normal levels are less than 4 ng/mL)

Δ Needle or aspiration **biopsy of the prostate** is used to **definitively diagnose** or rule out prostate cancer.

Δ Computed tomography (CT) scans, magnetic resonance imaging (MRI), and bone scans are used to assess for metastases from prostate cancer.

Therapeutic Procedures and Nursing Interventions

Δ There are several different methods of **removing the enlarged section of the prostate**.

- TURP via a resectoscope (closed procedure)

- Retropubic, suprapubic, or perineal approaches to remove prostate (open procedures)

Δ A **radical prostatectomy** (retropubic, suprapubic, or perineal approach) involves removal of the entire prostate gland, along with the seminal vesicles, the cuff at the bladder neck, and the regional lymph nodes.

Δ   Postoperative treatment includes placement of an **indwelling three-way catheter**.

- The catheter **drains urine and allows for instillation of a continuous bladder irrigation** (CBI) of normal saline (**isotonic**) or another prescribed irrigating solution in order to keep the catheter free of obstruction.

- The **rate of the CBI is adjusted to keep the irrigation return pink or lighter.** For example, if bright red (arterial) bleeding with clots is observed, the nurse should increase the CBI rate.

- If the **catheter becomes obstructed** (bladder spasms, reduced irrigation outflow), turn off the CBI and irrigate with 50 mL of irrigation solution using a large piston syringe. Contact the primary care provider if unable to dislodge the clot.

- Record the amount of irrigating solution instilled (generally very large volumes) and the amount of return. The difference equals urine output.

- The catheter has a **large balloon** (30 to 45 mL) that is kept pulled down by **traction** so that the balloon will apply firm pressure to the prostatic fossa to **prevent bleeding**. This makes the client feel a **continuous need to urinate**. Instruct the client to not void around the catheter as this causes bladder spasms.

Δ   If the client has a **suprapubic prostatectomy**, a **suprapubic catheter** – in addition to the urethral catheter – will be placed. Usually, it will be removed when residual urine measurements are less than 75 mL.

Δ   Monitor vital signs and urinary output postoperatively.

Δ   Administer/provide increased fluids.

Δ   Monitor for bleeding (persistent bright red bleeding unresponsive to increase in CBI, reduced hemoglobin levels) and report to the primary care provider.

Δ   If present, monitor the incision and change dressing as appropriate.

Δ   Administer **medications** as prescribed.

- Analgesics (surgical manipulation or incisional discomfort)

- Antispasmodics (bladder spasms)

- Antibiotics (prophylaxis)

- Stool softeners (avoid straining)

Δ **Discontinue CBI and catheter** as prescribed. Monitor urinary output. Initial voidings following removal may be redder and contain clots. The color of the urine should progress toward amber in 2 to 3 days. Instruct the client that expected output is 150 to 200 mL every 3 to 4 hr. The client should contact the primary care provider if unable to void.

Δ **Client Education**

- Avoid heavy lifting, strenuous exercise, straining, and sexual intercourse for the prescribed length of time, usually 2 to 6 weeks.

- Drink 12 or more glasses of water each day.

- Avoid caffeine and alcohol (overstimulation of the bladder).

- If urine becomes bloody, stop activity and rest. Increase fluid intake.

- Contact the provider for persistent bleeding or obstruction (less than expected output, distention).

- Following radical prostatectomy surgery, teach the client to perform perineal exercises to reduce urinary incontinence.

Complications and Nursing Implications

Δ **TURP Complications**

- **Urethral trauma**, **urinary retention**, **bleeding**, and **infection.** Monitor and intervene for bleeding. Provide antibiotic prophylaxis.

- Regrowth of prostate tissue and **reoccurrence** of bladder neck obstruction.

Δ **Radical Prostatectomy Complications**

- Irreversible **erectile dysfunction** due to pudendal nerve damage during the operation is possible. In certain circumstances, the surgeon may be able to perform a nerve-sparing prostatectomy. Initiate referrals as appropriate.

- **Refractory postoperative urinary incontinence** requiring implantation of an **artificial urinary sphincter** (AUS). This is a device that prevents incontinence and allows the client some control over bladder elimination pattern.

Meeting the Needs of Older Adults

Δ The incidence of prostate cancer increases accordingly with age.

Δ Surgery poses a greater risk for the older adult client. Assess cardiovascular, respiratory, and renal systems carefully prior to surgery. Monitor for postoperative complications.

Primary Reference:

Ignatavicius, D. D., & Workman, M. L. (2006). *Medical-surgical nursing* (5th ed.). St. Louis, MO: Saunders.

Additional Resources:

NANDA International (2004). *NANDA nursing diagnoses: Definitions and classification 2005-2006*. Philadelphia: NANDA.

Chapter 119: Prostate Surgeries

Application Exercises

1. Which of the following client findings suggest a need for prostate surgery? (Check all that apply.)

_____ DRE reveals enlarged prostate
_____ DRE reveals firm prostate with palpable irregularities
_____ Repetitive episodes of acute urinary retention
_____ Nocturia with fluid consumption after 2000
_____ Hematuria
_____ PSA of 3 ng/mL

Scenario: A nurse is caring for a client following a TURP.

---

2. In the immediate postoperative period, priority should be given to which of the following nursing actions?

A. Encouraging oral fluid intake
B. Administering antispasmodics
C. Monitoring the client's incision
D. Maintaining continuous bladder irrigation

3. Identify an appropriate nursing response if this client demonstrates the following findings.

Client Finding	Nursing Response
Output is brighter red and contains more clots.	
Volume of output decreases and client reports feeling an extreme need to urinate.	
Client reports a constant need to urinate.	

4. Calculate the client's urinary output for the past hour given the following values:

Irrigant input: 2,600 mL

Catheter output: 2,725 mL

5. The nurse should provide which of the following discharge instructions to the client. (Check all that apply.)

_____ Contact the provider if small clots are noted during urination.

_____ Restrict fluid intake to prevent incontinence.

_____ Avoid lifting objects heavier than 20 lb for at least 2 weeks.

_____ If urine becomes bloody, stop activity, rest, and increase fluids.

_____ Use stool softeners and avoid straining to have a bowel movement.

Chapter 119: Prostate Surgeries

Application Exercises Answer Key

1. Which of the following client findings suggest a need for prostate surgery? (Check all that apply.)

__x__	DRE reveals enlarged prostate
__x__	DRE reveals firm prostate with palpable irregularities
__x__	Repetitive episodes of acute urinary retention
_____	Nocturia with fluid consumption after 2000
__x__	Hematuria
_____	PSA of 3 ng/mL

   A normal PSA level is less than 4 ng/mL. Nocturia with fluid consumption after 2000 is not diagnostic of BPH.

   Scenario: A nurse is caring for a client following a TURP.

   ---

2. In the immediate postoperative period, priority should be given to which of the following nursing actions?

   A. Encouraging oral fluid intake

   B. Administering antispasmodics

   C. Monitoring the client's incision

   D. Maintaining continuous bladder irrigation

   Maintaining continuous bladder irrigation is a high priority nursing action. Obstruction poses several serious risks. Encouraging oral fluids, monitoring the incision, and maintaining client comfort are important but not the highest priority.

3. Identify an appropriate nursing response if this client demonstrates the following findings.

Client Finding	Nursing Response
Output is brighter red and contains more clots.	Increase CBI. Increase fluid intake. Contact the primary care provider if persistent.
Volume of output decreases and client reports feeling an extreme need to urinate.	Irrigate with 50 mL using a piston syringe (more pressure). Contact the provider if not able to resolve.
Client reports a constant need to urinate.	Explain the impact of catheter balloon size and traction. Rule out obstruction. Administer antispasmodics as prescribed.

4. Calculate the client's urinary output for the past hour given the following values:

Irrigant input: 2,600 mL

Catheter output: 2,725 mL

Catheter output – irrigant input = urinary output, so:

2,725 – 2,600 = 125 mL

5. The nurse should provide which of the following discharge instructions to the client. (Check all that apply.)

_____   Contact the provider if small clots are noted during urination.

_____   Restrict fluid intake to prevent incontinence.

__x__   Avoid lifting objects heavier than 20 lb for at least 2 weeks.

__x__   If urine becomes bloody, stop activity, rest, and increase fluids.

__x__   Use stool softeners and avoid straining to have a bowel movement.

The client should avoid heavy lifting for at least 2 weeks postoperatively. The client should stop activity, rest, and increase fluids if urine becomes bloody. Stool softeners may be used to avoid straining. Persistent bleeding and more than small clots is a reason to call the primary care provider. Small clots alone, however, do not require calling the provider. The client is encouraged to drink at least 12 or more glasses of water each day.

Unit 12   Nursing Care of Clients with Reproductive Disorders
Section: Nursing Care of Clients with Reproductive Cancers

Chapter 120:   Female Cancers
                 Contributor: Sharon Lytle, MS, RN, CNM

⟳ NCLEX-PN® Connections:

Learning Objective: Review and apply knowledge within **"Female Cancers"** in readiness for performance of the following nursing activities as outlined by the NCLEX-PN® test plan:

Δ   Assist with relevant laboratory, diagnostic, and therapeutic procedures within the nursing role, including:

   •   Preparation of the client for the procedure.

   •   Accurate collection of specimens.

   •   Monitoring client status during and after the procedure.

   •   Reinforcing client teaching (before and following the procedure).

   •   Recognizing the client's response (expected, unexpected adverse response) to the procedure.

   •   Monitoring results.

   •   Monitoring and taking actions to prevent or minimize the risk of complications.

   •   Notifying the primary care provider of signs of complications.

Δ   Recognize signs and symptoms of the client's problem and complete the proper documentation.

Δ   Provide and document care based on the client's health alteration.

Δ   Monitor and document vital signs changes.

Δ   Interpret data that need to be reported immediately.

Δ   Reinforce client education on managing the client's health problem.

Δ   Recognize and respond to emergency situations, including notification of the primary care provider.

Δ   Review the client's response to emergency interventions and complete the proper documentation.

Δ   Provide care that meets the age-related needs of clients 65 years of age or older, including recognizing expected physiological changes.

Breast Cancer

📖 Key Points

Δ   Breast cancer is the second leading cause of cancer deaths in women in the United States.

Δ   A combination of breast self-examination (BSE), clinical breast exam (CBE), and mammography is effective in detecting early breast cancer and reducing mortality rates.

Δ   An annual clinical breast exam and mammogram should be performed earlier for women at risk for breast cancer.

Key Factors

Δ   **Risk Factors**

- High genetic risk

  ◊   First-degree relative with breast cancer (parent, sibling, or child)

  ◊   Early age at diagnosis

- Female sex (less than 1% of males develop breast cancer)

- Age over 40

- Early menarche

- Late menopause

- First pregnancy after age 30

- Endometrial or ovarian cancer

- Early or prolonged use of oral contraceptives

- High-fat diet (possible risk)

- Low-fiber diet (possible risk)

- Excessive alcohol intake (possibly related to folic acid depletion)

- Cigarette smoking

- Exposure to low level radiation

- Hormone replacement therapy (HRT)

- Obesity

- History of endometrial or ovarian cancer

Diagnostic Procedures and Nursing Interventions

Δ **Mammogram**

- Prepare the client for mammogram; instruct the client to not use talcum powder or deodorant before the procedure.

- Mammograms are best done in the first 2 weeks of the menstrual cycle so that minimal cystic changes are present.

Δ **Biopsy: Definitive Diagnosis**

- Incisional biopsy is the surgical removal of tissue from a breast mass.

- Excisional biopsy removes the mass itself for histologic exam.

- Aspiration therapy is the removal of tissue or fluid from the breast mass through a large-bore needle.

- The choice of treatment depends on the stage and size of the tumor, as well as nodal involvement.

Therapeutic Procedures and Nursing Interventions

Δ **Surgical procedures** include lumpectomy (breast-conserving), wide excision or partial mastectomy, total mastectomy, modified radical mastectomy, radical mastectomy, and reconstructive surgery.

Δ **Adjuvant therapy** (radiation therapy, chemotherapy, or hormonal therapy) follows surgery to decrease the risk of reoccurrence.

Assessments

Δ Monitor for **signs and symptoms.**

- Skin changes (for example, peau d'orange)

- Dimpling

- Increased vascularity

- Nipple retraction or ulceration

- Enlarged lymph nodes

- Breast pain or soreness

Δ   **Assess/Monitor**

- Client's risk factors for breast cancer, especially gynecological/obstetrical, alcohol, and smoking

- Client's family history of breast cancer

- Client's history of breast self-examination and mammography

- Client's understanding and expectations of treatment

- Dressings, drains for indications of postoperative bleeding

- Circulatory status of affected arm

- Intake and output

- Vital signs

- Postoperative drainage

- Fluid collection or swelling at operative site

- Signs of infection

- Pain

- Signs of disturbed body image

- Need for prosthesis if the client elects not to have breast reconstruction

NANDA Nursing Diagnoses

Δ   Anxiety

Δ   Anticipatory grieving

Δ   Acute pain

Δ   Disturbed body image

Δ   Impaired skin integrity

Δ   Risk for infection

Nursing Interventions

Δ   **Screening**

- All women > age 20: Monthly breast self-examination (BSE) and annual clinical breast examination (CBE)

- Age 40: Baseline screening mammogram

- Age 40 to 50: Yearly screening mammograms

Δ **Chemoprevention**: Administration of selective estrogen receptor modifiers (SERMs), such as tamoxifen (Tamofen) and raloxifene (Evista), to women at high risk for breast cancer.

Δ Prepare the client for surgery, radiation, or chemotherapy, as indicated.

Δ **Postoperative nursing interventions** include:

- Administer pain medications as prescribed.

- Maintain surgical asepsis of dressings, incision, and drains.

- Support arm on operative side with sling while ambulating.

- Encourage the client to lie on the unaffected side postoperatively to relieve pain.

- Advise the client to avoid a dependent arm position. This position will interfere with wound healing.

- Encourage early arm exercises (for example, hand wall climbing) to prevent lymphedema and to regain full range of motion.

- Avoid administering injections, taking blood pressure, or drawing blood from the affected arm.

- Teach the client not to wear constrictive clothing and to avoid cuts and injuries to the affected arm.

- Teach/reinforce teaching regarding breast self-examination.

- Encourage the client to discuss reconstruction alternatives with the surgeon.

- Refer the client to home health care services for care of drains and dressings and for help with activities of daily living.

- Emphasize the importance of a well-fitting breast prosthesis for a client who has had a mastectomy.

- Instruct the client to report numbness, pain, heaviness, or impaired motor function of the affected arm to the surgeon.

- Provide emotional support to the client and family.

- Arrange for a visitor from Reach for Recovery to speak with the client.

- Refer the client to a community support group as appropriate.

Complications and Nursing Interventions

Δ **Tumor invasion** of lymphatic channels and seeding of cancer cells into the blood and lymphatic systems. The most common areas of metastases are the nearby bone, lungs, brain, and liver.

Cervical Cancer

Key Points

Δ   The incidence of cervical cancer in situ is increasing and affecting a younger population than in the past.

Δ   Early cervical cancer is generally asymptomatic. Symptoms do not develop until the cancer has become invasive.

Δ   Papanicolaou (Pap) tests are an effective screening tool for detecting the earliest changes associated with cervical cancer. Findings of a Pap smear are usually classified according to the Bethesda system.

Key Factors

Δ   **Risk Factors**

- Early sexual activity (before 18 years old)

- Multiple sexual partners, either self or male partner

- Male partner who had a female partner with cervical cancer

- Low economic status

- Hispanic, African-American, and Native-American heritage

- Chronic inflammation

- Infection with human papilloma virus (HPV), associated in 90% of cases

- History of sexually transmitted diseases (STDs)

- Infection with HIV

- Cigarette smoking

- Immunosuppression

- Intrauterine exposure to diethylstilbestrol (DES) during pregnancy

Diagnostic Procedures and Nursing Interventions

Δ   **Pap Smear** – microscopic examination of cervical cells

Δ   **Cervical biopsy** (definitive) is performed for cytologic studies when a cervical lesion is identified. Biopsy is usually performed during colposcopy as a follow-up to an abnormal Pap smear.

Therapeutic Procedures and Nursing Interventions

Δ   Unsatisfactory colposcopy findings or a positive biopsy necessitates **removal of the lesion** by conization, cryotherapy, laser ablation, or loop electrosurgical excision procedure (LEEP).

Δ   Clients with more extensive cancer may require a **total abdominal hysterectomy** or a more extensive pelvic surgery called exenteration.

Assessments

Δ   Monitor for **signs and symptoms.**

- **Painless vaginal bleeding**
- Watery blood-tinged vaginal discharge
- Leg pain (sciatic) or leg swelling
- Flank pain (hydronephrosis)
- Unexplained weight loss
- Pelvic pain

Δ   **Assess/Monitor**

- Pain level
- Vital signs
- Signs of infection
- Signs of disturbed body image
- The client's understanding and expectations of treatment

NANDA Nursing Diagnoses

Δ   Acute pain

Δ   Ineffective peripheral tissue perfusion

Nursing Interventions

Δ   Treat and reverse anemia as indicated.

Δ   Treat any pelvic, vaginal, or urinary tract infections.

Δ   Administer pain medications as prescribed.

Δ   Provide emotional support to the client and family.

Δ   Prepare the client for biopsy, cryosurgery, conization, laser therapy, LEEP, radiation, or surgery as indicated.

Δ   Teach the client signs and symptoms of infection.

Δ   Teach the client regarding home care following special procedures (vaginal discharge, pain, avoiding douches, avoiding sexual intercourse, safety precautions, and post-radiation treatments).

Δ   Refer the client to a community support group as appropriate.

Δ   Refer the client to counseling if depressed or expressing concerns over sexuality.

Ovarian Cancer

Key Points

Δ   The exact etiology of ovarian cancer is unknown; however, the more times a woman ovulates in her lifetime seems to be a risk factor since ovarian cancer is more prevalent in women with early menarche, late onset menopause, nulliparity, and in women who use infertility agents.

Δ   **Metastases** frequently occur before the primary ovarian malignancy is diagnosed.

Δ   The most reliable indicator of prognosis is related to the stage of the cancer at the time of diagnosis.

Key Factors

Δ   **Risk Factors**

- Over 40 years of age
- Nulliparity or first pregnancy after 30 years old
- Family history of ovarian, breast, or colon cancer
- History of dysmenorrhea or heavy bleeding
- High-fat diet (possible risk)
- Use of baby talc (possible risk)
- Hormone replacement therapy (HRT)
- Use of infertility drugs

Diagnostic Procedures and Nursing Interventions

Δ   **Pap Smear** – only abnormal in small percentage of clients with ovarian cancer.

Δ   **Staging** of ovarian cancer is determined at the time of exploratory laparotomy when the tumor is removed and examined by the pathologist.

Δ **Cancer antigen test** (CA-125 antigen) is better at measuring treatment than screening for presence of disease.

Δ "Second look" surgical procedure following treatment to determine if there is a residual tumor, or if the cancer has been successfully treated.

Therapeutic Procedures and Nursing Interventions

Δ **Primary interventions** are surgery, traditional chemotherapy, intraperitoneal chemotherapy, and pelvic and abdominal irradiation.

Assessments

Δ Monitor for **signs and symptoms.**

- Abdominal pain or swelling
- Abdominal discomfort (dyspepsia, indigestion, gas, distention)
- Abdominal mass

Δ **Assess/Monitor**

- Nutritional status
- Weight
- Pain status
- Laboratory data
- Urinary frequency and urgency
- Signs of urinary obstruction
- Signs of bowel obstruction
- Emotional status of the client and family
- Postoperative status
- Vital signs
- Abdominal incision
- Postoperative complications (shock, hemorrhage, pulmonary complications)
- Infection
- Side effects and toxic effects of chemotherapy
- Side effects and toxic effects of radiation therapy

NANDA Nursing Diagnoses

Δ   Acute pain

Δ   Ineffective peripheral tissue perfusion

Nursing Interventions

Δ   Provide pain control.

Δ   Teach the client regarding diagnostic tests.

Δ   Provide preoperative teaching and care.

Δ   Provide routine postoperative care.

Δ   Change dressings as ordered.

Δ   Provide pain relief as ordered.

Δ   Prepare the client for chemotherapy and radiation therapy.

Δ   Relieve unpleasant side effects due to chemotherapy and/or radiation therapy.

Δ   Encourage the client to express feelings about the cancer and fears of death.

Δ   Help the client and family to develop coping strategies.

Δ   Monitor the client's progress through the stages of grief.

Δ   Arrange for a visit with a cancer survivor if possible.

Δ   Provide information about cancer support groups.

Δ   Provide information about hospice care when appropriate.

Meeting the Needs of Older Adults

Δ   Breast cancer rates are expected to increase over the next 50 years due to the increase in the older adult population. BSE monthly, CBE yearly, and mammography every 1 to 2 years is recommended for women age 65 and older.

Δ   Increased risk of cervical cancer occurs with advancing age.

Δ   Women who develop ovarian cancer are usually over 40 years old.

Δ   Older adult clients are at greater risk of complications following surgery for cancer.

Primary Reference:

Ignatavicius, D. D., & Workman, M. L. (2006). *Medical-surgical nursing* (5th ed.). St. Louis, MO: Saunders.

Additional Resources:

Lewis, Heitkemper, and Dirksen (2004). *Medical-surgical nursing: Assessment and management of clinical problems* (6th ed.). St. Louis, MO: Mosby.

NANDA International (2004). *NANDA nursing diagnoses: Definitions and classification 2005-2006.* Philadelphia: NANDA.

Chapter 120: Female Cancers

Application Exercises

Scenario: A 47-year-old female client presents to the health screening clinic for the first time in 8 years. For the first time since the death of her husband 8 years ago, she is in a new relationship and is planning to resume sexual activity. Her medical history is significant for hypercholesteremia, which resolved with dietary changes and exercise. She lost 25 lb last year. Her body mass index is 25. She smokes three to four cigarettes daily. She engages in vigorous exercise four to five times a week. Family history is significant for the death of her mother at age 25 due to ovarian cancer. She has no siblings.

She was married for 3 years prior to the death of her husband and was unable to conceive during that time. The couple did not seek infertility treatment. The client has had one sexual partner in her lifetime. Her menstrual history is: menarche at age 12, regular 31 day cycles, gravida 0.

1. What assessment findings place the client at risk for cancers of the reproductive system?

2. What assessments and diagnostic procedures can the nurse anticipate the client will need to be prepared for?

3. What type of client education will be provided?

Chapter 120: Female Cancers

Application Exercises Answer Key

Scenario: A 47-year-old female client presents to the health screening clinic for the first time in 8 years. For the first time since the death of her husband 8 years ago, she is in a new relationship and is planning to resume sexual activity. Her medical history is significant for hypercholesteremia, which resolved with dietary changes and exercise. She lost 25 lb last year. Her body mass index is 25. She smokes three to four cigarettes daily. She engages in vigorous exercise four to five times a week. Family history is significant for the death of her mother at age 25 due to ovarian cancer. She has no siblings.

She was married for 3 years prior to the death of her husband and was unable to conceive during that time. The couple did not seek infertility treatment. The client has had one sexual partner in her lifetime. Her menstrual history is: menarche at age 12, regular 31 day cycles, gravida 0.

1. What assessment findings place the client at risk for cancers of the reproductive system?

   Female gender, age over 40, nullipara, previous history of obesity, cigarette smoking, ovarian cancer in a first-degree relative

2. What assessments and diagnostic procedures can the nurse anticipate the client will need to be prepared for?

   Complete head-to-toe physical examination including clinical breast examination, bimanual pelvic examination, and rectal exam. Diagnostic procedures will include Pap smear and mammogram. Serum studies – such as complete blood count, serum cholesterol, and thyroid profile – as well as urinalysis and stool for occult blood may also be performed if the client has not had these tests performed recently.

3. What type of client education will be provided?

Prior to the physical exam, the nurse will prepare the client by explaining what to expect and how she will be positioned during the exam. The client may be offered the opportunity to have a nurse remain present during the exam, rather than remain alone with the provider performing the exam. Some providers require the presence of a nurse during pelvic examinations.

Instructions will be provided for further laboratory work or diagnostic procedures. Information is provided about recommended health screenings such as BSE, CBE, mammograms, and Pap smears, and the client is encouraged to follow recommendations for health screening.

Also, the client is encouraged to stop smoking, continue regular exercise, follow a healthy diet, and maintain her normal weight.

Unit 12 Nursing Care of Clients with Reproductive Disorders

Section: Nursing Care of Clients with Reproductive Cancers

Chapter 121: Male Cancers

Contributor: Dana Bartlett, MSN, RN, CSPI

NCLEX-PN® Connections:

Learning Objective: Review and apply knowledge within **"Male Cancers"** in readiness for performance of the following nursing activities as outlined by the NCLEX-PN® test plan:

Δ   Assist with relevant laboratory, diagnostic, and therapeutic procedures within the nursing role, including:

  • Preparation of the client for the procedure.

  • Accurate collection of specimens.

  • Monitoring client status during and after the procedure.

  • Reinforcing client teaching (before and following the procedure).

  • Recognizing the client's response (expected, unexpected adverse response) to the procedure.

  • Monitoring results.

  • Monitoring and taking actions to prevent or minimize the risk of complications.

  • Notifying the primary care provider of signs of complications.

Δ   Recognize signs and symptoms of the client's problem and complete the proper documentation.

Δ   Provide and document care based on the client's health alteration.

Δ   Monitor and document vital signs changes.

Δ   Interpret data that need to be reported immediately.

Δ   Reinforce client education on managing the client's health problem.

Δ   Recognize and respond to emergency situations, including notification of the primary care provider.

Δ   Review the client's response to emergency interventions and complete the proper documentation.

Δ   Provide care that meets the age-related needs of clients 65 years of age or older, including recognizing expected physiological changes.

Testicular Cancer

Key Points

Δ **Testicular cancer** accounts for less than 2% of all cancers in men. It is, however, the most common malignancy in men 15 to 35 years old.

Key Factors

Δ The cause of testicular cancer is unknown.

Δ **Risk Factors**

- Undescended testis (cryptorchidism)
- Genetic disposition, possibly
- Metastases

Diagnostic Procedures and Nursing Interventions

Δ Tumor markers, alpha-fetoprotein (AFP) and human chorionic gonadotropin (hCG): Elevated in some forms of testicular cancer

Δ Ultrasonography: Determine if palpable mass is solid or fluid-filled.

Δ Computed tomography (CT) imaging scan, magnetic resonance imaging (MRI), chest x-rays, and bone scans: Evaluate the extent of the cancer.

Therapeutic Procedures and Nursing Interventions

Δ **Surgery** – the testis is removed (**unilateral orchiectomy**), and the client may also undergo a **radical retroperitoneal lymph node dissection** to stage the disease and remove some of the bulk of the tumor.

Δ For certain testicular cancers, radiation or chemotherapy may be used after surgery.

Assessments

Δ Monitor for **signs and symptoms.**

- Lumps and/or swelling of testes
- Evidence of metastasis (abdominal masses, gynecomastia, back pain)

NANDA Nursing Diagnoses

Δ   Sexual dysfunction

Δ   Dysfunctional grieving

Δ   Disturbed body image

Δ   Acute pain

Δ   Anxiety

Nursing Interventions

Δ   **Screening**

- Teach clients regarding testicular self-examination (TSE). Examine monthly after a shower. Look and feel for any lumps or change in the size, shape, or consistency of the testes.

Δ   **Postoperative Care**

- Arrange for sperm banking prior to treatment.

- Assess intake and output.

- Observe for signs and symptoms of infection (chills, fever, incisional pain or drainage). Instruct the client to report symptoms.

- Monitor pain and administer analgesics as needed. Monitor the client's response.

- Provide, or arrange for, counseling for the client's anxiety and reaction to sexual dysfunction and change in body image.

- Avoid heavy lifting and strenuous activity for a designated period of time.

Complications and Nursing Implications

Δ   Complications of testicular cancer involve the **change of body image** and the adjustment to the **change in sexual function**. Clients will have significant needs for counseling and psychological support.

Prostate Cancer

 Key Points

Δ   Prostate cancer is a common cancer in men after age 40.

Key Factors

Δ   **Risk Factors**

- Family history

- Heavy metal exposure

- History of vasectomy

- History of sexually transmitted disease (STD)

- Certain viruses

Diagnostic Procedures and Nursing Interventions

Δ   **Digital rectal exam (DRE)** – physical exam of the prostate for size and consistency. The client lies in a side-lying fetal position or bends over a table during the examination. Prostate cancer is indicated by **hard, palpable irregularities**.

Δ   **Prostate-Specific Antigen (PSA)** serum levels: Elevated with prostate cancer (normal levels are less than 4 ng/mL)

Δ   Needle or aspiration **biopsy of prostate** is performed to **definitively diagnose** or rule out prostate cancer.

Δ   CT scans, MRI, and bone scans are performed to assess for metastases from prostate cancer.

Therapeutic Procedures and Nursing Interventions

Δ   A **radical prostatectomy** (retropubic, suprapubic, or perineal approach) involves removal of the entire prostate gland, along with the seminal vesicles, the cuff at the bladder neck, and the regional lymph nodes.

Δ   **Radiation therapy** – external beam radiation therapy or implanted radioactive seeds.

Assessments

Δ   Monitor for **signs and symptoms.**

- Urinary hesitancy

- Recurrent bladder infections

- Urinary retention

- **Painless hematuria**

Δ Assess/Monitor

- Pain

- Intake and output

NANDA Nursing Diagnoses

Δ Acute pain

Δ Impaired urinary elimination

Δ Sexual dysfunction

Δ Disturbed body image

Nursing Interventions

Δ **Hormone therapy**, such as leuprolide acetate (Lupron). Monitor adverse effects, such as hot flashes.

Δ **Postoperative Care**

- Monitor for pain and administer analgesia as indicated. Patient-controlled analgesia is commonly prescribed.

- Elevate scrotum and penis and apply ice intermittently.

- Provide sequential compression device and/or antiembolic stockings.

- Monitor for deep vein thrombosis.

- Monitor urinary output (indwelling catheter).

- Instruct the client in catheter care.

- Administer antispasmodics as prescribed.

Complications and Nursing Implications

Δ A radical prostatectomy also has risk for the following complications:

- Irreversible **erectile dysfunction** due to pudendal nerve damage during the operation – in certain circumstances, the surgeon may be able to perform a nerve-sparing prostatectomy. Initiate referrals as appropriate.

- **Refractory postoperative urinary incontinence** requiring implantation of an **artificial urinary sphincter** (AUS) – this is a device that prevents incontinence and allows the client some control over his bladder elimination pattern.

Primary Reference:

Ignatavicius, D. D., & Workman, M. L. (2006). *Medical-surgical nursing* (5th ed.). St. Louis, MO: Saunders.

Additional Resources:

NANDA International (2004). *NANDA nursing diagnoses: Definitions and classification 2005-2006*. Philadelphia: NANDA.

Chapter 121: Male Cancers

Application Exercises

1. When instructing a client in testicular self-examination, the nurse should provide which of the following instructions? (Check all that apply.)

_____   Examine testicles while lying down.

_____   Examine testicles following a shower.

_____   Roll testes between fingers feeling for any lumps.

_____   Report changes in the size, shape, or consistency of the testes.

_____   Examine testes every 6 months.

2. Label each of the following symptoms as characteristic of prostate (P) or testicular cancer (T).

_____   Testicular lump

_____   Elevated alpha fetoprotein (AFP)

_____   Elevated prostate-specific antigen (PSA)

_____   Urinary hesitancy

_____   Recurrent bladder infections

_____   Urinary retention

_____   Painless hematuria

3. Label each of the following complications as possible for radical prostatectomy (P), orchiectomy with radical retroperitoneal lymph node dissection (T), or both (B)

_____   Disturbed body image

_____   Urinary incontinence

_____   Erectile dysfunction

4. What instructions should a nurse provide to a client who is incontinent following a prostatectomy?

Chapter 121: Male Cancers

Application Exercises Answer Key

1. When instructing a client in testicular self-examination, the nurse should provide which of the following instructions? (Check all that apply.)

_____	Examine testicles while lying down.
__x__	Examine testicles following a shower.
__x__	Roll testes between fingers feeling for any lumps.
__x__	Report changes in the size, shape, or consistency of the testes.
_____	Examine testes every 6 months.

Testicular self-examinations should be performed monthly following a shower. Any lumps or changes in the size, shape, or consistency of the testes should be reported to the primary care provider.

2. Label each of the following symptoms as characteristic of prostate (P) or testicular cancer (T).

__T__	Testicular lump
__P__	Elevated alpha fetoprotein (AFP)
__P__	Elevated prostate-specific antigen (PSA)
__P__	Urinary hesitancy
__P__	Recurrent bladder infections
__P__	Urinary retention
__P__	Painless hematuria

3. Label each of the following complications as possible for radical prostatectomy (P), orchiectomy with radical retroperitoneal lymph node dissection (T), or both (B)

__B__	Disturbed body image
__P__	Urinary incontinence
__P__	Erectile dysfunction

4. What instructions should a nurse provide to a client who is incontinent following a prostatectomy?

Encourage the client to perform Kegel exercises at every urination, decrease or eliminate the consumption of caffeine, and stop smoking.

Unit 12   Nursing Care of Clients with Reproductive Disorders
Section: Nursing Care of Clients with Select Reproductive Disorders

Chapter 122:   Benign Prostatic Hypertrophy (BPH)
                 Contributor: Sharon Lytle, MS, RN, CNM

NCLEX-PN® Connections:

Learning Objective: Review and apply knowledge within "**Benign Prostatic Hypertrophy (BPH)**" in readiness for performance of the following nursing activities as outlined by the NCLEX-PN® test plan:

Δ   Assist with relevant laboratory, diagnostic, and therapeutic procedures within the nursing role, including:

   •   Preparation of the client for the procedure.

   •   Accurate collection of specimens.

   •   Monitoring client status during and after the procedure.

   •   Reinforcing client teaching (before and following the procedure).

   •   Recognizing the client's response (expected, unexpected adverse response) to the procedure.

   •   Monitoring results.

   •   Monitoring and taking actions to prevent or minimize the risk of complications.

   •   Notifying the primary care provider of signs of complications.

Δ   Recognize signs and symptoms of the client's problem and complete the proper documentation.

Δ   Provide and document care based on the client's health alteration.

Δ   Monitor and document vital signs changes.

Δ   Interpret data that need to be reported immediately.

Δ   Reinforce client education on managing the client's health problem.

Δ   Recognize and respond to emergency situations, including notification of the primary care provider.

Δ   Review the client's response to emergency interventions and complete the proper documentation.

Δ   Provide care that meets the age-related needs of clients 65 years of age or older, including recognizing expected physiological changes.

✎ Key Points

Δ   Benign prostatic hypertrophy (BPH) is **the most common benign tumor in older men**. BPH develops to some degree in all older adult men.

Δ   **Conservative management** of BPH involves deferring treatment or "watchful waiting." If symptoms worsen, the client may undergo drug therapy or surgery.

Δ   More than 300,000 surgical procedures for BPH are performed yearly in the U.S. The goal of **surgical procedures** for BPH is to remove excess prostate tissue and thus eliminate symptoms.

Δ   The prognosis for men undergoing surgery for BPH is excellent.

Key Factors

Δ   **Risk Factors**

• Male gender

• Age over 50 years, 50%; age over 70 years, 80%

• Family history (predominantly first-degree relatives)

• Western cultural heritage

• Diet high in zinc, butter, and margarine, possible

• Caucasian

Diagnostic Procedures and Nursing Interventions

Δ   **Digital Rectal Exam (DRE)** – physical exam of the prostate for size and consistency. The client lies in a side-lying fetal position or bends over a table during the examination. Palpation reveals an enlarged elastic prostate if BPH (versus hard palpable irregularities with prostate cancer).

Δ   **Prostate-Specific Antigen (PSA)** serum levels: Elevated with BPH, prostatitis, and prostate cancer (normal levels are less than 4 ng/mL).

Δ   X-ray of kidneys, ureter, and bladder (KUB) are performed to outline the structure of the urinary tract system.

Δ   **Cystourethroscopy: Definitive visualization** of bladder neck obstruction and its impact on functioning.

Δ   Needle or aspiration **biopsy of prostate**: Definitively diagnose or rule out prostate cancer.

Δ   Urinalysis with culture: Rule out urinary tract infection.

Δ   Serum creatinine: Rule out renal insufficiency.

Δ   Post-void residual urine volume

Therapeutic Procedures and Nursing Interventions

Δ   There are several different methods of **removing the enlarged section of the prostate.**

- TURP – transurethral resection of the enlarged segment via a resectoscope (closed procedure)

- Retropubic, suprapubic, or perineal approaches to remove the prostate (open procedures)

- Newer surgical procedures include transurethral needle ablation (TUNA), balloon dilation of the prostate, transurethral microwave thermotherapy (TUMT) of the prostate, transurethral laser incision, transurethral electrovaporization of the prostate (TUVP), and insertion of prostatic stents.

Assessments

Δ   Monitor for **signs and symptoms.**

- Urinary frequency (small amounts)

- Nocturia

- Urinary hesitancy (difficulty starting stream)

- Dribbling after urination

- Bladder distention

Δ   **Assess/Monitor**

- Bladder distention after voiding

- Acute urinary retention

- Intake and output

- Signs of infection

- Postoperative condition if the client undergoes surgery:
    ◊ Hemoglobin and hematocrit levels for anemia due to blood loss
    ◊ Urinary catheter drainage for blood and clots
    ◊ Urinary catheter for kinking or obstruction
    ◊ Continuous bladder irrigation
    ◊ For hyponatremia (as a result of absorption of bladder irrigating fluid)
    ◊ For urinary retention following catheter removal

NANDA Nursing Diagnoses

- Δ   Impaired urinary elimination

- Δ   Risk for deficient fluid volume

- Δ   Risk for infection

- Δ   Acute pain

- Δ   Fear/anxiety

- Δ   Ineffective therapeutic regimen management

Nursing Interventions

- Δ   Encourage the client to void when the urge occurs.

- Δ   Instruct the client to drink 2,500 to 3,000 mL of fluid a day or as directed by the provider.

- Δ   Instruct the client to avoid drinking large quantities of fluid over a short period of time.

- Δ   Reinforce restriction of evening fluid intake.

- Δ   Instruct the client on a timed voiding schedule.

- Δ   Educate the client to use moderation in consuming alcohol, caffeinated beverages, and spicy foods.

- Δ   Teach the client to avoid medications that can cause urinary retention (anticholinergics, antihistamines, decongestants).

- Δ   Insert a urinary catheter to drain bladder if ordered.

- Δ   Provide routine preoperative and postoperative care if surgery is performed.

  - •   Maintain urinary drainage system following surgery.

  - •   If bleeding occurs, arrange for blood component therapy as ordered.

  - •   Remind the client to keep his leg straight if the catheter is taped to his thigh.

  - •   Remove indwelling catheter when ordered.

- Δ   Make an appointment for a follow-up visit with the primary care provider.

Δ   Administer **medications** as prescribed (conservative waiting approach).

- 5-alpha-reductase inhibitors, such as finasteride, to reduce the size of the prostate gland

- Alpha-adrenergic receptor blockers, such as doxazosin (Cardura), terazosin (Hytrin), and tamsulosin (Flomax), to block alpha$_1$adrenergic receptors, promote smooth muscle relaxation in the prostate, and facilitate urinary flow. Monitor for orthostatic hypotension and teach the client to change positions slowly.

Δ   Discuss alternative/complementary therapies with the client if appropriate. Herbal therapy such as saw palmetto may improve urinary symptoms, but long-term effectiveness is unknown. Advise the client to speak with the primary care provider before trying alternative treatments.

Complications and Nursing Implications

Δ   Untreated BPH can lead to serious complications.

- **Renal Failure** – urinary retention because of an occluded bladder neck can lead to backup of urine through the ureters into the kidneys (**hydronephrosis**), which can lead to renal failure.

- Overstretching of the bladder wall can result in **bladder muscle weakness**.

- Residual urine in the bladder poses a risk for **urinary tract infection** and possibly kidney infections.

- Monitor intake and output, residuals, and for evidence of reflux and/or infection.

Meeting the Needs of Older Adults

Δ   Older adult males have the following statistical incidence of BPH:

- 50% of males develop some degree of BPH by age 60.

- 90% of males develop microscopic evidence of BPH by age 85.

- 25% of males in the U.S. will have symptoms severe enough to require intervention by age 80.

Δ   When caring for an older adult client who may be disoriented, reorient the client frequently and remind the client not to pull on the catheter.

Δ   Monitor older adult clients for signs of infection following surgery because existing conditions may compromise their immune system and lower resistance to microorganisms.

Δ   Assess older clients following surgery for pneumonia and other complications of immobility. Have the client turn, cough, deep breathe, and ambulate as soon as possible.

Primary Reference:

Ignatavicius, D. D., & Workman, M. L. (2006). *Medical-surgical nursing* (5th ed.). St. Louis, MO: Saunders.

Additional Resources:

Lewis, Heitkemper, and Dirksen (2004). *Medical-surgical nursing: Assessment and management of clinical problems* (6th ed.). St. Louis, MO: Mosby.

NANDA International (2004). *NANDA nursing diagnoses: Definitions and classification 2005-2006*. Philadelphia: NANDA.

Chapter 122: Benign Prostatic Hypertrophy (BPH)

Application Exercises

Scenario: A 79-year-old male client was admitted to the acute care floor 4 days ago for treatment of bilateral lower lobe pneumonia. The client responded well to treatment with levofloxacin (Levaquin) 500 mg IVPB every 24 hr and methylprednisolone (Solu-Medrol) 60 mg IV every 6 hr. Vital signs are stable, and oxygen saturation is 97% on room air. Scattered crackles are present. Continuous intravenous fluids were discontinued 3 hr ago, and the client now has an intravenous lock. Discharge is planned following repeat chest x-ray the next morning.

The primary nurse notices that the client is urinating frequently, even though he no longer is receiving continuous intravenous fluid hydration. The client has consumed 350 mL of oral fluids in the last 3 hr. He has urinated four times in those 3 hr, 30 to 50 mL with each void.

1. What assessment findings suggest that the client needs further evaluation regarding urinary patterns?

2. What assumptions might the nurse make about the client's urinary patterns?

3. What additional assessments should the nurse make regarding the client's urinary patterns?

4. What additional actions will the nurse take following assessment of the problem?

Chapter 122: Benign Prostatic Hypertrophy (BPH)

Application Exercises Answer Key

Scenario: A 79-year-old male client was admitted to the acute care floor 4 days ago for treatment of bilateral lower lobe pneumonia. The client responded well to treatment with levofloxacin (Levaquin) 500 mg IVPB every 24 hr and methylprednisolone (Solu-Medrol) 60 mg IV every 6 hr. Vital signs are stable, and oxygen saturation is 97% on room air. Scattered crackles are present. Continuous intravenous fluids were discontinued 3 hr ago, and the client now has an intravenous lock. Discharge is planned following repeat chest x-ray the next morning.

The primary nurse notices that the client is urinating frequently, even though he no longer is receiving continuous intravenous fluid hydration. The client has consumed 350 mL of oral fluids in the last 3 hr. He has urinated four times in those 3 hr, 30 to 50 mL with each void.

1. What assessment findings suggest that the client needs further evaluation regarding urinary patterns?

   Urination four times in 3 hr, only 30 to 50 mL with each void – this suggests that the client may be experiencing urinary retention and voiding only overflow urine.

2. What assumptions might the nurse make about the client's urinary patterns?

   Because the client has consumed a total amount of oral fluid of 350 mL in 3 hr since discontinuation of intravenous fluid, the nurse may assume that the client is adequately hydrated.

   The client does have scattered crackles; however, this can be due to the infectious process rather than excess fluid volume.

   Voiding frequent small amounts of urine may indicate urinary tract infection or urine retention with overflow or urine.

3. What additional assessments should the nurse make regarding the client's urinary patterns?

History of urinary patterns:

    Frequency

    Hesitancy

    Amounts

    Nighttime voiding patterns

    Pain or burning with urination

    Sensation of bladder fullness after urination

Physical examination

    Palpation of bladder following urination

4. What additional actions will the nurse take following assessment of the problem?

Notify the primary care provider of the assessment findings.

Unit 12

Section:

Nursing Care of Clients with Reproductive Disorders

Nursing Care of Clients with Select Reproductive Disorders

Chapter 123:   **Cystocele and Rectocele**

Contributor: Dana Bartlett, MSN, RN, CSPI

🔄 **NCLEX-PN® Connections:**

Learning Objective: Review and apply knowledge within "**Cystocele and Rectocele**" in readiness for performance of the following nursing activities as outlined by the NCLEX-PN® test plan:

Δ   Assist with relevant laboratory, diagnostic, and therapeutic procedures within the nursing role, including:

- Preparation of the client for the procedure.

- Accurate collection of specimens.

- Monitoring client status during and after the procedure.

- Reinforcing client teaching (before and following the procedure).

- Recognizing the client's response (expected, unexpected adverse response) to the procedure.

- Monitoring results.

- Monitoring and taking actions to prevent or minimize the risk of complications.

- Notifying the primary care provider of signs of complications.

Δ   Recognize signs and symptoms of the client's problem and complete the proper documentation.

Δ   Provide and document care based on the client's health alteration.

Δ   Monitor and document vital signs changes.

Δ   Interpret data that need to be reported immediately.

Δ   Reinforce client education on managing the client's health problem.

Δ   Recognize and respond to emergency situations, including notification of the primary care provider.

Δ   Review the client's response to emergency interventions and complete the proper documentation.

Δ   Provide care that meets the age-related needs of clients 65 years of age or older, including recognizing expected physiological changes.

📖 Key Points

Δ   A **cystocele** is a protrusion of the bladder through the vaginal wall. It is caused by **weakened pelvic muscles and/or structures**.

•   For a cystocele with mild signs and symptoms, medical treatment can be tried. If this is not successful, surgery may be indicated.

Δ   A **rectocele** is a protrusion of the anterior rectal wall through the posterior vaginal wall. It is caused by a **defect of the pelvic structures or a difficult delivery or forceps delivery**.

•   For a rectocele with mild signs and symptoms, medical treatment may be tried. If this is not successful, surgery may be indicated.

Key Factors

Δ   **Risk Factors for Cystocele**

•   Obesity

•   **Advanced age (loss of estrogen)**

•   Chronic constipation

•   Family history

•   Childbearing

Δ   **Risk Factors for Rectocele**

•   Pelvic structure defects

•   Difficult childbirth

•   Forceps delivery

•   Previous hysterectomy

Diagnostic Procedures and Nursing Interventions

Δ   Cystocele

•   **Pelvic examination** reveals a bulging of the anterior wall when the client is instructed to bear down.

•   **Voiding cystourethrography** is performed to identify the degree of bladder protrusion and amount of urine residual.

Δ   Rectocele

•   **Pelvic examination** reveals a bulging of the posterior wall when the client is instructed to bear down.

•   **Rectal examination** and/or **barium enema** reveals presence of a rectocele.

Therapeutic Procedures and Nursing Interventions

Δ **Cystocele**

- Surgery for a cystocele is called an **anterior colporrhaphy**. Using a vaginal approach, the pelvic muscles are tightened.

Δ **Rectocele**

- Surgery for a rectocele is called a **posterior colporrhaphy**. Using a vaginal/ perineal approach, the pelvic muscles are tightened.

Δ In some cases, surgery for both a cystocele and a rectocele is needed; this is called an **anterior-posterior repair.**

Assessments

Δ Monitor for **signs and symptoms of a Cystocele.**

- Urinary frequency
- Urinary urgency
- Stress incontinence
- Urinary tract infection
- Sense of vaginal fullness

Δ Monitor for **signs and symptoms of a Rectocele.**

- **Constipation**
- Hemorrhoids
- Sensation of a mass in the vagina
- Pelvic pressure or pain
- Difficulty with intercourse

NANDA Nursing Diagnoses

Δ Urinary retention

Δ Risk of infection

Δ Urinary stress incontinence

Δ Constipation

Δ Altered body image

Δ Disturbed tissue integrity

Δ Sexual dysfunction

Nursing Interventions

Δ **Prevention**

- Avoid traumatic vaginal childbirth with an early and adequate episiotomy.

- Inform the client of measures to prevent atrophic vaginitis and of the advantages of prevention.

- Advise clients at risk to lose weight if obese.

- Instruct clients to eat a high-fiber diet and drink adequate fluids to prevent constipation.

Δ **Kegel Exercises** (tighten pelvic muscles for a count of 10, relax slowly for a count of 10, repeat in sequences of 15 in lying down, sitting, and standing positions)

Δ **Estrogen Therapy** – to prevent uterine atrophy and atrophic vaginitis. Preassess the client's risk for complications from hormone therapy (for example, cardiovascular or embolic history). Monitor for side effects of estrogen therapy (fluid retention, headaches).

Δ Weight loss and changes in diet may be helpful.

Δ **Vaginal Pessary** – removable rubber, plastic, or silicone device inserted into the vagina to provide support and block protrusion into vagina. Teach the client how to insert, remove, and clean the device. Monitor for possible bleeding or fistula formation.

Δ **Postoperative care** includes:

- Administer analgesics, antimicrobials, and stool softeners/laxatives as prescribed.

- Provide perineal care at least twice daily following surgery and after every urination or bowel movement.

- Apply an ice pack to the perineal area to relieve pain and swelling.

- Suggest that the client take frequent warm sitz baths to soothe the perineal area.

- Provide a liquid diet immediately following surgery followed by a **low-residue diet** until normal bowel function returns.

- Instruct the client on how to care for an indwelling catheter at home following surgery. Remind the client to thoroughly wash her hands before and after handling the catheter and to remove any crust or debris that has collected around the catheter.

- Recommend that the client drink at least 2,000 mL of fluid daily, unless contraindicated.

- Following removal of the catheter, instruct the client to void every 2 to 3 hr to prevent a full bladder and stress on stitches.

- Teach the client how to perform clean intermittent self-catheterization (CISC) techniques in the event that the client is unable to void. Instruct the client to:

  ◊ Assume a comfortable position.

  ◊ Separate the labial folds with the thumb and mid-finger of the nondominant hand.

  ◊ Wash the perineal area from the front toward the anus.

  ◊ Keep labial folds separated and insert catheter into the urinary meatus.

  ◊ Allow urine to flow until flow stops.

  ◊ Remove the catheter slowly.

  ◊ Instruct the client to keep the catheter clean, wash it carefully, and store it in a clean container after each use.

  ◊ Remind the client that CISC is only a temporary measure while she heals following surgery.

- Caution the client to avoid straining at defecation, sneezing, coughing, lifting, and prolonged sitting, walking, or standing following surgery.

- Instruct the client to tighten and support pelvic muscles when coughing or sneezing.

- Postoperative restrictions include avoidance of strenuous activity, weight lifting greater than 5 lb, and sexual intercourse.

Complications and Nursing Implications

Δ Residual urine in the bladder poses a risk for **recurrent bladder infections** and possibly kidney infections.

Δ **Constipation**

Δ Dyspareunia (painful sexual intercourse) is a possible surgical complication due to surgical alteration of the orifice.

Meeting the Needs of Older Adults

Δ   Cystocele and rectocele develop in older female clients, usually following menopause.

Δ   Older clients tend to overuse laxatives and enemas for the relief of constipation.

Δ   Older adults are more susceptible to postoperative complications.

Δ   Performing Kegel exercises and manipulating a pessary may be more difficult for older adults.

Primary Reference:

Ignatavicius, D. D., & Workman, M. L. (2006). *Medical-surgical nursing* (5th ed.). St. Louis, MO: Saunders.

Additional Resources:

NANDA International (2004). *NANDA nursing diagnoses: Definitions and classification 2005-2006*. Philadelphia: NANDA.

Chapter 123: Cystocele and Rectocele

Application Exercises

1. What instructions should a nurse provide a client who is wearing a pessary for conservative management of a cystocele or rectocele?

2. What instructions should the nurse provide to the client concerning Kegel exercises for conservative management of a cystocele or rectocele?

Scenario: A 65-year-old woman diagnosed with serious cystocele and rectocele is being discharged home with an indwelling catheter following an anterior/posterior repair. If the client has difficulty voiding following removal of the catheter, she will need to perform clean intermittent self-catheterization (CISC).

3. What measures can the client take to prevent urinary tract infection (UTI) related to the use of an indwelling catheter?

4. What instructions should the nurse provide to the client concerning CISC?

5. What signs and symptoms should the postoperative client report to her primary care provider following discharge?

Chapter 123: Cystocele and Rectocele

Application Exercises Answer Key

1. What instructions should a nurse provide a client who is wearing a pessary for conservative management of a cystocele or rectocele?

   Pessary users should: (a) immediately report any discomfort from the pessary to the primary care provider; (b) report to the provider if the pessary falls out; (c) report any change in color, amount, odor, or consistency of vaginal discharge; (d) report vaginal itching; (e) return for follow-up examinations within 3 days following initial insertion of the pessary; and (f) schedule re-examinations every 6 weeks thereafter.

2. What instructions should the nurse provide to the client concerning Kegel exercises for conservative management of a cystocele or rectocele?

   Instruct the client to contract the circum vaginal or perirectal muscles, starting with 10 repetitions and gradually increasing to 35 to 50 repetitions. The client should hold the contraction for 6 to 10 seconds followed by a 10-second relaxation period. Exercises need to be performed every day for 6 to 12 weeks.

Scenario: A 65-year-old woman diagnosed with serious cystocele and rectocele is being discharged home with an indwelling catheter following an anterior/posterior repair. If the client has difficulty voiding following removal of the catheter, she will need to perform clean intermittent self-catheterization (CISC).

3. What measures can the client take to prevent urinary tract infection (UTI) related to the use of an indwelling catheter?

   Instruct the client with an indwelling catheter to: (a) thoroughly wash hands before and after handling the catheter or drainage system; (b) drink at least 2,000 mL of fluid a day, unless contraindicated; (c) perform perineal care to remove any crust or debris from around the catheter itself; and (d) take antibiotics and urinary antiseptics as ordered.

4. What instructions should the nurse provide to the client concerning CISC?

Instruct the client to: (a) attempt to void prior to the catheterization; (b) if unable to void, wash hands thoroughly; (c) assume a comfortable position; (d) separate the labial folds with the thumb and mid finger of the nondominant hand; (e) wash the perineal area from front toward the anus; (f) keep labial folds separated and insert catheter into the urinary meatus; (g) allow urine to flow until flow stops; and (h) remove the catheter slowly.

5. What signs and symptoms should the postoperative client report to her primary care provider following discharge?

The client should report signs and symptoms of urinary tract infection, such as urinary frequency and urgency, burning on urination, fever, and cloudy, foul-smelling urine. She should also report constipation, since constipation can result in a fecal impaction.

Unit 13   Perioperative Nursing Care
Section: Diagnostic and Therapeutic Procedures: Surgical

Chapter 124:   Anesthesia
              Contributor: Kevin D. Hite, MSN, RN

↻   NCLEX-PN® Connections:

Learning Objective: Review and apply knowledge within "**Anesthesia**" in readiness for performance of the following nursing activities as outlined by the NCLEX-PN® test plan:

Δ   Perform/assist with relevant laboratory, diagnostic, and therapeutic procedures within the nursing role, including:

- Preparation of the client for the procedure.

- Reinforcement of client teaching (before and following the procedure).

- Accurate collection of specimens.

- Monitoring procedure results (compare to norms) and appropriate notification of the primary care provider.

- Monitoring the client's response (expected, unexpected adverse response, comparison to baseline) to the procedure.

- Monitoring and taking actions, including reinforcing client teaching, to prevent or minimize the risk of complications.

- Recognizing signs of potential complications and reporting to the primary care provider.

- Recommending changes in the test/procedure as needed based on client findings.

Δ   Recognize the client's recovery from anesthesia, if used.

Δ   Monitor therapeutic devices (drainage/irrigating devices, chest tubes), if inserted, for proper functioning.

Key Points

Δ   Anesthesia is **a state of depressed central nervous system (CNS) activity**, marked by depression of consciousness, loss of responsiveness to stimulation, and/or muscle relaxation.

Δ   Anesthesia is classified as general or local.

• **General anesthesia** – loss of sensation, consciousness, and reflexes. General anesthesia is the method used when the client is undergoing major surgery, one that will require complete muscle relaxation.

• **Local anesthesia** – loss of sensation without loss of consciousness. Local anesthetics block transmission along nerves. In turn, this provides for loss of autonomic function and muscle paralysis in a specific area of the body.

Key Factors

Δ   **Risk Factors for General Anesthesia Complications**

• Family history of malignant hyperthermia

• Respiratory disease (hypoventilation)

• Cardiac disease (dysrhythmias, cardiac output)

• Gastric contents (aspiration)

• Preoperative use of alcohol or illicit drugs

Δ   **Risk Factors for Local Anesthesia Complications**

• Allergy to ester-type anesthetics

• Alterations in peripheral circulation

Therapeutic Procedures and Nursing Interventions: General Anesthesia

Δ   The phases of general anesthesia are:

• **Induction** – preoperative medications given, IV lines initiated, placement to monitoring, airway secured.

• **Maintenance** – surgery performed, airway maintenance.

• **Emergence** – surgery completed, removal of assistive airway devices.

Δ   Anesthetics used during general anesthesia are classified as either **injectable or inhaled**. Inhaled anesthetics are volatile gases or liquids that are dissolved in oxygen, and injectable anesthetics are given intravenously.

• Examples of inhalation anesthetic agents include halothane (Fluothane), isoflurane (Forane), and nitrous oxide.

- Examples of intravenous anesthetic agents include benzodiazepines, etomidate (Amidate), propofol (Diprivan), ketamine (Ketalar), and droperidol plus fentanyl.

Δ **Inhalation anesthetics are eliminated** predominantly through **exhalation.** The rate of elimination is dependent upon pulmonary ventilation and blood flow to the lungs. Consequently, postoperative administration of oxygen and encouraging the client to take deep breaths are important interventions.

Δ During administration of anesthetics, **adjunct medications** are also given. These substances are used to achieve further reactions as listed below:

Adjunct Medication Class	Medications	Use
Opioids	Fentanyl (Sublimaze) Sufentanil (Sufenta)	Sedation and analgesia
Benzodiazepines	Diazepam (Valium) Midazolam (Versed)	Amnesia and anxiety reduction
Anticholinergics	Atropine Glycopyrrolate (Robinul)	Dry up excessive secretions—decrease risk of aspiration
Antiemetics	Promethazine (Phenergan)	Nausea and vomiting reduction—decrease risk of aspiration
Sedatives	Pentobarbital (Nembutal) Secobarbital (Seconal)	Amnesia and sedation
Neuromuscular blocking agents	Succinylcholine (Anectine) Vecuronium (Norcuron)	Muscle relaxation for surgery and airway placement

Δ **Nursing Responsibilities**

- Monitoring the airway and the client's oxygen saturation

- Drawing and reporting laboratory values as appropriate (ABGs, CBC)

- Constant monitoring of the client's cardiac status (rhythm, heart rate, blood pressure)

- Assessment of the client's temperature

- Monitoring of drains, tubes, catheters, and IV access throughout anesthesia and surgery

- Assessment of level of sedation and anesthesia (level of consciousness, vital signs)

- Notification of the surgeon and anesthesiologist if abnormalities are noted

Therapeutic Procedures and Nursing Interventions: Local Anesthesia

Δ   There are three main methods of administration of local anesthesia:

- **Topical** – applied directly to the skin or mucous membranes.

- **Local infiltration** – injected directly into tissues through which a surgical incision is to be made.

- **Regional nerve block** – injected into or around specific nerves. There are four types of regional nerve blocks:

    ◊   **Spinal** – injected into the subarachnoid space cerebral spinal fluid (CSF), providing autonomic, sensory, and motor blockade to the body below the level of innervation that the area of spine where the injection was made provides.

    ◊   **Epidural** – injected into the epidural space in the thoracic or lumbar areas of the spine. Sensory pathways are blocked, but motor function remains.

    ◊   **Bier** – intravenous injection of anesthetic into an extremity following mechanical exsanguination with a tourniquet, providing analgesia and a bloodless surgical site.

    ◊   **Peripheral** – injection of anesthetic into a specific nerve for analgesic and anesthetic use.

Δ   Examples of local anesthetic agents include procaine (Novocain) and lidocaine (Xylocaine).

Δ   Concurrent administration of a **vasoconstrictor**, usually epinephrine, is likely with local anesthetic administration in order to prolong the effects and to decrease the risk of systemic toxicity. This practice is avoided for distal injuries (for example, finger) due to decreased circulation. Prolonged vasoconstriction could lead to tissue necrosis.

Δ   **Nursing Responsibilities**

- Observation for systemic absorption (restlessness, excitement, seizures, tachycardia, tachypnea, hypertension)

- Monitoring the airway and the client's oxygen saturation

- Drawing and reporting laboratory values as appropriate (ABGs, CBC)

- Constant monitoring of the client's cardiac status (rhythm, heart rate, blood pressure)

- Monitoring of drains, tubes, catheters, and IV access throughout anesthesia and surgery

- Assessment of level of sedation and anesthesia (level of consciousness, vital signs)

- Notification of the surgeon and anesthesiologist if abnormalities are noted

- Assessment of motor function to ensure paralysis does not ensue (movement returns first, then sense of touch, pain, warmth, and finally, sensation of cold)

Complications and Nursing Implications

Δ Potential complications from use of anesthesia that the nurse should monitor for are:

Complication	Signs and Symptoms
Myocardial depression	Bradycardia, hypotension, cyanosis, edema
Anaphylaxis	Cardiac failure, allergic symptoms, abnormal vital signs
Malignant hyperthermia (for example, with administration of succinylcholine)	Tachycardia, tachypnea, hypercarbia, dysrhythmias
ANS system blockade (epidural and spinal)	Hypotension, bradycardia, nausea, vomiting
CSF leakage (spinal and epidural)	Headache

Δ The nurse should notify the surgeon and anesthesiologist, if any of the above signs and symptoms are noted.

Meeting the Needs of Older Adults

Δ Older adult clients are more susceptible to anesthetic agents than any other population. Medications have to be titrated carefully to better control the incidence of unwanted effects. Airway is the main priority in all situations, but cardiac problems can arise much more quickly in older adult clients. The nurse needs to pay special attention when an older adult is undergoing a procedure, because the client's condition can deteriorate quickly.

Primary Reference:

Ignatavicius, D. D., & Workman, M. L. (2006). *Medical-surgical nursing* (5th ed.). St. Louis, MO: Saunders.

Additional Resources:

Lewis, Heitkemper, and Dirksen (2004). *Medical-surgical nursing: Assessment and management of clinical problems* (6th ed.). St. Louis, MO: Mosby.

Lilley, L., Harrington, S., & Synder, J. (2005). *Pharmacology and the nursing process* (4th ed.). St. Louis, MO: Mosby.

NANDA International (2004). *NANDA nursing diagnoses: Definitions and classification 2005-2006*. Philadelphia: NANDA.

Chapter 124: Anesthesia

Application Exercises

Scenario: A 74-year-old male client is undergoing a bowel resection for removal of ischemic bowel. He has a medical history of diabetes mellitus, hypertension, and congestive heart failure (CHF).

1. What type of anesthesia would be expected for this procedure?

2. What special considerations need to be made in this case?

3. A 17-year-old male is having a knee arthroscopy performed. After administration of midazolam (Versed), the nurse notices the client's blood pressure has dropped to 86/40 mm Hg and his heart rate is 134 beats/min. Which of the following should the nurse anticipate after informing the surgeon of the vital sign changes?

   A. Administering naloxone

   B. Administering morphine

   C. Giving 500 mL NS bolus

   D. Stopping the procedure

4. After an anesthesiologist delivers nitrous oxide with a face mask, which of the following is the priority assessment?

   A. Oxygen saturation

   B. Blood pressure

   C. Heart rate

   D. Temperature

5. Which of the following is the most dangerous possible adverse effect of inhalation anesthetics?

   A. Hypertension

   B. Increased intracranial pressure

   C. Malignant hyperthermia

   D. Atrial tachycardia

Chapter 124: Anesthesia

Application Exercises Answer Key

Scenario: A 74-year-old male client is undergoing a bowel resection for removal of ischemic bowel. He has a medical history of diabetes mellitus, hypertension, and congestive heart failure (CHF).

1. What type of anesthesia would be expected for this procedure?

General anesthesia

2. What special considerations need to be made in this case?

Based on the client's age and cardiac history, special attention will need to be given to monitoring his vital signs and his heart rhythm. The client's CHF presents a high risk for pulmonary edema, so his oxygenation status will need to be carefully monitored. His blood glucose will also have to be monitored frequently to prevent complications of glycemic instability.

3. A 17-year-old male is having a knee arthroscopy performed. After administration of midazolam (Versed), the nurse notices the client's blood pressure has dropped to 86/40 mm Hg and his heart rate is 134 beats/min. Which of the following should the nurse anticipate after informing the surgeon of the vital sign changes?

    A. Administering naloxone

    B. Administering morphine

    C. Giving 500 mL NS bolus

    D. Stopping the procedure

A fluid bolus is appropriate to raise the client's blood pressure to maintain adequate cardiac output and tissue perfusion.

4. After an anesthesiologist delivers nitrous oxide with a face mask, which of the following is the priority assessment?

> **A. Oxygen saturation**
> B. Blood pressure
> C. Heart rate
> D. Temperature

Assessment of oxygenation is the priority with administration of a medication with CNS and respiratory depression effects.

5. Which of the following is the most dangerous possible adverse effect of inhalation anesthetics?

> A. Hypertension
> B. Increased intracranial pressure
> **C. Malignant hyperthermia**
> D. Atrial tachycardia

Malignant hyperthermia is a life-threatening risk with inhalation anesthesia (for example, succinylcholine). Prompt administration of 100% oxygen, dantrolene (skeletal muscle relaxant), and cooling blankets is vital to survival.

Unit 13   Perioperative Nursing Care
Section: Diagnostic and Therapeutic Procedures: Surgical

Chapter 125:   Conscious Sedation
Contributor: Kevin D. Hite, MSN, RN

⟲ **NCLEX-PN® Connections:**

Learning Objective: Review and apply knowledge within "**Conscious Sedation**" in readiness for performance of the following nursing activities as outlined by the NCLEX-PN® test plan:

Δ   Monitor the client following conscious sedation.

Δ   Perform/assist with relevant laboratory, diagnostic, and therapeutic procedures within the nursing role, including:

   •   Preparation of the client for the procedure.

   •   Reinforcement of client teaching (before and following the procedure).

   •   Accurate collection of specimens.

   •   Monitoring procedure results (compare to norms) and appropriate notification of the primary care provider.

   •   Monitoring the client's response (expected, unexpected adverse response, comparison to baseline) to the procedure.

   •   Monitoring and taking actions, including reinforcing client teaching, to prevent or minimize the risk of complications.

   •   Recognizing signs of potential complications and reporting to the primary care provider.

   •   Recommending changes in the test/procedure as needed based on client findings.

Δ   Recognize the client's recovery from anesthesia, if used.

Δ   Monitor therapeutic devices (drainage/irrigating devices, chest tubes), if inserted, for proper functioning.

📖 Key Points

Δ Conscious sedation is the administration of sedatives and/or hypnotics to the point where the client is relaxed enough that minor procedures can be performed without discomfort, yet the client **can respond to verbal stimuli**, **retains protective reflexes** (for example, gag reflex), is easily arousable, and (most importantly) **independently maintains a patent airway**.

Δ Only a qualified provider can administer conscious sedation. These include anesthesiologists, certified registered nurse anesthetists (CRNAs), attending physicians, or registered nurses (RNs) under the supervision of one of the previously mentioned providers.

Δ The **nurse must continuously monitor a client undergoing conscious sedation**. During the procedure, an RN must be present to monitor the client, with no other responsibilities during the procedure. This nurse is to remain with the client at all times before, during, and immediately after the procedure.

Key Factors

Δ **Procedures** that may require conscious sedation include, but are not limited to:

- All types of endoscopy, lumbar puncture, and cardioversion.

- Wound care: Suturing, dressing changes, incision and drainage of abscesses, and burn debridement.

- Minor surgical procedures: Dental, podiatric, plastic, and ophthalmic procedures; vasectomy.

- Placement of implanted devices, catheters, and tubes.

- Bone marrow aspiration.

- Reduction and immobilization of fractures.

- Removal of implanted devices and tubes.

Diagnostic and Therapeutic Procedures and Nursing Interventions

Δ **Common drugs** used for and during conscious sedation are:

- Opioids – morphine, fentanyl, hydromorphone, and meperidine (Demerol).

- Anesthetics – propofol (Diprivan).

- Benzodiazepines – midazolam (Versed), diazepam (Valium), lorazepam (Ativan).

Δ Dosages required for "light sedation" are highly individualized and require careful titration.

Δ During the procedure, the **following equipment needs to be present** within immediate reach for routine monitoring and in case deep sedation with respiratory depression occurs:

- Fully equipped crash cart, including emergency and resuscitative drugs, airway and ventilatory equipment, and defibrillator.

- **Electrocardiogram (ECG) monitor with display**

- **Noninvasive blood pressure (BP) monitor**

- **Oximetry monitor**

- Means to monitor body temperature

- Stethoscope

- **100% oxygen source and administration supplies**

- Airways and positive pressure breathing device

- Suction source and supplies

- IV supplies

Δ **Nursing Responsibilities before the Procedure**

- Obtain a full history, including allergies, medication usage, and preexisting medical conditions (for example, pulmonary disease). Any previous experiences with sedation or anesthesia need to be reported, especially any adverse reactions. Note the last dose of each medication, especially if it could alter the client's response (diuretic, antihypertensive, narcotic).

- Provide education about the procedure and the medications to be used.

- Perform a full assessment, including baseline vital signs, cardiac rhythm, and level of consciousness.

- Determine the last time the client ate or drank (generally NPO for 4 hr before the procedure).

- Establish IV access and keep-vein-open fluids.

- Verify informed consent.

- Attach monitoring equipment.

- Remove the client's dentures (in case intubation would become necessary).

Δ **Nursing Responsibilities during the Procedure**

- After the sedation is given, the monitoring nurse is to **continuously assess** the client (**level of consciousness, cardiac rhythm, respiratory status, vital signs**) and to watch the monitors.

- The monitoring nurse is to never leave the client's side. Other staff may be used to assist the provider with the procedure.

- Vital signs are recorded frequently throughout the procedure, as well as level of consciousness (usually Glasgow coma scale scores).

Δ   **Nursing Responsibilities after the Procedure**

- After completion of the procedure, the monitoring nurse continues to record vital signs and level of consciousness **until the client is fully awake and all assessment criteria return to pre-sedation levels.** Only then can the nurse remove the monitor and all emergency equipment from the bedside.

- Typical **discharge criteria** include:

   ◦   Level of consciousness as on admission.

   ◦   Vital signs stable for 30 to 90 min.

   ◦   Ability to cough and deep breathe.

   ◦   Ability to take oral fluids.

   ◦   No nausea, vomiting, shortness of breath, or dizziness.

Complications and Nursing Implications

Δ   Before, during, and after the procedure, emergency equipment is to remain at the bedside. Some complications that can arise from conscious sedation include:

- Airway obstruction: Insert airway, suction.

- Respiratory depression: Administer oxygen and reversal agents, such as naloxone (Narcan) and flumazenil (Romazicon).

- Cardiac arrhythmias: Set up 12-lead ECG, provide antidysrhythmics and fluids.

- Hypotension: Provide fluids, vasopressors.

- Anaphylaxis: Administer epinephrine.

Δ   Most hospitals and facilities require that for conscious sedation the RN needs to be certified in advanced cardiac life support (ACLS) or pediatric advanced life support (PALS) in case of emergency. In all instances of complications, the sedation needs to be stopped and care given to end the problem.

Meeting the Needs of Older Adults

Δ   Older adult clients:

- Are at greater risk of adverse reactions to sedation medications.

- May need to have surgical consent forms signed by a legal guardian.

- May be more fearful due to financial concerns and lack of social support.

- Have less physiologic reserve than younger clients, so care needs to be adjusted accordingly.

- Often have sensory limitations so the nurse must be alert to maintaining a safe environment.

Δ The nurse needs to pay careful attention to cardiac and respiratory status in the older adult client, as problems may arise more quickly.

Primary Reference:

Ignatavicius, D. D., & Workman, M. L. (2006). *Medical-surgical nursing* (5th ed.). St. Louis, MO: Saunders.

Additional Resources:

NANDA International (2004). *NANDA nursing diagnoses: Definitions and classification 2005-2006*. Philadelphia: NANDA.

To read the American Nurses Association's position statement on the role of the registered nurse (RN) in the management of clients receiving conscious sedation for short-term therapeutic, diagnostic, or surgical procedures, take the following link: *http://nursingworld. org/readroom/position/joint/jtsedate.htm*

Chapter 125: Conscious Sedation

Application Exercises

Scenario: An adult female is brought into the emergency department for episodes of paroxysmal supraventricular tachycardia (PSVT). After performing all other interventions, the provider decides to perform cardioversion and to use midazolam (Versed) to relax the client for the procedure.

1. What steps need to be completed before the Versed is given?

2. What equipment is needed at the bedside for the procedure?

3. Which of the following equipment is required at the bedside for conscious sedation? (Check all that apply.)

_____ Defibrillator

_____ Oxygen

_____ Suction

_____ Blood tubing

_____ Electrocardiogram (ECG) monitor with display

_____ Noninvasive blood pressure (BP) monitor

_____ Oximetry monitor

_____ Naloxone (Narcan)

4. A 68-year-old client is undergoing an endoscopy, which will require conscious sedation. Which of the following findings in her history indicates the need for further assessment?

A. Allergic to bee stings

B. Hypertension

C. Gastrointestinal bleed

D. Chronic obstructive pulmonary disease

Chapter 125: Conscious Sedation

Application Exercises Answer Key

Scenario: An adult female is brought into the emergency department for episodes of paroxysmal supraventricular tachycardia (PSVT). After performing all other interventions, the provider decides to perform cardioversion and to use midazolam (Versed) to relax the client for the procedure.

1. What steps need to be completed before the Versed is given?

   Obtain a full history, including allergies, medication usage, and preexisting medical conditions (for example, pulmonary disease). Any previous experiences with sedation or anesthesia need to be reported, especially any adverse reactions. Note the last dose of each medication, especially if it could alter the client's response (diuretic, antihypertensive, narcotic).

   Provide education about the procedure and the medications to be used.

   Perform a full assessment, including baseline vital signs, cardiac rhythm, and level of consciousness.

   Determine the last time the client ate or drank (generally NPO for 4 hr before the procedure).

   Establish IV access and keep-vein-open fluids.

   Verify informed consent.

   Attach monitoring equipment.

   Remove the client's dentures (in case intubation would become necessary).

2. What equipment is needed at the bedside for the procedure?

Fully equipped crash cart, including emergency and resuscitative medications, airway and ventilatory equipment, and defibrillator.

Electrocardiogram (ECG) monitor with display

Noninvasive blood pressure (BP) monitor

Oximetry monitor

Means to monitor body temperature

Stethoscope

100% oxygen source and administration supplies

Airways and positive pressure breathing device

Suction source and supplies

IV supplies

3. Which of the following equipment is required at the bedside for conscious sedation? (Check all that apply.)

x	Defibrillator
x	Oxygen
x	Suction
___	Blood tubing
x	Electrocardiogram (ECG) monitor with display
x	Noninvasive blood pressure (BP) monitor
x	Oximetry monitor
x	Naloxone (Narcan)

Blood administration is not a predicted intervention for complications associated with oversedation.

4. A 68-year-old client is undergoing an endoscopy, which will require conscious sedation. Which of the following findings in her history indicates the need for further assessment?

> A. Allergic to bee stings
>
> B. Hypertension
>
> C. Gastrointestinal bleed
>
> **D. Chronic obstructive pulmonary disease**

Chronic obstructive pulmonary disease poses a risk for possible airway compromise.

Unit 13   Perioperative Nursing Care
Section: Perioperative Nursing

Chapter 126:   Preoperative Nursing
                   Contributor: Kevin D. Hite, MSN, RN

↻ NCLEX-PN® Connections:

Learning Objective: Review and apply knowledge within "**Preoperative Nursing**" in readiness for performance of the following nursing activities as outlined by the NCLEX-PN® test plan:

Δ   Provide perioperative care to the client undergoing surgery.

Δ   Assist with relevant laboratory, diagnostic, and therapeutic procedures within the nursing role, including:

- Preparation of the client for the procedure.

- Accurate collection of specimens.

- Monitoring client status during and after the procedure.

- Reinforcing client teaching (before and following the procedure).

- Recognizing the client's response (expected, unexpected adverse response) to the procedure.

- Monitoring results.

- Monitoring and taking actions to prevent or minimize the risk of complications.

- Notifying the primary care provider of signs of complications.

Δ   Recognize signs and symptoms of the client's problem and complete the proper documentation.

Δ   Provide and document care based on the client's health alteration.

Δ   Monitor and document vital signs changes.

Δ   Interpret data that need to be reported immediately.

Δ   Reinforce client education on managing the client's health problem.

Δ   Recognize and respond to emergency situations, including notification of the primary care provider.

Δ   Review the client's response to emergency interventions and complete the proper documentation.

Δ   Provide care that meets the age-related needs of clients 65 years of age or older, including recognizing expected physiological changes.

Key Points

Δ   Surgery can take on many forms, including curative, palliative, cosmetic, and functional. Surgical procedures are performed on an inpatient, same day, or outpatient admission basis.

Δ   Preoperative care takes place from the time the client is scheduled for surgery until care is transferred to the operating suite. **Informed consent** is obtained by the provider, and at that time all risks and benefits are explained to the client or surrogate.

Δ   **Assessment of risk factors** is one of the major aspects of preoperative care. Preoperative care includes a **thorough assessment of the client's physical, emotional, and psychosocial status prior to surgery.**

Δ   **Preoperative teaching** includes instructions concerning:

   •   Pain management.

   •   Deep breathing and coughing techniques.

   •   Leg and foot exercises for prevention of thrombi formation.

Key Factors

Δ   **Risk Factors: Surgery**

   •   Infection (risk of sepsis)

   •   Anemia (oxygenation, healing impact)

   •   Hypovolemia from dehydration or blood loss (circulatory compromise)

   •   Electrolyte imbalance through inadequate diet or disease process (dysrhythmias)

   •   Age (older adults and infants are at greater risk)

   •   Pregnancy (fetal risk with anesthesia)

   •   Respiratory disease (COPD, pneumonia, asthma)

   •   Cardiac disease (CVA, CHF, MI, HTN, dysrhythmias)

   •   Diabetes (decreased intestinal motility, delayed healing)

   •   Liver disease (altered drug metabolism)

   •   Renal disease (altered elimination)

   •   Endocrine disorders (hypo/hyperthyroidism, Addison's, Cushing, diabetes mellitus)

   •   Immune system disorders (allergies, immunocompromise)

- Coagulation defect (increased risk of bleeding)

- Malnutrition (delayed healing)

- Obesity (impact on anesthesia, elimination, and wound healing)

- Use of some medications (antihypertensives, anticoagulants)

- Substance use (tobacco, alcohol)

- Family history (malignant hyperthermia)

- Allergies (latex, anesthetic agents)

Diagnostic Procedures and Nursing Interventions

Δ Urinalysis: Rule out infection

Δ Blood type and crossmatch: Transfusion readiness

Δ Complete blood count: Infection/immune status

Δ Hemoglobin and hematocrit: Fluid status, anemia

Δ Clotting studies (PT, INR, aPTT, platelet count)

Δ Electrolyte levels: Hypokalemia, hyperkalemia

Δ Serum creatinine: Renal status

Δ Pregnancy test: Fetal risk of anesthesia

Δ Arterial blood gas: Oxygenation status

Δ Chest x-ray: Heart and lung status

Δ 12-lead electrocardiogram: Baseline heart rhythm, dysrhythmias

Assessments

Δ **Preoperative Assessment**

- Detailed history (including medical problems, allergies, medication use, substance abuse, psychosocial problems, and cultural considerations)

- Anxiety level regarding the procedure

- Laboratory results

- Head-to-toe assessment

- Vital signs

NANDA Nursing Diagnoses

Δ   Deficient knowledge

Δ   Anxiety

Δ   Anticipatory grieving

Δ   Ineffective individual coping

Nursing Interventions

Δ   **Informed Consent**

- Once surgery has been discussed with the client or surrogate as treatment, it is the responsibility of the primary care provider to obtain consent after discussing the risks and benefits of the procedure. The nurse is **not** to obtain the consent for the provider in any circumstance.

- The nurse can clarify any information that remains unclear after the provider's explanation of the procedure.

- The **nurse's role is to witness the client's signing of the consent form after the client acknowledges understanding of the procedure.**

Δ   **Preoperative Teaching**

- Postoperative pain control techniques (medications, mobilization, patient-controlled analgesia pumps, splinting)

- Demonstration and importance of coughing and deep breathing

- Demonstration and importance of range of motion exercises and early ambulation for prevention of thrombi and respiratory complications

- Invasive devices (drains, catheters, IV lines)

- Postoperative diet

- Use of the incentive spirometer

- Preoperative instructions (avoid cigarette smoking for 24 hr preoperatively, medications to hold, bowel preparation)

Δ   **Preoperative nursing actions** may include:

- Verification that the informed consent is accurately completed, signed, and witnessed.

- If the client is undergoing bowel surgery, administration of enemas and/or laxatives either the night before or the morning of the surgery will be required.

- Regularly scheduled medications may need to be altered (hold antihypertensives, increase corticosteroids).

- Client will be **NPO for at least 6 to 8 hr** before surgery with general anesthesia and 3 to 4 hr with local anesthesia **to avoid aspiration**. Note on the chart the last time the client ate or drank.

- Skin preparation may include cleansing with antimicrobial soap and clipping of hair in areas that will be involved in the surgery.

- Removal of jewelry, dentures, prosthetics, makeup, nail polish, and glasses. These items can either be given to the family or locked away safely.

- Establish IV access.

- Administer preoperative medications (prophylactic antimicrobials, antiemetics, sedatives) as ordered by the primary care provider.

  ◊ Have the client void prior to administration.

  ◊ Monitor the client's response to the medications.

  ◊ Raise side rails following administration to prevent injury.

- Ensure that the preoperative checklist is complete.

- Transfer the client to the preanesthesia care unit.

Complications and Nursing Implications

Δ Complications during the preoperative period are usually related to the medications given preoperatively. These medications and their possible complications are listed below:

Medication Class	Possible Complications
Sedatives (benzodiazepines, barbiturates)	Respiratory depression, drowsiness, dizziness
Narcotics	Respiratory depression, drowsiness, dizziness
Intravenous infusions (NaCl, lactated Ringer's)	Cardiac abnormalities (especially in CHF), hypernatremia
Gastrointestinal medications (antiemetics, antacids, H_2 receptor blockers)	Alkalosis, cardiac abnormalities (certain H_2 receptor blockers), drowsiness

Δ For clients encountering severe anxiety and panic, reassurance will be necessary and sedation medications may be given.

Δ Be alert for any allergic reactions to medications given.

Meeting the Needs of Older Adults

Δ Older adult clients:

- Are at greater risk of adverse reactions to preoperative medications.

- May need to have surgical consent forms signed by a legal guardian.

- May be more fearful due to financial concerns and lack of social support.

- Have less physiologic reserve than younger clients, so care needs to be adjusted accordingly.

- Have sensory limitations, so the nurse must be alert to maintaining a safe environment.

- May have oral alterations that may pose problems during intubation.

- Perspire less, which leads to dry, itchy skin that becomes fragile and easily abraded. Precautions need to be taken when moving and positioning these clients.

- Have decreased subcutaneous fat, which makes them more susceptible to temperature changes. They need to be covered with lightweight cotton blankets when they are moving to and from the operating room.

Primary Reference:

Ignatavicius, D. D., & Workman, M. L. (2006). *Medical-surgical nursing* (5th ed.). St. Louis, MO: Saunders.

Additional Resources:

NANDA International (2004). *NANDA nursing diagnoses: Definitions and classification 2005-2006*. Philadelphia: NANDA.

Chapter 126: Preoperative Nursing

Application Exercises

Scenario: A 73-year-old male client is scheduled for surgery for the removal of ischemic bowel. He has a past medical history of hypertension, type 2 diabetes mellitus, and hypothyroidism.

1. Which of the following preoperative client findings should be reported to the client's primary care provider? (Check all that apply and identify rationale.)

_____ Potassium level of 3.9 mEq/L

_____ Sodium level of 145 mEq/L

_____ Creatinine level of 2.8 mg/dL

_____ Prothrombin time of 23 sec

_____ Glucose level of 235 mg/dL

_____ White blood cell (WBC) count of 17,850/mm³

2. What interventions must the nurse perform the night before the procedure? Which of these may be delegated to other staff?

3. The morning of the procedure, the nurse records the client's vital signs and completes an assessment. The nurse finds that the client's temperature is 38.4° C (101.1° F). What interventions should the nurse perform?

4. What are the nurse's responsibilities regarding informed consent for the procedure?

5. Identify tasks typically included on a preoperative checklist that the nurse must ensure are completed and documented in the client's chart.

6. The morning before a scheduled hysterectomy related to uterine cancer, the client informs the nurse that she does not want to go through with the procedure. Which of the following steps should the nurse take next?

    A. Inform the client that the surgery is necessary and that there is nothing to worry about.

    B. Notify the surgeon that the client is refusing surgery and needs to be sedated.

    C. Inform the surgeon of the client's statement so that the surgeon can talk with the client.

    D. Note the client's statement on the chart and reassess the client.

7. A nurse records a client's vital signs before transferring him to the preanesthesia unit for an exploratory laparotomy. The client's temperature is 39° C (102.2° F) orally. Which of the following should the nurse do next?

    A. Contact and inform the surgeon regarding the temperature.

    B. Transfer the client to the preanesthesia unit and notify the accepting nurse about the temperature.

    C. Administer 650 mg acetaminophen and recheck the temperature in 1 hr.

    D. Apply a cooling blanket and recheck the client's temperature in 30 min.

Chapter 126: Preoperative Nursing

Application Exercises Answer Key

Scenario: A 73-year-old male client is scheduled for surgery for the removal of ischemic bowel. He has a past medical history of hypertension, type 2 diabetes mellitus, and hypothyroidism.

1. Which of the following preoperative client findings should be reported to the client's primary care provider? (Check all that apply and identify rationale.)

_____	Potassium level of 3.9 mEq/L
_____	Sodium level of 145 mEq/L
__x__	Creatinine level of 2.8 mg/dL
__x__	Prothrombin time of 23 sec
__x__	Glucose level of 235 mg/dL
__x__	White blood cell (WBC) count of 17,850/mm³

Potassium and sodium levels are within normal ranges. Creatinine level is elevated, which indicates possible renal elimination problems. Prothrombin time is prolonged, which poses concern for increased risk of bleeding due to delayed coagulation. Glucose level is high and intervention is needed (for example, administration of insulin). WBC is elevated and possibly indicative of an ongoing infection that needs treatment prior to surgery.

2. What interventions must the nurse perform the night before the procedure? Which of these may be delegated to other staff?

Clipping hair around the surgical site, administration of an enema or laxative, assessment of the client's anxiety level, and addressing any cultural considerations are interventions the nurse should perform the night before the procedure. The RN may delegate clipping hair and administration of an enema. The RN should assess the client's anxiety level and address cultural concerns.

3. The morning of the procedure, the nurse records the client's vital signs and completes an assessment. The nurse finds that the client's temperature is 38.4° C (101.1° F). What interventions should the nurse perform?

The surgeon must be notified of the fever, and assessments for further signs of infection need to be performed. In addition, administration of an antipyretic may be warranted.

4. What are the nurse's responsibilities regarding informed consent for the procedure?

The nurse needs to make sure the client signed the consent without any sedation given prior, clarify any points that remain unclear about the procedure after the surgeon's explanation, and document the signing of the informed consent. Also, the nurse may need to witness the consent.

5. Identify tasks typically included on a preoperative checklist that the nurse must ensure are completed and documented in the client's chart.

Client's identification band on

Preoperative vital signs

Blood type

ECG and chest x-ray

Consent signed

History and physical assessment completed

Labs drawn and results noted

All makeup, jewelry, dentures, nail polish, glasses, and prosthetics removed

Time client was made NPO

When preoperative medications were given

Time client last voided

6. The morning before a scheduled hysterectomy related to uterine cancer, the client informs the nurse that she does not want to go through with the procedure. Which of the following steps should the nurse take next?

    A. Inform the client that the surgery is necessary and that there is nothing to worry about.

    B. Notify the surgeon that the client is refusing surgery and needs to be sedated.

    C. Inform the surgeon of the client's statement so that the surgeon can talk with the client.

    D. Note the client's statement on the chart and reassess the client.

The provider performing the procedure has the responsibility to obtain the client's consent. The nurse has responsibilities as a client advocate.

7. A nurse records a client's vital signs before transferring him to the preanesthesia unit for an exploratory laparotomy. The client's temperature is 39° C (102.2° F) orally. Which of the following should the nurse do next?

    A. Contact and inform the surgeon regarding the temperature.

    B. Transfer the client to the preanesthesia unit and notify the accepting nurse about the temperature.

    C. Administer 650 mg acetaminophen and recheck the temperature in 1 hr.

    D. Apply a cooling blanket and recheck the client's temperature in 30 min.

The surgeon needs to be notified. Additional assessments will likely be prescribed to investigate the possibility of an infectious process that needs to be treated prior to surgery.

Unit 13   Perioperative Nursing Care
Section: Perioperative Nursing

Chapter 127:   Intraoperative Nursing
                 Contributor: Kevin D. Hite, MSN, RN

NCLEX-PN® Connections:

Learning Objective: Review and apply knowledge within "**Intraoperative Nursing**" in readiness for performance of the following nursing activities as outlined by the NCLEX-PN® test plan:

Δ   Provide perioperative care to the client undergoing surgery.

Δ   Assist with relevant laboratory, diagnostic, and therapeutic procedures within the nursing role, including:

•   Preparation of the client for the procedure.

•   Accurate collection of specimens.

•   Monitoring client status during and after the procedure.

•   Reinforcing client teaching (before and following the procedure).

•   Recognizing the client's response (expected, unexpected adverse response) to the procedure.

•   Monitoring results.

•   Monitoring and taking actions to prevent or minimize the risk of complications.

•   Notifying the primary care provider of signs of complications.

Δ   Recognize signs and symptoms of the client's problem and complete the proper documentation.

Δ   Provide and document care based on the client's health alteration.

Δ   Monitor and document vital signs changes.

Δ   Interpret data that need to be reported immediately.

Δ   Reinforce client education on managing the client's health problem.

Δ   Recognize and respond to emergency situations, including notification of the primary care provider.

Δ   Review the client's response to emergency interventions and complete the proper documentation.

Δ   Provide care that meets the age-related needs of clients 65 years of age or older, including recognizing expected physiological changes.

Key Points

△ There are three areas of the surgical suite:

- **Unrestricted** – street clothes and scrubs, holding area and staff areas.
- **Semi restricted** – surgical attire required, corridors and support areas.
- **Restricted** – full surgical gear, operating room (OR).

△ The surgical suite is arranged so that **cross-contamination is prevented** from clean to sterile areas.

△ The **perioperative nurse** functions as **client advocate and educator** throughout the intraoperative experience.

△ Two nursing roles within the OR:

- **Scrub nurse** – monitoring of aseptic technique, handles surgical equipment for the surgeon, must remain sterile during the procedure.
- **Circulating nurse** – plans and coordinates intraoperative care, maintains documentation, reports off to the postanesthesia care unit (PACU) at transfer from the OR.

△ Other roles in the OR include surgical technicians, surgeon and assistants, anesthesiologist, and the nurse anesthetist.

Key Factors

△ **Risk Factors: General Anesthesia Complications**

- Family history of malignant hyperthermia
- Respiratory, liver, and/or renal problems (altered drug metabolism and elimination)
- Age (risks associated with age-related alterations in elimination)
- Cardiac problems (altered circulation, risk of dysrhythmias)

△ **Risk Factors: Positioning Complications**

- Age (older adults lose skin elasticity)
- Arthritis

Diagnostic Procedures and Nursing Interventions

△ **Radiology procedures** to verify placement may be performed during some surgical procedures. Measures to protect surgical staff from unnecessary radiation exposure should be employed.

Assessments

Δ The **perioperative nurse** performs an initial assessment after transfer from the preoperative area. The nurse should assess the client's identity, as well as assessing physical, psychosocial, and cultural client findings **for risk factors and considerations for the operative procedure**. Note advance directives (must be honored in the surgical environment).

Δ The **circulating nurse** performs frequent assessments of **client positioning** (functional position without pressure), maintenance of **sterile technique and a sterile field**, and of the client's **intake and output** throughout the surgical procedure.

NANDA Nursing Diagnoses

Δ Risk for perioperative positioning injury

Δ Impaired skin integrity

Δ Impaired tissue integrity

Δ Risk for infection

Nursing Interventions

Δ Last-minute questions are to be answered by the perioperative nurse prior to induction of anesthesia.

Δ A final chart review is to be performed by the nurse to note any changes or abnormalities that could affect the procedure.

Δ The nurse will assist with **positioning** the client for the surgery:

- Dorsal recumbent, prone, lithotomy, or lateral position as indicated by procedure and as directed by the surgeon.

- **Pad bony prominences** with gel pads or pillows (elbows, under knees, hips).

- **Maintain body alignment** with padded straps tight enough to prevent movement (loss of protective reflexes), but not so tight as to cause undue pressure.

- **Position so as to not impede circulation and respiratory expansion.**

- **Avoid pressure** against skin, bones, and nerves.

- Change the client's position at regular intervals.

Δ Promote electrical safety by properly placing grounding pads and checking equipment.

Δ The nurses and OR team prepare the OR for the procedure before the client is brought in.

Δ   The nurse ensures that all members in the room are scrubbed and sterile before the procedure begins.

- Remove jewelry.

- Keep short, clean natural fingernails.

- Control water flow with foot-operated handle.

- **Use antimicrobial solution** with **vigorous rubbing (friction) for 3 to 5 min.**

- **Rinse** with hands and arms positioned so that **water runs off rather than up or down arms.**

- Enter the OR with **hands higher than elbows** and dry hands thoroughly with sterile towel before gowning and gloving.

Δ   **The nurse monitors the surgical field and observes for breaks in sterile technique.** Areas of surgical attire considered sterile are from 2 inches below the neck to waist and from wrist to elbow.

Δ   The nurse, along with the anesthesiology team, monitors the client's heart rhythm and vital signs to be able to notify the surgeon if problems arise.

Δ   The nurse **keeps track of fluids used and calculates the estimated blood loss** (EBL). The nurse may assist with intraoperative autologous blood salvage and transfusion.

Δ   After the procedure is finished, the **circulating and scrub nurses will perform a count of all equipment, sponges, and towels** to ensure that nothing is left inside the client.

Δ   The circulating nurse reports off to the PACU nurse when transferring the client after the surgery.

Complications and Nursing Implications

Δ   Cardiac Arrest: Intervene per ACLS protocols.

Δ   Massive Blood Loss: Monitor blood loss and replace fluids and administer blood products as indicated.

Δ   **Anaphylactic reactions** that occur during surgery may be masked by anesthesia, so it is important for the nurse to be able to recognize a reaction when it occurs.

Δ   **Malignant hyperthermia** is an acute, possibly fatal reaction that can be caused in a small segment of the population **by certain anesthetics**. It can occur during induction (for example, with administration of succinylcholine) or hours into the procedure. It is characterized by **high body temperature and rigid skeletal muscles**. Other client findings include tachycardia, hypotension, cyanosis (increased CO_2 and decreased O_2), and myoglobinuria (protein in urine). Response to this emergency includes:

- **Stop administration** of the causative anesthetic agent.

- If the client is not intubated, then **intubate**.

- Ventilate with **100% oxygen**.

- Infuse **IV dantrolene** as prescribed (dosage based on the client's weight).

- Use cooling techniques and monitor body temperature.

- Monitor heart rhythm carefully and intervene as prescribed.

- Monitor urinary output for amount and for presence of blood or myoglobin. Administer diuretics as prescribed.

- End surgery as soon as possible.

Δ   **Positioning Complications**: Assess skin integrity prior to and following surgery. Take measures to prevent pressure and dislocation. Document skin assessments.

Meeting the Needs of Older Adults

Δ   The older adult client is more susceptible to reactions from anesthetics.

Δ   Communication abilities are often lessened in the older adult client, so the nurse must ensure that all conversations and questions are understood by the client.

Δ   Older adult clients have more risk factors for hypothermia, so warming blankets may be needed when transporting into and out of the OR.

Primary Reference:

Ignatavicius, D. D., & Workman, M. L. (2006). *Medical-surgical nursing* (5th ed.). St. Louis, MO: Saunders.

Additional Resources:

Lewis, Heitkemper, and Dirksen (2004). *Medical-surgical nursing: Assessment and management of clinical problems* (6th ed.). St. Louis, MO: Mosby.

NANDA International (2004). *NANDA nursing diagnoses: Definitions and classification 2006-2006*. Philadelphia: NANDA.

Chapter 127: Intraoperative Nursing

Application Exercises

1. Identify the surgical attire that must be worn at the client's bedside during surgery. (Check all that apply.)

_____ Scrub jacket

_____ Mask

_____ Eye protectors

_____ Sterile gown

_____ Sterile gloves

_____ Shoe covers

_____ Scrubs worn from home

2. Match each of the following surgical procedures to the anticipated client positioning.

_____ Lumbar laminectomy	A. Lateral
_____ Coronary artery bypass graft	B. Prone
_____ Dilation and curettage	C. Lithotomy
_____ Hip arthroplasty	D. Dorsal recumbent (supine)

3. Identify the potential harm to a client posed by each of the following acts of negligence within the operating room:

Act of Negligence	Potential Harm to Client
Metal hairpins left in the client's hair	
Surgical team member leaning against the client	
Inadequately strapping the client's extremity	
Not maintaining body alignment	
Prolonged pressure against a nerve	

4. Identify the steps that should be taken if the initial equipment and sponge counts come up wrong after the surgery is completed?

Chapter 127: Intraoperative Nursing

Application Exercises Answer Key

1. Identify the surgical attire that must be worn at the client's bedside during surgery. (Check all that apply.)

_____	Scrub jacket
__x__	Mask
__x__	Eye protectors
__x__	Sterile gown
__x__	Sterile gloves
__x__	Shoe covers
_____	Scrubs worn from home

2. Match each of the following surgical procedures to the anticipated client positioning.

__B__	Lumbar laminectomy	A. Lateral
__D__	Coronary artery bypass graft	B. Prone
__C__	Dilation and curettage	C. Lithotomy
__A__	Hip arthroplasty	D. Dorsal recumbent (supine)

3. Identify the potential harm to a client posed by each of the following acts of negligence within the operating room:

Act of Negligence	Potential Harm to Client
Metal hairpins left in the client's hair	Risk for electrical burn with use of cautery
Surgical team member leaning against the client	Tissue ischemia with potential development of pressure ulcer
Inadequately strapping the client's extremity	Joint dislocation (subluxation)
Not maintaining body alignment	Contracture, wrist drop, foot drop
Prolonged pressure against a nerve	Paralysis, loss of sensation

4. Identify the steps that should be taken if the initial equipment and sponge counts come up wrong after the surgery is completed?

The circulating and scrub nurses must count equipment and sponges prior to the start of surgery and again prior to wound closure. If initial counts following the surgery are incongruent, the counts should be repeated. If still off, the surgeon must be notified and measures taken to verify that no items are left inside the client. Counts must be documented on the client's surgical record.

Unit 13   Perioperative Nursing Care
Section: Perioperative Nursing

Chapter 128:   Postoperative Nursing
Contributor: Kevin D. Hite, MSN, RN

⟳ **NCLEX-PN® Connections:**

Learning Objective: Review and apply knowledge within "**Postoperative Nursing**" in readiness for performance of the following nursing activities as outlined by the NCLEX-PN® test plan:

Δ   Provide perioperative care to the client undergoing surgery.

Δ   Monitor the client for postoperative complications and intervene appropriately.

Δ   Assist with relevant laboratory, diagnostic, and therapeutic procedures within the nursing role, including:

- Preparation of the client for the procedure.

- Accurate collection of specimens.

- Monitoring client status during and after the procedure.

- Reinforcing client teaching (before and following the procedure).

- Recognizing the client's response (expected, unexpected adverse response) to the procedure.

- Monitoring results.

- Monitoring and taking actions to prevent or minimize the risk of complications.

- Notifying the primary care provider of signs of complications.

Δ   Recognize signs and symptoms of the client's problem and complete the proper documentation.

Δ   Provide and document care based on the client's health alteration.

Δ   Monitor and document vital signs changes.

Δ   Interpret data that need to be reported immediately.

Δ   Reinforce client education on managing the client's health problem.

Δ   Recognize and respond to emergency situations, including notification of the primary care provider.

Δ   Review the client's response to emergency interventions and complete the proper documentation.

Δ   Provide care that meets the age-related needs of clients 65 years of age or older, including recognizing expected physiological changes.

🎓 Key Points

Δ   Transferring the postoperative client from the operating room to the postanesthesia care unit (PACU) is the responsibility of the anesthesiologist. The circulating nurse will give report to the PACU nurse.

Δ   Postoperative care is usually provided initially in the **PACU**, where skilled nurses can closely monitor the client's recovery from anesthesia.

Δ   Initial postoperative care involves making assessments, providing medications, managing the client's pain, preventing complications, and determining when the client is ready to be discharged from the PACU.

Δ   During the immediate postoperative stage, maintaining **airway patency and ventilation are the main priorities for care**.

Δ   Postoperative clients who received **general anesthesia** require frequent assessment of their **respiratory status**. Postoperative clients who received **epidural or spinal anesthesia** require ongoing assessment of **motor and sensory function**.

Key Factors

Δ   **Risk Factors** (for postoperative complications)

- Immobility (respiratory compromise, thrombophlebitis, pressure ulcer)
- Anemia (oxygenation, healing impact)
- Hypovolemia (tissue perfusion)
- Older age (age-related changes)
- Respiratory disease (respiratory compromise)
- Immune disorder (risk for infection, delayed healing)
- Diabetes mellitus (gastroparesis, delayed wound healing)
- Coagulation defect (increased risk of bleeding)
- Malnutrition (delayed healing)
- Obesity (wound healing, dehiscence)

Diagnostic Procedures and Nursing Interventions

Δ   Complete blood count (infection/immune status)

Δ   Hemoglobin and hematocrit (fluid status, anemia)

Δ   Electrolyte levels (hypokalemia, hyperkalemia)

Δ   Serum creatinine (renal status)

Δ   Arterial blood gas (oxygenation status)

Δ   Laboratory tests (for example, glucose) based on procedure and other health problems

Assessments

Δ   **Assess/Monitor**

- **Continually for airway patency and adequate ventilation**
- Vital signs until stable (for example, every 15 min x 4; every 30 min x 4, every 2 hr x 4, every 4 hr for 1 to 2 days)
- For evidence of bleeding
- Client skin color and condition
- Mucous membranes, lips, and nail beds for cyanosis
- For hypothermia
- For signs of fluid and electrolyte imbalance
- For nausea and vomiting
- Drainage tubes for patency and proper function
- For after-effects of anesthesia
- Intake and output (I&O) every 15 min to hourly as directed in PACU
- For signs of hypervolemia and hypovolemia
- Bladder for distention
- Urinary catheters for patency
- Color, consistency, odor, and amount of urine
- Surgical wound, incision site, and dressing
- For pain
- For movement of extremities
- Level of consciousness
- Blood oxygen levels
- Electrocardiogram (ECG) readings

Δ   Monitor the client's recovery from anesthesia by using the **Aldrete Scoring System**. Each of the following five factors is given a score based upon the nurse's observations of the client. The five scores are totaled to determine the client's Aldrete Score.

ALDRETE SCORING SYSTEM		
Factor	**Assessment/Observation**	**Score**
Activity	Able to move 4 extremities	2
	Able to move 2 extremities	1
	Able to move 0 extremities	0
Consciousness	Fully awake	2
	Arousable	1
	Unarousable	0
Respiration	Breathe deeply and cough	2
	Dyspnea, hypoventilation	1
	Apneic	0
Color	Pink	2
	Pale	1
	Cyanotic	0
Circulation	BP within 20 mm Hg of preanesthesia level	2
	BP within 20-50 mm Hg of preanesthesia level	1
	BP not within 50 mm Hg of preanesthesia level	0

Δ Criteria indicating **readiness for discharge** from PACU include:

- Aldrete Score of at least 10.

- Stable vital signs.

- No evidence of bleeding.

- Return of reflexes (gag, cough, swallow).

- Wound drainage minimal to moderate.

- Urine output of at least 30 mL/hr.

NANDA Nursing Diagnoses

Δ Impaired gas exchange

Δ Ineffective airway clearance

Δ Ineffective breathing pattern

Δ Risk for infection

Δ Acute pain

Δ Altered tissue perfusion

Δ   Impaired tissue integrity

Δ   Impaired skin integrity

Δ   Nausea and vomiting

Δ   Urinary retention

Δ   Constipation

Nursing Interventions

Δ   On receiving the client from the anesthesiologist and receiving report from the circulating nurse, the PACU nurse immediately performs a full body assessment with priority given to airway, breathing, and circulation.

Δ   Maintain airway and ventilation.

- Keep an airway in place if the client is comatose.

- Administer humidified oxygen.

- Suction accumulated secretions if the client is unable to cough.

- Assist with coughing, deep breathing, and splinting.

- Encourage the use of an incentive spirometer.

- Reposition every 2 hr and ambulate early and regularly.

Δ   Client Positioning

- Position the client supine with head flat (prevent hypotension).

- Put the client on his side if unconscious or comatose (risk of aspiration).

- When the client is fully reactive, raise the head of the bed to facilitate respiratory expansion.

- Do not elevate the client's legs higher than placement on a pillow if the client has received spinal anesthesia.

- Do not put pillows under knees or use a knee gatch (decreases venous return).

- Elevate the client's legs if shock develops.

Δ   Monitor and maintain fluid status.

- Administer intravenous isotonic infusions (for example, lactated Ringer's and 5% dextrose with lactated Ringer's) and maintain a patent IV line.

Δ Monitor and manage pain.

- A preventive approach rather than an "as needed" approach is more effective in relieving pain. With a preventive approach, the medication is administered at prescribed intervals rather than when the pain becomes severe or unbearable. Monitor the client every 30 min for pain relief and respiratory rate.

- Provide continuous pain relief through use of a patient-controlled analgesia (PCA) pump. Epidural and intrathecal infusions are also available.

- Monitor for side effects, such as nausea (encourage the client to change positions slowly), urinary retention, and constipation.

- Provide analgesia 30 min before ambulation.

Δ Monitor renal function (output should equal intake).

- Monitor and report urinary outputs of less than 30 mL/hr.

- Ensure that the client who does not have a catheter voids at least 200 mL of urine within 6 hr after surgery.

- Palpate the bladder of the client following voiding to assess for bladder distention.

Δ Monitor and promote bowel function and oral comfort.

- Maintain the client on NPO (nothing by mouth) status until return of the gag reflex (risk of aspiration) and peristalsis (risk of paralytic ileus).

- Irrigate nasogastric (NG) suction tubes with saline as needed to maintain patency. Do not move NG tubes in gastric surgery clients (risk to incision).

- Provide ice chips and sips of water as permitted.

- Provide frequent oral hygiene.

- Monitor for bowel sounds x 4 and ability to pass flatus.

- Advance the diet as prescribed and tolerated (clear liquids to regular).

Δ Prevent and monitor for thromboembolism (especially following abdominal and pelvic surgeries).

- Apply pneumatic compression stockings and/or elastic stockings.

- Reposition the client every 2 hr and ambulate early and regularly.

- Administer low-level anticoagulants as prescribed.

- Monitor extremities for calf pain, warmth, erythema, and edema.

Δ   Monitor incisions and drain sites for bleeding and/or infection.

- Monitor drainage (should progress from sanguineous to serosanguineous to serous).

- Monitor the incision site (expected findings include pink wound edges, slight swelling under sutures/staples, slight crusting of drainage). Report signs of infection, including redness, excessive tenderness, and purulent drainage.

- Monitor wound drains (with each vital sign assessment). Empty as often as needed to maintain compression. Report increases in drainage (possible hemorrhage).

- Change wound dressings as required, using surgical aseptic technique.

- Use an abdominal binder for obese or debilitated clients.

- Encourage splinting with position changes.

- Administer prophylactic antibiotics as prescribed.

- Remove sutures or staples in 6 to 8 days as prescribed.

Δ   Promote wound healing.

- Encourage a diet high in calories, protein, and vitamin C.

- If the client has diabetes mellitus, encourage good glycemic control.

Δ   Provide discharge teaching.

- Medications (purpose, administration guidelines, adverse effects)

- Activity restrictions (driving, stairs, limits on weight lifting, sexual activity)

- Dietary guidelines, if applicable

- Special treatment instructions (wound care, catheter care, use of assistive devices)

- Emergency contact information and signs to report

Complications and Nursing Implications

Δ   **Airway Obstruction**: Monitor for choking, noisy irregular respirations, decreased oxygen saturation scores, and cyanosis and intervene accordingly. Keep emergency equipment at the bedside in the PACU.

Δ   **Hypoxia**: Monitor oxygenation status and administer oxygen as prescribed. Encourage the client to cough and deep breathe. Position the client to facilitate respiratory expansion.

Δ   **Hypovolemic Shock**: Monitor for decreased blood pressure and urinary output, increased heart rate, and slow capillary refill. Administer fluids and vasopressors as indicated.

Δ **Paralytic Ileus**: Monitor bowel sounds, encourage ambulation, advance the diet as tolerated, and administer prokinetic agents, such as metoclopramide (Reglan), as prescribed.

Δ **Wound Dehiscence or Evisceration**: Monitor risk factors (obesity, coughing, moving without splinting, diabetes mellitus, day 5 to 10). If wound dehiscence or evisceration occurs, call for help, stay with the client, cover with sterile towel or dressing moistened with sterile saline, do not attempt to reinsert organs, monitor the client for shock, and notify the primary care provider immediately).

Meeting the Needs of Older Adults

Δ Age-related respiratory, cardiovascular, and renal changes necessitate special attention to the postoperative recovery of older adults.

Δ Older adult clients are more susceptible to cold, so additional warm blankets in the PACU may be required.

Δ Responses to medications and anesthetics may delay the older adult client's return of orientation postoperatively.

Δ Age-related physiologic changes may affect an older adult client's response to and elimination of postoperative medications. Monitor closely for appropriate client response and possible adverse effects.

- Older adults perspire less, which leads to dry, itchy skin that becomes fragile and easily abraded. Use of paper tape for wound dressing may be appropriate, as well as lifting precautions.

- Take care to meet the nutritional needs of older adults in order to promote effective wound healing.

Primary Reference:

Ignatavicius, D. D., & Workman, M. L. (2006). *Medical-surgical nursing* (5th ed.). St. Louis, MO: Saunders.

Additional Resources:

Lewis, Heitkemper, and Dirksen (2004). *Medical-surgical nursing: Assessment and management of clinical problems* (6th ed.). St. Louis, MO: Mosby.

Lilley, L., Harrington, S., & Synder, J. (2005). *Pharmacology and the nursing process* (4th ed.). St. Louis, MO: Mosby.

NANDA International (2004). *NANDA nursing diagnoses: Definitions and classification 2005-2006*. Philadelphia: NANDA.

Chapter 128: Postoperative Nursing

Application Exercises

1. Interpret each of the following postoperative client findings and outline a plan for intervention.

Postoperative Client Finding	Interpretation & Intervention Plan
Stridor and snoring (PACU)	
Jackson Pratt (JP) drainage: 2 times output in previous hour	
Blood pressure 25% below preoperative blood pressure	
Ten minutes after use of PCA, client has pain rating of 8	
Erythematous swollen warm area on left calf; calf pain on dorsiflexion	
Urinary output for past 4 hr is 100 mL	
Sleeping, responds to command (PACU)	
pH 7.30, PaCO$_2$ 50 mm Hg	
Pulse oximetry reading of 96%	
Bowel sounds faint 24 hr after abdominal surgery	
Serosanguineous drainage beyond postoperative day 5	
White blood cell count of 9,800/mm^3 on postoperative day 1	
Wound edges: Pink with slight swelling under sutures, scant amount of crusted serosanguineous drainage on postoperative day 2	
Total Hgb level of 8.9 g/dL on postoperative day 2 following hip arthroplasty surgery	
Scant amounts of blood in nasogastric contents in the first 24 hr postoperative gastric or bowel surgery	
Crackles in lung bases bilaterally postoperative day 1 following abdominal surgery	

Chapter 128: Postoperative Nursing

Application Exercises Answer Key

1. Interpret each of the following postoperative client findings and outline a plan for intervention.

Postoperative Client Finding	Interpretation & Intervention Plan
Stridor and snoring (PACU)	Possible tracheal/laryngeal spasm or blockage (mucus, edema, tongue): Emergency equipment on standby, restore airway (reposition, intubation).
Jackson Pratt (JP) drainage: 2 times output in previous hour	Possible hemorrhage: Assess surgical site and vital signs, stat CBC, notify surgeon.
Blood pressure 25% below preoperative blood pressure	Cardiac depression, fluid volume deficit, shock, hemorrhage, or medication effects: Treat cause, monitor closely, provide fluids and/or vasopressors.
Ten minutes after use of PCA, client has pain rating of 8	Inadequate pain management protocol: Advocate for additional pain interventions, employ non-pharmacological comfort measures.
Erythematous swollen warm area on left calf; calf pain on dorsiflexion	Thrombophlebitis/deep vein thrombosis: Report findings to primary care provider promptly, maintain bedrest until thrombosis is ruled out or client is anticoagulated.
Urinary output for past 4 hr is 100 mL	Renal insufficiency: Promptly report hourly outputs of less than 30 mL/hr.
Sleeping, responds to command (PACU)	Expected finding following general anesthesia: Continue to routinely assess/monitor.
pH 7.30, $PaCO_2$ 50 mm Hg	Hypoventilation/respiratory acidosis: Encourage deep breathing, mobilize secretions (suction).
Pulse oximetry reading of 96%	Expected findings are 94 to 98%.
Bowel sounds faint 24 hr after abdominal surgery	Expected findings due to effects of general anesthesia: Encourage ambulation, administer prokinetic agents as prescribed.
Serosanguineous drainage beyond postoperative day 5	Possible indication of ineffective healing and risk for wound dehiscence/evisceration: Report findings, encourage the client to avoid forceful coughing and straining and to splint the incision with movement.
White blood cell count of 9,800/mm³ on postoperative day 1	No evidence of infection: Continue infection risk reduction interventions.

Postoperative Client Finding	Interpretation & Intervention Plan
Wound edges: Pink with slight swelling under sutures, scant amount of crusted serosanguineous drainage on postoperative day 2	**Expected findings of effective wound healing: Continue to monitor wound healing and to change dressings using proper technique.**
Total Hgb level of 8.9 g/dL on postoperative day 2 following hip arthroplasty surgery	**Surgical blood loss: Administer blood replacement products as prescribed, energy conservation measures, administer erythropoietin and/or iron supplements as prescribed, administer oxygen as prescribed.**
Scant amounts of blood in nasogastric contents in the first 24 hr postoperative gastric or bowel surgery	**Expected finding: Report increases or bright red blood, do not reposition nasogastric tube due to risk of disrupting sutures.**
Crackles in lung bases bilaterally postoperative day 1 following abdominal surgery	**Hypoventilation and ineffective airway clearance related to pain with coughing: Administer pain medication prior to coughing exercise, reposition frequently, encourage splinting with coughing.**